Global Gender Research

This book provides an in-depth comparative picture of the current state of global feminist social science research on women and gender issues. It familiarizes readers with an extensive range of salient issues, research methods, and leading authors from around the globe. Readers can compare and contrast the threads of similarity and difference in feminist concerns globally, gaining familiarity with the breadth of gender research, and understanding the national or regional contexts that produced it. Organized into four regional sections—on Africa, Asia, Latin America and the Caribbean, and Europe—each section is introduced by a synthetic essay on the socio-historical developments that shape contemporary gender questions for the entire region, as well as the relationship of these research questions to feminist activism and women's or gender studies. Subsequent chapters provide in-depth overviews of research in selected key countries within each region. Then, the editors illustrate the new wave of global gender research by concluding each section with translated samples of post-2000 research carried out in additional countries within the same region, and covering the diversity of important global topics—such as work, sexuality, masculinities, childcare and family issues, religion, violence, law and gender policies. The volume is also a research resource, providing extensive bibliographies and a listing of websites for International Women's Research Centers.

Christine E. Bose is Professor of Sociology; Women's Studies; and Latin American, Caribbean, and U.S. Latino Studies, at the University at Albany, SUNY. She has been Editor of *Gender & Society*, President of Sociologists for Women in Society, and a Fulbright Senior Scholar.

Minjeong Kim is an Assistant Professor of Women's Studies in the Interdisciplinary Studies Department at Virginia Tech. She was a 2007 Woodrow Wilson Dissertation Fellow in Women's Studies.

PERSPECTIVES ON GENDER

Edited by **Myra Marx Ferree,** University of Wisconsin, Madison

Black Feminist Thought by Patricia Hill Collins

Black Women and White Women in the Professions by Natalie J. Sokoloff

Community Activism and Feminist Politics Edited by Nancy Naples

Complex Inequality by Leslie McCall

Disposable Women and Other Myths of Global Capitalism by Melissa W. Wright

Feminism and the Women's Movement by Barbara Ryan

Fixing Families by Jennifer A. Reich

For Richer, For Poorer by Demie Kurz

Gender Consciousness and Politics by Sue Tolleson Rinehart

Grassroots Warriors by Nancy A. Naples

Home-Grown Hate Edited by Abby L. Ferber

Integrative Feminisms by Angela Miles

Laboring On by Wendy Simonds, Barbara Katz Rothman and Bari Meltzer Norman

Maid in the U.S.A. by Mary Romero

Mothering Edited by Evelyn Nakano Glenn, Grace Chang and Linda Rennie Forcey

Rape Work by Patricia Yancey Martin

Regulating Sex Edited by Elizabeth Bernstein and Laurie Schaffner

Rock-a-by Baby by Verta Taylor

School-smart and Mother-wise by Wendy Luttrell

Stepping Out of Line by Cheryl Hercus

The Social Economy of Single Motherhood by Margaret Nelson

Understanding Sexual Violence by Diana Scully

When Sex Became Gender by Shira Tarrant

Forthcoming
Negotiating the Global: Northeast Brazilian Women's Movements and the Transnational Feminist Public by Millie Thayer

Global Gender Research

Transnational Perspectives

Christine E. Bose and Minjeong Kim

EDITORS

Routledge
Taylor & Francis Group

NEW YORK AND LONDON

First published 2009
by Routledge
270 Madison Ave, New York, NY 10016

Simultaneously published in the UK
by Routledge
2 Park Square, Milton Park, Abingdon, Oxon OX14 4RN

Routledge is an imprint of the Taylor & Francis Group, an informa business

© 2009 Taylor & Francis

Typeset in Sabon by Swales & Willis Ltd, Exeter, Devon
Printed and bound in the United States of America on acid-free paper by
Sheridan Books, Inc

Library of Congress Cataloging in Publication Data
A catalog record has been requested for this book

ISBN10: 0–415–95269–7 (hbk)
ISBN10: 0–415–95270–0 (pbk)

ISBN13: 978–0–415–95269–9 (hbk)
ISBN13: 978–0–415–95270–5 (pbk)

CONTENTS

Foreword   x

Preface   xii

Acknowledgements   xiv

Map   xv

Note on Text Edits   xvi

1 Introduction to Transnational and Local Issues   1

CHRISTINE E. BOSE AND MINJEONG KIM

The major commonalities and differences in gender research across the globe are described, while also examining the social structures that help shape research questions

SECTION 1: AFRICA

2 Introduction to Gender Research in Africa   11

MARY JOHNSON OSIRIM, CHRISTINE E. BOSE, AND MINJEONG KIM

An overview on how political, social, and economic trends shape gender research across the African continent

3 Women's and Gender Studies in English-Speaking Sub-Saharan Africa: A Review of Research in the Social Sciences   16

AKOSUA ADOMAKO AMPOFO, JOSEPHINE BEOKU-BETTS, WAIRIMŨ NGARŨIYA NJAMBI, AND MARY JOHNSON OSIRIM

Health, education, gender-based violence, sexuality, globalization and work, and politics, the state, and NGOs are important themes in English speaking Africa's gender research

4 Trading Goes Global: Ghanaian Market Women in an Era of Globalization   41

AKOSUA K. DARKWAH

As formal sector occupations disappear under structural adjustment plans, educated women become transnational traders in the informal economy

5 Feminine Injustice   49

CONCEIÇÃO OSÓRIO AND EULÁLIA TEMBA

*Women who experience family violence do not find justice in the courts of
Mozambique, but a return to older consensual tribal methods does not work either*

6 Women, the Sacred and the State   56

FATOU SOW

The practice of Islam shapes family law even in a secular state like Senegal

SECTION 2: ASIA AND THE MIDDLE EAST

7 Introduction to Gender Research in Asia and the Middle East   67

MINJEONG KIM AND CHRISTINE E. BOSE

*An overview on how political, social, and economic trends shape gender research
across Asia and the Middle East*

8 Promising and Contested Fields: Advancing Women's Studies and
Sociology of Women/Gender in Contemporary China   73

ESTHER NGAN-LING CHOW, NAIHUA ZHANG, AND WANG JINLING

*The underlying themes of local-global interaction and "discipline building" link the
growth of both women's studies and the sociology of women/gender*

9 The Study of Gender in India: A Partial Review   92

BANDANA PURKAYASTHA, MANGALA SUBRAMANIAM, MANISHA DESAI, AND SUNITA BOSE

*Focusing on theory, methods, social movements and domestic violence, the authors
review dynamics of doing research in a diverse country*

10 Women's Studies in Iran: The Roles of Activists and Scholars   110

SHAHLA EZAZI

*Women's studies was recently established by a decree of the Ministry of Higher
Education, but activists and NGOs are more likely to be in touch with new global
gender research*

11 Masculinity and Anti-Americanism: Focusing on the Identity of KATUSA   125

INSOOK KWON

*Katusa soldiers' ideas on masculinity are shaped through their interactions with
U.S. counterparts and by masculinity models found among regular Korean military
conscripts*

12 Gender, Development and HIV/AIDS in Vietnam: Towards an
Alternative Response Model among Women Sex Workers   133

VAN HUY NGUYEN, UDOY SANKAR SAIKIA, AND THI MINH AN DAO

*Addressing gender and development issues adequately is key to combating the spread
of HIV/AIDS in Vietnam, especially among sex workers*

13 *Fufubessei* Movement in Japan: Thinking About Women's Resistance
and Subjectivity   141

Kɪ-ʏᴏᴜɴɢ Sʜɪɴ

*Women who want to keep their own family names at marriage are having an impact on
revising family law, even though they do not organize like a traditional social movement*

SECTION 3: LATIN AMERICA AND THE CARIBBEAN

14 Between the Dynamics of the Global and the Local: Feminist and
Gender Research in Latin America and the Caribbean   151

Eᴅɴᴀ Aᴄᴏsᴛᴀ-Bᴇʟᴇ́ɴ

*An overview on how political, social, and economic trends shape gender research
across Latin America and the Caribbean*

15 Relations in Dispute: Conflict and Cooperation Between Academia and
the Feminist Movements in Central America   158

Mᴏɴᴛsᴇʀʀᴀᴛ Sᴀɢᴏᴛ ᴀɴᴅ Aɴᴀ C. Esᴄᴀʟᴀɴᴛᴇ

*Academic–activist linkages are key to understanding the themes in Central
American gender research on topics including human rights, violence against
women, citizenship, political participation, economic inequality, gendered
identities, masculinities, and migration*

16 Puerto Rico: Feminism and Feminist Studies   178

Aʟɪᴄᴇ E. Cᴏʟᴏ́ɴ Wᴀʀʀᴇɴ

*Common gender research themes include women's employment, poverty, family
violence, and sexual and reproductive rights, with growing interest in the
intersectionalities of gender, race, nation, class, and sexuality*

17 Gender Studies in Cuba: Methodological Approaches, 1974–2007   196

Mᴀʀᴛᴀ Nᴜ́ñᴇᴢ Sᴀʀᴍɪᴇɴᴛᴏ

*Gender studies began only in the late 1980s, but researchers learned from the mistakes
of others; various methodological approaches are described for a sample of researchers*

18 Feminist Research and Theory: Contributions from the Anglophone
Caribbean   215

Rʜᴏᴅᴀ Rᴇᴅᴅᴏᴄᴋ

*Early emphasis on finding the local roots of feminism and describing women's realities
shifted to a more recent focus on cultural studies*

19 Trade Unions and Women's Labor Rights in Argentina 231

GRACIELA DI MARCO

Unionized workers in traditional and progressive unions are trying to move from a "specific structures" to a "main structure" model with the help of a union female quota law

20 In the Fabric of Brazilian Sexuality 239

MARIA LUIZA HEILBORN

Survey research on youth reveals gender differences and myths about liberal sexual attitudes

21 Citizenship and Nation: Debates on Reproductive Rights in Puerto Rico 248

ELIZABETH CRESPO-KEBLER

Feminists and nationalists created different discourses about citizenship, as illustrated in organizing around abortion and sterilization abuse

SECTION 4: EUROPE

22 Introduction to Gender Research in Europe 257

CHRISTINE E. BOSE AND MINJEONG KIM

An overview on how political, social, and economic trends shape gender research across Europe

23 Traveling Theories–Situated Questions: Feminist Theory in the German Context 261

GUDRUN-AXELI KNAPP

Feminist scholars in German-speaking Europe have developed a strong focus on feminist socio-historical theory, with a trajectory influenced by National Socialism, the unification of East and West Germany, and by broader European Union events; currently they are shifting from gender-class axes to a focus on the intersectionality of gender, class, race, sexuality, and nation

24 An Overview of Research on Gender in Spanish Society 278

CELIA VALIENTE

In the post-Franco era, gender studies has been shaped by feminist activism and state funding for research; and important themes include families, education, work, politics, sexuality, and men

25 At the Crossroads of 'East' and 'West': Gender Studies in Hungary 290

EVA FODOR AND ESZTER VARSA

Gender studies has many similarities with other former state socialist countries, but there are also differences in disciplines, institutionalization, the power of feminist NGOs, and other features

26 "The Rest is Silence . . .": Polish Nationalism and the Question of
Lesbian Existence 308

JOANNA MIZIELIŃSKA

*Polish nationalistic discourse avoids the question of homosexuality and makes it
invisible, largely due to the Church's role in the decline of communism, as shown in
analyses of the Catechism and the new Polish Constitution*

27 Collective Organizing and Claim Making on Child Care in Norden:
Blurring the Boundaries between the Inside and the Outside 315

SOLVEIG BERGMAN

*Nordic countries use a combination of insider and outsider strategies to achieve
child care support, but they vary in their usage of home care vs. institutional
support, and in how they support paternity leave*

28 Integrating or Setting the Agenda?: Gender Mainstreaming in the
European Constitution-Making Process 323

EMANUELA LOMBARDO

*Competing frames, norm-setting, and male-dominated institutions are reasons for
resistance to adopting gender norms in the EU constitution-making process, thus
shifting to an agenda setting approach*

Appendix: Websites of International Women's Research Centers 331

Contributors 347

Reprint Permission List 355

Index 358

FOREWORD

This volume is the most recent addition to a long-running series of "Perspectives on Gender" books that it has been my privilege to edit. Even as publishers have changed, the series has continued in its quiet way to add new and more diverse scholarship to illuminate the workings of gender in society. As editor for the series, I have grown intellectually through manuscripts with which I have worked. The authors have been kind enough to engage with me in a back-and-forth discussion of the substantive perspectives they offer as well as the issues of style and voice they present. I hope that readers also can recognize the collective energy in the series as well as the distinctive contributions of each individual book.

From the outset, the series was dedicated to the purpose of publishing the very best feminist scholarship on gender in the social sciences, understanding that this should be work that was advancing both the understanding of how inclusive of difference our perspectives need to be to capture what gender means and the ability to grasp the implications of social change in and for gender relations. The commitment to diversity initially was expressed in the range of topics from micro to macro analyses of gender transformations, the mix of quantitative and qualitative methods employed, and the strong emphasis on making sure that gender was seen as intersectional with race and class. The centrality of social change to the titles in this series has implied an emphasis on contested power relations, social movements, and historical transformations in work, family, and politics. Although the titles appearing in the series may seem an eclectic bunch, it should not be challenging to the reader of the list (on page ii) to recognize these two themes weaving though them.

Over the two decades that the series has been in existence, its complementary emphases on inclusivity and transformation have led to an ever increasing focus on the world outside the borders of the United States. The current volume is an excellent example of how — in me as well as in the authors submitting manuscripts, the reviewers and publishers responding to them, and the readers who turn to the books we collectively produce — the recognition has grown that we need to understand the world as a global unit in order to make sense of the social, economic, and political dimensions of gender relations. Moreover, we feminists have grown to understand more fully that each of us has a standpoint in this world, and that we need to draw in the scholars and scholarship located in many corners of the world to begin to form anything like an accurate view of the intersectional and transformative dynamics of gender.

I thus especially appreciate the cover illustration of this book. The "cat's cradle" game is known under many names in many parts of the world; it is cooperative rather than competitive; it is passed down across generations but open to innovations; and, as in the art of weaving to which it is so closely connected, the beauty of the whole arises from the relationships emergent from the simple, everyday materials. Seeing the patterns built and knowing how it is done enhances rather than detracts from appreciation of the complexity of the "world" of gender that is formed while leaving it to us to almost magically to "unweave" it and redo it differently. Christine Bose and Minjeong Kim have brought together many hands to weave a picture of a world of gender that is beautiful in its complexity, challenging in its mutability and impressive in the skills displayed in its creation. I hope that readers will follow the multiple threads of this volume and be inspired to put their own hands in to pick up the game themselves.

Myra Marx Ferree
Series Editor

PREFACE

CONCEPT FOR THIS VOLUME

The idea for *Global Gender Research: Transnational Perspectives* began when its co-editors, Christine E. Bose and Minjeong Kim were, respectively, Editor and Managing Editor for *Gender & Society*, the journal of Sociologists for Women in Society (SWS), between the years of 2000 and 2003. During that time, we felt it would be important to "internationalize" the journal and solicited a series of six review essays under the theme "International Perspectives on Gender Research," which covered countries from three continents.

We wanted the overviews to cover a wide range of topics and meet multiple objectives. Among them were 1) to analyze the historical or political background that shapes the trajectory of social science gender studies in each country, 2) to discuss the major theoretical and empirical issues that emerge in gender research organized by key topics, 3) to explore the relationship of gender research to women's activism, and 4) to describe the most typical research methods used. The original six articles provided the initial core for the current 28 chapter volume, but *Global Gender Research* now represents an expansion across countries and regions, adding many review chapters that have never been published, including exemplary research articles from each region, providing regional introductory essays, and a list of websites for gender research centers across the globe.

The development of this volume had some of the collective structure and organizing components that are typical of women's activism. We gathered together almost all of the fourteen co-authors of the original published essays, and members of this diverse group met each other for the first time during the 2004 Winter Meetings of SWS in Albuquerque, New Mexico. The team organized a plenary panel at the conference, but we also held several of our own meetings. The authors' enthusiasm for making all of these essays available, both in the United States and around the globe, turned these international scholars into a *de facto* international advisory board for this volume. The scholars had been energized by their own co-authored articles, and had unearthed a considerable amount of information, some of which they were not even previously aware of. They (and we) believed that pulling all the essays together, and extending them to cover additional countries was an important endeavor for gender studies/ women's studies in the social sciences worldwide. Subsequent authors who joined us also felt their review chapters were enhanced either by taking on co-authors or by interviewing feminist and gender studies scholars in their nations about the growth and development of gender research.

We, and our advisory group, expect this volume will help transform the social science disciplines and women's studies by truly bringing international native/indigenous gender scholarship to the United States, as well as to other countries. These advisors suggested several creative ideas to make this volume useful in their own countries and abroad, in particular pointing to additional countries that should be incorporated in this more expansive venue and in locating gender research centers within the countries they knew best. We are indebted to the efforts of all these scholars, and to the other women (and men) across the globe, who were ready to help us with "local knowledge" and contributed so much to this volume in response to our inquiring e-mails.

ACKNOWLEDGEMENTS

We had considerable technical assistance from many people in order to complete this project, and we want to thank them for their generosity. While many of them already are listed in our appendix of Contributors' Bio Sketches, they deserve special thanks. Edna Acosta-Belén, Yasir Robles, Kristen Bini, Marta Castillo (Marta Merajver-Kurlat), and Jacqueline Hayes contributed their excellent skills to the translation of articles that were originally in Spanish, Portuguese, or French. Graphic artist and medical illustrator at The Johns Hopkins University, Lydia Gregg (who also is Christine Bose's niece) contributed the eye-catching cover art; while GIS expert Jin-Wook Lee, working for the University at Albany's Center for Social and Demographic Analysis, created our extremely useful map of the countries covered by the chapters in this volume. Kim Tauches worked on an earlier edition of the listing of websites, and a whole network of international scholars helped ensure the accuracy (at least for this moment in time) of the web addresses that we have listed.

Other people were instrumental in getting this project off the ground and bringing it to fruition. We thank the Publications Committee of Sociologists for Women in Society (SWS) for making our initial efforts easier by waiving reprint fees for the original six articles. We are grateful to Myra Marx Ferree for seeing the wide-ranging contribution this book can make, and for accepting it as part of her Routledge book series—as well as for her excellent ideas on authors or centers to contact. And it has been a pleasure for Chris to work with Steven Rutter once again, but in a new context, as our current Routledge Acquisitions Editor. He has gently moved us along, while answering all our technical questions on everything from cover design to copyright issues.

We both also want to thank the people who have supported, nourished, and inspired us as we have written and edited these chapters. Minjeong Kim especially thanks her mother, Jae-sang Ye, who has been a feminist inspiration for her; meanwhile Chris Bose wants to thank Edna Acosta-Belén, who has given her many years of personal support and made generous contributions in translating, proof-reading, and writing a portion of this volume. Both of these women have believed in our vision of this book and changed many of their plans to accommodate our drive to complete it. Finally, we wish to thank each other—we have worked together in one capacity or another for nine years, always around global gender issues, and this volume represents the most recent culmination of that collaboration.

Christine E. Bose and Minjeong Kim
Albany, New York
July 2008

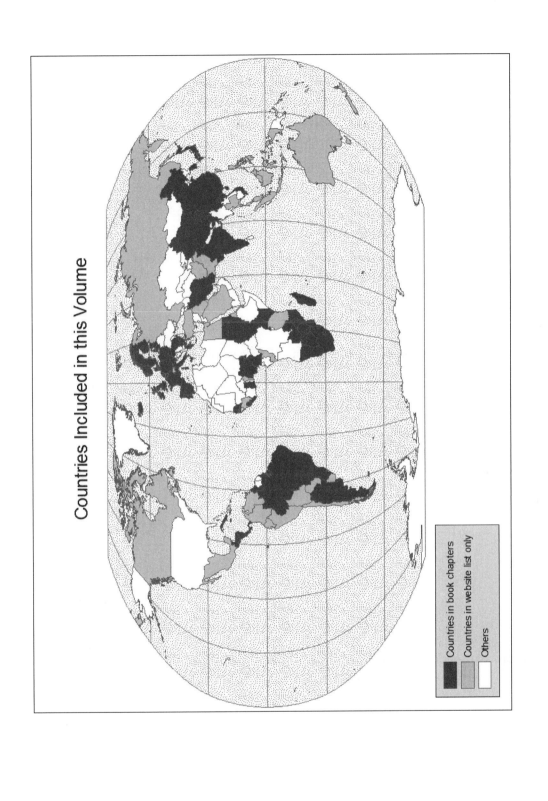

Countries Included in this Volume

Countries in book chapters
Countries in website list only
Others

NOTE ON TEXT EDITS

Many of the chapters in this volume are shortened versions of an original published piece. Where cuts have been made, ellipses have been inserted in the text to indicate where these have occurred.

. . .   indicates omission of a few words in a sentence

. . .   within a paragraph indicates omission of at least a whole sentence

. . .   at the end of a paragraph or above the first paragraph in the piece indicates that at least a
        whole paragraph has been omitted

CHAPTER 1

An Introduction to Transnational and Local Issues

Christine E. Bose and Minjeong Kim

Global Gender Research: Transnational Perspectives presents transnational and local views of social science gender and women's studies research by analyzing the historical, economic and political trends that shape the trajectory of these investigations around the world. We describe some of the major unique theoretical and empirical issues that emerge in gender and women's research in various countries and regions, as well as several common threads that are found across multiple regions. In doing so, we consider the intertwined relationship of gender research to women's and feminist social movements, and point out the most typical methods used in such research. Of course, in many countries gender and feminist perspectives are well integrated into the social science disciplines, particularly sociology, but in others, they are isolated in the interdisciplinary field of women's studies. Because we know that the category "women" encompasses a great diversity of experiences, understanding global variation is important in order to comprehend why some research questions (and feminist issues) are of greater concern in one locale versus another.

The four regions that we cover in this volume are Africa, Asia and the Middle East, Latin America and the Caribbean, and Europe—we chose these regional country groupings to match those used by the United Nations in their statistical summaries of women's status.

LINKAGES BETWEEN FEMINIST ACTIVISM AND ACADEMIC WOMEN'S STUDIES/GENDER RESEARCH

As Sagot and Escalante (Chapter 15) describe in this volume, when women's studies and gender research began during the mid-twentieth century "second wave" of feminism, just describing women's issues and conditions was enough to engage in dialogue and debate. In fact, as Ezazi (Chapter 10) notes, in some countries like Iran where gender issues are a critical topic of contention, that might still be true. Yet, on the whole, a panoramic view of the evolution of scholarship on women and gender issues reveals that research has evolved and become much more nuanced and sophisticated since the global pioneering stages of the early 1970s, basically aimed at unveiling, incorporating, and documenting the presence and contributions of women to the history and productive lives of their respective societies, and exposing the major sources of their oppression, as well as their most pressing conditions.

The overall process of inclusiveness and redefining or transforming knowledge on women's livelihoods and experiences has been accompanied by an engaged and persistent effort by many feminist and gender studies scholars to address and challenge the historical exclusions, biases, patriarchal power structures, and androcentric perspectives of the past, and confront the realities, conditions, and different forms of oppression that continue to shape women's lives and perpetuate their subordination in the present. They have introduced new perspectives and approaches that are now inescapably crucial to the analysis of a wide-range of differences in women's experiences, social, economic, and political conditions, and manifestations of feminism that rely on diverse visions and strategies in the pursuit of their claims for meaningful social change.

Even if one accepts the debatable notion that since the U.N. Decade for Women (1975–1985) feminism has become a global project of social transformation or a generalized consensus to liberate women from the subordinate and unequal conditions they experience in nearly all societies, most feminists would concur that whatever progress has been made in the recent past—in freeing women from full-time domestic work, in increasing their visibility and participation in the public sphere, and in addressing a whole gamut of critical women and gender issues—is still far from subverting or transforming the entrenched sexist and unequal power structures and relations that prevail all over the world. The latter continue to be reinforced by the prevailing hierarchical and polarizing relations between capital and labor, developed and developing countries and regions, and a globalized and more integrated capitalist system that continues to reproduce and perpetuate different forms of subordination. This system also promotes policies that, for the most part, are weakening national and regional power, and fostering the subordinate integration of developing countries into the world's dominant capitalist economies. Thus any advances or transformative changes in the status of women are more a result of their unrelenting articulation of demands and responses from state or institutional power structures that generally attempt to negotiate, co-opt, or accommodate them without any significant transformations in these male-dominated spaces.

The world is now caught up in new dynamics and forms of capitalist globalization that are only exacerbating socioeconomic inequalities, poverty, health problems, and environmental degradation, as well as generating a vast displacement of workers and unprecedented migration throughout different countries and regions of the planet. In confronting these critical issues feminist activism comes and goes in waves or spurts carried out by different generations of women making modest inroads at local or national levels, but without being able to forge a broader consensus about a bold and multifaceted women-focused agenda for change, in part because women's conditions and needs vary by the region, country, or locality in which they live. Even within the major metropolitan centers of world capital (such as in Europe, Chapters 22 to 28), where women have become a more visible presence in public life and have achieved notable progress in a few vital areas—such as education, political representation, and reproductive rights—they continue to fight to mainstream their agendas into public life, to develop policy that truly integrates work and family for both men and women, or to attain an income and overall status equal to that of their male counterparts. What this relative progress illustrates is that even when some women are able to penetrate the dominant patriarchal power structures sexism and patriarchy persist in myriad and constantly changing forms.

Still, as history demonstrates, struggling against the odds is an intrinsic part of women's movements for social justice and equality, and the assertion that women have come a long way since the suffragist movements would be hard to refute. Qualified progress has been made in some countries to combat violence against women, improve their health status, their rights to control their own bodies and express their sexuality, their access to jobs and education, and to other basic human rights, and in enacting new laws to protect their civil liberties and alleviate past discrimination. Equally important is how researchers and activists have brought a considerable level of legitimacy and innovative approaches to the analysis of women and gender issues. Notwithstanding, in many other ways the struggle towards eradicating prevailing gender inequalities is still largely a work in progress. Thus it would be a fallacy for the younger generations of women to simply assume that they have an easier path to full equality and liberation than women did just a few decades ago, as Reddock duly observes (Chapter 18). Indeed, as some of the Women's Studies pioneers in various nations enter international activism or official government positions in their home countries, they can leave a void in domestic activism (see Reddock, Chapter 18). On the other hand, since the early 1970s the proliferation of women's studies programs and gender-focused research, and the rise of transnational women's organizations and solidarity networks has allowed women to "connect" more easily with the realities and challenges faced by other women around the globe, and with the work that is being carried out to deal with some of the most pressing and vital issues, which despite some obvious common strands, vary significantly from the conditions found in a country's local communities and those that are of a broader national or international nature. But if there is an indisputable fact, it is that during the last four decades women and gender have become indispensable categories of analysis in conducting research or formulating public policies. Hampering this progress, however, are the expanding media technologies and the unrelenting ideological diffusion of gender relations debased by the implicit or explicit subordination of women or objectification and commodification of their bodies that continue to spread globally like a persistent and insidious pandemic. Yet, paradoxically, these same technologies are being used—albeit, not necessarily with the same reach or popular appeal—by organizations worldwide to engage in networking and in carrying out their respective messages for the improvement of different aspects of women's lives.

The United Nations' Division for the Advancement of Women (DAW) and its Commission on the Status of Women (CSW) have been around since 1946, but it was not until after the first Women's World Conference, held in Mexico in 1975, that they became more relevant and visible in formulating some semblance of "a global agenda" on women's rights and in fostering the proliferation and active participation of non-governmental organizations (NGOs) in this process, many of which had been successful in dealing with specific localized women's concerns. Overall, the four Women's World Conferences sponsored by the United Nations from 1975 to 1995 have had a significant impact in gathering data about the status of women around the world, and monitoring their progress in more measurable areas, such as demography, reproductive health, education, work, and political representation (Ashford and Clifton 2005). Agencies such as the United Nations Development Fund for Women (UNIFEM) have played an active role in promoting the goal of gender equality and in developing specific Millennium Development Goals (MDGs) that include decreasing the feminization of poverty, combating violence against women and epidemic diseases such as HIV/AIDS, and advocating for gender equality and the advancement of women. It is worth noticing that feminists and women's organizations in developing countries tend to be more aware of these international agencies and efforts than their counterparts in the United States. For example, Chow et al. (Chapter 8) describe the importance of the U.N. world conferences in helping to legitimize gender/women's studies in China.

The actual status of women's studies and women's research is quite diverse across regions and within regions, as described in the introductions to each regional section of this volume.

FEMINIST RESEARCH APPROACHES

Just as the countries of the world take different paths to activism, there are also differences in feminist research approaches, such as the choice of research methodology and style. As reflected in many of this volume's chapters, qualitative methods are common, while quantitative methods are utilized less frequently (for an exception, see Chapter 20). Indeed, some authors, such as Núñez Sarmiento, writing about Cuba (Chapter 17), argue that qualitative methods better assess women's true concerns and situations. In Cuba's case, lack of research funds for large-scale surveys also render the usage of in-depth interviews or participant observation more expedient. Evidently, a wide range of qualitative methods is used in gender research. For example, Darkwah's (Chapter 4) research on market women uses life histories, Crespo-Kebler's (Chapter 21) research on reproductive rights uses an historical approach, with a focus on the media, Nguyen et al. (Chapter 12) discuss HIV/AIDS using a policy perspective, and Lombardo (Chapter 28) uses a textual analysis of the European constitution to study gender mainstreaming. Qualitative methods have been critical both to unravel the complex issues in women's private and public sphere lives and to challenge the "objective" and "scientific" stance of quantitative studies. Recently, as qualitative methods have become important in the fields of sociology of gender and women's studies, feminists gradually call for more balance by integrating quantitative methods into feminist studies.

As the focus in feminist studies shifts from women to gender, research on men and masculinities is slowly gaining ground in this field. Valiente (Chapter 24) points out that men's studies in Spain is still in an embryonic state, but attention to the construction of masculinity demonstrates the significance of the intrinsic connection between gender (masculinity) and sexuality (heterosexuality). In addition, Reddock (Chapter 18) shows that applying an intersectionality approach to the analysis of masculinity reveals how gender relations are deeply complicated by racial and class inequalities. And, as an illustrative example, Kwon (Chapter 11) describes the contested masculinities of Korean and U.S. soldiers within complex military power relations that are shaped by the global hierarchies of race, class, education, and political economy.

In addition to research methods and agendas, language is another issue that emerges in feminist research and theorizing. It is undeniable that the feminist intellectual articulations drawn from Anglo-American contexts have had a significant impact on feminist studies in many other countries, often through the dynamics of the global political economy, as well as through transnational feminist linkages. As a result, one of the issues raised in feminist studies pertains to language and terminology. For example, as described in the case of China (Chapter 8), the term "gender" is novel in countries whose language is not rooted in a Latin or romance language system. In those countries, feminists deal with the issue of terminology either by inventing new terms or adapting existing ones, while also trying to avoid linguistic post-colonialism. As Knapp (Chapter 23) points out, language barriers can hinder feminist thoughts developed in non-English speaking countries from traveling back to feminists in the global North.

Language is not the only barrier that can block feminist work from being widely disseminated. Once the research is completed, the global economic status of a country, and its political climate or relative wealth/poverty, can limit the number of outlets in which to publish feminist/gender research. Consequently, research results may be published in the journals of more developed countries outside of the region, reducing local access to knowledge, which occurs for some of the research on Africa; or results may not be published until funds are available, which happened in some resource-poor time periods in Cuba; or research is distributed via the world wide web or in feminist magazines, rather than in poorly supported or non-existent local academic journals—in this case, allowing the research to reach a wide feminist activist audience. It is for this reason that we have included an Appendix on websites for women's research centers in many countries of the world.

GLOBAL TRENDS, REGIONAL TRENDS, AND OTHER DYNAMICS

Just as there is diversity among individual women, based on their intersecting axes of age, race or ethnicity, class, marital status, sexual orientation, religion, or other characteristics, gender research in any specific country will emphasize different issues depending upon that nation's economic, political, social, or cultural setting and history. As a result, one can think about there being transnational, regional, thematic, and unique national trajectories of global gender research.

First, some feminist/gender research concerns are worldwide—and the most universal and critical issue is violence against women. However, the form of violence that becomes a primary feminist activist and research concern may focus on various particular national issues including, wife beating, date rape or rape during war, military prostitution, genital mutilation, bride burning (when dowries are perceived as being too small), and many others.

Second, some feminist activist and research concerns are regional priorities. Many of these regional priorities are defined by economic conditions, such as the influence of neo-liberal reform in Latin America (Chapters 14 and 19), structural adjustment programs in Africa (Chapter 4), post-communist economic changes in Eastern Europe (Chapter 25), or integrating work and family life in Northern Europe (Chapter 27).

Third, some gender research concerns are based on cross-cutting themes that influence a few countries in many regions. For example, health issues such as the transmission of HIV/AIDS to women is especially important in segments of Africa, where infection rates are among the world's highest, or in southeast Asian countries like Thailand, which has had a significant sex tourism industry. Another example can be found in concerns over the connection of religion and the state. As described in Chapter 26, the role of the Catholic Church in transforming Poland from a socialist to a capitalist nation allowed the insertion of Catholic morality into the new post-communist national constitution. As a result, the existence of lesbians, gay, bisexual, or transgender individuals was denied—they have few rights and are rendered completely invisible. Another example can be found in the application of Islam to family law in Africa, as discussed in chapters on Islamic law in Mozambique (Chapter 5) and Senegal (Chapter 6), or its application to education and research in Iran (Chapter 10).

Finally, some research concerns draw on relatively unique national trajectories. For example, in Spain, due to Franco's strong emphasis on women's traditional role in the family during the mid-twentieth century, contemporary feminist researchers tended to avoid issues of the family and instead focused on women's work and politics in the early post-dictatorship years (Chapter 24). Or, in Brazil, researchers have challenged the myth of a national eroticized sexuality (Chapter 20).

There are also specific trajectories in the relationship of social science gender studies to national and transnational feminist movements. Many authors located in developing countries describe the influence of feminist thinking from the global North on activism and research in their own countries: they positively comment on the material support or intellectual influence that has been useful, while also noting problems with certain theories or strategies that do not always fit their own realities, which are shaped in different social, political and cultural contexts, or the biased representations of local women that reinforce western-, white-, or middle-class-centered perspectives. Thus, it is important to promote the circulation of transnational intellectual flows that can inform locally based women's studies and gender research (and vice versa), that connect local organizers and researchers in different nations to one another, and that undermine global patriarchal and capitalist power structures in all their forms. Just as global movements provide impetus for feminist research, the latter also provides the foundation on which activists can strategize and form transnational sisterhood.

Feminist activism can take many forms, as illustrated in these chapters, ranging from small local groups (Japan in Chapter 13), to national groups that function as non-governmental organizations advocating for women (India in Chapter 9), to the development of "national machineries for women" that have become increasingly common on the global stage (Europe in Chapter 28), especially outside of the United States.

A relevant example is the concept of "gender mainstreaming," first introduced in the 1985 Third Women's World Conference in Nairobi, which has been propelled since the 1995 Beijing Conference as a new intergovernmental strategy of the CSW. This approach has been especially popular in the European Union. The goal of this approach is to adopt a gender perspective in all its policies and programs, "assessing the impact on women and men of any planned action," but more importantly, promoting gender equality as its "ultimate goal" (United Nations 2002: 5). However, besides the customary conceptual debate about the benefits of having a major global initiative focusing on "gender" rather than "women," the other limitations in the implementation of gender mainstreaming are widely discussed, especially in Europe and Africa. As Lombardo describes (Chapter 28), the feminist political dilemma is how to strategically incorporate gender mainstreaming into policy-making, while maintaining feminist agendas that challenge patriarchal domination. She notes that it is easy to end up compromising feminist principles while working in the political arena, but that debates among scholars and practitioners on these issues should go on continuously.

ORGANIZATION OF *GLOBAL GENDER RESEARCH*

In order to cover all of the themes and issues described above, this volume explores research in four regions of the world, using several techniques to insure broad coverage, as well as concrete examples of research in a region and in many of its specific countries. Therefore, first, each regional section begins with an introductory essay that describes some of the socio-historical developments that have shaped key contemporary gender issues for the entire region (Chapters 2, 7, 14, and 22). Second, following each section introduction, there are chapters that provide a broad overview of research topics, important authors, and research methods in specific countries of that region. Next, the sections culminate in several chapters that are samples of post-2000 research carried out in additional countries within the same region. These countries were chosen to represent typical research within a region, but also with the objective of covering a wide variety of issues in the entire book. Finally, so that readers can find the most contemporary research in a broad spectrum of countries, we include a listing of Websites of International Women's Research Centers (Appendix 1) that incorporates all the countries covered in the articles, plus many additional ones. The world map that appears before this introduction symbolizes the breadth of our coverage by labeling countries discussed in the book's chapters in dark gray and additional countries that have only website listings in light gray.

We have intentionally chosen not to include essays on the sociology of gender in the United States, even as part of the section on the Americas. There are already many volumes entirely devoted to this subject, and U.S. sociology of gender or other feminist social science paradigms already are dominant and well known worldwide. We argue that the onus is on U.S. gender studies students and scholars to incorporate the kinds of original material and insights that these international perspectives present, and to diversify the coverage given in typical U.S.-based gender studies readers—rather than this book incorporating U.S. perspectives. Nonetheless, the United States is still present in many of these essays as a point of comparison by which some authors note similarities or differences with U.S. gender research and issues, or the influence of U.S. scholarship in their respective nations. Our intent is not to deny that the United States is an important part of the global picture, but rather not to use it as a standard by which to judge other countries' developments in gender studies. Our goal is to provide balance to material that is generally and predominantly U.S.-based by presenting the voices of scholars from around the world—rather than the usual voices of U.S. scholars describing the world. Thus, we expect that *Global Gender Research* will help shape and define the quickly emerging field that one might call global sociology of gender, global gender studies, or international women's studies by making use of indigenous gender/women's research from around the globe. As gender studies have "gone global," it could be argued that the United States is no longer the world leader in identifying the key global issues in this field. Indeed, some have argued that the African Union's formal stance on gender issues is among the most progressive (Adams 2006), and that African women can learn from the mistakes made by others.

Our goal in this volume is to help feminist scholars and students to be engaged in "feminist solidarity or comparative feminist studies" (Mohanty 2003) by learning about the status of a broad spectrum of women's experiences, their feminist movements and the issues that guide them, and gender/women's studies around the world.

REFERENCES

Adams, Melinda (2006) "Regional Women's Activism: African Women's Networks and the African Union," in M. M. Ferree and A. M. Tripp, *Global Feminism*, New York: New York University Press.

Ashford, Lori and Donna Clifton (2005) *Women of Our World*, Washington, DC: Population Reference Bureau.

Mohanty, Chandra Talpade (2003) *Feminism Without Borders: Decolonizing Theory, Practicing Solidarity*, Durham, NC: Duke University Press.

United Nations, Office of the Special Adviser on Gender Issues and Advancement of Women (2002) *Gender Mainstreaming: An Overview*, New York: United Nations.

SECTION 1

Africa

2 Introduction to Gender Research in Africa 11
   Mary Johnson Osirim, Christine E. Bose, and Minjeong Kim

3 Women's and Gender Studies in English-Speaking Sub-Saharan Africa:
   A Review of Research in the Social Sciences 16
   Akosua Adomako Ampofo, Josephine Beoku-Betts, Wairimū Ngarūiya Njambi,
   and Mary Johnson Osirim

4 Trading Goes Global: Ghanaian Market Women in an Era of Globalization 41
   Akosua K. Darkwah

5 Feminine Injustice 49
   Conceição Osório and Eulália Temba

6 Women, the Sacred and the State 56
   Fatou Sow

CHAPTER 2

Introduction to Gender Research in Africa

Mary Johnson Osirim, Christine E. Bose, and Minjeong Kim

The continent of Africa is extremely diverse, because of its varied climate and geography, religions, languages and cultures, but also because of a history of colonization by multiple European countries, beginning in the fifteenth century. During the late nineteenth century, Britain, Portugal, and France, as well as Germany, Belgium, Spain and Italy, attempted to claim and divide up among themselves the remaining African territory. Because the first three countries became the largest stakeholders, and their languages are still widely spoken in Africa, along with Arabic, Swahili, and other native languages, we have chosen three research articles to represent English, French, and Portuguese speaking Africa. These articles, respectively by Darkwah on Ghana, Sow on Senegal, and Osório and Temba on Mozambique, reflect some of the women's issues within each nation. However, these issues are not purely local, and they have been shaped by current nation-building efforts and transnational economic influences, as well as by the legacies of colonization and pre-colonial dynamics.

During the middle to late twentieth century, and especially from the late 1950s through the 1960s, many African countries achieved their independence. Nonetheless, some countries were independent earlier, and others had to wait until the 1970s and 1980s to achieve that status. A few island-nations remain colonies, even today. This means that most African nations are relatively "new" on the world stage, creating nation-building problems for many of them. To address such issues, the African countries have organized regionally, first through the Union of African States (1958–1962), then the Organization of African Unity (1963–2002), and now through the African Union. Most analysts agree that the formation of the African Union, as a nascent transnational body, has opened a unique opportunity for African women to shape their rights, and to do so based on their own experiences, but with full knowledge of what has or has not worked elsewhere. Therefore, it is not surprising that an important component in African social science gender research is the area of politics, the state, and empowerment for women. This is one of the many topics elaborated in this section's Chapter 3, on the largest group of African countries, entitled "Women's and Gender Studies in English-Speaking Sub-Saharan Africa," by Akosua Adomako Ampofo, Josephine Beoku-Betts, Wairimū Ngarūiya Njambi, and Mary Johnson Osirim.

In this introduction we discuss some of the regional and national dynamics that have shaped feminist social science gender research spanning Anglophone, Lusophone, and Francophone Africa. In addition to women's legal and political rights, already mentioned earlier, two other dimensions—women's equal access to paid work and to education—are almost always fundamental for developing countries like those in Africa, and are reflected in feminist research agendas. Other issues, like gender-based violence, or sexuality and health, are more universal concerns, but they take on unique shape in different countries. In the following sections, we address these research concerns and the conditions that make them important.

We also want to note that universities in Africa have experienced declining resources, especially due to economic restructuring, which tends to shrink the public sector. As a result, it is not always easy for feminist social scientists to publish their work at home. Over the past decade, however, the Annual Gender Institutes of the Council for the Development of Social Science Research in Africa (CODESRIA) and the creation of the journal, *Feminist Africa*, by the African Gender Institute at the University of Cape Town have facilitated the publication of gender studies research on the continent. In addition, not all feminist and gender scholars are university-based, and some work for feminist non-governmental organizations (NGOs).

POLITICS, THE STATE, AND EMPOWERMENT FOR WOMEN

This topic covers a broad range of issues, ranging from government bureaucracies and formal electoral politics to the law and social movements.

Similar to women in the European Union (EU), some feminists in countries of the African Union (AU) hope to achieve women's empowerment through "national machineries for women" which, like "gender mainstreaming" in the EU, are intended to increase the number of women in political office and put women's issues on national agendas. The gender research literature reflects disagreement about the usefulness of this activist approach. It has been advocated by feminists in some of the Anglophone African states such as Zimbabwe, Zambia, Ghana, and Uganda. However, similar to what Lombardo (Chapter 28) describes in Europe, other scholars argue that such national machineries have not addressed women's issues, developed feminist national agendas, nor transformed African (or European) states.

In the past, other approaches have been tried to increase women's representation in the state and place women's issues on policy agendas, including gaining power through the wives of male heads of state, assuring that women technocrats (or "femocrats") are appointed, or using affirmative action quota systems. Needless to say, the "wives" strategy, as described in literature on Kenya by Maria Nzomo or by Amina Mama for Nigeria, as well as others, is both class-biased and ineffective. For the latter strategy involving electoral gender quotas, which are fairly common in Europe, scholars such as Sylvia Tamale have described the often-cited case of Uganda.

Although the number of women in elected political positions has increased especially in Rwanda and throughout the continent, this has been insufficient in addressing women's rights and issues. Thus, some scholars (e.g., Amanda Gouws in South Africa) have argued that in order to see real transformation, transnational feminist networks (TFNs) are needed (along with local civil society organizations and social movements) to create democratic, transformative states that promote gender equality. However, other scholars (e.g., Shireen Hassim, also in South Africa), argue that TFNs that work with state institutions and local organizations tend to be "reformist–minded" and are likely to be co-opted by the state. As a result, there is little major change and there can be too much competition for scarce resources between local groups and TFNs.

Looking at national-based political movements, gender studies scholars also have written about the roles of women's organizations in promoting women's rights in various areas, as well as about women's past participation in liberation wars or nation-building struggles. For example, among the English-speaking nations, anti-colonial wars in Zimbabwe or South Africa provide good examples. Meanwhile, in Portuguese speaking Africa, early gender scholarship in the post-colonial period focused on women's roles in liberation movements in Angola, Mozambique and Guinea-Bissau. Some of these writings were autobiographical accounts of women's actual engagement with revolutionary organizing and building modern nation-states.

Women's and feminist social movements are an increasingly important area for gender studies scholars. Examples include Zimbabwe and Ghana, where Domestic Violence Acts were passed in the latter case as the result of a social movement, or Mozambique where Conceição Osório and Eulália Temba (see Chapter 5) describe women's rights in the context of domestic violence. Gender studies scholars also describe other important movements, including resisting globalization, neo-liberalism, and the power of multinational corporations, especially around oil companies in the Niger Delta.

The law, especially in its interactions with culture, is another key arena shaping women's empowerment. In scholarship from North Africa, the Horn of Africa, and some regions of Francophone and Anglophone West Africa, gender studies scholars have been very concerned with the relationship between women's rights and the state under Islam. In some nations such as Senegal (See Chapter 6 by Fatou Sow), the practice of Islam is central within a secular state. Issues of family law—marriage, divorce, death and inheritance, and legislation around the right of women to work—have been foci of activists and scholars. Nigeria is considered a secular state, but it is actually a federation of 36 states, and there are states in predominantly Muslim Northern Nigeria that historically have existed and functioned under Shari'a law for centuries. However, Shari'a law in Nigeria was extended from the areas of personal and family law in the late 1990s to include criminal law, where illicit sex and adultery have been criminalized. These issues became major concerns during the early 2000s for African gender studies scholars (e.g., Ayesha Imam or Charmaine Pereira) as well as for transnational feminist networks, such as Women Living Under Muslim Laws (WLUML). Researchers in Lusophone Africa have also written quite extensively about family law, bridewealth and polygamy. Scholars from Mozambique have written about the historical role of lobola (bridewealth), the impact of Christianity and the further changes in family law that came with liberation struggles and socialism.

WORK, EDUCATION, AND GLOBALIZATION

Throughout sub-Saharan Africa, work in agriculture, micro-enterprises, or other parts of the informal sector constitute the major areas of income earning for women—something much less common in Europe or North America. African gender studies scholars have addressed this issue over the past 25 years or so, as described in a section of Chapter 3 of this volume.

Although women's participation in the formal sector of African economies has generally increased during the past two decades, structural adjustment policies (SAPs), as part of globalization, posed serious challenges for women's economic and educational achievement. From the mid-1980s through the 1990s, structural adjustment policies were enacted in over 40 African nations. As the civil service and other formal sector occupations began to shrink during this period, more and more women turned to the informal sector to support themselves and their families. Even women who had tertiary level education began to turn to this sector to find alternatives to keep their families afloat, and more women became involved in transnational trade, as described by Akosua Darkwah for Ghana (see Chapter 4). Ironically, such informal transnational trade between Asia and West Africa became far more lucrative for Ghanaian women during adjustment and liberalization than remaining as teachers or working in other civil service jobs.

Economic adjustment and political crises have created other substantial problems for the African economy. They have contributed to a brain drain, including African women who left positions in universities, hospitals and other government bureaucracies to obtain more stable employment abroad. This was evident in most African nations, but perhaps especially in Zimbabwe, Liberia, Sierra Leone and Nigeria, although with the exception of Zimbabwe, less so now than in the past. In addition, economic crisis and globalization have led to increases in various forms of human trafficking and in the number of sex workers, including those leaving to practice their trade abroad and those engaged in such work locally. This has become an important means of making a living but, of course, has major consequences for sexually transmitted diseases, especially HIV/AIDS.

The growth in women's poverty is also related to displacement and refugee status caused by wars and various armed conflicts in Africa. Lusophone scholars have documented this for Angola and Mozambique. Violent struggles in the Horn and in West Africa also contributed significantly to the population of refugees in the United States, especially for such nations as Eritrea, Ethiopia and Liberia.

Gender inequality in formal education has a long history in Africa, and is linked to the vestiges of colonialism that persist, as well as to African patriarchy and contemporary economic issues. During colonialism and in its aftermath, those women who could receive formal education received less than their male counterparts and this was highly gendered. Women were taught basic arithmetic, reading, and home-economics-type courses, whether they lived in colonized settler nations (e.g., Kenya, Zimbabwe, South Africa) or non-settler environments (e.g., Nigeria, Ghana). More recently, structural adjustment programs in African countries led to increases in user fees (school fees for education) and, when coupled with African patriarchy, many young women were removed from schools. If families were poor or had low income, young women were removed from school before young men, since women had more limited prospects in the labor market, and male wage earners were still regarded as the breadwinners and thus, were needed to support parents in their old age.

African gender researchers now are turning their attention to gender inequality, not only in student access to education, but also in terms of access and resource issues for women faculty. One of the more recent issues of the journal *Feminist Africa* was dedicated to this topic. In one such article, Rudo Gaidzanwa from the University of Zimbabwe (who was a leader in their affirmative action program to increase the representation of women students in under-represented fields and of women faculty) talks about the increased alienation these days among faculty members. Not only have faculty members had to strike for basic needs (wages, benefits, etc.) but even the physical structure of the university and the types of engagement that used to exist (the healthy debates of political views) are now jeopardized in the university community because of Zimbabwe's crisis.

SEXUALITY, HEALTH, AND GENDER-BASED VIOLENCE

Sexuality is a key site of women's subordination, and it is an area that is receiving more attention in African gender research. Both European colonists (or European patriarchy) and African patriarchy have attempted to control African women's sexuality, particularly through the development of "customary law," as described in the politics section above. In many cases, women's bodies and sexuality have been described as "dirty" unless the discussion is about reproduction; and in particular, African gender studies scholars have written about women's distinctive initiation into becoming sexual adults in Uganda, Angola and other nations. Meanwhile, gay, lesbian, bisexual and transgendered issues have been most significantly addressed by gender studies scholars in southern Africa, particularly in South Africa and Zimbabwe. In the former case, scholarship on sexuality has occurred in conjunction with their more progressive constitution. However, debates about sexuality and sexual preference are not limited to that region.

Lack of many basic health resources renders reproductive health a critically important issue for women throughout the continent. And HIV/AIDS is still a critical public health issue, especially in parts of sub-Saharan Africa. It is clearly linked to issues of patriarchy, sexual freedom/control, gender-based violence, poverty, poor health care and labor migration. The highest rates of HIV/AIDS today are in southern African, especially Botswana, Zimbabwe and South Africa, but Nigeria also has a large number of persons with HIV/AIDS (the third largest in the world after India and South Africa) due to its status as the most populous nation in Africa (although a lower percentage of the overall population is infected as compared to its southern African neighbors). Not surprisingly, these are important areas of investigation for gender studies scholars in several African countries. Meanwhile, women have also had to deal with increased violence in periods of political crises and wars, such as in Rwanda, the Democratic Republic of the Congo, Zimbabwe and even Kenya, which experienced violence around its election results (December to January 2008), leading to an increase in rapes and beatings of women.

Despite the major challenges posed by economic and political crises in African states, gender studies researchers on the continent are making major contributions to scholarship by and about African women. In this regard, they are expanding the theoretical and empirical debates in global feminist and gender studies and contributing to the overall advancement of women.

CHAPTER 3

Women's and Gender Studies in English-Speaking Sub-Saharan Africa: A Review of Research in the Social Sciences

Akosua Adomako Ampofo, Josephine Beoku-Betts, Wairimū Ngarūiya Njambi, and Mary Johnson Osirim

HISTORICIZING WOMEN'S STUDIES AND GENDER STUDIES IN AFRICA

Since the 1980s, there has been a proliferation of women's and gender research in Africa (Lewis 2002; Mama 1995, 1996; Manuh 2001; Nzomo 1998; Pereira 2002). This outgrowth of scholarship can be attributed to several factors, including (but not limited to) the global North women's movement, "the influence of the [women and] development industry, national political [and economic] conditions, the crisis in African education and the emergence of state feminism" (Mama 1996: 4). Prior to this period, in the 1950s and 1960s, women's activism was linked to nationalist struggles for independence. In addition, gender, race, and class relations were already integral to struggles African women were engaged in when compared to their counterparts in the global North, who only began to acknowledge the centrality of these issues in the 1980s (Lewis 2002: 1).

In the 1970s and 1980s, feminist scholarship and activism began to gain a foothold in women and development debates. Many feminists were involved in establishing the Association of African Women for Research and Development (AAWORD) in 1977, with the purpose of "envisioning an agenda for African feminism" through scholarship and activism (Mama 1996: 6). African gender studies, especially in the southern region, are now even more focused on historical and critical political analysis. Much of this work has evolved out of women's involvement with liberation struggles, democratization, and neoliberal economic reforms.[1]

Current approaches to the study of women and gender in Africa are rooted in African feminist as opposed to global North feminist ethnographies and theories. African gender studies specialists are conversant with postmodernist and other current political debates, but some of them caution against overreliance on postmodernist discourses on difference, stressing the need to generate systematic evidence around issues that unify and create space for dialogue rather than confrontation and difference (Nzomo 1998: 13). These studies are closely integrated into wider political struggles and public debates about post independence nation building and globalization (Mama 1996; Manuh 2002). Their concerns center around imperialism, race, class, ethnicity, and geographical differences and they explore the interactions between these factors (Imam 1997; Lewis 2002).

This article provides an overview of some of the issues and contestations addressed since the mid-1980s by feminist and non-feminist scholars and activists based in English-speaking sub-Saharan Africa. Although we recognize that there is substantial scholarship on women and gender studies in Africa written in French, Portuguese, and other languages by African and Africanist scholars, given our regions of specialization and language limitations, we focus mainly on those studies written in English. Specifically, we examine those works that address women's issues written by continental scholars, as this area of feminist scholarship on Africa has been largely invisible and silent in feminist discourses in the global North. We also review African gender studies in the social sciences, which on the continent are largely concentrated in the fields of sociology, history, anthropology, political science, and education and approached from a multidisciplinary perspective. Topics are selected from issues ratified by African women in the African Platform for Action, the regional document prepared for the World Conference on Women in 1995. We identified common issues in feminist social science debates, including health, gender-based violence, education (mainly higher education, due to space limitations), globalization and work, and politics, the state, and nongovernmental organizations. Sexuality was added to the list of topics, given its growing importance in African feminist studies.

RECONCEPTUALIZING METHODOLOGICAL PARADIGMS

To understand the state of social science research in Africa, most scholars emphasize the impact of the economic and political crisis on funding and institutional support for higher education (Makandawire 1997; Sawyer 1994). Thus, many scholars focus on Women in Development consultancies and donor-driven research at the expense of independent theoretical and innovative empirical research (Imam and Mama 1994; Kassimir 1998; Mama 1997; Nzomo 1998). The productivity of African social scientists is also impeded by the shortage of current publications, few publishing outlets, heavy teaching and administrative responsibilities, a repressive and hostile intellectual climate, and patriarchal institutional cultures (Bennett 2002; Imam and Mama 1994; Manuh 2002; Pereira 2002; Prah 2002). Studies on women are also less likely to receive funding from governments, as demonstrated in the dearth of gender disaggregated data and the general failure to incorporate women and gender in development policies (Imam and Mama 1994; Manuh and Adomako Ampofo 1995; Tsikata 2001c).

As in the global North, social science scholarship on women and gender has revitalized African social science production in the past two decades (Imam et al. 1997). The notion that research methods and techniques are atheoretical has been challenged, as are the false ideas of scientific neutrality and the separation of politics, theory, and methods (Adomako Ampofo 2004; Imam and Mama 1994; Steady 1986; Tsikata 2001d). Marxist social science research has also been criticized for its hostile and/or dismissive treatment of feminist issues (Graham 2001; Imam 1997).

In examining research on women and gender, quantitative methods are still viewed as more scientific than qualitative methods, and large-scale social surveys and formal interview techniques are most widely used in disciplines like sociology (Imam et al. 1997). Qualitative methods are increasingly gaining preference because they foreground the experiences and voices of the research participants as well as incorporate other important factors that define the everyday life practices of women and men (Echo Magazine 2001; Gana Shettima 1998).

The use of various forms of historical methods, such as oral history and autobiographical and biographical studies, helped redefine conventional understandings of various historical events and processes (Lewis 2002). Many of the life history studies show

how the public sphere/private sphere dichotomy never accurately reflected the African experience and illustrate the distinctive ways in which women exercised agency in the pre-independence period by subverting conventional understandings of appropriate gender relations (e.g., Denzer 1995; Johnson-Odim and Mba 1997; Mbilinyi 1989; Mukurasi 1991; Shawulu 1990; Tsikata 1989).

In the area of theory, recent research in African gender studies takes a multidisciplinary approach, while integrating theory and practice with a view to restructuring power relations. Theory is also grounded in qualified generalizations that are context specific (Imam et al. 1997; Mama 2004).

CONFLICTS AND CONTESTATIONS IN WOMEN'S STUDIES AND GENDER RESEARCH IN AFRICA

At the center of questions regarding the relevance and application of research on women's and gender studies in Africa is how to name these concepts in ways that would "allow for a collective imagining of the concept" (Jita Allan 2001: 73). For example, while some African scholars have identified their work as "feminist," and recognize the relationship between activism and intellectualism in the liberation of women, many (especially male scholars who do studies of women) have rejected the term. Others have opted for the term "gender" or "women's" studies as more neutral (see critiques by Mama 1995, 1996 and Imam 1997 on this debate). Imam (1997), for instance, argues that as a discipline, women's studies have always had a political gender consciousness in their recognition of gender subordination. Despite the lack of consensus among scholars and activists about these concepts and in various efforts to foster transformative relations between women and men in Africa, the concept of gender remains a crucial rhetorical tool for some.

Also problematized are high-profile national programs launched by first ladies in the 1980s, such as those launched by the wives of Rawlings of Ghana and Babangida of Nigeria, to improve the lives of rural and marginalized women. African feminist scholars view this as the governmental appropriation of feminism for agendas that have very little to do with the liberation of African women (Abdullah 1993; Mama 1995, 1996; Tsikata 2001a). In the next section, we review social science research on the specific themes of (1) health, (2) gender-based violence, (3) sexuality, (4) education, (5) globalization and work, and (6) politics, the state, and nongovernmental organizations.

THEMES IN WOMEN'S STUDIES AND GENDER RESEARCH IN AFRICA

Health

Issues of women's health in Africa, particularly women's reproductive health, have been the focus of much research in both the social and biomedical sciences, and from a multidisciplinary perspective. However, this work has tended to take an instrumental, "developmentalist" approach, assuming that women's health is influenced by the trickle-down effect of modernization and democracy (Lewis 2002). Thus, women's issues have been constructed in biological terms with a focus on their reproductive health, highlighting the magnitude of maternal morbidity and mortality. Some scholars have pointed out that this approach is entrenched with cultural and Eurocentric stereotypes of women as mothers and wives and that it neglects the variety of women's health concerns (Boadu 2000) and their contributions as providers of health care services (Boadu 2000). Thus, women's studies scholars in Africa not only have sought to respond to the Western gaze and Eurocentric concepts but also have highlighted areas for critical enquiry such as the practices of traditional healers (Adomako Ampofo 2004; Machera 2004; Ratele 2004).

Recent studies on health have looked at how specific gendered traditions such as those within marriage institutions (e.g., early marriage, polygyny, seclusion, wife inheritance) and other cultural practices such as female genital cuttings influence women's maternal morbidity and their mortality and fertility behavior (Ezumah and Oreh 1999). They also address the importance of women's "status," measured primarily by education or reproductive behavior. However, the limitations of relying on structural measures to the neglect of other sources of power and authority such as seniority have been pointed out (Adomako Ampofo 2002; Tagoe 1995).

The establishment of the *African Journal of Reproductive Health* in 1993 made an important contribution toward highlighting the gendered dimensions of women's reproductive health, as did some continental and national organizations.[2] Before the International Conference on Population and Development held in Cairo in 1994, reproductive health policies in sub-Saharan Africa were linked to population policies and focused on lowering population growth, hence "helping" women to "control" their fertility. African feminist scholars have criticized the objectification of women and cultural hegemony that occurred when the population enterprise reached Africa (Adomako Ampofo 2002). For example, Adomako Ampofo (2004) has critiqued the demographic concept of "unmet need," pointing out that it neglects the centrality of notions of masculinity, and hence male dominance, in human reproduction. Using both quantitative and qualitative methods, she has questioned the (over) reliance on traditional knowledge, attitude, practice–style survey questions in the measurement of demographic concepts such as the "unmet need" (for contraception).[3]

Teenage pregnancy has largely been constructed as a health problem (Katapa 1998), with scholars noting the physical and emotional challenges of becoming a mother as well as the contradictions that arise from this new concept created by the recent gap between onset of menarche and marriage. Important work appears in the volume *Chelewa Chelewa* (Komba-Maleka and Lijestrom 1994) that grew out of the Teenage Girls and Reproductive Health Study Group's work at the University of Dar es Salaam. Although the authors paint unmarried girls who become pregnant as active agents who can succeed in their lives (Katapa 1998), they also point to the health risks of early, and often repeated, pregnancies that are associated with poverty, sexual exchange, and the failure to use family planning. On the other hand, Mbilinyi (1985) has suggested that in focusing on teenage pregnancies (with attendant issues of prostitution, induced abortions, and baby dumping), African feminists may have unwittingly promoted a "bad girl" image of the pregnant teen by neglecting the boys or men who make them pregnant and young women's rights to reproductive health information and services.

Inherent in feminist scholarly and activist discourse is the discussion of women's reproductive rights. Nonetheless, Ilumoka (2003) argues that the "rights discourse" requires scrutiny and that the field of reproductive rights (and human rights and women's rights) is an arena of struggle for African women to define their own agendas devoid of (ethnocentric) assumptions about the backwardness of African customs.

In much of Africa, women's right to reproductive health services, especially access to safe abortions, remains a concern. However, the issues continue to be hotly debated, and the subject of abortion remains contentious, revealing that there is no universal position for feminists across the African continent. Lewis (2002) points out how colonial authorities, especially in eastern and southern Africa, adopted campaigns to contain the population growth of Black people through the use of harmful injectibles and forced sterilization in Namibia and South Africa. Consequently, fertility control has been tainted with Malthusian images of enforced demographic control (Adomako Ampofo 2004; Lewis 2002). Bradford's (1991) work describes how the apartheid state urged white women to have babies while temporarily and permanently sterilizing Black women. Abortion was also used by the state, and by individual men, to control unwanted female fertility (Bradford 1991). So while abortion challenges patriarchal controls and reduces maternal mortality, patriarchy is also manifested in male-inspired abortions that seek to control women's bodies (Mpangile et al. 1998).

Research on women's experiences with, and responses to, HIV/AIDS is a vast and rapidly expanding field. Women's gender roles and the constructions of femininity and masculinity—such as behavior that sanctions polygyny, extramarital relations, and multiple partners for men as well as the enormous work burdens that many women confront—make women particularly vulnerable to HIV infection and result in poor care when they become infected (Adomako Ampofo 1998; Awusabo-Asare et al. 1993; Mbilinyi and Kaihula 2000). Particular attention has been paid to the perceptions of men's and women's sexual rights and whether women can refuse to have sex with their partners (Awusabo-Asare et al. 1993; Rajani and Kudrati 1996). Thus, Awusabo-Asare et al. (1993) points out that some women consider it hopeless to expect fidelity from their partners and feel unable to refuse to have sex with nonmonogamous partners. The general consensus is that many women lack control over their sexuality, are unable to refuse sex to nonmonogamous partners, are unable to insist on or negotiate condom use, and it is male dominance in sexual matters that increases women's vulnerability (Adomako Ampofo 1995;

Awusabo-Asare et al. 1993; Mbilinyi and Kaihula 2000; Rajani and Kudrati 1996). The link between women's economic dependence on men and their vulnerability has also been addressed. For younger women, this is compounded by the fact that many adult men actively seek younger partners who are perceived to be free of HIV (Rajani and Kudrati 1996). Rajani and Kudrati (1996) also point out that there has been an overemphasis on the role of adults to the neglect of potentially risky peer encounters. For example, among street children, rape is frequently used as an expression of power (Adomako Ampofo et al. 2004; Rajani and Kudrati 1996). There are other women's concerns around HIV/AIDS. Long's (1996) work conveys how gender also gives women the burden of responsibility for protecting and taking care of themselves, their partners, and their families. McFadden (1992) argues that the medicalization of AIDS prevents understanding of the sociocultural circumstances that invariably affect its transmission, its prevention, and the treatment of those infected.

Research on women's health and well-being has been politicized by linking it to gender-based violence, health care services, economic and political forces, and issues such as the control of women's sexuality. Thus, the effect of structural reforms on women's access to health care and their health-seeking behavior has received some attention (Emeagwali 1995; Manuh 1998). In this context, groups considered to be particularly vulnerable have received attention, such as women in conflict/war situations and refugee women. Theorizing around health is also expanding to include the link between women's social roles and their health and women's mental health (Boadu 2000). Boadu's (2000) work on the mental health of female doctors, nurses, and stone quarry workers in Ghana, for instance, highlights the fact that for women, health problems are dominated by psychosocial considerations such as social relationships, work, and mothering roles. The relationship between women's health and well-being and gender-based violence highlights the need for more comprehensive studies on how violence affects women's lives. The following section will examine key issues relating to gender-based violence in Africa.

Gender-Based Violence

Relatively unspoken of until the 1990s (Coker-Appiah and Cusack 1999; Mama 1997), gender-based violence is a widespread and escalating phenomenon in Africa. As in the global North, the relative silence is due to the fact that most victims do not report incidences of gender-based violence. Reported cases are rarely documented because they are viewed as a domestic and private matter. Most countries also do not have customary or statutory laws to protect women from violence, although there are laws against assault and some contexts of rape. Since the 1990s, there has been increasing pressure from women's nongovernmental organizations to institute legislation against gender-based violence in such areas as rape, wife battering, and sexual harassment (Armstrong 1990; Bennett 1999; Carol and Ofori-Atta 1998; Coker-Appiah and Cusack 1999; Ofei-Aboagye 1994).[4] A wealth of advocacy-oriented research based on country and regional case studies has been produced, particularly in South Africa, to support this effort. One of the accomplishments of this advocacy process has been that the Rwanda War Crimes Tribunal recognized gender-based violence as an instrument of genocide and a crime against humanity and tried such cases at the tribunal.

Violence is also being examined from a structural context, with emphasis on the historical, social, political, and economic conditions that foster it, allow women to tolerate it, and empower men to perpetrate abuses against women (Ibeanu 2001; Mama 1997; Odendaal 1993). For example, Mama (1997) explains how colonialism was both a violent and a gendered process that exploited preexisting social divisions within African culture. The coercive control of women that was endemic to colonialism—e.g., rape as a form of military conquest and the domestication of women—has continued in the post independence period and has been sanctioned by repressive political regimes. A structural perspective therefore broadens understanding of the connections between the physical, sexual, and psychological impacts of violence and such issues as access to resources, reconciliation, reintegration, and long-term peace building (Ibeanu 2001).

General themes covered in gender-based violence research in Africa are domestic violence (e.g., wife battering, assault of cowives in polygamous marriages, assault on maids and foster children by women employers/guardians, and assault on mothers and grandmothers), sexual violence (e.g., rape, incest, sexual harassment, and female genital cutting, the latter of which is generally perceived to be popularized and sensationalized in Western scholarship and lobbying; see Lewis 2002), traditional practices defined as violence (e.g., child marriage and accusation of witchcraft), and the role of the state in relation to violence (e.g., conflict situations, institutional violence, and economic violence).

Wife battering is the most prevalent yet underreported form of violence against women in Africa (Abane 2000; Atinmo 2000; Coker-Appiah and Cusack 1999; Gizaw 2002; Kuenyehia 1998; Machera 2000; Ofei-Aboagye 1994). In most countries, feminists describe it as a way of life for many women, irrespective of class and ethnic background (Abane 2000; Atinmo 2000; Carol and Ofori-Atta 1998; Coker-Appiah and Cusack 1999; Gizaw 2002). Cultural understandings of men's right to control women lead many societies to condone the physical disciplining of women and girls (Gizaw 2002; Machera

2000; Ofei-Aboagye 1994; Prah and Adomako Ampofo forthcoming). For example, a study of 50 women clients attending a legal aid clinic in Ghana found that women used the terms "beating" and "disciplining" interchangeably and accepted some level of beating as disciplining, although excessive beating was considered deplorable (Ofei-Aboagye 1994). Given that not all behaviors that are claimed to be tradition or culture are actually static or of value, some scholars advocate deconstructing their meanings and using historical analysis to investigate the origins of those practices that are oppressive (Imam 1997).

Rape is another problem that goes unreported because the rapists are usually known to the victims and because of the stigma associated with the victims and their relatives (Armstrong 1990; Carol and Ofori-Atta 1998; Coker-Appiah and Cusack 1999). As in the global North, females who are victims of rape are usually blamed and ridiculed for inviting attention through body language and dress. Thus, girls and women who have been raped are sometimes married off quickly to protect the family (Carol and Ofori-Atta 1998). Although there are laws against assault in many countries, forced sex within marriage is not viewed as rape (Coker-Appiah and Cusack 1999).[5] Rape is also linked to the growing pace of urbanization and widening class disparities in many African cities (Odendaal 1993).[6]

As in other parts of the world, in Africa women are victims of rape in conflict and war situations, such as the civil wars in Rwanda and Sierra Leone. Studies in Africa reveal that rape and the forcible abduction of women are strategies of war that are systematically used to assert power over ethnic groups, by overpowering "their" women (Turshen 1998). Ibeanu's (2001) study of the Ogoni sociopolitical and economic crisis in Nigeria in the 1990s is an example of how women are treated under conditions of civil conflict.[7]

The issue of the state's role in conflict-based violence against women in Africa has been further addressed in a number of studies. Feminist scholars are especially concerned with how the social construction of masculine aggression gains social acceptance through the state's complicity with the use of violence, either overtly or by its silence, during war and peacetime, and the adverse implications for women in those social spaces (Coker-Appiah and Cusack 1999; Imam 1997; Kuenyehia 1998; Turshen and Twagiramariya 1998). Most of the studies that address these issues are based on qualitative research. Topics addressed include the transmission of sexually transmitted diseases and HIV/AIDS, pregnancy as a consequence of rape, the gendered effects of displacement and dislocation, the vulnerabilities women refugees face during flight from their homes, and the psychological and economic implications for women who lose their husbands and lands in the aftermath of civil conflicts.

Studies have also examined how women are used by the legal system to reinforce gender stereotypes through the monitoring and policing of their activities, to the extent of criminalizing their activities as deviant. Tibatemwa-Ekirikubinsa's study *Women's Violent Crime in Uganda* (1999; cited in Lewis 2002) is based on case studies that show how gender biases are built into the legal system, resulting in a lack of legal recourse for women. To advocate for gender-equitable legislative reforms, several women's nongovernmental organizations, such as Women Living under Muslim Laws and Women and Law in South Africa, have conducted advocacy research studies designed to examine existing laws of particular countries and to establish what rights and practices exist so as to determine the impact of these laws.

African gender scholars are particularly active in advocating for legislative changes in how international instruments such as the Convention on the Elimination of All Forms of Discrimination against Women (CEDAW) and the African Charter on Human and People's Rights have addressed the particular plight of African women refugees and internally displaced women. For example, Oloka-Onyango (1996) points out that international laws have failed to establish adequate mechanisms to address the particular circumstances of women as refugees. He maintains that solutions to these problems can only be effective when there is "a comprehensive reconstruction of the basic premises of international, regional, and domestic human rights law to alter the status of women" (1996: 394).

In sum, much of the work on gender-based violence in Africa takes a structural perspective, emphasizing the connections between the physical, sexual, psychological, economic, social, and political processes at the local and global levels. The following sections build on these emerging research areas by focusing on sexuality and same-sex relationships.

Sexuality

Among the issues currently receiving researchers' attention are the misrepresentation and silencing of African female sexuality and the complex intersecting dimensions of gender, race, religion, and culture as well as same-sex relationships. However, some African feminist scholars and activists have suggested that a strong silence remains regarding the question of female sexuality within African women's and gender studies (McFadden 2001, 2003; Mama 1996; Sexuality 1996). They note that little research has been done regarding sexual desires, homoerotic desires, lesbian relations, and other sexual transformations, including those that may have followed the colonial and decolonization processes as well as impacts of the new global economy. As Mama points out, "Considering that sexuality has been a major area of interest within women's studies

internationally, the first question one asks in surveying African women's studies is why there are so few studies of sexuality" (1996: 39). Both Mama (1996) and Pereira (2003) suggest that these silences need to be understood given racist European fascinations with projecting hypersexuality onto Africans. Feminist scholars such as Mama (1996) and Imam (2001) have carefully addressed various historical records that contribute to the silence on African women's sexuality, such as colonial attitude, appropriation of reductive and sexist ideologies of the family and women's bodies by religious and nationalist movements, representations of HIV/AIDS, and practices of female genital cuttings in the global North. As Mama suggests, "In view of the constraining effects of [female genital cuttings] on female sexuality, one is left to ask, where is the research on traditions which empower women, which give them more, rather than less, control of their sexual and reproductive lives? Given the frequent claims to this effect, why is there not more research on aspects of indigenous cultures which empower women's sexuality?" (1996: 47).

Similarly, in her theorization of practices of Magnomaka and Bolokoli-kêla in Mali, Diallo (2003) questions the mainstream feminist model in the global North, which was used to explain female genital operation practices in Africa while maintaining a silence on other aspects of women's sexuality.[8] She describes the Malian practice of Magnomaka as one of enhancing "sexual pleasure" while another, Bolokoli-kêla, served to "hinder" women's sexuality.

Even with such strong silence, a number of studies have emerged recently in Africa that view sexuality from multiple theoretical and methodological approaches (see especially Ahanmisi 1992; Akitunde 2001; Diallo 2004; Gays and Lesbians of Zimbabwe 1999; Imam 2001, 2002; Kahyana 2002; Kerata Chacha 2002; Long 2001; McFadden 2003; Mama 1996; Muthien 2003; Muzaki

2002; Ratele 2004; Tadesse 1997). Such studies have looked at sexuality not only as an interdisciplinary question but also as an issue that cannot be separated from African women's racialized and gendered histories and other social, political, religious, and economic relations. They combine feminist theory with postcolonial theories and analyses of critical race, sexuality, and cultural studies to address the complexities of sexuality practices in Africa today, and they also explore practices of resistance and empowerment as important elements of female sexuality.

In examining the intersections of sexuality with gender, race, culture, and identity politics, some scholars have problematized orthodox disciplines and their essentializing notions of identity formations. For example, in one study of sexuality politics in contemporary South Africa, Ratele asks

> If questions about sex deserve any seriousness, even if it's only because many people around the world still find inter-racial, inter-ethnic, inter-cultural, or inter-religious coupling irritating or at best titillating, should critical scholars and activists not come out and advocate inter-group sex education as part of gender-conscious antiracism, multiculturalism, or religious and ethnic tolerance?
>
> (2004: 1)

A particular aspect of sexuality and identity that has not received much attention is homosexual relationships. A few writers have broken the silence and have urged scholars to seriously question practices of heteronormativity and to promote discussions about sexual orientation (Gays and Lesbians of Zimbabwe 1999; Long 2001; McFadden 2001; Machera 2000; Muthien 2003). These issues are addressed in the next section.

Same-Sex Relationships

There are several kinds of discussions of same-sex relationships in Africa. While some studies question notions that homosexuality in Africa is taboo and "unAfrican" (Muthien 2003; Tamale 2003; Yahaya 2003), organizations such as Gays and Lesbians of Zimbabwe focus on universal human rights standards and how they "can be used by sexual minorities to claim equality and freedom from discrimination" (Gays and Lesbians of Zimbabwe 1999: 1).[9]

Another important topic is the practice of woman-to-woman marriage. For example, building on an earlier study that looked at such marriage practices from the perspectives of the women involved (Njambi and O'Brien 2000), Kerata Chacha's study of woman-to-woman marriage in Tanzania presents it "as a system that radically disrupts the male domination and allows women to traverse gender barriers in order to gap up or rectify reproductive, social and economic problems—by examining it within the framework of colonial judicial systems against African customary law" (2002: 3). Perspectives among scholars vary on the issue of sexuality between such women, with no generalizable account possible, although the issue needs more careful study. Nonetheless, same-sex relationships should not necessarily be conflated with same-sex sexual relations. For example, see the pioneering work on woman-to-woman marriage in Nigeria by Amadiume (1987).

A number of gender and women's studies scholars have also looked at the relationship between religious (and/or traditional) practices and sexuality practices. These studies have problematized the fundamentalist religious views of female sexuality and have been critical of reductive approaches that tend to treat all cultural and religious practices as a single and interchangeable discourse. For example, in her studies of Muslim religious discourses on sexuality, Imam suggests, "Issues of divorce, seclusion, and even access to education all have implications for considerations of sexuality. That they vary points to the need to recognize and distinguish different Muslim discourses of sexuality" (2001: 18).

Education

This section addresses the history and theory of education and the role of education in the struggle for social justice and gender equality in Africa. Of particular importance to African feminist scholars and activists is the impact of imposed formal educational systems on African societies under colonialism. For example, Gaidzanwa (1997) explains how in Zimbabwe, colonial women's education was designed to prepare women as housewives and subsistence farmers. In contrast, education in precolonial African societies served a conceptual and practical purpose designed to fit the needs of the social and physical environment. While recognizing the existence of gender hierarchies in various social and political contexts, women did participate at very complicated intellectual levels in leadership positions, such as in spiritual belief systems; in state matriarchal political systems; in secret societies; and through everyday activities, in agriculture, family management, trade, and health care provision (Assie-Lumumba 1997, 2001).

Several scholars have also analyzed the unintended effect of the colonial educational system in creating critical and subversive minds that challenged its own presence. For example, middle-class women's organizations such as the Forum for African Women's Education and the Association of African Women for Research and Development have played significant roles in demanding more gender equity in education throughout the continent (Assie-Lumumba 2001; Etta 1994; Gaidzanwa 1997).

The effects of gender discrimination at the primary, secondary, and tertiary levels are key issues in postcolonial research on women and education in Africa (Assie-Lumumba 2001; Gaidzanwa 1997; Katapa and Ngaiza 2001; Mbilinyi 1998; Prah 2002; Tamale

and Oloka-Onyango 2000). Empirical studies in different regions focus on gender disparities in specific contexts measured by access, completion rates, attainment levels, curriculum content, and feminization of certain fields. Studies suggest that while much has been done by many governments to rhetorically and legislatively support regional and international conventions and declarations to redress gender disparities in education, most have failed to implement these intentions strategically and programmatically, especially at the tertiary level (Etta 1994; Meena 2007; Mondoh and Mujidi 2006). According to some there is a need for skill and capacity building to mainstream gender in core development sector areas like education (Meena 2007), while others stress that to avoid negative political consequences for marginalized groups, it is necessary to critically examine the factors that determine which aspects and categories of the educational system are expanding (Gaidzanwa 1997). Others point to the increasing dependency of African governments on external donors, leading to loss of autonomy over the process of educational reforms (Mlama 2007).

In analyzing patterns of gender inequity in education, studies have also explored the interlocking impact of race, class, ethnicity, and regional differentiation on women's lives. For example, South African women represent diverse race and class categories with implications for their positioning in the educational and labor market structure. While significant strides have been taken through affirmative action policies to address both race and gender inequities in education, women still dominate low level administrative and non-professional positions in the labor market, years after the dismantling of apartheid (Higgs 2007; Moja 2007). Similarly, negative parental attitudes and cultural practices adversely impact enrollment and retention rates for girls in rural regions of many African countries.

Gender scholars also draw attention to specific factors that exacerbate educational problems for girls, especially those in secondary school. These are early marriage, teenage pregnancy, sexual violence at the primary and secondary school levels, domestic and agricultural responsibilities, the feminization of certain forms of employment, and potential unemployment. Some scholars also question the effects of discriminatory policies that condone punitive attitudes toward young women's sexuality, such as when pregnant schoolgirls are expelled from secondary school whereas the men or boys who father their children are not held accountable (Assie-Lumumba 1997; Etta 1994; Moja 2007). The rising HIV/AIDS pandemic in Africa has also affected the educational sector in regard to the large numbers of teachers who are dying as well as orphans without support for schooling. Young girls are particularly vulnerable to the disease as a result of rape and coerced sex and their school drop-out rates are higher than male counterparts because of increased domestic responsibilities in taking care of sick parents, and siblings after the death of parents (Mlama 2007).

The impact of neoliberal reforms, especially structural adjustment programs (SAPs), is also pertinent. The general consensus is that SAPs have weakened the state's ability to provide basic education to its citizens (Mbilinyi 1998). Some observe that the growing privatization of primary and secondary schools and the adverse effects of severe government cutbacks have kept many poor children away from school and have had a disproportionate effect on women and girls (Assie-Lumumba 1997; Etta 1994; Gaidzanwa 1997; Katapa and Ngaiza 2001; Kwesiga 2002; Mbilinyi 1998; Otunga 1997). For example, despite the expansion of free or subsidized primary education, there are fewer girls relative to boys entering secondary schools, and the potential applicant pool for women entering university,

and ultimately professional and administrative careers, remains small, especially in scientific institutions (Assie-Lumumba 1997; Gaidzanwa 1997; Kwesiga 2002; Namuddu 1993; Prah 2002).

Some attention has also been given to the need for women's strategic involvement in educational administration and decision making (Mama 1996; Manuh 2002; Prah 2002). Gaidzanwa's (1997) combined qualitative/quantitative study on Zimbabwe reveals that women are concentrated in middle- and lower-level academic positions and that most of them are white. Women are also underrepresented in important committees and as chairpersons of departments. Prah's (2002) study of women faculty at the University of Cape Coast in Ghana concludes that the concerns and needs of women faculty are largely ignored because of their low statistical and political visibility in the workplace. In particular, some study participants complained of male bias in opportunities for career advancement, such as grants, scholarships, and fellowships.

In an effort to redress gender inequity in African higher education institutions, affirmative action programs have been instituted. Studies in Uganda suggest that there is resentment and resistance toward these programs and misogynist attitudes toward women as intellectually less capable than men (Kasente 2002; Kwesiga 2002). Others feel that affirmative action is still a numbers game designed to allow a limited number of women to gain access to higher educational institutions while they continue to be hostile environments for women (Mama 1996; Manuh 2002).

Sexual harassment and sexual violence are also endemic problems affecting women students at all educational levels, including women faculty and staff (Gaidzanwa 1997; Hallam 1994; Jelil Ladebo 2003; Kwesiga 2002; Mejiuni Fashina 2000; Phiri 2000; Tamale and Oloka-Onyango 2000). In higher education institutions, some of the key debates pertain to understandings of sexual harassment in situations where students commonly have relations with and marry university staff. Pereira (2002) suggests that distinctions should be made between the concepts of sexual harassment and sexual corruption, the latter being applied to women students who solicit their male lecturers for grades, course entrance, and examination questions. What seems pertinent to understanding these problems is the need for more contextually grounded definitions and concepts that reflect the complexity of gender-based dynamics as manifested in such issues as sexual harassment cases and affirmative action programs (Bennett 2002).

Finally, the emergence of women and gender studies programs in several African universities since the 1990s is significant (Moja 2007; Kasente 2002; Odejide 2002). Although these programs are growing, they remain confined to women students and faculty and have a limited impact on the mainstreaming of gender issues in universities (Tamale and Oloka-Onyango 2000). Nonetheless, there are a number of universities in Uganda, Tanzania, Nigeria, and Ghana that are involved in mainstreaming gender equity concerns, such as affirmative action programs, strengthening women's academic presence and research status, addressing sexual harassment problems, lobbying national policy makers, and maintaining liaisons with the wider women's movement (Bennett 2002). Some argue that with the development of state-coordinated initiatives to promote gender and development, these programs might lose their political force and end up servicing mainstream or conservative gender training and advocacy (Awe, cited in Mama 2000). Whatever the outcome, most studies make it clear that women and gender studies programs provide the critical knowledge base presently needed to harness skill development for gender mainstreaming and to prepare a critical mass of people who can

positively influence educational reforms that promote gender equality (Mlama 2007).

Work and Globalization

During the past 15 years, African gender researchers have significantly expanded the scholarship on women and work in the region (Afonja 1990; Darkwah 2002, 2007; Gana Shettima 1998; Mama 1996; Manuh 1994, 1997; Rutenge Bagile 2002–2003). While they have analyzed the changing roles that women occupy in the formal and informal sectors, many scholars have recently shifted their attention to the effects of SAPs on African women (Fall 1999; Garba and Garba 1999; Nzomo 1995; Pereira 2003; Rutenge Bagile 2002–2003).[10] Previously, they found that African women made important strides in the professions, business, and government, but the majority of African women remained concentrated in agriculture and the microenterprise (informal) sector.

Generally, these scholars concur on several major issues. First, women have been and continue to be engaged in both productive and reproductive labor, which differed in various historical periods and geographical locations. Second, a gendered division of labor exists between women's and men's work. Third, women's labor still remains invisible and devalued yet indispensable to state economies. Finally, women's work has substantially increased in the recent period of economic crisis and adjustment beginning in the mid-1980s (Adepoju 1994b; Magubane 2001; Mama 1996; Manuh 1994, 1997; Masinde 1993; Mbilinyi 1992, 1994; Rutenge Bagile 2002–2003). Mbilinyi (1992) notes that in Tanzania, many women do not prioritize sharing their work with men, even though wives remain responsible for domestic tasks, because they have access to domestic workers or other dependents to do housework. These choices make social transformation less likely.

Some feminist scholars examining women and work engage in critical political analysis and apply the intersectionality perspective in their studies. Using a political economy lens, Benjamin (2001) adds race and imperialism/capitalism to the intersecting factors of gender and class in explaining the position of many working-class women in South Africa. Zimbabwe and South Africa are among the most highly industrialized nations on the continent and have provided more opportunities for formal-sector employment. However, due to South Africa's agreement with the World Trade Organization requiring lower tariffs on clothing and textiles, thousands of women in these sectors have recently lost their jobs in an effort to compete with lower priced imports (Benjamin 2001). During the past 15 years, scholars have noted the loss of about 2.5 million formal-sector positions for women due to economic crises (Adepoju 1994a).

Although most studies of work on the African continent examine women's position in the contemporary period, some scholars trace women's productive and reproductive labors over time. While women's labor was a major component in many precolonial societies, women did not command the labor of others and were not equal to men (Afonja 1990; Mama 1996). During the colonial period, an ideology of domesticity combined with modern capitalism to exclude African women from the formal sector (Mama 1996). Although independence for African states signaled greater educational opportunities for some women, occupational inequality persisted for most women.

Gender scholars highlight women's current participation in formal-sector positions while also acknowledging that men still far outdistance women in such jobs. During the past two decades, women's labor force participation rates have increased most noticeably in the public sector. Research from Kenya documents that women comprised about 21 percent of all employees in the public and the private sector, but about 75 percent of women in public employment were clustered in low-wage, low-status positions (Nzomo 1995). Women in the private sector are concentrated in low-salaried fields such as sales, service, and clerical work, while at the upper end of the spectrum they are clustered in primary and secondary school teaching and nursing (Adepoju 1994b; Mama 1996; Manuh and Adomako Ampofo 1995; Nzomo 1995). Some women have entered medicine, law, business, and academia, but overall, their participation in these areas remains low (Mama 1996). The lack of education and training, gender-segregation in the labor market, lack of access to critical resources, patriarchal cultures, and heavy reproductive burdens limit women's formal-sector employment (Adepoju 1994a; Magubane 2001; Mama 1996).

Most African women work as farmers and/or farm laborers and as entrepreneurs and workers in the microenterprise sector (Manuh and Adomako Ampofo 1995). Women in subsistence agriculture bear the responsibilities for farming and daily farm management particularly due to male labor migration to urban areas (Adepoju 1994b). Despite women's heavy workloads, women often lack the authority to make major decisions (Farah 1989). Muro (1989) argues that agriculture is in decline partly because of the failure to acknowledge women as primary producers. Within formal waged work, women constitute a high proportion of the agricultural laborers. Mbilinyi (1991) observes that the employment of more women as farm workers in Tanzania illustrates the efforts of owners to increase profits because women are often seasonal workers, earning lower salaries than men earn. Women occupy dual roles in agriculture and the microenterprise sector, since women market about 60 percent of the food crops in Africa (Magubane 2001).

During the past two decades, the microenterprise sector has become an increasingly important socioeconomic and political phenomenon (Darkwah 2002; Mama 1996; Rutenge Bagile 2002–2003). More research has been conducted on women's work in this sector than on any other area within African economies. This scholarship is a response to the major increase in the numbers of women and men involved in informal work in the wake of economic crisis and SAPs. In fact, Munguti, Kabui, and Isoilo (2002) stated that poor Kenyan women enter the microenterprise sector as a coping strategy during economic crises. Gender segregation persists since women are concentrated in areas such as food processing, trading, and sewing (Adepoju 1994b; Mama 1996).

Rutenge Bagile (2002–2003) reports that for some women, entering the microenterprise sector improves their economic status, while for others, it means greater burdens. Women still experience discrimination in their lack of access to credit, lack of access to property, low levels of social capital, and police harassment. Moreover, women encountered increased domestic violence since some men felt disempowered by women's financial independence and their enhanced role in decision making (Prah and Adomako Ampofo forthcoming; Rutenge Bagile 2002–2003).

Gender studies scholars have increasingly drawn our attention to the impact of globalization on women's status (Darkwah 2002, 2007; Fall 1999; Magubane 2001; Munguti et al. 2002; Pereira 2003). Most of these scholars agree that globalization and the International Monetary Fund-imposed SAPs have led to the growing feminization of the labor market in low-level positions, an expansion in sex work, an increase in women's workloads, and further feminization of poverty. With the adoption of SAPs in about 40 African nations, governments have retrenched public-sector workers and decreased spending on education, housing, and health care.

Some researchers note that globalization

has created both benefits and problems for African women. Discussing Ghanaian women's engagement in transnational trade, Darkwah (2002, 2007) shows how trade liberalization advantaged women by streamlining access to imported goods such as clothing. She also illustrates how the later devaluation of the Ghanaian cedi jeopardized their position. On the other hand, in Kenya and Uganda, trade liberalization produced some benefits for women, including increased access to employment in nontraditional, export-oriented goods, such as flowers and fruit (Pheko 1999). While trade liberalization provides access to employment for women, these advantages may be limited to the low-wage sector of the labor market (Pheko 1999).

The AIDS epidemic, as well as globalization, has influenced a renewed interest in the subject of sex work and the ambiguities around it. Some accounts portray women's agency and their own positive self-perceptions (Adomako Ampofo 1999, 2007; Mbilinyi and Kaihula 2000; Tekloa 2002), pointing out that for most women, prostitution is an economic strategy selected in the face of increasingly limited economic options. Contrary to some Afrocentric perspectives that seek to portray prostitution as a legacy of colonialism, research in gender and women's studies shows that even though colonialism brought with it the proliferation of urban centers and a cash economy—both of which significantly disrupted power and gender relations, thereby promoting commodified sexual exchanges—forms of commodified sex existed before colonial interventions (Adomako Ampofo 2001; Tekloa 2002). Complex social and gender relations are involved in prostitution. For example, Mbilinyi and Kaihula (2000), in their work in rural Tanzania, show how many rural households depend on women's incomes following men's loss of incomes in agriculture and the formal sector.

Qualitative studies, which create space for

research subjects to be located in their work, also have provided insights into the conditions and experiences of sex work, pointing to the variations by age, status, and location. While older women rarely refer to risks inherent in the work, the younger women's stories are full of fears and insecurities arising from abuses—gang rape, refusal to wear condoms, clients who try to avoid payment, and offensive sexual acts. There is also rivalry and competition. Madams are accused of cheating young protégéés out of money or stealing clothing and jewelry, while the latter say they provide assistance, care, and support (Tekloa 2002).

There are other significant concerns around sexual exploitation, especially trafficking in women and child prostitution, which some argue is based on severe poverty and the ways in which globalization makes human beings easy goods to transport and trade in (Adomako Ampofo 2002). Studies in which sex workers are interviewed frame entry into sex work in economic terms—the failure of a business, nonsupport from partners, the need to care for dependents—and as a stopgap. Scholars point to the failure of the state in discussions of women's struggles for survival, and in the final section, we address issues of the state and nongovernmental organizations.

Politics, the State, and Nongovernmental Organizations

During the past two decades, there has been considerable research on the impact of emerging states and state policy on women's status. Gender scholars have explored the contributions of African women to the continent's liberation wars as well as post independence states' opportunities for women in elected and appointed offices, women's participation in civil society organizations, and the development of feminist politics. While political crises and war characterized many African states in the 1980s and 1990s, Africa also witnessed the establishment of many dynamic nongovernmental women's organizations that offered hope during political turmoil. Through many of these nongovernmental organizations, women resisted structural adjustment and other policies that opposed their needs and struggled for basic human rights (McFadden 2001; Pereira 2003).

Some research on African states has explored women's relationship to independence movements. Despite their commitment to the independence of their nations, as illustrated in their participation in the Zimbabwean liberation war, African women continued to experience subordinate status during the postcolonial period. Working within the intersectionality paradigm, feminist scholars note how the nexus of imperialism, race, class, and gender severely limited women's position, especially during the process of nation building in the newly independent African states (Lewis 2002; McFadden 2001; Nzomo 1993). McFadden (2001) acknowledges that the neocolonial state sought to retard women's basic human rights through the reestablishment of traditional courts and statuses in the legal systems of Zimbabwe and South Africa. Such actions speak to the collusion between men of different classes and races to exclude women from democratic practices and institutions that women fought so courageously to build.

Other feminist scholars have examined how postcolonial states fail women. For example, Nzomo (1993) notes how the patriarchal state largely ignores women's human rights regarding rape, domestic violence, and sexual harassment. Other scholars have explored how the patronizing nature of the postcolonial state created a "femocracy" (Abdullah 1993; Mama 1995, 1996, 2000). Mama defines femocracy as "an antidemocratic female power structure, which claims to exist for the advancement of ordinary women, but is dominated by a small clique of women whose authority derives from their being married to powerful men" (1995: 41).[11] Nzomo (1993) pays similar attention to the emergence of the women's movement in Kenya as symbolized by the National Council of Women of Kenya, which she describes as "muzzled and ineffective." As noted earlier, when discussing national programs launched by African first ladies, scholars studying state-sponsored feminism recognize that the intersection of gender and class can limit the position of poor women in masculinist regimes while enhancing the status of upper-class women (Mama 1995, 1996, 2000; Nzomo 1993; Tsikata 2000).

One way to rectify the underrepresentation of women in politics is through affirmative action, reserved-seat policies such as that adopted by Uganda guaranteeing at least 39 women district representatives in its parliament (Tamale 1999). To discover if these officials were actually representing women's interests, Tamale (1999) interviewed 40 female and 15 male legislators and concluded that even when affirmative action candidates believe they are representing women's interests, they largely speak for educated middle- and upper-class women because members must have completed upper secondary school to occupy a seat. Problems have also been noted in this system at the local level in Uganda where women are elected in a separate process after the conclusion of regular elections (Ahikire 2003). In fact, women's representation remains most challenging at the local levels throughout the continent where affirmative action is largely absent and male privilege is strongest (Hassim 2006). Today, at least ten African nations have used a quota system to increase the number of women in their legislatures. Some feminist scholars have noted that quotas when combined with a proportional representation list system can make a difference in the number of women in African parliaments (Gouws 2004). On the other hand, Hassim (2006) discovered that in southern Africa,

proportional representation gives significant power to party leaders who may choose women who will not challenge the status quo by pursuing feminist policies leading to broader social transformation.

Given these problems, some African scholars think that increasing the numbers of women in elected office is not the best method for improving the status of most women. International treaties combined with activism have been more effective for advancing women's position. African feminist activists and scholars have participated in local and global movements and shared information on women's human rights, particularly concerning sexual rights and reproductive health, customary laws and practices, and economic rights (McFadden 2001; Nigerian NGO 2001). Some studies have highlighted the role of international treaties in advancing African women's human rights. Tamale (2001) has discussed the importance of CEDAW and the African Charter for Human and People's Rights as treaties that can empower women[12] but that have been underutilized because many women feel alienated from such legal instruments. An example of what can be, but rarely is, done is the suit brought by Sarah Longwe against the Intercontinental Hotel in Lusaka, Zambia, for denying entrance to women unaccompanied by men. The judge stated that a court could look to treaties such as CEDAW and the African Charter, which has now been incorporated in national statutory laws, if a matter was not covered under domestic legislation (Tamale 2001).

Although some African women have been successful in applying CEDAW to their cases, feminist scholars and nongovernmental organization activists have drawn our attention to nations whose implementation of CEDAW has been ineffective. Discussing the work of Nigeria's nongovernmental organization CEDAW coalition, Lewis and Imam (2001) have concluded that the Nigerian government inadequately depicted their implementation of CEDAW and also failed to accurately report on the status of Nigerian women, particularly the discrimination of customary laws against women with regard to marriage, family law, and the administration of property (Nigerian NGO 2001).

A series of studies on national machineries in Africa explores the role of international treaties and policies on the status of women. The researchers pointed to some of the major problems in state efforts to implement the treaties when they set up various national machineries such as women's bureaus (Chisala and Nkonkomalimba 2000; Dambe 2000; Mama 2000; Tsikata 2000; Wangusa 2000; Zimbabwe Women's Resource Centre and Network 2000). They noted a lack of political commitment, under-resourcing, ambiguous locations in the state apparatus, and competition from the organizations of first ladies.

Nonetheless, some important achievements were observed among the bureaucracies for women such as the efforts of the Ministry of Community Development and Women's Affairs in Zimbabwe to promote equal pay for equal work (Zimbabwe Women's Resource Centre and Network 2000). In Botswana, they improved gender awareness and the lessening of stereotypes, while in Uganda, the state funded increased research on inheritance, rape, justice, and equity for women (Dambe 2000; Wangusa 2000). The Gender in Development Division offered sensitization workshops to introduce gender analysis to ministries in Zambia (Chisala and Nkonkomalimba 2000).

The past two decades have seen remarkable increases in the number of women's nongovernmental organizations. Even when some African regimes have attempted to silence women in the political realm, women continue to respond to state policies and strive for their full human rights through civil society organizations (Tsikata 2001b). Pereira describes the current focus of such organizations as "the denial of women's

human rights, restricted access to justice, the need for reproductive health, struggles for legal rights and literacy and against human trafficking" (2003: 793–794). Groups such as BAOBAB for Women's Human Rights have drawn international attention in their efforts to inform women of their rights under state, religious, and customary laws.[13] Women's nongovernmental organizations in Zimbabwe and Nigeria and voluntary development organizations in Ghana have been credited with assisting in poverty alleviation, health education, and literacy in local communities (Imam et al. 1992; Manuh 1989; Zimbabwe Women's Resource Centre and Network 2000). Moreover, Pereira (2003) notes that Nigerian women's organizations have expressed resistance to multinational oil corporations, the state, and more generally, globalization.

Women's non-governmental organizations in several African nations, including Tanzania, South Africa and Ghana, have also formed broad-based coalitions with other civil society groups to press their concerns with the state for gender equality, equity and sustainable development in the form of Women's Manifestos. Gender studies scholars have indicated that in such nations as Ghana, these documents were the result of a very inclusive process bringing together women from all regions of the country, trade union groups, NETRIGHT (the coalition for women's rights in Ghana) and the Coalition for the Domestic Violence Bill among others (Mama 2005). These Manifestos are directed at government agencies, political parties and elected officials to promote their accountability on gender justice.

CONCLUSION

In this article, we have pointed to the ways in which scholarship and activism on women in all regions of Anglophone sub-Saharan Africa have been conducted on the continent, and we have discussed some of the key areas that research has been focused on. For gender scholars on the continent, there is a close synergy between research and activism in their work, which differs from their Africanist colleagues working mainly outside the continent. Furthermore, while the African researchers cited in this article are based on the continent, many of them also work in the diaspora. For scholars on the continent, the guiding principle in social science research on women and gender in sub-Saharan Africa is that it must remain sensitive to the social contexts and complexities of women's and men's lives and linked to action to promote gender equity and social change. However, given the present political, social, and economic climate in Africa, the major challenge to women's studies and gender research is the survival of its feminist activist variants instead of deradicalized studies of women and gender, as presented in research, training, and policy planning in the academic institutions.

One of the most significant calls among the works reviewed here is the need to recognize the many cultures and multiple identities that need to be studied and understood. African gender researchers are becoming more sensitive to the ways in which class, race, and age, as well as colonialism and imperialism, affect and intersect on gendered social relations. Although these scholars are beginning to explore the impact of other social differences such as ethnicity, religious fundamentalism, and sexual orientation on women's status, gaps in the literature still remain in these areas. In particular, religious differences are of increasing importance in assessing women's position in African societies, however, because of space limitations, we had to exclude this area from our review. Aspects of indigenous cultures that empower women are also underrepresented in research. The process of increasing the visibility of continental scholarship is hampered by the state of the academy and publishing in

Africa, along with the fact that most of the research continues to be carried out by scholars in the global North. In addition, scholars do very little cross-referencing of their own works. New initiatives such as the Strengthening Gender and Women's Studies for Africa's Social Transformation, at the University of Cape Town, serve as a means to create more enabling environments for institutions and individuals to become more self-reliant by means of the World Wide Web, electronic journals, and listservers that enable scholars on women and gender on the continent to network among themselves, to access works by other African scholars that otherwise would have been overlooked, and as Lewis (2002) indicates in her review essay, provide a basis to establish links where conversations have not begun.

NOTES

The four coauthors contributed equally to the production of this article. We acknowledge with gratitude Chris Bose, whose initiative inspired this series of articles, International Perspectives on Gender Studies, and whose editorial comments were most helpful. We also wish to thank the two anonymous reviewers, Ayesha Imam, N'Dri Assie-Lumumba, and Philomena Okeke for their comments and suggestions and Jennifer Kent for providing research assistance.

1. Although both groups of feminist scholar/activists are not mutually exclusive, among those associated with the establishment of AAWORD are Simi Afonja, Bolanle Awe, Nina Mba, Molara Ogundipe, Filomena Steady, Fatou Sow, N'dri Assie Lumumba, Zenebeworke Tadesse, Christine Obbo, Achola Pala Okeyo, and Nawal El Sadaawi. Those associated with the second phase of research and activism are Amina Mama, Ayesha Imam, Charmaine Pereira, Maria Nzomo, Rudo Gaidzanwa, Patricia McFadden, and Takyiwaa Manuh, to name a few.
2. Examples are continental organizations such as Amanitare based in Zimbabwe and national organizations such as the Women's Health Project in South Africa and the Empowerment and Action Research Center in Nigeria.
3. The need for comparative fertility data on a global scale prompted the creation of demographic surveys that measure individuals' knowledge,

attitudes, and practices related to a range of reproductive issues.

4. Some of these organizations are the Gender Studies and Human Rights Documentation Center in Ghana, Women and Law in West Africa, the Tanzania Media Women's Organization, the Emang Basadi Women's Organization in Botswana, and BAOBAB for Women's Human Rights.

5. For example, since the 2002 drafting of a domestic violence bill by the attorney general's department in Ghana and massive work by a coalition of women's groups to publicize the bill, there continue to be statements, some even by the minister of women's and children's affairs, that marital rape is a "foreign" concept.

6. For example, in Namibia, Odendaal (1993) has suggested that there are links between the rate of unemployment, population growth, youth crime, and an emerging middle class of Black Namibians and the increasing incidence of rape crimes.

7. This was a time when the state, oil companies, and people in the Ogoni region were engaged in a violent civil conflict over the distribution of profits and other resources from the wealth produced from the mining of crude oil. Many women became the victims of rape and were ostracized and verbally abused by their husbands, relatives, community leaders, and local women's organizations. Many women were also abandoned and forced into arranged marriages.

8. According to Diallo (2003), feminist writers and activists who have theorized about "female genital mutilation" have emphasized that the practice is an expression of patriarchal control and oppression of women.

9. See Long's (2001) study on other parts of Africa regarding issues of same-sex relationships in which she describes the legal framework that criminalizes homosexuality in Egypt. Long describes the physical and psychological torture and severe beatings by police that gay people in Egypt are subjected to when they have consensual sex and offers some recommendations for action to be implemented by the Egyptian government. Tamale (2003) also describes ways in which the patriarchal state makes it difficult for "sex outlaws" of any kind to fight for basic human rights.

10. The International Monetary Fund and the World Bank generally impose structural adjustment programs on nations that are experiencing economic crisis and are unable to pay their debts to commercial banks, foreign governments, and the World Bank. Structural adjustment programs are designed to enable these nations to qualify for new World Bank and International Monetary Fund loans. To qualify for more loans, however, nations have to meet several conditions that generally include currency devaluations, the adoption of a free market economy, and major reductions in state expenditures.

11. Femocracy was apparent in the establishment of the Better Life Programme for Rural Women in Nigeria in the late 1980s. However, femocracy is also about the bureaucratization of feminism through women's (state) machineries.

12. Tamale discusses several landmark cases wherein these treaties have been used to provide women with "broader and more comprehensive protection than domestic laws" (2001b: 100).

13. BAOBAB is the actual name of the organization, not an acronym. It is based in Lagos, Nigeria, and has been working closely with individuals convicted under the new Sharia criminal legislation in Nigeria passed since 2000.

REFERENCES

Abane, Henrietta (2000) "Towards research into wife battering in Ghana: Some methodological issues" in F. Oyekanmi (ed.) *Men, women and violence*, Dakar, Senegal: CODESRIA.

Abdullah, Hussaina (1993) "Transition politics and the challenge of gender in Nigeria," *Review of African Political Economy* 56: 27–41.

Adepoju, Aderanti (1994a) "The demographic profile: Sustained high mortality and fertility and migration for employment" in A. Adepoju and C. Oppong (eds.) *Gender, work and population in sub-Saharan Africa*, Portsmouth, NH: Heinemann.

—— (1994b) "Women, work and fertility in Swaziland" in A. Adepoju and C. Oppong (eds.) *Gender, work and population in sub-Saharan Africa*, Portsmouth, NH: Heinemann.

Adomako Ampofo, Akosua (1995) "Women and AIDS in Ghana: 'I control my body (or do I)?' Ghanaian sex workers and susceptibility to STDs, especially AIDS" in P. Makwina-Adebusoye and A. Jensen (eds.) *Women's position and demographic change in sub-Saharan Africa*, Liège, Belgium: Ordina Editions.

—— (1998) "Framing knowledge, forming behaviour; African women's AIDS-protection strategies," *African Journal of Reproductive Health* 2, 2: 151–174.

—— (1999) "Nice guys, condoms and other forms of STD protection: Sex workers and AIDS protection in West Africa" in C. Becker, J. P. Dozon, C. Obbo, and M. Touré (eds.) *Vivre et penser le Sida en Afrique/Experiencing and understanding AIDS in Africa*, Paris: CODESRIA, IRD, Karthala.

—— (2001) "The sex trade: Globalisation and issues of survival in sub-Saharan Africa," *Research Review* 17, 1: 27–43.

—— (2002) "Does women's education matter? A case

study of reproductive decision making from urban Ghana," *Ghana Studies* 5: 123–157.

—— (2004) " 'By God's grace I had a boy': Whose 'unmet need' and 'dis/agreement' about childbearing among Ghanaian couples" in S. Arnfred (ed.) *Rethinking sexualities in contexts of gender*, Uppsala, Sweden: Nordic Africa Institute.

—— (2007) "My cocoa is between my legs: Sex as work among Ghanaian women" in S. Harley (ed.) *Women's labor in the global economy: Speaking in multiple voices*, New Brunswick: Rutgers University Press.

Adomako Ampofo, Akosua, Osman Alhassan, Francis Ankrah, Deborah Atobrah, and Moses Dortey (2004) "Report on the child sexual exploitation in Accra study," Accra, Ghana: Unicef/Institute of African Studies.

Afonja, Simi (1990) "Changing patterns of gender stratification in West Africa" in I. Tinker (ed.) *Persistent inequalities: Women and world development*, New York: Oxford University Press.

Ahanmisi, Osholayemi (1992) *Strength in weakness: Bini women in affinal relations*, Lund, Sweden: Lund University.

Ahikire, Josephine (2003) "Gender equity and local democracy in contemporary Uganda: Addressing the challenge of women's political effectiveness in local government," in A. M. Goetz and S. Hassim (eds.) *No shortcuts to power*, London: Zed Press.

Akitunde, Dorcas Olu (ed.) (2001) *African culture and the quest for women's rights*, Ibadan, Nigeria: Institute of Women in Religion and Culture.

Amadiume, Ifi (1987) *Male daughters, female husbands: Gender and sex in an African society*, London: Zed Books.

Armstrong, A. (1990) "Women and rape in Zimbabwe. Human and People's Rights Project," Monograph no. 10. Maseru, Lesotho: Institute of Southern African Studies, National University of Lesotho.

Assie-Lumumba, N' Dri (1997) "Educating Africa's girls and women: A conceptual and historical analysis of gender inequality" in A. Imam, A. Mama, and F. Sow (eds.) *Engendering African social sciences*, Dakar, Senegal: CODESRIA.

—— (2001) "Gender, access to learning and production of knowledge in Africa" in Association of African Women for Research and Development (AAWORD) (ed.) *Visions of gender theories and social development in Africa: Harnessing knowledge for social justice and equality*, Dakar, Senegal: AAWORD.

Atinmo, Morayo (2000) "Sociocultural implications of wife beating among the Yoruba in Ibadan City, Nigeria" in F. Oyekanmi (ed.) *Men, women and violence*, Dakar, Senegal: CODESRIA.

Awusabo-Asare, Kofi, John K. Anarfi, and D. K. Agyeman (1993) "Women's control over their sexuality and the spread of STDs and HIV/AIDS in Ghana," *Health Transition Review* 3 (Suppl. issue).

Benjamin, Saranel (2001) "Masculinisation of the state and the feminization of poverty," *Agenda* 48: 68–74.

Bennett, Jane (1999) "Research review: Gender-based violence, poverty alleviation and peace negotiation in South Africa," Oxford, UK: OXFAM/IDRC.

—— (2002) "Exploration of a 'gap': Strategizing gender equity in African universities," *Gender and Women's Studies E-Journal* 1. Available from http://www.feministafrica.org/01-2002/jane.html.

Boadu, J. Nana Aba (2000) "The health of working mothers in Accra: A case study of doctors and nurses at the Kolre-bu Teaching Hospital and workers at North Gbawe Stone Quarry," M.Phil. thesis, Institute of African Studies, Accra, Ghana.

Bradford, Helen (1991) "Her body her life: 150 years of abortion in South Africa," Paper presented at the Conference on Women and Gender in Southern Africa, University of Natal, Durban, South Africa, January 31 to February 2.

Carol, Henry D. R., and Nana Ama Ofori-Atta (1998) "Violence against women in the Gambia" in K. Akua (ed.) *Women and law in West Africa: Situational analysis of some key issues affecting women*, Legon, Ghana: Women and Law in West Africa.

Chisala, Victoria, and Mpala Nkonkomalimba (2000) *The Zambian national machinery for women and other mechanisms*, Accra North, Ghana: Third World Network-Africa.

Coker-Appiah, Dorcas, and Kathy Cusack (1999) *Breaking the silence and challenging the myths of violence against women and children in Ghana: Report of a national study on violence*, Accra, Ghana: Gender Studies and Human Rights Documentation Center.

Dambe, Regina Thea Maaswai (2000) *The national machinery for the advancement of women: The Botswana experience*, Accra North, Ghana: Third World Network-Africa.

Darkwah, Akosua (2002) "Trading goes global: Market women in an era of globalization," *Asian Women* 15: 31–49.

—— (2007) "Work as a duty and as a joy: Understanding the role of work in the lives of Ghanaian female traders of global consumer items" in S. Harley (ed.) *Women's labor in the global economy: Speaking in multiple voices*, New Brunswick: Rutgers University Press.

Denzer, Laray (1995) *Constance Cummings-John: Memoirs of a Krio leader*, Ibadan, Nigeria: Humanities Research Center.

Diallo, Asitan (2003) "Paradoxes of female sexuality in Mali: On the practices of Magnonmaka and Bolokolikela" in S. Arnfred (ed.) *Rethinking sexualities in contexts of gender*, Uppsala, Sweden: Nordic Africa Institute.

—— (2004) "Paradoxes of female sexuality in Mali: On the practices of 'Magnonmaka' and 'Bolokoli-Kela' " in S. Arnfred (ed.) *Rethinking sexualities in contexts of gender*, Uppsala, Sweden: Nordic Africa Institute.

Echo Magazine (2001) "Issue topic: Female genital mutilation," Dakar, Senegal: Newsletter of the Association of African Women for Research and Development.

Emeagwali, G. (1995) *Women pay the price: Structural adjustment in Africa and the Caribbean*, Trenton, NJ: Africa World Press.

Etta, Florence E. (1994) "Gender issues in contemporary African education," *Africa Development* 19, 4: 57–84.

Ezumah, Nkoli, and Kate Oreh (1999) "Socio-cultural factors affecting the reproductive health of women at Obukpa, Nsukka in Enugu State, Nigeria," *Tropical Journal of Medical Research* 3: 80–87.

Fall, Yassine (1999) "Globalization, its institutions and African women's resistance" in Y. Fall (ed.) *Africa: Gender, globalization and resistance*, Dakar, Senegal: AAWORD.

Farah, Amina A. (1989) "Research priorities and support needs for women in agriculture in the Sudan" in Z. El-Bakri and R. M. Besha (eds.) *Women and development in Eastern Africa: An agenda for research*, Addis Ababa, Ethiopia: OSSREA.

Gaidzanwa, Rudo B. (1997) "Gender analysis in the field of education: A Zimbabwean example" in A. Imam, A. Mama, and F. Sow (eds.) *Engendering African social sciences*, Dakar, Senegal: CODESRIA.

Gana Shettima, Abba (1998) "Gendered work patterns in the endangered Sahelian rural environment: Exploring three layers of exploitation," *Africa Development* 23, 2: 163–183.

Garba, Abdul-Ganiyu, and P. Kassey Garba (1999) "Trade liberalization, gender equality and adjustment policies in sub-Saharan Africa" in Y. Fall (ed.) *Africa: Gender, globalization and resistance*, Dakar, Senegal: AAWORD.

Gays and Lesbians of Zimbabwe (1999) *Sexual orientation and Zimbabwe's new constitution: A case for inclusion*, Harare, Zimbabwe: GALZ.

Gizaw, Blen (2002) *Some reflections on criminalizing domestic violence against women with emphasis on Ethiopia*, Addis Ababa, Ethiopia: Center for Research Training and Information on Women in Development (CERTWID), Addis Ababa University.

Gouws, Amanda (2004) "Women's representation: The South African electoral system and the 2004 election," *Journal of African Election* 3: 2.

Graham, Yao (2001) "Changing the united brotherhood: An analysis of the gender politics of the Ghana Trades Union Congress" in D. Tsikata (ed.) *Gender training in Ghana: Politics, issues and tools*, Accra, Ghana: Woeli.

Hallam, R. (1994) "Crimes without punishment: Sexual harassment and violence against female students in schools and universities in Africa," Discussion paper no. 4, Africa Rights, London.

Hassim, Shireen (2006). *Women's organizations and democracy in South Africa: Contesting authority*, Scottsvile: University of KwaZulu Natal Press.

Higgs, Philip (2007) "The current status of, and legislation of redress gender inequalities in South Africa" in N. A. Lumumba (ed.) *Women and Higher Education in Africa: Reconceptualizing gender-based human capabilities and upgrading human rights to knowledge*, Abidjan: CEPARRED.

Ibeanu, Okechukwu (2001) "Healing and changing: The changing identity of women in the aftermath of the Ogoni crisis in Nigeria" in S. Meintjes, A. Pillay, and M. Turshen (eds.) *The aftermath: Women in post-conflict transformation*, London: Zed Books.

Ilumoka, Adetou (2003) "Advocacy for women's reproductive and sexual health and rights in Africa: Between the devil and the deep blue sea," Paper presented at the Institute of African Studies/Nordic Africa Institute workshop on Research, Activism, Consultancies: Dilemmas and Challenges, Institute of African Studies, Legon, Ghana, October.

Imam, Ayesha (1997) "Engendering African social sciences: An introductory essay" in A. Imam, A. Mama, and F. Sow (eds.) *Engendering African social sciences*, Dakar, Senegal: CODESRIA.

Imam, Ayesha M. (2001) "The Muslim religious right ('fundamentalists') and sexuality" in P. B. Jung, M. E. Hunt, and R. B Alakrishnan (eds.) *Good sex: Feminist perspectives from the world's religions*, New Brunswick, NJ: Rutgers University Press.

—— (2002) "Of laws, religion and women's rights: Women's rights in Muslim laws (Sharia)" in *Islamization in secular Nigeria: Implications for women's rights*, London: Women Living under Muslim Laws.

Imam, Ayesha, and Amina Mama (1994) "The role of academics in limiting and expanding academic freedom" in M. Diouf and M. Mamdani (eds.) *Academic freedom in Africa*, Dakar, Senegal: CODESRIA.

Imam, Ayesha, Amina Mama, and Fatou Sow (eds.) (1997) *Engendering African social sciences*, Dakar, Senegal: CODESRIA.

Imam, Ayesha, Nema Ngur-Adi, and Joy Mukubwa-Hendrickson (1992) *The WINdocument: Conditions of women in Nigeria and policy recommendations to 2,000 AD*, Zaria, Nigeria: Ahmadu Bello University Press.

Jelil Ladebo, Olugbenja (2003) "Sexual harassment in academia in Nigeria: How real?" *African Sociological Review* 7, 1: 117–130.

Jita Allan, Tuzyline (2001) "Feminist scholarship in Africa" in C. R. Veney and P. T. Zeleza (eds.) *Women in African studies scholarly publishing*, Trenton, NJ: Africa World Press.

Johnson-Odim, Cheryl, and Nina Mba (1997) *For women and nation: Funmilayo Ransome-Kuti of Nigeria*, Champaign: University of Illinois Press.

Kahyana, Danson (2002) "Ugandan Asians, identity and the literacy medium," Paper presented at CODESRIA 10th General Assembly Africa in the New Millennium, Kampala, Uganda, December 8–12.

Kasente, D. (2002) "Institutionalizing gender equality in African universities: Case of women's and gender studies at Makerere University," *Feminist Africa Intellectual Politics* 1: 91–99.

Kassimir, Ron (1998) "Talking points for the panel on social science research funding in Africa: Views from the field," Paper presented at the International Symposium on Globalization and the Social Sciences in Africa, Graduate School for Humanities and Social Sciences, University of Witwatersand, Johannesburg, South Africa, September 14–18.

Katapa, Rosalia (1998) "Teenage mothers in their second pregnancies" in M. Rwebangira and R. Liljestrom (eds.) *Haraka, Haraka ... Look before you leap: Youth at the crossroad of custom and modernity*, Uppsala, Sweden: Nordic Africa Institute.

Katapa, Rosalia, and Magdalena Ngaiza(2001) "Debt in Tanzania: Are women silent or concerned?" in AAWORD (ed.) *Visions of gender theories and social development in Africa: Harnessing knowledge for social justice and equality*, Dakar, Senegal: AAWORD.

Kerata Chacha, Babere (2002) "Travesting gender and the colonial madness: Same-sex relationship, customary law and change in Tanzania, 1890–1990," Paper presented at CODESRIA 10th General Assembly Africa in the New Millennium, Kampala, Uganda, December 8–12.

Komba-Maleka, Betty, and Rita Lijestrom (1994) "Looking for men" in Z. Timba-Masabo and R. Lijestrom (eds.) *Chelewa Chelewa: The dilemma of teenage girls*, Oslo, Norway: Scandinavian Institute of African Studies.

Kuenyehia, Akua (1998) "Violence against women in Ghana" in A. Kuenyehia (ed.) *Women and law in West Africa: Situational analysis of some key issues affecting women*, Accra, Ghana: Women and Law in West Africa, Human Rights Study Center, Faculty of Law, University of Ghana.

Kwesiga, Joy (2002) *Women's access to higher education in Africa: Uganda's experience*, Kampala, Uganda: Fountain.

Lewis, Desiree (2002) "Review essay: African feminist studies: 1980–2002," *Gender and Women's Studies Africa*. Available from http://www.gwsafrica.org/knowledge/africa%20review/history.html.

Lewis, Tolulope, and Ayesha Imam (2001) "NGO's

CEDAW report for Nigeria: Foreword," Lagos: Nigerian NGO Coalition for a Shadow Report to CEDAW.

Long, Lynellen (1996) "Counting women's experiences" in L. Long and M. Ankrah (eds.) *Women's experiences with HIV/AIDS: An international perspective*, New York: Columbia University Press.

Long, S. (2001) *Egypt: Torture and inhuman and degrading treatment based on sexual orientation*, Geneva: World Organization against Torture.

Machera, Mumbi (2000) "Domestic violence in Kenya: A survey of newspaper reports" in F. Oyekanmi (ed.) *Men, women and violence*, Dakar, Senegal: CODESRIA.

—— (2004) "Opening a can of worms: A debate on female sexuality in the lecture theatre" in S. Arnfred (ed.) *Rethinking sexualities in contexts of gender*, Uppsala, Sweden: Nordic Africa Institute.

Magubane, Zine (2001) "Globalization and the South African women: A historical overview" in AAWORD (ed.) *Visions of gender theories and social development in Africa: Harnessing knowledge for social justice and equality*, Dakar, Senegal: AAWORD.

Makandawire, Thandika (1997) "The social sciences in Africa," *African Studies Review* 39, 2: 15–37.

Mama, Amina (1995) "Feminism or femocracy? State feminism and democratization in Nigeria," *Africa Development* 20, 2: 37–58.

—— (1996) "Women's studies and studies of women in Africa during the 1990s," Working paper series 5/96. Dakar, Senegal: CODESRIA.

—— (1997) "Postscript: Moving from analysis to practice?" in A. Imam, A. Mama, and F. Sow (eds.) *Engendering African social sciences*, Dakar, Senegal: CODESRIA.

—— (2000) *Feminism and the state in Nigeria: The national machinery for women*, Accra North, Ghana: Third World Network-Africa.

—— (2004) "Critical capacities: Facing the challenge of intellectual development in Africa," Inaugural lecture, Prince Claus Chair in Development and Equity, Institute of Social Studies, April 28. Available from http://www.gwsafrica.org/knowledge/amina.html.

—— (2005) "In conversation: The Ghanaian Women's Manifesto Movement," *Feminist Africa* 4.

Manuh, Takyiwaa (1989) "A study of selected voluntary development organization in Ghana" in P. McFadden and N. Sow (eds.) *Women as agents and beneficiaries of development assistance*, Dakar, Senegal: AAWORD.

—— (1994) "Changes in women's employment in the public and informal sectors in Ghana" in P. Sparr (ed.) *Mortgaging women's lives: Feminist critiques of structural adjustment*, London: Zed Press.

—— (1997) "Ghana: Women in the public and informal sectors under the economic recovery program" in

N. Visvanathan et al. (eds.) *The women, gender and development reader*, London: Zed Books.

—— (1998) "Women in Africa's development," Briefing paper no. 11 (April), Africa Recovery, United Nations Department of Public Information.

—— (2001) "On teaching gender in an African university," Paper presented at the Conference on Africa after Gender, University of California at Santa Barbara, April 20–21.

—— (2002) "Higher education, condition of scholars and the future of development in Africa," *CODESRIA Bulletin* 3/4: 42–48.

Manuh, Takyiwaa, and Akosua Adomako Ampofo (1995) "Population and women's issues," in *Analysis of demographic data. Vol. 2: Detailed analysis reports*, Accra: Ghana Statistical Service.

Masinde, Catherine K. M. (1993) "Women's access to and control of productive resources in Kenya" in W. Mukabi-Kabira, J. Adhiambo-Oduol, and M. Nzomu (eds.) *Democratic change in Africa: Women's perspective*, Nairobi, Kenya: AAWORD/ACTS.

Mbilinyi, Marjorie (1985) "Struggles concerning sexuality among female youth," *Journal of Eastern African Research and Development* 15: 111–123.

—— (1989) "Women's resistance in 'customary marriage': Tanzania's runaway wives" in A. Zegeye and S. Ishemo (eds.) *Forced labour and migration*, London: Hans Zell.

—— (1991) *Big slavery: Agribusiness and the crisis in women's employment in Tanzania*, Dar es Salaam, Tanzania: Dar es Salaam University Press.

—— (1992) *Review of women's conditions and positions in Tanzania: Issues and methodology*, Dar es Salaam: Tanzania Gender Networking Programme.

—— (1994) "The role of NGOs in promoting the economic advancement of rural women" in Summary report CIRDAFRICA/IFAD workshop. Arusha, Tanzania: Centre on Integrated Rural Development for Africa.

—— (1998) "Searching for utopia: The politics of gender and education in Tanzania" in M. Bloch, J. A. Beoku Betts, and B. R. Tabachnick (eds.) *Women and education in sub-Saharan Africa: Power, opportunities, and constraints*, Boulder, CO: Lynne Rienner.

Mbilinyi, Marjorie, and Naomi Kaihula (2000) "Sinners and outsiders: The drama of AIDS in Rungwe" in C. Baylies and J. Bujra (eds.) *AIDS, sexuality and gender in Africa: Collective strategies and struggles in Tanzania and Zambia*, London: Routledge.

McFadden, Patricia (1992) "Sex, sexuality, and the problem of AIDS in Africa" in R. Meena (ed.) *Gender in southern Africa: Conceptual and theoretical issues*, Harare, Zimbabwe: SAPES.

—— (2001) *Patriarchy: Political power, sexuality and globalization*, Port Louis, Mauritius: Ledikasyon Pu Travayer.

—— (2003) "Sexual pleasure as feminist choice," *Feminist Africa* 2 Available from http://www.feministafrica.org/index.php/sexual-pleasure-as-feminist-choice.

Meena, Ruth (2007) "Women's participation in higher levels of learning in Africa" in N. A. Lumumba (ed.) *Women and Higher Education in Africa: Reconceptualizing gender-based human capabilities and upgrading human rights to knowledge*, Abidjan: CEPARRED.

Mejiuni Fashina, Olutoyin (2000) "Academic freedom and female academics in Nigeria" in E. Sall (ed.) *Women in academia: Gender and academic freedom in Africa*, Dakar, Senegal: Council for the Development of Social Science Research in Africa.

Mlama, Penina (2007) "The significance of Higher Education in gender and education reforms in Africa" in N. A. Lumumba (ed.) *Women and Higher Education in Africa: Reconceptualizing gender-based human capabilities and upgrading human rights to knowledge*, Abidjan: CEPARRED.

Moja, Teboho (2007) "Politics of exclusion in Higher Education: The inadequacy of gender issues in the globalization debates" in N. A. Lumumba (ed.) *Women and Higher Education in Africa: Reconceptualizing gender-based human capabilities and upgrading human rights to knowledge*, Abidjan: CEPARRED.

Mondoh Omondi, Helen and Jedidah Mujidi (2006) "The education of girls in Kenya: Looking back and still looking forward," *CODESRIA Bulletin* 1 & 2: 58–60.

Mpangile, G. S., M. T. Leshabari, S. Kaaya, and D. Kihwele (1998) "Abortion and unmet need for contraception in Tanzania: The role of male partners in teenage induced abortion in Dar Es Salaam," *African Journal of Reproductive Health* 11, 2: 108–121.

Mukurasi, Laeticia (1991) *Post abolished: One woman's struggle for employment rights*, London: Women's Press.

Munguti, Kaendi, Edith Kabui, and Mabel Isoilo (2002) "The implications of economic reforms on gender relations: The case of poor households in Kisumu Slums" in A. Tamboura Diawara (ed.) *Gender, economic integration, governance and methods of contraceptives*, Dakar, Senegal: AAWORD.

Muro, Asseny (1989) "Priority areas of research on women and development in agriculture in Tanzania" in Z. El-Bakri and R. M. Besha (eds.) *Women and development in Eastern Africa: An agenda for research*, Addis Ababa, Ethiopia: OSSREA.

Muthien, Bernedette (2003) " 'Why are you not married yet?' Heteronormativity in the African women's movement," *Women's Global Network for Reproductive Rights Newsletter* 79, 2. Available from http://www.wgnrr.org.

Muzaki, Sarah (2002) "Cultural turbulence at its most:

Uganda's 'guyz' and 'chiks' neither 'here' nor 'there' ", Paper presented at CODESRIA 10th General Assembly Africa in the New Millennium, Kampala, Uganda, December 8–12.

Namuddu, Katherine (1993) "Gender perspectives in the transformation of Africa: Challenges to the African university as a model to society," Paper presented at the 8th General Conference and 25th Anniversary Celebration of the Association of African Universities, University of Ghana, Legon, January 18–23.

Nigerian NGO Coalition for a Shadow Report to CEDAW (2001) *NGOs CEDAW report for Nigeria*, Lagos: Nigerian NGO Coalition for a Shadow Report to CEDAW.

Njambi, Wairimu N., and William E. O'Brien (2000) "Revisiting 'woman–woman marriage': Notes on Gikuyu women," *National Women's Studies Journal* 12, 1: 1–23.

Nzomo, Maria (1993) "Engendering democratization in Kenya: A political perspective" in W. Mukabi-Kabira, J. Adhiambo Oduol, and M. Nzomo (eds.) *Democratic change in Africa: Women's perspective*, Nairobi, Kenya: AAWORD.

—— (1995) *Women in top management in Kenya*. Nairobi, Kenya: African Association for Public Administration and Management.

—— (1998) "Gender studies in Africa at crossroads?: Some reflections," Paper presented at the International Symposium on Social Sciences and the Challenges of Globalization in Africa, Johannesburg, South Africa, September 14–18.

Odejide, Abiola (2002) "Profile of Women's Research and Documentation Center, Institute of African Studies, University of Ibadan, Nigeria," *Feminist Africa Intellectual Politics* 1: 100–107.

Odendaal, A. (1993) "Violence and social control of women in Namibia" in K. K. Prah (ed.) *Social science research priorities for Namibia*, Dakar, Senegal: CODESRIA.

Ofei-Aboagye, Rosemarie O. (1994) "Domestic violence in Ghana: An initial step," *Columbia Journal of Gender and Law* 4, 1: 1–16.

Oloka-Onyango, J. (1996) "The plight of the larger half: Human rights, gender violence and the legal status of refugee and internally displaced women in Africa," *Denver Journal of International Law and Policy* 24, 2–3: 349–394.

Otunga, Ruth N. (1997) "School participation by gender: Implications for occupational activities in Kenya," *Africa Development* 22, 1: 39–64.

Pereira, Charmaine (2002) "Locating gender and women's studies in Nigeria: What trajectories for the future?," Revised version of paper presented at the 10th General Assembly of CODESRIA, Africa in the New Millennium, Kampala, Uganda, December 8–12.

—— (2003) "Configuring 'global,' 'national,' and 'local' in governance agendas in Nigeria," *Social Research* 69, 3: 781–804.

Pheko, Mohau (1999) "Privatization, trade liberalization and women's socio-economic rights: Exploring policy alternatives" in Y. Fall (ed.) *Africa: Gender, globalization and resistance*, Dakar, Senegal: AAWORD.

Phiri, Isabel A. (2000) "Gender and academic freedom in Malawi" in E. Sall (ed.) *Women in academia: Gender and academic freedom in Africa*, Dakar, Senegal: CODESRIA.

Prah, Mansah (2002) "Gender issues in Ghanaian tertiary institutions: Women academics and administrators at Cape Coast University," *Ghana Studies* 5: 1–20.

Prah, Mansah, and Akosua Adomako Ampofo (forthcoming) "Punishment and discipline of women and children in Ghana" in K. Cusack and T. Manuh (eds.) *Violence against women in Ghana*, Accra, Ghana: Gender and Human Rights Documentation Centre.

Rajani, Rakesh, and Mustafa Kudrati (1996) "The varieties of sexual experience of the street children of Mwwanza, Tanzania" in S. Zerdenstein and K. Moore (eds.) *Learning about sexuality: A practical beginning*, New York: Population Council/Women's Health Coalition.

Ratele, Kopano (2004) "Kinky politics" in S. Arnfred (ed.) *Rethinking sexualities in contexts of gender*, Uppsala, Sweden: Nordic Africa Institute.

Rutenge Bagile, Astronaut (2002–2003) "Increased social economic and gender inequality under globalization: The case of women in the informal sector" in A. Tamboura Diawara (ed.) *Gender, economic integration, governance and methods of contraceptives*, Dakar, Senegal: AAWORD and AFARD.

Sawyer, Akilagpa (1994) "Ghana: Relations between government and universities" in G. Neave and F. A. van Vught (eds.) *Government and higher education relationships across three continents: The winds of change*, Paris: IAU Press and Pergamon.

Sexuality (1996) *Agenda: Empowering women for gender equity*, Issue 28.

Shawulu, R. (1990) *The story of Gambo Sawaba*, Nigeria: University of Jos.

Steady, Filomena C. (1986) "Research methodologies and investigative frameworks for social change: The case for African women," Research on African Women: What Type of Methodology? Seminar. AAWORD occasional paper series 1.

Tadesse, Zeneworke (1997) "Gender relations, constitutional change and cultural/religious identity in Ethiopia," Paper presented at Cultural Transformations in Africa: Legal, Religious and Human Rights Issues, Addis Ababa, Ethiopia, March 11–13.

Tagoe, Eva (1995) "Maternal education and infant/child

morbidity in Ghana: The case of diarrhea. Evidence from the Ghana DHS" in P. Makinwa and A.-M. Jensen (eds.) *Women's position and demographic change in sub-Saharan Africa*, Liège, Belgium: IUSSP.

Tamale, Sylvia (1999) "Towards legitimate governance in Africa: The case of affirmative action and parliamentary politics in Uganda" in E. K. Quashigah and O. C. Okafor (eds.) *Legitimate governance in Africa*, Amsterdam, the Netherlands: Kluwer Law International.

—— (2001) "Think globally, act locally: Using international treaties for women's empowerment in East Africa," *Agenda 50*: 97–104.

—— (2003) "Virgin brides are dinosaurs from a dead culture," *Monitor Newspaper*, October 15.

Tamale, Sylvia, and J. Oloka-Onyango (2000) " 'Bitches' at the academy: Gender and academic freedom in Africa" in E. Sall (ed.) *Women in academia: Gender and academic freedom in Africa*, Dakar, Senegal: Council for the Development of Social Science Research in Africa.

Tekloa, Bethlehem (2002) *Narratives of three prostitutes in Addis Ababa*, Adis Ababa, Ethiopia: Centre for Research Training and Information on Women in Development, Addis Ababa University.

Tsikata, D. (1989) "Women's political organizations 1951–1987" in E. Hansen and K. Ninsin (eds.) *The state, development and politics in Ghana*, Dakar, Senegal: CODESRIA.

Tsikata, Dzodzi (2000) *Lip service and peanuts: The state and national machinery for women in Africa*, Accra, Ghana: Third World Network.

—— (2001a) "Gender equality and development in Ghana: Some issues which should concern a political party" in D. Tsikata (ed.) *Gender training in Ghana: Politics, issues and tools*, Accra New Town, Ghana: Woeli.

—— (2001b) *Gender training in Ghana: Politics, issues, and tools*, Accra, Ghana: Woeli.

—— (2001c) "Introduction" in D. Tsikata (ed.) *Gender training in Ghana: Politics, issues and tools*, Accra, Ghana: Woeli.

—— (2001d) "The politics of policy-making: A gender perspective" in D. Tsikata (ed.) *Gender training in Ghana: Politics, issues and tools*, Accra, Ghana: Woeli.

Turshen, Meredith (1998) "Women's war stories" in M. Turshen and C. Twagiramariya (eds.) *What women do in wartime: Gender and conflict in Africa*, London: Zed Books.

Turshen, Meredith, and Clotilde Twagiramariya (1998) *What women do in wartime: Gender and conflict in Africa*, London: Zed Books.

Wangusa, Hellen (2000) *The national machinery for women in Uganda*, Accra North, Ghana: Third World Network-Africa.

Yahaya, Hanifatu (2003) "The reality of homosexuality in Ghana: A case study of homosexuality in Accra," Social work dissertation, University of Ghana, Department of Sociology.

Zimbabwe Women's Resource Centre and Network (2000) *The national machinery for women in Zimbabwe: An NGO assessment*, Accra North, Ghana: Third World Network-Africa.

CHAPTER 4

Trading Goes Global: Ghanaian Market Women in an Era of Globalization

Akosua K. Darkwah

Much of the writing on African women's economic activity focuses on the traditional economic endeavors associated with African women such as farming and trade in local foodstuffs or manufactured cloth (Gladwin 1991). For Ghanaian women especially, their trading activities have been documented since the mid-1800s (Cruickshank 1853; Daniell 1856; Robertson 1983; Clark 1994; Chamlee-Wright 1997). Informal sector activities such as farming and trade have been seen as the preserve of the uneducated African woman (Robertson 1995). Educated African women took advantage of the opportunity that education provided them to work in the formal sector where jobs were more befitting of women with such skills and paid more. With the adoption of structural adjustment programs in many parts of Africa that have shrunk the public sector, and the generally low wages available to workers in both the existing public sector jobs and the now burgeoning private sector jobs, some educated African women are parlaying the trading skills they acquired as children or learning to trade as adults to make substantial incomes as traders of global consumer items. However, their lives as transnational traders are not without challenges of their own. The life histories of two such women are presented below.

AKYAA

In the 1950s, Akyaa's mother owned a shop at Makola market, Ghana's largest consumer goods market, selling canned food items, which she bought from the large expatriate firms located in the country. As a child, Akyaa helped out in her mother's shop by assisting her make and collect orders as well as price the items for sale. Akyaa discovered quickly that she could make her weekly allowance grow by buying sweets off of her mother and selling them during break time at grade school.

During her years in boarding school, Akyaa continued to amass wealth by buying and selling sweets.... Her mother often commented that she acted like an adult because she had financial resources of her own that she had acquired through her own efforts. As a teenager, Akyaa was able to procure clothing in fashion at the time, even when her mother refused to provide her with the financial resources to buy items because she disapproved of her clothing choices. Akyaa continued to trade throughout her secondary school years at boarding school and on to university. By the time Akyaa started university in the late 1960s, she could afford to buy herself a round trip ticket to and from London during school vacations.

After university, Akyaa undertook a master's degree in social administration. Though she had traded all her life, business administration was not a career choice that she sought to undertake. The general perception at the time was that tertiary education was to provide women with the opportunities to break away from the selling mold that the majority of Ghanaian women, with no other job options, were forced to take up as income-earning ventures. . . . For Akyaa, a woman with tertiary education, trading was simply not an option. After earning her degree, Akyaa began to work at the newly created center for civic education as a research assistant helping to collect and collate data on civic issues in Ghana. Then came the coup d'état of 1972, which resulted in the dissolution of the center where she worked. Six months pregnant at the time, Akyaa chose not to bother with finding a job only to have to proceed on maternity leave. She doubted that she would have been successful at finding one anyway. . . . Akyaa rented the vacant shop from her parents and stocked it with items that she purchased from the major departmental stores located in the heart of the city. Trading for a living, an option she had initially rejected, now became the alternative to staying unemployed.

When her daughter was three, Akyaa left her shop in the care of employees and took on a full-time job in the formal sector, working in one of the port cities in Ghana. Akyaa was dissatisfied with the amount of money she made working in the formal sector and sought ways to increase her earnings. While working at the port city, she took advantage of her proximity to a major fishing center in the country and started selling fish at home. She would wake up at 3 am to clean and repackage three cartons of fish, which she would then leave to be sold by her shop assistants later in the day. She remembers the drudgery of that period quite clearly. . . . For a while then, Akyaa worked full-time in the formal sector and part-time in the informal sector while fulfilling her responsibilities in the domestic sphere as well.

Akyaa, who had visited London on several occasions during her years of tertiary education, continued to do so when she took time off from work. While there, she bought children's wear to sell back in Ghana in an attempt to further increase her income. . . . She picked children's clothing because she had a young daughter to clothe at the time. Over time, she added items that mothers would need to care for infants. She eventually was the first person to run a real mother-care shop (a one-stop shop for children's needs) in the capital city.

Another item, a lot of which Akyaa bought during her trips, was artificial flowers. . . . At the time, as they were unavailable on the Ghanaian market, her friends would borrow them on occasion only to have some of them lost or damaged. Embarrassed, some of these friends would give her money to replace the damaged/lost ones or to buy them some of their own. She discovered then that it was a lot cheaper to buy the flowers in bulk and so she began to do so even as she continued with the sale of mother-care items.

She switched over completely to the sale of floral items when she discovered flowers in the inner chamber of the wholesaler from whom she bought her mother-care items. The wholesaler decided to give the items to her at a really cheap price, so she bought all of it and sold it alongside the mother-care items. When she ran out of them, her customers started pestering her for more. . . . In a conversation with a fellow Ghanaian she met on the plane, . . . she was given a list of wholesalers in one particular trading estate located on the outskirts of London, where she could purchase floral items.

On her next trip, Akyaa went to that trading estate and set up a permanent relationship with one of the wholesalers there. She stuck with that wholesaler for a number of years. That changed, however, when she accidentally discovered a wholesaler with more varieties of floral items for sale. . . . She took note of the location of this newly discovered trading estate, visited it the following day and found her new wholesaler. At this point, Akyaa quit the sale of mother-care items, concentrating instead on floral items.

Akyaa received free training in floral arrangements from her wholesalers, which she modified to suit the conditions of the Ghanaian market. She removed items from boxes to increase their attractiveness and made samples of bouquets so that potential customers had a variety of items to choose from. . . .

Throughout the 1970s, Akyaa continued to work in the formal sector, subsidizing her income with the proceeds from her trading activities in the informal sector. The increasing state antagonism towards traders, combined with her educational background, did not make the option of trade as a full-time career seem lucrative and worthy of a woman with tertiary education. . . .

State–trader relationships in Ghana from the time of independence through the 1960s and 1970s were characterized by state neglect of the potential role of traders in Ghana's economic development (Chamlee-Wright 1997) and antagonism of various sorts (Darkwah 2002). Two incidents in 1979 made this relationship even more tenuous. First, military personnel looted Makola market, on June 4th, the day of the 1979 coup d'état against the Akuffo regime. Then in August of the same year, the military regime of the time, the Armed Forces Revolutionary Council (AFRC), embarked on a "housecleaning exercise" to rid the nation of its corrupt citizenry. Traders, who were blamed for the high prices of items, were one of the main targets of this "housecleaning exercise." . . . The solution to this food scarcity then was to eliminate the traders who were the middlemen in this marketing chain so that the farmers could sell their produce directly to the consumers (Fraker and Harrel-Bond 1979). . . . While traders in food items were accused of instilling fear in the producers, traders in consumer items were accused

of creating artificial shortages by hoarding goods and then selling them at exorbitant prices. . . .

The idea that the shortages of items in the country were due to hoarding on the part of the traders had its antecedents in a report commissioned in 1964 by the first president of the country. The Abrahams' report on trading malpractices blamed the shortages of items and the high prices of available goods on hoarding practices by the traders. . . . Scholars writing about this issue, however, are of a different opinion (Steuer 1973). For these scholars, the hoarding practices of the traders were in reaction to . . . ill-conceived government policies [which] lay at the heart of the food and consumer item shortages on the market. . . .

Despite the scholarly interpretation of the cause of the crisis, the state meted out punishment to the traders whom they blamed for the crisis. Women who were caught hoarding items were subject to punishment, which ranged from public flogging to death in some extreme cases (Robertson 1983). In its attempts to preserve its image as the military government that had come into power to deliver the masses from the hands of the corrupt state officials and citizenry, the military government took its intimidation of traders to new heights when on August 18th, 1979, after soldiers had plundered money and goods worth millions of cedis at the Makola market, the market was blown up with dynamite (Robertson 1983). . . . The impact of the losses of 1979 on traders was substantial. . . . Two decades later, memories of those events, particularly the destruction of the markets, still linger on as evidenced by occasional referrals to that incident and the emotion with which the incident is recounted.

At the time of the destruction of Makola, Akyaa's shop, run by employees, was situated at the extreme periphery of Makola market. . . . [H]er proximity to the site made her fully aware of the precariousness of trade as a full-time career. . . .

Akyaa's dual participation in the formal and informal sector was to change, however, as her second child, who was born in 1975, grew older. Ama had a terrible case of asthma, which had her hospitalized frequently, sometimes twice or thrice a week. . . . It was then that she decided it made more sense for her to run a flexible schedule, which would allow her to take care of her daughter without the constraints that employment in the formal sector imposed on her. The floral shop that she had set up to subsidize her income now became her sole source of income. Luckily for Akyaa, her decision to trade on a full-time basis coincided with the state's adoption of structural adjustment programs. Among other things, the state abolished import and price controls and allowed for the introduction of private foreign exchange bureaus, all of which made transnational trade in global consumer items relatively easy. As a result, since 1985, there has been a steady growth in the distributive trade sector of the economy (Aryeetey 1994). Like others in the distributive sector, the increasing spirit of cooperation on the part of the state made it possible for Akyaa to reap substantial financial rewards from trading on a full-time basis.

Akyaa's husband was at first opposed to the idea that his wife, who had a Master's degree in administration, was selling items at the market. Now he sees that it paid off in two main ways. First, it provided the family with a sizeable amount of income. Second, and perhaps more important, trading at the market paid off in terms of their daughter's health. She is now a healthy lawyer of whom they are both very proud. At fifty-five, Akyaa is thinking about ways of ensuring that she would be guaranteed a decent amount of income during her retirement years. Having worked for most of her life in the informal sector, she does not have access to the state-funded retirement fund that workers in the public sector do. . . . She is therefore considering turning her profits over the coming years into treasury bills (certificates of deposit), the proceeds of which she can live on once she quits the trading business.

AFARIWAA

Afariwaa is a thirty-one year old university graduate who has chosen to trade in clothing instead of using the skills she acquired in university because trading provides her with both flexibility and more money than she would receive in the formal sector. She sets her own hours, she does not have to answer to anybody if she feels too tired or sick to show up at work at the appointed time and, besides, trading at the market pays much more than she ever made working in the formal sector. As she put it, "What more could one ask for?"

She was introduced to trading by her older sister, Oparibea, who ran a shop of her own at Makola. She spent the summer before she finished university putting her sister's books in order. She tallied up all the monies owed to her sister by various people and discovered that people owed her sister to the tune of . . . $10,000. Her sister was quite aware of the fact that many of the people with whom she conducted business owed her quite substantial amounts of money. However, she was oblivious to exactly how much money was owed to her. She made a fairly decent income even with the outstanding debts. In those days (1991), trading was quite profitable. . . . The transnational traders wholesaled their items out to women who could pay half the price of the items at one go. . . . Since the transnational traders sold the items at about three times their original cost, they made 150 percent profit, even when the wholesalers paid only half the amount.

Once Afariwaa discovered how much money her sister had locked up with her debtors, she decided to do something about it. She spent one week going from shop to shop collecting the money owed to her sister. . . . Thanks to Afariwaa, Oparibea was able to increase her working capital for her next trip from 15 to 25 million cedis.

Oparibea could not believe how helpful her sister was in aiding her to recoup her locked up capital. During the ensuing vacations, Oparibea took Afariwaa along with her on buying trips . . . to show her the ropes of transnational trading.

After university, Afariwaa fulfilled her government-mandated year of national service, a concept introduced by the Rawlings government, by working at the National Council on Women and Development, then Ghana's national machinery for women. However, she spent Saturdays helping her sister out at the shop. She discovered during this period that daily sales at her sister's shop far exceeded the monthly salary she received at her place of employment. By the time Afariwaa was finished with her national service, Oparibea was pregnant and therefore unwilling to make the long distance journeys to Asia herself. She asked her younger sister to undertake the trips on her behalf; which she willingly did. . . .

[Afariwaa] grew up in an economic environment that was quite different from the one in which Akyaa had grown up in . . . changed by the introduction of structural adjustment programs. Key among these changes was the reduction in the public sector to rid this sector of its underemployed workforce and reduce government expenditure. The Ghanaian state cut 15 percent of public sector jobs in the late 1980s using a last in–first out policy (Boateng 2001). As a result, while only 21 percent of civil service employees were women, 35 percent of those who were laid off were women (Haddad et al. 1995). By the time Afariwaa was old enough to enter the job market . . . the educated population could not expect life-long careers in the formal, public sector as had been the case when Akyaa was growing up. The private sector in both the formal and informal sectors of the economy was seen as a more favorable option for those with tertiary education. It provided higher incomes and, unlike the public sector, one felt relatively more secure about one's tenure in a job.

Afariwaa took on her job at the shop with a certainty that it was a much wiser option than seeking work in the formal sector. . . . She kept the accounts meticulously and helped her sister figure out the prices of each item she brought back. . . . Afariwaa helped Oparibea out at her shop until Oparibea got wind of a shop available for lease at Makola market. To show her appreciation to Afariwaa, Oparibea paid a ten-year lease on the shop and gave her sister $4,000 as her start-up capital to begin her own life of transnational trading. . . . Afariwaa was expected to create a niche market of her own both in terms of the items she bought for sale and the various trading relationships that she set up to sell her items.

Afariwaa started running her own shop in 1996. Like her sister, she specialized in the sale of clothing items. Her sister, who has a lot more capital than she does, sells a much wider variety of clothing than Afariwaa. Oparibea also purchases her clothing from the United States and Asia unlike Afariwaa who purchases her clothes strictly from Asia. In addition, Oparibea's shop is located in the section of Makola nearest the car park, which the market women consider as the shopping area for the Ghanaian elite who are unwilling to walk too far from their cars to purchase items. Generally, Oparibea's goods sell at higher prices than Afariwaa's. . . .

Initially, Afariwaa traveled to both the United States and Thailand to purchase her items. Since 1998, however, she has focused solely on Thailand as her [purchasing] market for the clothing items she sells. The turning point for her, she says, came with the Asian financial crisis of late 1997/early 1998. With the Ghanaian cedi stable against the dollar and the Thai baht devaluing at an alarming rate, she made a huge profit on her trip that year. . . .

For the last six years, Afariwaa has made her living by buying global consumer items from Pratunam market in Thailand and retailing them at Makola market in Ghana. . . . The heart of the market though is the tiny stalls and shops out in the open area leading to and around the Tower. The scene there is strikingly similar to the Makola market. . . . The market consists primarily of small stalls and shops, though they are not as small as those in Makola. Clothes hang from every available space and goods are lined up in front of the shops just as one would find at Makola. The streets have hordes of people. . . .

Despite the quite obvious similarities, there is a crucial difference between Makola market and Pratunam market. This market serves as an outlet for the numerous clothing factories scattered around the country that produce items for the global market. At Pratunam, people from various racial backgrounds could be found either shopping for themselves or, more likely, to retail in distant countries. Pratunam market serves as the biggest exporter of wholesale clothes. While most of the shops offer items at retail prices, their appeal, at least from the perspective of transnational traders like Afariwaa, lies in the wholesale prices that they offer. Items attract wholesale prices once one buys either three, six, or a dozen depending on the item and the shop. Usually, the minimum required is three items for which one can expect to pay rock bottom prices. . . .

Financial transactions at Pratunam market are also far more formalized than is the case at Makola. Each of the shops at Pratunam provides receipts to which a business card is attached after final payments are made. . . .

Like Akyaa who changed careers to accommodate the needs of her daughter, Afariwaa also finds herself having to rearrange her work schedules as she attempts to balance her role as a trader with that of her role as a mother. Traders make at least two trips a year to coincide with the two peak purchasing seasons of the Ghanaian calendar: Christmas and Easter. Ideally, traders should make their trips two months prior to the celebration of these festivities. . . . Exactly when trips are made depends on the traders' ability to secure alternative living arrangements for their children since very few fathers are willing to take on child-care responsibilities. . . . For Afariwaa, whose children are both beneath the age of five, this is especially crucial. There have been occasions when she has had to reschedule purchasing trips so that her travel plans do not conflict with the travel plans of the sister in whose care her children are put while she travels.

. . . Afariwaa's husband . . . is not particularly pleased that his wife chooses to sell in the market. . . . For now though, Afariwaa is happy with the flexibility that trading provides. She does concede, however, that once her two boys aged three and four are older, she will embark on a graduate degree and move out of working in the informal sector. Afariwaa's desire to eventually return to work in the formal sector is also shaped by the fact that the increasing devaluations of the Ghanaian cedi vis-à-vis other currencies makes trading in global consumer items less lucrative than it was in previous years. . . . The increasing prices, in the face of relatively stagnant salaries, decrease the purchasing power of Ghanaian citizens resulting in lower sales overall. A general refrain from transnational traders these days is that "business is slow especially when compared to previous years." In the face of declining sales, traders like Afariwaa, who are relatively young and have tertiary education, may take advantage of their training to opt out of trading.

CONCLUSION

In the last two decades, "globalization" has become a nebulous term frequently used in the social science literature to refer to global changes in a variety of areas. . . . In Ghana, the most evident process subsumed under the term "globalization" is the country's adoption of a structural adjustment program. Arguably, Ghana is one of the few countries in the world that consistently maintained a structural adjustment program.

Specific aspects of the program, such as the retrenchment policies, limited employment opportunities in the formal public sector for educated Ghanaians. Prior to its introduction, educated Ghanaians could count on careers in the formal public sector, but the imposition of these policies eroded this possibility. As such, this category of prospective employees needed to look elsewhere for employment. Fortunately, while retrenchment policies closed off some employment opportunities, other aspects of the structural adjustment program, such as the trade liberalization policies, opened new avenues for income generation. Trade liberalization policies streamlined import procedures and made importing less cumbersome. . . . [Furthermore,] [t]ime–space compressions, made possible by changes in transportation and telecommunication technologies, aided the efforts of these Ghanaians. Innovations in transportation and telecommunication reduced travel distances between hitherto far-off places and lowered the cost of communication across continents.

However, other aspects of structural adjustment policies, specifically currency devaluations, made the opportunities for income generation through the importation of global consumer items short-lived. If the Ghanaian cedi remained stable while the currencies of other countries devalued, as was the case during the East Asian financial crises, the economic fortunes of traders in global consumer items were secure. On the other hand, traders lost money if the Ghanaian cedi devalued while the currencies of other countries remained stable. The severe devaluation of the Ghanaian cedi over the last two years (2000–2002) has heightened traders' awareness of the financial insecurities inherent in the trade of global consumer items. Consequently, those traders who, because of their educational backgrounds, have other career options are choosing to opt out of the trade in global consumer items.

The two life histories presented above illustrate the impact of globalization in general and structural adjustment policies, in particular, on one segment of the Ghanaian female population. These life histories show the Janus-faced nature of structural adjustment policies which close some avenues to wealth creation while creating opportunities for others. Yet, there are limits to the extent to which one can rely on these newly available income-generating opportunities as a source of steady income.

REFERENCES

Aryeetey, Emmanuel (1994) "Private Investment under Uncertainty in Ghana," *World Development* 22, 8: 1211–1221.

Boateng, Kwabia (2001) "Employment and Incomes under the Structural Adjustment Programme in Ghana" in A. Y. Baah (ed.) *The Social Dimension of Structural Adjustment in Ghana*, Accra: Hallow Ads Limited.

Chamlee-Wright, Emily (1997) *The Cultural Foundations of Economic Development: Urban Female Entrepreneurship in Ghana*, London: Routledge.

Clark, Gracia (1994) *Onions Are My Husband: Survival and Accumulation by West African Women*, Chicago: University of Chicago Press.

Cruickshank, Brodie (1853) *Eighteen Years on the Gold Coast of Africa Including an Account of the Native Tribes and Their Intercourse with Europeans*, London: Hurst and Blacket.

Daniell, William, F. (1856) "On the Ethnography of Akkrah and Adampe, Gold Coast, Western Africa," *Journal of the Ethnological Society* 4: 1–32.

Darkwah, Akosua, K. (2002) "Going Global: Ghanaian Female Transnational Traders in an Era of Globalization," Unpublished Ph. D. Dissertation, University of Wisconsin-Madison.

Fraker, A., and B. Harrell-Bond (1979) "Feminine Influence," *West Africa* (November 26): 2182–2186.

Gladwin, Christina, H. (1991) *Structural Adjustment and African Women Farmers*, Gainesville: University of Florida Press.

Haddad, Lawrence, Lynn R. Brown, Andrea Richter,

and Lisa Smith (1995) "The Gender Dimensions of Economic Adjustment Policies: Potential Interactions and Evidence to Date," *World Development* 23, 6: 881–896.

Robertson, Claire (1983) "The Death of Makola and Other Tragedies," *Canadian Journal of African Studies* 17, 3: 469–495.

—— (1995) "Trade, Gender and Poverty in the Nairobi Area: Women's Strategies for Survival and Independence in the 1980s" in R. L. Blumberg, C. A. Rakowski, I. Tinker and M. Monteon (eds.) *Engendering Wealth and Well-being: Empowerment for Global Change*, Boulder, CO: Westview Press.

Steuer, M. D. (1973) "After the Crisis Longer Term Prospects for the Economy of Ghana," Inaugural Lecture Pamphlet, Accra: Ghana Universities Press.

CHAPTER 5

Feminine Injustice

Conceição Osório and Eulália Temba

This chapter is about the system of the administration of justice in Mozambique, carried out by the Project "Legal Situation of Women" in 1998 and 1999. . . . In 25 years, the country went from an exclusively state-controlled justice system to a context of re/surfacing of old and new means of conflict resolution where previous spaces of mediation have gained visibility, multiplying and opening up new spaces for litigation. We are trying to analyze if this has brought qualitative changes for women's access to justice or if, on the contrary, old subalternarities have been reinforced in a context where the roles and functions of women have not been reevaluated. . . .

THE DOMINANCE OF PATRIARCHY

The creation of national independence was based on a political model which wanted to be revolutionary within the traditional socialist system. This implied, on the one hand, rupture with the colonial past of stratification and, on the other hand, the traditional forms of social organization. . . .

The social relations of gender and the destruction of its structural elements (e.g., dowries and polygamy) led to the concealment of signs of gender inequality, without questioning this inequality. This means that, from a political point of view, the Basic Law (Constitution of the Popular Republic of Mozambique, 1975) gave visibility to gender equality and evoked women's participation in the political arena. However, women's social role continued to be centered on the androcentric model. In other words, gender equality was represented only in a complementary basis, without questioning male dominance.[1]

However, if the destruction of the elements of the traditional gender inequality (such as dowries and marriages) had strengthened in some way the continuous submission of women to the patriarchal model[2] ("bureaucratically" breaching with the old forms of social cohesion), emancipation only occurred in political discourse. On the other hand, the social participation of women legitimizes and rejects the violation of their rights.[3]

. . . [T]he Law of the Judiciary Organization of 1978 (Law No. 12/78, December 2) attempted to be compatible with the level of justice found in the political order instituted in 1975 and created Popular Tribunals, opening access of judicial activity to the citizens that have been elected by the popular assemblies. . . .

[However] the reorganization of the judiciary system[4] (accenting a normative conception of the law) ended the popular tribunals, and introduced community courts (that are not part of the judicial system), while rehabilitating traditional or religious forms of power, as forms of conflict resolution. . . .

The objective of our work, studying

women's access to justice, is to deepen the analysis of how the ... changes imply alterations in the social relations of gender, in the direction of the transgression of the traditional role of the woman, and the solution to the conflicts in which women are involved. ...

... [T]he differences between groups and statutes only modify the way in which the subordination is exercised. ... When we refer to access to justice, we not only take into account the formal aspects, but also the mechanisms that control such social access. ...

The creation of the popular courts, up until the middle of the 1980s (when the economic war, politics and the inefficacy of the political system began to intervene with its function), reflect the revolutionary concept of justice, widening its access to all.[5] Simultaneously, they fill the space denied by the traditional instances of conflict resolution. ...

For women, this situation has double consequences: in the name of the law and political discourse, it allows them to "appear" in a space that was not recognized as theirs in the past. The nature of the conflicts and the solutions, [however], found in the instances of justice continue to consecrate the dominance of a model that subordinates women. ...

CONFLICTS: PRODUCTION AND REPRESENTATION

... The effect of the war and the economic crisis (including changes in political strategies), lead, on the one hand, to the destruction of blood relations and, on the other hand, to the sprouting of new ways of belonging (social networks of inter-help).[6] ...

Although the impact of the change in the family set-up has not had the same intensity across the country, the results from the research of the last years lead to the conclusion that the war, the programs of structural adjustment, and the reduction of the state's

role has contributed to the diversification of social organizations throughout the country. ...

... The war and the economic crisis lead to the destruction of the traditional family and to the sprouting of many families constituted basically of children and women, leading to, even in rural areas, women having to look for the means to family survival in the public sphere.

The presence of a woman in the work force, caused by economic need, concretizes some of the conflicts that structure gender relations. In particular, combining women's traditionally sanctioned roles of mother and wife with their presence in the work force, considerably multiplies women's activity. Their presence in the public sphere for a wage (in contrast to what happens with their domestic tasks) provokes alterations in the mechanisms of control surrounding the subalternarity of women.

While the work of peasant women (about 91 percent of the active population of the country) (PNUD 1998) is considered as part of domestic work, and therefore, socially not valued, ... their presence in the labor market unchains representations and practices of transgression of the social constructions of the feminine. ...

[I]f the "emergence" of women in the labor market creates the potential for contradictions and conflicts in the patriarchal model to appear (allowing the modification of some of the mechanisms of control and submission),[7] then analysis of these conflicts (both old and new) is basically understood in the same way that other family conflicts are understood; and the family is a field of power production. When the contradictions are recognized, they emerge as a conflict or contribute to creating change in the patriarchal model. ...

All the [legal] conflicts presented by women have a situation of systematic and permanent violence as a base. However, the violence itself, even with physical damage, does not appear as reason for presenting a complaint.

Especially in rural areas, but also in urban ones, violence against women structures social gender relations. The naturalization of this violence is more efficient when women themselves recognize men's right to impose punishment. . . .

. . . [T]he increase in conjugal violence (in the context of men's unemployment and associated with alcoholism) does not correspond to the increase in female complaints (at least in a formal manner). In recent years, [however], complaints have increased in frequency about aggression by men who are not part of the women's family. This situation shows not only the legitimacy (allied to the fear and the shame) of conjugal violence but also reveals the rejection of male violence, without its recognition.

For this reason, complaints about violence are almost always made in situations of a husband's abandonment of the house and are systematically accompanied by the request for a food pension or divorce.

The request for food pension is only made when there are small children, not only because the woman is unaware of the law, but because she has a negative impression of her rights. Divorce has constituted one of the main types of litigation presented by women in the formal courts.[8] Whereas, men do not need a divorce to be recognized as legitimate proprietors of marital property,[9] and for them, public complaint against a woman is considered un-prestigious for the male power. . . .

Compared to the past, the number of divorce cases has increased in the entire country, even though this means that, in traditional society or traditionalized urban areas, the women's families have to "take them back."

However, as in the past, due to the negative representation of divorced women, a divorce case presented by a woman is always the product of abandonment and maltreatment and, rarely, of the woman's desire to separate.

About 90 percent of separated women told us: "he beats a lot, but that is not the problem . . . he did not give money for the house . . . he took his clothing to the house of his lover . . . he always beats, but the real problem is when he does not provide money for food . . ."

The regulation of paternal power constitutes one of the new conflicts produced by the combination of an old phenomenon—a continued absence of marriages and registration of children—with a new phenomenon—discouragement of traditional marriages in the post independence period and an increase in the number of illegitimate children. . . .

[O]n the one hand, most of the conflicts produced between couples do not correspond (quantitatively) with the number of cases directed to the system. . . .

On the other hand, the prohibition against polygamy in the recent past was reversed when a new political system was installed in the country, and then the practice of polygamy was resumed without respecting the traditional norms and rituals that limited the number of wives. This happens because some of the mechanisms of legitimization were broken, therefore socially permitting men to have four or five women, outside of the norm enforced by tradition.

A consequence of this situation was the systematic abandonment of the women, since there were no social sanctions; and, as a result, increasing numbers of children are not integrated into families. In other words, none of the families (paternal or maternal) has the moral obligation to protect them.

Furthermore, social and economic instability has contributed to an increased number of premature marriages. As a result, marriage loses its main purpose to reinforce family alliances, but instead emphasizes its mercantile nature.

Child abuse cases are found in great numbers in hospitals, but there is no real justice under the law, because most cases reported in health centers are perpetrated within the family circle. In the case of abuse against children aged 4 to 5, the explanations socially "justify" it as "acts of momentary madness" and the abuse cases of older children, age 10 to 12 years, are explained as "provocation" by a young girl, or because "the men are like that."[10]

The situation of social disorder, in opposition to the order established with independence, still leads to the emergence of new forms of violence against women. In this case, they are accusations of witchcraft against old women, most of whom are poor and widows, as a way to remove the threat of hunger and disasters that threaten the community. . . .

The witches of the past, who were feared because of the forces that they could unleash, have been replaced by the poor slandered women of today, who can be easily accused of "killing their husbands," and expelled from their lands and their houses. . . .

ACCESS TO JUSTICE AND CONFLICT MANAGEMENT

. . . We have therefore to consider two factors influencing women's access to justice: on the one hand, there is the social model, which places women in the private space that removes the possibility and the recognition that they can exercise their rights (which in many cases they are unaware of); and, on the other hand, there are material factors and issues of social representation by the agents who generate the conflicts. . . .

Conflicts that are produced within the scope of the family (with the exception of criminal court cases) are excluded from the legal corpus, strengthening the patriarchal representation in the justice system. For this reason, physical violence against women is socially identified as being a private matter that must be solved in the scope of the family.

As a result of this situation, even when a divorce case involves direct brutal beating, the complaint can never be presented as a crime against the husband, discouraging the accusation of violence in the first place. . . .

. . . [I]n the District of Angónia in the Province of Tete, . . . [an informant said:] "it is an act of shame by any women who presents a complaint of physical abuse against her husband because it is the men's right to punish women. Therefore any woman would be seen negatively after presenting such a complaint . . ."

This type of representation of masculine violence is found in all the studied regional zones, which reflects a justice system that is based on a social model that grants men the legitimacy of women's domination and control. Therefore, women's access to justice is mainly through informal instances, either with the police or traditional courts.

. . . [Moreover,] . . . the more rural the area, the more it is influenced by traditional forms of power. . . .

In the southern part of Mozambique, where the political power was established with some effectiveness, the structure of the party in power, like the Grupo Dinamizadores (Dynamist Group) and the OMM, becomes the place where litigation is presented. In this region, the traditional authorities were, as we previously affirmed, incorporated into (or adjusted to) the party's exercise of political power, thus lessening conflicts between different forms of power.

Many traditional courts in the south of the country have ethnic/family links with the controllers of the state, easing the struggle for decision making.[11] This ambiguity (the traditional chiefs make judgments using their double role: as head chiefs and secretaries of village) allows for their rulings to be tied to the regular tribunals.

In the north of the country, the marginalization of the traditional authorities in the post-independence period and after the peace accords enabled these authorities to become the legitimate representatives of the traditional order, demanding the management of conflicts in their communities.

In these areas, the traditional authorities are second to the family in power. They are the most important figures in conflict resolution. Their decisions are never the object of last resort to other situations. . . .

. . . [W]e can also see that the access to justice can be produced in very different ways within one province (like Gaza): while, in the provincial capital, the OMM is the place par excellence for the presentation of marital conflicts, but in the districts, such as in Guijá, the organization of the women does not have any visibility in the arbitration of the litigations. . . .

Currently, the multiplication of organizations, such as AMETRAMO (Association of Traditional Doctors), the churches and sects, that are mostly managed by the same people who are elected judges in the communitarian and district courts, allows the development of strategies on the part of the population that, independently of the conflicts, appeal to one or another situation in function of social recognition. . . .

In regards to the formal justice system, the social representation of the conflicts by the justice agents and the social stature of the litigants determine (as in the court cases where professional judges exist) the form in which the conflicts are managed.

The complexity of the procedures and the insufficient number of legal professionals (about 150 in all the country, of which two-thirds are in Maputo), and the content of the law (i.e., difficulties of interpretation and application) lead to corruption in the judicial system, transforming justice into an arbitrary field. . . .

The long delay in the production of sentencing is proof of the interaction of different and plural factors in the exercise of the administration of justice. . . .

This wait (almost like waiting for Godot) has supplemental effects in the case of the women who continue to be subjected to multiple forms of violence. If, against all odds (and at times against themselves), they bring their complaints about the long delays in the resolution of their cases to the public, that wait only reinforces the inequality, and the disappointment makes them accept that, indeed, nothing will be done. . . .

The articulations between the formal and informal levels of justice are not uniform in all the country. . . .

In the south of the country, for example, our research showed that the OMM, the police and the communitarian courts, have exchanged information and it seems that there is a search for consensus, independent of the content of the law. In the center of the country, mainly in Sofala, the traditional authority and other forms of authority exclude themselves, rivaling the recognition on the part of the populations. . . .

According to the law, the communitarian courts have only one function—advisement, but they mostly function as decision makers. The same situation occurs with traditional authorities and with women's organizations. . . .

. . . The women's organizations, in general (with prominence given to the OMM), are the key places for the presentation of complaints. The majority of the conflicts presented to them have to do with a husband's abandonment of the house, coupled with physical and psychological violence by him.

Because the OMM was created in the context of an ideological political orientation in which the patriarchal model is not questioned, the forms of conflict management seek to articulate the traditional norm with the theoretical principles of the revolutionary order.

This means that there is an attempt to end the physical violence against women, as long as women accept the masculine superiority (for example if the husband finds another woman, first she must accept the other woman and find a way to distribute the goods and the attention for the two households). . . .

The same women, when in front of the police or a female judge, look for legitimacy in the masculine model. In other words, they adopt the aggressiveness and rigidity of a male and at the same time erase their femininity, becoming the "other" to be heard and recognized.

No differences were found in the observation of the judgments in which the parties involved (as mediators, defendants or complainants) were women. Women do not carry with them ways to subvert the hierarchical model. Instead, they submit themselves to the exclusion of the feminine condition. On behalf of equality, and to be in the masculine space, women have to lose their differences.

However, when looking for justice, such as from the police, women are not expected to break any subordinate norm. . . .

The same situation is found in the court system that looks to a judge for social legitimacy and makes women obey. To achieve such a purpose, the courts use a language or legal codes that women cannot understand, and such language intimidates them and further naturalizes women's inferiority. . . .

The guilt, the humiliation, and the desire for justice all are mixed together and the result, for the most part, is violent. This violence is evident when the courts deny their rights. By not recognizing the rights of women as human rights, and by positively representing women as being *calm, patient, maternal*, the justice system and its agents notably contribute to the victimization of women. . . .

This means that because women are poorer and have fewer qualifications, abandonment by their long-time partners leaves them in absolute misery. In areas of matriarchal organization in the north of the country, where marriages take a traditional form, this allows for principles to be more favorable to women. However, the situation is now becoming closer to the southern regions of the country where the economic crisis and displacements do not allow for the restoration of their traditional norms.

It is interesting to note how the biggest myth of women's freedom in a matriarchal system falls to the ground once the components of gender relations are closely analyzed. In fact, if we can find a greater capacity for women to find (and to abandon without having any social sanctions imposed on her) a partner (because traditionally it was her family that would do it), the matrilineal organization, which continues to center around the masculine figure since it does not contain the marital rituals that exist in the south, it becomes easier, in situations of social disruptions, to end marital relations without holding the men responsible or the men's family accountable for both women and their children's financial support.

STILL LOOKING FOR JUSTICE

. . . Today, the traditional family is particularly affected (by instability in the old social order), destructuring the ways that used to legitimize the marital alliances as well as how the roles and functions were organized.

On the one hand, this destruction allows for women to assume functions in the public sphere (especially in the informal market), making possible the rupture with the mechanisms of traditional control. On the other hand, the disappearance of structural rituals has increased the social vulnerability of the women (as is the case in the reduction of traditional marriages). . . .

. . . For these reasons, the rehabilitation of traditional forms and the emergence of a set of spaces for conflict resolution (churches, healers, etc.) do not modify the social relations of power on their own. These power relations continue to be guided by the social mechanisms that are fixed in keeping women in a subordinate position. . . .

The fight for women's access to justice aims, in our view, not to recuperate the old consensual forms to manage conflicts (because such social consensus excluded the rights of the women as human beings), but for a re-conceptualization of justice and of the cultural, social, and political models that configure it. . . .

NOTES

Editors' Note: This article was translated from the Portuguese original version by Yaser S. Robles.

1. Women's anthem in Mozamique, which places "women as the faithful partners of the men," is a clear example of how a discourse that intends to honor women as subjects is fundamentally a recognition of their subordination.
2. The administrative "abolition" of dowries in the first years of national independence resulted in the elimination of an important factor for the "protection" of women's rights. In other words, what those in power understood (in their modernity), as a mere economic phenomenon, that they translated as a purchase or sale of women, had a structural social function and was a stabilizer. The direct consequences of the destruction of these elements of social cohesion was the increasing abandonment or expulsion of women from their homes when they were not purchased through dowries and, as a result, there was an elimination of all social responsibility for the fulfilment of legitimizing rituals.
3. In the first years of independence, the OMM (Women's Organization of Mozambique) was acknowledged as the result of women's discontent.
4. Law number 10/92 of June 5, 1992.
5. Under revolutionary justice, the problems created by the autonomy of the justice system from the system of political domination no longer existed because the justice system became an integral part of the political arena.
6. Teresa Cruz e Silva conducted an interesting study about the emergence and structuration of new social webs of inter-help in the town of Mafalala during the period of change.
7. Evident are two new conflicts in the tentative realm of social control: one refers to the gains women have had in the work force, and the other is over her reproductive rights, or lack of it, as she is forced to reproduce indefinitely.
8. A divorce implies civil marriage, the legal recognition of traditional unions.
9. In most areas of the country, even in matriarchal areas, it is believed that when a woman gets married, she must "go to the husband's house."
10. Cases of child abuse happen most of the time as a result of the advice of healers to people who are looking to "end their bad luck."
11. The use of the local language (and the forms of communication used) in the encounters with the population was one of the main elements used by the Party leaders and the state to reject the credibility of the traditional authorities in the south of the country.

REFERENCES

Constitution of the Popular Republic of Mozambique (Constituição da República Popular de Moçambique) (1975).

Cruz e Silva, Teresa (2000) "As redes de solidariedade como intervenientes na resolução de litígios: o caso da Mafalala," in B. S. Santos et al. *Conflito e Transformacão social : uma paisagem das justiças em Moçambique*, Relatório de pesquisa, Maputo/Coimbra: CEA/CES (mimeo).

Judiciary Organization of Mozambique (Organização Judiciária de Moçambique) (1978).

PNUD (1998) *Relatório de Desenvolvimento Humano*, Maputo: United Nations Development Programme.

WLSA Mozambique (Women and Law in Southern Africa Research and Education Trust) (1998) *Famílias em Contexto de Mudança*, Maputo: WLSA, Mozambique.

—— (1999) *Administração da Justiça em Moçambique*, Maputo: WLSA, Mozambique.

CHAPTER 6

Women, the Sacred and the State

Fatou Sow

. . . Senegal is a secular state. The separation of church and state was written into all constitutions that have governed the country since 1960. Even so, periodically, there is a discussion between those who support secularity as the hallmark of the Republic and those arguing for its abolition, noting the Muslim identity of the majority of Senegalese citizens. This discussion was very heated at the time of the development of the new constitution (2001), several months after the Democratic Senegalese Party took power and at the time when a large coalition of forces opposed the Socialist Senegalese Party. The legal tradition inherited from French colonization finally prevailed: Senegal remained a secular state. Political institutions and legal documents that have governed the country for forty years do not, as a whole, make specific reference to religious obedience or to Islam, the dominant religion, as a source for governance. This is not the case in the Islamic republics of Mauritania, or of the Sudan, nor of certain states in the north of Nigeria who avow themselves to be Islamic in spite of the unconstitutionality of such a declaration in the context of the Nigerian Federation. . . .

. . . [W]e will explore, on the one hand, the multifaceted demands of women for more equality in family rights over the last four decades (1970–2000) and, on the other, the accusation of their being anti-Islamic. . . . The debate surrounding Islam and women's rights is often denounced as an imported polemic of western feminism and is aggravated by the recurring anti-Muslim discourse. The attacks against the World Trade Center in New York in September 2001 and the sharp American counter-attack against Muslim "fundamentalists," accused of terrorism, did nothing but poison and muddle the controversy that was already difficult to define. The atmosphere surrounding the international media campaigns denouncing extreme cases, such as hand amputation as punishment for theft in Mauritania in the 1980s, and the death penalty as punishment for adultery and illegitimate pregnancy among Hausa women in northern Nigeria at the beginning of the twenty-first century, testify to the intensity of peoples' passion. . . .

Here, Islamic politics is a throwback to the usage of religion as a political argument, either by the society itself, notably in its brotherhoods and religious associations, or by the state where legislative power is inspired from the Koran for the family code, all while using Muslim communities and their leaders as electoral pawns for the acquisition or the maintenance of political power. In an equally ambiguous context, secularity and religion come together and become the subject of periodic debate.

Muslim communities in colonial Senegal expressed a bitter hostility toward the civil code due to the Judeo-Christian values that they felt it implied (e.g., monogamy) despite the secularization that this initiative represented. From the time of Durand Valentin (elected in 1848), Carpot (1904), Blaise Diagne (1914) and Lamine Guèye (1946), the French parliamentary representatives have supported their electors' position to maintain the *shari'a*, which was rethought as a way of managing family relationships according to their customs. Colonial authorities were thus led to recognize decisions made about the family by the Muslim court presided over by a Qadi. However, this appeal for theological and judicial order that was as much a religious affirmation as it was an affirmation of identity in the face of colonial presence became a call to religion, and has become more and more difficult to contest in contemporary Senegal. In this context, the debate rarely turns toward an analysis of these changes and of contemporary social aspirations but is reduced to a controversy about their religious character. . . .

This article is a two-fold study about women, laws and Islam in Africa. First, it originates from an ensemble of research on women and social gender relationships in Senegalese society. Second, it is of a collective nature, initiated by the group, "Women Living under Muslim Laws (WLUML)." It studies the impact of Islam on laws that affect gender relationships in both family and social contexts. This study assumes the particular importance of religion, because it is an unavoidable dimension in the lives of Muslim women. "The parameters of a woman's life are determined by a combination of formal statuary provisions and of informal customs that can each be based in religion, the traditional customs of the region and in other sources such as colonial regulations or universal tendencies" (Women Living under Muslim Laws 1994: 7). Now, a close examination reveals that all of these provisions are part of an unequal social hierarchy between the sexes. . . .

THE DEBATE BETWEEN SECULARITY AND RELIGION IN SENEGAL

The Koran is the word of God revealed to the prophet Mohammad and is considered to be the code of religious, moral and social conduct for all Muslims. It is the fundamental source for Islamic law. . . . Facing the need to consider new questions about the historical and political evolution of Muslim communities, Ulemas, legal scholars, had to turn to the *sunnah* as a secondary legal source. The *sunnah* gathers oral traditions (*hadith*), bringing back practices from the time of the Prophet Mohammad and his followers. Over the course of many centuries, the *ijtihad*, as a practice of reflection and interpretation, enabled discussing, (re)constructing, and reinforcing Muslim discourse to allow certain adaptations and to accord a certain flexibility in the context of local customs. It authorizes people qualified by their Koranic learning to reason and establish links, which are not always explicit, between Koranic text and the rules of the *shari'a*. . . . The *shari'a*, as "an ensemble of cultural and social tradition (in the wide sense) drawn from the Koran and the *sunnah*" (Ramadan 2001: 64), organizes and regulates various aspects of the religious and social life of followers including fasting and dress codes as well as marriage, divorce, widowhood, and inheritance. This is at the heart of the current debate surrounding Islam and modernity because its enforcement is criticized due to its opposition to social "modernization."

The term "Islamic fundamentalism" lends itself to the greatest controversy today since it has a more marked political meaning due to the sheer activity of the movement.

Islamists belong to a politico-religious, conservative fundamentalist wave of Islam. Their major goal is a total Islamization of laws, government and other institutions. Islamism is often associated with fundamentalism, the concept that first emerged with the protestant movements in the 1920s in the

United States. This movement is associated with a scrupulous respect for the Bible in the face of an American society in the midst of great political and social transformation. It was a way of reaffirming their racial and religious identity. . . . Today, we must qualify fundamentalists or extremists into groups that are as heterogeneous as the Wahhabi, the Taliban, Hezbollah, the Muslim Brotherhood, Pentecostals, Adventists, or American tele-evangelists, the Hassidic Jews or the Catholic fundamentalists of Monsignor Lefebvre, the former French archduke of Dakar from 1948–1962. . . .

Surrounding the debate over secularity versus religion, two positions can be observed that willfully oppose one another in Senegalese politics.

The first is that secularity is at the root of democracy, no matter what the religion. "The governing of the city and of politics can only be secular." These were the terms expressed by the former President of Senegal, Abdou Diouf at the time of his nomination as secretary general of the Francophone Organization at the Bayreuth summit on October 20, 2002. . . .

Secularity was, and still is, a force in all political, judicial, economic and financial Senegalese institutions. France, "the oldest daughter of the church," set the tone in all its former colonies. All discrimination based on religion is unconstitutional and no political party should have its roots in religion. At no time should constitutional, commercial, or penal rights be influenced by Islamic law. Legal provisions coming from the *shari'a* (or in the mindset of the *shari'a*)[1] only apply to the family. Colonial authority gave in to this communitarian demand and juxtaposed civil rights with Islamicized African customs. [A]fter independence, the new authority maintained this even if they reinforce secular culture by obliterating Muslim tribes. . . .

The second position in the debate surrounding secularity versus religion, more than questioning the idea of secularity, desires a greater religious participation in politics. . . .

Questions concerning the family are at the heart of the Senegalese debate on secularity and the return to the *shari'a*. At no time is the governing of the state or of business closely examined by Islamic religious associations. As in the Islamic republic of Mauritania, these debates do not put commercial law, banking practices (interest rates), constitutional law or penal law into question. It is in a private context that the secularity/religion debate is most tangible, with family law at the root of the conflict. In this case, the return to *shari'a* is a political position that engages leaders of religious associations and Arabic scholars who target the shaping of women and children. This is their way of participating in politics and constructing a legitimate base.

WOMEN, THE STATE, AND THE SACRED

Numerous Muslim societies are still state-controlled by written legislation and unwritten codes that are derived from interpretations of the Koran, but which overlap with local customs, and which are openly or tacitly accepted. These interpretations vary according to the place and context and can have a considerable impact on the lives of women and on their civil rights.

The resurgence of Muslim discourse in a Senegal that practices old Islam, which is deeply rooted in the culture and "the peaceful," contributed to the expansion of numerous feminine *dahira*.[2] Certain "fundamentalist" movements (*Jama'atu Ibaadu Rahman, dahira* of Madina Gounas) favored wearing the headscarf in several categories of the population, a practice until then, unknown, particularly in urban or student circles. In the same vein, Islamic social pressure came to the point of stopping men and women from shaking hands as was the common practice. [M]ore and more ostentatious religious practices can be witnessed. For example, employees interrupt service and leave meetings under the pretext of praying on time. . . .

A few examples of the debate on women's rights illustrate the collusion between politics and religion that reinforces the patriarchal system.

Access to school has become a basic right. Colonial schools enrolled sons of chiefs or hostages, two or three generations before making place for women. In spite of the progress accomplished in educating girls, in the 1990s, Senegal had to establish a program specifically for this purpose along with the support of international organizations like UNICEF. The objective of the SCOFI (*Scolarisation des Filles* [Education of Girls]) program is not only to organize enrollment campaigns, but to keep girls in school. Today, campaigns are still necessary so that girls are not withdrawn as minors either to do domestic work, to be put on the job market, or to be married. . . .

Since April 2002, the teaching of religion in all public schools has been officially allowed, under pressure from Islamic associations. At the time of the 1982 general state of education convention, with the advent of President Abdou Diouf, the question of whether or not to teach religion was a thorny one. It was a matter of clearly introducing the teaching of religion, particularly of the Koran, following the example of private Catholic institutions. In order for Muslim students to learn the Koran, there were special hours reserved in the afternoon, after their heavy curricular work. This recommendation has not been upheld for fear of infringing upon secularity. We have the same concerns today. It is obvious that studying religion is an important part of education as long as it does not promote tendencies that infringe on secularity, for example, seeing girls forced to wear a headscarf during Koran classes, imposing a dress

code, dissolving co-ed schools, respecting hours of prayer, etc.

The law repealing female genital mutilation was the subject of an immense protest within Senegalese society before its adoption in February 1999. Excision, which was one part of the issue, was generally presented as an African cultural initiation practice. In regions where excision is practiced, it is a marker of femininity. It took more than thirty years of international controversy to be able to work out this law. In the midst of the debate, cultural and religious arguments were brandished against western feminists and their African colleagues whose belated protests could only be attributed to the west.[3] Muslim communities such as Hal Pulaar, Soninke and Mandeng have adhered to the argument that unexcised women were impure and could not pray, which would greatly ostracize them. It was certainly the revelation of the harmful medical consequences of these practices, and also the fact that they alter sexual pleasure, which proved to be very important in helping to pass the law.

Undoubtedly, the impact of religion is most important in laws pertaining to the family. Senegalese women are often accused of undermining the word of God when they try to advance their own democratic civil rights, rights that are denied or not applicable, in spite of the clear-cut provisions in the current constitution.

Senegal depended on the former French civil code and the Koran in 1973 in order to promulgate the first civil code of the new independent state. This code was sharply contested within the heart of the Muslim community from the time of its enactment in 1973. People mobilized against its openness and some even spoke of the code as against the *shari'a* and its rules, thus against Muslims and their faith. It was accused of being a women's code. Twenty-five years later during the 2000 presidential elections, one of the religious candidates, without a doubt the most excessive, went as far as to promise to completely suppress the law in order to reestablish the *shari'a*. His remarks were penalized by a poor electoral showing, proving the popular repudiation of his ideas. This code, denounced by its opponents as being pro-woman, has a particularly patriarchal position in many of its articles. Each demand that women made, in order to eradicate the discriminatory provisions, was denounced by men as being anti-religious . . .

Nevertheless, the family code is based on the principles of forgiveness and the protection of women as affirmed by the Koran. It reflects a push toward judicial modernization of Senegalese society down from its highest levels. It was approved by President Leopold Sedar Senghor who legislated on both administrative and territorial reform and about the national domain that he wanted to protect for community use. It is true that the code protected women. It most notably obliged spouses to register their marriage with the state to assure a woman's consent. It was aimed at reducing excessive polygamy that occurs due to the simple concessions that women make to maintain their own household, their spouse and their children. It was the logic of matrimonial options. Polygamy was abolished in other Muslim countries, such as Turkey, Tunisia, and the Ivory Coast. In Iraq, one must ask for permission to have a polygamous marriage before a court of law. Only a judge can declare a divorce and fix reciprocal obligations and conditions of child custody, of alimony or child support, etc.

Constraining provisions are still maintained in the civil code, supposedly for women. Certain injustices were corrected in response to women's demands, always expressed through the media. Polygamy comes out of a singularly masculine initiative, even if it is negotiated by the family code and could not be abolished. This also holds true for the unequal share of inheritance between girls and boys. This is done in the name of the *shari'a*, a legal text that should

not be confused with the Koran. Yet, the Senegalese people should know that:

> If polygamy is widespread in Senegal, according to the results of EDSIII (1997), it concerns 45.5% of married women. One can even observe a slight reduction in the frequency of these unions as the percentage was 48.5% in 1978. This drop is probably linked to education and urbanization. There are people without formal education and rural women in the same proportions (48–49%) who are in polygamous unions. In 1992, 50.5% of women without formal education, 32% with a primary school education and 29% with secondary or more education were engaged in polygamous relationships. In 1997, their percentages were respectively 49.4%, 34.4%, and 27.1%. Women without instruction constitute the only group in which the frequency of polygamy does not seem to have dropped (49–50%). At the same time, the percentage of women in a polygamous relationship diminished with the degree of urbanization. Within a rural context, the drop is from 50% to 48% from 1978 to 1997. It drops more drastically in the cities with the total dropping from 46% to 41% for the same period.
>
> (Sow et al. 2000: 198)

This is to underline that even if polygamy is a legal and religious practice, Senegal is also a monogamous country.

Still within the subject of discrimination toward women in the family code, we can cite the former right of the husband to forbid his wife from working if he finds it to be something that could taint the family honor. This clause, which could only be brought into question with the intervention of a judge, took ten years to be abolished in 1984. It was the eve of the last conference of the world decade of women in Nairobi, when Maimouna Kane, minister in charge of women's issues, was given a real voice in the government. In spite of this, journalists (men) from the local media who had just gained freedom of speech used this newfound right to slander the cause. They used headlines accusing women of seeking out prostitution if they exercised the conjugal veto at their disposal. Today more and more Senegalese households need the salaries of all family members to survive and they cannot do without that of the wife. The right of the man to authorize his wife to leave the country, whatever her professional status, became obsolete with the abolition of the right of any and all Senegalese citizens to leave the country when Abdou Diouf was elected president in 1981. Surprisingly, certain consulates, including that of France continue in their own way to require a marriage certificate and an affidavit certifying the resources of the husband. Single people have no chance of obtaining a visa because of their marital status. Finally the demands of women fostered negotiations leading to changes in the family code in 1984, giving rights over the location of the conjugal household that previously were the domain of the marital authority.

People who oppose the law most dread the fundamental right of a woman to have control over her own body, her own sexuality, and her own fertility. Fertility control that allows women to use contraceptive methods regularly provokes reactions. International agencies, such as the UNFPA (United Nations Population Fund) which encourages family planning, have been accused of wanting to depopulate the planet and of having fooled the Senegalese and their religious guides into acting against divine will.[4] Contraception does indeed give women the power to control their own fertility: to choose to have or not to have children, how many children to have, the number of years between births, etc. . . . Furthermore, unlike Christianity, Islam allows parents to choose the number of years between births and even to have an abortion in extreme cases. This is the position of religious leaders who, in spite of everything, do not believe that women should have rights over their own sexuality and fertility. More than a desire to have a child; maternity is an obligation of marriage. . . . Sterile women

will be marginalized because they do not contribute to the "fabrication" of a lineage that all men "should" have in order to assert their masculinity and the social power that they must establish. In high society, as in numerous African societies, "accumulating children is a sure way to gain prestige" (Échard 1985: 40). This prestige is seated in a woman's body, where sexuality and fertility are controlled by the societal rules defined by each group: virginity, circumcision, surveillance, marriage, submission to the desires of their spouse, management of fertility, etc. The difficulty does not lie in discussing fertility in medical terms, but in terms of the basic rights of those who carry, give birth to, and raise the children to decide whether or not to have them, and how many to have . . .

The current debate surrounding parental authority is another example that illustrates the collusion between politics and religion to reinforce the patriarchal system. . . . The . . . parental authority law has been up for review since 2001. The question has been debated in families, in the print media, and during the course of secular or religious debates on radio or television. The law wants to remedy the current paternal authority situation, under which the father is legally the only family member responsible for his children, and instead calls for parental authority. Currently, maternal authority is only legal if the father is deceased or declares his own incapacity to take this responsibility, in which case he must make a declaration before a judge.

The demand for parental authority nevertheless is only one thing among many that discriminates against married women. Professional associations and women's unions also denounce the discriminatory character of the income tax and the difficulty of taking care of one's family with regard to social security. Taxes are personal and taken out at the source by the employer. A woman earning an income cannot, as her husband can, benefit from tax breaks based on the number of children she has. She is automatically considered to be single and without children. She cannot take over her spouse and children's health insurance, since she is not the head of the family. Those individuals or Islamic groups that find fault with . . . this proposed law on parental authority, openly accuse women of wanting to reject marital authority. . . . Here, the family code is only respecting Koranic limitations that reinforce the power of men over women.

More than the abolition of paternal power and marital authority, what is contested is the recognition and the establishment of genuine equality between men and women. This equality was guaranteed by all constitutions from the time of independence; it is reinforced by the 2001 constitution, voted in by the majority of the Senegalese people. Many articles in it, for example on access to education, to land or to jobs, make explicit mention of equality between men and women. Two articles of the family code are responsible for the numerous constraints that affect women within the family and which often have repercussions in the public sector. The articles affirm that the man is the head of the family and that his wife owes him submission and obedience. The anti-constitutionality of these two articles was denounced by Senegalese women, whose position was reinforced by measures contained in the new constitution that was voted into law during transparent elections. . . .

The African Charter for Human Rights, accepted in 1993, took decades to put into practice and had no particular provision or specific protocol for women. On July 11 2003, the African Union adopted an additional protocol for this Charter on Human Rights as they relate to women. This resulted from a continent-wide struggle by women. The protocol recognizes the rights of women to equal pay for equal work, and the right to maternity leave in both public and private sectors. It affords special protection for handicapped or distressed women, elderly women, widows, women in prison, etc. However, it is in the domain of sexual and reproductive rights where gains are most remarkable, notably the right to abortion in the case of rape and incest, the abolition of female genital mutilation, and protection against physical and sexual violence. The protocol still has to be ratified by the states.

The family that religious and political leaders glorify no longer exists even in rural contexts. The climate has changed under the impact of various social transformations, not all negative, since the time of independence. Urbanization, education, new economic activities, and political and legal changes also have contributed to transforming the Senegalese family. Some would like men to cling to masculine domination; as a last resort, they conjure up, not the spirit of the holy book, but instead use literal interpretations. . . . The undeniable social reality is that more and more women are heads of households. . . .

CONCLUSION

The debate about forced secularity against an aggressive and intolerant "re-Islamization" of African and Senegalese societies is essential when we fight for equality between the sexes and the advancement of the position of women. Links between the state and religion, politics and the sacred are complex in a society where religion and culture are profoundly intertwined. The religious bedrock, whether it is Islamic, pre-Islamic or Christian, remains inextricably linked to daily life. The resurgence of Muslim discourse in the world had considerable impact, whereas secularity or laicism, as a baseline principle of the law, was accused of "progress." [W]omen are stuck between the state, whose responsibility is to guarantee equality between its citizens, and a religious elite, whose main concern is to maintain and support an immutable patriarchal hierarchy. Family is the last bastion to take. Only secularization of the state and of laws can resolve this conflict.

NOTES

Editors' Note: This article was translated from the French original version by Kristen Bini.

1. The provisions laid out are not a strict application of the *shari'a*.
2. *Dahira* is a group of followers linked to a brotherhood, and united to run mostly religious and cultural activities. A *dahira* can be composed of all men, all women, mixed gender, or a group of young people. It ends up structuring itself as a formal organization with decision-making and deliberative groups.
3. Debates were organized during world conferences of women, notably the ones in Copenhagen (1980) and Nairobi (1985). In Africa, the inter-African Committee fights traditional practices that affect women and children's health by promoting sensitivity campaigns on these issues.
4. Results of the 1994 Cairo conference were strongly decried. See *"Le Musulman"*, Journal of the *Jama'atu Ibaadu Rahmane* 47: 4–5.

REFERENCES

Échard, Nicole (1985) "Même la viande est vendue avec le sang" in N. Matthieu (ed.) *L'Arraisonnement des femmes, essais en anthropologie des sexes: Cahiers de l'homme*, Nouvelle Série XXIV, Paris: Éditions de l'École des Hautes Études en Sciences Sociales.

Ramadan, T. (2001) *Islam. Le face à face des civilisations. Quel projet pour quelle modernité?* Lyon: Éditions Tawhid.

Sow, F., M. M. Guèye, A. Touré and N. Diakhaté (eds.) (2000) *Les Sénégalaises en chiffres*, Dakar: PNUD.

Women Living under Muslim Laws/Femmes sous lois musulmanes (1994) "Femmes et lois, Initiatives dans le monde musulman," *Débats tirés de la réunion internationale: Sur le chemin de Beijing: Femmes, lois et statut dans le monde musulman*, December 11–12, Lahore (Pakistan).

SECTION 2

Asia and The Middle East

7 Introduction to Gender Research in Asia and the Middle East   67
   Minjeong Kim and Christine E. Bose

8 Promising and Contested Fields: Advancing Women's Studies and
   Sociology of Women/Gender in Contemporary China   73
   Esther Ngan-ling Chow, Naihua Zhang, and Wang Jinling

9 The Study of Gender in India: A Partial Review   92
   Bandana Purkayastha, Mangala Subramaniam, Manisha Desai, and Sunita Bose

10 Women's Studies in Iran: The Roles of Activists and Scholars   110
    Shahla Ezazi

11 Masculinity and Anti-Americanism: Focusing on the Identity of KATUSA   125
    Insook Kwon

12 Gender, Development and HIV/AIDS in Vietnam: Towards an
    Alternative Response Model among Women Sex Workers   133
    Van Huy Nguyen, Udoy Sankar Saikia, and Thi Minh An Dao

13 *Fufubessei* Movement in Japan: Thinking About Women's Resistance
    and Subjectivity   141
    Ki-young Shin

Introduction to Gender Research in Asia and the Middle East

Minjeong Kim and Christine E. Bose

According to the country groupings used in the United Nations' statistical reports on the worlds' women, Asia includes a very broad spectrum of nations located in Eastern Asia (for example, China, Japan, and Korea), Southeast Asia (e.g., Singapore, Thailand, Vietnam, the Philippines, Singapore, etc.), Southern Asia (e.g., India, Pakistan, Afghanistan, etc.), Central Asia (e.g., Uzbekistan, etc.), and the Middle East, which they consider Western Asia (e.g., Iraq, Lebanon, Saudi Arabia, Turkey, etc.). Clearly the geographic, cultural, and demographic landscape of the Asian continent is immense, and in a short volume it is not possible to discuss each of these countries in detail. However, Asia is an important region, where more than 60 percent of the world's population lives, and it includes the world's two largest countries, China and India, each of which we cover in depth. Although race and ethnicity, culture and language, history, religion and the social, economic and political structures are different across East Asia, South Asia, Southeastern Asia, and the Middle East, transversal cultural flows are maintained through regional links. U.S. readers may be aware of military conflicts in the Middle East, the growth of women's microenterprises in India, the One-Child policy in China, or other gendered practices in this region, but this section provides an overview of what social science feminist and gender researchers have considered their important issues.

As in Africa and Latin America, many countries in Asia were encroached upon by colonial powers, especially by Britain, France, Russia, the United States, and Japan, whose influence was at full strength beginning in the eighteenth century. These colonial powers tried to "modernize" or westernize some of the Asian and Middle Eastern nations, transforming their political structures, sometimes affecting their cultural patterns, and also intensifying internal conflicts and those among nations. New ideologies, especially Marxism and socialism, had a major impact on countries like China or Vietnam, and helped introduce feminist thought to the region as well.

While women have organized politically in many countries, such as India, since the early twentieth century, it was not until the 1970s and the 1980s that a new wave of women's movements and the inception of women's studies or gender studies emerged in these regions within geographically and historically specific contexts. Women's studies and the sociology of gender now are established as academic disciplines in many Asian countries, as reflected in our list of international gender research center websites (see Appendix). The process of developing gender studies usually has started with inquiries on sex differences, but moves on to incorporate feminist perspectives that examine various patriarchal practices and institutions.

This book section includes review essays on gender research in two of the largest Asian countries, China in East Asia and India in South Asia, as well as on Iran, which sits on the border between Southern Asia and the Middle East. The Asian region comprises nations in many different stages of economic development, and therefore this section also includes research articles on gender issues in a developed country—Japan, on one of the newest industrialized economies—South Korea, and on the developing nation of Vietnam.

While many Asian countries are still "developing," some countries achieved remarkable economic improvement during the Cold War Era, which also changed women's roles and gender relations in the countries. Despite its devastating defeat in the Pacific War (1941–1945), Japan soon entered the ranks of the Global North, differentiating itself from other Asian countries. By the mid-1980s, several newly industrializing countries (NICs) had experienced an "economic miracle"—including Hong Kong and Singapore, whose success was based on international trade, and South Korean and Taiwan, whose growth was based on export-oriented industrialization (EOI) (Chow 2002). Then, by the early twenty-first century, these countries were elevated to core positions in the Asian economy, turning their attention to investment in the newest NICs, such as China, India, the Philippines, and Thailand, which began to expand their economic capacity in the global economy by implementing export-oriented industrialization. The industrialization process often creates gendered issues as it strategically relies on the underpaid labor of women who migrate from rural to urban areas for such jobs. For example, in South Korea, the exploitation of women workers sparked women's (and labor) movements, and paved the way for women's intellectual endeavors, while in China, women's migration for urban jobs is often temporary, and they return to the countryside to marry. Alternatively, some countries like the Philippines "export" women's labor within the region, encouraging women to migrate overseas to be contract workers in transnational corporations' assembly lines, in domestic work, and in entertainment or sex work. Both forms of women's migration have become critical issues in the field of global gender research and women's transnational mobilization.

While many Asian countries transformed their social, economic and political systems, practices, and ideologies, to varying degrees in the second half of the twentieth century, and increased their interactions with the West, some countries in the Middle East fortified their nationalist position against western involvement in regional politics, which culminated in resurging forms of Islamic fundamentalism. While countries in the Middle East, such as Saudi Arabia, the United Arab Emirates, Qatar, Kuwait, and Iran, have maintained their economic standing based on the export of oil and oil-related products, nationalist, fundamentalist Islamic movements in some countries have calcified rigid gender relations and men's control over women in the name of the religion. In recent years, women's situation in Islamic countries has raised critical global women's issues, challenging both patriarchal ideology and western feminism. As Ezazi shows (Chapter 10), women living under Islamic regimes continue to make efforts to challenge oppressive social and legal inequalities based on their own articulation of the situation, translations of the religious texts, and strategies for action. Her descriptions of women's family problems mirror some of the descriptions for the African nations of Mozambique (Chapter 5) and Senegal (Chapter 6).

Among the common women's issues in many, but not all, of the Asian countries are the important topics of militarization, sex work, and family structure. These are universal gender issues, but they have been especially pronounced in Asia and the Middle East. As described below, the chapters by Kwon (Chapter 11), Nguyen, Sankar Saikia, and Dao (Chapter 12), and Shin (Chapter 13) discuss these familiar issues from new directions, presenting richly complex global gender issues.

MILITARIZATION AND THE WORLD GENDER ORDER

Global militarization is maintained not only by political conflicts, but also by the weapons industry and military science academies. Militarization promotes masculine traits, such as aggressiveness and violence, and this masculinity is mobilized in order to maintain the hierarchy of nation-states, shaping "the world gender order" (Connell 1998). Therefore, global interactions among the states complicate local gender relations in which the power matrices of race, ethnicity, class, nationality, and gender are both challenged and reinforced.

The U.S. military has been present in Asia since World War II. During the Cold War era, some of the conflicts that had begun during the modern colonization period exploded into wars, such as the Korean War (1950–1953) and the Vietnam War (1959–1975), and these full-blown conflicts justified the expansion of the U.S. military power in the region. Militarization in Asia has made violence against women and militarized prostitution into primary political issues. One notable example is the issue of the so-called "comfort women," women from the Philippines, South Korea, China and Russia who were forced into militarized prostitution for Japanese soldiers during the Pacific War.

In Chapter 11, Kwon studies the effects of U.S. militarization on the construction of masculinities. She shows how the Korean conscripts in the U.S. army, called KATUSA, struggle both with other Korean soldiers' practices of military masculinity and the image of "hegemonic masculinity" (Connell 1995) projected through white U.S. soldiers. This highlights complex gender relations among the U.S. men and women soldiers, Korean soldiers in the U.S. army and the Korean army, and Korean women—college students and sex workers—shaped by their race, class, and sexuality as well as the hierarchy of nation-states. Kwon's empirical research sheds light on the complex shape of the world gender order.

OLD PROBLEMS IN NEW TERRAINS: SEX WORK

Sex work has been an issue of contention in some Asian countries. Asian governments such as those in the Philippines, Thailand, and South Korea used sex tourism as an industrial strategy to earn foreign currency. With rapid economic development, the South Korean government withdrew its support for and control over sex tourism and the industry declined while sex tourism continues to be become a significant source of currency in Thailand. Sex tourism now has expanded to other regions, including Latin America and Eastern Europe. In conjunction with the websites that promote sex tourism, there is a continuing commercialization of sex work and the objectification of women of racial and ethnic minorities.

Despite its ubiquity, sex work remains illegal in many countries, leaving sex workers vulnerable in many ways, including abusive treatment by violent clients and pimps, social discrimination and stigmatization, law enforcement, and health issues. Nguyen, Sankar Saikia, and Dao (Chapter 12) show how these issues affect sex workers in Vietnam, with a focus on HIV/AIDS. After opening its markets to capitalist countries in the mid-1980s, Vietnam has achieved rapid economic development. At the same time, the authors contend that as the gap between the rich and the poor widens, many poor women turn to sex work for their livelihood. Without education or institutional protection, many sex workers contract HIV/AIDS. Though the country has not become a destination of sex tourism, these long-standing problems surrounding sex work emerge in this new developing country.

Sex work has been a critical topic among feminists in Asia, where researchers argue against using a "women as victim" versus "women's agency" framework that reflects a Madonna/whore dichotomy (Kempadoo and Doezeman 1998). The chapter's authors argue that while it is important to address the immediate issues of sex workers, including the objectification of women's sexualized bodies, the expression of women's sexuality, and the protection of sex workers, it is more important not to be diverted from the root causes that push women into the occupation, which include poverty, gender inequality, and patriarchy.

PATRIARCHY IN FAMILY SYSTEM

In many Asian countries, marriage is still a social and cultural norm that is expected of all men and women above some "appropriate" age. Indeed, many Asian countries have very high marriage rates. As homosexuality is still invisible or marginalized in most Asian countries, family structure remains based on heterosexual marriage, and patriarchal ideology is embedded in various aspects of family, ranging from custom to family law. In recent years, feminist scholars and activists in Asia and Africa have addressed and challenged the role of the state in reinforcing patriarchal practices by examining family policies and laws. A wide range of legal issues have been raised, including family names, the family registration system, inheritance rights, polygamy, rights to divorce, and marital violence, to name a few.

In Iran, unequal rights between husbands and wives are blatantly enforced. Ezazi describes (in Chapter 10) how Iranian family law brings women under the control of men. Men retain most legal rights not only around issues of marriage and divorce, but also for women's personal rights, such as making travel decisions for themselves.

It is also important to understand the underlying patriarchal culture that works with the seemingly neutral family policies to reinforce gender inequality. Family names are an important gender issue that is included even in the U.N. Convention on the Elimination of All Forms of Discrimination Against Women (CEDAW), which requires husband and wife to have the personal right to choose a family name. In Japan, as described by Shin (Chapter 13), people can choose either the husband's or wife's family name. However, the majority (98 percent) of married couples choose the husband's family name upon marriage because the family registration system (*koseki*) in Japan requires representation by only one family name. Thus, the patriarchal notion that a man has to be a head of a household overshadows a woman's right to keep her last name.

The deep-seated patriarchal culture places married women in a subordinate status within the larger family structure, and sometimes subjects women to marital violence ranging from wife battering to rape. In India, as shown by Purkayastha, Subramaniam, Desai, and Bose (Chapter 9), married women sometimes are subject to violent treatment, that can go as far death, for not meeting their husband's family's dowry expectations despite the legal system that criminalizes assault and murder.

Thus, gender researchers feel that it is important to deal with both the legal and cultural aspects of the gendered family system to address unequal gender relations and patriarchal practices in heterosexual marriages and families.

TRANSNATIONAL ACTIVISM AND RESEARCH: LINKING THE LOCAL WITH THE DIASPORA

A common theme across the three research overview chapters is the role of transnational women's activism and diasporic scholars in shaping women's and gender studies at a national level. Chow, Zhang and Wang (Chapter 8) point out that the 1995 Beijing World Conference on Women provided a critical point for Chinese scholars to reinforce the global legitimacy of policy, activism, and research centering on women. In addition, the Chinese Society for Women's Studies, a U.S.-based feminist organization, provided concrete support by facilitating dialogues among Chinese feminist scholars inside and outside of the country.

The 1995 Beijing World Conference on Women also was instrumental for Iranian feminists in facilitating structural changes and furthering their local agenda. Ezazi (Chapter 10) illustrates how the importance of this event compelled the Iranian government to establish a Women's Bureau, which later played a role in establishing women's studies programs and a Master's Degree in Women's Studies that has been offered since 1995. Nonetheless, given government restrictions on publishing, it is politically difficult for Iranian scholars to maintain direct links with scholars in the Diaspora.

Purkayastha, Subramaniam, Desai, and Bose (Chapter 9), who are Indian-born feminist scholars based in the United States, also attest to the importance of transnational collaboration. They describe how the relationship between Indian-resident activists and scholars and those of Diaspora is a significant, yet complex, one. Diaspora scholars often draw on the work of Indian feminist scholars to question theoretical constructs and methodological traditions that are created and constructed in the West. Scholars collaborate with feminist activists to bring changes both in society and academia, for example by pointing out the lack of shelters for domestic violence and rape survivors, or by challenging male-oriented perspectives in academic research and school textbooks. Many Indian feminist researchers do not adhere to the demarcations of academic disciplines but use an interdisciplinary approach to exploring the issues of exploitation and inequality, as they are simultaneously shaped by gender, caste, region, and religion.

In addition to the actions of transnational organizations or events, national organizations, such as the All India Democratic Women's Association or the All-China Women's Federation, and feminist publications, like *Zanan* magazine in Iran or *Manushi* in India, have been leading forces for feminist research efforts. These organizations and publications reflect an interface between the global and the local. For example, Indian feminists made significant contributions to feminist thought that had an impact on feminist theorizing in the West, and several Indian publications have been significant vehicles for international feminist social and intellectual movements.

However, these collaborative efforts are not without challenges. Some scholars in the Diaspora over-emphasize local women's "agency" in order to challenge western views of Third World women as powerless victims. But this representation can underestimate the weight of the structural oppression women experience in their native countries. Presenting issues, struggles, and perseverance from local women's perspectives, and not losing sight of the power of state, cultural, and societal institutions is a balancing act that feminist researchers must continue.

REFERENCES

Chow, Esther (2002) *Transforming Gender and Development in East Asia*, New York: Routledge.
Connell, R. W. (1995) *Masculinities*, Berkeley and Los Angeles: University of California Press.
—— (1998) "Masculinities and Globalization," *Men and Masculinities* 1, 1: 3–23.
Kempadoo, Kamala, and Jo Doezeman (1998) *Global Sex Workers: Rights, Resistance and Redefinition*, London and New York: Routledge.

CHAPTER 8

Promising and Contested Fields: Advancing Women's Studies and Sociology of Women/Gender in Contemporary China

Esther Ngan-ling Chow, Naihua Zhang, and Wang Jinling

This chapter navigates the rise and development of women's studies and the sociology of women/gender, two relatively new, interrelated academic fields, in the People's Republic of China (PRC).[1] Drawing from significant contemporary publications and research written primarily in Chinese by indigenous and diasporic Chinese scholars, we articulate the major contributions in the discipline building and transformation of local knowledge on gender and feminist scholarship to a non-Chinese-speaking readership. English materials are used if they are deemed relevant to the discussion. Women's and gender studies in China are multidisciplinary and promoted by various actors, including academicians, research staff of the All-China Women's Federation (ACWF), staff of the Chinese Academy of Social Sciences (CASS) at various levels, and of the Party schools as well as activists in women's nongovernmental organizations (NGOs).[2] Given China's vast land with great social, economic, geographic, and ethnic diversity, it is impossible to navigate and cover all studies of women and gender issues there. Hence, our review is specifically about the development of women's studies in general and sociology of women/gender in particular, reflecting the intellectual effort of scholars and activists to create these two fields in China.

The challenge of translating simple English terms such as "women" and "women's studies" into Chinese is of particular importance.

The translated meanings of terms such as "feminism," "gender," and "NGOs" are still hotly debated among Chinese scholars (J. Wang 2000a, 2000b; Z. Wang 1998; Naihua Zhang 2001). The same problems occur when Chinese scholarship is translated into English. For example, different terms are used in China to refer to women's studies, each with minute differences in emphasis and connotation and with implications for theory and research. Here, we refer to "women's studies" broadly to encompass an academic discipline as well as other research activities on women outside of academia.

We first discuss the historical, social, and political factors that gave rise to the emergence and development of women's studies there. Likewise, we examine the field of sociology of women/gender in China in terms of its process of knowledge development, academic positioning, content, research methodology, and discipline building. Third, we demonstrate how the theoretical perspectives of these two fields have evolved in a dynamic and dialectical interplay between Marxism and feminism in China today. Finally, we provide an updated development of these two fields from 2003 to 2008.

THE DEVELOPMENT OF WOMEN'S STUDIES

Because the development of women's studies is intricately related to the establishment of the sociology of women/gender, the two underlying themes—local–global interaction and "discipline building" (*xueke jianshe*)—emerge in its development, and we discuss them to show the social contexts and dynamic processes that have opened up an intellectual space for knowledge production and transformation of this new field.

Local Development and Global Influence

Public discussion of women's issues begun with the Reform Movement of the mid-1890s and the New Cultural Movement of the May Fourth Era (1915–1925), introduced Western ideologies, including Marxism, socialism, and feminism, and provided impetus for the rise of the first-wave women's movement in modern China. Before and after the founding of the People's Republic of China (PRC) in 1949, the Chinese Communist Party (CCP) made major efforts to promote women's liberation. The official ideology on women was based primarily on Marxist analyses of "the woman question," thus laying the theoretical foundation for studying women's issues today.

The current wave of women's studies in China germinated in the urban-based women's movement of the mid-1980s (Wesoky 2002; Zhang and Xu 1995). The field, rather than being an outgrowth of the women's movement as in the West, developed as an integral part of the Chinese women's movement. In less than two decades, women's studies has become one of the most dynamic influences on various academic fields including sociology and on the women's movement in China. Its development can be divided generally into two periods—a first stage of initiation and consolidation from the early 1980s to the early part of 1993 and a second stage of expansion and internationalization from the second half of 1993 onward. The line is drawn at 1993 to emphasize the impact on the field's development when China hosted the United Nations' Fourth World Conference on Women (FWCW) in 1995. The word "internationalize-tion" is used to shed light on China's effort to "connect to the international track" (*yu guoji jiegui*) and its incorporation into the transnational women's movement.

In the first period, the initial effort to study women's issues was made by research-oriented organizations within and outside of the ACWF (Yi 2000). Under the ACWF's leadership, various research associations were established at the provincial and municipal levels, bringing interested scholars and professional women together to study women's issues. The ACWF began with the study of marriage and the family in the early 1980s, but women's issues soon developed into other areas of inquiry. Within the academy, the first women's studies group was formed in 1985, led by Li Xiaojiang of Zhengzhou University, a pioneering scholar who later established China's first women's studies center at her university in 1987. In spite of the Tiananmen Square incident in 1989 that caused considerable setbacks in other disciplines, the field of women's studies took off and consolidated itself (Lin et al. 1998). By the early half of 1993, the so-called one institute and four centers became the leading force behind women's studies in China—the ACWF's Institute of Women's Studies and four women's studies centers, respectively, at Zhengzhou University, Hengzhou University, Beijing University, and Tainjin Normal University, with a women's studies center at the Central Party School added later. Chinese scholars' interaction with their overseas counterparts had also expanded from indirect, sporadic exchanges between 1985 and 1989 to direct, organizational ones with collaborative projects in the 1990s (Du 1996; Tan 1995). Also established by 1993 were the supporting networks for women's studies, as more NGOs joined forces. More than 40 women's magazines and newspapers, mostly within the ACWF system, were published; among these are the *Chinese Women's News* and *Collection of Women's Studies*, China's only journal focusing on women's research at that time.

In the same period, efforts were made to study women's practical issues, informed by the CCP's "Marxist perspective on women." Practical research was done in response to many problems women faced, such as unemployment, migration, maternity benefits, divorce, domestic violence, crime, and sex trafficking of women (Chow 2003; B. Liu 1999). The central concerns for women's condition and status became the topics of several large surveys (Tan 1995). For example, how women can improve their quality (*suzhi*) and circumstances for capability building (*funu chengcai*) were focal points of study, reflecting the concerns with women's problems and their liberation within the Marxist framework, whether the obstacles were women themselves or society. This period further examined and critiqued the Marxist perspective on women, resulting in a few publications on Marxist theories and the history of the Chinese women's movement (ACWF 1986, 1988, 1989; Luo 1986; Tao 1991).

The second period was marked by China's active preparation in 1993 for the 1995 FWCW conference and its mobilization of people to participate in the NGO forum that resulted in a surge of women's studies centers in universities. In less than two years' time, from September 1993 to May 1995, 18 women's studies centers were added to the original 5, with another 13 established by December 1999. Women's studies centers also found their way into the Chinese Academy of Social Sciences (CASS) and other social research institutions. This expansion signaled a significant shift in the development pattern of women's studies institutions in China, from concentration in the ACWF system in the 1980s to growth in academia in the 1990s (Du 2000; Yi 2000). This politically triggered expansion, however, produced

great variations among the women's studies centers. While more established centers remain vibrant, some centers existed in name only without actual teaching or research projects; some lacked critical feminist perspectives; some became inactive afterward; and some offered few courses, including, at worst, those with "women" titles, which were in fact selling commercialized "femininity."[3] This phenomenon led scholars to refocus on discipline building at the end of the 1990s.

Compared to the first period, the second was distinguished by the increased influence of the international women's movement and transnational organizations. Direct exchange intensified between Chinese scholars and activists with their counterparts and institutions such as the Chinese Society for Women's Studies (CSWS) (see Ferguson 1997; Wong 1995). The world concerns of women specified by the Beijing Declaration and the United Nations Platform for Action introduced new research topics for women's studies in China, framed by the theoretical and analytical perspectives in the international documents (i.e., the new language and perspective of gender). Study of women and the mass media and, even more so, study, service, and intervention in domestic violence against women experienced rapid growth in China. Concepts and perspectives such as gender, development, reproductive health, human rights, environment, AIDS and poverty alleviation provided rather new analytical categories for examining women's issues in a changing China (Du 2001; B. Liu 1999).

Increased external funding coming into China also directed Chinese women scholars and activists to empirically based projects on these topics. This helped boost research on rural women, which had been scant in the first period (Gao 1999), and resulted in a growing field of "women and development." Research on practical problems or issues affected by the 1995 conference dominated the early years of the second period, but more recently, theoretical concerns and discipline building have gained special attention.

Constructing the Discipline

When research on women's issues was taking off in the early 1980s, the term "women's studies" was introduced to China from the West in three different versions of Chinese translation: *Funuxue* (women's studies), *funu yanjiu* (women's research or research on women), and *nuxingxue* (literally, female studies) (Du 2001). The interest in this new field sparked a debate over whether to establish *funuxue* in China (Wei-dong Wang 1988; Z. Wang 1998). Despite the objection to adopting *funuxue* by a high-ranking theorist in the ACWF who disdained its Western, bourgeois origin and wanted to distinguish it from "theoretical studies of women's issues" in China, the establishment of *funuxue* took hold. "*Funuxue*" became the preferred term to refer not only to studies done in academic settings but also the collective effort to research women's issues in China generally, perceived as an academic discipline that promised a modern, scientific approach to women's issues. The term "*funu yanjiu*" later caught on and was used for women's studies centers established in the universities and research institutions, although quite a number of these research units associated with the ACWF, which were established between 1985 and 1987, named themselves *funuxue* (J. Li 1992).

As the word *xue* means "a branch of learning" (i.e., as "ology" in English), discipline building became a topic of heated discussion from the outset of women's studies in China. At that time, the focus of discipline building was to envision and conceptualize: What would this discipline be like, what should its guiding theoretical framework be, and what should be included in it? On one hand, this discussion began with Li Xiaojiang's (1987) work that perceived women's studies as a cluster of existing disciplines with women added as a subject of study (e.g., women's history, women's sociology). She viewed this as making women's studies part of the "human science" guided by Marxist theory on women. She considered women's studies a way to examine the whole existence of humanity from the perspective of a "sexed being" (*youxing*).

On the other hand, He Zhengshi (1987) of the Women's Federation of Henan Province regarded the problems women face as the subject of women's studies aimed at facilitating women's liberation. She thus considered women's studies to be part of the social sciences, with Marxism as the theoretical base. Her framework provides an example of how some researchers tried to reconcile Marxism with *funuxue*. Xiong et al. (1992) of the ACWF edited a collection of essays reflecting a decade's theoretical research on women since the 1980s. The essays on "female disciplines" include women's anthropology, population studies, sociology, psychology and literature. Although a few "women" courses were offered, the teaching of women's studies did not get much emphasis in this early period.

Concern with discipline building was revived in 1998 at a conference organized by the Women's Studies Center at Beijing University and gained momentum with a series of conferences afterward devoted solely to this topic (Northeastern Normal University 2002; X. Sun 1999). At this time, the teaching of women's studies in third-tier educational institutions was a major concern. Responding to China's tenth five-year plan (2001–2005) which emphasized education as the base for development, the ACWF expanded its degree-/diploma-conferring programs geared toward women in addition to its traditional task of training women cadres (Gu 2007). It has 65 colleges and schools with 2,000 faculty and staff, recruits an average of 20,000 students, and trains

30,000 female cadres annually (Gu 2007). Its central school, established in 2001 and now named China Women's College, has a women's studies department, offering a four-year B.A. degree. In 2000–2004, it extended a pre-master's degree program in women's studies in conjunction with the Chinese University of Hong Kong and the University of Michigan.

Discipline building, an important component of knowledge production, aimed at incorporating women and gender courses in both undergraduate and graduate programs, requires three major ingredients: Transforming curriculum, teacher quality, and instructional material. Of all the efforts toward discipline building at the present stage, the multiyear "Developing China's Women/Gender Studies Project" (2000–2006) funded by the Ford Foundation—led by Du Fangqin, a feminist historian in China with Wang Zheng (a diasporic scholar in the United States) as consultant along with other leading Chinese scholars—most decidedly marks a new phase of discipline building of women's studies in China. This project's special emphases are (1) a commitment to make feminism and gender the theoretical bases and the principal analytical concepts of women's studies; (2) an engagement with scholarship from outside China through a series of reading/discussion seminars to evaluate the relevance of this scholarship to the Chinese context; (3) curriculum building and faculty development by combining scholarship with teaching practice inside and outside China for theory building, curriculum development, and pedagogy; and (4) multidisciplinary and interdisciplinary approaches targeting three disciplines: history, sociology, and education. Each discipline features its own seminar with textbooks and syllabi produced for each, and together these disciplines share a general understanding of feminist ideas, theoretical frameworks, and methodological approaches, forming a common ground for teaching women's studies courses in general. This project represented the first organized effort to bring different disciplines together systematically to make women's studies an independent and interdisciplinary field, serving as a springboard for further developing women's studies in Chinese universities.[4]

Both Du and Wang reserve the term "*funuxue*" exclusively for feminist teaching and research in universities in China and abroad, using "*funu yanjiu*" for the rest of research activities on women in China, which they lament are becoming studies of "any issues related to women" (Du 2001; Z. Wang 1998, 2000). They share others' view of emphasizing curriculum transformation and knowledge production at the institutes of higher education as important for furthering the field.

DEVELOPING SOCIOLOGY OF WOMEN/GENDER

In this section, we discuss how the sociology of women/gender positioned itself in the reinstated sociology discipline and examine various aspects of this subfield's development, knowledge production and transformation through research and teaching. Disciplinary characteristics and their theoretical foundation shared by both women's studies and the sociology of women are discussed in the subsequent sections.

Academic Positioning and Development

Introduced to China at the end of the nineteenth century, sociology had developed itself as a discipline in the country by the 1930s (Lu 2000). The Chinese government disbanded it in 1952, accusing it of being a "false science of the bourgeoisie" and replacing it with the study of Marxism. In 1979, amid the intellectual renaissance sparked by China's economic reform, sociology was restored. At that time, a so-called sociology of women was nonexistent in China. The Institute of Sociology was established within CASS in 1980, followed by the first sociology department established at Shanghai University (K. Wang 1989; H. Zheng 1989). Scholars from both CASS at the national, municipal, and local levels and institutions of higher education reconstructed sociology as a discipline. For state funding purposes, the Institute of Women's Studies at the ACWF was grouped under sociology. The early researchers involved in China's sociology of women were people from diverse academic backgrounds who switched from their previous training in other disciplines.

Linking up with women's studies in the mid-1980s, sociology was considered an all-inclusive field best suited to studying women's changing roles, status, and problems in the post-reform era. Sociology specializes in studying economic development and social change, making it very appropriate for examining how macro-dynamic forces transform social institutions, individuals, ideology, and culture; for examining social problems and inequality; and for informing the state and social policy. Scholars began by adding "women" to the inquiry and studying the nature, extent, and prevalence of "women as problems" and practical solutions. In 1986, for example, Wang Jinling's important research on the maternal protection and childbearing of employed women workers led to public debates in seven cities and a change to the new provision of maternal benefits by locally established funding programs rather than through employers, thus reducing their reluctance to hire women (Meng 1995). More than 500 cities and counties adopted a program. Research in this period tended to be more descriptive than analytical and more pragmatic, oriented toward problem solving to inform policy rather than theory building.

By the early 1990s, the discipline of sociology gradually regained its scientific status and these scholars, preoccupied with the use of scientific methods, conducted large-scale studies and examined the impact of socioeconomic transformation on women's changing roles. (e.g., Meng 1995; J. Sha 1995; L. Sha 1995; Tao and Jiang 1995; Tong 2000; Xin 1993). Four major research priorities on women, though rather narrow, were occupational segregation, job choices, paid employment, and unpaid household labor and reproduction.

The pressure to do pure research demanded that women scholars use sociological theories and methods to study women's issues while maintaining a critical edge and challenging the main-/male-stream of sociology effectively. Two investigations by Li Yinhe (1989, 1991), a woman sociologist at CASS—the first on women's mate choices and selection, and the second on marriage and sexuality in China—were well received by mainstream sociologists as fine examples of using sociological methods to systematically examine women's issues.

The study of women in sociology made few inroads into the mainstream sociology in China, and only a few articles appeared in top publications such as *Sociological Research* and *Annual of Sociology*. Most revealing was a 1994 debate in *Sociological Research* concerning equality between men and women. Using a functionalist perspective, Zheng Yefu (1994) argued that the quest for equality promoted by the state disrupted the traditional gendered division of labor, resulting in "the robbery by the weak from the strong." Sun Liping (1994) proposed women returning home as a way to solve the labor surplus problem and to restore traditional gender relations. These young male rising stars received strong criticism from women scholars, who argued that sexist ideology prevented them from seeing women's interests as valid, and subjected women to the "societal interest" of economic growth and efficiency.

China's growing economy and hosting of the FWCW conference greatly sped up and expanded academic exchanges between Chinese women's scholars and their counterparts, facilitating the introduction of, mostly Western, feminist scholarship into China and allowing research on women to break into mainstream sociology. At the end of 1994, women sociologists were able to get support from CASS to hold its first research seminar on women's issues. More research on women appeared in the journal *Sociological Research*, which also inaugurated a special column, "Gender and Development," in 1999 (volume 5). The *Annual of Sociology* published in 2000 featured its first article on preliminary explorations of feminist sociology (Wu 2000).

Standpoint and Content

One of the most significant contributions of the sociology of women is its insistence on focusing on women first and then gender. According to Wang Jinling (2000b), the standpoint of sociologists in China can be generally classified into two main categories—gender neutral and women centered. Those sociologists who are trained in the positivist tradition insist on maintaining objectivity and gender neutrality. Proponents of a women-centered standpoint argue that pure objectivity and gender neutrality do not exist, for the individual cannot completely separate herself or himself from values and subjectivity. They insist that women should be the central focus of analysis, treated as the subject rather than the object of study. Wang Jinling observed that these two standpoints coexist presently in sociological research on women in China.

The adoption of gender and feminist perspectives helped enrich studies on diverse women's identities, experiences, discourses, cultures, labor participation, domestic violence, reproductive health, human rights, and development. In the midst of debate on whether gender should be incorporated into Chinese women's studies, the concept

had already reached rural women, who had received "gender training" (Gao 1999; Tan and Li 1995). Although development studies is generally dominated by neo-liberalism, the gender and global South perspectives of transnational feminist scholarship and practice have penetrated China, as reflected in the presence of gender and development (GAD) units locally. As the result of the active involvement of organizations such as Oxfam, some influences of European feminist thought are present in this field.

In terms of content, Wang Jinling (2000a) has identified 10 substantive areas in the sociology of women/gender in China: social stratification, socialization, employment, cultural education, health, public policy, marriage and family, crime and deviance, development, and comparative and historical studies. A two-volume anthology, *Sociology of Women: Indigenous Research and Experiences*, published by Wang and Zhao (2002) gives an overview of scholarly development, illustrating what has been done and what needs to be done in this field.

To take social stratification as an example, the Marxist framework dominates class analysis in China. The gender dimension remains at the margin of stratification analysis and has yet to interrogate the definition, power structure, social differentiation, resource allocation, class formation, and mobility in studying stratification within Chinese mainstream sociology. A few studies have directly addressed the intersection of gender with class, ethnicity, age, and sexuality, but the pragmatic concern with problem solving dilutes efforts devoted to theorizing about patriarchy embedded deeply in gender stratification.

Some research attention has extended to diverse kinds of women from the rural areas (Du 1993; Gao 1994; Jin 1998), the peripheral provinces, and the ethnic minority regions (He 1998; Yan and Song 1991). Departing from the exclusive focus on Han majority women as research participants, some important works have focused on the socioeconomic development, culture, education, health (HIV/AIDs), marginalization, poverty alleviation, and empowerment of Mosuo, Miao, Yi, and Naxi ethnic women and their communities (He 1997, 1998; He and Qiao 1995; Yan and Song 1991; X. Zhang 1997). For instance, Zhao (2002) analyzed five vibrant programs—training, natural resource management, population mobility, gendered institutional studies, and agricultural technological development —of an NGO in one ethnic minority area of Yunan province, using feminist perspectives to critique development theories and practices and using indigenous experience to inform feminist thinking.

Research Method

The emphasis on women as the subject of study has resulted in different research methods being adopted by women's researchers in China. Quantitative methodology using survey sampling and statistical analysis has been used in some large-scale research, such as in the national women's status surveys (Research Institute of ACWF and State Statistical Bureau 1998, 2001). Various qualitative approaches (such as interviews, field observation, oral history) informed by feminist perspectives entered the mainstream sociological journals in the early 2000s (Du 1998a; Jin and Liu 1998; J. Liu 2002; Wang and Zhao 2002).

From the mid-1990s onward, participatory research gained importance in China, with women as social actors, researchers, and practitioners collaborating as partners to integrate theory, method, and practice and to improve women's living conditions. This bottom-up approach was effective in making known the viewpoints and voices of diverse grassroots women and in deriving research topics and agendas based on their gender needs and interests. This approach is sensitive to the rights and obligations of research

participants and connects research with action. The goal is both to study and to empower and intervene.

For example, the Center for International Development at Beijing Agriculture University used a participatory approach in a project studying rural women's involvement in agricultural development. Working with these women, the researchers looked into local resources to understand rural women's needs and problems and to explore ways to set up mechanisms for their self-development and capacity building (X. Li 1994). Li Yinhe and Tan Shen undertook a massive study of migrant women workers (CASS 2000) and devoted the second stage of this project to the practical aspects of gender consciousness raising, skills acquisition, and educational training for migrant women workers. The research on sex workers (1997– 2000) by Wang Jinling et al. (1998) identified the worker's needs and proposed skills training, counseling, hotline programs, and self-help booklets to assist these women in finding alternative ways to earn a living.

MARXIST THEORY AND FEMINIST PERSPECTIVES

This section examines the historical interplay and tension between the Chinese Marxist tradition and the influence of Western feminism to illustrate how the two fields have evolved in the dynamic process of theoretical knowledge production.

Marxist Theory and Women's Liberation

From the beginning, the theoretical foundation of women's studies and the sociology of women/gender in socialist China has been grounded in the historical interaction between Marxism and feminism in changing sociopolitical contexts over time. While Marxism is the theoretical mainstay of almost all disciplines, the introduction of

Western feminism has created strains with the official Marxist line in balancing theories imported from the West with indigenous thinking and practice in China.

Our central point is that Marxist theory has been used to serve the political interest of the CCP in keeping women's concerns under state/party control in various sociopolitical circumstances at different historical times. The CCP's official theoretical framework is a set of views and assumptions about women and women's liberation, articulated by the leaders of the CCP and the ACWF. This framework originated from three sources: May Fourth Feminism,[5] Marx and Engels' critique of the family, and the nationalist discourse. May Fourth feminism arose because women became emblematic of the oppression of the "old society," and their liberation was closely linked to broader issues of nationalism in the face of Western imperialism, liberalism, colonialism and modernity. The nation's survival assumed a higher priority than women's liberation, revealing how individuals were always subordinate to the larger collectivity, whether it had a nationalist or a communist ruling party.

The Marxist theoretical framework on women further developed in subsequent years based on the CCP's experiences and practice. After the founding of the PRC in 1949, Marxist-inspired women's liberation for the "new society" was formally institutionalized. In 1978, this stance was specified as "Chairman Mao's theory and line on women's liberation" by then-ACWF Chairwoman Kang Keqing (1978), and it was renewed in 1990 by former CCP general party secretary Jiang Zemin (1990) as the Marxist perspective on women (Marxist "funuguan"). This perspective finds the roots of women's subordination and oppression in private ownership and the class system, considering public ownership, centralized state power, women's participation in production outside the home, and collectivizing housework necessary conditions for eradicating

the roots of women's oppression and realizing their emancipation. It specifies the path to women's liberation as beginning with a proletariat class struggle for the establishment of socialism and communism, including setting up women's organizations under CCP leadership and addressing women's needs in order to mobilize them to participate in the revolutionary struggles (Jiang 1990; Kang 1978; Luo 1986).

The Marxist perspective on women is not only the theoretical foundation of the Chinese communist state ideology and political discourse on women but also the guiding principle for everyday practices supporting women's liberation (Shaanxi Women's Federation 1991). Since the state claimed that women's liberation and equality were achieved with the arrival of socialism in 1956, the official discussion of political struggle for gender equality was presumed over. When Chinese Marxism was adapted to local conditions, inconsistencies sometimes arose between theory and practice. Women's problems, if any, were often considered to be residual of the old feudal society, and it was assumed that incidences of inequality would disappear with women's full liberation. The political priority of national liberation allowed the CCP and the state a major role, limiting the abilities of the women's movement to achieve its goals and leaving women's cultural, psychological, and individual liberation not fully addressed.

Challenge to Marxism from Within: Incorporating Women's Perspective

Against this historical backdrop, women scholars and activists began critical examination of the CCP's theoretical and practical approaches to women. In general, they do not see the Marxist perspective on women as simply the official, state ideology to be abandoned but rather view it as complex, fluid, and viable for both political/ideological and academic/theoretical purposes. At the political/ideological level, for the CCP and the leadership of the ACWF, the Marxist perspective on women as the banner of women's liberation has to be upheld, and hence discourse on women has been and still is a state-sponsored dominant theme. When increasing problems for women occurred during the reform era, the ACWF became the most important negotiator with the state on behalf of women. The idea that "socialism with a Chinese character" needed to guarantee the material base of women's equality in employment, political participation, and social benefits gained government support for women's rights and entitlements. The ACWF has thus maintained its institutional and ideological continuities as a state bureaucracy by upholding the Marxist banner of women's liberation and serving both the state and women's interests simultaneously (Liu 2006).

At the theoretical/academic level, the official line has always been that the Marxist perspective on women has to be the same basic theory (scholars' theoretical resources, *lilun ziyuan*) and guiding principle for women's studies as for all academic disciplines. The ACWF has legitimized this official theoretical position academically and mainstreamed it into everyday discourse and practice.

This theory and socialist revolution are indeed part of Chinese women's lived experience and their social and historical legacy, with both positive and negative effects. On one hand, the women's movement pioneer cohort of Mao's era, particularly those in the ACWF and scholars in academic settings, were trained in this theoretical tradition. Many of them still hold to this orthodoxy, and some have even regarded the Marxist perspective as a standpoint for resisting a postcolonial impact on women's studies in China (X. Li 1995). On the other hand, Li Xiaojiang (1989) had a heated debate about ACWF's functions and openly questioned

the necessity for its existence. She contended that there are "three forbidden areas" of discussion in women's studies: Class (separating women's from class oppression), sex (incorporating sexuality in research on women), and feminism (including feminist thoughts). Without entering these areas, she said, women's self-consciousness could not be effectively raised. Other Chinese intellectuals have contended that the ACWF's persistence has closed up the social space for Chinese women's spontaneous activism and have demanded that it be reopened. While Marxism as an analytical framework has contributed greatly to supporting Chinese women's liberation and research on women, this state-sponsored theory and practice remains a site of women's struggle for fuller liberation in China.

Since economic reform in 1978, the field of women's studies has gradually transmitted Western feminist thinking to the ACWF, academic institutions, and other women's organizations. Mounting gender inequality and problems surfacing in social, economic, and political life as a result of the free-market rationality of capitalist development either contradicted or canceled the CCP's early policy of gender equality. At the micro level, while economic reform in China had been a catalyst of social change improving conditions for women in education and employment, women still lagged behind in many aspects of social life. A few critics began to challenge the Marxist assumption of the material base of women's liberation, but these voices and writings did not carry a feminist label (e.g., X. Li 1988, 1989; Z. Wang 1997). Some who embraced Western feminism became intellectual interrogators of gender-blind Marxism as well as moral voices of social conscience, advocating a revisionist stand promoting women's identity, self-realization, interest and equality (Lin et al. 1998).

The views of Chinese feminists and those of their Western counterparts have achieved some consonance on the following four issues. First, Marxist economic determinism gave primacy to class analysis under which women's issues are subsumed. The fact is that Chinese women's liberation has not been fully achieved despite a prolonged socialist revolution that has sought to eliminate private property, to overthrow the bourgeois class, and to install the proletarian class as leader of the state. Second, Western feminism emphasizes the importance of studying patriarchy, both public and private, as it shapes the hierarchical structure of gender power relationships that oppresses women. The Maoist slogan "women holding half the sky" created a myth of sameness between the genders. Women in socialist China used to believe, and some still do, that they were rather liberated in comparison to previous generations of women living under a patriarchal-feudal system. Yet they still face traditional gender role ideology and sexism. Third, Western feminism's critical analysis of the state–gender relationship parallels Chinese scholars' critique of Chinese women's liberation under socialism as a state-sponsored project underlined by a paternalistic discourse. These scholars argue that women's liberation under socialism has fostered women's dependency on the state and hindered their self-development, further reinforcing ruling ideology and a state power structure that oppress them. Finally, like their Western feminist counterparts, Chinese scholars and activists have engaged in feminist consciousness-raising. Their feminist awakening from both within and without led to their questioning the ruling power of the state and of women's interests enmeshed within it, particularly as the state lowered the priority it had been giving women in favor of economic growth, modernization, and development.

More broadly, the responses of Chinese intellectuals, officials, and activists to Western feminism varied greatly. Some perceived it to be a homogeneous entity, while others saw its diversity. Some disdained its hegemonic, imperialist, bourgeois nature, while others recognized its utility as a new theoretical challenge to the validity of a Marxist perspective on women. Of central importance was an emerging interest in essentializing gender differentiation and discourses on femininity. Reclaiming a feminine self through dress, appearance, social roles, behavior, and occupation since the 1980s, especially among the younger generation, signaled the birth of femininity discourse in post-Mao China. Wang Zheng (1998) keenly observed that women's resentment of the de-sexed approach of the Maoist era and the official version of gender equality that held up men as the standard for women played a large role in the zeal for a "feminization of women." Although Li was seriously criticized later for her limited analysis, she and other Chinese intellectuals represented the early effort to challenge the Marxist and Maoist theoretical status quo and to foster female consciousness and self-realization (X. Li 2000). However, as Wang Zheng (1998) reported, some Chinese scholars felt the need to explore other theoretical feminist frameworks (Bao 1995).

Perceiving Western feminism as a potential threat, some Chinese scholars resisted the Westernization of women's studies. The ACWF deployed its legitimate influence over state leaders by reinserting Marxist theory of women in the CCP agenda. On March 8, 1990, Jiang Zemin, then the general secretary of the CCP, reiterated that the entire party and society should establish the Marxist perspective on women in promoting social development in China. This proclamation culminated in a joint publication by the ACWF and the Shaanxi Women's Federation in 1991, *An Introduction to the Marxist Theory of Women*, representing one of the most important theoretical works on the Marxist theory of women and feminism in contemporary China. Women scholars, officials, and activists, for both political and strategic reasons, neither abandoned the Marxist theory of women entirely nor accepted Western feminism instantaneously, instead awaiting an opening of intellectual space at an appropriate time and place.

From Women's to Gender Perspectives

Adopting the concept of gender and gender analysis is perhaps one of the most significant developments in women's studies and sociology of women/gender. Gender analysis has become a powerful analytical tool and a critical perspective for a large number of scholars, resulting in some highly regarded scholarly work (B. Liu 1999). Beginning in 1992, more direct, intense scholarly exchanges outside China expanded theoretical frontiers within the country, opening intellectual space for Western feminism.

Three main driving forces set the stage for this intellectual trend. The Chinese Society for Women's Studies, Inc. (CSWS), a U.S.-based feminist organization formed in 1989, played an important role in this regard. First was the "Engendering China" conference held at Harvard University in 1992, at which a group of women's studies scholars from China participated in an academic conference abroad for the first time (Gilmartin et al. 1994). The Chinese scholars shared mutual interests with their Western counterparts in critiquing ethnocentrism, orientalism, and the cultural imperialism of conventional knowledge in the West. The second crucial event was the 1993 Tianjin International Conference, "Chinese Women and Development—Status, Health, and Employment," which was organized by the CSWS and the Center for Women's Studies at Tianjin Normal University. At this seminar, gender became a key concept for discussion and greatly aroused the interest of Chinese scholars (Du 1993). Two feminist publications, including one on critiques of Western feminist thought, were the fruitful outcomes of these conferences (Bao 1995; Du 1993).

The third momentous event was the 1995 FWCW and the NGO Forum, which had several significant outcomes for developing women's research and studies in China in the 1990s. First, the official use of the feminist concept of gender was legitimized internationally, not restricted to Western use in terms of language and perspective. The concept mainstreamed into feminist discourses in the academic disciplines and grassroots activism. Two ACWF publications, *China Women's News* (*Zhogguo Funubao*) and the journal *Collection of Women's Studies*, adopted the feminist concept of gender. Second, the ideas and agendas of the international women's movement embedded in the FCWF documents have shaped the official Chinese gender rhetoric and policy. Huang Qizao (1996: 14) explicitly stated that "to incorporate gender into policy making, we have to begin gender analysis before a policy, a law, a program, and a project are made." Third, new concepts of women's empowerment, sustainable human-centered development, women's rights as human rights, women and the environment, and gender-based violence against women were inspired by global feminisms. Fourth, while hosting the FWCW was a politically expedient opportunity for the Chinese government to showcase its supposedly progressive policies, the positive effects on women included government funding, resources, and support for women's projects and programs internally and externally, which furthered the development of women's studies and the production of gender knowledge in China.

However, incorporating the gender and feminist perspectives in China has raised some important questions. We name a few here: How is gender different from sex, femininity, and sexuality? What is (are) Chinese feminism(s) and what are their indigenous characteristics? How has nationalism, and now socialism with a capitalist twist, benefited or not benefited women? How do gender interests intersect with class and other interests? In what way does patriarchy enter into gender analysis? How can men's subjectivities and masculinities be incorporated in such an analysis? Is the CCP's Marxist perspective on women a form of Marxist feminism? Is it a form of state feminism? Is the marriage between Marxism and feminism a happy or unhappy one and why? Presently, there are no definitive answers to the above questions, and they are still under debate and exploration.

The term "gender" appears to be difficult to translate into Chinese for it has no direct Chinese equivalent and is often confused with sex and femininity. For example, "sociology of women" has been translated as "female sociology." CSWS publications have clearly recommended translating "gender" as *shehui xingbie* (literally meaning "social sex") to separate it from sex and femininity linguistically (Bao 1995; Hom and Xin 1995; Z. Wang 1998). Some scholars have argued for using *nuquan zhuyi* (women's rights-ism) to refer to Western feminism and *nuxing shuyi* (female-ism) for Chinese women's experience to emphasize the differences in agenda and context of the two women's movements. While some scholars prefer to use neither term, still others have chosen to put them together with a slash. Various translations no doubt have implications for gender theory, method, analysis, and even praxis in China. Studying patriarchy and masculinity has just begun, and more work needs to be done. It should further recognize that women's positioning in society depends greatly on their relative situations in gender relations vis-à-vis men, forming a gender hierarchy that is often compounded by class, ethnicity, age, region, sexual orientation, and disability.

As of 2008, Marxism as an intellectual theory with analytical power and the capability for macro, systematic analyses of women's liberation remains central in women's research in China. On one hand, Lin et al. (1998: 112) have pointed out that Chinese scholars have increasingly appreciated Marxism as a scientific inquiry rather than a state ideology, which has often subordinated women to nationalism and class interests. On the other hand, as Chinese scholars and researchers have increasingly embraced the feminist concept of gender as a social and cultural construction, research concerning women has been broadened and repositioned in the gender context for analysis, negating the narrowly focused discourse on femininity (Lin et al. 1998; B. Liu 1999).

As early as 1993, Du Fangqin (1993) took a "gender–woman angle of view" not only to eliminate bias and prejudice against women but also to enrich human understanding and to produce an inclusive system of knowledge. Some Chinese scholars also have turned to gender and development theory to dispel the myth of equating economic growth with women's liberation and class struggle with women's liberation, shifting the blame from women for lagging behind in the market economy to gender bias. Few scholars who hold to the Marxist perspective on women would want to admit to being feminists or desire their works to be labeled Marxist or socialist feminist. Although neither claims to use Marxist or socialist feminist theories, Jin Yihong's (2000) study of the impact of depeasantization of rural women and men in Jiangsu Province and Du Fangqin's (1998b) work on the historical formation of gender systems in China are prime examples of combining Marxist class with gender analyses. More scholars are exploring the ways in which Marxism interplays with feminism, interrogating the tendency to view them as an either–or approach, juxtaposing one against the other.

DEVELOPMENTS IN THE TWENTY-FIRST CENTURY: 2003–2008

Since an earlier version of this review was first published, women's studies and the sociology of women/gender fields have been blossoming, as evidenced by increased gender mainstreaming, institutionalization of women's studies in higher education, discipline building, theoretical critiques, and innovative research. Gender mainstreaming is the process of implementing and assessing changes toward gender equity through different mechanisms, including legislation, policies, programs, projects, research, and teaching. Along with the ACWF, researchers, scholars, policy advocates, and activists in women's movements have worked to integrate gender sensitivity and the equal entitlements of women into law and state policy-making. Growing efforts also have channeled the study of women and gender into the mainstream of social sciences research in major universities, research academies, and NGOs. This research has demonstrated its usefulness in shaping state policy, particularly in the regulations pertaining to domestic violence and to equal rights in retirement age for women civil workers. Various initiatives (J. Wang 2007) have led to research with gender as a new focus (i.e., gender-based violence, women's relations with the law, media, economic development, public policy, technology, marriage mobility and even religion) and have launched research in neglected areas (i.e., women' rights, political participation of rural women, and girl children). These rich research agendas have deepened understanding of the engendering processes in everyday life and contributed to women's movement activism in pursuing gender equality, societal harmony and sustainable development in China.

Discipline building continues to have the goal of integrating women's and gender perspectives, curriculum, teaching and faculty development into mainstream academia in China (Chen 2006; J. Wang 2005). Internal and external funding sources (such as the Ford Foundation) have continuously supported projects to develop women's/gender studies and centers at major universities, first in the coastal region and now in outlying areas such as Hunan Women's University, Guangxi University, and Guizhou University. By June 2006, university-level women's/gender studies institutions were offering 250 courses. About a dozen women's/gender studies programs have academic degrees at the Masters level (Du and Wang 2008). Thus far, no doctoral degree program on women's studies is offered, but graduate students can take a few courses on women/gender studies and combine their gender interests in working on their Ph.D. dissertations in other disciplines.

After a few years of negotiation, in 2006, a group of women sociologists launched the formation of a sociology of women/gender subfield within the Chinese Sociological Association. The group's initiatives mobilized hundreds of sociologists to meet at its subsequent planning meeting, and the Sociology of Women and Gender Research Committee (SWGRC) was inaugurated on September 16, 2007 in Hangzhou, with an executive board that is chaired by Wang Jinling. Under the rubric of Marxist perspectives on women, this newly established organization is developing diverse perspectives to actively conduct scientific study, teaching, and practical applications in sociology of women/gender, and it has developed a strong network to connecting members in cyberspace.

In China, many women's studies units and research centers have flourished. When the Chinese Women's Research Society (CWRS) was formed in 1999, it recruited 180 core members from multiple disciplines to strengthen the institutionalization of women's/gender studies programs and research centers in China. By 2005, there were about 30 women's studies and research programs located within the ACWF at the provincial level, 9 at the Chinese Academies of Social Sciences (CASS), and 50 at major universities (Tan et al. 2005: 98). In 2006, the ACWF identified 21 women's studies units to develop into the so-called "Women/Gender Studies Research and Training Bases" in China from the four organizational entities, that is—ACWF, CASS, academic universities and colleges, and Chinese Communist Party schools for cadres (Gu 2007). These bases signify a strong network formed among women's studies and research units to offer gender training, to unify resources and solidarity, to develop research and teaching education and to advance the scientific study of women/gender among them.

In addition, the CWRS organizes activities and holds annual meetings to advance research on women/gender. *The Almanac of Chinese Women's Studies (2001–2005)* published in 2007 by the Women's Studies Institute of China (WSIC), the research arm of the ACWF, summarizes the significant women's research achievements, especially on employment, migration, political participation, grass-root rural women, education, health and poverty (B. Liu 2007).

The link between theory and practice remains as the foundation of women's studies and sociology of women/gender in China. On the one hand, Chinese researchers at the ACWF continue to study Marxist theory on women as an official theoretical position. Other scholars and researchers have become more critical about imported ideas of Western feminism and sought alternative thinking. Increasing research, centered on comparative studies, for example, with other Asian countries (e.g., South Korea and India, see Du 2005), have also explored the unique Chinese characteristics of women's localized research with global perspectives (Chow 2007; Ding 2007; Du and Wang 2008; B. Liu 2005; Wei 2006). On the other hand, there is an active push for gender mainstreaming from below by various women's NGOs and grassroots organizations. For example, NGOs within the Gender and Development (GAD) field are effective in applying gender perspectives in theoretical explanations and interventions in rural community develop-

ment projects and in popularizing gender training as a vehicle to raise consciousness and disseminate gender ideas.

While the top-down approach is prominently employed in gender mainstreaming, the empowering force of gender mainstreaming with a bottom-up approach should be acknowledged as well. How to move gender mainstreaming effectively beyond national policies, and how to affect fundamental social and cultural changes to uproot structural inequality in Chinese society remains an open question for future pursuit.

CONCLUSION

Our aim has been to show how various historical and sociopolitical contexts have greatly shaped the emergence and the development of women's studies and the sociology of women/gender in China. We emphasize the relationships between the changing social structure and the processes and outcomes of knowledge production, demonstrating how these relationships mask the interests of a ruling ideology, justify existing unequal power relationships between women and men, support institutional arrangements, and perpetuate gender inequality and injustice in society.

We also discern several features that have uniquely characterized women's studies and sociology of women/gender in China. Among these are the legacy of Marxism, the influence of the CCP's Marxist perspective on women, the paramount role of the state, the peculiar institutional settings, the practical orientation in research toward solving women's problems, the indigenous nature of women's research, the close ties to national and international women's movements, and the multidisciplinary and interdisciplinary orientations of the two fields. All of these have made the two fields stand out as dynamic intellectual spaces, holding promise for future development. At the same time, they have been contested theoretically, methodologically, and substantively, in various changing sociopolitical circumstances, as is well illustrated by the tense interplay between Marxism and feminism in different historical contexts in China. This tension should be interpreted not as an either–or approach, but as a reflection of the demand to find ways that the two theories can complement and embrace one another, or simply coexist in knowledge production through research, teaching, and praxis in China.

Entering the new millennium in China, women's studies and the sociology of women /gender, though still in their early formation, have undergone a shift from applied, policy-oriented fields for solving women's problems to more theoretically relevant and empirically grounded fields incorporating a gender perspective. The prevalent attitudes among these scholars are well expressed by Du Fangqin (2001: 36), quoting Adrienne Rich: "We are not the 'woman question' asked by somebody else, we are the women who ask the questions." Chinese scholars and activists alike have been questioning social hierarchies as systems of domination, gender construction, power relationships, structural gender inequality, social identity, human agency, and subjectivity of women in producing and transforming knowledge. These queries in research on women and gender have great potential both for developing the two fields in China and for contributing to the epistemology of global feminisms.

NOTES

This article is dedicated to our beloved deceased colleague, Bao Xiao Lan, who had inspired us to work for the advancement of feminist scholarship in China. The first two authors are primarily responsible for writing this chapter, but it is the result of intensive collaboration, reflecting not necessarily one view but a plurality of views. Special thanks go to Du Fangqin, Liu Bohong, Ma Yuanxi, Tan Shen, Wu Xu, Wang Zheng, Christine E. Bose, and anonymous reviewers who offered constructive comments and thoughtful suggestions on different versions of this paper. Thanks also to Elaine Stahl Leo and Maria Eugenia Verdaguer who provided helpful reviews of and editorial support to the article.

1. For political and practical reasons, the term "feminist sociology" has not been widely adopted. Because the incorporation of a gender perspective is still in transition, we use a slash to combine "sociology of women" with "gender."

2. With respect for the differences in name-ordering customs in China and the United States, we follow the Chinese pattern, placing the last name first and the first name last for the Chinese scholars cited in the main text.

3. Personal communication with Wang Zheng, in July 2003.

4. Thus far, 11 major universities or colleges in China offer a total of 28 women and gender courses in sociology, among which 16 are at the M.A. level.

5. According to Wang Zheng (1997: 149), "May Fourth feminism refers to Chinese male intellectual's promotion of feminism and the emergence of a women's emancipation movement in the decade between 1915 and 1925."

REFERENCES

All references are written in Chinese except when otherwise indicated.

All-China Women's Federation (1986) *Historical materials of Chinese women's movement: 1921–1927*, Beijing, China: People's Press.

—— (1988) *Cai Chang, Deng Yingchao, Kang Keqing: Selected works on issues of women's liberation*, Beijing, China: People's Press.

—— (1989) *History of Chinese women's movement: New democratic revolution period*, Beijing, China: Chunqiu.

Bao, Xiaolan (1995) *An introduction to Western feminist scholarship*, Beijing, China: Sanlian Bookstore.

Chen, Fang (2006) "Thoughts on the development of women's studies in China," *Collection of Women's Studies* 72: 35–41.

Chinese Academy of Social Sciences (CASS) (2000) *Peasant migration and gender: Women workers and their rural migration project*, Zhengzhou, China: Central China Peasants' Press.

Chow, Esther Ngan-ling (2003) "Gendered migration, human security, and citizenship: The case of factory workers in south China," Paper presented at the annual meeting of the American Sociological Association, Atlanta, GA, August. [In English]

—— (2007) "Critical globalization studies and women/gender," Included in the Net of Women's/Gender Studies, http://www.chinagender.org. [In English]

Ding, Juan (2007) "The summary of the China's Unique Socialist Women's Theoretical Inquiry," in B. Liu (ed.) *Almanac of Chinese Women's Studies (2001–2005)*, Beijing, China: All China Women's Federation. [In English]

Du, Fangqin (1993) "Introduction," in the Women's Studies Center of the Tianjin Normal University (ed.) *Chinese women and development: Status, health, and employment*, Zhengzhou, China: Henan People's.

—— (1996) "Ten years' overview: Exchange of Chinese women's studies with foreign scholars", *Reprinted Materials from Newspapers and Journals: Women's Studies* 3:20–23.

—— (1998a) *Daughters of the mountains: Experiences, voices, and needs—Northern China volume*, Guizhou, China: Guizhou Ethnicity Press.

—— (1998b) *Historical and cultural exploration of gender in China*, Tainjin, China: Tainjin Academy of Social Sciences Press.

—— (2000) "Opportunities and mission: Paths and prospects of women's studies centers in universities," *Reprinted Materials from Newspapers and Journals: Women's Studies* 3:16–20.

—— (2001) "Local women's studies reflected in a global perspective—China's experience: An unfinished process," *Reprinted Materials from Newspapers and Journals: Women's Studies* 3:33–42.

—— (2005) "Understanding, comparison, and sharing: The rise of Asian Women's Studies: Critique of the Asian Women's Studies Collection," *Collection of Women's Studies* 67:76–80.

Du, Fangqin and Jun Wang (2008) "The discipline building of women's/gender studies in China in the past three decades," in L. Zhang (ed.) *Report on the development of women's education in China, 1979–2008*, Beijing, China: Social Sciences Documentary Press.

Ferguson, Ann (1997) "Two women's studies conferences in China: Report by an American feminist philosopher," *Asian Journal of Women's Studies* 1:161–71. [In English]

Gao, Xiaoxian (1994) "Trends in rural labor change and feminization of agriculture in contemporary China," *Sociological Research* 2:83–91.

—— (1999) "Women's development in China: Analysis and reconsideration of practice," *Reprinted Materials from Newspapers and Journals: Women's Studies* 3:13–17.

Gilmartin, Christina K., Gail Hershatter, Lisa Rofel, and Tyrene White (1994) *Engendering China: Women, culture, and the state*, Cambridge, MA: Harvard University Press. [In English]

Gu, Xiulian (2007) " 'Have a clear view of the situation, make clear the tasks, strive to open up': A new prospect for Women's Federation's work in education and training," *Chinese Women's Movement* 9:9–15.

He, Zhengshi (1987) "Sketch of theoretical framework of women's studies," *Selected Materials from Newspapers and Journals: Women's Organizations and Activities* 2:26–28.

He, Zhonghua (1998) *Daughters of the mountains: Experiences, voices, and needs—Southern China volume*, China: Guizhou Ethnicity Press.

He, Zhonghua, and Qiao Hengrei (1995) *Research on current state of women in Yunnan*, Kunming, China: Yunnan Education Press.

Hom, Sharon K., and Xin Chunying (1995) *English–Chinese lexicon of women and law*, Beijing, China: CTPC and UNESCO. [In English]

Huang, Qizao (1996) "Incorporate gender perspective into mainstream decision making," *Reprinted Materials from Newspapers and Journals: Women's Studies* 4:14.

Jiang, Zemin (1990) "The whole party and society should have Marxist perspectives on women", *People's Daily* 8 March.

Jin, Yihong (1998) "Rural women in the process of depeasantization" in Jin Yihong and Liu Bohong (eds.) *Chinese women and development at the turn of the century: Theory, economics, culture, and health*, Nanjing, China: Nanjing University Press.

—— (2000) *The decline of patriarchy: Gender in the modernization process of rural areas in southern Jiangsu province*, Chengdu, China: Sichuan People's Press.

Jin, Yihong, and Liu Bohong (1998) *Chinese women and development at the turn of the century: Theory, economics, culture, and health*, Nanjing, China: Nanjing University Press.

Kang, Keqing (1978) "Noble tasks for the Chinese women's movement in the new era" in the All-China Women's Federation (ed.) *Mobilizing women of all ethnic groups to carry out the new long march*, Beijing, China: People's Press.

Li, Jing-zhi (1992) "Research units within the women's federation system" in Xiong Yu-mie, Liu Xiaozong, and Qu Wen (eds.) *Decade of women's theoretical studies in China: 1981–1990*, Beijing: Chinese Women's Press.

Li, Xiaojiang (1987) "Historical and logical categories of Marxist theory on women," *Selected Materials from Newspapers and Journals: Women's Organizations and Activities* 2:15–28.

—— (1988) *The exploration of eve*, Zhengzhou, China: Henan People's Press.

—— (1989) *Gender gap*, Beijing, China: Sanlian.

—— (1995) *Toward women: Report of women's studies in the new era*, Zhengzhou, China: Henan People's Press.

—— (2000) "Moving in-between the margin and the center," *Chinese Female Culture* 1:43–54.

Li, Xiaoyun (1994) *Research on women and rural development*, Beijing: Chinese Commerce Press.

Li, Yinhe (1989) "Standard of mate selection in contemporary China," *Chinese Social Sciences* 2.

—— (1991) *Sexuality and marriage of Chinese*, Zhengzhou, China: Henan People's Press.

Lin, Chun, Liu Bohong, and Jin Yihong (1998) "Women's studies in China" in A. Jagger and I. Young (eds.) *A companion to feminist philosophy*, Oxford, UK: Basil Blackwell. [In English]

Liu, Bohong (1999) " '95 World Conference on Women and Chinese women's studies," *Reprinted Materials from Newspapers and Journals: Women's Studies* 2:13–18.

—— (2005) "Globalization and Women's Health in China," *Yenan Ethnic University Bulletin* 4: 37–41.

—— (2007) "Conclusion" in B. Liu (ed.) *Almanac of Chinese Women's Studies (2001–2005)*, Beijing, China: All China Women's Federation.

Liu, Dao Xiao (2006) "When do national movements adopt or reject international agendas? A comparative analysis of the Chinese and Indian women's movements," *American Sociological Review* 71: 921–942. [In English]

Liu, Jun (2002) "A study of feminist methodology," *Collection of Women's Studies* 1: 34–40.

Lu, Xueyi (2000) "50 years of sociology in new China" in the Institute of Sociology, the Chinese Academy of Social Sciences (ed.) *China year book of sociology: 1995–1998*, Beijing, China: Social Science Document Press.

Luo, Qiong (1986) *Basic knowledge of issues concerning women's liberation*, Beijing, China: People's Press.

Meng, Xianfan (1995) *Chinese women in the wave of reform*, Beijing: Chinese Women's Press.

Northeastern Normal University, Center for Female Research (2002) "Summary of seminar on women's studies curriculum and teaching in Chinese universities," *Collection of Women's Studies* 11:62–68.

Research Institute of ACWF and State Statistical Bureau (1998) *Gender statistics in China: 1990–1995*, Beijing: China Statistical.

—— (2001) "Report on the major statistics of second survey of social status of Chinese women," *Collection of Women's Studies* 5:4–12.

Sha, Jicai (1995) *Research on women's status in contemporary Chinese family*, Tianjin, China: Tianjin People's Press.

Sha, Lianxiang (1995) *Development and conflict of roles of Chinese women*, Beijing, China: Ethnicity Press.

Shanxi Women's Federation (1991) *An introduction to the Marxist theory on women*, Beijing: Chinese Women's Press.

Sun, Liping (1994) "Reconstructing gender roles and relations," *Sociological Research* 6:65–68.

Sun, Xiao-mei (1999) "Establishment and development of women's studies discipline in Chinese Women's College" in the Institute of Women's Studies of the All-China Women's Federation (ed.) *Collection of papers for 50 years of theorizing Chinese women seminar*, Beijing: All-China Women's Federation.

Tan, Lin (1995) "New development in women's studies," *Reprinted Materials from Newspapers and Journals: Women's Studies* 2:7–15.

Tan, Lin, and Li Jianxin (1995) *Women and sustainable development*, Tianjin, China: Tianjin Science and Technology Press.

Tan Lin, Wu Jing, and Li Yan-ni (2005) "Chanel women/gender studies into the mainstream of China's social sciences research," *Collection of Women's Studies* 69:96–100.

Tao, Chunfang (1991) *Introduction to Marxist perspective on women*, Beijing: Chinese Women's Press.

Tao, Chunfang, and Jiang Yongping (1995) *Introduction to the status of Chinese women*, Beijing: Chinese Women's Press.

Tong, Xin (2000) "Production and reproduction of inequality in gender relations: Analysis of domestic violence in China," *Sociological Research* 1:102–11.

Wang, Jinling (2000a) "Chinese sociology of women in view of the discipline," *Academic Journal of Zhejiang* 1:66–72.

—— (2000b) "Women's studies within the field of sociology: 15 years' construction and development Zhejiang," *Research Journal* 1:51–64.

—— (2007) "From margin to mainstream: Development of Sociology of Women/Gender 2001–2005," *Reprinted Materials from Newspapers and Journals: Women's Studies* 1:110–18.

Wang, Jinling and Jie Zhao (2002) *Sociology of women: Indigenous research and experiences*, Shanghai, China: Shanghai People's Press.

Wang, Jinling, Gao Xueyu, and Jiang Ming (1998) "Gender analysis of commercial sex traders," *Zhejiang Academic Journal* 3:53–59.

Wang, Jun (2005) "Women's studies in the perspective of disciplinary institution," *Collection of Women's Studies* 69: 101–103.

Wang, Kang (1989) "Reconstruction of sociology in mainland China" in the Institute of Sociology, the Chinese Academy of Social Sciences (ed.) *China year book of sociology: 1979–1989*, Beijing: China Encyclopedia.

Wang, Wei-dong (1988) "Several issues in the exploration of women's studies," *Selected Materials from Newspapers and Journals: Women's Organizations and Activities* 5: 31–35.

Wang, Zheng (1997) "Maoism, feminism, and the UN Conference on Women: Women's studies research in contemporary China," *Journal of Women's History* 8:126–52. [In English]

—— (1998) "Research on women in contemporary China" in G. Hershatter, E. Honig, S. Mann, and L. Rofel (eds.) *Guide to women's studies in China*, Berkeley: Institute of East Asian Studies, University of California. [In English]

—— (2000) "Application of the concept of gender in China," *Reprinted Materials from Newspapers and Journals: Women's Studies* 2: 3.

Wei, Guo-ying (2006) "Development in leaps and bounds and local experience: Review of women's studies development in ten years," *Collection of Women's Studies* 70: 33–40.

Wesoky, Sharon (2002) *Chinese feminism faces globalization*, New York: Routledge. [In English]

Wong, Yuenling (1995) *Reflections and resonance: Stories of Chinese women involved in international preparatory activities for the 1995 NGO Forum on Women*, Beijing, China: Ford Foundation. [In English]

Wu, Xiaoying (2000) "Exploration of feminist sociology" in by the Institute of Sociology, the Chinese Academy of Social Sciences (ed.) *China yearbook of sociology: 1995–1998*, Beijing, China: Social Science Document Press.

Xin, Tong (1993) *Analysis of crimes committed by women*, Beijing, China: Gold City Press.

Xiong, Yu-mie, Liu Xiaocong, and Qu Wen (1992) *A decade of women's theoretic studies in China: 1981–1990*, Beijing: Chinese Women's Press.

Yan, Ruxian, and Song Zhaolin (1991) *Matrilinal system of Naxi ethnic group in Yongning*, Kunming, China: Yunnan People's Press.

Yi, Ying (2000) "Preliminary review of women's studies organizations in modern China," *Collection of Women's Studies* 2:34–38.

Zhang, Naihua (2001) "Searching for 'authentic' NGOs: The NGO discourse and women's organizations in China" in P.-C. Hsiung, M. Jaschok, and C. Milwertz (eds.) *Chinese women organizing: Cadres, feminists, Muslims, queers*, Oxford, UK: Berg. [In English]

Zhang, Naihua, with Wu Xu (1995) "Discovering the positive within the negative: The women's movement in a changing China" in A. Basu (ed.) *The challenge of local feminisms: Women's movements in global perspective*, Boulder, CO: Westview. [In English]

Zhang, Xiao (1997) *Research on oral history of Miao women in Xijiang*, Guiyang, China: Guizho People's Press.

Zhao, Jie (2002) "Our footprints: Reflections on theory and practice of Yunnan GAP group in activities and projects," Paper presented at the Gender and Development Seminar, Xian, China.

Zheng, Hongsheng (1989) "Chinese society in transition and Chinese sociology in development" in the Institute of Sociology, the Chinese Academy of Social Sciences (ed.) *China year book of sociology: 1979–1989*, Beijing: China Encyclopedia.

Zheng, Yefu (1994) "Sociological reflection of equality between men and women," *Sociological Research* 2:108–13.

CHAPTER 9

The Study of Gender in India: A Partial Review

Bandana Purkayastha, Mangala Subramaniam, Manisha Desai, and Sunita Bose

This article provides a brief introduction to contemporary thinking and controversies surrounding the study of gender in India. That said, we need to begin with several caveats. First, India is a multilingual country, and what is written in English represents a minuscule portion of the ongoing debates on the subject. Second, it is very difficult to draw a neat boundary around what constitutes "Indian." A number of scholars from around the world have written extensively on gender with reference to India. Many scholars were born in India and live in that country. Other scholars were born in India, live in other parts of the world, but continue to maintain active research links in India. Yet others, such as Gail Omvedt, were not "born Indian" but have lived and worked in the country for decades. Moreover, we could not rely on our ability to identify "Indian" writing based on any particular style of presentation. Some scholarship focusing on gender in India is published in countries such as the United States and, therefore, reflects the norms of the peer review process in these societies. Other work may be published in India and reflects those publication criteria, but the ideas may, at times, closely follow similar work done in other countries. Many scholars publish in more than one country, complicating the choice about which of their work is "Indian." Here, we follow a general rule: We focus primarily on scholars who are natives or primarily based in India and/or who have

written first for Indian audiences. We also restrict ourselves to contemporary work. We include work that would not be considered "academic" in the United States. However, our collective experience suggests that these "nonacademic" publications are important sites in which gender has been conceptualized. The role of the public intellectual remains much more vibrant in India than it is in the United States; thus, academic debates and controversies are expressed in multiple platforms. Nor do we confine ourselves to the work of scholars who identify with feminism. Indeed, some of the leading scholars, as we will discuss later, disavow the title. In sum, what is presented here reflects some of our own biases in terms of what we know the best and the need to keep the length of the article within acceptable limits. All of us are located in U.S. universities but maintain active research links in India. We originate from different parts of India, and English is the only language common to all of us. Thus, we are very aware of how our knowledge of gender literature in India is limited by our linguistic and regional–cultural competencies, as well as by our scholarly interests. The field of gender in India is too vast, too complex, and too contested, with historical roots traversing several centuries, to describe within a single review. This essay, then, simply provides a glimpse of the field of gender in India.

The contemporary study of gender in

India arose within a specific socio-historical context: the establishment of a nation-state in 1947 after two centuries of British colonialism. The nationalist movement to overthrow the British included a significant component of resistance at the level of symbolic representation and formal knowledge construction, and these knowledge systems inspire some of the work on gender. Post-independence social change driven by ideas of development within the current phase of globalization, in which state and international economic and political interests often intersect to erode local autonomy, has spawned work from Marxist, socialist, and a variety of other gender perspectives. The current theoretical controversies, methodologies, and analyses of gender illustrate how Indian perspectives on multiple inequalities intersect with similar knowledge developed in other countries. The article begins with a brief overview of some of the theoretical issues on gender; this is followed by a discussion of methodologies and preferred methods of data collection. The next two sections provide a glimpse into two arenas of study—gender and social movements and gender and domestic violence. These topical sections illustrate some of the issues raised under previous headings, including the close relationship between activism and the production of knowledge. The topical areas are linked in the sense that the rise of the autonomous women's movement, which has focused on violence against women, generated the research on such violence. Overall, the four sections provide a glimpse of the type of work being done, who contributes to the understanding of gender, and how different frameworks are used for studying different gender topics. The conclusion indicates other important areas that were not described in this article and briefly points to the similarities and differences of this scholarship with that of selected countries around the world.

WOMEN AND GENDER: THEORETICAL ISSUES

More than a century of women's formal organizing (R. Kumar 1993), as well as the multilingual, multicultural nature of Indian society, has led to the development of different perspectives on gender, intersectionality, and power inequalities.[1] At least three overlapping dimensions are relevant for understanding how gender is conceptualized in the Indian context. First, there is a tension between scholars who have foreground gender and those who adopt a more intersectional approach. Second, the epistemological roots of work on gender are not inevitably based on feminism. Third, there is a considerable emphasis on the role of the nation-state and international structures in fostering gender inequalities.

A key issue in the research on gender is the ongoing debate, beginning in the mid-1970s, between scholars who foreground gender (e.g., Butalia 1993; Ray and Basu 1999) and those who emphasize the intersection of class, religion, caste, age, sexuality, and gender (e.g., Datar 1993; Dietrich 1992; Gandhi and Shah 1992; Kelkar 1992; R. Kumar 1993; Omvedt 1993; I. Sen 1990; Sood 1990). These authors have collectively argued that women qua women make up an empty theoretical category; their work emphasizes the interaction of class, gender, caste, religious, and regional specificities as key for understanding the conditions of women and men. Many of the methodological dilemmas (discussed in the next section) arise from the need to properly capture intersectionality instead of privileging gender as a shared similarity between women.

The disagreements between the groups are increasingly recognized and are the subject of scholarship. For instance, John (1996) described the growing participation of women in the communal movements and the dilemma of reconciling, from a feminist perspective, their clearly stated communal position and their ability to change gender relations at some level (see also T. Sarkar 1991; Tharu and Niranjana 1994). Other controversies involve scholars who work within the intersectional approach but may emphasize class or caste as the fulcrum of intersecting axes and disagree about whose standpoint should define the theoretical center of the women's movement—the class/gender scholars (e.g., Datar 1999) or the scholars representing the dalit ("the downtrodden") women (e.g., Rege 1998).

The second overlapping dimension that influences the direction, language, and emphases in gender work is the different epistemological bases of gender scholarship. Some of the gender scholarship is rooted in the more widely understood notions of feminism. Work by Sangari and Vaid (1989) or Kannabiran (2005), which delves into the regional, class, and caste variations of patriarchal practices, are examples of this genre of scholarship. Most of the quantitative literature on violence against women (described later in this review) is also based on a feminist perspective.

However, a significant portion of the work on gender is not drawn from feminism (or from feminism alone) but from other strands of philosophical and political thinking on broader issues of social justice. For instance, the work of Madhu Kishwar (1999a), the editor of *Manushi*, is based on a rejection of westernized "isms." Writings by Vandana Shiva (1993, 2005) and Ela Bhatt (2005), the founder of the revolutionary Self-Employed Women's Association [SEWA]), are grounded in the Gandhian principles of nonviolence and local autonomy. Madhu Khanna's (2002) writings on Tantra are derived from more androgenous conceptions of humans, and the celebration of a female principle in matters of religion. These scholars have questioned the excessive importance attached to "feminist principles, such as public–private dichotomy, or the sexual division of labor as the source or

cause of women's subordination" (Mazumdar and Agnihotri 1999: 235), and the taken for granted assumptions about men and women that are derived solely from Judeo-Christian theology.

While much of the resistance to the label feminism has been interpreted in some feminist literature as cultural relativism and anti-Westernization, the theoretical controversy is more complex. For many of the scholars who reject a feminist epistemology, their unease arises from how sharp distinctions are drawn between men and women, and between "woman" as an identifiable, embodied individual and woman defined through multiple relationships, in the dominant strands of feminist scholarship in Euro-America. Like the reservations expressed by many of the race–gender scholars in the United States, such dichotomization is unacceptable to many Indian scholars. Given local forms of knowledge that are based on more holistic conceptions of individuals in collectivities, these scholars choose either to draw from non-feminist perspectives or to meld the two without privileging feminism. Some of the philosophical conflicts among scholars who work in the areas of environment, work, law, community, and sexuality are apparent in an edited collection by Menon (1999). The writings on sexualities (Menon 2007, Vanita 2002) also reflect different starting points for understanding gender, "queerness" and heteronormativity.

The third overlapping dimension that is important for understanding the nature of gender scholarship in India is the conscious interrogation of national and international structures in the creation of local gender inequalities. Scholars such as Gandhi and Shah (1992) or Menon and Bhasin (1996), have interrogated the nature of the state and state formation processes. The intersections of communities, the state, and the status of women of different religious, ethnic, linguistic, and cultural backgrounds have been the focus of a significant strand of gender research. Chakravarti (1990) and Hasan (1994), among others, have described the constructions of such communities as they are forged in response to national and international processes. Laws that govern community life, and how these reflect class and religious biases, are the subject of scholarship by researchers such as Agnes (1995, 1999).

The interaction of international processes—colonialism, neocolonialism, and the current phase of "globalization"—with national agendas, and how these have further marginalized millions of women, is another arena of gender scholarship (Bagchi 1996; Chatterjee 1992; Poonacha 1995). The role of global processes in enhancing gender divisions in occupations is described by scholars such as Susmita Sen (1999) and Banerjee (1989), who have documented the emergence of occupational segregation. Mazumdar and Agnihotri (1995) have pointed to the new structures of global power that are relatively anonymous, often work without controls, and negatively affect power residing in local communities. Some of the literature on violence against women (reviewed later) also uses this perspective.

In sum, because gender is conceptualized from multiple epistemological bases and/or from different nodes of intersectionality, it encompasses a variety of approaches, methods, emphases, and analytical strategies. As the next three sections indicate, the methodologies and areas of study are marked by variety rather than by one unified perspective on gender.

RESEARCH APPROACHES: FIELDWORK AND METHOD

Methodological approaches to research in the area of gender in India emerge from a wide variety of disciplines, including sociology, history, and economics. These multidisciplinary bases, as well as the various sources of gender theory described above, lead to the use of a variety of approaches for studying gender. Though some of the work reflects the same dilemmas voiced by gender scholars in Euro-America (including insider–outsider and power issues in research), the different context of research means that the salient issues appear differently. Two issues are highlighted in this section: fieldwork, especially the dilemmas of objectivity, action, and the position of researcher, and the methods used for gathering data and information. These discussions provide the background for understanding what is written about specific gender topics and the type of data that is used for drawing conclusions.

Fieldwork

While fieldwork and ethnography are often used synonymously in the United States, in India, the terms include varying degrees of participant observation, such as structured or semi-structured interviews, and may involve survey interviews for quantitative analysis. A structural difference needs to be kept in mind: Unlike in developed countries, fieldwork conditions in developing countries, especially in rural areas, can be physically demanding because of the lack of infrastructure and poor transportation and communication facilities. Traveling to collect data is a lengthy and time-consuming process. It requires significant cultural competencies on the part of researchers. In addition, large-scale, geo-coded templates are not available to conduct random-sample surveys for creating large, quantitative data sets.

Fieldwork entails the active involvement of the researcher in the production of knowledge, and this process often upholds power differences between the researcher and researched (Subramaniam 2008). Power is discernible in at least two interrelated dimensions. First, there are power differences stemming from the different social locations of the researcher and the researched (not simply in terms of gender and class but also in caste, religion, nationality, life chances, and rural/urban backgrounds). Second, there is power exerted during and after the research process, such as defining the research relationship, having unequal exchanges and exploitation, and defining what constitutes "peoples' voices."

Using dichotomous categories such as insider–outsider to describe the relationship between the observer and the observed does not wholly capture the process of studying groups or societies within national boundaries or outside these boundaries, especially in multilingual countries such as India. First, simply because a researcher shares the gender and ethnicity of his or her participants does not automatically qualify him or her as an insider. Common and shared positions due to linguistic similarities or caste, religion, race, class, gender, or nationality do not always lead to common understandings (N. Kumar 1992). Often, other issues such as crossing caste lines (Dua 1979; N. Kumar 1992; Srinivas et al. 1979) and restricting expectations of others (Gupta 1979) are relevant. The constant balancing between the "similarities" (being Indian and with work experience in India) and "differences" (upper class and upper caste) locates scholars in positions that require constant negotiations of their identities (e.g., N. Kumar 1992). Second, the politics of location influences what is portrayed as the "subjects' voices" (see Karlekar 1995). For instance, John (1996) questioned interpretations of terms and phrases (such as what constitutes co-optation) by those who are unfamiliar or unexposed to the local and national social context. The point is that even though these issues sound similar to gender research dilemmas in Euro-American societies, places such as India pose completely different levels of challenge because of the variations in complex inequalities and social meaning.

Considering linguistic differences in field-work illustrates some of these issues, especially if the research focuses on the poor and/ or is conducted in rural areas. Since a number of languages are spoken in India and there is significant variation across states and regions, knowledge of the language spoken in the area of research can facilitate direct communication between the researcher and the researched. A limited knowledge of the language (for instance, understanding but not speaking it) can be helpful if field-workers or interpreters are fluent in both the local language and the one into which the interviews are being translated. Research scholars, such as John (1996), have raised concerns about compromise in accessing information, such as when interpreters are hired or when using preconceived concepts such as power, gender, or empowerment that can take on entirely different meanings and social implications in different languages. Thus, including "multiple voices" in the interests of generalizability (or international-izing) may create significant problems of data quality (John 1998).

Highlighting issues of local conditions (e.g., poor telephone and road infrastructure, especially in small towns and rural areas), language, and culture does not minimize the significance of structural issues in undertaking research. Structural features of Indian society such as caste and religion have an impact on sampling, the micro or macro scope of research (see, for instance, All India Democratic Women's Association [AIDWA] 2002; International Center for Research on Women 2000), and how variables are operationalized and results are interpreted (for instance, Jejeebhoy 1998, 2000; Subramaniam 2001).

Method

The methods used for gender research in India can be categorized into three broad, somewhat overlapping, streams. The first stream, historical analysis, focuses on the changing construction of gender relations and, has therefore, relied on particular events or on historical secondary documents (such as Butalia 1993; Chakravarti 1993, 1996; Omvedt 1998; Rao 1999; Suresh 1998; Talwar 1999). A second approach is the analysis of specific cases, such as the caste-based atrocity in Sirasgaon described by Anupama Rao (1999) or Kalpana Kannabiran's (1996) analysis of a particular rape in the book *Embodied Violence*. Quantitative analyses form the basis for the third approach. The third approach has dominated two areas of research: demography and feminist economics, especially the impacts of micro-finance projects on women's status and/or empowerment (for instance, B. Agarwal 1994; Basu 1992; Dreze and Sen 1997). Scholars such as Bina Agarwal (1985, 1994) have helped reassess the measure and definition of "work," highlighting the gender-based division of labor in the Indian context.

However, more recently, larger studies covering several states have been undertaken. AIDWA, together with the Indian School for Women's Studies and Development, conducted an 18-state survey of adolescent girls of marriageable ages and their parents/guardians (nearly 10,000 respondents) using their grassroots contacts. The International Center for Research on Women also conducted a three-year research project, beginning in 1997, on domestic violence in partnership with researchers from a wide range of Indian academic and activist organizations. These efforts are indications of a shift from focusing on only micro-level studies to considering broad-based data and documentation seen as essential to targeting the state for change.

Secondary analysis of data has been minimal because of the paucity of large-scale surveys (such as the Virginia Slims or General Social Survey in the United States). Instead, compiled data or information on women and related issues are often published. Examples include the *Status of Women, 2001* report published by the National Commission for Women (Gopalan

2002) and the *Report of Unnatural Deaths with Special Reference to Dowry Deaths* by the Bureau of Police Research and Development (Gautam and Trivedi 1986).

While no specific evidence is available about a division in quantitative versus qualitative approaches, theoretical arguments are more frequently made in the context of qualitative analysis (John 1998). *The Indian Journal of Gender Studies*, which has been published since the early 1990s, features both qualitative as well as quantitative analysis of gender-related issues (see, for example, Karlekar and Kasturi 2002). Scholars who adopt a case-based approach (as evident in the next section) are often activists at the local/grassroots level and so often draw from their experiences for their gender-related arguments. Such scholarship has generally been descriptive. Qualitative methods are being increasingly used in gender and family studies such as in research focusing on domestic violence (Srinivasan 1997; Burton et al. 2000).

Historical analyses, including textual analysis, have received substantial attention in gender research in India. Among the methods used are feminist historiography (Sangari and Vaid 1989), essays structured around a historical perspective to assess the context and provide referential meanings (e.g., N. Kumar 1992), and discursive textual analysis "where the very existence of a text is evidence of the consciousness being looked for" (N. Kumar 1992: 14). In addition, life histories and oral histories have been used as particularly compelling and unobtrusive ways to study unempowered women.

The emphasis on historical and case methods arises from two related causes. First, scholars working in the area of gender and trained in specific disciplines do not necessarily view the choice of a particular set of methods and methodology as critical for conceptualizing and theorizing. The aim seems to be to reflect women's voices rather than be occupied with statistics that mask the reality of how processes and structures influence the daily lives of a variety of disadvantaged groups. Part of this emphasis has to do with the primary intention to recover and appreciate (and often re-present in another language) the work of women researchers and theorists. Others such as Sangari and Vaid (1989: 1) argue that "given the regional, class and caste variation of patriarchal practices and their diverse histories, it is necessary to have specific studies in order to build an adequate theoretical basis."

A second reason is the lack of resources, time, funds, and labor to undertake elaborate quantitative analysis. India's diversity in geographical terrain (rural/urban, physical infrastructure) and the numerous languages spoken in the country make designing research studies, which can be interpreted similarly across regions, a formidable task. In addition, constraints on the availability of field-workers make data gathering even more challenging.

A significant point related to research in India that is rarely mentioned and discussed is regulation of procedures for the use of human subjects. Institutional Regulatory Board (IRB) procedures pertaining to ethics and use of human subjects enforced in the U.S. are not of much concern in India. Social science based research, unlike medical research, is perceived as not directly inflicting harm on respondents or as being intrusive. This issue needs to be discussed particularly in the wake of increasing interest in international and comparative research.

Overall then, the research methodologies adopted point to the interactive relation between the researcher, the researched, and the context, in a way that reflects the diversity of voices. While much of the research may not conform to the positivist notions of objectivity, in many cases, the methodologies and methods of data collection are designed to provide grounded data and theory rather than generalizable objective data. The emphasis, as described in the next section, is on research to foster social change.

WOMEN'S MOVEMENT SCHOLARSHIP IN INDIA

This section focuses on women's movement scholarship produced by activists and scholars writing and living in India.[2] Most of the authors are activists and/or activist scholars themselves, and their analysis tends to be movement driven rather than a literature-driven analysis, and the objective, as pointed out in previous sections, is to collect grounded data to construct meaningful theory. The discussion that follows is based on the following books: Datar (1993), Dietrich (1992), Gandhi and Shah (1992), Radha Kumar (1993), Omvedt (1993), and Sen (1990).

These authors analyze the contemporary women's movement in India that various scholars date from the early to mid-1970s. The autonomous women's movement, one part of the contemporary movement, reached its peak in the 1980s when it made public the various forms of violence against women and made gender and patriarchy important categories of analysis along with class, caste, and religion. But by the end of the 1980s, the success they had enjoyed in the early part of the decade—in seeking legal reforms, raising public consciousness, and starting women's centers that enabled abused women to seek legal, medical, and emotional support—was challenged in parts of the country by the increasing Hinduization of politics as well as by their lack of connectivity with the different types of rural movements.

Activists and Activist Scholars

All the authors are active in different parts of the women's movements. Gabriele Dietrich, Gail Omvedt, and Ilina Sen are all involved with poor women's movements—Dietrich in urban Tamil Nadu, Omvedt in rural Maharashtra, and Sen in rural Madhya Pradesh. Nandita Gandhi, Nandita Shah, and Radha Kumar are involved mostly with urban autonomous groups that are small, informally structured, and made up primarily of educated, middle-class women. The authors' locations in various parts of the contemporary movements influence their preferences for participatory methods of research and the thematic content and analysis of movement scholarship. Because they all work in collaboration with other progressive movements, they conclude that the women's movement needs to go beyond "women's issues" (violence, reproduction) and provide women's perspectives in all the struggles of poor women in urban and rural areas, including issues of development, ecology, and religion.

These authors also focus on the relationship between poor women's movements and urban, autonomous feminists.[3] While they acknowledge the contributions of the autonomous movement, they also critique these feminists' emphasis on urban locations and small groups, which has led to the exclusion of the majority of women living both in urban and rural areas. In addition, the movement has been criticized for its alienation from party politics, its reliance on foreign funding for developing service-based nongovernmental organizations (NGOs), and for organizing conferences that exclude most women. In some ways, the lines between the work more focused on gender and the intersectional work (as described in the theoretical section) are getting blurred.

One example of such a successful linkage is the movement of rural women who have been deserted by their families (Datar 1993). The campaign focuses on widowed, unmarried, divorced, and deserted women and centers on the issue of being single in a society that places a premium on marriage. The campaign highlights the social and economic distress of these women and works for their rights to land ownership, ration cards, employment, social security, and, most important, acceptance for them as single women with a right to live a life of dignity, free from social stigma and with financial and social security. As with most rural campaigns, it stresses economic as well as social issues and politicizes women who are marginalized in rural society.

By contrast, the focus of most autonomous activist authors is on the campaigns of the urban, autonomous movement. Thus, Gandhi and Shah (1992) and R. Kumar (1993) focused on how the need for "autonomy" arose from the subordination of women's issues in the movements to resolve class and caste inequalities in the 1960s, when most activists came of age and honed their political skills. Gender and patriarchy were absent in these analyses. To address these absences, women activists began to meet in small groups in the mid- and late-1970s to discuss these silences and the relevance of feminist analyses in the Indian context. Autonomy was thus an attempt by women to organize themselves, outside of party and left movement politics, to address women's issues without subordination to other issues and organizations.

The autonomous activist authors focus on the limitations of their strategies and on the rich discussions in the movement around autonomy, organization, "case work" versus consciousness raising, and foreign funding. Foreign funding, particularly the NGOization of the movement, is an issue raised by all the books, and it has become an even more dominant issue today than at the time when these books were written (Alvarez 1999). The autonomous activist authors particularly reflect on their work on violence against women and on ways to articulate alternatives. For example, Flavia Agnes's chapter in Datar (1993) explores the dilemmas and the limitations of the anti-rape campaign as it evolved over the years. She argues that the weakest point of the campaign was the lack of support given to the individual victims of rape, the difficulties of working with individuals and maintaining a political campaign, and the differences in the attitudes and values between activists and the woman and her family who seek help from women's groups for "traditional and accepted solutions." She laments the lack of any rape crisis centers even after a decade-long struggle, as well as the absence of a new framework that would seek solutions outside a patriarchal understanding.

Thus, women's movement scholarship in India is often a dialogue and reflection among activists and activist scholars on movement issues, strategies, and the need for articulating alternatives.

Movement-Driven Analysis

The analysis in most of these works is driven, implicitly or explicitly, by a search for meaningful categories that can facilitate the organizing effort of the movement. The lack of explicit dialogue between academic literature and movement scholarship might seem problematic from a U.S. academic perspective. However, it frees the authors to develop organic analytical categories that are more likely to feed back into the movement. This is even the case for scholars who do engage the academic literature, such as Omvedt, Dietrich, and Sen.

Omvedt (1993), for example, used the new social movements perspective, but it gets completely transformed in her intersectional analysis of the nationalist and socialist roots of the Indian women's movements, along with the anticaste, farmer's, and environmental movements. Her main argument is that these "new" social movements present a challenge to both nationalist and Marxist visions of change in India and, in the process, are reinventing revolution. What makes them new is that "they have been explicitly antisystemic in their ideologies, looking towards a casteless, nonpatriarchal, nonlooting, sustainable society; they are involved, in their own view, in inherent conflict with the social order" (Omvedt 1993: 318).

The new model of politics, unlike the earlier nationalist or Marxist ones, focuses on the relations of exploitation rather than relations of production. It redefines exploitation to include issues of caste, gender, rural livelihoods, and the environment; it develops new participatory and nonhierarchical organizations; and it articulates new understandings of development that question the industrial/capitalist international model and provide community-based alternatives based on equality and justice.

Omvedt (1993) went on to show how rural women are at the forefront of new alternatives as they are reworking issues of gender, caste, ecology, and rural livelihoods through their focus on stree-shakti, "women's power," rather than women's oppression, which was the focus of both Marxists and feminists. She demonstrated how rural women are developing this stree-shakti through an alternative model of development based on biomass production, renewable energy sources, and skilled employment in rural areas, seeking property rights as well as political power at the local level.

Similarly, Dietrich (1992), writing about religion, argued that feminists, influenced by secular humanist values and the patriarchal elements of Hinduism and other religions, have been unwilling to take on religion proactively and, as a result, find themselves only reacting to Hindu nationalists' mobilization of religious dogmas, in the supposed empowerment of women. Mrinal Pande (1996), in her insightful book *Devi*, made a similar argument about the feminist stance on goddesses. Despite the appropriation of Kali as the name of the most visible feminist press in India, the feminist distance from religion alienates them from the vast majority of Indian women for whom goddesses are a source of strength, meaning, and joy.

Furthermore, Dietrich argued that by focusing only on critiquing religious personal laws, without providing alternatives, feminists are unable to reach a majority of Indian women. And it is only when the women's movement has a base among all women that it can effectively counter Hindu nationalism and religious violence as SEWA has done in Ahmedabad, because it has both Hindu and Muslim women working in the movement. Dietrich also critiqued the autonomous women's movement for not dealing specifically with untouchability and its romanticization of low-caste and dalit cultures. Her reflections on ecology and development highlight two issues. One is how to "draw on women's vital experiences and skills to reverse the situation of oppression," and the other is to

> work out the connection between the ecological and the cultural crises caused by development based on a neo-colonial, capitalist, patriarchal model (with its internationally based power) that violently assaults the base for human material and spiritual survival, and is destructive of both nature and culture.
>
> (Dietrich 1992: 95)

Borrowing from the work of Shiva and Mies, Dietrich focused on the concept of production of life, which integrates production and reproduction and captures both material and spiritual dimensions. The focus is on recapturing shakti for the livelihood of the urban poor with whom Dietrich worked. Thus, women's movement scholarship in India is driven by organic categories that move back and forth from activism to analysis.

The political–economic terrain in India shifted dramatically beginning in the 1990s with the liberalization of the Indian economy, the adoption of structural adjustment programs, the rise to power of the Hindu nationalist party, and the emergence of regional caste-based parties at the center of rising communal violence in the various states. The women's movement's responses to these events have been multiple and have met with varied successes. Chief among them, are the ways in which Indian feminists and activists are at the forefront of shaping transnational women's movements through their engagement in the World Social Forum, and creating Feminist Dialogues with feminists and movements from Asia, Africa, Latin America, and the U.S. Some of these developments can be followed in publications such as *Manushi*, the National Women's Movements Conference Reports, *Samya Shakti*, *Lokayan Bulletin*, and reports of the Indian Women's Studies Association, Center for Women and Development Studies, and the S.N.D.T University Women's Studies Research Unit. But globalization, NGOization, ecological destruction, and religious fundamentalism are issues that continue to pose challenges to women's movements worldwide.

The women's movement scholarship in India highlights the need for movement-driven analyses that can contribute to activism as well as to the production of grounded theories. This is evident in the next section because the women's movement in India brought to the foreground issues of violence against women that had previously been silenced or ignored.

SCHOLARSHIP ON VIOLENCE AGAINST WOMEN

The research presented in this section on violence against women in India primarily arose from the work of autonomous feminist organizations. As with most other gender issues in India, there are two distinct strands of scholarship evident in the literature. The social movement-related scholarship, as discussed in the previous section, is driven by activist scholars who use writing as their platform to publicize various aspects of violence and to push for change. Second, there is a more "academic" scholarship that provides a historical and sociological analysis of the issues.

Most feminist literature in India defines violence against women as any form of coercion, power, or control perpetrated against a woman by her intimate partner or his extended kin and includes physical, sexual, verbal, and mental abuse. In its broadest sense, the definition of violence against women in India also includes topics such as sex-selective feticide (a recent form of violence), female infanticide, and discrimination against women (R. V. Bhatt 1995; Jaising 1995; Kelkar 1992). A substantial scholarship is available in this area, but this review is limited to rape, dowry deaths, and wife battering—a choice that is shaped by the problems that lately have been in the public eye and by this chapter's page limitations.

Movement-Driven Analysis

Much of the scholarship on rape and dowry deaths is written by scholars in social movements. In the 1980s, dowry deaths were on the rise and began to be increasingly reported in the media. Dowry itself is an issue among the upper- and middle-level castes. Poverty and the notion of associating specific rituals and practices with caste categories made dowry a less controversial issue among the lower castes. But this does not imply the nonexistence of other forms of violence against women from the lower castes. Violence against dalits and women in particular, which has steadily climbed since 1994, is an extreme form of the intolerance against lower castes and tribes. One particular form of this violence is the use of rape by upper caste men to control and intimidate lower caste women.

A major purpose of the movement-driven scholarship is to present violence against women as a social justice issue (arising from intersecting marginalizations) in a format that is accessible to people outside academia.

One way of doing this is to state the magnitude of the problem: National statistics such as 5,000 dowry deaths (Jaising 1995; Nelson 1996) or 20,000 rapes every year (Kelkar 1992) are used to increase consciousness about the pervasive nature of violence against women in India. The activist scholars are also publicly vociferous in debating the official numbers as gross under-reports—dowry deaths could be as high as 12,000 per year (Nelson 1996), and it is possible that only a quarter of rape cases are reported every year (Kelkar 1992) because of the shame and dishonor that it brings to the victim and her family.

Analysis of rape and dowry deaths is often based on case studies and investigative reporting. The journal *Manushi* often highlights individual rape cases or experiences of women's organizations dealing with victims of violence (D. Agarwal 1998; Kishwar 1999b; Verghese 1997). It is interesting to note that these reports are not generally based on a feminist theoretical approach. For example, as described above, Madhu Kishwar of *Manushi* has distanced herself from feminism, even while she publicizes violence against women in her journal. In an interview with an NGO that deals with victims of violence, there is even a token bone thrown to "objectivity" by discussing incidences of men being battered by their wives and the fallout from that (Kishwar 1999b).

In addition to cases reported in journals, there is the occasional book that is written primarily from a social movement standpoint, although there may be some crossover to the academic side in terms of the analysis. An example of this is Sushma Sood's (1990) edited collection, *Violence against Women*. This book includes articles on everything from wife battering to female infanticide to violence against elderly women. The chapters are written by social activists, doctors, and lawyers, all of whom are involved with women's rights in India. Most of the chapters end with the authors providing practical suggestions on how to improve women's status in India, including pushing for social and legal changes. Analysis of existing laws and their implementation is often used by the activist scholars to highlight the injustices being perpetrated against women. For example, organizations that work with victims of domestic violence point out that it is hard to pursue court cases. The police are biased, evidence is not preserved, and judges are unsympathetic. Even dying women in the hospital try to protect their husbands because of the shame or because of the children (Kishwar 1999b). In response to these activist scholars and a resultant public outcry, some changes were made to the Indian penal code in the 1980s to make prosecution easier in matters of custodial rape cases and dowry deaths (Jaising 1995; R. Kumar 1993; S. Prasad 1999; L. Sarkar 1994). These changes have led to some convictions but have not fully addressed the problem (Jaising 1995; L. Sarkar 1994). All the articles dealing with the legal process provide excerpts from judgments that show how often the judiciary's sympathies lie with the accused (Agnes 1993).

Academic Analyses

Most of the academic analyses of violence against women, which are from a feminist perspective, focus on the cultural and structural context of violence. The research varies from case studies to analyses of data from quantitative surveys. Some scholars provide a complex analysis based on a combination of sociocultural-, economic-, and individual-level factors (Kelkar 1992; Keonig et al. 2006; B. Prasad 1990; Sinha 1989). In recent years there has been an emphasis on the link between violence and reproductive or sexual health, including the risk of HIV/AIDS (Collumbien and Verma 2003; S. Desai 2005; Stephenson et al. 2005). Some analyze the historical roots of violence as condoned by the ancient texts, scriptures, and religion (Kumari 1989; Sood 1990). In general, violence is explained in terms of a patriarchal Indian society as a method of controlling women who have subordinate status. For example, one analysis of rape explains it in terms of the strict controls over women's sexuality that are necessary to protect patriarchy and patriarchal property rights (Agnes 1990); others may point to mass rapes of lower caste women by upper caste men (Maydeo 1990) or of rural and tribal women by policemen and army personnel as multiple methods of subduing women (Kelkar 1992).

Analyses of wife battering (ranging from slaps and kicks to broken bones and murder) show how some physical abuse is justified by batterers and their families as culturally appropriate ways of maintaining authority and control over a woman's behavior (Dhruvarajan 1989; Krishnan 2005; Mahajan 1990; Mukhopadhyay and Garimella 1998). Based on their regional research, scholars such as Sinha (1989), who looked at Bihar, Jejeebhoy (1998), who looked at Tamil Nadu and Uttar Pradesh, and Mahajan (1990), who studied Punjab, concluded that cultural justifications grounded in patriarchal relations include disobedience, shirking household duties, or a wife's bad temperament. Conflict with or disrespect shown to her parents-in-law (Mahajan 1990; Mohan 1990), doubts about a wife's fidelity (R. V. Bhatt 1995; Lata 1990; Parihar 1990), or disobeying the husband (Heise et al. 1994) may be other cultural reasons. Often, parents-in-law are involved in the process (Sinha 1989). While a common myth in India is that only the lower classes indulge in violence against women, researchers have found plenty of evidence to the contrary. Only the degree of secrecy varies by class/caste hierarchy (Sinha 1989; Sood 1990), and sometimes the exact form of emotional or physical abuse is different (Bhatti 1990; Verma and Pandey 1989).

A type of violence that may be unique to

India is dowry-related violence. Most of the research points to cultural reasons. For instance, after marriage, the young bride goes into a household where, in addition to her husband, she has to live with her parents-in-law and often siblings-in-law. In such a situation, a woman faces multiple subordinate status as a wife, daughter-in-law, sister-in-law, and mother. Patrilocal residence and patriarchal family structures place the wife at the bottom (Mahajan 1990). Any and all of her household's members can take it on themselves to chastise the bride for perceived infractions. In the case of dowry deaths, the mother-in-law and the husband's siblings have been found culpable in many cases (B. Prasad 1990).

A second type of analysis of dowry deaths looks at the intersections of local cultures and cultures of globalization. Scholars have shown the connection between globalization, increasing consumerism, and increasing dowry demands (see B. Prasad 1990). The custom of dowry has increased among all groups in India—Hindu, Muslim, and Christian (Bala 1989). "Dowry free" states or regions are reporting a shift toward a "pan Indian" model of marriage traditions that includes exchange of dowries (AIDWA 2002). Even the lower castes have switched from bride-price to dowry (Bhat and Halli 1999). According to Rajni Parliwala, who is involved in the analyses of the AIDWA study, "dowry encapsulates contemporary and intensifying inequalities and oppressions—gender, class, caste—it encapsulates the materialist and consumerist desires of today, the new religion of liberalization: It encapsulates the new orthodoxies of primordial identities and cultural justifications which ruling ideologies propagate" (AIDWA 2002: 1).

A large dowry is a status symbol (B. Prasad 1990). In addition to cash and jewelry, the groom's family demands cars, scooters, TVs, and refrigerators. Brides who fail to bring in an adequate dowry face intense verbal and physical abuse, sometimes leading to death. Dowry deaths are often referred to as bride burning because the favorite form of murder is to pour kerosene over the victim and set her on fire, thereby allowing the culprits to later claim that it was a kitchen accident (Jaising 1995; Nelson 1996).

While most of the analyses on rape and dowry deaths are based on qualitative assessments or case studies, research on wife battering in India has generated some quantitative analysis, perhaps because battering does not have as serious legal and social consequences. Typically, the emphasis in these studies is on individual-level characteristics (although these can be conditioned by structural or societal characteristics). Most authors conclude their analyses of violence against women with sections on strategies for change. Interestingly, although the social movement literature documents and advocates collective solutions, in which women's groups publicly humiliate the perpetrators of violence through public campaigns in their neighborhoods or workplaces, and public stripping and parading of men through villages (R. Kumar 1993) as a way of sending a strong message to the community, this strategy is not often mentioned in the academic literature as a way to initiate change. The academic literature focuses more on women's education, crisis intervention, and shelters. Given the emphasis on cultural causes, many solutions focus on the normative level, with the emphasis on documenting the consequences of patriarchal cultural relations in society. Few study the causes of interregional variations in violence or specific intervening variables such as relative access to legal or community redress that lead to more or less violence.

CONCLUSION

This brief review provides a glimpse into the nature of Indian scholarship on gender and is, perhaps, marked by what we have not been able to include here. If we confine ourselves to work published in English alone, work, employment, and wages; theorizing and constructing valid indicators of empowerment and development; work on consequences of development; control of resources; religions/religious communities and gender; gender in the construction of nations; gender outcomes of the partition of India; communities and individuals as political actors; gender and the environment; women's histories and cultural customs; gender and resistance; and dalit feminism are among some of the major themes that were not discussed here. If we broaden our perspective to include work based on a social justice model, the themes would multiply, as they would if we considered the broader field of "women's writing." Even a quick examination of the websites of some feminist Presses—Women Unlimited, Kali for Women, Stree—or the *Indian Journal of Gender* illustrates the variety of work being done. The writing on gender is not confined to women, though they make up the bulk of the authors. Nor is it confined to English, though, given India's population, the English -language publication market is large enough for publishers such as Sage Publications and Oxford University Press to consider the subcontinent a separate market. However, the writing in regional languages, which commands less global attention, is equally important and provides insightful sources for understanding how the intersection of global, national, and local processes affects people's gendered lives (excellent examples of such work are by Mahasweta Devi, Nabaneeta Deb Sen, or Chitra Deb). Many regional languages have very vibrant debates, controversies, research reports, and activist writings on gender, and their roots can be traced through centuries. Oral, and often alternative, traditions are other sources shaping gender resistance and social change.

In some regards, there are similarities between the writing on gender in India and the writing on gender in other parts of the world. Themes such as violence against women, which are now global issues, tend to be framed most often in terms of patriarchy, whether they are written in the United States, Argentina, or India. India shares with other ex-colonies around the world a research tradition questioning the role of the nation as well as entities with global spheres of influence such as colonial and neocolonial states and multinational corporations. It shares with other countries that have many cultures, religions, and significant indigenous populations the simultaneous existence of alternative understandings of gender: This is reflected in the research. The rise of right-wing fundamentalist organizations has been a global phenomenon through the past few decades of the twentieth century. The feminist, womanist, and social justice research on gender in India is, as in the United States, in political conflict with those with an ultra-rightist agenda. A difference is that while questions about the nature of citizenship and multiculturalism are beginning to frame debates about nations in societies such as the United States, this type of research has longer roots in India. Given the multicultural, economically diverse nature of the country, and the variety of contexts within which gender hierarchies are understood, studied, and challenged, it is likely that the research will remain multifaceted: It will be conducted at multiple levels, exist at many linguistic and geographical levels, and affect, in diverse ways, those who are touched by it.

NOTES

The order of the authors reflects the sections they have written and is not intended to reflect the extent of their contributions. Comments may be directed to Bandana Purkayastha (bandana.purkayastha@uconn.edu), who wrote the introduction, conclusion, and the section on theory, or any of the section authors: Mangala Subramaniam (mangala@purdue.edu) on methodology/methods, Manisha Desai (manisha.desai@uconn.edu) on gender and social movements, and Sunita Bose (boses@newpaltz.edu) on gender and violence.

1. A sense of this variety can be understood if we keep in mind that at least 21 major languages and thousands of language-like dialects are spoken in India (and states may have different official languages); that seven major religions are officially recognized by the constitution, and practices such as marriages and inheritance, which arise from religious beliefs and practices, are protected by "personal laws;" and that candidates from 169 political parties contested the 2000 national elections.

2. The Indian scholarship is not being presented out of any romantic notion of the "authentic" or the "local" but because their location and audience shape what they write about as well as how they write, providing a different perspective than the ones available in writings by scholars in U.S. academies. Many of these scholars are part of global networks that clearly undermine any attempts to demarcate the local from the global. For an excellent review of scholarship on the women's movements in India by scholars primarily writing in U.S. academies, see Kalpagam (2000).

3. In the Indian context, autonomous feminist groups emerged in the mid-1970s in response to women activists' experiences of subordination of women's issues in other left groups and movements. Therefore, these are groups of women and for women, and they are autonomous from any political parties or movements (M. Desai 1989).

REFERENCES

Agarwal, Bina (1985) "Work participation of rural women in the Third World: Some data and conceptual biases," *Economic and Political Weekly* 20, 51/52: A155–64.

—— (1994) *Gender and command over property: An economic analysis of South Asia*, Cambridge, UK: Cambridge University Press.

Agarwal, Deepa (1998) "Judgement galore yet justice eludes a child victim of rape," *Manushi* 106, May/June: 28–31.

Agnes, Flavia (1990) "Wife beating: Changes in social structure crucial to combat the problem" in S. Sood (ed.) *Violence against women*, Jaipur, India: Arihant Publishers.

—— (1993) "The anti-rape campaign: The struggle and the setback" in C Datar (ed.) *The struggle against violence*, Calcutta, India: Stree Publications.

—— (1995) "Redefining the agenda of the women's movement with a secular framework" in T. Sarkar

and U. Butalia (eds.) *Women and the Hindu right*, New Delhi, India: Kali for Women.

—— (1999) *Law and gender equality in India*, New Delhi, India: Oxford University Press.

All India Democratic Women's Association (AIDWA) (2002) "Report of AIDWA on the workshop on expanding dimensions of dowry," September 1–2, New Delhi, India.

Alvarez, Sonia E. (1999) "Advocating feminism: The Latin American feminist NGO 'boom'," *International Feminist Journal of Politics* 1 (2): 181–209.

Bagchi, Jashodhara (1996) "Ethnicity and the empowerment of women: The colonial legacy" in K. Jayawardena and M. Alwis (eds.) *Embodied violence: Communalising women's sexuality in South Asia*, New Delhi, India: Kali for Women.

Bala, Krishna (1989) "Marriage and violence: An analysis of cruelty related to the practice of dowry" in N. Sinha (ed.) *Women and violence*, New Delhi, India: Vikas Publishing House.

Banerjee, Nirmala (1989) "Working women in colonial Bengal: Modernization and marginalization" in K. Sangari and S. Vaid (eds.) *Recasting women: Essays in Indian colonial history*, New Brunswick, NJ: Rutgers University Press.

Basu, Alaka (1992) *Culture, the status of women, and demographic behaviour*, Oxford, UK: Clarendon.

Bhat, P. N. Mari, and Shiva S. Halli (1999) "Demography of bride price and dowry: Causes and consequences of the Indian marriage squeeze," *Population Studies* 53: 129–148.

Bhatt, Ela (2005) *We are poor but so many: The story of self-employed women in India*, New York: Oxford University Press.

Bhatt, Rohit V. (1995) "Violence against women in Asia and reproductive health" in H. Wallace (ed.) *Health care of women and children in developing countries*, Oakland, CA: Third Party Publishing.

Bhatti, Ranbir Singh (1990) "Socio-cultural dynamics of wife battering" in S. Sood (ed.) *Violence against women*, Jaipur, India: Arihant Publishers.

Burton, Barbara, Nata Duvvury and Nisha Varia (2000) *Justice, change, and human rights: International research and responses to domestic violence*, Synthesis Paper. A report of the International Center for Research on Women and The Center for Development and Population Activities.

Butalia, Urvashi (1993) "Community, state, and gender: On women's agency during partition," *Economic and Political Weekly* 28, 17: WS12–24.

Chakravarti, Uma (1990) "Whatever happened to the Vedic Dasi? Orientalism, nationalism and a script for the past" in K. Sangari and S. Vaid (eds.) *Recasting women: Essays in Indian colonial history*, New Brunswick, NJ: Rutgers University Press.

—— (1993) "Conceptualizing Brahmanical patriarchy

in early India: Gender, caste, class and state," *Economic and Political Weekly* 28, 14: 579–585.

—— (1996) "Wifehood, widowhood and adultery: Female sexuality, surveillance and the state in 18th century Maharashtra" in P. Uberoi (ed.) *Social reform, sexuality, and the state*, New Delhi, India: Sage.

Chatterjee, Partha (1992) "The nation and its women" in R. Guha (ed.) *A subaltern studies reader: 1986–1995*, Minneapolis: University of Minnesota Press.

Collumbien, Martine and Ravi K. Verma (2003) "Wife beating and the link with poor sexual health and risk behavior among men in urban slums in India," *Journal of Comparative Family Studies* 34, 1: 61–74.

Datar, Chhaya (1993) *The struggle against violence*, Calcutta, India: Stree Publications.

—— (1999) "Renderings of feminism in Maharashtra: Is it a more emancipatory force?" *Economic and Political Weekly* October 9.

Desai, Manisha (1989) "From affiliation to autonomy: The rise of the women's movement in Western India," Ph.D. Dissertation, Washington University in St. Louis, MO.

Desai, Sapna (2005) "HIV and domestic violence: Intersections in the lives of married women in India," *Health and Human Rights* 8, 2: 140–168.

Dhruvarajan, Vanaja (1989) *Hindu women & the power of ideology*, Granby, MA: Bergin & Garvey.

Dietrich, Gabriele (1992) *Reflections on the women's movement in India*, New Delhi, India: Horizon Books.

Dreze, Jean, and Amartya Sen (1997) *Indian development: Selected regional perspectives*, Delhi, India: Oxford University Press.

Dua, Veena (1979) "A woman's encounter with Arya Samaj and untouchables: A slum in Jullundar" in M. N. Srinivas, A. M. Shah, and E. A. Ramaswamy (eds.) *The field worker and the field: Problems and challenges in sociological investigation*, Delhi, India: Oxford University Press.

Gandhi, Nandita, and Nandita Shah (1992) *The issues at stake: Theory and practice in the contemporary women's movement in India*, New Delhi, India: Kali for Women.

Gautam, D. N., and B. V. Trivedi (1986) *Unnatural deaths of married women with special reference to dowry deaths: A sample study of Delhi*, New Delhi: Bureau of Police Research and Development, Ministry of Home Affairs, Government of India.

Gopalan, Sarala (2002) *Towards equality: The unfinished agenda. Status of women in India—2001*, New Delhi, India: National Commission for Women.

Gupta, Khadija Ansari (1979) "Travails of a woman fieldworker: A small town in Uttar Pradesh" in M. N. Srinivas, A. M. Shah, and E. A. Ramaswamy (eds.) *The fieldworker and the field: Problems and challenges in sociological investigation*, Delhi, India: Oxford University Press.

Hasan, Zoya (1994) *Forging identities: Gender communities and the state in India*, New Delhi, India: Kali for Women.

Heise, Lori L., Jacqueline Pitanguy, and Adrienne Germain (1994) "Violence against women: The hidden health burden," World Bank discussion papers, Washington, DC: World Bank.

International Center for Research on Women (2000) *Domestic violence in India. A summary report of a multi-site household survey*, Washington, DC: International Center for Research on Women.

Jaising, Indira (1995) "Violence against women: The Indian perspective" in J. Peters and A. Wolper (eds.) *Women's rights, human rights*, New York: Routledge.

Jejeebhoy, Shireen (1998) "Wife-beating in rural India: A husband's right? Evidence from survey data," *Economic and Political Weekly* 33, 15: 855–862.

—— (2000) "Women's autonomy in rural India: Its dimensions, determinants and the influence of context" in G. Sen and H. Presser (eds.) *Women's empowerment and demographic processes: Moving beyond Cairo*, Oxford, UK: Oxford University Press.

John, Mary (1996) *Discrepant dislocations: Feminism, theory and postcolonial histories*, Berkeley: University of California Press.

—— (1998) "Feminisms and internationalisms: A response from India," *Gender & History* 10, 3: 539–548.

Kalpagam, Uma (2000) "The women's movement in India today—New agendas and old problems," *Feminist Studies* 26: 645–660.

Kannabiran, Kalpana (1996) "Rape and the construction of communal identity" in K. Jayawardena and M. Alwis (eds.) *Embodied violence: Communalising women's sexuality in South Asia*, New Delhi, India: Kali for Women.

—— (ed.) (2005) *The violence of normal times*, New Delhi, India: Women Unlimited.

Karlekar, Malavika (1995) "Search for women's voices: Reflections on fieldwork, 1968–93," *Economic and Political Weekly* 30, 17: WS30–37.

Karlekar, Malavika, and Leela Kasturi (2002) "Women's studies in India: Crisis or renewal? Introduced by Mary John," *Indian Journal of Gender Studies* 9, 2.

Kelkar, Govind (1992) *Violence against women*, New Delhi, India: Manohar Publications.

Keonig, Michael A., Rob Stephenson, Saifuddin Ahmed, Shireen J. Jejeebhoy, and Jacquelyn Campbell (2006) "Individual and contextual determinants of domestic violence in North India," *American Journal of Public Health* 96, 1: 132–138.

Khanna, Madhu (2002) "The goddess-woman question in Sakta-Tantras" in D. Ahmed (ed.) *Gendering the Spirit*, London: Zed Books.

Kishwar, Madhu (1999a) *Off the beaten track:*

Rethinking gender justice for Indian women, New Delhi, India: Oxford University Press.

—— (1999b) "When homes are torture chambers: Vimochana's work with victims of domestic violence," *Manushi* 110: 17–24.

Krishnan, Suneeta (2005) "Do structural inequalities contribute to marital violence? Ethnographic evidence from rural South India," *Violence Against Women* 11, 6: 759–775.

Kumar, Nita (1992) "Introduction" in N. Kumar (ed.) *Women as subjects: South Asian histories*, Charlottesville: University Press of Virginia.

Kumar, Radha (1993) *The history of doing: An illustrated account of movements for women's rights and feminism in India 1800–1990*, London: Verso.

Kumari, Madhu (1989) "Patriarchy and violence against women in India" in N. Sinha (ed.) *Women and violence*, New Delhi, India: Vikas Publishing House.

Lata, P. M. (1990) "Violence within family: Experiences of a feminist support group" in S. Sood (ed.) *Violence against women*, Jaipur, India: Arihant Publishers.

Mahajan, A. (1990) "Instigators of wife battering" in S. Sood (ed.) *Violence against women*, Jaipur, India: Arihant Publishers.

Maydeo, Anjali (1990) "Domestic violence: The perspective and experiences of an activist group" in S. Sood (ed.) *Violence against women*, Jaipur, India: Arihant Publishers.

Mazumdar, Vina, and Indu Agnihotri (1995) "Changing terms of political discourse, women's movement in India, 1970s–1990," *Economic and Political Weekly* 29 July.

—— (1999) "The women's movement in India: Emergence of a new perspective" in B. Ray and A. Basu (eds.) *From independence towards freedom: Indian women since 1947*, New Delhi, India: Oxford University Press.

Menon, Nivedita (1999) *Gender and politics in India*, New Delhi, India: Oxford University Press.

—— (ed.) (2007) *Sexualities*, New Delhi, India: Women Unlimited.

Menon, Ritu, and Kamla Bhasin (1996) "Abducted women, the state and questions of honor" in Kumarti Jayawardena and Malathi Alwis (eds.)*Embodied violence: Communalising women's sexuality in South Asia*, New Delhi, India: Kali for Women.

Mohan, Vidhu (1990) "Is there hope for battered wives?" in S. Sood (ed.) *Violence against women*, Jaipur, India: Arihant Publishers.

Mukhopadhyay, Swapna, and Surekha Garimella (1998) "The contours of reproductive choice for poor women: Findings from a micro survey" in S. Mukhopadhyay (ed.) *Women's health, public policy and community action*, New Delhi, India: Manohar.

Nelson, Toni (1996) "Violence against women," *World Watch* 9: 33–38.

Omvedt, Gail (1993) *Reinventing revolution: New social movements and the socialist tradition in India*, New York: M. E. Sharpe.

—— (1998) "The anti-caste movement and the discourse of power" in T. V. Sathymurthy (ed.) *Region, religion, caste, gender and culture in India*, Delhi, India: Oxford University Press.

Pande, Mrinal (1996) *Devi: Tales of the goddess in our time*, New Delhi, India: Penguin.

Parihar, Lalita (1990) "Battered wife syndrome: Some socio-legal aspects" in S. Sood (ed.) *Violence against women*, Jaipur, India: Arihant Publishers.

Poonacha, Veena (1995) *Gender in human rights discourse*, Womens; Studies Research Center, Mumbai: SNDT University

Prasad, B. Devi (1990) "Dowry related violence towards women: A sociological perspective" in S. Sood (ed.) *Violence against women*, Jaipur, India: Arihant Publishers.

Prasad, Shally (1999) "Medicolegal response to violence against women in India," *Violence against Women* 5: 478–506.

Rao, Anupama (1999) "Understanding Sirasgaon: Notes towards conceptualizing the role of law, caste, and gender in a case of atrocity" in R. S. Rajan (ed.) *Signpost: Gender issues in post-independence India*, New Delhi, India: Kali for Women.

Ray, Bharati, and Aparna Basu (eds.) (1999) *From independence towards freedom: Indian women since 1947*, New Delhi, India: Oxford University Press.

Rege, Sharmila (1998) "Dalit women talk differently: A critique of difference and towards a dalit feminist standpoint position," *Economic and Political Weekly* 33, 44: WS39–46.

Sangari, Kumkum, and Sudesh Vaid (1989) *Recasting women: Essays in Indian colonial history*, New Delhi, India: Kali for Women.

Sarkar, Lotika (1994) "Rape: A human rights versus a patriarchal interpretation," *Indian Journal of Gender Studies* 1, 1: 69–89.

Sarkar, Tanika (1991) "The woman as communal subject: Rashtra sevika samiti and the Ram janmabhoomi movement," *Economic and Political Weekly* 26, 35: 2057–2062.

Sen, Illina (1990) *A space within the struggle: Women's participation in people's movement*, New Delhi, India: Kali for Women.

Sen, Susmita (1999) *Women in late colonial India*, Cambridge, UK: Cambridge University Press.

Shiva, Vandana (1993) "The Chipko women's concept of freedom" in M. Meis and V. Shiva (eds.) *Ecofeminism*, London: Zed Books.

—— (2005) *Earth Democracy*, London: Zed Books.

Sinha, Niroj (1989) *Women and violence*, New Delhi, India: Vikas Publishing House.

Sood, Sushma (ed.) (1990) *Violence against women*, Jaipur, India: Arihant Publishers.

Srinivas, M. N., A. M. Shah, and E. A. Ramaswamy (1979) *The fieldworker and the field: Problems and challenges in sociological investigation*, Delhi, India: Oxford University Press.

Srinivasan Shobha (1997) "Breaking rural bonds through migration: The failure of development for women in India," *Journal of Comparative Family Studies* 28: 89–102.

Stephenson, Rob, Michael A. Koenig, and Ahmed Saifuddin (2006) "Domestic violence and contraceptive adoption in Uttar Pradesh, India," *Studies in Family Planning* 37, 2: 75–86.

Subramaniam, Mangala (2001) "Translating participation in informal organizations into social empowerment: Women in rural India," Ph.D. Dissertation, University of Connecticut, Storrs.

—— (2008) "Negotiating the field in rural India: Location, organizational structure, and identity salience" in M. Huggins and M.-L. Glebbeek (eds.) *Danger in the field*, New York: Rowman and Littlefield.

Suresh, V. (1998) "The dalit movement in India" in T. V. Sathymurthy (ed.) *Region, religion, caste, gender and culture in India*, Delhi, India: Oxford University Press.

Talwar, Vir Bharat (1999) "Feminist consciousness in women's journals in Hindi: 1910–1920" in K. Sangari and S. Vaid (eds.) *Recasting women: Essays in Indian colonial history*, New Brunswick, NJ: Rutgers University Press.

Tharu, Shasi, and Tejaswini Niranjana (1994) "Problems for contemporary theory of gender," *Social Scientist* 22: 93–117.

Vanita, Ruth (2002) *Queering India: Same-sex love and eroticism in Indian culture and society*, New York: Routledge.

Verghese, Sudha (1997) "Justice denied: The suspicious death of Deepa Murmu," *Manushi* 98: 17–19.

Verma, Jyoti, and Madhu Pandey (1989) "Violence in everyday life" in N. Sinha (ed.) *Women and violence*, New Delhi, India: Vikas Publishing House.

CHAPTER 10

Women's Studies in Iran: The Roles of Activists and Scholars

Shahla Ezazi

Although the women's movement has a long tradition in Iran, women's studies is a relatively new subject in Iranian universities. It was first established as an MA degree and a multidisciplinary field of study in 1999, with the first students attending classes beginning in September 2000.

Despite the fact that there was a negative attitude toward the new discipline, at present more than 10 universities all over the country offer it. This new subject has raised the general attention to women's issues as a field of study, a new discourse has developed, students from other disciplines are doing research in this field, and the negative academic milieu is slowly changing. Women's studies is now being seen as an academic discipline, and many instructors feel obligated to learn more about feminist theories and use a gender approach in their projects.

This chapter is about the situation of women's studies in Iran and its impact on society. First, I will give a brief history of the women's movement in Iran and its demands, both before and after the Islamic revolution. The next section is on the social context that made it possible to establish this discipline. I also will describe the position of this subject in universities, the types of gender approaches and the methodology used by social scientists, the most important areas of study from instructors and activists' viewpoints, and the contribution of universities to addressing women's problems. For this purpose, I interviewed 10 university instructors and about 15 activists to evaluate their gender understandings.

A BRIEF HISTORY OF THE WOMEN'S MOVEMENT IN IRAN

Background

Iran has experienced different regimes in its long history. The first Iranian revolution, over 100 years ago, had the goal of obtaining a constitution. The women's movement began in 1906, after that Constitutional Revolution, which triggered many modern political ideas. Shortly after the revolution some women sent a letter to the parliament, asking permission to establish women's own associations. The influential religious leader of the time, Modaress, responded that women should not have any associations for social and political affairs and that they could not demand equality in society because they are under the guardianship of men, and men should take care of women's rights (Khosro-Panah 2002).

Although the Constitutional Revolution was concerned with modern ideas of government and the social order, traditional attitudes towards women still prevailed. It was a common belief that women were entitled to fewer societal rights than men. The active women of that time, most of them young women from high status and religious families, demanded rights to education, especially primary education for girls, to organize associations, and for suffrage. They also asked for changes in family relations and opposed polygamy. They wrote articles about the ideal relationships in the family, and personal and social health (Khosro-Panah 2002).

In 1925, Reza Shah gained power and his regime tried to modernize Iran. This modernization project provided an opportunity for many women to convince the new regime to pay attention to women and give them equal rights with men. They achieved some of their objectives between 1925 and the revolution in 1979. For example, women received suffrage in all elections and, through the "Family Protection Law," gained more family rights, including women's right to divorce, while limitations were placed on men's divorce rights and on polygamy. The "Women's Organization," which was close to the royal court, implemented charity activities and tried to promote women's participation in public life, especially by urging changes in discriminatory laws (Ahmadi-Khorasani and Ardalan 2003).

Women were active in all these periods. They were successful in many endeavors and used the opportunity to gain more basic education, and even more higher education. By 1978, 30 percent of all students were women and girls. There was no visible difference between men and women in society, and women were portrayed as modern European or American women. Many women studied in Tehran universities and also in western countries.

With the Islamic revolution in 1979, the regime became an ideological one. Its strongest criticisms were towards the modernization ideas of the former Shah's regime, especially around the image of women in society. The new woman's image was supposed to be an Islamic one, and a new dress code and Islamic ethics were implemented. The regime also was against women's rights:

It repealed the Family Protection Law and removed women lawyers from judge positions in the courts. Opposition groups did not protest against these actions. Even when women demonstrated against being forced to wear a veil and the new dress code, other groups did not support them.

The regime managed to control women in the public sphere in other ways, too. The new sex divisions in society limited university entrance for women students, as well as their selection of fields of study, and it restricted job opportunities for women. Changes in the penal code made women worth half as much as men in official law court regulations, such as being a witness, in inheritance, and in "blood for blood" compensation. In these cases, it takes two women's testimony to be equal to that of one man (Ebadi 2002; Kar 1997). During this period, the leftist groups and other parties in Iran did not pay any attention to women's protests against these changes. Shortly after the revolution, the war between Iran and Iraq began and lasted for eight years; and, when the war ended in 1991, the reconstruction period started, preceding economic changes in society. Women's voices were ignored throughout these periods.

During this period, a new social group, "the new middle stand," as well as new intellectual groups came into being (Bashirieh 2002). Both of them had demands in the areas of the economy, culture, society, ideology and politics. There was a struggle between defenders of the traditional discourse, mainly expressed by clerics, and intellectual groups that were promoting democracy and civil society. Some new groups were established in this period, consisting of academicians, students, specialists, artists, authors, and other intellectuals who were involved in the modern higher education system. The core of this group consisted of intellectuals who were interested in western thought and believed in a mix of Islam and Marxism, though other schools of thought, such as hermeneutics, postmodernism, and liberalism, were common too. Their most common characteristic was a criticism of tradition, power relations, and governance (Bashirieh 2002).

In 1997, the Reform period started in Iran. In this era, intellectual groups found an opportunity to achieve some of their demands. The numbers of critical newspapers, articles, and books expressing new ideas rapidly increased. New discourses on civil society, citizenship, democracy and freedom were introduced. Despite these changes, the Reformist regime was not really interested in freedom and equality or in a real civil society. Many events were witnessed that normally are uncharacteristic of a government that claims to support civil society. For example, more than 10 newspapers, critical of the regime, were unexpectedly closed, and a demonstration of university students was brutally suppressed. In spite of advocating an ideology of tolerance and dialogue, the regime apparently limited its tolerance to its own devoted groups.

Changes in Social Situation After 1995

Some change in the social situation happened after 1995. Following its participation in the U.N. Beijing conference, the Iranian government was compelled by international attitudes to make changes in critical aspects of women's lives—many women's bureaus were established in ministries, and women could independently establish NGOs and other civic organizations. The regime understood that women's movements around the world had established their political standing and, because the government wanted to have a good image in the international community, they tried to allow Iranian women the opportunity to resume their own activism. Gradually, social problems affecting women, that the government had tried to hide for a long time, began to surface. Women's collective activities at various levels

and individual women's attempts to change their own lives enabled the public to become aware of women's oppressive situation and the extent of their problems in Iran, including violence in the family, runaway girls, prostitution, and the prevalence of drug addiction and HIV/AIDS.

In this period, women focused on publicizing women's issues, using ideas and concepts drawn from a gender analysis. Empowerment for women was the goal of many NGOs, as well as of the Women's Bureau, a government-affiliated institution. The branch offices of the Women's Bureau, including the offices set up in the Ministry of Education and the Ministry of the Interior, carried out positive activities within the government framework. They invited women from other provinces to workshops about gender related issues, so that they could go back and hold the same workshops and speeches at the provincial level.

I also want to draw attention to a very critical response initiated at the individual level. Faced with a situation that is oppressive, girls and women in Iran have made individual choices and undertaken activities to change their situation. These responses straddle a wide range of approaches. On the one hand, many young women have tried to improve their life chances through university education. The number of women students in universities has increased, and by 2007, about 70 percent of all students were women (Ezazi 2007). In part, this is because they have few job opportunities with a high school degree. One can hope that this increase in the number of women attending universities will positively affect the number of women in management positions in future.

On the other hand, some girls run away to escape from their miserable home lives, while other women ask for divorce. Indeed, there is some research on runaway girls in Iran (Moazami 2004), indicating that generally they are from violent families. In the most critical situations, women even commit suicide, and the suicide rate in some regions, especially by setting fire to oneself, is very high. This overall picture reflects the current contradiction between modernity and tradition in Iranian society. The imposed image of women in the Islamic Republic is a very traditional one, but young women who are exposed to a possibility of personal improvement find it hard to identify with this image. Instead of following the traditional way of life, they try to reject the authority of their fathers, brothers or husbands. Iranian women try to make decisions about their own lives because, in my judgment, they want to be independent, believe in equality, and desire basic human rights; they want more freedom in the family and in the schools. If they fail to realize these rights legally, they choose other ways, which can lead them to either positive or negative strategies.

SOCIAL CONTEXT AND WOMEN'S STUDIES

In 1997, social change encouraged men and women close to the regime to offer the Ministry of Higher Education the opportunity to open a new degree program under the name of Women's Studies. According to them, the goal of the program was to help with the analysis of women's situation under Islam, with an emphasis on the empowerment of women in Islam. In brief, the program aimed to present a new positive picture of women. The stated objective of this discipline was "to introduce the role and status of women in the world from an Islamic perspective ... to develop a scientific approach towards women's problems for improving public attitudes in terms of social and cultural aspects" (Moshakhesate koli barname motaleate zanan [General Specification of the Program and Outline] 1998: 1). It was argued that a program aimed to help students gain a "moderate gender approach" was needed.

Many scholars wrote articles in *Zanan* magazine about the establishment of this program. Their main subject was whether the new program was intended to change the existing social situation (Ezazi 2001) or to avoid reality (Moti 2001). Another *Zanan* article considered whether the program would improve, or merely justify, the existing situation for women (Shaditalab 2001). These articles were written by women who had played a large role in the education and teaching of subjects related to the new women's studies program, but they were never asked for their input before starting it. These scholars believed that the new discipline, based on university-provided syllabi, was aimed only to teach students that women were beneficiaries of the Islamic republic. Women's studies scholars were not told who created this syllabus, but could only suspect that it was a committee in the Higher Education Ministry. The syllabus did not even include sections that would give students the opportunity to discuss the real, current situation of Iranian women and their problems. Each educational group had the opportunity to change the syllabus, to a limited degree, but that needed the agreement of the faculty, and also of the university.

The most important criticism was about the androcentric approach of this program. Although some courses, such as psychology of women or women and literature, were offered, students could not understand the logic of this discipline. There were no courses on new theories, appropriate research methods, or the women's movement. They studied different subjects, but without understanding the relationship between them or the origins of gender inequality and the submission of women.

By the time the students admitted to the program had finished their first term, it became clear that changes were needed. Different universities made revisions in the subjects and syllabi. However, the changes only happened in faculties where lecturers were familiar with women's studies courses. After the first semester, for instance, faculty at Alame and Alzahra Universities gained a better understanding of the challenges regarding the courses and syllabi and tried to change some of their content accordingly. Alame Tabatabee University changed some courses, partly because their course syllabi overlapped with others. They were able to add a few new and more important subjects, such as "Introducing Women's Studies" and "Feminist Theories and the Women's Movement," while other subjects were replaced. For example, English was offered instead of Arabic, and "Qualitative Research Methodology" took the place of "Statistics." In other universities, especially at the provincial level, with no active women to push for changes, they offered the women's studies curriculum unchanged. In Spring 2008 there were just ten or twelve universities teaching this subject, out of which only two or three have implemented a feminist agenda in their curriculum.

THEORIES AND METHODOLOGY

Most of the universities in Iran are too conservative to be open to new ideas and theories, and neither a critical theory nor feminism is desired. The most prominent theories taught in courses are functionalist ones, and most of the instructors are followers of consensus theories, although there are some exceptions to the rule. New ideas, such as postmodernism or post-structuralism, including the ideas of Foucault, Derrida, or other thinkers, are discussed but to a lesser extent.

Sociology courses seldom teach or talk about feminism. Male colleagues are sometimes against these theories and think it is unscientific to use such theories or feminist research methods when doing surveys. In such a milieu, gender related issues are not the prime subjects of research and all

students, including female students, learn male-centered theories. The social problems that are discussed as important belong to the public sphere, and most research projects neglect women. While researchers use the variable sex to categorize men and women, they rarely pay attention to unequal power relations between men and women or carry out socio-economic and political analyses of gender.

After women's studies was established, the need for new theories and methodology became evident. Despite the resistance of graduate committees at each university, critical scholars tried to convince the committees' faculty that it was essential to offer other topics and methodologies. Thus, it proved possible to receive official approval from the committees to introduce other women-related subjects and methodologies. Now, students from different fields of study (such as cultural studies and even sociology) are interested in working on women's issues. Some of their topics include the effects of religious gatherings on women's awareness, women's attitudes towards abortion, violence against women, power relations in the family, the women's movement, the effects of mothering on women's identity, and gender stereotypes and their affect on women's attitudes towards housework. Feminist theories were often used, and very diverse methodologies, ranging from questionnaires to in-depth interviews, observation, and focus group discussions, were applied.

Women's studies, as a new subject in Iranian universities, caused some positive changes. The most significant contribution of this field to the social sciences is its ability to describe women's situation in Iran and reveal their problems, as well as different aspects of women's lives. However, only a few analyses or surveys have been produced about the causes of inequality. It is assumed that lack of social theory in this regard is a reflection of the social status of academicians. A scholar told me, "Of course, we develop our own theories about women in Iran. We are capable of producing some theories, but I think everybody avoids expressing these theories because of the dangers it is associated with." That is to say, living in a totalitarian regime makes it dangerous to express ideas about critical issues such as women's problems.

The lack of original theory is not solely the weakness of women's studies; other fields of study with more history than women's studies, such as sociology, have not been able to produce their own indigenous theory, either. But it is still possible to collect ideas about the actual situation in Iran from the written works of scholars in women's studies, sociology, or other fields, who have different ideas.

There may be another reason for a reluctance to produce theory; gender inequality is so deep in Iran that most of the efforts aim to identify the problems women face, and try to improve the situation in every possible way, leaving no time for theory development. Most scholars and activists do not hold influential positions, so their efforts are focused on convincing persons in decision-making positions about the negative effects of gender inequality. This advocacy happens in different ways; some try to raise the issues of social and psychological effects on individuals, families and even on social behavior. Other activists and scientific NGOs organize speeches, lectures, seminars and gatherings to inform the public and the regime about the consequences of gender inequality.

It is assumed that the prime goal of these activities is to obtain equality for all women in Iran through changes in the legal system. This does not mean that legal rights are the only reason for women's subordination. Cultural attitudes and social norms are also important. Yet, the preliminary efforts are aimed to show the prevalent gender inequality instead of theorizing it. Shirin Ebadi (2002) and Mehrangiz Kar (1997) have written many books and articles about this problem and have made the discriminatory character of the law clear. Current family law brings women under the control of men; women do not have any legal rights and can lose custody of their children. The right to divorce belongs only to men, without their being obliged to give any reason. Men are regarded as the heads of the family and also enjoy the right of being married to more than one wife at the same time (polygamy). Furthermore, basic decisions, like a family's place of residence or permission for wives to obtain travel permits, are made by men.

WOMEN'S STUDIES IN IRAN: ITS ISSUES AND IMPACT

Gender Approach in Women's Studies in Iran

In this section, I describe the gender theories used and the research methods most frequently applied by scholars, based on information I gathered from instructors and activists who are involved in Women's Studies programs.

Participants include 10 Assistant Professors, all with Ph.D.s, working at three universities in Tehran (Tehran University, Alame University, and Azad University). They are senior faculty members, whose age ranged from 40 to over 60. As most of them are sociologists, they have at least 15 years of teaching experience in the social sciences; and they have also taught courses on women and family or have taught in the Women's Studies program. In addition, two of them have held decision-making positions: one is the director of an educational group, and the other is the former director of the Women's Center Program. Some are also directing non-governmental scientific women's NGOs or are members of such NGOs.

Half of the instructors had studied for their undergraduate, graduate, and Ph.D. degrees in Iran, while two of them had gained their MA and Ph.D. degrees outside the country. Three interviewees were abroad during the late 1960s and were influenced by new ideas and concepts on women, while only one lecturer received her Ph.D. degree after 1990. All of them said that they had become interested in women's issues since their university days and were motivated to write about women and work on related subjects.

The topics the instructors have been working on varied, including subjects such as: family in general, and power relations in the family; divorce; mate selection and marriage; violence in the family; women and development; women's poverty; women's health and reproductive health; women in family law; women's portrayal in television and school books; working women; young women in Iran; social movements; law; and the everyday life of women. The subjects they work on reflect the main problems for women in Iran and they are all somehow related to the common underlying issues of violence, the legal system, and poverty.

I also interviewed five activists. Many of them were aged between 30 and 40, younger than the instructors, and all have some university education. Most of them graduated from universities in the social sciences, though a couple had gained degrees in women's studies. These interviewees all had published articles on women in magazines, and a few are journalists or have their own weblogs. Those with women's studies degrees were able to judge the quality of the courses and share their experience of social activism.

Almost all my interviewees confirmed that functionalism is the most common theory used in university programs, and that quantitative research methods are quite widespread. One interviewee said, "Tehran University is a very traditional university. Some professors have been working there for over 30 years. They do not let the younger generation of professors get in. They just repeat themselves and are closed to new ideas. They teach the theories of Parsons, perhaps Merton, and nothing more. They are

focused on quantitative research methods. Tehran University is traditionally against flexibility." Others think that the textbooks are very old and "classic," and that new theories are not presented. However, as younger instructors teach new theories and discuss them with the students, some were exposed to these ideas. One person said, "I think the modernist approach is very common in our universities, but I, myself, believe in a postmodern approach because it enables us to understand the differences and other variables that generate inequality."

Their types of gender approach varied because, although all the instructors are teaching, their capacities are not the same. Some are very well informed about contemporary feminist theories and methods, while others are not familiar with gender concepts. Some do not even believe themselves to be specialists in women's issues, because they had written their theses about women years ago but were not familiar with new theories. Moreover, they worried that women and gender and feminism are seen as interchangeable, and they did not want to be labeled as feminists.

Iranian academies still hold a very negative attitude towards feminism; most colleagues, even the open-minded ones, are indifferent. Some argue that certain groups of feminists are too radical and their demands are not rooted in realities. Others, who are close to the regime and dominant politicians, use feminism as an insulting term. This group understands feminism to be pornography, lesbianism, and abortion. They contend that feminists want to destroy the family and encourage deviant behavior in young girls and society. According to this official version of feminism, it is regarded as dangerous to be a feminist. Some interviewees avoided giving me a direct answer about their perspectives on gender issues because, I believe, while they were well informed about gender, they preferred not to share their views due to university conservatism. Instead, they tried to give me a picture about their research topics and the methodology they were using.

Impact of Gender Studies

I organized several roundtables and group discussion sessions to collect the views of these instructors, students, and activists about women's issues. Based on these discussions, I describe some of the characteristics of a gender approach in Iran.

The problems of women in Iran are very diverse and deep. The first investigations focused on general gender inequality by providing evidence of the formal problems in the legal system, education, and in cultural norms and values. The existing inequality has become a part of academic and social discourse. Now, many other hidden problems are the subject of official discussions, including violence, men's power, and the superior–inferior positions of men and women.

While sociology pays attention to sex differences, many scholars at these group discussions use a gender approach to draw the attention of students to social problems from a women's standpoint. Much of their research uses women-only samples and relies on interviews or observations as their methodology. Women's studies deals with problems that affect women's lives and encourages students to learn more about these problems in order to make changes in the society.

The most crucial problem has been violence against women, and many research projects were developed to address it (Ezazi 2002; 2004; Moazami 2004; Moti 2003; Shaditalab 2004, 2005). Students also show interest in other problems, such as power relations in the family; women's health, including infertility; and the issues of different groups of women, such as young women and urban women. While gender differences are still important, other variables related to inequality, such as culture, ethnicity, and age, as well as women in marginalized positions, have slowly caught the attention of scholars and students (Moti 2003; Shaditalab 2005). Most academicians think that, after a period of concentration on women's issues, it is now important to look at men because women's problems are related to men. We have to be concerned about both sexes to change social norms and attitudes, since men, as well as women, suffer from the prevalent cultural impositions and men's support is needed to improve the status of women. Men, especially young men, are no longer considered to be women's enemies, as their attitudes toward gender studies have changed. My respondents argue that it is a matter of a social paradigm that pits them against each other and not all women are victims all the time.

Following in the footsteps of active women scholars who conducted research on women's issues and published their findings, the faculties of anthropology, history, law, political science, medical sciences, and health services are now adopting a gender approach in their research projects. A network of different faculty with a focus on gender studies is slowly getting formed.

Almost all the instructors and activists that I interviewed thought that the discipline of women's studies had contributed to the advancement of the women's movement, mainly outside of academia, although this contribution significantly depends on the instructors and the way they teach. If instructors are not positive about feminism, they do not assign students to work on women's issues. Many former students, who are now active in their own institutions, have developed a different outlook towards women's problems. However, more effort is needed to improve the generally unfavorable attitude of universities towards women's studies courses, and more institutionalized university-activist connections would be useful.

NGO activists and independent feminist women also have contributed to gender studies. Their activism involves publishing books and writing articles.[1] The first women's publishing house, Rooshangaran and Women's Studies, has been active for over 20 years, and it now specializes in women's books. *Jense-Dovom* and *Fasl-e Zanan* (literally, and respectively, meaning *Second Sex* and *Time of Women*, with Noushin Ahmadi-Khorasani as the editor of both) translated and published many articles on gender and feminist issues. *Zanan* magazine also has published extensively on women-related issues for the last 15 years, and it was the first publication to include the works of Iranian Diasporic scholars.

Other activists have translated books, some of which are selected as textbooks for women's studies courses. The Women's Studies Group of the Iranian Sociology Association also undertook a translation project, inviting many activists to help with the translation of a reader on feminist theories, which was later published. The most frequently translated works are written by American or European second-wave feminists. Unfortunately, no translated books from any third-world feminists have been published; and only a few articles from third-wave feminists have been translated and published in women's magazines.

In recent years, the characteristic activism of women's NGOs has attracted many young women, and also men, to their rank and file, and they are actively engaged in organizing campaigns to demand more rights for women. Also some of the scientific NGOs, such as the Women's Studies Group of the Iranian Sociology Association, the Independent Researchers on Women's Issues, and Historian Women Scholars, increasingly focus on research about women. Most of them are affiliated with universities yet manage to advocate for the women's cause with their publications, seminars, and workshops. Ultimately, they aim to link activism and the academy together.

Challenges

Although many research projects investigate women's status in Iran, only a few of them study the country's hierarchical power structure. I believe this is a very important issue to be carefully studied in order to understand the root of women's oppression. Studies on violence can be used as a model because they have examined many different variables that influence social problems, including the level of men and women's education, men's addiction, and husbands' unemployment. However, they neglect the effects of the social and legal systems that give men the power and permit, or even encourage, them to control their wives.

Some research projects have shown the effects of gendered legal inequalities on women's lives. The most important research in this field is on violence against women, both in the private and public spheres. In the recent years, Shahla Ezazi's (2002) study on domestic violence and Fateme Ghasemzade's (2003) research on child abuse in families have galvanized the interest of other academics and students who studied such topics for their research projects and theses. The Center for Women's Participation and the Ministry of the Interior collaborated with each other to conduct a national survey (Shaditalab 2004) on domestic violence in Iran. Despite the lack of a gender framework underlying some of the research, many investigations have demonstrated the significance of these problems related to women in the family. Subsequently, the Women's Bureau tried to establish shelters for battered women. However, this proved to be very difficult because, under the law and "Shari'a," a husband has the right to control his wife, to the extent that she is not allowed to stay overnight anywhere without his consent. However, some efforts were made to protect battered women, although these were too restricted to be useful for women's safety.

There are other projects that deal with

violence against women: for example, in 2004 Shahla Moazemi examined the issue of women who were convicted of killing their husbands. In her report she contends that women suffering from their husband's abuse sometimes react to these assaults violently and end up killing their aggressor. Moazemi (2004) also conducted a project on runaway girls, which she writes about as another indicator of the prevalence of domestic violence. Gradually, other aspects of domestic violence are being studied, such as rape and incest in the family.

Violence against women in public is another critical subject. It ranges from sexual abuse on the streets to rape and murder. In 2003, the Women's Studies Group of the Iranian Sociology Association held a seminar on public violence against women, and it was reported that several students did their theses about sexual abuse in the public sphere, including on city streets. Another hidden problem is the prevalence of female circumcision in some regions of Iran, which garnered students' interest for their thesis research. However, the graduate committee did not approve this thesis topic on the grounds that theses on women's "sexual problems" are not good for our university's image. I also learned that one thesis was written about this subject but was not published.

Nowadays, no one can deny the occurrence of violence against women, which was once a latent problem. Newspapers and women journalists write articles about these problems, and various NGOs and students groups hold seminars on the International Day Against Violence. Although no legal changes were made, some changes can be observed in different sectors. Courses on domestic violence have been offered for judges, school directors, and the police staff, and social workers are now concentrating on the issues related to domestic violence. The most noteworthy consequence of these efforts is that women do not feel guilty anymore, and they go to the police and law courts to complain about the violent behavior of their husbands. Some Iranian women no longer believe that they should keep silent about this phenomenon.

NGOs have taken many actions to raise awareness on the issue of domestic violence. They have held workshops, seminars, and most notably, they have supported the victims of violence in courts of law. They also have made efforts to find them space in private shelters, help them with job searches or domestic tasks, and to empower them. There are some NGOs that help women to establish their own cooperative businesses, and these small businesses provide women with a little income. However, the significance of these endeavors is in their ability to provide women with an opportunity to be together and find a peaceful secure place to work in. They are also instrumental in strengthening the self-reliance of women.

In addition to making legal changes, it is crucial to bring about changes in cultural attitudes and social norms. For example, a major representation of gender inequality is found in the media, especially in school textbooks and on television. Many research projects focus on the portraits of women in textbooks as well as on television (Ezazi 1991; Hejazi 2006). These studies have described the effects of gender socialization on school children and the paradox between women's images and real women's lives. After a long period of campaigning, the Ministry of Education finally revised the school textbooks and, as a result, prejudice against women is less represented. However, in April 2008, the new Minister of Education suddenly announced his own decision that, because boys and girls are different, the school texts for them should be different too. Simply put, girls have to learn women's work and boys must learn men's work.

Many published research papers focus on the images of women on television (Ezazi 2003; Ravadrad 2003). In spite of revisions in the content of TV serials that favor women, many programs still highlight the role of women exclusively in the family, ignoring women's contributions in workplaces and society. Such programs are biased against women in the public sphere and do not respect the value of education for women. In these TV shows working women are portrayed as aggressive mothers and as wives who often mistreat their children, instead of supporting them. There even are TV soap operas that propagate polygamy. The reason given for having a new wife is normally portrayed as the fault of the first wife who fails to meet her husband's expectations.

Feminization of poverty is another important issue for women's studies in Iran. Some scholars argue that women's access to financial sources is an essential indicator of gender equality. The first studies were about working women, the effects of financial independence on women's lives, the problem of the double burden between work and family, and the value of housework (Jazani 2004). Other projects looked at the gendered labor market and used statistical data to substantiate economic inequality (Afshari 2002; Noroozi 2002) or focused on the situation of marginalized women, such as female household heads, and described their financial situation and the poverty among them. Many scholars also examined the situation of rural women with the goal of finding ways to empower them (Forouzan 2003; Moti 1999; Shaditalab 2005).

Family-related issues, including mate selection, power relations in the family (Ezazi 2004; Ghandehari 2004), or divorce and the role of women, were other important topics related to women. Many women's studies students have selected additional topics, such as the situation of mothers, housework, and the political and social participation of women, for their theses.

Some scholars have conducted historical investigations and, in recent years, the Historian Women Scholars NGO has held seminars on women. Among these authors are Etehadieh (1983), who wrote a history of the Ghajar dynasty, and Katayoon Mazdapoor (2002) and Banafshe Hejazi (1991), who examined other historical aspects of women's status. The everyday life of women also draws the attention of some researchers, who started writing on such topics as women's health, sport, nutrition, and leisure time.

Scholars Outside Iran: Theories and Methodologies

Since the Islamic revolution, many Iranians have left the country to live in Europe and North America. Most of them had higher education, some had studied abroad, and many of them now hold respectable positions in universities or other well-known organizations. Some of them are very active in women's affairs, teaching, writing, and carrying out research about women in Iran. The number of books published abroad about Iran is substantial and some of the books, especially those on social movements and the constitutional revolution, have been translated into Farsi. However, books and articles about the women's movement have yet to be translated.

I believe developing relationships between the two groups of women—those who are actively involved in women's issues in Iran and the others who work abroad—is desirable. In the last few years, our colleagues abroad were allowed to visit Iran, and scholars and activists from Iran could take part in seminars or workshops held abroad. As a result, the exchange between these two groups has increased.

It is important to grasp a picture of the theoretical exchange between these groups, so I asked my interviewees if they were familiar with the publications and theories of women living outside Iran. This section gives an account of their views on this issue. But before I go further, I would like to express my gratitude to Diasporic Iranian women scholars for their endeavors on behalf of women in Iran. Those of us who know how essential, and at the same time difficult, it is to raise issues about Iranian women's issues and bring them to the attention of foreign universities and international organizations, acknowledge their efforts. We are thankful for their involvement in campaigns and for their support to our movement.

Despite the fact that research by Iranian women scholars working abroad is very relevant to academicians, university instructors in Iran are less familiar with it than are women activists who are in frequent contact with Diasporic scholars. Only a few instructors assign their students any translated articles by Iranian scholars living abroad. It is through activists' efforts that non-academic journals on women (and websites) have published the Farsi version of many Diasporic scholars' works. Yet, while some activists said they had learned much from Diasporic scholars, there are no articles from the Diaspora in Iranian scientific journals. Nevertheless, the scholars that I interviewed did comment on the ideas and methods of Diasporic scholars.

The interviewees pointed out they were not familiar with the ideas of Diasporic scholars due to the language barrier. Since their works were not translated into Farsi, and not everyone in Iran is able to read and understand English, the students and instructors cannot easily be familiar with Diasporic discourses. A few women had obtained works by Diasporic scholars and the interviewees noted that *Zanan* magazine had been the source of their knowledge in this regard. In addition, the respondents argued that some of the Diasporic scholars consider Islam as the origin of women's inferior position in society, which reduces the accessibility of Diasporic scholars' works since the publication of books expressing these ideas is forbidden in Iran.

The research by Diasporic scholars is also ignored because many of them develop theories based on conclusions drawn from research projects conducted in the Middle East, North Africa, and West Asia, in countries like Afghanistan or Morocco. The interviewees commented that those theories do not fit the Iranian context, because Iran is very different country with a very different history. They felt that it was inappropriate to shape theories based on selected Muslim countries and apply them to others.

Most of the Diasporic scholars do not have close relationships with Iran. Some visit Iran for a short time and are amazed by what women are doing; they interpret it as the power of women in a Muslim country. During these visits, they inquire about women's experiences during the revolution or the war. They collect data that provide only a partial view of women's reality in Iran and, in my view, this is not enough to begin theorizing. It is true that women are active in Iran, despite the difficulties, but they are paying a high price for their activism.

One of the most important characteristics of the women's movement in Iran is its independence of all political parties. Women, regardless of their political affiliations, cooperate with each other. Granted that there are some differences among them, but they avoid taking sides politically. The interviewees observed that Diasporic scholars are influenced by political trends, such as by leftist groups, so they try to explain everything from a single standpoint. Some interviewees consider this kind of explanation inappropriate for Iran. Others are afraid of leftist ideologies, and believe that radical ideas are not acceptable in Iran and, therefore, it is not worth becoming familiar with such theories.

Yet, there are other Diasporic scholars who emphasize the positive aspects of Islam and think that women will benefit from "ideal Islam." Interviewees also commented critically about such scholars, because they found it paradoxical that non-resident scholars, living in other countries under the protection of different legal systems and with many advantages, defended Islamic laws. In their opinion, this was the reason that Diasporic researchers sometimes interpreted a phenomenon like "temporary marriage" as a solution for the poor or believed that polygamy could not easily be practiced in Iran.

Temporary marriage is a short-term marriage based on a contract, for a fixed time period and amount of money. It can last for an hour, a day, a week, or even longer. The man must pay the woman for this marriage, and this payment is called "Mahrieh." There are no limitations on this marriage, and many wealthy men use temporary marriage, although they also are married. In the past, a man needed the willingness or permission of his first wife for polygamy, or for having a second wife, but this was unnecessary for a temporary marriage. However, in April 2008, Parliament tried to eliminate the required permission of the first wife for a second marriage. This means that men could have as many wives as they want, and the first wife has no legal right to protest. She can ask for divorce but normally, because she does not have any other financial support, she is forced to stay in this polygamous family situation. Therefore, the women's movement in Iran disagrees with both premises of the Diasporic scholars' argument, and does not find such practices to be positive aspects of Islam.

I was surprised that the interviewees all agreed on this analysis of temporary marriage, as developed within the women's movement in Iran. Both secular and Muslim activists in Iran concur in this respect, and they have both reacted more or less negatively to Diasporic scholars' theories on these topics. I attribute native scholars' critical views towards Diasporic research to their lack of deep understanding, which necessitates further dialogues between scholars in and outside Iran.

CONCLUSION

The women's movement in Iran began over 100 years ago, concurrent with the spread of modern ideas. It achieved some of its demands, but there are still other objectives to attain. I find it problematic that after so many years, women still need to make the same demands as their grandmothers did.

Although numerous researchers have investigated women's problems for many years, it is only in about the last 10 years that Iranian universities have shown interest in establishing women's studies programs. The altering social situation provided the grounds for this change, but the efforts of all our women predecessors, who worked in difficult times, should be acknowledged.

Both activists and academicians played a great role in the women's movement. Because of the conservative character of universities, only the activists and instructors who were closer to the reformist regime could initiate the idea of a women's studies program. Gradually this change has touched even those universities with less gender sensitivity. The obviously positive aspect of offering women's studies courses at universities is that students are now more encouraged to pay attention to women's problems.

Another achievement of women's studies courses is the increase in the number of research projects on women. This does not mean that all researchers have taken a gender approach to women's problems, but as they try to analyze their data it is likely that such an approach will be adopted out of necessity. Many attempts have been made to show the critical gender inequality in Iranian society and, more generally, to achieve human rights. Consequently, women's studies has tried to emphasize the different variables that affect the lives of women, especially women with less access to resources.

Research has focused on a variety of variables, including legal changes, modern cultural trends versus traditional ones, power relations in society and the economy, the division of labor in society and the family, and family relations. I suggest that more attention should be given to the power hierarchy in the wider society and its impact on women's lives. It is time to develop feminist theories that fit the Iranian context to explain all these aspects of women's subordination.

Each group of women has done its best for women's issues. The academicians investigate crucial new aspects of women's lives, the activists try to mainstream gender equity and also help by means of publications and translations. In this paper, I have been able to touch on some, but not all, of these efforts without going deeper, but I hope that I have given a picture of the problems and issues we are facing, and of what women in different positions are doing.

Postscript

The situation in Iran has been changing very rapidly. After Ahmadinejad, changes have been happening daily, and it is really difficult to follow them. When this chapter was originally drafted in Fall 2007, there was just a little possibility to have an impact, but by Spring 2008 the possibilities have become very limited. In May 2008, the regime closed the magazine, *Zanan*, and many NGOs are closed too or are having difficulties doing their work. Many activists are in jail or awaiting trial, and many of them have received very harsh sentences. All public activities are now forbidden and internet websites are being filtered. No one knows what these changes mean, but the Education Minister has already asked for separate books and texts for primary school children, based on gender. The new government has been making decisions without any discussion with specialists, and it is difficult and unclear how to incorporate all these rapid current changes, or any possible future changes, into this chapter.

NOTES

1. However, due to strict censorship by the Iranian government, the publications of some feminist authors, such as Fateme Mernisi and Nawal al-Sadawi, are banned.

REFERENCES

Afshari, Z. (2002) "Eshteghale Zanan va refahe khanevade (Women's employment and family welfare)," *Pajouheshe Zanan* 2, 1: 69–86.

Ahmadi-Khorasani, N. and P. Ardalan. (2003) *Senator (Senator)*, Tehran: Tooseeh.

Bashirieh, H. (2002) *Dibachei bar jameeshenasi siasi Iran (An introduction to the political sociology of Iran)*, Tehran: Negahe Moaser.

Ebadi, S. (2002) *Hoghoughe zanan dar jomhourie eslamie Iran (Women's rights in the Islamic Republic of Iran)*, Tehran: Ganje Danesh.

Etehadieh, M. (1983) *Khaterate Tajolsaltane (Memoires of Tajolsaltane)*, Tehran: Nashre Terikh.

Ezazi, S. (1991) "Tazade myane amouzesh va parvaresh va jamee (Contradiction between education and society)," *Faslname Olome Ejtemaie* 1/2: 55–79.

——(2001) "Motaleate zanan: Emkane taghvieat ya taghir mogheiate ejtemai (Women's Studies: Possibility to strengthen or to change the existing social situation)," *Zanan* 79: 37–40.

——(2002) *Khoshoonate khanevadegi: Zanane kotak khorde (Family violence: Battered women)*, Tehran: Saly Publication.

——(2003) "Mogheiete Zanan dar majalate jameeshenasi (Women's position in journals of sociology)," *Pajouheshe Zanan* 4, 1: 86–111.

——(2004) "Sakhtare ejtemaie va khoshounat aleyhe Zanan (Social structure and violence against women)," *Refahe Rjtemaie* 14, 4: 59–96.

——(2007) "Sarorate estefade az roykarde jensiaty (The necessity of using a gender equality approach)," *Talim va Tarbiat* 22, 3: 33–58.

Forouzan, S. (2003) "Zanane sarparaste khanevade: emkanat va chaleshha (Female-headed housholds: Opportunities and challenges)," *Pajouheshe Zanan* 5, 1: 35–58.

Ghandehari, P. (2004) *Zanan va ghodrat (Woman and power)*, Tehran: Pajouheshkade Mardomshenasi.

Ghasemzade, F. (2003) "Koodakane khiabani Tehran (Tehran street children)," *Refahe ejtemaie* 7, 2: 249–266.

Hejazi, B. (1991) *Zan be zene tarikh (Women in history)*, Tehran: Shahrab.

Hejazi, E. (2006) "Behsazi tasvir zanan dar ketabhaye darsi ebtedaie (Improving the image of women in elementary school text books)," *Faslname talim va tarbiat* 22, 3: 121–146.

Jazani, N. (2004) *Arzeshe kar khanegi (Value of domestic chores)*, Tehran: Markaze omore Zanan.

Kar, M. (1997) *Hoghooghe siasi zanane Iran (Political rights of Iranian women)*, Tehran: Rooshangaran.

Khosro-Panah, M. H. (2002) *Ahdaf va faaliate zanane Iran (Goals and struggles of Iranian women)*, Tehran: Payame Emrooz.

Mazdapoor, K. (2002) "Gise ou sorkh va biniesh as gel (Her hair is red and her nose from clay)," *Zanan* 92: 36–42.

Moazami, S. (2004) "Jormshenasie khooshoonate khanevadegi va shooharkoshi dar sistan va baloochestan (The criminology of domestic violence and spousal murder in Sistan and Baluchestan)," *Refahe ejtemai* 2, 2: 39–54.

Moshakhasate kolie barname motaleate zanan (General Specification of the Program and Outline) (1998) Tehran: Vezarate farhang va amoozeshe ali.

Moti, N. (1999) "Zanan bedoone mardan (Women without men)," *Zanan* 55: 9–13.

—— (2001) "Motaleate zanan: Talighe vagheiyat (Women's studies: Suspension of reality)," *Zanan* 80: 36–37.

—— (2003) "Grouhhaye zanan dar harkat be soye tavanmandsazi (Women's group on the move to empowerment)," *Women's Research* 1, 6: 7–22.

Noroozi, L. (2002) "Tahlile jensiaty bazare kare Iran va zaroorate baznegari dar farname sevome tooseh (Gender analysis of Iran's labor market and the need for reforms in the third development plan)," *Pajouheshe Zanan* 1, 2: 9–28.

Ravadrad, A. (2003) "Mosharekate zanan dar radio va television (Women's participation in radio and television)," *Pajouheshe Zanan* 1, 5: 167–196.

Shaditalab, J. (2001) "Motaleate zanan : taghir ya tasbiete vaze mojoud (Women's studies: Change or justification of existing situation)," *Zanan* 83: 30–31.

—— (2004) *Tarhe meli khoshoonate khanevadegi dar Iran (National Survey on violence against women in Iran)*, Tehran: Markaze omoure mosharekate zanan.

—— (2005) "Faghre daramadi faghat yek janbe az faghre zanane sarparaste khanvar (Income poverty, only one aspect of female-headed housholds' poverty)," *Refahe ejtemaie* 17, 4: 227–248.

CHAPTER 11

Masculinity and Anti-Americanism: Focusing on the Identity of KATUSA

Insook Kwon

This research focuses on the masculinity of a unique organization of soldiers, KATUSA[1] (Korean Augmentation to the United States Army). KATUSA is a part of the Korean draft system, but it differs in form and content from the general South Korean draft military service. A close look at the experience of South Korean conscripts in KATUSA—where the personnel are managed by Koreans, but the right of command belongs to the Americans—reveals their ambiguous status. Their masculinity is in conflict with that of the U.S. soldiers, but it also has a complex relationship to the masculinity of general Korean conscripts. Scrutinizing these two comparisons helps us to comprehend the role of nation, ethnicity, sexuality, class, and education in forming the norms of masculinity.

In-depth interviews were conducted with 15 post-conscripts, whose years of military service ranged from the late 1970s to the early 2000s. Interviews were held between June and November in 2004 and lasted for two to three hours each. Due to the rapid economic growth of the Korean economy in the last 30 years, which changed the balance of economic and national power between Korea and the United States, interviewees were chosen to cover three decades. Interviewees are indicated using a number, according to the time of their conscription (i.e., Interviewee 1 in 1978; Interviewee 2 in 1982; Interviewee 6 in 1991; and Interviewee 15 in 2000).

MASCULINITY AS A CONTESTED SITE

In general, all the interviewees show strong anti-U.S. sentiments and claim that they have been discriminated against. Most KATUSA conscripts believe that the discrimination directed towards them by U.S. army personnel is a price they have to pay as citizens of a lesser world power that relies on the United States, a major economic, political and military power. Their sense of inferiority, however, has not been constructed only in comparison to the U.S. economic and military superiority; it also is based on their acknowledging the U.S. army as rational, modern, and well equipped, and thus as an advanced military institution.

KATUSA conscripts' sense of inferiority, as members of a nation that has a less-advanced military organization, conflicts with their feelings of superiority towards the U.S. private soldiers on a personal level. This sense of superiority has been most often noted as the prevalent element in determining the KATUSA conscript's identity in his personal relations with American soldiers. It is rooted in the educational and social class gap between the KATUSA conscripts and the privates who enlisted as soldiers in the U.S. army during those decades. Whereas the U.S. army is perceived as having been composed of members of the lower or working class and ethnic minorities, KATUSA conscripts pride themselves as being elites from prestigious universities and, as a result, consider themselves superior as individuals. Their consciousness as citizens of a less powerful nation, combined with their individual sense of superiority, transforms into a tension experienced through individual discrimination. In the army, most of the KATUSA conscripts felt discrimination for the first time in their lives. As men who had been free from discrimination based on race, gender, or education in Korean society, in the army they are treated by U.S. soldiers as a racial "other," or as a minority in terms of their masculinity.

The fact that they are discriminated against through the use of racist remarks or personal disregard by U.S. enlisted soldiers, whose educational level seems less than their own or even than the average Korean standard, intensifies their tension, which is expressed in two ways. One way is through fostering Korean hegemonic masculinity, stressing men's roles and position within the nation, and maintaining the logic of sacrifice for the sake of establishing a national and masculine identity. The second way is to confirm their sense of national superiority by redefining and demonstrating their masculinity in opposition to that of U.S. enlisted soldiers, who they consider weak, by engaging in various activities, such as physical exercise, or through temperate living.

Culturally Different Masculinities

KATUSA solders' simultaneous rejection of American soldiers' masculinity norms and retention of Korean ones, represents an effort to revive sentiments of national pride, which are continuously undermined, but also is a concrete form of anti-American sentiment.

The collective consciousness of being different from U.S. soldiers is well expressed within the KATUSA's group culture, which tries to formulate and maintain a separate identity as Korean soldiers in the following five ways. First, this identity physically manifested with a separate culture that exists among the KATUSA even among those living in the same barracks.

> In fact, most conscripts don't hang out with the U.S. soldiers. First of all, the Americans live in separate barracks, and hanging out with U.S. soldiers is interpreted as extracting oneself from the rule system of the Korean KATUSA. As a junior, you don't really have free time even in the afternoon. The senior always has an eye on you so going out with the Americans to have a drink at a bar would be unimaginable. Totally forbidden. As a result, even though you become a senior later on, your relations are limited to the Korean conscripts. It means you have almost no contact with the American soldiers.
>
> (Interviewee 14)

Second, a strict rank-based military culture exists among KATUSA conscripts, which is a replica of the regular Korean army. Many interviewees pointed out that this distinguishes the KATUSA from the general U.S. army, where no strict formalities of rank seem to exist among enlisted or "private" soldiers.[2] Among U.S. enlisted men, there is no salutation; and such private soldiers, including the deputy commanders, only bow to the officers. Among officers, the junior officer only salutes the senior and they are not required to salute indoors, either with a hand motion or using catchwords (Oh 2002). However, among the private soldiers at KATUSA the rank hierarchy is strictly followed and formal salutations are made to the privates first class and the sergeants who are in charge of setting military discipline.

Third, the role of military discipline differs considerably between the KATUSA and the U.S. army. While KATUSA soldiers view military discipline in the American army as merely observing rules and criteria for promotion decisions, military discipline among the KATUSA is a means of enforcing an oppressive hierarchical order to maintain a strict and vigorous group culture (Oh 2002;

Pak and Oh 2003). Interviewee 11, who experienced the army in the mid 1990s, remembers the KATUSA as a place where military discipline prevailed more strictly than in the general Korean army.

> Rules are much stricter at the KATUSA than at the general Korean quarters. In fact there were constant reports of suicide during my stay at the army. (Why was it so strict?) It is because the combat unit is expected to meet the U.S. standards despite their physical inferiority. To overcome that, mental power is demanded which of course isn't that easy. Moreover, seniors insist on it to sort of keep our Korean cultural identity. However, those were just meaningless rules that meant nothing.
>
> (Interviewee 11)

Fourth, diverse cultural tools are employed to sustain their identity as Korean soldiers. Group behaviors, such as singing the Korean national anthem, formal salutations, and using disciplinary punishment in the Korean way, reveal the strong need of the KATUSA conscripts to maintain their national identity. These patterns of behavior were based on the training methods used at the *Nonsan* military training center, where KATUSA conscripts shared their first military experience with their counterparts in the Korean army before being assigned to their posts, or on disciplinary methods generally known to exist in the Korean army.

Fifth and finally, this method of establishing their identity as Korean soldiers was generally accepted and maintained. For example, the disciplinary methods that are known to be most severe, which would be unacceptable to American soldiers, were acquiesced to as Korean ways by the KATUSA. Although there might be some exceptions, such as challenging extremely violent cases of disciplinary action (Interviewee 12) or not enforcing strict discipline on juniors as a senior (Interviewees 2 and 3), a certain degree of discipline generally had

been maintained as a way to establish their identity as Korean soldiers.

> (What is the main rationale behind this maintaining a stronger military discipline than the U.S. soldiers?) The rationale is very simple. It is because we are Korean soldiers. Everything gets explained through this logic. Because we are not Americans, we don't need to follow their rules. As Koreans, we are asked to obey the Korean way of military life, such as following certain disciplines and rules that resemble those of the Korean army. This is the sort of rationale in openly demanding that we should sustain this kind of culture.
>
> (Interviewee 7)

Although most interviewees participated in the efforts that were made to establish an identity as Koreans in the KATUSA, ironically they also showed little respect and even resented the general Korean soldiers for their extremely strict military culture. While Interviewee 4, for instance, who joined the KATUSA in 1986, had expressed much frustration about the fact that they were not perceived as part of the Korean army, he also held a cynical view of the general Korean army's way of doing discipline and claimed the superiority of the U.S. way.

This raises the question of why the KATUSA, a group composed of conscripts from leading universities[3] who are, at minimum, potential candidates for a Bachelor's degree, and who tend to hold a critical evaluation of the quality of the general Korean army, were so eager to keep the Korean military tradition throughout the 1980s and 1990s, until the present. In fact, the U.S. army tried to get rid of the severely violent elements of the Korean army culture[4] (Interviewee 12). Why then have the KATUSA maintained this oppressive military culture despite the fact that they have been despised by the U.S. soldiers for it and they consider it to be wrong themselves?

The fundamental reason can be traced back to the fact that former KATUSA conscripts have been subjected to derisive assessments from other Koreans for having attended an "easy-going" army where the lifestyle was comparably more relaxed and conscripts were given more free time. This severely undermined their masculinity, which is often boasted about by other Korean men whose military experiences are replete with extreme physical challenges. According to Hyukbum Kwon (2004: 33), "Within a strong nationalistic group culture, 'the individual' gains a negative meaning, thus conceived as a synonym to 'egoism'." The respondents reported that they decided to join the KATUSA, even after their second and third attempts at the KATUSA exam, for their personal interest or sense of achievement and to pursue a relatively comfortable military life. However, the KATUSA chose to maintain aspects of the Korean military culture in order to emphasize how their nationalist masculinity differentiated them from the U.S. soldiers, and to defend against and free themselves from the negative stereotypes of the KATUSA, which reflect selfish masculinity. In other words, the Korean military culture presented an alternative to the potential loss of their identity as Korean soldiers in relation both to the U.S. and the general Korean army, which represents "proper military masculinity."

Seeking a Different Sexuality

All interviewees remarked how the U.S. soldiers were sexually active both with Korean women and their American female colleagues. However, the Korean conscripts did not seem to be much affected by the sex culture of the American soldiers and actually noted that they followed a separate sex culture themselves.

> In my opinion, the KATUSA conscripts seem to be sexually castrated. The Korean soldiers (in the regular Korean army) must have been as sexually active as the Americans. Actually, I

didn't really envy them for that. Well, I can't totally deny that I wished to sleep with women myself. However, I can't say that I envied that kind of way of life.
>
> (Interviewee 6)

The interviews revealed that the KATUSA conscripts' discourse on sex and sex life focused on differentiating themselves from the Americans by stressing "that we were different from them."

> The biggest difference between us and the Americans is their view on sex. For example, it doesn't matter if you are a dentist who attended medical school and currently are a captain in the army. No matter how well you are educated, in relations with women they are all the same. They know no shame. They even exchange women among themselves.
>
> (Interviewee 3)

According to the above comments, it seems that sexuality functioned as a way of confirming a differentiated masculinity for the KATUSA conscripts; and this strategic choice was affected by the differences in their own sense of sexual propriety and social class.

KATUSA soldiers' critical attitudes toward American sexuality are also related to the U.S. soldiers' sexual relationships with Korean women. All interviewees confessed their contempt toward Korean women who dated American soldiers and actually lamented that the majority of those who went out with U.S. soldiers were university students.

> What really bothers me is that American men need to take much less effort to have a one-night stand with a woman than we have to do. Although it has much changed these days, in the old days, women preferred students studying abroad or foreigners. That really pissed me off. Why are women more hospitable to foreigners, whereas their attitude toward Korean men is quite harsh? I really don't like that aspect of Korean women.
>
> (Interviewee 13)

Interviewees expressed feelings of anger and jealousy about the fact that the American soldiers, especially white Americans, enjoyed too much privilege thanks purely to their nationality and race. In their view, white American soldiers did not deserve such popularity among educated Korean women.

I hate American soldiers playing with Korean women. (Why?) It doesn't feel good. [laughs] It feels like being conquered. It can't be good to see foreigners come to your country and Korean women cling to them.

(Interviewee 15)

Interviewees regarded Korean women's dating of American soldiers as evidence of Korea's (and their) position as a less powerful nation, symbolizing Korea's occupation by a foreign force and a disgrace to the nation's pride. To them, the female body symbolizes national territory (McClintock 1995), and protecting women and children along with the nation seems to be part of the masculine identity of male soldiers (Enloe 1988; Cock 1993). In addition, from the perspective of military masculinity, Korean women's preference for American men tends to eclipse the Korean soldiers' norms of military masculinity. Consequently, the men felt emasculated and that the Korean military component of that masculinity needed to be strengthened.

Another reason the KATUSA conscripts might critique the Korean women is that they chose to date American soldiers despite their perceived lower class and lesser education, and the men assume this is in order to enjoy a western lifestyle that is less patriarchal or possibly as an opportunistic choice to utilize or improve their English skills. Therefore, the KATUSA soldiers' criticisms seem to reflect an underlying uneasy feeling about these women's expression of sexual desire and their possible challenge to Korean patriarchal rules. Paradoxically, KATUSA conscripts' refusal to acknowledge women's

expression of desire, through their relationship with American soldiers, can explain why they do not discuss with confidence why they chose to join the KATUSA. Although the KATUSA soldiers did not say so, I argue that the Korean women's decision to date U.S. soldiers is comparable to that of the conscripts who wanted to have a relatively easy military life—both groups can feel their status elevated through their association with the U.S. superpower, and obtain an opportunity to improve their English.

Considering that the interviewees with service in both the 1980s and 1990s maintained a cynical view of women who dated American soldiers, this criticism cannot be purely based on the Korean society's traditional emphasis on female virginity, which has significantly changed especially since the 1990s. Instead it reflects the fact that sexual relationships between men of a major world power and women of a lesser power have always been condemned from masculine and nationalist perspectives.

In contrast, the interviewees showed almost no emotional response to the idea of sexual relations with prostitutes. In most cases, they said that they had not really paid attention to this practice or considered it seriously before and refused to talk further.

It is also true that there is not much information available regarding prostitution.

I don't know really about it. We, KATUSA conscripts, don't go to those places and I don't know about the American soldiers either. Probably they go.

(Interviewee 9)

I infer from this comment that prostitution was a topic that was avoided or neglected among the KATUSA soldiers and between them and the U.S. soldiers. Only Interviewee 8 commented on this topic, indicating that the comparatively negative attitudes towards Korean women students who dated Americans versus their indifferent attitudes towards Korean prostitutes who met with American men, left him with a guilty conscience. All the other interviewees had no comments on prostitution, which I think is a reflection of their taking prostitution for granted as a form of masculine sexuality that transcends the boundaries of nation and ethnicity. If Interviewee 8 is correct, then KATUSA conscripts deem Korean women university students to be respectable members of Korean society and that the association of their sexuality with American soldiers poses threats to Korean masculinity, but that they do not consider Korean women prostitutes as worthy of their protection. Alternatively, it could be that the theme of prostitution is perceived with too much shame for the men of this less powerful nation, signifying their failure to protect their own women.

Rejection of American Soldiers' Physical Norms of Masculinity

In commenting on the norms of military masculinity, Dongheun Lee (2002) mentions that men's masculinity tends to take on a competitive form. This suggests that conscripts might try to conform to the image of a muscular soldier, who is superior and resolute, while the gentle officer would be seen as inferior and, therefore, challengeable by his more masculine subordinates. However, I found that this image was not applicable. Contrary to the common assumption that U.S. soldiers' masculinity would be considered superior, due to their physical size and strength, Korean soldiers presented a considerable number of rationales that negated this idea and even stressed the superiority of the Korean male.

> Well, it depends on what are the criteria to determine superiority. For instance, it's undeniable that the American soldiers are better in lifting and holding heavy things. But in cases of long marching, it isn't necessarily physical strength that counts. (Do you mean that mental strength counts more?) Yes, it partly stems from the seniors' pressure, and also due to the will to keep your pride.
>
> (Interviewee 11)

Actually, the Korean conscripts had a strong collective will not to lose to American soldiers and, on average, had a better performance record in long-distance running and marching than the American soldiers. Moreover, interviewees hardly associated the characteristics of a Rambo-like muscular body with the norms of masculinity. This was mainly due to the fact that they attended the army at a time when people were less interested in shaping bodies than nowadays, but also due to the Korean culture that more highly values an individual's intellectual capabilities than physical ones, especially in relation to masculinity. Therefore, the fact that the KATUSA had benefited from being part of the elite in Korean society, combined with their stereotypical and racist images of "the big and dumb black soldier," fostered their sense of superiority over their American counterparts.

CONCLUSION

Because of the two types of comparisons they made and conflicts they experienced— between being citizens of a lesser economic and military power and their anti-American sentiments, combined with their ambivalent relationship to the general Korean military— these KATUSA conscripts came to stress a sense of sacrifice for the sake of the nation, but they also questioned their own identity. As a result, the conscripts were relatively silent regarding their army experience, even though they had the opportunity to experience the more advanced American military system and study English. Excluding Interviewee 12, all interviewees confessed that they never mentioned to others they had served at the KATUSA. Interviewee 4, for example, noted that he never even told his current close friends about his military life at the KATUSA.

> Because I didn't join the Korean army, I can't share the same experience with other Koreans. It means that I will get teased for having joined the KATUSA for the rest of my life. People usually don't know that a combat unit exists at the KATUSA. (Do you get teased for having been a KATUSA?) Yes, I can't tell anyone about it. (Wouldn't you rather get recognized as an elite person by others?) No, I don't think so. They will call me a fake soldier for having had an easy military life.
>
> (Interviewee 15)

Korean men, who are obligated to serve in the military as long as they are physically fit, realize their masculinity through personal sacrifice and commitment to military service. Notwithstanding the personal reasons for their choice, a form of "hegemonic masculinity" (Connell 1995)[5] decides how these former soldiers see themselves as men in Korean society.

The KATUSA's version of anti-Americanism enhances a Korean form of "hegemonic masculinity" among them, involving a heightened nationalistic male consciousness. The politics of hegemonic masculinity not only sets the standards of masculinity, but also reinforces its power through discriminating against or marginalizing people who do not meet these standards. At a global level, the inferiority complex of being citizens of a secondary power, along with the anti-U.S. sentiments based on the KATUSA's experience of discrimination by U.S. soldiers, tends to enforce a strong sense of national identity and a common effort to construct a masculinity that differs from that of the American soldiers. Also, at a personal level, their sense of superiority, rooted in the educational and class differences between the KATUSA conscripts and U.S. enlisted privates, enhances

their anger at the discrimination against them, and develops into anti-Americanism. These are the main motivations for the KATUSA to maintain a separate Korean military culture and sexuality. My research on the KATUSA conscripts shows how military masculinities have competed, cooperated, and been chosen in a multi-raced military or a multi-nation military. It also shows us how important it is to achieve a global perspective in studying masculinities.

NOTES

The article was translated and edited from the original Korean version by the author.

1. Since its establishment in the 1950s, the KATUSA has consisted of 4,800 soldiers, which is around 1/8 of the total size of the U.S. forces stationed in South Korea, and, so far, around 160,000 Korean men have served in the KATUSA. Entrance into the KATUSA is highly competitive and the recruitment screening itself is considered to be as difficult as passing a major state exam, such as the Bar exam, gaining its notorious name of "KATUSA state examination." Since 1982, the KATUSA has gained its reputation for being an army comprised of potential elites with strong academic backgrounds from prestigious universities.

2. The terminology "private soldier" refers to the American "GI" or enlisted person, and includes the ranks of Private, Private First Class, and Specialist, unlike the Korean army terminology that includes Sergeant. During much of this time the U.S. army was based on the draft system, and was different from the Korean military where you automatically get promoted after a certain amount of time. U.S. soldiers' promotion is based on performance and it usually takes 7–8 years to become a sergeant (Oh 2002).

3. Of course not all were from leading universities. Although most conscripts recruited through the central recruitment system were students at top universities in South Korea, those recruited through the platoon system mostly were students or graduates from general universities.

4. Interviewee 8 explains the reason why U.S. soldiers and KATUSA conscripts came to share barracks. "Some barracks are occupied by the KATUSA conscripts only, however, because the U.S. soldiers disliked the atmosphere of disciplinary punishment among the Koreans, rules were

changed that required us to share barracks with the American soldiers."

5. Connell defined hegemonic masculinity as the form of masculinity that is most domineering and considered to be ideal among the various norms of masculinities during a specific time, which functions as the basic element to sustain the structure of power and privilege in the nation, society, and organization (Connell 1995).

REFERENCES

Cock, Jacklyn (1993) *Women & War in South Africa*, Cleveland: The Pilgrim Press.

Cornell, R. W. (1995) *Masculinities*, Berkeley and Los Angeles: University of California Press.

Enloe, Cynthia (1988) *Does Khaki Become You*, London, Winchester, North Sydney and Wellington: Pandora.

Kwon, Hyukbum (2004) *Breaking Away from Citizenship: Nation, Progress, and the Individual*, Seoul: Samin Press.

Lee, Dongheun (2002) "The Male-centered Aspect of the Military Culture and Gender Equal Education," Masters Thesis at Yonsei University.

McClintock, Anne (1995) *Imperial Leather: Race, Gender and Sexuality in The Colonial Contest*, New York and London: Routledge.

Oh, Seong-sik (2002) "Post-conscript Seong-sik Oh's Understanding the English of the KATUSA," *Monthly Chosun's Total Guide Book of the Military*, Seoul: Monthly Chosun Press.

Pak, Jeong-cheol and Sung-hwan Oh (2003) *Do You Know the KATUSA*, Seoul: Lisu Press.

CHAPTER 12

Gender, Development and HIV/AIDS in Vietnam: Towards an Alternative Response Model among Women Sex Workers

Van Huy Nguyen, Udoy Sankar Saikia, and Thi Minh An Dao

INTRODUCTION

The HIV/AIDS epidemic continues to grow in many parts of the world and threatens development processes. Globally, a total of 30 million HIV/AIDS cases were documented in 1997 (Cohen 1998) and by the year 2005, there were an estimated 40.3 million people living with HIV/AIDS (PLWHA), close to 5 million of whom were newly infected and 3.1 million died from AIDS within that year, which means that this crisis pervades every part of the world (UNAIDS and WHO 2005). The UNAIDS projections reveal an upward future trend, with about 14,000 newly infected cases every day and 95 percent of these in developing countries (Swiss Centre for International Health 2005).

The epidemic used to be predominant among men in most nations in its earlier stages, but now women are bearing the brunt of the epidemic and make up almost half of the HIV/AIDS infected population globally (WHO 2003; UNAIDS 2004b). There is ample evidence to suggest that populations most affected by HIV/AIDS are those that have been socially and/or economically marginalized by income, employment, education, culture, power, gender and other socioeconomic aspects (Commonwealth Secretariat 2002). As a consequence, marginalized people are at greater risk of infection, isolation and in bearing the heavy responsibilities of caring for themselves and others,

which may result in early death. . . . HIV/ AIDS in Vietnam presents a complex picture. Since the first case reported in 1990 (McNally 2002), each subsequent year saw about 1,500 new cases, spreading to all 61 provinces of Vietnam in 1999, bringing the total to a cumulative 76,180 PLWHA till 2003 (Hien et al. 2004). However, the actual cumulative number was estimated to soar up to 160,000 cases at the end of 2002 (Policy Project Vietnam 2003). By the end of 2003, there were 11,659 AIDS cases and 6,635 AIDS-related deaths (Hien et al. 2004) and most of these were among people who were poor, less educated, and jobless (An 2004). The epidemic has not affected the general population in a major way as yet and is to be mainly found among high-risk behavior groups. The infection rate in the general population was just over 0.3 percent (Ministry of Labor, Invalids and Social Affairs and UNICEF 2005), but it is quite alarming in the high-risk groups such as sex workers and injecting drug users (IDUs) who comprise 21.6 percent (Agence France-Presse 2001) and 32 percent (Hien et al. 2004), respectively. While HIV infection among IDUs largely affects men, among sex workers it is found mainly among women.

. . . The number of women suffering HIV was below 50,000 cases before 2001 and increased to nearly 100,000 cases by 2005. Among female HIV/AIDS carriers, women sex workers predominate, with a dramatically growing trend. The rate of HIV among Vietnamese female sex workers rose from 2.8 percent in 1998 to 21.6 percent in 2001 (Agence France-Presse 2001). These women work in different categories of sites of the sex industry—bars, karaoke bars, the street, and call lines and some frequently move from one place to another to avoid the police (USAID, FHI and NASB 2001).... Too often they lack not just information, but the social and economic power to exercise control over their bodies and lives. There is growing evidence that poverty and gender issues are making women sex workers more vulnerable to the HIV/AIDS infection....

Overall, HIV/AIDS in Vietnam has become a gendered issue of utmost concern. In most studies on the subject, much attention has been focused on patterns and behavioral factors of HIV/AIDS transmission, while dimensions of gender and development remain neglected. Little attention has been given to these aspects in formulating HIV/AIDS control policies.... This paper initially explores some of the existing gender and development dimensions crucial to HIV/AIDS in Vietnam. Based on the significant published materials and policy documents relating to HIV/AIDS in Vietnam, this paper critically reflects on Vietnam's recent reactions to HIV/AIDS and suggests a better response model to the epidemic, especially as it impacts women sex workers in Vietnam.

A GENDER AND DEVELOPMENT PERSPECTIVE FOR HIV/AIDS AMONG WOMEN SEX WORKERS IN VIETNAM

Economic Reform

During the late 1970s and early 1980s, due to the serious economic crisis, Vietnam initiated a reform policy, called "Doi moi" in 1986. This led to a transition from central planning to a free-market economy for development, which had a positive impact on economic growth. However, it also fueled the spread of HIV/AIDS in Vietnam as suggested in the trends.

... While economic growth took place rapidly, with GDP (Gross Domestic Product) increasing from USD 78 in 1984 (UN 2001) to USD 156 in 1992, and to USD 400 in 2001 (Chien 2003), HIV/AIDS grew dramatically from one case in 1990 (immediately after reform) to about 2,500 cases by 1993 and 5,000 cases by 1999 (World Bank and Vietnam Ministry of Health 2001). The reasons for this increase in HIV/AIDS, alongside the growth in GDP are complex, and are mainly attributed to a widening gap between the rich and poor as a result of the reform.... Also, income gaps vary significantly by gender and region (Chien 2003). Females had much lower income levels than males: they had only 70 percent of the income of males. The largest income gap observed was between rural and urban areas: the top 20 percent of the urban population had income levels 23 times of the bottom 20 percent of the rural population in 1996. These disparities and socioeconomic inequalities drove many poor (about 700,000) people from the rural areas to migrate to urban areas each year to seek job opportunities (Australian National University 2003). In these migration streams, females outnumbered males (Tung et al. 2000). However, rural girls and women, without education and vocational skills, could not find job opportunities in the competitive urban environment. So they largely resorted to prostitution in the attempt to find a source of income (Tung et al. 2000). Because of their poor education and knowledge regarding HIV/AIDS prevention, together with the expansion and attraction of tourism and the service industry, migrants, many of whom were women, indulged in risky activities. For instance, they had sexual relations without using condoms and shared needles to inject themselves with drugs.... (Starink and de Bruin 2001; Tung et al. 2000). Ultimately, economic reform ... creat[ed] a growing surge of rural-to-urban migration, . . . exacerbating the transmission of HIV/AIDS.

Institutional Factors

. . . The legal policies see sex work as "social evils" (Tung et al. 2000; Rekart 2001). . . . As the infections are viewed as a "social evil," the solutions generated mainly seek to fight these, while prevention and care services have not received much attention. Police are actively mobilized to capture female sex workers when they find evidence of commercialized sex. For example, if police find condoms inside rooms of hotels, inns, or guest houses, the establishments are charged with sexual solicitation. Such places, therefore, do not make condoms available. Consequently, female sex workers cannot acquire condoms when they need them and are forced to take risks. . . . While the more affluent sex workers work through phone or call lines and avoid the police, . . . [t]hose who work on the street are . . . also IDUs and have nowhere else to operate from. Consequently, in both types of situations, women sex workers are discouraged from seeking and accessing prevention and treatment services. . . .

Moreover, if arrested and sent to rehabilitation centers, methods of education largely concentrate on labor re-education and ideological re-education rather than focusing on the need to reduce the risk of HIV/AIDS through counseling, testing and referral. After being released from these centers, those identified as having HIV do not care adequately about taking risks, while those who do not have the infection, think they can continue to take what they think is a little risk. . . . [T]he vulnerability of these groups to HIV/AIDS infection does not appear to reduce, despite the arrests.

Cultural Factors

. . . In Vietnam, some cultural norms and stigma as well as the unequal power and bargaining position of women, especially of sex workers, make them socially vulnerable to HIV/AIDS infection. . . . The cultural context also implies that gender inequality is deeply ingrained in social norms and has an impact on the bargaining position of women, both within and beyond the family. Unable to negotiate safer sex for themselves, they often keep silent and are powerless to ensure their own safety and survival. As such, if their husbands/partners have not used condoms when having sex, women too would be unable to use them (McNally 2002; UNAIDS 2004a), especially in cases where sexual services are paid for by the men. So, if the female sex workers try to persuade clients to use condoms, they risk losing them and the opportunity of earning something. Feudal opinions accept multiple sex partners for men, but not for women. In addition, it is more socially acceptable for men to marry girls who are virgins. If a girl is identified as . . . a non-virgin, she finds it difficult to get married. . . .

The greater the number of partners men have, the greater the risk for women of getting HIV. . . . Moreover, if the husband gets HIV/AIDS from multiple sex partners, they are blamed less so than women. An HIV-positive woman would have a major problem in disclosing her HIV status and continue receiving support from family and society. However, if a woman got HIV from her husband, she would suffer a lesser stigma than one who contracted HIV from prostitution (Rekart 2001; McNally 2002). . . . Once women suffer from HIV/AIDS, they face triple jeopardy—they are rejected by their husbands, especially if they are sex workers, they become unacceptable in their communities, and are discouraged from accessing health care. In both groups of women—female sex workers and women living with HIV/AIDS—familial and social vulnerabilities heighten various risks and reduce their survival opportunities. . . .

IMPACT OF THE HIV/AIDS EPIDEMIC

The impact of HIV/AIDS in Vietnam is multi-level and multidimensional. In the sphere of family, as women are expected to fulfill all productive, reproductive, and community tasks, they carry a triple burden, especially when their family members are suffering from the disease. Most (74 percent) women also undertake the burden of care-giving to family members afflicted by HIV/AIDS (UNDP 2004). For women suffering from the disease, the burden is further multiplied. . . . While being ill themselves, they continue to provide care for their husbands, family members, and/or sick children (Tallis 2002). This often means that they do not have time to care for themselves adequately, . . . which potentially affects their own health infections such as tuberculosis and pneumonia which also exacerbate their disease and risk of death. Families whose members suffer HIV/AIDS are more likely to be poor, since their household earnings decline and medical expenses increase (Policy Project Vietnam 2003). In 2004, about 126,000 Vietnamese people had either become newly poor or had fallen deeper into poverty because of HIV/AIDS and this trend continues to increase over time (UNDP 2004). For women-headed households or families, where both parents have HIV/AIDS, the poverty burden multiplies because of the loss of livelihood. Fifty percent of HIV carriers reported losing their jobs as a result of their health status being known (UNDP 2004). Therefore, poverty and disease apparently become tremendous challenges before them.

In communities where stigma and discrimination prevail, both women sex workers and PLWHA, and even their family members, face the multiple disadvantages of stress, social isolation and unemployment. Only one-third of PLWHA are accepted by their communities . . . (Policy Project Vietnam 2003). Fifty percent of non-HIV/AIDS workers did not want relationships with infected workers as they believed that the latter are responsible for their own sinful behavior (Global Nomads Group 2003). The impact of HIV/AIDS affects not just adults, but children and youth as well. They are required to stay home or stop their education to care for AIDS-infected family members (Policy Project Vietnam 2003). There are about 22,000 orphaned children in Vietnam as a consequence of parents who have died from AIDS. Once orphaned, children become heads of households at a very early age, which adversely affects their behavioral development and future opportunities. . . . The social and economic burden at the national level was believed to be heavy when women got HIV/AIDS. . . . Their absence and the cost of replacing workers with HIV/AIDS reduced the economic productivity of both public and private workplaces (Policy Project Vietnam 2003). . . .

TOWARD AN ALTERNATIVE RESPONSE MODEL

In an attempt to search for a better response model to HIV/AIDS among women sex workers in Vietnam, it is crucial to revisit Vietnam's current responses to the epidemic to pinpoint their strengths and weaknesses. . . . [T]he Vietnamese government made important decisions to mobilize organizations and individuals throughout the country, from the central to the grassroots levels, to participate in a prevention and control program. . . . In addition, legal documents against HIV/AIDS were issued by the Vietnam Ministry of Health (2002). . . . [T]hese measures aimed to propagate and educate on adherence to national traditions of morality, healthy lifestyles, and faithful loving, via a multi-sectoral approach. To expand responses to HIV/AIDS, the Vietnamese government has set up some initial centers for HIV/AIDS prevention and control at central and provincial levels (Long et al.

2000).... Consistent with the increase in HIV/AIDS, the government increased its budget allocation for HIV/AIDS prevention and care (Hien et al. 2004). There have been diverse activities targeting HIV/AIDS prevention—information-education-communication (IEC), life skills education for young people, harm reduction interventions among vulnerable groups, sentinel and behavioral surveillance surveys, blood safety and safe medical services, care and support for PLWHA, sexually transmitted disease (STD) treatment, prevention of mother-to-child HIV transmission, voluntary counseling and testing, and self-help groups for PLWHA (Hien et al. 2004). Moreover, Vietnam has received great assistance from the international community ... (Hien et al. 2004).

Overall, Vietnam has made some good efforts to launch three major groups of solutions: 1) social solutions ..., 2) technical solutions ..., and 3) financial solutions.... However, what are lacking in the existing interventions in Vietnam are responses that can address the root causes of the issue, such as poverty, education, job[s] and gender-sensitive initiatives.... The following sections discuss several potential initiatives that can make a difference.

Promoting Political Will

Because of the repressive legal policies against "social evils," women sex workers fear arrest, which pushes them towards undertaking risks and contracting HIV/AIDS (Starink and de Bruin 2001). Because of the repressive legal policies against "social evils," women sex workers fear arrest, which pushes them towards undertaking risks and contracting HIV/AIDS (Starink and de Bruin 2001). Also, because of cultural norms and legal policies, women sex workers fear being socially stigmatized and excluded from their families, making it difficult for the intervention programs to reach such groups (Starink and de Bruin 2001). These vulnerabilities make access to health services difficult for female sex workers, which in turn creates gendered inequities in health care. Thus, political will should be exercised to create an equal legal framework for the marginalized groups. In particular, there is need to fight social stigmas about female sex workers and HIV/AIDS-positive people.... In addition, there is need to change some repressive cultural norms and help commercial sex workers to challenge the social vulnerabilities they face regarding HIV/AIDS. Women sex workers and those living with HIV/AIDS need to be sympathized with and deserve a normal life, just like other people in society, as strongly stated by a Vietnamese president, Mr. Tran Duc Luong (Associated Press 2004). Such political initiatives would improve their self-esteem and confidence, encouraging them to change their behavior and not undertake risks. Since culturally given norms regarding gender generate health-related behaviors and health status (King and Mason 2001), improving on these would have a positive outcome.

Education, Job Opportunities and Gender Equity

Since women sex workers are disadvantaged by social position, poor education, joblessness, and low income, they are forced to enter the sex industry as a means of survival and income generation.... Thus, women sex workers need to be empowered to ensure gender equality in terms of class and power. Such change requires response from all sectors of society acting together—government, civil society and the private sector—which therefore calls for multi-sectoral collaboration, through education, health services, employment, and so on (Commonwealth Secretariat 2002). The education sector needs to improve female sex workers' access to education, as this would help them to gain the skills necessary to make decisions for, and to gain control over their own lives (Commonwealth Secretariat 2002).

The labor sector can promote job opportunities for female sex workers so that they can find alternative sources of income, instead of opting to enter commercial sex. . . . The Vietnamese government should redistribute socioeconomic resources, including income, among social classes, prioritizing this for women. For instance, Mackenbach et al. (2002) emphasize that basic redistribution of socioeconomic resources, using upstream solutions, can improve social equality and address the root causes of inequalities in health. Better access to education and income resources can improve women's confidence and capacity to protect their health (Campbell 2003) and is a basic ingredient for reducing poverty and gender disparities in health (King and Mason 2001). . . .

Prevention and Health Promotion

. . . Because of repressive legal policies and cultural norms, specific prevention and health promotion programs referred to as mid- and down-stream solutions are necessary to address these issues. Vietnam should follow internationally recognized models of peer education, condom-use promotion, and needle and syringe exchange—as suggested by Hien et al. (2004), because they would be appropriate to the current context of Vietnam and can help sex workers give up their risky behaviors. Peer education, which incorporates gender issues, would create a better understanding of how gender-related norms may increase risky sexual behaviors, and help young people think and act in more equalitarian and responsible ways (WHO 2003). Further, peer education would help to increase the access of women sex workers to prevention services, which would ensure confidentiality. Thereby, women sex workers themselves would act as providers of information regarding prevention to their peers. . . . Promoting condom-use would also be necessary for reducing risky behaviors. Since men are more powerful and in better bargaining positions regarding whether or not to use condoms, female condom-use should be encouraged. . . . A needle and syringe exchange program can reduce risks for female sex workers in the injection of drugs, as this would discourage needle-sharing in this group and would slow down the spread of the epidemic remarkably (Hagard 1988). Thailand is well known as an example of success in reducing HIV/AIDS transmission by promoting the above models—peer education, condom use promotion, and needle and syringe exchange (Hien et al. 2004; Ruxrungtham et al. 2004). With these three preventive models, knowledge would be improved and the high-risk behaviors of women sex workers can be reduced to mitigate the epidemic among this group. . . . [I]t is practically important here to examine the barriers challenging such a model in order to break them down.

Barriers to Change

There are three major challenges confronting the change process. First, . . . the strategies of promoting change would be fairly hard to undertake, unless the political environment is favorably disposed towards them. . . . In Vietnam legal policies are well documented in state institutions, while people's beliefs, perceptions, and behaviors are well rooted in cultural norms. Therefore, any change in these arenas would touch culturally and politically sensitive issues and need time and great effort on the part of the government and the whole society.

Second, based on the above review of areas [th]at require change, it is apparent that . . . a combination of three models—upstream, midstream and downstream (Murphy 2004), in other words, a comprehensive primary health care approach is required (Wisner 1988). . . . However, since resources available for this approach are usually limited, financial barriers are a major challenge (Walsh and Warren 1979).

Finally, limited capacity building for female sex workers is also a barrier to change. Although the models try to mobilize the participation of women sex workers in a number of ways, their lack of knowledge and skills may limit their authentic participation in addressing these issues that concern them greatly. Although compatibility in knowledge between interveners and the community of women sex workers is assumed, in reality the imbalance in knowledge affects their participation (Fowler 1998).

CONCLUSION

The HIV/AIDS situation in Vietnam shows that poverty, socioeconomic and gender-related inequalities are the main factors in transmitting the disease. At the same time, the epidemic also entrenches such inequalities. This clearly implies a two-way relationship between them. However, previous and recent research in Vietnam has not addressed this crucial aspect adequately. . . . This paper is an attempt to lead to increased awareness of the gender and cultural dimensions of the epidemic. . . . A good policy to combat the epidemic among women sex workers must be an initiative that considers both gender and development issues. We suggest the following: promoting political will, improving education, increasing job opportunities to enhance gender equality and strengthening prevention measures for health in future intervention agendas. Gender-specific strategies—both practical and strategic gender approaches—should be integrated to challenge cultural norms and transform gender relations. Through such initiatives, women would be empowered and given more voice both within and beyond their familial spheres to improve and gain control over their lives. . . . Such policy initiatives would not only be useful in the Vietnamese context, but also to many other developing countries where women sex workers and other marginalized groups are confronted with multiple vulnerabilities. . . . [A] new alternative response model, which addresses gender and development issues adequately, would be key for Vietnam in combating the spread of HIV/AIDS. Although the suggested model may face several obstacles of culture, politics, limited resources, and capacity building, the success stories from several Asian countries in combating HIV/AIDS throw valuable light on the way chosen by Vietnam to break down these barriers and to develop such a new model. . . .

REFERENCES

Agence France-Presse (2001) *Vietnam-Prostitute-AIDS: Vietnam Reports Explosion of HIV Infection among Prostitutes*, http://www.aegis.com/news/afp/2001/AF0103C2.html (accessed March 18, 2006).

An, D. T. M. (2004) *Survey Methods to Constructing a Preventive Model of Opportunistic Infections for HIV/AIDS-affected People in Bavi Rehabilitation Centre*, Unpublished, Hanoi, Vietnam.

Associated Press (2004) *Vietnam's President Visits HIV/AIDS Ward*, http://www.utopia-asia.com/aidsvie.htm (accessed October 1, 2008).

Australian National University (ANU) (2003) *Vietnam: a Transition Tiger? Poverty, Location and Internal Migration*, Canberra: ANU E Press.

Campbell, C. (2003) *Letting Them Die: Why HIV/AIDS Prevention Programmes Fail*, Bloomington: Indiana University Press.

Chien, T. T. T. (ed.) (2003) "Economic Growth, Income Gap, and Health," in *Equity- and Development-Oriented Vietnam Health Reform*, Hanoi: Medical Publisher.

Cohen, D. (1998) "Poverty and HIV/AIDS in Sub-Saharan Africa," The SEPED Conference Paper Series, Copenhagen, Denmark.

Commonwealth Secretariat (2002) *Gender Mainstreaming in HIV/AIDS: Taking a Multisectoral Approach*, London: Commonwealth Secretariat and Maritime Centre of Excellence for Women's Health.

Fowler, A. R (1998) "Authentic NGDO Partnerships in the New Policy Agenda for International Aid: Dead End or Light Ahead?" *Development and Change*, 29: 137–159.

Global Nomads Group (2003) *HIV/AIDS in Vietnam*,

http://www.gng.org/currents/vietnam/vie_hiv.html (accessed April 4, 2006).

Hagard, M. (1988) "Theory into Practice: Health Promotion Programmes for Specific Groups," in WHO (ed.) *AIDS Prevention and Control (World Summit of Ministers of Health on Programmes for AIDS Prevention)*, Oxford: Pergamon Press.

Hien, N. T., N. T. Long and T. Q. Huan (2004) "HIV/AIDS Epidemics in Vietnam: Evolution and Responses," *AIDS Education and Prevention*, 16, Suppl.: 137–154.

King, E. M. and A. D. Mason (2001) "Summary," in World Bank (ed.) *Engendering Development: Through Gender Equality in Rights, Resources and Voice*, New York: Oxford University Press.

Long, H. T., N. T. Hien and N. V. Dinh (2000), "Epidemiological Surveillance of HIV/AIDS Infection in Vietnam," *Journal of Practical Medicine* 382: 5–12.

Mackenbach, J. P., M. J. Bakker, M. Shito and F. Diderichsen (2002) "Strategies to Reduce Socioeconomic Inequalities in Health," in J. P. Mackenbach and M. J. Bakker (eds.) *Reducing Inequalities in Health: A European Perspective*, London: Routledge.

McNally, S. P. (2002) "HIV in Contemporary Vietnam: An Anthropology of Development," unpublished Ph.D. Thesis, Australian National University, Melbourne, Australia.

Ministry of Labor, Invalids and Social Affairs and UNICEF (2005) *Situation of Families and Children Affected by HIV/AIDS in Vietnam*, Hanoi: UNICEF.

Murphy, B. (2004) "In Search of the Fourth Dimension of Health Promotion: Guiding Principles for Action," in B. Murphy and H. Keleher (eds.) *Understanding Health: A Determinants Approach*, Melbourne: Oxford University Press.

Policy Project Vietnam (2003) *The Socioeconomic Impact of HIV/AIDS in the Socialist Republic of Vietnam*, http://www.policyproject.com/pubs/country reports/VIET_SEI.pdf (accessed April 4, 2006).

Rekart, L. M. (2001) "Sex in the City: Sexual Behavior, Societal Change, and STDs in Saigon," *Sexually Transmitted Infections* 78, Suppl. 1: 47–54.

Ruxrungtham, K., T. Brown and P. Phanuphak (2004) "HIV/AIDS in Asia," *The Lancet*, 364, 9428: 69–82.

Starink, M. and de Bruin, L. (2001) *Mobility and Vulnerability: An Explorative Study among Female Sex Workers in Ho Chi Minh City, Vietnam*, http://www.un.org.vn/undp/projects/vie98006/RSex.htm (accessed October 1, 2008).

Swiss Centre for International Health (2005) *HIV/AIDS Background Information for International Cooperation*, http://www.sdc-health.ch/priorities_in_health/communicable_diseases/hiv_aids/hiv_aids_-_

ubersichtspapier_fur_die_internationale_zusammenarbeit (accessed October 1, 2008).

Tallis, V. (2002) *Gender and HIV/AIDS: Overview Report*, http://www.bridge.ids.ac.uk/reports/CEP-HIV-report.pdf (accessed April 4, 2006).

Tung, N. D., N. T. Son and N. T. Trung (2000) *Population Mobility, Prostitution and Factors Related to HIV Transmission on Vietnam's Main Transportation Routes*, http://www.unaids.org.vn/resource/topic/mobilepop/mobilecswvietnam.doc (accessed March 18, 2006).

UN (United Nations) (2001) *Report Results of the Survey on High Risk Factors of Drug Abuse among Groups of Female Prostitutes in Vietnam*, http://www.unaids.org.vn/resource/topic/sexwork/csw-du.pdf (accessed March 18, 2006).

UNAIDS and WHO (2005) *AIDS Epidemic Update*, http://www.unaids.org/epi/2005/docJEPIupdate2005_pdf_en/epi-update2005_en.pdf (accessed March 30, 2006).

UNAIDS (2004a) *UNAIDS Praises Vietnam for Adopting National AIDS Strategy*, http://data.unaids.org/Media/Press-Releases02/PR_VietNam-18Oct04_en.pdf (accessed October 30, 2008).

—— (2004b) *Executive Summary: 2004 Report on the Global AIDS Epidemic*, http://www.unaids.org/bangkok2004/GAR2004_html/ExecSummary_en/ExecSumm_00_en.htm (October 1, 2008).

UNDP (2004) *Impact of HIV/AIDS on Household Vulnerability and Poverty in Vietnam* http://www.undp.org.vn/undpLive/digitalAsset/2/2930_hiv.pdf (accessed October 30, 2008).

USAID, FHI and NASB (2001) *HIV/AIDS Behavioral Surveillance Programme Vietnam, 2000*, http://www.fhi.org/NR/rdonlyres/e5vdojxh3pqriv2ntgp2hpw7m7zts675u5dxdjs4hcm6izmnz2in7qovnbm7hyzzr4khdw5ulphd3c/BSSVietnam2000.pdf (accessed October 1, 2008).

Vietnam Ministry of Health (VMOH) (2002) Systematization of Documents on HIV/AIDS Prevention and Control, Hanoi: VMOH.

Walsh, J. and K. S. Warren (1979) "Selective Primary Health Care—An Interim Strategy for Disease Control in Developing Countries," *New England Journal of Medicine* 30, 18: 967–974.

WHO (2003) *Gender and HIV/AIDS*, http://www.who.int/entity/gender/documents/en/HIV_AIDS.pdf (accessed October 30, 2008).

Wisner, B. (1988) "GOBI versus PHC? Some Dangers of Selective Primary Health Care," *Social Science and Medicine* 26: 963–969.

World Bank and Vietnam Ministry of Health (2001), *Vietnam Growing Healthy: A Review of the Health Sector*, Hanoi: WB and VMOH.

CHAPTER 13

Fufubessei Movement in Japan: Thinking About Women's Resistance and Subjectivity

Ki-young Shin

. . . Women in Japan live in a palpable discrepancy between the ideal of legal equality and the reality of gendered family life. . . . Virtually all social relations in Japan seem to be practiced on the basis of visible gender norms: nonetheless, formal legal equality is widely proclaimed. In such a society, where everyday family life is not seen as an arena that "rights claims" apply to, and the realization of gender equality in daily family life is not considered a constitutional concern, how do Japanese women negotiate their formal legal equality and the contradictions they are experiencing in their family life? . . . This paper is part of my attempt to answer these questions through conversing with Japanese women in the family law reform movement.

The family law reform movement is not one single organized movement. Two pillars of this reform movement are "marital family naming" and "discrimination against children born out of wedlock." In many cases in contemporary Japan, these two problems are interlocked. Here . . ., however, I will mainly focus on the Japanese women's movement to keep their family name in marriage, that is, to refuse to change their names to their husband's. This movement called *"fufubessei"* —literally meaning "husband's and wife's different surnames"—has gained significant currency among the Japanese public since the 1980s.

By studying the women's movement to keep their own names, I would like to bring to light particular ways in which the family name shapes women's relationship to the family and the state. Through their involvement with, and challenge to, the state family law in the movement, women forge new subjectivities, from which the possibility of social change was entailed, if not always intended by them. I will suggest that a subtle reading of women's struggles over the family name reveals an intertwined relationship between the Japanese family system (*ie*) and the state's construction of gendered family through law. Starting from women's agency in the movement to resist the state law, I believe, is the best way to illustrate how cultural and state power is exercised in women's lives (see Abu-Lughod 1990). It is thus my deliberate effort to approach this task by reading social problems from women's standpoint and understanding social change from women's movements. . . . I aim to demonstrate how everyday legal mobilization for marital naming comes to be an important site for the contestation of Japanese women's gender norms and the state ideal of "the Japanese family."

FAMILY, FAMILY NAME, AND FAMILY LAW: HOLLOW "CHOICE" OF FAMILY NAME

When the new Constitution was put into effect in 1946 in post-war Japan, Articles 14 and 24 declared the equal status of men and women before the law and, most importantly, equality in family life.[1] The Japanese Civil Code was amended the next year in accordance with these Constitutional articles. The legal status of women was revised to be equal to that of men. They came to be entitled to the same rights to inheritance; freedom of marriage; custody rights; etc. Two articles, however, bore seeds of future controversy: marital naming and discrimination against "illegitimate" children in inheritance. . . . [The] Japanese Civil Code Article 750 stipulates that a married couple decides either husband's or wife's family name as their family name upon marriage. . . . It looks as if the family name were chosen upon a couple's consent to what they freely decide as equal beings. However, in practice, . . . about 98 percent of Japanese women take their husband's names in marriage. Recently, enforcement of one single family name against one's own will upon marriage was declared unconstitutional in other countries.[2] The fact that 98 percent of Japanese women take their husband's names in marriage, when the couple must decide either of their names as family name, means that the state authority de-facto forces almost all wives to change their names as a prerequisite of marriage registration.

However, the question of a couple's marital naming goes much further than the liberal feminist concerns of formal gender equality in marital naming. The social, economic, and political functions of family name in Japan are very specific in which family name functions far beyond an expression of individual citizen's private identity or representation of moral bond among family members. The meaning of family name needs to be understood in its relation to the cultural function of the Japanese family institution (ie) and Japanese state's family registration system (koseki). The family name, I argue, is a symbolic metaphor that embodies the cultural power of the Japanese family, ie, and the state governance of population grouped into a legal family institution, koseki. Particular meanings and functions of family name in contemporary Japan become evident by shedding light on women's resistance to the compulsory change of marital name. . . . .

Family name is not only a cultural symbol of Japanese family, ie, but it also is a label of one legal family unit. The marriage is not legally recognized unless the couple registers their marriage at the local government office with their chosen marital family name. Based on the registered family name, a new family register (koseki) is created for each newly established family. A family created through marriage has one family name and only one family register. Koseki is a modern invention of the Japanese state. . . . It was designed to facilitate the authority to keep track of the history of each family, the subjects' civil status change, and their familial relations. People are obliged to report their change of status to the local state authority which is accountable for the management of koseki. Every person, at birth, "enters" her or his parents' family register. . . . An offspring of a legally married couple is recognized as "legitimate" and recorded as either first daughter, second daughter, or so on, in accordance to one's order of birth among siblings. Those who are born to a non-married couple or a single mother will be assumed as "illegitimate" and recorded as "female" or "male" instead of first daughter, second daughter, or so on. In so doing, koseki keeps a detailed record of the legal status of each nuclear family member on one piece of paper from birth, adoption, marriage, divorce, to death. Koseki has been widely used as an efficient tool for people's background checks, their ethnicity, their original caste, etc. It is managed and used mainly by the state, but private companies and families[3] are also common viewers of koseki for background checks of their employees and marriage partners.

Koseki is filed for each family, not for each individual . . . Koseki is a way of governance to prevent any individual subjectivity in family law where one's subject position is only allowed as a family member in a hierarchically ordered relation to the head of family (the so-called "standard person"). Except for the standard person who is usually a male elder, other family members are positioned as wife, first son, second son, first daughter, etc. after him. Thus, *koseki* imposes order on citizens in their familial hierarchy with a male standard person at its top. It is a detailed map of Japanese citizens through which the subjects become legible to the state (Foucault 1991; Scott 1998). It categorizes people as legitimate and illegitimate, good family and bad family, deserving citizens and undeserving citizens, and so on.[4] Through this powerful legal tool, the Japanese state penetrates into the very private sphere of family life for "the management of population in its depths and its details" (Foucault 1991: 102)....

... Current family law was supposed to dismantle the old hierarchical Japanese family system and establish a democratic family system based on the assumption of liberal rights-bearing individuals. However, by preserving the family registration system *koseki* and most of its cultural functions, the fundamental structure of the old family remains alive in a modified form.... The "choice" of one family name has been, in fact, sustained by women's relinquishing their names, and those of their families. When women attempt to restore their rights to choose their family name, the option of choice turns out to be an illusion....

JAPANESE WOMEN'S POLITICS OF RESISTANCE IN *FUFUBESSEI* MOVEMENT

... In this section, I will demonstrate that the family name further serves as a contested cultural and legal terrain where various forms of women's resistance take place. These forms of resistance may not aim to bring about a swift social change at any structural level; however, they pose a radical challenge to the ways in which Japanese think about the right form of family and women's positions in it. It suggests that mobilizing from the margin can constitute a force to problematize the hegemonic discourses of the "natural," "customary," and "cultural" Japanese family, at which the possibility of social change can be located. The change and reform which resulted from this movement might differ from what women in this movement wished for, yet it is this movement that initiates the first wave of larger-scale social change....

Local *Fufubessei* Groups: A Cultural Space

The very strong presence of the Japanese state permeating daily life is coupled with a critical sense of deprivation of subversive space for those social groups in opposition to the state's cause. Their own space, out of the reach of the state, allows them to generate and articulate alternative discourses.... Women talk and share their experiences in this space, whose discourses have come to be viewed as subversive of the current Japanese family norm. This space constitutes various forms of local meetings in which both members and visitors can freely participate. In addition to group meetings, newsletters and internet chat rooms, websites, and emails also serve as a discursive space among larger groups. These meetings were getting organized in the mid-1980s through the early 1990s, when women in many different regions began to protest the fact that the Japanese Civil Code forces women to change their names upon marriage. Those women who came to perceive it as odd and unfair to wives began to organize small local meetings to talk about what it means to them to be pressured to change their names against their own will....[5] These spontaneous meetings developed into the local *fufubessei* movement groups as the participants organized meetings on a regular basis and the number of the participants increased. Spreading quickly all over Japan throughout the 1990s, these local groups drew high media attention and the conservatives regarded *fufubessei* as a serious threat to Japanese traditional family values. *Fufubessei* meetings are voluntarily and independently organized. They only have a loose network among local groups to share information on their activities, local experience, and the developments regarding law reform in the Diet. All of them were led by local women who were lawyers, school teachers, civil servants working at various local government divisions, and quite a number of housewives.

The Japanese women's family law reform movement urges rethinking about commonly known social movements. . . . [Surprisingly,] it was not organized by any sort of effective network among members based on strong leadership at the center, and it is not defined as a sustained interaction with elites, opponents, and authorities. It is a diffuse and de-centered form of women's movement in its network and leadership. What is most conspicuous about the Japanese women's *fufubessei* movement is that the participants do not attempt to make direct interactions with elites, opponents, and authorities that Tarrow (1998) seems to emphasize for contentious politics. To the contrary, it is critical for Japanese women in the movement to preserve their space out of the reach of the opponents and the state: not to confront them. These particular forms of movements resonate with what women's movement theorists argue about the gendered opportunity structure, "as an outgrowth of the way nation-states constructed their politics on gendered lines, women are institutionally disadvantaged in contests waged on 'men's' terrain. Women thus are more likely to organize outside the formal polity, in the community and grassroots contexts that are gendered female." (Ferree and Mueller 2004: 598; see also, Molyneux 1998; Offen 2000). . . . The gendered aspect of social

movements certainly applies to the Japanese women's movement. Local group leaders confine their roles as helpers to reach out and consult those who are in trouble with a family name change. They facilitate information-sharing and candid talks among women in distress, and provide consultation on how to deal with the family naming problems. These meetings are the social space that the movement participants create together. The movement is not aimed at mobilizing the general populace for collective political action. . . .[6] This pseudo-private feminine space claims to be safe and non-political so that even housewives, the so-called least political subject in Japan, can freely participate. The discourse of participants is replete with their activities being non-political and even anti-political. . . .

This space is expanded through the newsletters that most local groups publish. They use newsletters to report their meetings and share new information they have collected. Members of the group write their stories and express gratitude to others. They encourage each other in their cause and remind each other of their rights to names. Many "secret" methods to take advantage of legal loopholes are exchanged. The group meetings are also for studying domestic and foreign family laws and they often invite outside family law specialists to give talks.

Through these activities, those who participate in the meetings could find . . . *nakama*—a Japanese term for those in the same group who have the same minds toward the same goal and who could work together with a strong sense of solidarity. *Nakama* is more than just a friend and colleague in the group, but one who is able to read the other's mind and work for a particular purpose together. Though the inter-group network among local groups is weak, solidarity among members of each local group is strong; for the most part, the *bessei* movement is dependent on the individual connection among *nakamas*. . . . For those women who are isolated in private relations, the local groups appear to provide a shared public space. . . . They share their concerns, anger, and stress from family and workplace, and also brainstorm ways out of legal straitjackets. The motivations of the participants vary greatly; from the family responsibility of the only daughter to continue the family name . . ., emancipation from the traditional role of a daughter-in-law in Japan, a sense of lost identity as an independent person, political protest against the Japanese family system, to economic disadvantage and inconvenience that change of name may cause. They all come and talk about these problems together despite sometimes radically conflicting motivations. . . .

Legal Mobilization in Everyday Life: Subversive Individuality

More and more women who resist the dominant gender identity that the Japanese family institution embodies are experimenting with a new form of marriage by "not registering their marriage" with the state. These women perceive resistance to family name change as a way to emancipate themselves from the oppressive gender identity which *ie* and *koseki* enforce. A woman in coupled living, without registering her marriage, has been commonly viewed as having an illegitimate relationship with her partner so that she cannot or is not eligible to register her coupled life legally. This type of coupled living is seen as temporary at best. However, women's deliberate "choice not to register" reverses this negative connotation of the unregistered marriage and passive women's agency. Their bold choice is a public statement . . . that they are choosing to live as individual selves. They outspokenly refuse to mold themselves into the gender identity that the marriage registration system constitutes. Those women search for a new selfhood based on individuality in opposition to their familial subjectivities, challenging the only forms of subjectivities available to married

women. These women, in interviews, often define their individuality by refusing certain expected familial positions as follows: . . .

I don't want to be restricted to the traditional familial responsibility. Legal marriage equals the traditional role of *yome* (daughter in law) even today. If I change my family name, I am going to be obliged to look after parents-in-law, but only parents-in-law, not my parents. I am opposing this social custom.

. . . Being a housewife reduces her identity to a care giver of her family. A normal housewife should not be so selfish to insist on her self-identity as an independent individual from her family. A career woman may want to keep her family name, since she has a career on which changing the family name would make an adverse impact. However, housewives do not have such "good reasons." Her identity as housewife excludes her, not only from other social identities, but also from being an individual identity separate from her family. Women's assertion of individuality in this social, cultural context is radical, hence needs to be read as resistance. . . . They say: . . .

I like to have an equal relationship with my partner.

My name and my family name are [an] important part of my identity. I don't want to change it. I feel myself taken away.

. . . Her separate family name symbolically signifies her individuality as a separate but equal individual from her husband. By not registering their marriage with the state, a couple has two separate *kosekis*, one for each, which in turn symbolizes their individual identities. Her separate family register proves that she never "entered" the husband's family. She uses the very controlling system of the state's family register in order to assert her individuality. In doing so, she takes advantage of the state's legitimacy to support for her separate selfhood from her husband's family. Cohabitation without marriage is still uncommon in Japan, yet in her survey study on non-registered Japanese couples, Yoshizumi (1997) finds distinct characteristics of newly emerging Japanese non-registered couples. She finds that Japanese non-registered cohabitation is predominantly women-led and intentionally chosen as a form of resistance to the conventional marriage institution. This is significantly different from Sweden and the U.S. where cohabitation is exercised in many cases as a prior stage of marriage or experimental coupled life (Yoshizumi 1997). . . .

The *bessei* movement represents an everyday form of resistance movement. By articulating subversive individuality and not registering their marriage to the state, yet claiming it as legitimate family life, women endeavor to carve out a new familial subjectivity. However, in many situations, they have to negotiate their individuality with other identities. Most women living coupled but unregistered confront a serious challenge when they decide to have children. . . . Japanese family law institutionalizes discrimination against children born out of wedlock, both in terms of a discriminatory record on *koseki* and in inheritance rights. A woman in an unregistered marriage, therefore, faces a tough decision whether she should insist on her individuality/her name and make her children legally illegitimate as a result. The law pressures unmarried women with children to take moral responsibility for their children's legal status. These women are seen as selfish for sacrificing children's welfare in order to keep their family names; motherhood is posed in opposition to women's individuality in Japanese family law.

. . . Many couples under this moral pressure often decide to register their marriage and create a new family register. Women submit to the pressure to change their names for the children's legal status. However, even when a couple is registered as married, the wife continues to use her old family name in her daily life from the workplace to her child's school.[7] That is, a wife uses two names: one is her legal *koseki* name and the other is her daily name. Her new family name is used for the cases where only a legal family name is accepted—for identification such as a passport, salary roster, insurance cards, and most bank accounts.[8] However, two names cause tremendous inconvenience to the wife, and confusion in her public identity. Above all, keeping two names does not solve the fundamental problem of marital naming; in fact, she did change her name legally.

Many women who already have registered their marriage and changed their names attempt to experiment a bolder manipulation of the law's formality: paper divorce. They choose divorce on paper while still living as a couple. Ironically, Japanese Civil Law leaves the decision of marriage and divorce completely to the couple's free will. . . . Legal divorce is simple and easy: all the divorcing parties need is to fill out the form for divorce with each party's seal on it, and submit the form to the local census office. As the local census office accepts it and updates a couple's family register, divorce is confirmed. . . . The wife reinstates her family name legally through paper divorce with her actual marriage life continuing. . . . These couples often repeat marriage and divorce several times whenever a couple is required to prove their marital status as legal spouse. When needed, they register their marriage by submitting a piece of paper filled out to the local government office, then they divorce again once the need is exhausted. Most women that I met in local women's meetings either practiced paper divorce or seriously considered this possibility. One woman who lived with her partner for years without registration told me about her plan for paper divorce. When her partner was to be sent to another country by the company he worked for, she would have to prove their relationship as husband and wife to get a visa as a dependent (wife).... [T]heir situation made her seriously consider marrying him and later divorce on paper when they came back to Japan....

The resistance these women are exerting is, however, not without difficulties.... Marriage means "entering husband's family register" to the extent that "entering one's family register" (*sekini hairu*) is used interchangeably of the word "marriage" in everyday conversation. It is implied that a woman who does not enter the husband's family register refuses to become a genuine member of the husband's family and furthermore is unwilling to take care of the parents-in-law in the future. In addition, these women are confronting moral sanction that they are "bad mothers" by making their children illegitimate and refusing to take care of the old and even the dead ancestors in the family tomb. The various ways in which women in the movement struggle to keep their family names illustrate Japanese women's agency in resistance as they deal with all these layers of power relations.

WHAT HAVE THEY ACHIEVED? THE QUESTION OF "SUCCESS"

As Cott argues, regarding the American marriage institution, that family law is the state institution that "uniquely and powerfully influences the way differences between the sexes are conveyed and symbolized" (2000: 3).... Starting from Cott's argument that marriage is the primary way the state controls gender relations, I further attempted to follow Japanese women's strategies to challenge the state family law. Their movement mobilizes little political activism, partly because women who participate in it have different motivations and there is no central leadership to manage the differences.... Under the circumstances where women struggle against the state family law, yet ask for state support for law reform, it is difficult to identify clear power-holders that they have to fight against. Moreover, their identity as married women deprives them of a belief that they could make any significant influence on politics. However, their movement nonetheless triggered a meaningful shakeup that led to a break in the present gender norms....

At the moment, the family law reform seems to be stalled in Japan. From the perspective of the law reform movement, the *fufubessei* movement would be a failed movement, since the law still remains in place. However, the broader influence on social institutions this movement has made speaks for its success. Now it is not surprising that many major workplaces allow women to continuously use their old names after marriage. In 2001, for the first time, all Japanese Ministries in government acknowledged married women's use of old names. Furthermore, the 2002 government opinion poll demonstrated a dramatic change in public opinion in favor of *fufubessei*. For the first time, public tolerance towards married women's use of old names surpassed the opposition. Social norms on women's position in family have gradually but surely been changing.... Japanese in most major cities now perceive this choice as interesting, but not odd or immoral as it used to be seen. The success of the *bessei* movement lies in this change of the family paradigm in Japanese society. Women's resistance to marital naming is beginning to persuade Japanese society of the injustice of a gendered family system....

NOTES

This study was funded by [a] 21 Century Center of Excellence (COE) research fellowship, Ochanomizu University. [An] earlier stage of this study had also been assisted by [a] Japan–Korea Cultural Foundation Research Fellowship (April 2003 to September 2004) and [a] Chester Fritz Grant for International Study and Exchanges, Graduate School of University of Washington (October 2002–December 2002).

1. Article 14 declares the general principle of equality regardless of gender, religion, and social status, while Article 24 specifically protects equality within family. This Article 24 is evaluated to be very advanced in terms of proclaiming gender equality even among those constitutions in liberal democratic societies.

2. Most recently, the Thai Constitutional Court declared enforcement of the same family for a married couple, against their will, as unconstitutional in June 2003. In Turkey, married women can keep their family names since the 2001 Civil Code revision.

3. This is possible, for *koseki* is in principle public.

4. At the same time, it is a marker for Japanese citizenship that draws a line against others of foreign origin who are not entitled to create *koseki*.

5. According to my interviewees, the direct motivation was more complex. Some said these groups were organized to put pressure on the Ministry of Justice where the bureaucrats had already been considering family law revision. Some later groups were also organized after they heard about other *fufubessei* groups' activities. Nonetheless, virtually all local groups were organized independently and voluntarily.

6. Student movements, including anti-Vietnam demonstrations in the 1960s, were subdued and cracked down on violently by the government. Also women's liberation movements in the 1970s were portrayed as extremely radical movements. The failure of major social movements in Japan contributed to creating the dangerous image of social movements and significantly cut down their legitimacy as a way of making political demands.

7. This may be similar to many western societies, where married women customarily change their names, but then keep their own separate names for professional purposes. However, in Japan, it has more than a "professional" meaning, since women's work is not seen as very professional in the first place, and many housewives who practice *fufubessei* do not have careers.

8. Broad currency of *fufubessei* has expanded the acceptance of women's separate names. Now many insurance cards are issued with women's separate names.

REFERENCES

Abu-Lughod, Lila (1990) "The Romance of Resistance: Tracing Transformations of Power through Bedouln Women," *American Ethnologist* 17, 1: 41–55.

Cott, Nancy F. (2000) *Public Vows: A History of Marriage and the Nation*, Cambridge, MA and London, England: Harvard University Press.

Ferree, Myra Marx and Carol Mueller (2004) "Feminism and the Women's Movement in A Global Perspective" in D. A. Snow, S. A. Soule, and H. Kriesi (eds.) *The Blackwell Companion to Social Movements*, Malden, MA: Blackwell.

Foucault, Michel (1991) "Governmentality" in G. Burchell, C. Gordon, and P. Miller (eds.) *The Foucault Effect: Studies in Governmentality*, Chicago, IL: University of Chicago Press.

Molyneux, Maxine (1998) "Analyzing Women's Movements" in C. Jackson and R. Pearson (eds.) *Feminist Visions of Development: Gender, Analysis, and Policy*, London and New York: Routledge.

Offen, Karen M. (2000) *European Feminism:1700–1950: A Political History*, Berkeley, CA: Stanford University Press.

Scott, James C. (1998) *Seeing like a State: How Certain Schemes to Improve the Human Condition Have Failed*, New Haven, CT: Yale University Press.

Tarrow, Sydney G. (1998) *Power in Movement: Social Movements and Contentious Politics*, Cambridge, England and New York: Cambridge University Press.

Yoshizumi, Kyoko (1997) *Kindai Kazoku o Koeru: Hihoritsukon Kapuru no Koe (Beyond the Modern Family Institution: Voices of the Common Law Marriage Couples)*, Tokyo, Japan Aoki Shoten.

SECTION 3

Latin America and the Caribbean

14 Between the Dynamics of the Global and the Local: Feminist and
    Gender Research in Latin America and the Caribbean   151
    EDNA ACOSTA-BELÉN

15 Relations in Dispute: Conflict and Cooperation Between Academia and
    the Feminist Movements in Central America   158
    MONTSERRAT SAGOT AND ANA C. ESCALANTE

16 Puerto Rico: Feminism and Feminist Studies   178
    ALICE E. COLÓN WARREN

17 Gender Studies in Cuba: Methodological Approaches, 1974–2007   196
    MARTA NÚÑEZ SARMIENTO

18 Feminist Research and Theory: Contributions from the Anglophone
    Caribbean   215
    RHODA REDDOCK

19 Trade Unions and Women's Labor Rights in Argentina   231
    GRACIELA DI MARCO

20 In the Fabric of Brazilian Sexuality   239
    MARIA LUIZA HEILBORN

21 Citizenship and Nation: Debates on Reproductive Rights in Puerto Rico   248
    ELIZABETH CRESPO-KEBLER

Between the Dynamics of the Global and the Local: Feminist and Gender Research in Latin America and the Caribbean

Edna Acosta-Belén

In searching for commonalities and differences among the nations that comprise the Latin American and Caribbean regions, a number of historical, social, economic, and political realities stand out. For the Latin American nations, territories largely colonized by the Spanish, but also by the Portuguese (Brazil) and French (Haiti), independence did not materialize until the early decades of the nineteenth century. In contrast, for the great majority of the Caribbean islands, colonized by the Spanish (e.g., Cuba, the Dominican Republic, Puerto Rico), British (e.g., Jamaica, Barbados), French (e.g., Haiti, Martinique, Guadeloupe), and Dutch (e.g., Aruba, Curaçao), sovereignty did not come until after the second half of the twentieth century. Even after independence, for some of the countries in both regions and, to this day, their decolonization process continues to be hindered by a number of factors: pervasive political instability and authoritarian regimes, their neocolonial dependency on foreign-capital investment and foreign loans to sustain their economies, their subjection to the global policies of international financial regulatory agencies, such as the World Bank, the International Monetary Fund (IMF), and the World Trade Organization (WTO), their exposure to the multiple effects that multinational corporations have over their populations' livelihoods, the widespread poverty, social inequality, and health problems that afflict a large portion of their populations, and the social, racial, and gender marginality endured by a substantial majority of their citizens, especially those of indigenous and black racial origin. Thus the long history of first, European and, subsequently, U.S. domination of these countries' economies through the presence of powerful transnational corporations, along with numerous U.S. military interventions, are all part the experience of colonialism, neocolonialism, and imperialist domination that is so crucial in understanding these regions.

The Caribbean played an important strategic military role for the United States, especially after the Spanish–Cuban–American War of 1898. The United States also solidified its presence by securing the rights to the Panama Canal in the early 1900s by creating a favorable U.S. investment environment with easy access to a low-waged labor force, by "policing" the region in order to protect its own interests and, in the second half of the twentieth century, by waging war against the perceived spread of socialism or communism in the hemisphere (including, for example, the 1983 invasion of Grenada by U.S. marines or the CIA's covert activities that led to the 1973 overthrow of Salvador Allende's duly elected government in Chile).

The historical context for these regions must also include the economic exploitation by powerful U.S. corporations. Among the more recent corporate abuses are Coca-Cola's support of anti-union paramilitary death squads in Colombia, Wal-Mart's reliance on their suppliers' use of sweatshop workers in Nicaragua and elsewhere, the water pollution and health problems caused by Newmont Mining in Peru, or the monopolizing of local water systems and water price gouging in many Latin American countries by the French Suez water company. These corporate actions, many of which have targeted women as workers or family health-care providers, fueled social activism and resistance to these conditions.

The precarious survival conditions faced by the great majority of workers, and thus large numbers of women, and the ways in which they organize to struggle against them, rarely have been imbued with the dramatic or radical bent of many of the social and political movements that characterize these regions' history. To a large extent, the latter have focused on destabilizing or overturning authoritarian and violent military or civilian regimes, struggling against the class domination of the ruling oligarchies that sustain them, organizing workers to protest exploitative corporate labor practices, and demanding some degree of social justice from the state for the impoverished and disenfranchised populations of their respective countries. On the whole, the indigenous or black racial profile of some of these populations underscores an additional crucial dimension of the marginality and exclusion experienced by sizeable or, in some cases, majority sectors of the population of these societies. In many of their wider social and political movements, along with those that focus specifically on strategic women's or gender issues, large numbers of women have been willing to take risks by fighting human rights violations and the violence of military regimes—such as the *Madres de Plaza de Mayo* and the *Comadres* of El Salvador—or less recognized collective efforts of women seeking solutions to everyday critical survival problems. Among the latter forms of activism, a few key areas stand out:

- Women joining in the efforts to resist neoliberalist and neostructuralist globalization policies and free trade agreements developed by international agencies and pushed by the leading capitalist countries upon the developing countries with little regard to their impact on the peoples' livelihoods or their local communities (see Chapter 19 by DiMarco);
- Devising new ways of making a living, largely in the informal economic sector, but also in factories, sweatshops, and the service sector, and struggling for the daily survival of their families when facing the most adverse economic conditions;
- Actively joining the battle in defense of their reproductive and health rights, and against the spread of HIV/AIDS and different manifestations of domestic and state violence (see Chapter 21 by Crespo-Kebler);
- Making gender equality and women's rights a fundamental aspect of development programs;
- Continue articulating and pressing specific demands to their governments at a time when most states are increasingly retreating from their social responsibilities to their citizenry; and,
- Engaging in consciousness raising and in different ways of empowering women from all social sectors to advance their status and assert their fundamental citizen rights.

Regarding the particular circumstances that have influenced women's organizing and research in the Latin American and Caribbean regions, it is important to point out that the capitalist structural adjustment and neoliberal policies of the new "world order," proclaimed by the leading industrialized powers after the disintegration of the socialist bloc, contributed to creating what is known in Latin America as the "lost decade." The coined term captures the despairing socioeconomic realities confronted by most of the countries in the region during the 1980s: unprecedented high levels of foreign debt and inflation, very low rates of economic growth and productivity, rampant unemployment and underemployment, the weakening of labor unions, and increased migration from rural to urban areas and to other countries. Ironically, the economic crisis was also an intense period of feminist organizing in order to meet the basic daily survival needs of their families, or to denounce the pervading persecution and violence of thousands of dissidents and innocent citizens who were tortured, murdered or disappeared under U.S.-sanctioned military regimes. From the 1970s to the 1990s, different manifestations of violence overwhelmed countries such as Argentina, Brazil, and Chile, while Guatemala, El Salvador, and Nicaragua were engulfed in civil war. The 1980s also marked the beginning of a process of democratization and return to civilian rule in a few of those countries, after the predominance of violence and human rights violations throughout the hemisphere. But, war and violence in Central America, which lasted until the 1990s, brought about a large exodus of displaced populations, especially women and children, seeking refuge in neighboring countries, as well as in the United States, where the proportion of the Latino population from Central and South America increased from 1980 through the late 1990s. As a result, researchers in Latin America and the United States are now focusing on new issues of women's migration.

The 1989 Washington Consensus of neoliberal economic reform policies to be prescribed and applied to Latin American countries by the IMF and the World Bank were intended as a "shock and rescue" operation that would lead these nations out of their devastating economic crisis. But, fundamentally, these neoliberalist and the subsequent neostructuralist structural adjustment policies promoted by the dominant capitalist economies through their international agencies went beyond Latin America and represent the core of the globalization processes that are often replicated in other developing countries (Leiva 2008). Another agent in the globalization processes has been the World Trade Organization (WTO)—a successor to the post-World War II General Agreement on Tariffs and Trade (GATT)—created in 1995 to liberalize and regulate free trade at a global scale. Because of the expanding control of the global economy by the most powerful industrialized nations, WTO critics see it as another form of "policy imperialism" or "market fundamentalism" that glorifies the benefits of the classic laissez-fare capitalist system, without being critical about how to curb its excesses and rapacious nature. As the WTO encourages states to privatize vital social services (e.g., education, health, and retirement benefits), the burden for these services is shifted to individuals and their households—especially to women. The most obvious results are the widening gap between the rich and the poor, the weakening of the middle classes, the intensification of poverty, a growing precariousness of labor, the undermining of democratic principles by transnational corporate profit and privilege, as well as the effects of unfettered capitalism.

Today, about 70 percent of the Latin American population still receives incomes of less than $3,000 a year. Yet, despite the dire socioeconomic conditions faced by a large majority of contemporary Latin American and Caribbean countries, modest inroads have been made in some nations in linking the activist agendas of many women's and feminist movements with those of women and feminist researchers, making their research more relevant and useful in defining specific initiatives for change in the conditions and policies that perpetuate their subordination. From the work of scholars and grassroots activists a great deal has been learned about the impact of neoliberalist and neostructuralist policies on their households and communities, and about the sexual division of labor of peasant and urban proletarian workers, in different occupational areas, and in the formal and informal sectors of the economy. Feminist scholars also have produced important work to document a global sexual division of labor fostered by transnational corporations, which relied on and exploited women's work. In Latin America, this type of work is exemplified by the *maquiladoras* located in export-processing zones (EPZs) in countries such as Brazil, Costa Rica, Colombia, Mexico, and Peru, in addition to those factories located in several Caribbean islands and U.S.–Mexican border free trade zones, which are mostly garment and electronics industries that primarily employ women (Ward and Pyle 1995). The case of women workers at Ciudad Juárez, considered to be the *maquiladora* capital of Mexico, also epitomizes all the gender and social inequalities engendered by globalization and neoliberalism (see Staudt 2008). For the last decade and a half, Juárez has become a symbol of femicide and a site for the most brutal manifestations of violence against women. The murders, mutilation, and rape of more than 550 women in the border region (hundreds more are still missing)—a rampage that began in 1993—and the disregard and inability of both Mexican and U.S. authorities to put an end to the fear produced by these hideous crimes, stirred mother's and relatives of the victims, as well as feminist activists across borders to organize in denouncing them, and in underlining the failure of law enforcement officials in dealing with these atrocities. Grassroots groups such as *Amigos de las Mujeres de Juárez* (Friends of the Women of Juarez), *Justicia para Nuestras Hijas* (Justice for Our Daughters), *Nuestras Hijas de Regreso a Casa* (Our Daughters On Their Way Home), and *Casa Amiga* (Friends' House), along with the campaigns supported by the influential U.S.-based National Organization for Women (NOW), also captured international attention and widespread media coverage by linking the women of Juárez's murders to other prevailing forms of violence and human rights violations against women.

Through the work of researchers and activists a great deal also has been learned about the multiple sources of Latin American and Caribbean women's oppression inside and outside the household, as well as different forms of women's collective activism and survival strategies in order to deal with these conditions—from self-help and advocacy groups, to strikes and demonstrations, national and international conferences, or smaller *encuentros* (gatherings) that occasionally resulted in ardent *encontronazos* (clashes) that underscored the wide diversity of experiences and priorities among women. Major professional organizations, such as the Latin American Studies Association (LASA) and the Caribbean Studies Association (CSA) have played an important role in promoting and disseminating feminist and women's research and activism in the many nations that comprise these regions. All of these forms of collective participation and organizing accentuated the inescapable and complex class, racial, ethnic, and political differences that characterize the populations of the many nations that comprise these regions. As a whole, these different forms of activism have played a vital and positive role in opening up the dialogue and debate on the multiplicity and complexity of the different conditions and experiences behind the category woman, and in contributing to purge the concept from its essentialist propensities.

Also worthy of notice is the higher profile of Latin American and Caribbean women in public life and their representation in high-level government posts, including the presidency of their country. In 2008, two Latin American nations have a woman president, Michelle Bachelet in Chile and Cristina Fernández de Kirchner in Argentina, and women cabinet ministers and legislators are also on the increase. In the past, women also have been heads of state in Nicaragua, Bolivia, Panama, Dominica, and Guyana. Additionally, for the first time in its history, in 2007 the Caribbean Congress of Labour (CCL), a regional trade union federation that involves 17 different countries, elected a woman, Trinidadian Jacqueline Jack, as president.

Chant (2003) points to some general indicators of change that reflect an expansion of institutional support for women throughout Latin America. These include a decline in fertility and illiteracy rates, rising levels of education and employment, and changing traditional gender relations that come from the weakening of patriarchal control within the household. The latter in turn contributes to increases in divorce rates and in the number of female-headed households.

The chapters included in this section confirm that women's struggle for equality and social justice or the envisioning of feminist utopias, takes place on multiple fronts that do not necessarily come together into an all-inclusive or sweeping coherent project for women's liberation or for the overall improvement of women's conditions. Chapters 15 to 18 provide comprehensive reviews of feminist research and activism in the Hispanic and Anglophone Caribbean, as well as a similar assessment for Costa Rica and other Central American countries.

Alice Colón Warren (Chapter 16) focuses on Puerto Rico, a country that because of its colonial relationship with the United States was subject to a massive U.S.-led industrialization and modernization process in the late 1940s and 50s, becoming a U.S. showcase for democracy and development model for other countries in the hemisphere. Colón Warren notes that in recent decades neoliberal policies in Puerto Rico have resulted in an exodus of U.S. industries and a reduction in U.S. federal assistance programs and in the island's public employment sector, all of which in turn have had a negative impact on women's employment levels and poverty rates. She also underscores the veil of silence that has existed on the island around issues of race and sexuality, pointing to the daring efforts of women scholars and activists in bringing these issues to the fore. Finally, she emphasizes the importance of pursuing comparative studies of Puerto Rican women on the island and within the U.S. diaspora, as well as with women in other Caribbean and Latin American nations.

An interesting comparison is provided using the experiences of living under the Cuban socialist government, as Marta Núñez Sarmiento (Chapter 17) describes the late arrival in the mid-1980s of gender and women-focused research as part of a government rectification process aimed at dealing with sex discrimination in the island's labor force. In this case, the national *Federación de Mujeres Cubanas* (Federation of Cuban Women) played an important role in the process. Furthermore, Cuban scholars' interests in issues of women and gender began by participating in international women's conferences, discussing their work and establishing connections with other gender scholars throughout the world. Núñez Sarmiento offers some valuable methodological insights based on her own research, stressing the need for gender scholars to practice participatory and action research, rely on the use of multiple methods, and be committed to producing research that contributes to social change.

Rhoda Reddock (Chapter 18) documents how feminist scholarship has flourished within the Anglophone Caribbean nations, but also within their respective diasporas, while the activism of women's movements has somewhat declined in comparison to the 1970s and 1980s. The work of researchers at the University of the West Indies, through its Centre for Gender and Development Studies, has been a key factor in promoting a link between scholarship and activism, while other organizations, such as the Caribbean Association for Feminist Research and Action (CAFRA), have fostered a regional network of researchers and activists. CAFRA was initially founded to challenge the anti-feminist stance of socialist and leftist political organizations, which often viewed feminism as "divisive" or a distraction from other broader political and social agendas, but it has diversified its objectives. This pattern, of promoting gender and women's studies through feminist research centers/institutes or through national feminist organizations, rather than primarily through university-based degree programs, is typical of Latin America and the Caribbean.

Turning to Central America, the conflict and cooperation between feminist academics and activists is an underlined theme of Monserrat Sagot and Ana C. Escalante's (Chapter 15) review of the work of these two important sectors of the women's movement. According to the authors, and based on data collected from interviews, there is a lack of articulation between research produced within the walls of the academy and the agendas of women's NGOs, which contributes to a perception of scholars as elitist or to some extent "disconnected" from the realities faced by less privileged women. Nonetheless, the authors reassert the strategic value of women's studies academic programs "for promoting the production of knowledge from a women's perspective and for transforming traditional constructions of scientific knowledge" (p. 172).

The next three chapters in this section, authored by Graciela Di Marco (Chapter 19), Maria Luiza Heilborn (Chapter 20), and Elizabeth Crespo-Kebler (Chapter 21), provide specific research examples of topics that have been part of the agendas of feminist or gender-focused research and movements—including women's trade union organizing, and issues surrounding sexuality and reproductive rights.

Crespo-Kebler frames Puerto Rico's debates on reproductive rights around important contemporary feminist issues of citizenship and nation. Because of its colonial relationship with the United States, feminism on the island was frequently viewed through the lenses of a conservative nationalist/anticolonial patriarchal discourse. The author criticizes the tendency to see women as victims, depriving them of their agency, and the application of universalizing paradigms to the analysis of gender or women's conditions, calling for a more sustained critique of the category "woman."

The effects of neoliberal policies in Argentina during the 1990s is critical to Di Marco's analysis of trade unions and women's labor force participation in that country, producing, as the author notes, "internal ruptures" (p. 231) in union organizing. She focuses on a comparative analysis of two unions that emerged from the opposition to the labor flexibilization policies brought on by structural adjustment policies, describing the ways in which women participated and struggled for their rights within these organizations. She also underscores the importance of the 2004 Trade Union Law on Female Quotas that mandated that union positions should have 30 percent representation by women workers, but concludes that there is what she calls "an implicit conservative consensus" (p. 236) or alliance among union men that keeps women from reaching the most powerful positions, no matter what form of participatory structure a union has.

For a long time, discussions of sexuality issues were largely taboo in Latin America and the Caribbean. Heilborn (Chapter 20) breaks this barrier with a quantitative study that focuses on sexual behaviors of Brazilians, in an effort to deconstruct the myths about their sexuality, especially the popular notion of an "erotized national identity" (p. 239). Relying on the results of a survey of three different Brazilian cities, she dispels the myth and stresses significant differences between the sexual practices of Brazilian women and men. Other authors, such as Balderston and Guy (1997), Quiroga (2000), and Cruz-Malavé and Manalansan (2002), also have contributed to the growth of scholarly research on sexuality. Indeed, women's and gender studies, and the subsequent flourishing of queer and LGBT studies, opened up the gates to the in-depth analysis of the experiences of lesbians, gays, bisexuals, and transgender populations, and to the societal attitudes and prejudices against them.

As a whole, the chapters in this section show an important shift in women's and gender scholarship, which is not merely focusing on different forms of women's subordination or the patriarchal power structures that contribute to their oppression, but the ways in which they exert their agency in seeking solutions to pressing problems and creating new organizational spaces for advocacy, empowerment, and collective action.

REFERENCES

Balderston, Daniel and Donna Guy (eds.) (1997) *Sex and Sexuality in Latin America*, New York: New York University Press.

Chant, Sylvia (2003) *Gender in Latin America*, New Brunswick, NJ: Rutgers University Press.

Cruz-Malavé, Arnaldo and Martin Manalansan (eds.) (2002) *Queer Globalizations: Citizenship and the Afterlife of Colonialism*, New York: New York University Press.

Leiva, Fernando I. (2008) *Latin American Neostructuralism: The Contradictions of Post-Liberal Development*, Minneapolis, MN: University of Minnesota Press.

Quiroga, José (2000) *Tropics of Desire: Interventions from Queer Latin America*, New York: New York University Press.

Staudt, Kathleen (2008) *Violence and Activism at the Border: Gender, Fear, and Everyday Life in Ciudad Juárez*, Austin: University of Texas Press.

Ward, Kathryn B. and Jean Larson Pyle (1995) "Gender, Industrialization, Transnational Corporations, and Development: An Overview of Trends and Patterns" in Christine E. Bose and Edna Acosta-Belén (eds.) *Women in the Latin American Development Process*, Philadelphia: Temple University Press.

CHAPTER 15

Relations in Dispute: Conflict and Cooperation Between Academia and the Feminist Movement in Central America

Montserrat Sagot and Ana C. Escalante

To Silvia Chavarría,

dear friend and a founder of women's studies in Costa Rica

Changes in the condition of women undoubtedly represent some of the most important milestones of social development in the twentieth century. However, this process has been neither easy nor linear. Every appeal for women's equality has been questioned and contested; every manifestation of the feminist movement has been ridiculed, discredited, opposed, defined as dangerous, or even repressed. But, every victory has had a dramatic impact on the lives of the women who witnessed it and every advance has translated into rights for future generations.

In Central America, like in other parts of the world, the development of systematic studies on women and gender relations established within the academy has been closely related to the contemporary feminist movement over the last 30 years. Nonetheless, the emergence of feminism as a social movement, as well as feminist intellectual production in the Central American region followed a difficult path due to the conditions of poverty, the presence of authoritarian military regimes, the systematic violation of human rights, and the armed conflicts that shattered the lives of a large majority of women during the 1970s and 1980s.

The first initiatives to promote reflection about the conditions faced by Central American women and about gender relations from a feminist perspective surfaced from different fronts, almost simultaneously, in the 1980s. First, in academic institutions, feminist perspectives had gained some prestige and acceptance, and even become institutionalized spaces for academic inquiry. Also, during this period, international organizations in the region and even some governments, initiated studies aimed at collecting data that would assist them in formulating public policies, largely due to the influence and demands of feminists occupying official posts, but also in accordance with the recommendations that came out of the United Nations Decade for Women (1975–1985), and the Convention on the Elimination of All Forms of Discrimination Against Women (CEDAW). Finally, although with fewer resources, women's organizations began to carry out their own research in order to have more effective tools for their daily practice and for the political work they were pursuing.

During this initial stage, university spaces dedicated to the study of women and gender relations were created by linking universities with women's organizations, which, to a certain extent, contributed to closing the gap between activism and academic work.

Indeed, the academic analysis of women's conditions has propelled the contemporary feminist struggle in the region, as much as feminist activism has enriched the academy (Careaga 2002).

Cognizant of this relationship, university women's and gender studies programs were established as interdisciplinary projects with two main types of goals: academic, to make visible and study the specific conditions of women and of gender relations; and political, attempting to eliminate social injustice and discrimination. Thus the feminist movement created the conditions for the development of women's studies.

Considering this context, our main objective here is to analyze the complex relationships between the feminist movement and academic spaces in the Central American region. In pursuit of this objective, first we provide an historical overview, emphasizing the junctures and more important events that defined the development of feminist studies. Then we analyze the main topics of feminist research within the social sciences, particularly in Costa Rica—the most developed country in the region—as well as the gaps and problems confronted by those who have been engaged in these tasks at the universities. Finally, the chapter analyzes the relationships between feminism as a social movement and as an academic endeavor, especially in university settings.

Our methological strategy is primarily grounded on reviewing and analyzing secondary sources about feminist scholarly production in the region, in addition to information gathered by the first author from interviews, in person and by phone, with key informants[1] from all the Central American countries. The women interviewees were selected because they have played the double role of being researchers and activists. All of them have lives that reflect the main characteristic of women's and gender studies in the region; that is, the close, albeit complex, relationship between academic research spaces

and the political practice of the feminist movement.

CENTRAL AMERICA AND WOMEN'S STUDIES

The First Attempts

The 1980s marked the beginning of a process throughout the world, in conjunction with the end of the U.N. Decade for Women, of expanding knowledge regarding women and gender relations. Topics never before explored or documented in Central America, such as the participation of women in politics, accounts of the everyday lives of women, and violence against women, were brought to light. During this period, those initiatives had supranational support for the first time because of the Nairobi Strategies documents.

The first important academic meeting in Latin America addressing the topic of women's life conditions took place in Argentina in 1974. The Torcuato de Tella Institute of Buenos Aires organized a conference with the theme "Feminist Perspectives in the Social Sciences" (Stimpson 1998). Then, in 1977, El Colegio de México sponsored the "First Central American–Mexican Seminar on Women's Research." Although it had a local focus, Costa Rica, also held a "Symposium on Female Education" in 1972 promoted by the country's Committee of Cooperation within the Commission of Inter-American Women (CIM) of the Organization of American States (OAS).

Most of Central America experienced a period of war and the systematic violation of human rights during the 1970s and 1980s. These conditions also provoked a serious weakening of public universities and even an exodus of many women academics, from countries such as Guatemala, El Salvador, and Nicaragua, who went into exile. Therefore it is not accidental that Costa Rica, a country that did not experience intense conflicts, provided relatively stable social and economic conditions which allowed for the first major development of women's studies. In Nicaragua, following the 1979 Sandinista Revolution in Nicaragua, the creation of these kinds of programs was allowed as a result of the new conditions that fostered women's participation in all areas of the country's social life (Palacios 1999).

In Central America, the first research and spaces devoted to intellectual feminist discussion on the condition of women emerged simultaneously in universities and women's organizations. The first publications dedicated to the analysis of women's lives emerged in the early 1980s from two Costa Rican feminist associations: *Ventana* (Window), a journal stemming from a group with the same name and *Mujer* (Woman), a journal of the Center for Feminist Information and Action (CEFEMINA).

Simultaneously in 1981, the School of Social Work at the Universidad de Costa Rica (University of Costa Rica) organized the "First Latin American Seminar on Women's Research," which brought together academic sectors, state institutions, and nongovernmental agencies. The seminar emphasized the importance of incorporating and strengthening women's studies as a discipline at universities, promoting and enhancing research, as well as courses and social action projects concentrated on the needs and interests of women. As part of this process, in 1984, the Social Science faculty at the University of Costa Rica dedicated the *Eugenio Fonseca Tortós Lectures* to the theme of "Women and Society" and the First University Congress on Women was organized. Although the Congress was held at the University of Costa Rica, it was organized by by CEFEMINA, in alliance with a group of university feminists, who favored the exchange between activists, academics, and others committed to promoting the development of a just and equal society.

Even before these events occurred, about midway through the 1970s, the first studies

on women's realities had emerged in Costa Rica. The first publications produced by the School of Social Work were on the participation of university women in national politics, and on societal opinions surrounding the "liberation of women" (Solano 1975). These early publications also included Mirta González's work (1977a; 1977b) on the sexual division of labor and papers by Eugenia López (1977) on the double exploitation of women. Much of the initial research was centered on the theme of work, corresponding to research trends of the time and the Marxist influence within the social sciences, prompting studies of exploitation and reproduction of the work force (Sagot 1991b)

During the first half of the 1980s, the tendency to focus on the theme of work continued in the region, with a particular focus on the work of rural women (CIERA 1984). Fundamentally, "the central theme of the first works revolved around the quantification of female oppression; for instance, making visible the levels of female poverty and the discrimination of women in the workplace" and the discrimination in other spheres (Vázquez 2001: 177).

However, women's participation as citizens or in social movements was rarely addressed, and, even less was written on the problems within women's daily lives or gender relations.[2] The absence of research around these topics helped perpetuate the invisibility of women as social actors and neglected daily life and the interplay of relations that come out of it. In spite of the omission in intellectual discussion, Central American women were actively participating in the war, in the union and peasant movements, and in struggles for daily survival prevalent during this period throughout the region (Sagot 1991a).

The stories of these women were detailed only in what is known as *testimonial literature*, which played an important role during this period. Margaret Randall (1980) was one of the first to compile the stories of

Sandinista women in her work *We're all awake*. This was followed by the well-known story of Rigoberta Menchú, written by Elizabeth Burgos (1983), along with other narratives of women combatants or participants in different social movements.

This type of document should be an obligatory reference for women's studies scholars in the region since testimonials uncover conditions of oppression and convert personal stories into public knowledge. However, in the process of advancing more structured types of knowledge, this form of research and writing has been substantially lost or forgotten (Vázquez 2001).

During the second half of the 1980s a process of institutional expansion in the production of knowledge about women was initiated throughout Central America. For example, in 1986, the Universidad Centroamericana (Central American University or UCA) in Nicaragua integrated a career track into Sociology entitled "Women, Family and Society," making the university a pioneer in the field; and in Panama, in 1983, a group of feminist academics along with community activists, created the Workshop for Women's Studies at the Universidad de Panamá (University of Panama).

The term "women's studies" was used for the first time in the academic environment during the celebration of a "Seminario de Estudios Sobre la Mujer" (Women's Studies Seminar) held by the Social Sciences faculty, and co-sponsored by the University at Albany, State University of New York (SUNY) and the University of Costa Rica (González and Guzmán 1998). This joint effort allowed the development of an intellectual relationship between Costa Rican academics and those from the United States, which strengthened and gave legitimacy to the establishment of women's studies as an academic discipline within Costa Rican universities.

As a result of an initiative supported by the Consejo Superior Universitario de Centroamérica (Council of Central America's Universities or CSUCA), the first postgraduate courses were offered at the Universidad Nacional de Costa Rica (National University of Costa Rica) in 1987. The Programa Interdisciplinario de Estudios del Género (Interdisciplinary Gender Studies Program or PRIEG) was established at the University of Costa Rica, and the Centro de Investigación en Estudios de la Mujer (Center of Women's Studies or CIEM) at the National University. At the end of this decade, CSUCA promoted a series of regional courses, research projects, and a scholarship program for graduate theses, aimed at developing women's studies in all Central American universities. During this period there was a presence of women scholars from the United States and Europe who actively collaborated in these initiatives, either teaching some of the courses offered, promoting the emerging university programs, or supervising some of the first student theses.[3]

Moreover, resulting from a program sponsored by CSUCA, the Facultad Latinoamericana de Ciencias Sociales (Latin American School of Social Sciences or FLACSO), and the University for Peace, a report entitled *Central American Women* was published in 1989. The work was a two volume series that compiled all available statistical data at the time, and analyzed the effects of armed conflict on women in the region (García and Gomáriz 1989).

Regional Peace-Making Process and the Expansion of Women's Studies

In the 1990s, Central America began a peacemaking process that included the electoral defeat of the Sandinistas in 1990 and, consequently, the end of the Contra War; the signing of the Peace Agreements in El Salvador in 1992; the end of the "War without a war" in Honduras; and the beginning of talks to end the conflict in Guatemala. These processes resulted in the expansion of civil society and the appearance of a large number of women's organizations, which received financial backing from international cooperation agencies in Europe, Canada, and the United States in order to work towards gender equality.

In 1991, with the support of NORAD (The Norwegian Agency for Development Cooperation), a gender studies program was established at UCA in Managua and by 1993 women's studies was officially institutionalized with the establishment of the regional Master's degree in women's studies (National University-University of Costa Rica), the first graduate program of its kind in Latin America, which was initially supported by a Dutch International Cooperation Agency.

In the process of institutionalizing women's studies, which has progressed at varying rates within each Central American country, feminist organizations were primary catalysts. Women's studies arose out of the struggles, social needs, and, interests of women's organizations that have been the engine for social change. Other important actors in this process included European partners, Spain in particular, and although seemingly paradoxical, the Catholic affiliated universities, primarily because much of the resistance against authoritarianism and oppression during the periods of war and conflict was concentrated in these institutions.

For example, the first gender studies program in Guatemala was prompted by the actions of the Guatemalan Foundation, a women's NGO, in conjunction with various Spanish universities and the catholic Universidad Rafael Landívar (Rafael Landívar University). According to my Guatemalan interviewees, the alliance *sui generis* with a Catholic university was an alternative strategy in a context where the public university was lost during the war and converted into a mediocre and authoritarian space that did not offer the possibility for new and progressive approaches. At the start of 2003,

FLACSO-Guatemala began its own program, a graduate degree in gender studies, with a multicultural focus, developed especially for members of women's organizations with the intention of strengthening their education and linking their experiences as militants with theoretical reflections.

Prior to that, in 2001, FLACSO-Guatemala organized the first *"Encuentro Mesoamericano de Estudios de Género"* (Mesoamerican Gathering on Gender Studies), coordinated by Walda Barrios-Klee, which attracted over 1,000 academics and activists from Central America and beyond. The success of this Encuentro, whose objective was to assess the "state of the art" for gender studies in the region, demonstrated the extent of the field's development, the acceptance and legitimacy that it had achieved, as well as the possibilities for dialogue between social movements and the various faces of academic feminism (Barrios-Klee 2002).

In El Salvador, the Jesuit Universidad Centroamericana José Simeón Cañas (Central American University José Simeón Cañas or UCA) made some attempts at creating a degree in gender studies in the early 1990s. Again, the major impetus for these initiatives also originated in a women's organization, *Mujeres por la Dignidad y la Vida* or *Las Dignas* (Women for dignity and life). Starting in 1994, *Las Dignas* initiated the School of Feminist Debate, in an effort to create an educational system with different levels, which has drawn the active participation of hundreds of women. In 1998, *Las Dignas* and other feminist organizations promoted the launch of a graduate degree program in gender relations in conjunction with the University of Girona of Cataluña. In 2004, the organization signed an agreement with the Universidad de El Salvador (University of El Salvador) for the creation of a Center for Gender Studies established by the President's office, which offered a diploma in gender and education.

In Honduras, the first center, the Centro de Estudios de la Mujer–Honduras (Center for Women's Studies–Honduras or CEM–H) was founded by the women's movement in 1987, including a group of feminist academics that had not found a suitable atmosphere within the University to develop their activities. Since that time, it has produced some of the most relevant gender research in the country. Also, at the Universidad Nacional Autónoma de Honduras (National Autonomous University of Honduras or UNAH), the Latin American Graduate Program in Social Work has become a prominent force by incorporating material on gender relations into its curriculum. Starting in 2000, the Universidad Pedagógica Nacional Francisco Morazán (National Pedagogy University Francisco Morazán) established a Diploma and a Master's in Gender and Education, with the help of the Canadian International Cooperation Agency and other international organizations, truly institutionalizing these studies within the Hondurean university system.

In Nicaragua, as previously mentioned, the Sandinista Revolution helped create a space within civil society where women's organizations played a critical role in the process of social transformation, which also facilitated the development of social research on women and gender inequality. Within the university setting, the Catholic affiliated Universidad Centroamericana (Central American University or UCA) is a pioneer in the field. With support from the Spanish Cooperation Agency and the Ford Foundation, UCA developed a Master's in Gender and Development, which was established through the joint efforts of university administrators and women's organizations. Also since 1988, the Universidad Autónoma de Nicaragua (Autonomous University of Nicaragua or UNAN) created a women's studies program that coordinated various activities including training, debates, and seminars dedicated to the discussion of problems faced by women during the pre- and post-war period.

In Panama, the Workshop on Women's Studies gave birth to the Interdisciplinary Commission of Women's Studies at the University of Panama in 1987. After a long struggle with the university, feminist academics finally received institutional recognition through the establishment of the Institute for Women (Instituto de la Mujer de la Universidad de Panamá or IMUP) in 1995. By 1999, the Institute offered two degrees: one in Domestic Violence and a Master's in Gender and Development, partially backed by international support (Pan American Health Organization and the European Community).

During the second half of the 1990s, women's and gender studies solidified their institutional standing in Central American universities. In this period, in addition to securing a prestigious, recognized, and regionally accredited Master's in Women's Studies (UCR–UNA), other programs were created at the Institute of Women Studies at the National University of Costa Rica, the Center for Women's Studies Research at the University of Costa Rica (formerly Programa Interdisciplinario de Estudios del Género, PRIEG), the Institute of Women's Studies at the University of Panama, and the Interdisciplinary Gender Studies Program at UCA–Nicaragua. These institutions developed systematic activities in teaching, research, and outreach, and were also in charge of supporting the victims of sexual harassment at the university.

The process of institutionalization also has resulted in the production of Presidents' reports about the State of Gender Equality at the Universidad de Costa Rica (2001 and 2007), Universidad de Panamá (2002), and Universidad Nacional de Costa Rica (2008). In the first report about the University of Costa Rica, the President, Dr. Gabriel Macaya, states: "I understand this assessment as an instrument that can allow us, throughout the university community, to . . . revise sexist practices and beliefs anchored in the past, and thus to agree on action towards change and the search for social justice (Rectoría Universidad de Costa Rica 2001: 7).

CURRENT TRENDS IN WOMEN'S AND GENDER STUDIES

In the field of feminist studies, Costa Rica stands out for several reasons. First, it is the Central American country where social, economic, and political conditions have best fostered the development of these studies in academic settings. Second, Costa Rican academics have researched topics that were rarely investigated in other countries of the region, such as women's literature, magic and witchcraft, abortion, and female and male subjectivities and identities. Last, since the 1990s, Costa Rica has produced more than 50 percent of all the Central American research papers, and the majority of the academic publications on women and gender topics, primarily due to the better material conditions that its universities and other sites of academic production had enjoyed (Aguilar 1995; González 1997). After the consolidation of women's studies as a recognized university discipline, Costa Rican research in this field became ample and diverse. Just between 1995 and 2000, Mirta González (2007) detected more than 350 studies and publications, including books, articles, and graduate theses.

Given the diversity of published research in Costa Rica, our analysis of the current trends in women's and gender studies must be selective. We chose the included works based on two criteria. First, we primarily discuss studies in the social sciences published since 1995. The works that appeared earlier were mentioned only if they were very relevant or they had a significant impact in the construction of knowledge. Second, only published

studies with an open feminist standpoint or using gender as the principal category of analysis were included. In the remainder of this section, we cover research on history, human rights, violence against women, citizenship rights and political participation, economic inequalities, female and male identities, masculinities, and migration.

One of the most important developments in feminist studies since the 1990s has been in the field of *history*. Eugenia Rodríguez (2002b) states, paraphrasing a statement by Asunción Lavrin, that writing women's history is a vital task because "history gives us the memory of what has been done and what needs to be done" (202). Feminist historians engaged in two fundamental tasks—rescuing the memory and the voice of women from invisibility and uncovering how gender-based power relations have been constructed in Costa Rica.

Recent historical studies have covered a wide range of topics in their attempt to demonstrate the long trajectory of women's participation in the public sphere, such as in independence movements, civil wars, social and revolutionary movements, the suffragist struggles, the expansion of women's education, migratory processes, the ideological redefinition of gender, and the construction of Costa Rican thought (Alvarenga 2005; Barahona 1994; Calvo 1989; Mora 2000; Murillo 1997; Prada 2005; Putnam 2002; Rodríguez 1998, 2002a, 2002b, 2003a). Among these, Grace Prada's (2005) work is worth mentioning because she rescued from oblivion activist women who helped forge women's and feminist thought, and laid a foundation for the democratic lifestyle that has characterized Costa Rican society.

In the realm of historical feminist studies, research on women's participation in the labor force, especially in urban areas, stands out, including the works of Iván Molina and Steven Palmer (2000) about the endengering of educational training, and those of Virginia Mora (2003) on urban women's social and labor participation in the 1920s. This was a critical period when the female population amplified its presence in the public sphere, which, according to the author, compelled women to question their place in society and to struggle for a redefinition of citizenship that subsequently led to the suffragist movement.

Another interesting research area is on the particularities of Costa Rican family history. These studies have helped to demystify the presumed stability and harmony within the family, and revealed the violent and abusive relationships that can be found within this institution. Other family studies have addressed the changing models of family, marriage and gender relations in the private sphere, as well as the ways in which women have resisted tradional patterns of family organization, and confronted different manifestations of violence (Rodríguez 2000, 2003b, 2006).

In Costa Rica, there has been an important push to do research on the various issues related to *women's human rights*. Some of the contributions in this area have analyzed how patriarchal law has supported the gender structure; a structure that is, at the same time, maintained and supported by the juridical system, which excludes women and denies them their rights as citizens who are endowed with a whole range of human rights. In this area, the pioneering work of Alda Facio (1992) *Cuando el género suena cambios trae* (When gender is brought to the fore, it brings change) and other feminist studies are directed toward democratizing the law and counteracting the discriminatory mechanisms built into the patriarcal juridical system (Arroyo 2003; Calvo 1993; Caravaca and Guzmán 1995).

Another prominent area of research in Costa Rica has been *violence against women*, since violence has been identified as one of the major problems in Central American societies. Feminist research has clearly responded to social demands, particularly from the women's movement and studies have revealed its different manisfestations, and offered the critical elements needed for theoretical and methodological reflection, which can bring a better understanding of the magnitude and effects of such a complex problem. The seminal works of Edda Quirós and Olga Barrantes (1994) and Cecilia Claramunt (1997) about domestic violence, as well as those of Gioconda Batres (1997) on incest, and Ana Carcedo and Karin Verbaken (1995) on the different manifestations of violence against women in the Central American context are noteworthy.

In addition, innovative studies have introduced new perspectives to deal with the issue of violence against women. For example, a study sponsored by the Panamerican Health Organization examined the path followed by women who endured intrafamily violence, yielding a model for responding to the health needs of battered women in all Central American countries (Carcedo and Zamora 1999; Sagot and Carcedo 2000). Also, in Costa Rica, the first research on femicide was conducted, which helped clarify the different scenarios, deeply determined by gender, in which men and women are murdered (Carcedo and Sagot 2002).

During the last few years, this problem has led to studies about particular forms of violence against women, such as commercial sexual exploitation of children and different forms of child abuse, sponsored by international agencies such as UNICEF and the International Labor Organization (Claramunt 1998; Claramunt and Pardo 2006; Sagot 1999). The participation of United Nations' agencies represents an important factor in the production of knowledge on violence against women and girls. They developed collaborative agreements with universities in order to produce high quality research, enhanced by the theoretical and methodological foundations generated within the academy.

Finally, as part of the most recent efforts,

there are analyses of public policies and social responses to violence. Some of this work involves the analysis of laws, the ways in which states and international agencies face the problem of violence, and how violence against women affects the security of the citizenry and denies their rights. One of the main conclusions is that there has been progress, but that the states are not capable—and many times do not even have the will—to guarantee women a life free of violence (Arroyo 2003; Carcedo 2006; Carcedo and Molina 2003; Ramellini 2003; Sagot 2006).

Yet, there have been important studies that document the process of women asserting their *citizenship rights*, and the obstacles they face in their ascent to elective posts and other spaces of political participation. This tradition started early in Costa Rica with the publication of Ana Sojo's 1985 book, *Mujer y política: Ensayo sobre el feminismo y el sujeto popular* (Women and politics: an essay on feminism and the popular subject). In this text, and consonant with the popular insurrections in Central America during that period, Sojo (1985) studies the relationship between women's liberation struggles and those of other actors. She argues that the "popular subject," a category frequently used by Marxists during this period, is a heterogeneous subject, and that asymmetrical power relations are deployed in a vast field of relations that go beyond the economic.

Similarly, Elsa Moreno Cárdenas (1995) published a study that documented the political participation of women in the State's power circles, in political parties, and in social and women's organizations in Costa Rica. At the Central American regional level, the research conducted by the Programa Regional La Corriente (1997; La Corriente Regional Program) on the process of constructing Central American women's movements was an important landmark. In particular, the study on Costa Rica carried out by Lorena Camacho and Lorena Flores (1997) characterized the women's and feminist movements, as well as the diverse expressions and modalities of organizing adopted in the country. The authors conclude that the second half of the 1980s was a key period in the construction of the Costa Rican women's movement, evidenced by the emergence of new organizations and, in general, a greater presence of women in the public sphere.

The process of reforming the Electoral Code to incorporate compulsory political participation quotas, promoting women's access to decision-making posts (1990–1999), generated a new line of research on the so-called politics of differentiation toward equality. Notable in this area are the works of Rosalía Camacho, Silvia Lara, and Ester Serrano (1996) on the minimum quotas of women's participation as tools of affirmative action, as well as the assessments carried out by Rosalía Camacho (1998) and Isabel Torres (2001) regarding the effectiveness of the mechanisms that were being incorporated into the Costa Rican political system to guarantee representational parity of women in decision-making posts.

Some of the literature produced on this theme includes the book *Un siglo de luchas femeninas en América Latina* (A century of feminist struggles in Latin America), edited by Eugenia Rodríguez (2002a), which is a selection of papers presented and discussed at the 1999 International Congress on the 50 Years Before and the 50 Years After the Conquest of the Women's Vote in Costa Rica: 1900–1999, and the anthology *Las mujeres y el poder* (Women and power) edited by Linda Berrón (1997). Women's participation in local governments is another important theme that is exemplified in Lily Quesada's works on the presence of women in constructing local development agendas (1998b), and her compilation of life stories of women leaders in different urban communities (1998a) also stands out.

In the last few years, collective efforts were

made to analyze the experiences of women who participate in traditional political spaces (Cobo et al. 2002) as well as the construction of new leadership and a political culture among women (Camacho, Martínez and Robert 2003; Díaz et al. 2006). Lastly, Costa Rican feminists have examined women's contributions to important contemporary social struggles, such as the one against capitalist globalization, and the construction of a democratic society that takes into consideration the goals of sustainable human development (Escalante Herrera 2001).

The activities that preceded the Fourth Women's World Conference (Beijing 1995) led to an important process of knowledge construction on the impact of structural adjustment and economic inequality among women in the region. Several pioneer research initiatives were undertaken on such topics as democratization, Central American development and integration (Fletcher and Renzi 1995), poverty (Pérez and Pichardo 1995), and Central American families (Fauné 1995). These studies inaugurated a new line of research on the impact of the different macrostructural processes in the organization of gender relations, and women's economic and social rights.

Among the most important works dealing with this theme are Wim Dierckxsens's (1999) analysis on the impact of structural adjustment among Costa Rican women workers, and an anthology of studies on women's employment within the context of globalization (Garita et al. 2000), carried out by the Women's Forum for Central American Integration. Similarly, the process of signing a Central America–U.S. Free Trade Agreement has generated a series of studies that depict economic conditions in Costa Rica in the context of free trade from a gender perspective (Pérez Echeverría 2005; Trejos 2006).

Finally, the social and labor conditions of women within the so-called "new economy" have been analyzed by other researchers, a few of them associated with the Women's Economic Agenda Regional Program of the United Nations. They conclude that the future of this new economy increasingly lies in the hands of women, but they are still facing major conditions of inequality in a context characterized by the absence of protective mechanisms or social policies that promote their welfare (Flórez-Estrada 2007; Martínez Franzoni 2008).

Another important area of feminist research has been the construction of female and male *gender identities*. In this area, scholars have explored the construction of gender throughout Costa Rican history, and gender relations within specific contexts, such as at the workplace or in sports. Among the important studies that provide a historical perspective are Carmen Murillo's (1997) work on the culture of men who participated in railroad construction in nineteenth-century Costa Rica, Alfonso González's (2005) writings on men and women during the postwar period, Roxana Hidalgo's (2004) research on nineteenth- and early twentieth-century women in the public sphere, and the writings of Mercedes González (2007) on the construction of women's madness in Costa Rica during the early twentieth century.

Examples of the construction of identitites in specific contexts are found in Carlos Sandoval's studies about maquiladora assembly line workers and construction workers (2007), and on how soccer can produce national identities based on exhaulting a hegemonic, xenophobic, and racist masculinity (2006), as well as in Roxana Hidalgo and Laura Chacón's study (2001) on conceptions of maternity and the construction of women's identity among those women accused of infanticide.

The topic of identities leads to a very important line of research about *masculinities*. These studies have been conducted primarily by men, but in most cases reflect a feminist theoretical framework and standpoint. Titles such as *El género es también asunto de hombres; reflexiones sobre la masculinidad patriarcal y la construcción de una masculinidad con equidad de género* (Gender is also an issue for men: Reflections on patriarchal masculinity and the construction of a masculinity with gender equity) by Gustavo Briceño and Edgar Chacón (2001), and *¿Son posibles otras masculinidades?: supuestos teóricos e implicaciones políticas de las propuestas sobre masculinidad* (Are other masculinities possible?: Theoretical notions and political implications of propositions about masculinity) by Mauricio Menjívar (2004) illustrate the research trends in this area.

In work on masculinities in Costa Rica, several studies have been useful in bringing a comprehensive view of the Central American region, and in providing comparative analyses among the different nations that constitute it. The most important publications with a regional perspective include the book, *Masculinidades en Centro América* (Masculinities in Central America) edited by Alvaro Campos and José Manuel Salas (2002), and their study *Explotación sexual comercial y masculinidad: un estudio regional cualitativo con hombres de la población general* (Commercial sexual exploitation and masculinity: A qualitative regional study with men of the general population) (2004). Lastly, several important studies about paternity have provided valuable information about male experiences, beliefs, and practices as they relate to human reproduction and sexual roles (Menjívar 2002; Rivera and Ceciliano 2004; Valladares 2006).

In Central America, the armed conflicts, conditions of extreme poverty, and increased inequalities among countries, have generated conditions of considerable vulnerability and social exclusion that have pushed millions of people into *migration*. Women are not secondary subjects in these processes; on the contrary, they have become actors in their own right. Because of the better economic and political conditions in Costa Rica, the country has become an important receiver of Central American immigration, especially from Nicaragua. This has led to important research analyzing sex differences in the migratory process. Among the topics studied are the experiences of women adolescents in Nicaraguan migration to Costa Rica (Cranshaw and Morales 1998); the vulnerability and violence faced by women involved in these processes (Loría 2007), the experiences of immigrants in the sexual tourism networks (Rivers-Moore 2007), and the hypersexualization of Nicaraguan immigrants in the construction of difference and otherness within Costa Rican society (Masís and Paniagua 2007).

Finally, in Costa Rica there are other areas that have been researched from a feminist perspective that have had a significant impact in the construction of knowledge about women and gender relations. Among these areas are education (Mirta González 1990), women's literature (Cubillo 2001; Macaya 1992), communication (Aguilar and Picado 2004; Córdoba and Faerron 1997), magic and witchcraft (Brenes and Zapparoli 1991), and sexual work and prostitution (Gamboa 2006; Marín 2007; Schifter 1997). A review of the major trends in the most recent feminist studies produced in Costa Rica cannot conclude without mentioning the anthology *The Costa Rican Women's Movement: A Reader* (1997), edited by Ilse A. Leitenger, which brought together academics and activists for the first time in one single text to offer a panoramic view of the diverse manifestations of feminism and the women's movement in the country. Even though the text was published only in English, it continues to be a mandatory reference for anyone interested in learning about the particularities of feminist political and academic activism in Costa Rica, since the volume includes the voices of the founding members of the main women's organizations, of activists, artists, and all the scholars that at the time had made some contribution to the development of women's studies in Costa Rica.

RELATIONS IN DISPUTE

Women's studies within the university environment reflects the connections between feminism as a political movement and as an academic manifestation. In this sense, despite the limitations, gender and women's studies programs in Central America have become a kind of "academic arm" of the feminist movement. In some cases, as already outlined, the creation of academic spaces was promoted by women's organizations outside the universities. Different from other academic projects, these programs attempted to eliminate the separation between theory and practice and, even with some limitations and difficulties, also have tried to maintain a commitment to the process of social transformation.

The existence of these programs represents a major challenge to the university and to the traditional ways social research is conducted. Their very presence within the universities of the region has changed the traditional forms of inquiry, the topics that are addressed, and the worldviews that are privileged.

As part of this process, Central American women began to tell their own stories, a process with strong inherent political connotations, involving implicit and explicit epistemological critiques of the social conventions and themes of traditional scientific research. At the same time, daily life experiences, which were previously excluded from scientific research, have been transformed into a field of inquiry that provides the necessary elements for the construction of alternative theories and interpretations regarding social life. However, when women's studies is situated in academic spaces it is always a territory in dispute. On the one hand, it is confronted by those at the university who accuse academic feminists of not being scientific or objective and of producing ideology in place of scientific knowledge. On the other hand, the feminist movement, on many occasions, reproaches academics at the universities for enjoying the rewards of academic privilege. Furthermore, movement members discuss the possibility of cooptation of women's studies by the university's institutional system, as well as the potential loss of feminist principles, accusing academics of taking more from the feminist movement than they give in return.

Questions arise regarding how and where academics are situated when they write the results of their research, and how they can present the voices of people they have studied without distorting, exploiting, or using them for their own benefit. Because it is clear that even if someone maintains a strong political and ethical commitment to feminism as a movement of social transformation, when researchers access the lives of women this, in turn, contributes significantly to the prestige they enjoy in the academic world, resulting from their research (Lincoln 1995).

In relation to the construction of studies analyzing women and gender relations in Central America, it is important to point out that given the nearly total invisibility of the female population in prior scientific work, in the beginning, it seemed like it was enough to just define "women" and their conditions as the objects of study. However, this resulted in "women" being treated as a homogenous population, stationary in time and space. Furthermore, many times, it was implied that since feminist researchers share some social and cultural characteristics with other women, they had the ability to fully understand their realities and speak for any woman in almost the same voice, without distortion. In other words, included in the premise, but not explicitly stated, was the idea that feminist researchers were "insiders" in any women's group and therefore could understand their reality, as if women's realities were unified or analogous.

Moreover, the essentialism that these positions entail raise the question of who speaks for whom, or how we situate ourselves as researchers in relation to the women we are studying and their lives. This is a common problem for every researcher faced with a social group they do not belong to (Olesen 2000). Nevertheless, within the field of women's and gender studies in the region, this frequent problem is overlooked and has not been sufficiently discussed or openly presented as a situation demanding constant attention and vigilance.

Additionally, in Central America, academics have only begun to incorporate criteria acknowledging differences based on race, class, age, religion and sexual orientation into research and university coursework. This only has been addressed as part of a formal discourse and an abstract discussion, yet not through integration or the utilization of these elements as analytical or explanatory factors. There is, in this sense, a tendency towards a discursive and real exclusion of the experiences of black women, indigenous women, older women, lesbians, and even girls. In fact, within academic spaces, themes related to the experiences of black, younger, or indigenous women have only begun to be addressed recently (Careaga and Campbell 2002; Loría 2000; Sagot 2004).

FEMINISM AS A SOCIAL MOVEMENT AND WOMEN'S STUDIES

With the purpose of analyzing the relationship between feminism as a social movement and women's studies as its academic branch, Sonia Alvarez's (1998) definition of feminism as "a discursive field of intervention/action" becomes very useful. According to Alvarez, more than a social movement, in the classical sense, which entails massive manifestations in the street, mobilizations, etc., the feminist movement is more a "political domain," extending beyond organizations and groups.

Alvarez (1988) also argues that feminists, who are scattered throughout that political domain, constantly engage, not just in "traditionally political" battles, but also in disputes over meanings or in discursive battles, such as the definitions of citizenship, development, or human rights. Furthermore, women who act within the feminist domain relate with each other in a variety of public, private and alternative spaces, using a variety of methods and modes of communication.

On the other hand, within the Central American region one can identify, at least, four different groups of people that participate in the field of women's and gender studies: the "pioneers," who studied about women and their conditions before the formal development and institutionalization of these type of studies; the "ideologues," in a Gramscian sense, dedicated to women's and gender studies due to their relationship with feminism as a social movement; the "latecomers," who are not yet familiar with the history and the political and academic process of feminism; and those who "joined the bandwagon," because women's and gender studies appear in fashion, are useful for their careers and for economic benefits.[4] According to my interviewees, some Central American feminists call the last group "gender workers."

In other words, not every person dedicated to women's and gender studies can be considered a participant in the feminist domain. And this is one of the most important critiques made by feminists who develop their practice in spaces outside the university. Because of those different points of reference and positions, at times it is difficult to build a true community of knowledge production in order to confront the misogynist and disqualifying attacks that occur within universities.

In that sense, aside from facing critiques from activists within civil society, academics also face criticisms within their university. As part of this "backlash," particularly since women's studies was institutionalized and consolidated in universities, misogynist men have found allies in some women academics who claim they are using a "gendered perspective," but dedicate themselves to discrediting and questioning feminist studies and scholars who do it.

For example, in Central American universities some researchers have challenged the findings and conclusions regarding domestic violence, by presenting facts about the supposed benefits obtained by women in violent relationships or their level of psychological violence against men; or about the supposed culpability of women in fostering irresponsible fathers, as a form of vengeance against men who do not want to commit or get married to them.

In spite of the conflicts and contradictions, feminists outside of the university setting have recognized the contributions of those dedicated to women's studies and gender relations within the academy. According to these feminists, academics help legitimate many feminist battles by bringing university support and the added value of scientific knowledge, methods, and techniques. In other words, academic research carried out at the university has developed empirical evidence showing the fairness of feminist political demands.

In addition, the existence of formal women's studies programs legitimate those who have studied, debated and developed a feminist perspective for years, yet without academic support. As some Guatemalan and El Salvadoran interviewees described, many women within the feminist movement need diplomas and academic certificates to participate in the work world, and women's and gender studies programs at the universities have aided this process. Many women within the feminist movement needed the theories and methodological support available at the university in order to improve their education and enable them to integrate their experiences as activists with theory.

In the opinion of the activists interviewed, the development and formalization of women's and gender studies has allowed for a deeper level of systemization of existing information, providing theoretical backing to ideas already outlined by the feminist movement. As one of the interviewed activists said, with the presence of academics in different political spaces and by incorporating them into the struggle, the feminist movement achieves a stronger and more grounded approach to the issues and, therefore, gains credibility. In this sense, this relationship with the academy has offered the feminist movement a stronger interlocutory capacity to interact with other sectors, particularly with the state and international agencies, since feminist academics are regarded as "experts." In other words, they convey a message to society that women's and gender studies and, therefore feminists' demands, have social legitimacy since they are recognized as areas of knowledge within the university.

Despite the acknowledgement of these valuable contributions, feminists outside the university also outline a series of important criticisms. In the first place, according to the activists interviewed, there is not an articulated connection or an explicit relationship between academics and the movement, since the moments of convergence are determined by particular political conjunctures, and not by long-term strategic alliances. From this perspective, minus a few exceptions, as in the case of *Las Dignas* and the University of El Salvador, there are no organic linkages between academic programs and feminist organizations. The existing linkages are mostly among specific persons, which makes those ties weak and temporary.

According to the interviewed activists, the majority of people dedicated to women's or gender studies are not involved in the political activities of the movement, with the exception of "the ideologues," who currently represent a minority. As a result, there is a rift between academic knowledge and political action. In addition, there are not sufficient spaces for encounters between academics and activists to share cumulative knowledge, since many academic spaces are elitist and remain isolated from the realities of everyday life, not only from the women's movement, but also from women in general.

Also, a significant portion of the research carried out by academics is not articulated with the agendas of non-governmental women's organizations or with public policy for gender equality. According to the interviewed activists, women's organizations and their struggles are seldom transformed into topics of relevant academic research. As a consequence, many scholars are not familiar with the activities of the feminist movement, their organizations, their history, their struggles, or their leaders. As one interviewee stated, "We are not asking that academics become activists, but to ignore the movement and its struggles is an atrocity." For this reason, many of the interviewees argue that academic spaces take more from the feminist movement than they give back, since there is no intentionality to build joint political action to pursue feminist goals in society at large.

Finally, according to the activists, women's studies programs and particularly the so-called "gender equality" programs have experienced a de-politicization. In these spaces, the concept of gender has lost its explanatory capacity, as a result of less rigorous use and, in some cases, has actually been presented as an alternative approach to feminism. Therefore, many programs embedded in the university have lost a feminist commitment and inspiration and have forgotten the objective of building a better world for women and for humanity in general.

CONCLUDING REMARKS

From the previous perspective, women's and gender studies in academic spaces have been transformed into a territory of conflict. On the one hand, they have to face critiques from inside universities and from conservative sectors. On the other hand, despite the recognition made by activists of the important contributions of those programs situated within universities, many activists are also staunch critics of these programs, accusing those involved of simply being "academics" or elitists. Although these critiques have a concrete base and constitute a serious challenge to the development of programs at Central American universities, it also means that academics have to deal with the attacks from those who are supposed to be their main allies and the very reason for the existence of women's studies academic programs.

Regardless of the challenges and difficulties, women's studies in university settings within Central America continues to be an important strategy for promoting the production of knowledge from a women's perspective and for transforming traditional constructions of scientific knowledge. In fact, these programs have contributed to the production of less falsified, partial, and perverse narratives and representations of social reality and of women's participation in constructing that reality. The contributions of women's studies to all areas of inquiry have provided a different reading of the past and present in the Central American region. Despite existing gaps or the criticism they have generated, the field also has helped problematize traditional ways of doing research, to rescue the historical memory of women, and to unveil realities that had been hidden by the sexist regime.

However, the tension between the academy and the feminist movement persists. The old belief about the possible cooptation of women's studies by the academic *doxa* continues, as does the old belief that women's and gender studies are trivial, lack objectivity, or are too radicalized for the university setting. Regardless of the limitations posed by academic institutions in studying the realities of women and in the development of a political feminist project, I continue to believe in the revolutionary potential of the feminist academics' world vision, as part of a historically oppressed group (Sagot 1994). In this sense, within Central American universities these programs, although characterized by privilege, continue to be fundamental spaces for the creation of alternative knowledge about women and gender relations in order to support the construction of a feminist utopia.

NOTES

Authors' Note: We wish to thank Edna Acosta-Belén for her generous help in the translation and revision of several sections of the chapter.

Editors' Note: This article was translated from the original Spanish version by Edna Acosta-Belén, with Jacqueline Hayes.

1. Key informants include: Walda Barrios-Klee, FLACSO, Guatemala; Lorena Camacho, Las Panchas, Costa Rica; Ana Carcedo, CEFEMINA, Costa Rica; Almachiara D'Angelo, MUSAVIA, Nicaragua; Gilda Parducci, Las Dignas, El Salvador; Margarita Puerto, Universidad Pedagógica Nacional "Francisco Morazán," Honduras; Daysi Flores, Red de Mujeres Jóvenes de Honduras (Young Women's Network–Honduras); and Urania Ungo, University of Panamá.

2. The exception are some studies carried out in Costa Rica on violence between partners, sexuality, and abortion, and some studies on the productive and reproductive role of women in Nicaragua (Vázquez 2001).

3. Among the most prominent names are Helen I. Safa, Sara Sharrat, Lourdes Benería, Helga Jiménez, Ana Falú, María Luisa Tarrés, and Ilse Leitenger.

4. This classification is based on findings of Catharine R. Stimpson (1998) for the United States, with some modifications in order to apply it to the Central American reality.

REFERENCES

Aguilar, Ana Leticia (1995) "Investigaciones sobre la mujer en Centroamérica," *Malabares* 2: 3–7.

Aguilar, Thaís and Hilda Picado (2004) *Un buen trato a los malos tratos periodísticos*, San José, Costa Rica: Centro de Investigación en Estudios de la Mujer–Servicio de Noticias de la Mujer (SEM).

Alvarenga, Patricia (2005) *De vecinos a ciudadanos. Movimientos comunales y luchas cívicas en la historia contemporánea de Costa Rica*, San José, Costa Rica: Editorial de la Universidad de Costa Rica–Editorial de la Universidad Nacional.

Alvarez, Sonia (1998) "Feminismos Latinoamericanos," *Estudos Feministas* 6, 2: 265–284.

Arroyo, Roxana (2003) *Aplicabilidad de la normativa sobre violencia contra la mujer en Centroamérica: un análisis comparado para América Central*, Heredia, Costa Rica: Publicaciones Universidad Nacional.

Barahona, Macarena (1994) *Las sufragistas de Costa Rica*, San José, Costa Rica: Editorial de la Universidad de Costa Rica.

Barrios-Klee, Walda (2002) "Los avatares de los estudios de género y la posibilidad de un feminismo plural" in G. Careaga (ed.) *Feminismos contemporáneos: retos y perspectivas*, México: Programa Universitario de Estudios de Género (PUEG–UNAM).

Batres, Gioconda (1997) *Del ultraje a la esperanza: tratamiento de las secuelas del incesto*, San José, Costa Rica: Instituto Latinoamericano de Naciones Unidas para la Prevención del Delito (ILANUD).

Berrón, Linda (ed.) (1997) *Las mujeres y el poder*, San José, Costa Rica: Editorial Mujeres.

Brenes, May and Mayra Zapparoli (1991) *De que vuelan, vuelan . . .! Un análisis de la magia y la brujería en Costa Rica*, San José, Costa Rica: Editorial Costa Rica.

Briceño, Gustavo and Edgar Chacón (2001) *El género también es asunto de hombres: reflexiones sobre la masculinidad patriarcal y la construcción de una masculinidad con equidad de género*, San José, Costa Rica: Unión Mundial para la Naturaleza (UICN).

Burgos, Elizabeth (1983) *Me llamo Rigoberto Menchú y así me nació la conciencia*, Havana, Cuba: Casa de las Américas.

Calvo, Yadira (1989) *Ángela Acuña, forjadora de estrellas*, San José, Costa Rica: Editorial Costa Rica.

—— (1993) *Las líneas torcidas del derecho*, San José, Costa Rica: Instituto Latinoamericano de Naciones Unidas para la Prevención del Delito (ILANUD).

Camacho, Lorena, and Lorena Flores (1997) "Un movimiento de mujeres en desarrollo.Costa Rica" in Programa Regional La Corriente (ed.) *Movimiento de mujeres en Centroamérica*, Managua, Nicaragua: Centro Editorial de la Mujer.

Camacho, Rosalía (1998) *Sintonizando la conciencia, el voto y los puestos de decisión. Las mujeres y la política en Costa Rica*, San José, Costa Rica: Fundación Arias para la Paz y el Progreso Humano.

Camacho, Rosalía, Silvia Lara and Ester Serrano (1996) *Las cuotas mínimas de participación de las mujeres: un mecanismo de acción afirmativa. Aportes para la discusión*, San José, Costa Rica: Centro Nacional para el Desarrollo de la Mujer y la Familia.

Camacho, Rosalía, Juliana Martínez and Anne Robert (2003) *Mujeres en movimiento: liderazgos transformadores para construir buenos gobiernos en Centroamérica*, San José, Costa Rica: Editorial de la Universidad Estatal a Distancia.

Campos, Alvaro and José Manuel Salas (eds.) (2002) *Masculinidades en Centro América*, San José, Costa Rica: Instituto Costarricense de Masculinidad, Pareja y Sexualidad.

—— (2004) *Explotación sexual comercial y masculinidad: un estudio regional cualitativo con hombres de la población general*, San José, Costa Rica: Organización Internacional del Trabajo (OIT).

Caravaca, Adilia and Laura Guzmán (1995) *Violencia de género, derechos humanos y democratización: perspectiva de las mujeres*, San José, Costa Rica: Programa de Naciones Unidas para el Desarrollo (PNUD).

Carcedo, Ana (2006) *Seguridad ciudadana de las mujeres y desarrollo humano*, Cuadernos de Desarrollo Humano No. 2, San José, Costa Rica: Programa de Naciones Unidas para el Desarrollo (PNUD).

Carcedo, Ana and Giselle Molina (2003) *Mujeres contra la violencia, una rebelión radical*, San José, Costa Rica: Embajada Real de los Países Bajos–CEFEMINA.

Carcedo, Ana and Montserrat Sagot (2002) *Femicidio en Costa Rica, 1990–1999*, San José, Costa Rica: Instituto Nacional de las Mujeres–Organización Panamericana de la Salud.

Carcedo, Ana and Karin Verbaken (1995) *La paz comienza en casa: la violencia contra las mujeres en Centroamérica y la cooperación holandesa*, San José, Costa Rica: Centro Feminista de Información y Acción (CEFEMINA).

Carcedo, Ana and Alicia Zamora (1999) *Ruta crítica de las mujeres afectadas por la violencia intrafamiliar en Costa Rica*, San José, Costa Rica: Organización Panamericana de la Salud.

Careaga, Gloria (2002) "Los estudios feministas en América Latina y el Caribe" in G. Careaga (ed.) *Feminismos contemporáneos: retos y perspectivas*, México: Programa Universitario de Estudios de Género (PUEG–UNAM).

Careaga, Gloria and Epsy Campbell (eds.) (2002) *Poderes cuestionados: sexismo y racismo en América Latina*, San José, Costa Rica: Fondo de Naciones Unidas para las Mujeres (UNIFEM).

CIERA (Centro de Investigaciones y Estudios de la Reforma Agraria) (1984) *La feminización de la fuerza de trabajo asalariada en el agro y sus implicaciones en la producción, reproducción y organización sindical*, Managua, Nicaragua: CIERA.

Claramunt, Cecilia (1997) *Casitas quebradas: el problema de la violencia doméstica en Costa Rica*, San José, Costa Rica: Editorial de la Universidad Estatal a Distancia.

—— (1998) *Explotación sexual en Costa Rica: análisis de la ruta crítica de niños, niñas y adolescentes hacia la prostitución*, San José, Costa Rica: Fondo de Naciones Unidas para la Infancia (UNICEF).

Claramunt, Cecilia and Rogelio Pardo (2006) *Explotación sexual comercial de niños, niñas y adolescentes: del compromiso a la acción*, San José, Costa Rica. Organización Internacional del Trabajo (OIT).

Cobo, Rosa, Alda Facio and Margarita Penón (2002) *La política sí es asunto de mujeres: testimonios y reflexiones en torno a la participación política de las mujeres*, San José, Costa Rica: Fundecooperación.

Córdoba, Ligia and Ana Lucía Faerron (1997) "Comunicación con perspectiva de género: escuchando voces de mujeres," *Revista de Ciencias Sociales* 76: 111–117.

Cranshaw, Marta and Abelardo Morales (1998) *Mujeres adolescentes y migración entre Nicaragua y Costa Rica*, San José, Costa Rica: Facultad Latinoamericana de Ciencias Sociales (FLACSO).

Cubillo, Ruth (2001) *Mujeres e identidades. Las escritoras del Repertorio Americano (1919–1959)*, San José, Costa Rica: Editorial de la Universidad de Costa Rica.

Diaz, Cecilia, Ana F. Torres and Lily Quesada (2006) *Pensar la cultura política desde las mujeres*, San José, Costa Rica: Centro de Estudios y Publicaciones Alforja.

Dierckxsens, Wim (1999) "El impacto del ajuste estructural sobre las mujeres trabajadoras en Costa Rica" in I. Siu, L. Guzmán and W. Dierckxsens (comp.), *Antología Latinoamericana y del Caribe: Mujer y género. Período 80–90*, Managua, Nicaragua: Universidad Centroamericana.

Escalante Herrera, Ana C. (2001) "La contribución de los movimientos de mujeres contemporáneos a la construcción de la democracia costarricense: mirando hacia el futuro" in J. Rovira Mas (ed.) *La democracia de Costa Rica ante el siglo XXI*, San José, Costa Rica: Editorial de la Universidad de Costa Rica.

Facio, Alda (1992) *Cuando el género suena, cambios trae. Una metodología para el análisis de género del fenómeno legal*, San José, Costa Rica: Instituto Latinoamericano.

Fauné, María Angélica (1995) *Mujeres y familias centroamericanas: principales problemas y tendencias*, San José, Costa Rica: PNUD.

Fletcher, Sylvia and María Rosa Renzi (1995) *Democratización, desarrollo e integración Centroamericana: perspectiva de las mujeres*, San José, Costa Rica: PNUD.

Flórez-Estrada, María (2007) *Economía del género. El valor simbólico y económico de las mujeres*, San José, Costa Rica: Editorial de la Universidad de Costa Rica.

Gamboa, Isabel (2006) "Los burdeles de la isla: relaciones erótico-afectivas entre mujeres," *Revista de Ciencias Sociales* 88: 77–85.

García, Ana Isabel and Enrique Gomáriz (1989) *Mujeres*

centroamericanas ante la crisis, la guerra y el proceso de paz, San José, Costa Rica: Facultad Latinoamericana de Ciencias Sociales (FLACSO).

Garita, Nora, Epsy Campbell and Ana Elena Badilla (2000) *Exluidas . . . pobres y desempleadas. Mujeres, empleo e integración centroamericana*, San José, Costa Rica: Fundación Arias para la Paz y el Progreso Humano.

González, Alfonso (2005) *Mujeres y hombres de la posguerra costarricense: (1950–1960)*, San José, Costa Rica: Editorial de la Universidad de Costa Rica.

González, Mercedes (2007) *La construcción cultural de la locura femenina en Costa Rica: 1890–1910*, San José, Costa Rica: Editorial de la Universidad de Costa Rica.

González, Mirta (1977a) *La mujer y el trabajo*, San José, Costa Rica: Escuela de Ciencias del Hombre, Universidad de Costa Rica.

—— (1977b) "La mujer en Costa Rica: división del trabajo, salarios y distribución en puestos administrativos," *Revista de Ciencias Sociales* 14: 31–44.

—— (1990) *El sexismo en la educación: la discriminación cotidiana*, San José, Costa Rica: Editorial de la Universidad de Costa Rica.

—— (1997) "Necesidades de investigación en Estudios de la Mujer en Centroamérica," *Actualidades en Psicología* 13: 3–53.

—— (2007) "Producción académica en Estudios de la Mujer (1996–2000)," *Revista de Ciencias Sociales*, Universidad de Costa Rica (In press).

González, Mirta and Laura Guzmán (1998) "Estudios de la Mujer en Costa Rica: de la democracia electoral a la democracia real" in G. Bonder (ed.) *Estudios de la Mujer en América Latina*, Washington, DC: Organización de Estados Americanos.

Hidalgo, Roxana (2004) *Historias de las mujeres en el espacio público en Costa Rica: ante el cambio del siglo XIX al XX*, Cuadernos de Ciencias Sociales No. 132, San José, Costa Rica: Facultad Latinoamericana de Ciencias Sociales (FLACSO).

Hidalgo Roxana and Laura Chacón (2001) *Cuando la feminidad se trastoca en el espejo de la maternidad: conversaciones con mujeres penalizadas por cometer infanticidio, una interpretación psicosocial*, San José, Costa Rica: Editorial de la Universidad de Costa Rica.

Leitenger, Ilse A. (ed.) (1997) *The Costa Rican Women's Movement: A Reader*, Pittsburg, PA: The University of Pittsburg Press.

Lincoln, Ivonna (1995) "Estándares para la investigación cualitativa: criterios emergentes de calidad en la investigación cualitativa-interpretativa," Paper presented at the American Educational Research Association meetings, San Francisco, CA.

López de Piza, Eugenia (1977) "La labor doméstica como fuente importante de valor de plusvalía en los países dependientes," *Revista de Ciencias Sociales* 14: 19–30.

Loría, Rocío (2000) *Complementariedad entre géneros u ocultamiento de la violencia: relatos de mujeres ngäbe de Conte Burica*, San José, Costa Rica: Departamento de Antropología, Universidad de Costa Rica.

—— (2007) "Vulnerabilidad a la violencia en la inmigación: mujeres nicaragüenses y panameñas en el tránsito migratorio hacia Costa Rica" in C. Sandoval (ed.) *El mito roto: inmigración y emigración en Costa Rica*, San José, Costa Rica: Editorial de la Universidad de Costa Rica.

Macaya, Emilia (1992) *Cuando estalla el silencio: para una lectura femenina de textos hispánicos*, San José, Costa Rica: Editorial de la Universidad de Costa Rica.

Marín, Juan José (2007) *Prostitución, honor y cambio cultural en la provincia de San José de Costa Rica: 1860–1949*, San José, Costa Rica. Editorial de la Universidad de Costa Rica.

Martínez Franzoni, Juliana (2008) *Domesticar la incertidumbre en América Latina. Mercado laboral, política social y familias*, San José, Costa Rica: Editorial de la Universidad de Costa Rica.

Masís, Karen and Laura Paniagua (2007) "Chistes sobre nicaragüenses en Costa Rica: barreras simbólicas, mecanismos de control social, constructores de identidad" in C. Sandoval (ed.) *El mito roto: inmigración y emigración en Costa Rica*, San José, Costa Rica: Editorial de la Universidad de Costa Rica.

Menjívar, Mauricio (2002) *Actitudes masculinas hacia la paternidad: entre las contradicciones del mandato y el involucramiento*, Colección Teórica No. 2, San José, Costa Rica: Instituto Nacional de las Mujeres (INAMU).

—— (2004) "¿Son posibles otras masculinidades? supuestos teóricos e implicaciones políticas de las propuestas sobre masculinidad," *Revista Reflexiones* 83, 2: 97–106.

Molina, Iván and Steven Palmer (2000) *Educando a Costa Rica: alfabetización popular, formación docente y género (1880–1950)*, San José, Costa Rica: Editorial Porvenir.

Mora, Virginia (2000) "Mujeres, política y ciudadanía: las reformistas en la campaña electoral de 1923," *Revista de Historia* 38: 115–141.

—— (2003) *Rompiendo mitos y forjando historia: mujeres urbanas y relaciones de género en Costa Rica a inicios del siglo XX*, Alajuela, Costa Rica: Museo Histórico Cultural Juan Santamaría.

Moreno Cárdenas, Elsa (1995) *Mujeres y política en Costa Rica*, San José, Costa Rica: Facultad Latinoamericana de Ciencias Sociales (FLACSO).

Murillo, Carmen (1997) "Hombres, trenes y espacios públicos," *Revista de Ciencias Sociales* 76: 89–105.

Navarro, Marysa and Catharine R. Stimpson (1998)

¿Qué son los Estudios de Mujeres? Argentina: Fondo de Cultura Económica.

Olesen, Virginia (2000) "Feminisms and qualitative research at and into the millennium" in N. K. Denzin and Y. S. Lincoln (eds.) *Handbook of Qualitative Research*, California: Sage Publications.

Palacios, Martha (1999) "Balance de los Estudios de Género en la Universidad Centroamericana" in I. Siu, L. Guzmán and W. Dierckxsens (comp.), *Antología Latinoamericana y del Caribe: Mujer y género. Período 80–90*, Managua, Nicaragua: Universidad Centroamericana.

Pérez, Laura y Arlette Pichardo (1995) *Pobreza en el istmo centroamericano: perspectiva de las mujeres*, San José, Costa Rica: PNUD.

Pérez Echeverría, Laura (2005) *Las mujeres en la agenda económica y la apertura comercial. El caso de Costa Rica*, San José, Costa Rica: PNUD

Prada, Grace (2005) *Mujeres forjadoras del pensamiento costarricense. Ensayos femeninos y feministas*, Heredia, Costa Rica: Editorial Universidad Nacional.

Programa Regional La Corriente (1997) *Movimiento de mujeres en Centroamérica*, Managua, Nicaragua: Centro Editorial de la Mujer.

Putnam, Lara Elizabeth (2002) *Migración, género y etnicidad en el Caribe costarricense (1870–1960)*, San José, Costa Rica: Centro de Investigaciones Históricas de América Central.

Quesada, Lily (1998a) *Historias de vida de mujeres líderes de Alajuelita y Pavas*, San José, Costa Rica: Colectiva Feminista Pancha Carrasco.

—— (1998b) *Mujeres y participación política. Construyendo la agenda local de las mujeres del Cantón de Alajuelita*, San José, Costa Rica: Colectiva Feminista Pancha Carrasco.

Quirós, Edda and Olga Barrantes (1994) *¿Y vivieron felices para siempre? Manifestaciones y efectos en las mujeres de algunas formas de violencia en la vida cotidiana*, San José, Costa Rica: Ministerio de Cultura Juventud y Deportes, Dirección General de Publicaciones.

Ramellini, Teresita (2003) "El posicionamiento de la violencia intrafamiliar como un problema de salud pública" in X. Bustamante (ed.) *100 años de Salud. Costa Rica, siglo XX*, San José, Costa Rica: Organización Panamericana de la Salud.

Randall, Margaret (1980) *Todas estamos despiertas: testimonios de la mujer nicaragüense hoy*, México: Siglo XXI Editores.

Rectoría Universidad de Costa Rica (2001) *Balance de la Equidad de Género en la Universidad de Costa Rica*, San José, Costa Rica: Sección de Publicaciones, Universidad de Costa Rica.

Rivera, Roy and Yajaira Ceciliano (2004) *Cultura, masculinidad y paternidad: las representaciones de los hombres en Costa Rica*, San José, Costa Rica: Facultad Latinoamericana de Ciencias Sociales (FLACSO).

Rivers-Moore, Megan (2007) " 'Son machistas, las tratan mal': masculinidad transnacional comparativa en el turismo sexual" in C. Sandoval (ed.) *El mito roto: inmigración y emigración en Costa Rica*, San José, Costa Rica: Editorial de la Universidad de Costa Rica.

Rodríguez, Eugenia (2000) *Hijas, novias y esposas. Familia, matrimonio y violencia doméstica en el Valle Central de Costa Rica (1750–1850)*, Heredia, Costa Rica: Editorial Universidad Nacional.

—— (2003a) *Dotar de voto político a la mujer*, San José, Costa Rica: Editorial de la Universidad de Costa Rica.

—— (2003b) *Los discursos sobre la familia y las relaciones de género en Costa Rica (1890–1930)*, San José, Costa Rica: Editorial de la Universidad de Costa Rica.

—— (2006) *Divorcio y violencia de pareja en Costa Rica (1800–1950)*, Heredia, Costa Rica: Editorial Universidad Nacional.

—— (ed.) (1998) *Entre silencios y voces: género e historia en América Central (1750–1990)*, San José, Costa Rica: Centro Nacional para el Desarrollo de la Mujer y la Familia.

—— (ed.) (2002a) *Un siglo de luchas femeninas en América Latina*, San José, Costa Rica: Editorial de la Universidad de Costa Rica

—— (ed.) (2002b) *Mujeres, género e historia en América Central durante los siglos XVIII, XIX y XX*, San José, Costa Rica: UNIFEM–Plumsock Mesoamerican Studies.

Sagot, Montserrat (1991a) "Women, political activism and housing: the case of women's struggle for housing in Costa Rica," Unpublished Ph.D. Dissertation, Department of Sociology, The American University: Washington, DC.

—— (1991b) "Estudios sobre la mujer y la sociología costarricense" in I. Wing Ching (ed.) *En torno a la discusión sociológica en Costa Rica*, San José, Costa Rica: Departamento de Sociología, Universidad de Costa Rica.

—— (1994) "Marxismo, interaccionismo simbólico y la opresión de la mujer," *Revista de Ciencias Sociales* 63: 129–140.

—— (2004) "La invisibilidad de las niñas y las adolescentes: trabajo doméstico y discriminación de género," in *Una mirada de género al trabajo infantil doméstico*, San José, Costa Rica: Organización Internacional del Trabajo (OIT–IPEC).

—— (2006) "La paz comienza en casa: las luchas de las mujeres contra la violencia y acción estatal en Costa Rica" in N. Lebon and E. Maier (eds.) *De lo privado a lo público. 30 años de lucha ciudadana de las mujeres en América Latina*, México: Latin American Studies Association–UNIFEM–Siglo XXI Editores.

—— (coord.) (1999) *Análisis situacional de los derechos de las niñas y las adolescentes en Costa Rica*, San José, Costa Rica: Fondo de Naciones Unidas para la Infancia (UNICEF).

Sagot, Montserrat and Ana Carcedo (2000) *La ruta crítica de las mujeres afectadas por la violencia intrafamiliar. Estudios de caso en diez países*, San José, Costa Rica: Organización Panamericana de la Salud.

Sandoval, Carlos (2006) *Fuera de juego: fútbol, identidades nacionales y masculinidades en Costa Rica*, San José, Costa Rica: Editorial de la Universidad de Costa Rica.

—— (2007) *Sueños y sudores en la vida cotidiana. Trabajadoras y trabajadores de la maquila y la construcción en Costa Rica*, San José, Costa Rica: Editorial de la Universidad de Costa Rica.

Schifter, Jacobo (1997) *La casa de Lila: un estudio de la prostitución masculina*, San José, Costa Rica: Instituto Latinoamericano de Prevención y Educación en Salud.

Sojo, Ana (1985) *Mujer y política. Ensayo sobre el feminismo y el sujeto popular*, San José, Costa Rica: Departamento Ecuménico de Investigaciones.

Solano, María Alejandra (1975) "Liberación de la mujer y trabajo social," Thesis for Ge degree of Licenciatura in Social Work, San José, Costa Rica: Universidad de Costa Rica.

Stimpson, Catharine R. (1998) "¿Qué estoy haciendo cuando hago estudios de mujeres en los años noventa?" in M. Navarro and C. R. Stimpson (comp.) *¿Qué son los Estudios de Mujer?* Argentina: Fondo de Cultura Económica.

Torres, Isabel (2001) *La aplicación de la cuota mínima de participación de las mujeres: ¿ficción o realidad? Un diagnóstico para Costa Rica*, San José, Costa Rica: Fundación Arias para la Paz y el Progreso Humano.

Trejos, María Eugenia (2006) *La mujer trabajadora frente a los embates del TLC*, San José, Costa Rica: Friedrich Ebert Stiftung.

Valladares, Blanca (2006) *Guía para reflexionar acerca de mitos y realidades sobre las maternidades y paternidades*, San José, Costa Rica: Instituto de Investigaciones Psicológicas.

Vázquez, Norma (2001) "Recuperar el feminismo para entender el género" in E. Gaviola and L. González (eds.) *Feminismos en América Latina*, Guatemala: Facultad Latinoamericana de Ciencias Sociales (FLACSO).

CHAPTER 16

Puerto Rico: Feminism and Feminist Studies

Alice E. Colón Warren

A Hispanic Caribbean, racially mixed colony; a colonial U.S. jurisdiction, with greater poverty and inequality than the federal states; and at the crossroads between the North and Latin America, Puerto Rico is an interesting arena to explore the intersections of gender, class, race, sexuality and nationality that have characterized recent trends in women's mobilization and have been revealed by the latest feminist post-structural, postmodern, and postcolonial theorizing. In the context of its relationship to U.S. feminism, Puerto Rican feminist mobilization and feminist studies led those in other Latin American and Caribbean countries in its second wave movement emerging in the 1970s. Yet, even when the Island's stunted development has framed a focus on class inequalities, especially with regard to women's employment and poverty, it was only in the 1990s that other differences such as race and sexualities were addressed as notable bases for activism and analyses. In addition, issues of gender and their relation to the state and nationality must be deepened in a context of regional and transnational integration.

I explore some of the shared political, social, economic and cultural matrices that have been the context for feminist organizing and studies in Puerto Rico since the 1970s. Taking the broadest possible definition of feminist outlooks, I discuss some of the main contributions of social science analyses that have documented women's struggles and questioned women's unequal status in Puerto Rico, including studies on education and the media, legal and historical studies, and social and political approaches. Given space limitations, I cannot cover all the discussions on gender, women, and feminism published during this period, even without including the important related work on Puerto Rican women in the United States or the growing body of work on masculinities in Puerto Rico, contributing to a more complete understanding of gender issues (García Toro et al. 2007; Ramírez 1993). The references cited here serve as examples of the topics discussed and of the key authors.

PUERTO RICO AND PUERTO RICAN WOMEN: CONTEXT AND BACKGROUND ON THE WOMEN'S MOVEMENT

The political and economic transformations beginning in early twentieth century in Puerto Rico propelled changes in women's status, reproduction, and the family, which challenged the most traditional definitions of femininity and paved the way for feminist organizing. After 400 years under Spanish rule, the colonial transfer of Puerto Rico to the United States in 1898 accelerated its immersion into capitalist, modernizing strategies, becoming a model for the emerging new international division of labor and a "showcase of democracy" after World War II, and leading in transformations towards high-tech industries and services under accelerated globalization. Puerto Rico pioneered the trends of women's proletarianization and employment in Latin America and the Caribbean. The tobacco and needle trades of the first decades of the twentieth century and the subsequent labor-intensive manufacturing, social services, commerce, and public administration fields facilitated women's increasing involvement in dominant economic sectors as well as a moderate employment expansion (Acevedo 1987; Colón Warren 1998; Ríos 1993).

Puerto Rican upper-class and working-class suffragists achieved women's right to vote earlier than in most other Latin American and Caribbean countries (Barceló Miller 1997, 1998; Jiménez Muñoz 1997, 1998). Women reformers also impelled expanded schooling, housing, health, birth control, and other social services, pushing the state to create policies focusing on the status of women and the domestic sphere beyond those imposed by U.S. programs (Azize and Avilés 1990; Briggs 2002; Burgos Ortiz 1998; Colón Warren 2002). Dramatic improvements in social and economic indicators after World War II have placed the Island closer to the demographic trends of developed countries, with increasing women's education surpassing that of men by the 1990s (Colón Warren 1998, 2002).

Feminist groups emerging since the second wave of feminist organizing in the 1970s brought issues to the forefront of public discussion such as sexism in education and the media, discrimination, women's health and reproductive rights, and even violence against women earlier than in other Latin American and Caribbean countries. Among other measures, a ban on sex discrimination in the Puerto Rican Constitution in the 1950s, still pending in the United States at that level, was followed in the 1970s and thereafter by laws against employment discrimination, reforms in family law equalizing marital partners, laws against sexual harassment and domestic violence, and the creation of the Commission for Women's Affairs, presently called the Office of the Women's Advocate (Alegría Ortega 2003; Colón Warren 2002). The legalization of abortion, achieved through the Roe v. Wade decision of the U.S. Supreme Court in 1973, also received the support of the then budding Puerto Rican feminist groups (Colón et al. 1999; Crespo Kebler 2001b).

Violence against women and reproductive health and rights remain as important foci for feminist mobilization. However, throughout the 1990s there were neo-conservative reactions against advancing women's rights, some related to an even more evident backlash in the United States. Organized groups and individuals have lobbied to amend the law against domestic violence since its enactment and there is increasing resistance to its implementation (Vicente 2003). Modeled on similar groups in the United States, other organizations such as Pro Vida (Pro-Life) and Morality in Media, as well as representatives of the Catholic Church, have repeatedly—albeit unsuccessfully—attempted to restrict the right to abortion, have opposed the use of condoms, and marriage between people of the same sex, and have insisted on abstinence as the focus of sexual education (Laboy Llorens 2003).

Sharing reformist or more leftist visions, but also in the context of continuing poverty and social conflict, feminist mobilizations on the Island usually have incorporated issues of class and concerns for national development and structural transformation. High levels of joblessness and poverty—even if not as visible as in other Latin American countries—have also been a continuing and defining characteristic of Puerto Rican society since the beginning of U.S. intervention, so that gender discrimination in the labor market and the situation of broad sectors of working-class and poorer women have been on the agenda of feminist organizing. At the beginning of the twenty-first century, economic prospects are unclear, as industries continue leaving the Island and neo-liberal policies of economic restructuring, privatization, and cuts in state employment, U.S. federal funds, and public services impact women's employment and poverty. Since the 1980s, feminists have organized against privatization and neoliberal policies, and have worked on projects promoting the personal and economic development of poor women, particularly female heads of family and victims of domestic violence.

Poverty and national subordination have also been central in Puerto Rican women's activism regarding reproductive health and rights. With support from women reformers, poor Puerto Rican women were the objects of the first experiments in population control, initially enacted on the Island under the New Deal programs of the 1930s, since then open to public discussion and controversy. Particularly contentious was the dramatic increase in women's sterilization, including about a third of reproductive age women by the 1960s and 45 percent of reproductive age women living in couples by 1995 (Briggs 2002; Colón et al. 1999; Crespo Kebler 2001b; Dávila 1997). By the 1970s, feminists criticized abuses in the implementation of population control programs, while elaborating a perspective on women's health and rights that allowed for the defense of women's access to all safe forms of contraception, including abortion (Colón et al. 1999; Laboy Llorens 2003).

In the face of homogenizing visions of the Puerto Rican nation that ignored gender inequality, feminists argued that all women faced conditions of oppression and they demanded autonomy from other struggles. However, since the 1980s non-white and Third World feminists insisted that women were not a homogeneous group and that they did not face gender subordination equally.

Differences not only in terms of class and nation, but of race and sexualities gained salience in women's demands and mobilizations. In Puerto Rico, during the 1990s there was notable diversification of issues and identities. Coalitions against violence toward women and for reproductive rights incorporating service, research, and even government organizations, as well as autonomous feminist-identified groups diversified their outlooks, focusing on the needs of specific groups such as women on welfare, young women, and lesbians. Perhaps more important, women's and feminist perspectives that are organized around particular interests of race, ethnicity, and sexualities have appeared among women who were less directly linked to identifiable feminist groups. These included organizations of Black women such as Unión de Mujeres Puertorriqueñas Negras and the Grupo de Identidad de la Mujer Negra, Centro de Apoyo a la Mujer Dominicana, and a parallel movement for sexual rights incorporating homosexuals, lesbians, bisexuals, transgender, and transsexuals (Laboy Llorens 2003; Rivera Lassén 2001).

I argue that the political, cultural, and social matrices in Puerto Rico have led to the silencing of race and racism and of topics regarding sexuality, delaying women's organizing and also feminist studies around these issues. The response to a strong Catholic tradition and the power of the clergy, despite the prevailing separation of Church and State, has been to ignore controversial issues, unless forced to an open discussion. Since the 1990s, open debates have been impelled whenever the most conservative groups have promoted measures that would undermine women's access to abortion or restrain demands to end discriminatory legislation against gay, lesbian, transsexual, or transgendered persons.

On the other hand, the particular exclusions suffered by Black women and the ways in which racism is enmeshed with gender subordination had also been virtually ignored in feminist organizing. The functioning of race and racism in Puerto Rico, as in other Latin American countries, includes mechanisms of denial, while also celebrating the racial mixture of our population. The dichotomous racialization that is imposed by dominant (white) sectors in the United States on African Americans, as well as on colonized populations and "unassimilated" migrants (Briggs 2002; Santiago-Valles 1999a, 1999b), contrasts with the hierarchy of racial mixture in Puerto Rico. On the Island, race ranges along a continuum from white to Black, running through a variety of categories related to the presence of particular phenotypical traits, such as mulatto, trigueño (lighter skinned or as a euphemism for Black), or grifo (tight, curly hair), through which racial identification is evaded while maintaining white as superior (Jorge 1986). In this context of racial mixture and denial of racism, race has only recently become a more salient issue of general social mobilization and for feminists on the Island, even though many come from poorer origins and are phenotypically mulatto or Black.

It also is important to reincorporate discussions of our national status and identity. Although I will not discuss the situation of Puerto Ricans in the Diaspora, it is important to consider how migration has also impinged on the lives of Puerto Rican women both in the United States and on the Island. A growing literature (e.g., Ortiz 1996) has shown how women have been part of the Island's migration to the United States, both as family members and as workers and political actors in their own right (see also Toro-Morn 1995; Torruellas et al. 1996; Whalen 1998). Puerto Rican women's labor allowed the survival of the garment industries remaining in the Northeast after the 1950s, and they contributed to the building of the Boricua (Puerto Rican) community as leaders in education, social services, and social mobiliza-

tions (Muñiz 1996; Ortiz 1996; Sánchez-Korrol 1996). As shown by Alicea (1997) migration affects the lives of Puerto Rican women at both ends and should be recognized in our discussions regarding those in the Island.

THEORETICAL AND METHODOLOGICAL DEVELOPMENTS

Methodology

Since the 1970s, feminist mobilizations have been accompanied by the development of projects and research initiatives on women's studies at diverse universities and campuses in Puerto Rico. The gender research projects at the Social Science Research Center, as well as the Programa de Estudios de Género, are among the more recently established centers promoting feminist research at the Río Piedras campus of the University of Puerto Rico, and follow upon the previous Centro de Estudios, Recursos y Servicios a la Mujer. The Pro Mujeres program located in the Cayey campus as well as Mujer y Salud and Salud Pro Mujer at the Medical Sciences campus are also part of the University of Puerto Rico system. The Interamerican University was important in coordinating efforts for the creation of the Centro de Investigación y Documentación de la Mujer early in the 1980s, and presently includes the Centro Interdisciplinario de Investigación y Estudios del Género. The former Governor's Commission for Women's Affairs, now the Office of the Women's Advocate, also carries out a research and publication program. These institutionalized efforts have provided a base for an important part of the research reviewed here, while the presence of women's studies groups at other universities and campuses and an increasing number of individual researchers undertaking gender issues in their investigations will also be noted. The colloquiums organized by the network named Congreso Universitario para los Asuntos de las Mujeres y los Géneros have been a forum for meeting among all interested investigators.

Many researchers, if not all, stand out because of their strong relationship to feminist groups, to activism, and to policy developments, as well as for their academic contributions. Feminist academic materials published since the 1970s have focused on issues such as sexism in socialization, education, and the media; equality in occupational and educational opportunities; and women's unequal status in political participation and legislation, all directed at changing policies, practices, and pedagogical visions. From the 1990s forward, discussions of androcentrism and women's difference, theoretical work and studies on educational equity (Martínez Ramos 2003); the law and judicial decisions (Torres Viada 2002); the social sciences (Pro Mujer 1990), and the media (Valle Ferrer et al. 1996) also have analyzed women's subordination to male perspectives as the norm in knowledge, science, laws, and pedagogical practices. Initially influenced by neo-Marxist historical materialism and European social history in the 1970s, and later including poststructuralist outlooks, a continuing body of historical work has provided class and political analyses of women's participation in the Puerto Rican historical processes. Incorporating insights of socialist and radical feminism, the 1980s also shifted the focus to power structures in gender relations, particularly in marital relations, stressing violence against women as an expression of such male control. Research on violence against women not only reinforced feminist critiques but was part of lobbying efforts and even propitiated changing gender definitions among women participants in research activities (Vicente 1999).

In terms of research techniques and methods, only a few studies have used quantitative analyses. Most of the social–psychological or sociological–anthropological studies have been based on smaller, non-representative samples and have used a more qualitative approach, even when some have incorporated quantitative descriptions. As has been common in many feminist methodological discussions, qualitative techniques were in fact presented by Martínez et al. (1988) as an alternative to what was criticized as the dominant, quantitative, positivistic methodologies that did not facilitate a critique of prevailing patriarchal structures and visions.

While prioritizing qualitative research, authors have developed discourse analyses of language and culture on the Island. Content analysis of interviews, group discussions, the media, and other texts have been undertaken by considering discourse and language in their relation to material conditions and power structures. From diverse perspectives, studies have analyzed both latent and explicit language—what it reveals and what it obliterates—as underlying and constituting the simultaneous presence and resistance to hegemonic codes, both at rational and emotional, affective levels (Alegría Ortega 2005; Martínez Ramos 2002; Muñoz Vázquez and Fernández Bauzó 1988; Silva Bonilla 1981).

With these theoretical assumptions on the nature of consciousness and ideological codes, participatory research with similarities to Paulo Freire's pedagogy was developed as a methodological innovation. In many of these studies, gathering information was done in discussion groups or workshops involving a dialogue directed at problematizing participants' definitions of gender relations on issues such as divorce (Muñoz Vázquez and Fernández Bauzó 1988), sexual harassment (Martínez et al. 1988), domestic violence (Silva Bonilla et al. 1990), teachers' definitions as women and professionals (Martínez Ramos 2003), and since the 1990s, the experience of racism among Puerto Rican girls and women (Franco Ortiz and Ortiz Torres 2004; Franco Ortiz and Quiñones Hernández 2005).

Theoretical Developments in Intersectionality: Gender, Nation, Class, Race, and Sexuality

In terms of general theoretical outlooks, Puerto Rican feminist scholars appear to have followed a trajectory familiar in U.S. feminist research from liberal, socialist feminist, radical to poststructuralist or postmodern or postcolonial. This is not surprising because of the exposure that the Island's academics have to U.S. intellectual production. However, they also have been influenced by European, Latin American, and other Third World social science and feminist theorizing. For some authors, the shifting, contested construction of gender makes it questionable to consider "men" or "women" as plausible categories, and the breaking down of such binary gender definitions is precisely the way of resisting women's subordination (Román 2004; Vale 2003). Without necessarily assuming that particular view, feminist analyses have become more complex, considering diversity in the shifting constitution of gender. As in feminist organizing, race and sexualities are only more recently growing as a body of work, and the analyses of differences and intersections must be further developed.

In diverse ways, research throughout the 1990s has provided the framework to consider gender as contested, shifting, discursive relationships, mutually constituted through the struggles and resistance of diverse groups of men and women immersed in other social positions/identities.

First, moving beyond the documentation of women's presence in history, recent studies have come to question the androcentric visions or essentialist notions in social analyses, such as the idea of a homogeneous gender or national identity. Suárez Findlay (1999), Barceló Miller (2000), Crespo Kebler (2001a, 2001b), Jiménez Muñoz (1997, 1998), and Rivera Lassén (2001) have shown how national culture and modernizing social projects in diverse historical periods have been defined in relation to traditional images of motherhood and the subordinate status of women. As one unfortunate result, nationalist-oriented authors sometimes described changes in gender relations and the growth of feminism as foreign or imperial impositions. Alternatively, Jiménez Muñoz (1997) has suggested that the alliance of Puerto Rican suffragists with U.S. feminists and state functionaries could entail contradictions by reinforcing the established colonial power and also advancing the status of Puerto Rican women.

Other feminist social scientists have discussed the conflictual nature of the solidarity among workers and deconstructed the idea of a feminist sisterhood among all women. With diverse emphases, for example, Barceló Miller (1997) and Jiménez Muñoz (1997, 1998) have questioned the labor movement's touted support for women's organizing and suggested more complex and nuanced interpretations than previous investigations that privileged the role of working-class feminists. At the same time, these authors, in considering the role of professional women's feminist organizations in the struggle for women's enfranchisement, discussed these groups' class and political biases and the types of negotiations that limited their cross-class alliances with working-class suffragists.

Second, Suárez Findlay's work (1999) suggests that merely deconstructing the homogeneity of women or other social categories may not tell the whole story. It is important to show not only how gender definitions vary across social categories but also how other social hierarchies are gendered and hegemonic definitions are mutually constituted in relation to each other. Even when taking on modernizing projects of social reform presumed to benefit working-class and poorer women, upper-class women simultaneously reinforced their privileged position when their own definition of respectability was built in reference to the "less respectable" lower classes, on whom they imposed their own class/racial codes of femininity, hygiene and mothering, and social stratification (Suárez Findlay 1999).

Third, researchers have recognized that mobilization does occur, although perhaps halfheartedly (Barceló Miller 1998), among members of groups subjected to the same, if also different and contradictory, axes of oppression—be it gender, nation, class, or race. To the extent that gender is the basis of inequality, for example, it also has been the basis for women's collective action when their common interests have been identified as more important than their conflicts and differences. The challenge remains to analyze gender definitions and relations in their mutual, conflicting constitution with other social hierarchies and identities and the conditions under which gender inequality can become the source of mobilization.

Sharing in the cultural silencing of these issues, studies on sexuality and sexual rights until recently have been relatively limited, although analyses of the construction of female bodies and the possibilities for women's resistance have become part of post-structuralist discussions (Figueroa Sarriera 1994, 1999; Vale 2003). Studies have shown the particular conflicts and dilemmas lived by lesbian women in relation to feminist and gay organizing. Rivera Lassén and Crespo Kebler (2001) have discussed the presence of lesbians in feminist groups during the 1970s, the silencing of sexual orientation because it might reinforce opposition to feminism, the stigma attached to lesbians by other feminists, and the process through which lesbianism became more open. Negrón-Muntaner's (1992) articles on the gay movement in Puerto Rico during the 1970s analyzed its class and gender differences, its affinities and tensions with feminist organizations, and its alliances with North American organizations against homophobic practices on the Island.

As already mentioned, race rarely has been incorporated explicitly in people's subjective definitions or academic discourses. Since the early twentieth century, this denial of race and racism has been a way of solidifying what was discussed as a homogeneous Puerto Rican identity, existing in opposition to the United States culture, while simultaneously reproducing racial hierarchies. Obliterating race is also an avoidance of the identification with Blackness, that not only covers up racist practices, but ignores or folklorizes Black identity and culture in what remains a white definition of Puerto Ricanness. Racial definitions and divisions in Puerto Rico, thus, have been ignored, obscured, or distorted in much of the academic work, especially in relation to the situation of Black women.

Among the notable exceptions since the early 1980s are Ramos Rosado's (1999, 2005) pioneering discussions of Black women's depictions in Puerto Rican literature and the analyses of sexism and racism in language by Picó and Alegría (1983). Jorge (1986) analyzed how the gradations in Puerto Rican racial categories and the possibilities to "mejorar la raza" (improve the race), have allowed for a person's whitening in Puerto Rican society through intermarriage, as well as through socioeconomic mobility, but are less likely particularly for women who are most evidently phenotypically Black. Research published in the 2000s has also shown how gendered beauty canons intersect with race among Black girls and women who suffer from rejection and discrimination due to their physical traits, as Blackness is displaced onto those deemed darker even in the most intimate family relations (Franco Ortiz and Ortiz Torres 2004; Franco Ortiz and Quiñones Hernández 2005). Suárez Findlay (1999) discusses how class, race and gender categories are mutually constituted, based not only on phenotypical traits but on behavior, as women's respectability or "acting Black" became integral components of class/racial divisions in Puerto Rico.

It is important to continue analyzing the

racial categories and relations in Puerto Rico considering that they are constituted both by U.S. racializing practices and by internal racial codes and relations. Such analyses should consider the particular conditions, relations and practices that are created by the different gradations of Blackness, and identify the particular weight and meaning of color and racial categorizations in the Puerto Rican social hierarchy in relation to class and gender definitions.

SALIENT ISSUES IN CONTEMPORARY FEMINIST SOCIAL SCIENCE RESEARCH

This section discusses the most salient themes in research on Puerto Rican women, including women's employment and poverty, family relations and violence, and sexual and reproductive rights, noting both advances and the need for further work on the aforementioned parameters.

Economic Development, Women's Work, and Poverty

Analyses of the impact of capitalism on women's economic activity have incorporated the view that gender construction is shifting, contested and diverse. Studies show how the gendered definitions of women as household and remunerated workers in Puerto Rico have been historically imposed through conflicts between men and women, between men and capitalism that demanded female labor, and even between women in diverse familial and employment positions. For example, Baerga (1993a, 1999) documented how the labor movement's defense of the privileged position of craft workers and their skills was partly based on their definition of men as the main breadwinners, devaluing women and their productive and reproductive work in the household. However, she also documented the conflicts between women in different employment positions: those in the

home needle trades defended the need to improve their working conditions, while both men and women in organized labor sought the total elimination of home production. The needs of men and capitalism did not perfectly meld either: U.S. industrial investments and colonial power and the Puerto Rican state acting with relative autonomy imposed economic strategies that led to continuing, although moderate, female labor demand that paralleled increasing male unemployment during the subsequent industrial strategies on the Island (González 1993; Ríos 1993).

Studies illustrate how late twentieth-century economic strategies simultaneously propelled the economic participation and advancement of some white-collar women, even if they are all in lower ranked professional jobs and administrative assistance or sales positions, while also increasing their distance from other women who are in lower ranked occupations or are displaced from work by industrial flight and the move to technologically advanced production (Colón Warren 1998). Acevedo (1987, 1999) thus suggested we must counter analyses that pose dichotomous alternatives when they stress either women's marginalization and exploitation in the labor market or the positive aspects of their employment. Neither can we assume that women in general serve as a labor reserve, if by this we mean that they join the workforce only intermittently and to displace male workers.

The position of women as low-paid workers should be researched as it was shaped in different historical moments and for women in diverse family and life cycle positions (Acevedo 1993; Baerga 1993b). Women's particular positions in household structures (such as their age, life cycle, and marital status) and their family responsibilities have impinged on their availability as a labor supply and also have had an impact on changing definitions of female labor demand. For example, Baerga (1993b, 2000) shows how male unemployment and lower female employment in tobacco industries made married women the most important labor supply for the household needle trades in the beginning of the twentieth century. Acevedo (1993) for her part has shown how, with the movement of garment industries out of Puerto Rico, remaining factories appear to have maintained what is now their relatively older, married, female labor supply, a change from what has been posed as the ideal, young, single maquila worker in other countries.

Among the few and more sophisticated statistical analyses (Acevedo 1987, 1993), Enchautegui (2004) has shown how women receive lower earnings for their levels of skill and education compared to men, even considering their unequal occupational distribution. Such use of women as lower paid labor is not a mere reproduction of their position in the domestic sphere but is also related to gendered definitions in the labor market that keep women segregated in female-dominated job spheres (Acevedo 1987, 1999; Colón Warren 1998; Enchautegui 2004; Ríos 1993). For example, Safa (1995) and Pérez Herrans (1996) documented how paternalist workplace practices, the lack of unions' response to women's needs, as well as the pressures and rewards of family networks and responsibilities continue reinforcing traditional feminine identities and distance women from labor organizing. This gendering of jobs has also been analyzed as contested, shifting and mutually constituted with class identities. For example, Casey (1996) discussed how women sometimes consider the growing sphere of administrative assistant jobs as upward mobility and professionalization for them, while retaining a content of femininity. She also showed how these definitions were contested by women workers who recognized the dead-end nature and lower pay of their jobs, leading them to a labor militancy not usually identified as female or higher status.

Race and gender have been enmeshed in these processes of labor supply and demand and the constitution of particular job spheres. Merino Falú (1996) has highlighted the role of Black and mulatto women in domestic work, and Matos Rodríguez (1998) has shown how they differed in status from "whiter" seamstresses in the nineteenth century. Crespo Kebler (2005) has shown how, given their historical immersion in domestic services, Black women were actually more likely to have already been employed at the turn of the century, while it was white women who were disproportionately attracted to the emerging industries linked to agro-industrial production. Yet Black women were recruited not only into lower status jobs, but also responded to the increasing demand for teachers at the turn of the century (Merino Falú 2005). Still, as discussed by Ríos González (2005), Black women remain discriminated against in the labor market even with similar education and in similar occupations.

Finally, it has been important to investigate how trends in women's employment and non-employment affect poverty and socioeconomic stratification in Puerto Rico, especially the particular situation of an increasing number of female family heads (Colón Warren 1998). Different from the United States, poverty affects a high proportion of married couples who are the majority of poor families on the Island. The prevalence of poverty among Puerto Rican female family heads is still much higher than among married couples, related to the Island's endemic joblessness (Colón Warren 1998; Safa 1998). An analysis of the impact of cuts in social benefits becomes particularly relevant. Studies have documented how, in a context of declining employment and without offering them the training and social support needed to obtain adequate jobs, welfare reform has pushed many female family heads off the rolls but not out of poverty. Despite more sensitive treatment by service providers than may be evident in the United States, critical analyses have shown the class and gender biases of welfare reform, particularly in the context of Puerto Rican endemic unemployment (Fernós 2003; Hernández Angueira 2001; Nieves-Rosa, 2007).

High tech manufacturing, commerce, and technological services, and to a lesser extent the development of a tourist industry that has been geared to wealthier travelers, remain central among the present economic strategies. Future analyses should be directed at exploring the intersections of gender, race, class, family status, the social construction of sexualities, and other characteristics in the constitution of the particular sectors of the labor market, and how they may have been re-shaped during the shift to technologically advanced and service industries. It would also be important to study these intersections in the processes of job displacement, considering which particular groups have been most affected and how they differ in resources for adjusting to unemployment. For example, it is important to consider how these intersections operate in the informal economy, which is a fairly common type of work in Puerto Rico even though it is uncounted in official statistics, and has a similar gender segregation as the formal economy (Petrovich and Laureano 1986). In addition, it would be useful to analyze these intersections in the patterns of welfare benefits usage and in the effects of reductions in the rolls, including the quality of services provided and the possibilities of beneficiaries' employment.

Family Relations and Violence against Women

Studies of marital relations have documented how women's ascribed roles and definitions of femininity have been shifting and contested. As in other places, women's employment and advancements have not led to a redefinition and redistribution of women's responsibilities at home. Nonetheless, Muñoz Vázquez and Fernández Bauzó (1988) and Safa (1995) have suggested that advances in women's education and employment, and struggles for their rights during this period have resulted in a social acceptance of the need for their employment, in greater equity in a number of aspects (such as child rearing, fertility control, and family budgets), and in their lessened acceptance of men's control, unfaithfulness, or violence. Such resistance may not be without tensions and contradictions. Crespo (1994) analyzed what became a very familiar phrase on the need for women's education, "*estudia por si tu marido te sale un sinvergüenza*" (study in case your husband turns out to be a scoundrel). This expression shows that marriage remains women's ideal as long as men respond to "legitimate" authority, but also that male domination can be challenged especially since women are encouraged not to accept men's irresponsible or oppressive behavior.

Women's advances and challenges to dominant gender roles and definitions, such as have taken place in Puerto Rico, can lead to more equitable intimate partner and family relations, especially among higher status couples, but also to increasing family conflict until more fully democratic patterns are accepted. Class–gender intersections have been researched in this respect, with specific reference to the situation of men in family relations. Safa (1995) contextualized this by suggesting that when men's employment declines and men's authority is undermined, women's employment may allow them to leave what they deem as undesirable relations. According to Muñoz Vázquez and Fernández Bauzó (1988), economic instability may intensify such marital conflict, particularly if lower strata men, with less access to other forms of power, resort to more authoritarian behavior.

Marital tensions, including domestic violence, have been explained as expressions of prevailing gender hierarchies, with authors analyzing the forms of domination, structures and norms that provide for such victimization predominantly against women (Silva Bonilla et al. 1990; Vicente 1999). Later critiques, however, underscored how stressing women's subjection to violence may reproduce dominant stereotypes and dichotomous gender definitions of men's aggressiveness and women's weakness and passivity (Román 1999; Román et al. 1999). Studies have shown that women are not exempt from expressing violent behavior, albeit with different frequency, intensity and bound by gendered meanings, nor are they passive victims of violence. Questioning gender essentialist views, Valle Ferrer (1999) has analyzed the experiences of women suffering violence by documenting the diverse forms of coping used by survivors, depending on their appraisal of the stakes in the battering and of their control of the situation, as well as their experiences with violence as children.

Research has also shown the importance of class, race and other social contexts in shaping the propensity of men's violence in domestic relations and for women's resistance to it. A study published in 2006 showed that men convicted of domestic violence in Puerto Rico tended to have low education, be younger, and more likely to be in consensual unions than the general male population. Acknowledging the class and gender biases of the penal system and that violence among the higher classes tends to be less visible, the authors hypothesized that male control of lower class, younger men in more open relationships could be more challenged than those of older or higher status men, so that more open violence may become a means of exerting authority (Colón, Burgos and García 2006). As indicated by Valle Ferrer (2002) we must do more research incorporating ethnicity, national origin, race, class, sexual orientation, or other categories that make the axes of oppression and violence more complex among women.

It is just as important to consider non-heterosexual family and intimate partner relations. A volume of the *Juridical Journal*, published in 2002 by the Interamerican University, includes academic analyses of sexual rights, although the discussion is still predominantly legal (Braulio Martínez 2002; Ortiz Camacho 2002; Sánchez De León 2002). In particular, violence among homosexual intimate partners must be further investigated. Recent investigations have shown the need to analyze unequal power in these conflictive relations without comparing them to heterosexual gender definitions (Toro Alfonso and Rodríguez 2005).

Furthermore, it is important to analyze domestic violence against women in the context of broader political, social, and economic relations. The above-mentioned research on convicts showed that domestic violence was only weakly related to other criminal and violent activity, suggesting its particularity as part of a socially condoned pattern of gender inequality (Colón, Burgos and García 2006). Research by Santiago-Valles (1994), however, has suggested that violence against women was related to conditions of social crises and intensified subjection among the lower classes during the first decades of the twentieth century in Puerto Rico. We need more analyses that elaborate the particular linkages between gender conflict and the broader trends in social violence in our society.

Sexual and Reproductive Health and Rights

The various studies on reproductive health and rights allow us to consider how shifting definitions of femininity are intertwined with national, class, and racial definitions.

Population policies have indeed been immersed in the economic structures that are part of prevailing colonial relations, with their gendered class and racial overtones promoting birth control as part of middle-class values. Since the beginning of the birth control movement in Puerto Rico in the 1920s and 1930s, nationalist sectors, including some feminists, without necessarily rejecting birth control, have considered population control as an imperialist imposition, while using a definition of Puerto Rican culture that depicted Puerto Rican women as victims of a coercive sterilization abuse (Briggs 2002; Colón et al. 1999; Crespo Kebler 2001a, 2001b). Yet, there were also middle-class feminists and women reformers who defended birth control as a means of dealing with illegitimacy, child abandonment, and maternal and child health by opening reproductive options for poor women (Briggs 2002; Colón et al. 1999). Women's employment and reduced fertility in a small, nuclear, presumably more democratic family were part of the ideal image of modern family, middle-class aspirations and upward mobility (Colón Warren 2002). Briggs (2002) showed how this hegemonic definition carried its racial/class counterpart: the irresponsible over-breeders, "demon mothers," who made Puerto Ricans responsible for the Island's underdevelopment and whose existence was used to explain the causes of poverty found in the Island's colonial, economic, and political structures.

Even while denouncing repressive population control policies, since the 1980s, critical feminist analyses have demanded the advancement of women's options for fertility regulation as part of their sexual and reproductive rights. In this respect, analysts have reinterpreted the high rates of sterilization in Puerto Rico as active responses to the conditions in which women undertake reproductive decisions, using neo-Malthusian policies on their own terms (Crespo Kebler 2001a, 2001b; Lugo Ortiz 1999). Transcending dichotomous interpretations of sterilization as either abusive or freely chosen, López (1998) interpreted such active responses as elements of resistance that must still focus on the constraints that gender oppression and poverty impose on reproductive freedom. A broader definition of reproductive rights therefore suggests that it is important to continue research on the conditions that define sexual practices and childbearing patterns among Puerto Rican women of diverse social and racial categories, enabling and constraining their reproductive options.

Furthermore, even after its legalization, abortion in Puerto Rico remains publicly condemned and silenced in order to appease the church and other opposing forces, although it is clandestinely accepted as a personal decision by women and people in general. Given the silence and stigma attached to abortion, there is greater ignorance with regard to the extent of its practice and even its legality in the Island (Azize and Avilés 1997; Dávila 2001). Research by Azize and Avilés (1992) demystified the characterization of women resorting to abortion as young, immoral, irresponsible, or not desiring motherhood, by showing that the majority of these were adults who were or had been married, who had children, were religious, had practiced contraception, and had undergone abortion very early in their pregnancies. Other research indicated that attitudes towards abortion vary with interpretations of motherhood, and are related, among other factors, to women's class-based aspirations of fulfilling additional roles and expectations for their children (Colón et al. 1999). Further analyses of abortion should be undertaken in relation to the diverse women's reproductive options, constraints and patterns throughout their life cycle, including the meaning they attribute to childbearing and motherhood. Such research should help break down the silence and illegitimacy that constrain its practice in Puerto Rico.

SOME AREAS FOR FURTHER RESEARCH

In this review, I have suggested the need for further investigation of the shifting, disputed, mutual constitution of social categories and how they come to be played out in the study of particular topics in feminist studies.

Racial categorizations and sexualities are only beginning to be more explored in Puerto Rico and must be incorporated in the analyses of gender definitions and relations. Besides those mentioned in the text, there are other areas that also would merit more intersectional investigation.

As in other countries, feminist strategies and the relationship of feminism to power and the state have been an area of recurrent debate. Organized feminist activism has, in many instances, been geared to legal advances, and at various points, feminists have had linkages with state institutions, including the present Office of the Women's Advocate. In this context, Román (1993) and Román, Vargas, and Hernández (1999) have argued that laws against domestic violence open up private and personal lives to greater intervention and criminalization by the state. While recognizing the state's reproduction of prevailing power structures, others (Colón Warren 2002; Vicente 1999, 2003) have argued that it cannot be ignored as an arena of struggle in which the interests and definitions of the diverse social sectors are disputed, and where spaces are open for sub-ordinate groups' advancements. The balance of feminist involvement in state policies and power structures needs further investigation, as it has varying effects on the lives of diverse sectors of women.

In this respect, political participation and access to the highest levels of decision making remain among the strongest knots of gender inequality. Analyses by Gallart (1998) and by Muñoz Vázquez (1996) have recognized women's increasing participation in political parties as well as labor and social movements, and how these have been a means of introducing their particular interests and styles in leadership and activism. Miranda's (1994) and Alegría Ortega's (2000) research has documented how stereotypes and gender roles still hinder women's involvement and leadership in electoral politics and social movements. Continuing study of the conditions constraining and enabling the political participation and social mobilization of diverse groups of women is on the agenda.

Finally, while homogenizing views of nationality need to be questioned, it is still true that Puerto Rican women are immersed in a situation of national subordination that, in some instances, may have advanced their struggles, but that also imposes the United States' policies as limits (Alegría Ortega 1998–1999; Colón et al. 1999; Fernós 2003). Discussions of the lives of Puerto Rican women require that we continue analyses of nationality in the context of colonial relations, and of our relations with other countries in a globalizing world.

Complicating the discussion of nationality issues, economic and social globalization have placed Puerto Rican women on the Island in a relationship with those in the United States, as well as in a Latin American and Caribbean context. There is need to continue analyses of the continuities and ruptures, similarities and differences, and the mutual influences between Puerto Ricans on the Island and in the Diaspora. The increasing contacts will force researchers to continue addressing issues such as hybridism, borders, and transnational families, communities, and identities, which have been much more common in migration literature in the United States.

Intensified globalization will also impel the consideration of Latin America and the Caribbean as still another identity and subject position. The Caribbean Association for Feminist Research and Action (CAFRA) and the organization of women and activists from the South, Development Alternatives with Women for a New Era (DAWN), are but two of the transnational groups in which Puerto Rican feminists have participated. Publications on Puerto Rican women in relation to the rest of the Caribbean have begun relatively recently and most remain national in focus (Baerga 1993a; Colón and Fabián

1995; Colón and Reddock 2004; Hernández Angueira 1995; Quiñones 2000; Safa 1995). Future research should call for comparisons among nations, as well as to the analysis of the connections and hierarchies among them that affect the lives of diverse women in our countries, as well as provide for the continuing advancement of women's organizing as a regional and international movement.

NOTES

My acknowledgments to the 2000–2003 editor of *Gender & Society*, Christine Bose, for asking me to write this analysis of Puerto Rican feminist studies. Her comments and editing provided direction to this chapter. I also acknowledge the excellent suggestions by the journal's reviewers, who helped to improve the final content, which, nonetheless, remains my full responsibility.

REFERENCES

Acevedo, Luz del Alba (1987) "Políticas de industrialización y cambios en el empleo femenino en Puerto Rico, 1947–1982," *Homines* 4: 40–69.

—— (1993) "Género, trabajo asalariado y desarrollo industrial en Puerto Rico: La división sexual del trabajo en la manufactura" in M. del Carmen Baerga (ed.) *Género y trabajo: La industria de la aguja en Puerto Rico y el Caribe Hispano*, San Juan: Editorial Universidad de Puerto Rico.

—— (1999) "Género y trabajo en Puerto Rico" in F. Martínez (ed.) *Futuro económico de Puerto Rico*, Río Piedras: Editorial de la Universidad de Puerto Rico.

Alegría Ortega, Idsa E. (1998–1999) "Challenge of diversity," *Lola Press* November/May, 48–49.

—— (2000) "Nudos de género en las elecciones del 2000," *Mujeres en Marcha*, October 2.

—— (2003) "Ideología y política pública: la representación de las mujeres" in L. M. Martínez Ramos and M. Tamargo López (eds.) *Género, sociedad y cultura*, San Juan, Puerto Rico: Centro Interdisciplinario de Investigación y Estudios del Género, Universidad Interamericana de Puerto Rico, Recinto Metropolitano.

—— (2005) "No todo es armonía: Género y raza en la serie de televisión *Mi familia*" in I. E. Alegría Ortega and P. N. Ríos González (eds.) *Contrapunto de género y raza en Puerto Rico*, Río Piedras, Puerto Rico: Centro de Investigaciones Sociales, Universidad de Puerto Rico.

Alicea, Marixsa (1997) "A 'chambered nautilus': The contradictory nature of Puerto Rican women's role in the social construction of a transnational community," *Gender & Society* 11, 5: 597–626.

Azize, Yamila, and Luis A. Avilés (1990) "Los hechos desconocidos: Participación de la mujer en las profesiones de salud en Puerto Rico (1898–1930)," *PRHSHJ* 9, 1: 9–16.

—— (1992) *La realidad del aborto en Puerto Rico*, Cayey: Pro Mujer, Colegio Universitario de Cayey, Universidad de Puerto Rico.

—— (1997) "Abortion in Puerto Rico. The limits of colonial legality," *Reproductive Health Matters* 5, 9: 55–65.

Baerga, María del Carmen (1993a) "El género y la construcción social de la marginalidad del trabajo femenino en la industria de la confección de la ropa" in M. del Carmen Baerga (ed.) *Género y trabajo: La industria de la aguja en Puerto Rico y el Caribe Hispano*, San Juan: Editorial Universidad de Puerto Rico.

—— (1993b) "Las jerarquías sociales y las expresiones de resistencia: Género, clase y edad en la industria de la aguja en Puerto Rico" in M. del Carmen Baerga (ed.) *Género y trabajo: La industria de la aguja en Puerto Rico y el Caribe Hispano*, San Juan: Editorial Universidad de Puerto Rico.

—— (1999) " 'A la organización: A unirnos como un solo hombre . . .': La Federación Libre de Trabajadores y el mundo masculino del trabajo," *Journal of the Historical Research Center* (Universidad de Puerto Rico) 11: 219–52.

—— (2000) "La lucha por el derecho al trabajo y la subsistencia de la unidad doméstica: Las trabajadoras a domicilio de la aguja, 1930–1940" in *Ponce, 1898, Panoramas*, Ponce, Puerto Rico: Museo de Arte de Ponce, Fundación Puertorriqueña de las Humanidades, Museo de la Historia de Ponce.

Barceló Miller, María de Fátima (1997) *La lucha por el sufragio femenino en Puerto Rico*, Río Piedras, Puerto Rico: Huracán/CIS.

—— (1998) "Halfhearted solidarity: Women workers and the women's suffrage movement in Puerto Rico during the 1920s" in F. Matos Rodríguez and L. C. Delgado (eds.) *Puerto Rican women's history: New perspectives*, Armonk, NY: M. E. Sharpe.

—— (2000) "Nociones de género en el discurso modernizador en Puerto Rico, 1870–1930," *Revista de Ciencias Sociales* 8: 1–27.

Braulio Martínez, Mildred (2002) "Matrimonio sin género: La legalización de las relaciones entre personas del mismo sexo," *Revista Jurídica Universidad Interamericana de Puerto Rico, Facultad de Derecho* 36, 3: 517–532.

Briggs, Laura (2002) *Reproducing empire: Race, sex, science, and U.S. imperialism in Puerto Rico*, Berkeley: University of California Press.

Burgos Ortiz, Nilsa M. (1998) *Pioneras de la profesión*

de trabajo social en Puerto Rico, Hato Rey, Puerto Rico: Publicaciones Puertorriqueñas Editores.

Casey, Geraldine J. (1996) "New tappings on the keys: Changes in work and gender roles for women clerical workers in Puerto Rico" in A. Ortiz (ed.) *Puerto Rican women and work: Bridges in transnational labor*, Philadelphia: Temple University Press.

Colón, Alice, and Ana M. Fabián (1995) *Mujeres en el Caribe: Desarrollo, paz y movimientos comunitarios*, Río Piedras: Instituto de Estudios del Caribe y CERES del Centro de Investigaciones Sociales, Universidad de Puerto Rico.

Colón, Alice and Rhoda Reddock (2004) "The changing status of women in the contemporary Caribbean" in B. Brereton, T. Martínez Vergne, R. A. Romer and B. Silvestrini (eds.) *General History of the Caribbean. Vol. V*, The Caribbean in the Twentieth Century, Paris: UNESCO Publishing and London: Macmillan Caribbean.

Colón, Alice, Nilsa Burgos and Víctor García (2006) *La violencia en la relación de pareja: Estudio de personas convictas por Ley 54*, San Juan, Puerto Rico: Oficina de la Procuradora de las Mujeres.

Colón, Alice, Ana Luisa Dávila, María Dolores Fernós, and Esther Vicente (1999) *Políticas, visiones y voces en torno al aborto en Puerto Rico*, Río Piedras: Centro de Investigaciones Sociales, Universidad de Puerto Rico.

Colón Warren, Alice (1998) "The feminization of poverty among women in Puerto Rico and Puerto Rican women in the Middle Atlantic region of the United States," *Brown Journal of World Affairs* 5, 2: 262–282.

—— (2002) "Asuntos de género en la discusión pública a través del siglo veinte en Puerto Rico," *Revista Jurídica Universidad Interamericana de Puerto Rico, Facultad de Derecho* 36, 3: 403–432.

Crespo, Elizabeth (1994) "Puerto Rican women: Migration and changes in gender roles" in R. Benmayor and A. Skotes (eds.) *Migration and identity*, New York: Oxford University Press.

Crespo Kebler, Elizabeth (2001a) "Ciudadanía y nación: Debates sobre los derechos reproductivos en Puerto Rico," *Revista de Ciencias Sociales* 10: 57–84.

—— (2001b) "Liberación de la mujer: Los feminismos, la justicia social, la nación y la autonomía en las organizaciones feministas de la década de 1970 en Puerto Rico" in A. I. Rivera Lassén and E. Crespo Kebler (eds.) *Documentos del feminismo en Puerto Rico: Facsímiles de la historia, Vol. 1, 1970–1979*, San Juan: Editorial de la Universidad de Puerto Rico.

—— (2005) "¿Y las trabajadoras domésticas dónde están? Raza, género y trabajo" in I. E. Alegría Ortega and P. N. Ríos González (eds.) *Contrapunto de género y raza en Puerto Rico*, Río Piedras, Puerto Rico: Centro de Investigaciones Sociales, Universidad de Puerto Rico.

Dávila, Ana L (1997) *Puerto Rico. Reproductive health survey, 1995/1996. Preliminary report*, San Juan: Escuela Graduada de Salud Pública, Recinto de Ciencias Médicas, Universidad de Puerto Rico.

—— (2001) "El aborto: ¿Cuándo algunas veces, cuándo casi nunca? ¿Cuál es el sentir de las puertorriqueñas en la Isla y en la Diáspora al comienzo de la década de los ochenta?" in A. Colón and E. Planell (eds.) *Silencios, presencias y debates sobre el aborto en Puerto Rico y el Caribe Hispano*, San Juan: Proyecto Atlantea, Intercambio Académico Caribe-Universidad de Puerto Rico.

Enchautegui, María (2004) *Amarres en el trabajo de las mujeres: Hogar y empleo*, San Juan: Estado Libre Asociado de Puerto Rico, Oficina de la Procuradora de las Mujeres.

Fernós, María Dolores (2003) "Género, clase y poder en las políticas sociales" in L. M. Martínez Ramos and M. Tamargo López (eds.) *Género, sociedad y cultura*, San Juan, Puerto Rico: Centro Interdisciplinario de Investigación y Estudios del Género, Universidad Interamericana de Puerto Rico, Recinto Metropolitano.

Franco Ortiz, Mariluz and Blanca Ortiz Torres (2004) "Desenmascarando experiencias de racismo cotidiano con niñas jóvenes en Loíza, Puerto Rico," *Identidades* 2, 2: 18–43.

Franco Ortiz, Mariluz and Doris Quiñones Hernández (2005) "Huellas de ébano: Afirmando cuerpos de mujeres negras" in I. E. Alegría Ortega and P. N. Ríos González (eds.) *Contrapunto de género y raza en Puerto Rico*, Río Piedras, Puerto Rico: Centro de Investigaciones Sociales, Universidad de Puerto Rico.

Figueroa Sarriera, Heidi (1994) "¿Cuál cuerpo? ¿Qué mujer? Heterutopías feministas ante el encuadre 'high tech'" in H. Figueroa-Sarriera, M. Milagros López, and M. Román (eds.) *Más allá de la bella (in) diferencia. Revisión postfeminista y otras escrituras posibles*, Río Piedras, Puerto Rico: Publicaciones Puertorriqueñas.

—— (1999) "Hibridación: Lo femenino al filo de la perversión," *Bordes* 7: 26–31.

Gallart, Mary Frances (1998) "Political empowerment of Puerto Rican women, 1952–1956" in F. Matos Rodríguez and L. C. Delgado (eds.) *Puerto Rican women's history: New perspectives*, Armonk, NY: M. E. Sharpe.

García Toro, Víctor, Rafael L. Ramírez and Luis Solano Castillo (2007) *Los hombres no lloran. Ensayos sobre las masculinidades*, San Juan, Puerto Rico: Ediciones Huracán.

González, Lydia Milagros (1993) "La industria de la aguja de Puerto Rico y sus orígenes en los Estados Unidos" in M. C. Baerga (ed.) *Género y trabajo: La industria de la aguja en Puerto Rico y el Caribe Hispano*, San Juan: Editorial Universidad de Puerto Rico.

Hernández Angueira, Luisa (1995) "En yola y al margen: Reflexión teórica y metodológica en torno al género y la migración," *Caribbean Studies* 28, 1: 223–244.

—— (2001) *Mujeres puertorriqueñas, "welfare" y globalización*, Hato Rey, Puerto Rico: Publicaciones Puertorriqueñas.

Jiménez Muñoz, Gladys (1997) " 'So we decided to come and ask you ourselves': The 1928 U.S. congressional hearings on women's suffrage in Puerto Rico" in F. Negrón Muntaner and R. Grosfoguel (eds.) *Puerto Rican Jam*, Minneapolis: University of Minnesota Press.

—— (1998) "Literacy, class, and sexuality in the debate on women's suffrage in Puerto Rico during the 1920s" in F. Matos Rodríguez and L. C. Delgado (eds.) *Puerto Rican women's history: New perspectives*, Armonk, NY: M. E. Sharpe.

Jorge, Angela (1986) "The Black Puerto Rican woman in contemporary American society" in E. Acosta-Belén (ed.) *The Puerto Rican woman. Perspectives on culture and society*, New York: Praeger.

Laboy Llorens, Isabel (2003) "Los derechos reproductivos" in L. M. Martínez Ramos and M. Tamargo López (eds.) *Género, sociedad y cultura*, San Juan, Puerto Rico: Centro Interdisciplinario de Investigación y Estudios del Género, Universidad Interamericana de Puerto Rico, Recinto Metropolitano.

López, Iris (1998) "An ethnography of the medicalization of Puerto Rican women's reproduction" in M. Lock and P. A. Kaufert (eds.) *Pragmatic women and body politics*, Cambridge, UK: Cambridge University Press.

Lugo Ortiz, Lourdes (1999) "Relatos de la esterilización: Entre el acomodo y la resistencia," *Revista de Ciencias Sociales* 6: 208–226.

Martínez, Lourdes, Ruth Silva Bonilla, and Idsa Alegria (1988) *El hostigamiento sexual de las trabajadoras en sus centros de empleo*, Río Piedras: CERES-CIS, Social Science Research Center, University of Puerto Rico.

Martínez Ramos, Loida M. (2002) "En el salón me dijeron 'mami': Reflexiones en torno a las mujeres, la educación y la búsqueda de alternativas pedagógicas al sexismo," *Homines* 20, 1: 322–332.

—— (2003) "Currículo(s) y género (s)" in L. M. Martínez Ramos and M. Tamargo López (eds.) *Género, sociedad y cultura*, San Juan, Puerto Rico: Centro Interdisciplinario de Investigación y Estudios del Género, Universidad Interamericana de Puerto Rico, Recinto Metropolitano.

Matos Rodríguez, Félix (1998) " 'Quién trabajará?' Domestic workers, urban slaves, and the abolition of slavery in Puerto Rico" in F. Matos Rodríguez and L. C. Delgado (eds.) *Puerto Rican women's history: New perspectives*, Armonk, NY: M. E. Sharpe.

Merino Falú, Aixa (1996) "El gremio de lavanderas de Puerta de Tierra" in A. Gaztambide Géigel and S. Álvarez Curbelo (eds.) *Historias vivas: Historiografía puertorriqueña contemporánea*, San Juan, Puerto Rico: Asociación Puertorriqueña de Historiadores and Editorial Postdata.

—— (2005) "La mujer puertorriqueña negra en la educación (1900–1930). Notas para su estudio" in I. E. Alegría Ortega and P. N. Ríos González (eds.) *Contrapunto de género y raza en Puerto Rico*, Río Piedras, Puerto Rico: Centro de Investigaciones Sociales, Universidad de Puerto Rico.

Miranda, Dolores S. (1994) "Experiencias de mujeres en luchas comunitarias en Puerto Rico: Conflictos y perspectivas" in H. Figueroa-Sarriera, M. Milagros López, and M. Román (eds.) *Más allá de la bella (in) diferencia. Revisión postfeminista y otras escrituras posibles*, Río Piedras, Puerto Rico: Publicaciones Puertorriqueñas.

Muñiz, Vicky (1996) "Resistencia y afirmación de identidad: Las mujeres puertorriqueñas luchan contra el desplazamiento en un barrio de la ciudad de Nueva York," *Revista de Ciencias Sociales* 1: 156–177.

Muñoz Vázquez, Marya (1996) "Gender and politics: Grassroots leadership among Puerto Rican women in a health struggle" in A. Ortiz (ed.) *Puerto Rican women and work: Bridges in transnational labor*, Philadelphia: Temple University Press.

Muñoz Vázquez, Marya, and Edwin Fernández Bauzó (1988) *El divorcio en la sociedad puertorriqueña*, Río Piedras, Puerto Rico: Huracán.

Negrón-Muntaner, Frances (1992) "Echoing Stonewall and other dilemmas: The organizational beginnings of a gay and lesbian agenda in Puerto Rico, 1972–1977," *El Centro* Winter: 76–95 and Spring: 98–115.

Nieves-Rosa, Limarie (2007) *Economic restructuring, public policies and gender: The experiences of poor women in Puerto Rico*, San Juan, Puerto Rico: Oficina de la Procuradora de las Mujeres.

Ortiz, Altagracia (1996) " 'En la aguja y el pedal eché la hiel': Puerto Rican women in the garment industry of New York City, 1920–1980" in A. Ortiz (ed.) *Puerto Rican women and work: Bridges in transnational labor*, Philadelphia: Temple University Press.

Ortiz Camacho, Marta Enid (2002) "Los derechos de las madres lesbianas en las adjudicaciones de custodia y patria potestad," *Revista Jurídica Universidad Interamericana de Puerto Rico Facultad de Derecho* 36, 3: 565–596.

Pérez Herrans, Carmen (1996) "Our two full-time jobs: Women garment workers balance factory and domestic demands in Puerto Rico" in A. Ortiz (ed.) *Puerto Rican women and work: Bridges in transnational labor*, Philadelphia: Temple University Press.

Petrovich, Janice, and Sandra Laureano (1986) "Towards an analysis of Puerto Rican women in the formal economy," *Homines* 4: 70–81.

Picó, Isabel, and Idsa Alegría (1983) *El texto libre de prejuicios sexuales y raciales*, Río Piedras: Centro de Investigaciones Sociales, Universidad de Puerto Rico.

Pro Mujer (1990) *Hacia un currículo no sexista*, Cayey: Pro Mujer, Colegio Universitario de Cayey, Universidad de Puerto Rico.

Quiñones, María Isabel (2000) "Quincalleras transisleñas: Estrategias para entrar y salir de 'lo global'," *Revista de Ciencias Sociales* 9: 28–51.

Ramírez, Rafael (1993) *Dime capitán. Reflexiones sobre la masculinidad*, Río Piedras, Puerto Rico: Huracán.

Ramos Rosado, Marie (1999) *La mujer negra en la literatura puertorriqueña*, Río Piedras: Editorial de la Universidad de Puerto Rico, Editorial Cultural, Instituto de Cultura Puertorriqueña.

—— (2005) "Reflexión en torno a las mujeres puertorriqueñas negras y el movimiento feminista en Puerto Rico" in I. E. Alegría Ortega and P. N. Ríos González (eds.) *Contrapunto de género y raza en Puerto Rico*, Río Piedras, Puerto Rico: Centro de Investigaciones Sociales, Universidad de Puerto Rico.

Ríos, Palmira N. (1993) "Gender, industrialization and development in Puerto Rico" in C. E. Bose and E. Acosta-Belén (eds.) *Women in the Latin American development process*, Philadelphia: Temple University Press.

Ríos González, Palmira (2005) "¿Majestad Negra? Raza, género y desigualdad social en Puerto Rico" in I. E. Alegría Ortega and P. N. Ríos González (eds.) *Contrapunto de género y raza en Puerto Rico*, Río Piedras, Puerto Rico: Centro de Investigaciones Sociales, Universidad de Puerto Rico.

Rivera Lassén, Ana Irma (2001) "La organización de las mujeres y las organizaciones feministas en Puerto Rico: Mujer Intégrate Ahora y otras historias de la década" in Ana Irma Rivera Lassén and Elizabeth Crespo Kebler (eds.) *Documentos del feminismo en Puerto Rico: Facsímiles de la historia, vol. 1, 1970–1979*, San Juan: Editorial de la Universidad de Puerto Rico.

Rivera Lassén, Ana Irma, and Elizabeth Crespo Kebler (2001) *Documentos del feminismo en Puerto Rico: Facsímiles de la historia, vol. 1, 1970–1979*, San Juan: Editorial de la Universidad de Puerto Rico.

Román, Cynthia V., Brenda Liz Vargas, and Frances Hernández (1999) "De la violencia doméstica a la violencia domesticada," *Bordes* 7: 12–18.

Román, Madeline (1993) *Estado y criminalidad en Puerto Rico*, San Juan, Puerto Rico: Publicaciones Puertorriqueñas.

—— (1999) "Ardientes cuadriláteros," *Bordes* 7: 8–11.

—— (2004) "Vínculos apasionados: Volver sobre la pregunta, ¿qué es ser mujer?" *Identidades* 2, 2: 81–89.

Safa, Helen I. (1995) *The myth of the male breadwinner. Women and industrialization in the Caribbean*, Boulder, CO: Westview.

—— (1998) "Female-headed households in the Caribbean: Sign of pathology or alternative form of family organization?," *Brown Journal of World Affairs* 5, 2: 203–214.

Sánchez De León, Carmen Margarita (2002) "La construcción del género y la orientación sexual," *Revista Jurídica Universidad Interamericana de Puerto Rico, Facultad de Derecho* 36, 3: 433–440.

Sánchez-Korrol, Virginia (1996) "Toward bilingual education: Puerto Rican women teachers in New York City schools, 1947–1967" in A. Ortiz (ed.) *Puerto Rican women and work: Bridges in transnational labor*, Philadelphia: Temple University Press.

Santiago-Valles, Kelvin A. (1994) *"Subject people" and colonial discourses: Economic transformation and social disorder in Puerto Rico, 1898–1940*, Albany: State University of New York Press.

—— (1999a) " 'Higher womanhood' among the 'lower races': Julia McNair Henry in Puerto Rico and the 'burdens' of 1898," *Radical History Review* 73: 47–73.

—— (1999b) "The sexual appeal of racial differences: U. S. travel writing and anxious Americanness in turn of the century Puerto Rico" in R. Scott-Childress (ed.) *Race and the production of modern American nationalism*, New York: Garland.

Silva Bonilla, Ruth (1981) "El lenguaje como mediación ideológica entre la experiencia y la conciencia de las mujeres trabajadoras en Puerto Rico," *Revista de Ciencias Sociales* 23, 1–2: 21–50.

Silva Bonilla, Ruth M., J. Rodríguez, V. Cáceres, L. Martínez, and N. Torres (1990) *Hay amores que matan: La violencia contra las mujeres en la vida conyugal*, Río Piedras, Puerto Rico: Huracán.

Suárez Findlay, Eileen J. (1999) *Imposing decency: The politics of sexuality and race in Puerto Rico, 1870–1920*, Durham, NC: Duke University Press.

Toro Alfonso, José and Sheilla Rodríguez-Madera (2005) *Al márgen del género: La violencia doméstica en parejas del mismo sexo*, San Juan, Puerto Rico: Ediciones Huracán.

Toro-Morn, Maura I. (1995) "Gender, class, family, and migration: Puerto Rican women in Chicago," *Gender & Society* 9, 6: 712–726.

Torres Viada, Frank C. (2002) "Una mirada a la igualdad de género: Modelos y acercamientos teóricos al interior de nuestro Tribunal Supremo," *Revista Jurídica Universidad Interamericana de Puerto Rico, Facultad de Derecho* 36, 3: 673–696.

Torruellas, Rosa M., Rina Benmayor, and Ana Juarbe (1996) "Negotiating gender, work, and welfare: Familia as productive labor among Puerto Rican women in New York City" in A. Ortiz (ed.) *Puerto*

Rican women and work: Bridges in transnational labor, Philadelphia: Temple University Press.

Vale Nieves, Otomie (2003) "De la construcción a las construcciones: el género que se desborda" in L. M. Martínez Ramos and M. Tamargo López (eds.) *Género, sociedad y cultura*, San Juan, Puerto Rico: Centro Interdisciplinario de Investigación y Estudios del Género, Universidad Interamericana de Puerto Rico, Recinto Metropolitano.

Valle Ferrer, Diana (1999) "Validating coping strategies and empowering Latino battered women in Puerto Rico" in A. Roberts (ed.) *Battered women and their families*, New York: Springer.

—— (2002) "Domestic violence in Latino cultures" in L. R. Paglicci, A. R. Roberts, and J. S. Wodarsky (eds.) *Handbook of violence*, Hoboken, NJ: Wiley.

Valle Ferrer, Norma, Bertha Hiriart, and Ana María Amado (1996) *El abc de un periodismo no sexista*, Santiago, Chile: Editorial FEMPRESS.

Vicente, Esther (1999) "Beyond law reform: The Puerto Rican experience in the construction and implementation of the Domestic Violence Act," *Revista Jurídica de la Universidad de Puerto Rico* 68, 3: 553–633.

—— (2003) "Violencia en las relaciones de pareja: discusiones y repercusiones" in L. M. Martínez Ramos and M. Tamargo López (eds.) *Género, sociedad y cultura*, San Juan, Puerto Rico: Centro Interdisciplinario de Investigación y Estudios del Género, Universidad Interamericana de Puerto Rico, Recinto Metropolitano.

Whalen, Carmen Teresa (1998) "Labor migrants or submissive wives: Competing narratives of Puerto Rican women in the post–world war era" in F. Matos Rodríguez and L. C. Delgado (eds.) *Puerto Rican women's history: New perspectives*, Armonk, NY: M. E. Sharpe.

CHAPTER 17

Gender Studies in Cuba: Methodological Approaches, 1974–2007

Marta Núñez Sarmiento

This article aims at organizing the Cuban gender studies jigsaw puzzle, emphasizing only its methodological approaches and its gender perspectives. I also describe the social and historical context prevailing in Cuba 25 years ago, to understand the moment when the majority of Cuban researchers started studying gender issues—mainly about women—and to explain why we started many years after our colleagues from Latin America, the United States, Canada, and Western Europe. In Cuba, there was no boom of social research on gender; instead what happened was a sort of flow of studies in this direction, which we all slowly decided to join. The reasons for doing so are found at the macro social level as well as at the individual level of the professional and emotional needs of researchers.

Beginning in 1985, I focused my research on Cuban women in traditional and nontraditional jobs, as well as on images of women in the Cuban mass media. Lately I have engaged in topics concerning gender and politics, as a way to confirm the usefulness of the gender approach in matters transcending gender relations. Since 1973, I have been teaching methodology and methods of sociological research at the University of Havana. The intersection of these subjects in research and teaching helped me to develop an in-depth interview for the 26 researchers in my sample asking them to focus on items concerning methodological approaches and

methods that are linked to the gender perspectives they use in their studies.

The Appendix to this article lists some of the works on gender written by the researchers I interviewed, printed in a few Cuban journals, in many foreign publications, and in books, or still unpublished as of 2007. The bulk of our studies were ready to go to press in the 1990s, in the midst of the Cuban crisis, when printing facilities were very limited and several publications were temporally closed. For the sake of brevity, I listed only three works from each researcher.

Before describing my methods, I want to clarify several important research issues. First, writing this article was a highly collaborative experience because the colleagues I interviewed changed the questions I posed and added others I had not imagined. Second, I focus on the methodological approaches used by these scholars to study gender relations. I did not study the contents of their works, although I am familiar with most of them. I see this as the next research step, and it is open to anyone who wishes to use the articles and books listed in the Appendix. Third, I am not a specialist in gender theory and did not ask about theory during the interviews, nor did I focus on the difficulties in trying to apply the results of these studies. Fourth, I include only Cuban social scientists specializing in gender relations and living in Havana though they are from different disciplines and age groups. Most have specialized in gender issues, while others do not focus solely on these topics but pay attention to gender relations throughout their research. Finally, in preparing this article, I was inspired by the articles written during the second half of the 1990s by Cubans Mayda Alvarez (1995), Luisa Campuzano (1996), Nara Araújo (1996), Norma Vasallo (1995), and North American Carollee Bengelsdorf (1997), dealing with gender studies in Cuba.

SAMPLE AND METHOD

From May to July of 2001, I interviewed 26 scholars. I intentionally selected my sample to include several disciplines and research topics, different sex and age groups and professionals working in academia, government, international institutions, and non-governmental organizations. The key informants are among the most important specialists dealing with gender in Cuba, but my sample is biased. I did not include some well-known scholars who strongly contributed to developing gender research and teaching in Cuba. I am thinking of Cuban professors and writers Graciela Pogolotti and Adelaida de Juan, Cuban journalist Mirta Rodríguez Calderón, Cuban psychologist and professor Patricia Ares, and North American anthropologist John Doumoulin. My interviewees mentioned their names, as well as those of Cuban writers Vicentina Antuña and Mirta Aguirre (also a poet), Dominican essay writer Camila Henríquez Ureña, and Argentine sociologist Isabel Larguía, who are no longer among us, but who taught in Cuban academia with a gender perspective. I believe there are strengths in working with intentional samples like the one used here.

Studies of this sort, require deep professional and personal empathic relations between those who ask questions and those who respond, and they favor exchanges among equals rather than focusing on the famous. People in my sample followed the basic guidelines in my questionnaire, but felt they could change some of the questions, cut out others, and include topics I had not considered. It made me rethink methodological matters dealing with gender research and start dealing with others we had not previously thought about. Eventually, I decided to become part of the sample, so that I exchanged my views with those I interviewed. I did so because they wanted to know my own answers; I also felt the need to dissent from their opinions or to agree with them. I wanted to turn the in-depth interviews into actual dialogues to avoid problems that Bourdieu ([1973] 1987) identified long ago. He stated that sociological interviews usually do not favor the free flow of ideas for the interviewer controls the question-making process, leaving the interviewee to merely answer the questions. Therefore, information runs only in one way: from the respondent to the researcher guiding the interview, from the commanded to the person in command.

The guilt I felt for not following the rules of orthodox methodology vanished when several persons in the sample said that researchers must engage the rules of gender perspectives in the sense that they must understand their own subjectivities to explain the subjectivities of the persons they are studying. It is a matter of understanding our own ideologies from a scientific point of view, of controlling their inclusion throughout the research process, so that we are able to avoid imposing our own views on those persons we are investigating.

I asked the interviewees to focus on the social and personal settings in which they became involved in gender studies, the motivations leading them to do so, the most distinctive methodological traits composing their gender perspectives, the methods that they generally have used in the course of their research, and the non-Cuban authors who have influenced their studies. Finally, I asked them to summarize the ideas they would suggest to Cuban social scientists engaging in gender studies. This article organizes their analytical and critical thoughts on the ways they approach their topics, highlighting their methodological views.

I interviewed 22 women and 4 men. In 2001 their ages ranged from 23 to 65 years old: 3 of them were in their 20s, 1 was in her 30s, 6 were in their 40s, 9 were in their 50s, and 7 were in their 60s. There are 21 whites and 5 Blacks. Occupationally, 6 are sociologists, 5 historians, 4 in arts and letters, 2 lawyers, 3 psychologists, 3 demographers, 1 biologist, 1 engineer, and 1 psychiatrist. Sixteen have Ph.D.s and 7 hold master's degrees, which they completed in Cuba, the former USSR, the former German Democratic Republic, Chile, Romania, Hungary, and Mexico. There are 13 full professors, 2 assistant professors, 3 full researchers, and 3 assistant researchers, which are the highest teaching and research ranks in Cuba.

Several of them hold decision-making posts: the director of the Center for Studies on Population and Development at the National Statistics Office of Cuba and also of the National Census of 2002, the editor-in-chief of the journal *Revolución y Cultura* and the head of the Women's Studies Program at the Casa de las Américas, the head of the Women's Studies Center at the Federation of Cuban Women, the directors of the Women's Studies Programs at the University of Havana and the Cátedra Gertrudis Gomez de Avellaneda. Others head or have headed departments and research teams at the university and centers belonging to the Academy of Sciences.

The interviewees deal with the following topics within gender relations: the history of Cuba in the nineteenth and twentieth centuries (families, Black female slaves, and women underground and guerrilla fighters during the 1950s); the role of women in history, culture, and the shaping of Cuban identity during the nineteenth and twentieth centuries, emphasizing the way they were represented in literature, history, political documents, and all types of texts; women in population and development studies in Cuba; gender and empowerment; women and race; traditional and nontraditional women's jobs; images of women and men in mass media; rural women; homosexuals; female prostitution in the nineteenth century and today; women and health, health policies, and reproductive health; middle-aged women; women, generations, and youth; women in comparative and family law; and differences related to gender in the life standards of people suffering stigmatized illnesses (e.g., HIV, tuberculosis, and leprosy).

In reporting my results, I do not use pseudonyms. Indeed, I have the scholars' permission to use their names.

THE SOCIAL AND PERSONAL CONTEXT FOR CUBAN RESEARCHERS IN THE 1980s, THE 1990s, AND SINCE 2000

The majority of the researchers in this sample started focusing their studies on gender relations, mainly on women, in the middle of the 1980s or early in the 1990s. Therefore, I decided to reconstruct the social and personal conditions of that period to help the reader understand why they decided to begin then.

The epistemological decision to understand how people act according to their social and economic contexts comes from my Marxist formation and from the gender perspective. In taking this approach, I feel close to standpoint epistemology, as defined by Nancy Naples (2003).

The three researchers who were younger than 30 became familiar with gender topics in the course of their undergraduate studies during the 1990s. This explains why they wrote their bachelor's and master's degree theses on gender relations. They began dealing with these themes at a younger age than the rest of my informants and with a wider gender-sensitive culture around them.

In the midst of the 1970s, the three demographers and the sociologist who taught demography were the first specialists in the sample to acknowledge the differences revealed in statistical data when using the variable *sex*. But they started using a gender approach only at the beginning or middle of the 1980s. Next came the specialists who, early in the 1980s, wanted to study women in Cuban literature of the nineteenth and twentieth centuries. The rest started investigating gender relations during the second half of the 1980s or early in the 1990s.

I cannot explain yet why the process of entering the field of gender studies evolved this way. It may have had to do with the professions of the scholars in my sample. What were the social contexts related to women when gender studies began developing in Cuba, and what were the personal settings of the researchers? Cuban women's social and economic development became evident around 1985–1986. Women composed 38 percent of the labor force and 56 percent of all professional and technical workers in the state civil sector (*Anuario Estadístico de Cuba 1986* 1987: 199). Increased female representation in education was visible, with 52 percent of all university graduates and 54 percent of upper-secondary-level graduates being women (*Anuario Estadístico de Cuba 1986* 1987: 521–522). Indeed, women workers had higher educational levels than men in the same jobs.

At the political level, the rectification process, which expanded from late 1984 until 1988/1989, was aimed at correcting sex discrimination, especially as suffered by women workers. This was one of the reasons for the massive construction of nurseries, houses, and new schools. In 1986, the Third Congress of the Communist Party of Cuba declared the need to promote women, Blacks, and youth to decision-making positions.

The Fourth Congress of the Federation of Cuban Women in 1985 evidenced the rise of women's participation in all spheres of life. This organization urged Cuban specialists (women and men) to attend international events where they could compare the situation of Cuban women with those of women in other countries. Such events included the preparatory meeting of Latin American and Caribbean representatives for the United Nations Conference in Nairobi on the Decade of Women (Havana in 1984), the international meeting of Women on the Foreign Debt (Havana in 1985), and the United Nations Conference for the Decade of Women (Nairobi in 1985). The 1997 National Plan of Action of the Cuban Government to Supervise the Platform of Actions for the Advancement of Women, which was agreed on at the UN 1995 Beijing Conference, has guided Cuban government institutions in their quest to promote women's participation in all aspects of life, mainly at their jobs and in managerial positions.

The presence of Cuban scholars at international conferences on women grew beginning in 1985. Through the Federation of Cuban Women, Cuba was represented in the meetings of the Convention for the Elimination of all Forms of Exploitation on Women at the United Nations headquarters in New York. In the course of these and other meetings, Cuban delegates were able to give and get feedback regarding the implementation of social policies benefiting women in Cuba. Cuban scholars dialogued with their colleagues from Latin American, American, Canadian, and Western European universities and became acquainted with their women's studies programs. They were attracted by the feminist trends of thought aimed at unveiling and explaining inequalities between men and women, especially questions related to the feminization of poverty. At the same time, the United Nations Fund for Population

Activities promoted studies on population and development, underlining the need to use sociological approaches to analyzing demographic data.

The Federation of Cuban Women coordinated social research programs on Cuban women with Cuban and foreign scholars, thus mobilizing a revival of sociological research in Cuba, not only in reference to women. For example, in 1987, a study of women workers was carried out at the Celia Sánchez Manduley textile factory in Santiago de Cuba; another study was carried out between 1986 and 1989 by American anthropologist Helen Safa (1989) and the Federation of Cuban Women in the Ariguanabo textile factory, 40 kilometers southwest of Havana; and a third comparative study was carried out from 1987 to 1988 on women's employment in five countries of the Americas. Participants in the 1988 National Seminar on the Implementation of the Nairobi Strategies for Women in Cuba (held in Havana) developed multidisciplinary reflections on the situation of Cuban women.

The Cuban women's organization created the Center for Studies on Women in the mid 1990s, which has developed research on topics of empowerment, domestic violence, mass media, family and the use of gender perspectives in community development projects. Since the turn of the century, the National Center for Sexual Education has focused more intensely on non-heterosexual sexual orientations, as part of the promotion of an inclusive sexual ethics in the Cuban population.

In 1991, Cuban scholars and the Federation of Cuban Women jointly created the Women Studies Program at the University of Havana, as well as women and family programs in other Cuban universities. The federation created houses for women and the family at municipal levels and the Center for Research on Women of the Federation of Cuban Women, Casa de las Américas, the Cuban Union for Artists and Writers, the Institute of Literature and Linguistics, and the Union of Cuban Journalists created permanent spaces to discuss gender matters among Cuban and foreign specialists. Since 1986, scientific conferences organized by Cuban universities and the Academy of Sciences have created working groups to discuss gender issues, and these are usually the best attended sessions. Beginning in 2000, Master's Degree programs on Gender and on Sexuality were organized by the Women's Studies Program at the University of Havana and the National Center for Sexual Education.

In Cuba's crisis of the 1990s, the so-called special period, the basic role played by Cuban women was acknowledged, thanks to the creative ways in which they implemented strategies to survive with very few resources. Nonetheless, differences between men and women openly appeared in terms of access to empowerment and youth-related issues. Prostitution reappeared, and although it had new traits in comparison to other periods of Cuban history, it worried and still worries Cuban citizens. Since the year 2000, the decision-making abilities of Cuban women acquired new forms of empowerment, mainly through their growing participation in leading managerial positions at their jobs as well as at the higher levels of the State, the Parliament and the Party. For example, in 2008 women head "hard core" ministries such as Foreign Investment, Finances, Basic Industry, Agriculture, Justice and Audit.

Nevertheless, during the first eight years of this century several socio-demographic indexes related to women exhibited the same trends as in the previous years: low birth rates, an aging population, insufficient population growth and the feminization of external migration.

Social scientists in my sample lived through all these experiences inside Cuba, and they studied them, having difficulty balancing matters of involvement and detachment. During the second half of the 1980s and the beginning of the 1990s, the specialists I interviewed had fully developed their personal and professional lives, excluding the three younger specialists. Personally, they had raised children, had changed their marital status or stayed with their original partner, and had lost their parents or were taking care of them. They had lived through processes that made them make constant decisions. Engaging feminism and/or gender studies was one of them. As professionals, they had accomplished a considerable amount of research in their specialized topics. Since they studied matters in which they were interested and which were connected to their previous research, they created a permanent process of feedback between feminist knowledge and the outcomes of that knowledge, such as the methodology of social research, the social history of Cuba, comparative and family law, or relations among rural workers.

The curriculum vitae of these scholars shows that over the past 25 years, they have developed a very wide array of contacts on gender issues with colleagues around the world, have discussed papers at conferences, joined organizing committees for international scientific events, taught in foreign universities, joined international multidisciplinary research teams, received scholarships from outstanding scientific agencies, and worked as experts for the United Nations and other international agencies.

I have more to do in order to work out the intertwining of these three levels—what happens at the level of society as a whole, in their professional environments, and their personal lives—not to mention what is happening at the global level concerning gender studies. All this would enable me to explain, more comprehensively and sociologically, how each of these levels has placed its stamp on the research process of these Cuban scholars. The reader should also consider the fact that feminist trends were stigmatized in Cuba for many years, and prejudices toward them still persist. It is necessary to consider these facts in analyzing why we in gender studies engaged so late compared to our colleagues from other countries.

DISTINCTIVE TRAITS OF CUBAN RESEARCHERS' GENDER PERSPECTIVE

Practically all the scholars interviewed confessed that during their research process, they do not spend much time defining what a gender approach means, either in terms of theory or methodology. This does not mean that they lack methodological or theoretical knowledge in terms of gender. They are well read, well trained, and they are widely experienced in deciding how to approach their subjects, to collect the required information, to organize their own databases, and to infer knowledge from them. Therefore, when I asked them to define their gender perspectives, their answers were very rich.

Practically everyone started using a gender approach in their research intuitively. This was true even for those who began studying gender relations in the 1990s. Some wanted to bring out matters concerning women who were marginalized, concealed, invisible, or discriminated against. For example, Luisa Campuzano, Susana Montero, and Mirta Yáñez studied women in Cuban literature during the nineteenth and the twentieth centuries to help redefine the history of literature and the way women perceived this process. As early as the 1970s, Juan Carlos Alfonso, Sonia Catasús, Alfonso Farnós, and Niurka Pérez noted interesting differences coming out of their demographic data when controlling for the variable sex, although then they lacked a gender approach. Others suffered at the end of their research, for they acknowledged losing precious information because they had omitted gender-related topics. This happened to María Isabel Domínguez at the end of the 1980s when she was studying generations and youth. She confessed, "I felt terribly upset, because for five years of research I had gathered loads of information, which I couldn't fully work out, because I hadn't used a gender approach from the beginning."

Once the scholars engaged the gender perspective in a scientifically conscious way, they kept enriching its definition. I have grouped their widely ranging definitions of gender perspectives into five components. First, everyone agrees on a broad definition of this concept: to approach society understanding that men and women not only have biological sex but that societies assign them different roles. This is based in the knowledge that the social and economic realities of gender relations, as well as the conceptions that have tried to explain them, have to be approached by understanding that the identities of women and men have been constructed in the contexts of historically specific societies which have imposed cultural patterns assigning human beings differentiated gender roles. This means that a scientist researching gender topics must understand the economic, social and ideological relations which shape the socioeconomic structure of each society, globally and locally, including (and emphasizing) those which explain how cultural patterns mould gender identities. This should be practiced in all stages of social research, from constructing gender-oriented statistics to the inclusion of gender relations as a permanent object of study.

Some of the specialists proposed revising the dichotomous definition of gender, which allows only for the masculine and the feminine. This is biased by societies that are based on patriarchal culture, and therefore, a scientific definition of gender ought to include homosexuals who may follow neither set of norms. The majority also differentiated among sex, gender, and sexual orientation. Luis Robledo believes that:

> while studying everyday lives among homosexuals, I found out that sexual orientations

are not directly related to the traditional gender identities they assume or are given by society. For example, men working as dancers or beauticians are easily labeled by Cubans as gays.

Almost all scholars felt that identifying gender perspectives only with women was a limited view. All of the specialists believe it is time to study men, too. For example, according to Juan Carlos Alfonso, a researcher gains knowledge when analyzing the impact of men's and women's behaviors in the divorce process: Usually, women decide to divorce and get through the process quickly, while men encounter divorce with fears.

Second, the respondents agreed that the use of a gender perspective is a scientific imperative for all the social sciences. Without it, it is impossible to understand either social processes in Cuban history or contemporary events. The scientific significance of this perspective lies in the use of a historical perspective to understand contemporary phenomena. Consequently, those of us who studied survival strategies developed by Cuban women during the crisis of the 1990s had to acknowledge the survival abilities and the sense of creativity that are part of Cuban culture, inherited mainly from African slaves and their offspring. Digna Castañeda's article on women slaves' working conditions in colonial Cuba contributed to understanding this heritage.

The gender perspective also helps one understand the subjectivities both of those who are studied and of the researchers. Many of the specialists in the sample admitted that they stopped feeling guilty and uncomfortable for having incorporated their own subjectivities and emotions in the course of their studies. It is not a matter of denying one's own or others' ideologies, for it is impossible to do so, but to be capable of understanding how they operate in each person's everyday research activities. Those who study violence, because to some extent, they were subject to it, have to pull out of their subjectivities all feelings and emotions linked to their own violent experiences to attain the difficult balance between involvement and detachment. This is the only way to produce valuable reflections from life experiences of one's own. Whenever you practice these rationalizing procedures concerning subjectivities, all persons involved in the research process will be able to participate in it in a creative way that will enhance everyone's self-esteem.

There is another scientific quality in the gender perspective: It admonishes us to admit differences in society and to study them, take others into account, and promote constant comparisons. This approach analyses general and global levels of society as well as the individual level. The gender approach is an inclusive one for it underscores the need to understand gender as linked to all other structures of a given society: class, generation, political concepts, and ideological concepts, among others. These scholars see the gender perspective as a Marxist perspective, for it implies a feminist commitment to pursue social justice for all and not only for women. In the words of Luisa Campuzano, "It is Marxist because it is engaged in the feminization of equality and criticizes those trends of thought that allow only one-sided flows of equity, for example, trends which do not acknowledge differences in their aspirations for equity." Susana Montero considers that "the gender approach is a non-dogmatic one since it does not accept fixed or established truths. It promotes discussing and questioning everything and affirms its dislike for any imposition of power towards researchers' thoughts."

Third, the scholars concurred that a gender perspective has to do with politics and power. It helps to understand the structures of inequalities between men and women by revealing sexist traits in political decision-making, along with social and legal policy-making and their actualization in everyday life. It helps to disentangle the network of repressions and power, at the societal and personal levels, and consequently paves the way toward equity. Luisa Campuzano believes that the gender perspective is more a political than a methodological one: It means that each person has been affected by ideological schemes linked to given societies. She and other researchers think that it is also a political and revolutionary position as it seeks to unveil the hidden structures that explain the ways people think and act to help change them for new and more just attitudes.

Fourth, according to the social scientists I interviewed, the gender perspective is a methodological concept with multiple definitions, for the reality it focuses on is ontologically diverse. In addition, when you approach society with a gender perspective, you do it with different views, according to your profession and your personal life experiences. It is a definition opened to new knowledge that will be gathered in the future, and consequently, it undergoes a constant process of construction.

Finally, these researchers feel that people using the gender approach must assume it as part of their identities in the same way they accept their race and their birthplace. Mirta Yáñez said she had to incorporate it "as one of my essences." Specialists feel that you have to practice it in your daily personal and professional lives. You cannot study women's employment and the double shift and then accept a sexist division of labor at home. Consequently, scholars using gender approaches must practice ethics that represent the goals of justice and equality. They take full responsibility for those research processes dealing with gender, which begin by studying gender relations and end up by analyzing society as a whole.

MOTIVATIONS FOR STUDYING GENDER ISSUES

The main incentive that led all my respondents toward gender studies was their goal of attaining social justice and erasing discrimination toward women and also toward homosexuals. Practically all of them sense that there is a need to study men in order to understand their role in the social and individual networks that have marginalized women and homosexuals. They also want to unearth the social, spiritual, and physical problems suffered by men, caused by the roles that society assigned them. The desire to struggle against the nobody-ness assigned to women at many levels of society flourished based on discrimination experienced by several of the women over the course of their lives. Historians Gladys Marel García, Sonnia Moro, and Elvira Díaz Vallina, who fought in the underground movement against Batista in the 1950s, were compelled to prove that they were as good as the men they fought with. Two other graduates from arts and letters were annoyed by the lack of information on Cuban literature written by women and by the low representation of women in literary anthologies and on prize juries. Several women acknowledged that they were motivated to join gender studies by their feminist involvement. According to Luisa Campuzano, it is their broad conception of feminism, an inclusive one, that respects differences and pursues an understanding of equality that does not erase the differences between genders.

The second motivation to focus on gender topics was the need to create a comprehensive scientific approach to society. They were experienced scholars in their fields of knowledge who, at a certain point in their careers, admitted the need to include a gender view in their scientific approach in order to understand society both globally and individually. Historian María del Carmen Barcia used the gender perspective in her studies of the role of Cuban families in Cuban social history of the twentieth century. Digna Castañeda worked with it when she studied the role of women slaves in the labor force during the nineteenth century in Cuba and the Caribbean. Lawyer and sociologist Olga Mesa applied the gender approach in her studies of comparative law to understand why, although there is legal equality for men and women in Cuba today, many subtle and even open inequalities persist.

According to these scholars, one of the basic scientific traits of a gender approach is that it does much more than merely diagnose: It searches for diversities they can compare to find commonalities, and it helps them attain a comprehensive understanding of society without leaving out individualities. Therefore, all researchers using this perspective start focusing on gender matters and end up by studying the social environment as a whole. In the 1970s, sociologist and demographer Juan Carlos Alfonso became acquainted with a huge amount of social and demographic information in the Department of Demography where he started working. He admitted that all the data analyses had been impeccably calculated, but they lacked "sociological imagination." He began noting the gender differences that arose when he analyzed the data using the variable *sex*. "Imagine what happened when I used the gender approach many years later." As a way to explain this idea, he referred to the rich information one can infer when one analyzes fertility not just as an issue concerning women. You have to understand the social and economic settings where women and their partners are living and you have to question how men's behaviors affect the reproductive process.

When Cuban organizations started publishing statistical data on women, many of the researchers in the sample were interested in explaining the different behaviors among men and women. They mentioned the volumes *Mujeres en cifras* (Women in numbers)

(1975), *La población de Cuba* (The population of Cuba) (1976), the *Statistical Yearbooks on Cuba* (which stopped being published in 1988 due to the crisis and reappeared in 1996), and the *Statistical Profile of the Cuban Woman in the Threshold of the XXI Century* (1999). Researchers have had permanent access to gender oriented statistical figures published by the National Statistics Office of Cuba since the end of the 1990s. An example of this is the "Information for Population and Development Studies with a Gender Perspective" published in 2005. They also referred to other publications edited by the Federation of Cuban Women beginning in the mid-1970s, with data on women.

Specialists also began using a gender approach because of its usefulness in pointing out small, omitted, and forgotten things of everyday life and understanding their meaning in society. One case concerns women agricultural workers in the town of Guanímar, whom I studied in 1992. They used jokes to challenge their male coworkers, hammering on their sexual impotence. Men usually were unable to defend themselves against these jokes, and they always retreated. I inferred that this could be a way in which women workers used their power. In another example, in her book *Reyita*, Daysi Rubiera (1997) told the story of her mother, a Black woman born of slave parents. Using the method of life history and paying attention to the most insignificant details of Reyita's life, the author embodied the intricate network of gender, class, and race in Cuba in the first half of the twentieth century.

The youngest specialists I interviewed, who started studying gender in the 1990s, were motivated to transcend the limits of research on women to be able to focus on men and homosexuals. They wanted to dig more deeply into the differences among sex, gender, and sexual orientation and to elaborate on the hypothesis that says that patriarchal cultures constructed the men–women dichotomy, leaving out homosexuals. They were willing to unveil the misconception that homosexuality is a social pathology. This is why Gryska Miñoso studied differences in criteria on the quality of life among HIV patients and why Luis Robledo wrote his master's degree thesis on homosexuals in Cuba.

During the 1990s, specialists in the sample started studying gender relations or continued doing so, thanks to their participation in discussions carried out by several multidisciplinary groups among Cuban women. They usually invited foreign specialists. For example, there have been workshops organized by the Women's Studies Program at the University of Havana, Casa de las Américas, the Federation of Cuban Women and its Fe del Valle school, the Union of Writers and Artists of Cuba, the Union of Cuban Journalists, the Martin Luther King Jr. Center, the program Gertrudis Gómez de Avellaneda of the Institute of Literature and Linguistics, and Magin (a Cuban non-governmental organization of mass media specialists). As a result, reading foreign authors who specialize in gender matters and getting to know them personally has been a third and permanent source of motivation to develop gender studies. My informants mentioned the fact that they have learned much from working together with foreign specialists in Cuba or abroad. Throughout these exchanges, both parties benefited. They referred to the Mexican scholar Elena Urrutia and her Interdisciplinary Program for Gender Studies at El Colegio de Mexico; to the Brazilian sociologist Mary García Castro and the American anthropologist Helen Safa, who headed the Ariguanabo textile factory research project on women; to the American economist Carmen Diana Deere and Colombian economist Magdalena León de Leal for their studies with rural working women; to Dominican sociologist Magaly Pineda; and to anthropologists Dolores Juliano and Verena Stolcke from Barcelona. Several respondents began studying gender topics because they were asked by Cuban organizations to help them do so.

Once they started, they could not stop. Only one of these specialists was already a feminist when she was invited, and the rest engaged feminism later.

IMPORTANT NON-CUBAN SCHOOLS OF THOUGHT AND METHODOLOGIES

One important question I asked was, which are the non-Cuban schools of thought and authors, especially focused on methods and methodology that have influenced you the most? Which are the methods you primarily use?

At the end of the eighteenth century, Don José Agustín Caballero recommended that intellectuals in Cuba practice an "elective" approach. He urged his students to extract knowledge from all readings and experiences that could help them understand their realities, wherever they came from. All these scholars have widely practiced electivism. They named it a non-dogmatic approach, illustrated electivism, and also referred to it as the infinite capacity to absorb all wisdom that contributes to understanding reality in an intelligent and committed way. These specialists studied Marxism in the course of their careers, their master's degree programs, and their doctorates, and they have used it to implement their methodological perspectives. They became acquainted with the Soviet Marxist handbooks but preferred to draw out methodological hints from the works of the classics and contemporary Marxist authors. A solid academic education plus all the vital experiences she attained living in Cuba and working as a professional led Mirta Yáñez to exclaim, "I practice Marxism with a historical and logical perspective, from Havana, and from my perspective as a middle-aged woman who is always trying to keep her condition as a science fiction writer."

All the sample members favor constructing their own information and reflecting on it, for the purpose of drawing their own conclusions. Historian Maria del Carmen Barcia writes social history or historical sociology following recommendations she derived from the works of Charles and Louise Tilly: She analyzes data she has personally collected and opposes those who use ideas written by others, later adding a theoretical framework also picked up from other authors.

In matters concerning methods, practically all researchers I interviewed claimed to use both quantitative and qualitative methods but favored the use of the latter. They use socio-demographic information to understand the social and historical settings where the persons they study live. They compare statistical data concerning people in their samples with macro socio-demographic information to be able to locate similar and different traits in their behaviors, leading them to draw conclusions, for example, the age of women when they have their first child, the type of family they live in, their marital status, and race. These researchers combine quantitative and qualitative methods for the purpose of identifying people they study in demographic terms, mainly to measure their quality of life.

They privilege qualitative methods for two reasons: First, to analyze the subjectivities of people, as well as other facets of their lives, when questions contained in surveys are unable to disclose this. Second, qualitative methods are cheaper in terms of material and human resources, at least in Cuba. The crisis of the 1990s drastically cut down the possibilities of printing questionnaires and mobilizing huge numbers of interviewers.

The specific qualitative methods used vary according to the researchers' professions. Historians use procedures of historical anthropology and of micro history. While studying families in the nineteenth century, Maria del Carmen Barcia applied methods of "formal and informal sociability" worked out by Maurice Agulhon (1983). Formal sociability methods study the associations constituted through contracts, while informal sociability refers to the integration of networks, including families, individuals, and civil society, and links between the public and private spheres. She also mentioned James Casey (1990), whose works define families by their internal coherence, their capability of permanence, and their ability to be open to external environments. Casey broke the home-family link widely used by demographers. Many of them also refer to Michel Foucault's methods for analyzing the diverse and unseen levels of empowerment not included in the political sphere. They always analyze documentary sources and secondary ones. When they study contemporary history, oral history allows historians to explore subjectivities of the persons they are interviewing. This is a procedure that requires empathy among researchers and their research participants. Niurka Perez, who lived with a Nicaraguan family for one month, declared,

> It also permits everyone involved in the research process to uncover their affections, and it is a method which facilitates the need of people to be heard. When used properly, it is difficult to find persons who are not willing to talk.

The researchers I interviewed are familiar with the methodological aspects of work by other scholars including Mexicans Eugenia Meyer and Marcela Lagarde and with those of American sociologist Marietta Morrissey and historian Rebecca Scott.

Scholars specializing in women in literature approach literary texts focusing on their contents and the social and historical environments where they were produced. They also consider the intertextual and intra-textual relations, as well as the biography of the authors they study. They privilege reading and gaining experiences from those foreign authors who practice a critical social view and who analyze race, gender, and class. They mentioned North American and European scholars bell hooks (writer), Jean Franco (literary critic and former president of the Latin American Studies Association), Mary Louise Pratt (literary critic and Latin Americanist), Julia Kristeva (whose literary criticism focused on semiotic theory), Elaine Showalter (feminist critic and literature scholar), and Latin American authors Silvia Molloy (Argentine literary critic), Elena Urrutia (Mexican gender scholar), Aralia López (essay writer and professor), Marlyse Meyer (writer), and Rosario Ferré (Puerto Rican author). They also referred to Italian Luisa Murano and the philosophers of the Diotima group from Verona.

Susana Montero has used idiothematic analysis (*análisis idiotemático*) to search for the diverse expressions arising from women and men as readers. She submitted literary texts written by women to male and female readers and found out how differently they interpreted those texts according to their gender. For example, men saw historical perspectives, myths, and elements of continuity in them. Women brought out the semantics of denial, the intentions of breaking with traditional feminine discourses, and the purpose of denying social rules.

Sociologists and anthropologists use participant observation because it reveals even the smallest significant behaviors of men and women. It also helps researchers become involved in the social process they are observing. These scholars feel that investigations must start with observation methods because it is a way to become acquainted with those parts of society they are studying. These methods are useful in designing research projects because they enrich the visions of social scientists and they help decide on the appropriate sample. For example, in the exploratory phase of his research on homosexuals, sociologist Luis Robledo visited several gay groups in Havana until he decided which of them he would invite to participate in discussion groups. In studies carried out by Niurka Pérez with women agricultural workers and peasants in rural communities, by Gryska Miñoso with HIV patients, and by María Isabel Domínguez in her studies of young women, observation methods served to decide which groups would be given questionnaires, which would do in-depth interviews, and finally, which people might be the subjects of life histories. Sociologists, economists, and anthropologists in the sample have read North American sociologist Maria Patricia Fernández-Kelly, anthropologist Helen Safa and economist Carmen Diana Deere (both of whom are past presidents of the Latin American Studies Association), Colombian economist Magdalena León de Leal, and Brazilian María Aparecida Morais to become acquainted with the use of observation methods.

Researchers who have practiced observation techniques with their equals or people similar to themselves (gays, professional women, middle-aged women) admit that it has been easier to develop empathetic links with these persons. But they are conscious of the risk of committing themselves to these persons, as well as the danger of developing transference and counter-transference. Both mistakes could block their vision and limit their capability to observe how others behave. In depth interviews provided them with information that people transmit only when they trust their interviewers. Therefore, they became acquainted with such traits as sexual behaviors and problems arising from relations between subordinates or with topics of violence. They mentioned learning in-depth interview techniques from authors such as Brazilian sociologist Mary

Garcia Castro, Cuban-American Yolanda Prieto, and American anthropologist Helen Safa.

The sociologists and anthropologists I studied also have used group interviews, discussion groups, and techniques related to popular education. They use them to complement other methods of collecting information, to submit final reports, and to give feedback to persons who have been studied, including the conclusions and the recommendations of the research. Ana Violeta Castañeda said that these methods "contribute to the research/action and participation processes, for they favor an open flow of reflections, where participants speak from their realities. Their subjectivities can be analyzed and, with this new knowledge, they can transform their environments." Among the sources they have consulted for these methods are texts produced by the Research Center for Women's Action, headed by Magaly Pineda in the Dominican Republic, and the Center for Women's Studies in Chile and the works of Brazilian educator Pablo Freire.

Sociologists have used content analysis to reveal the images of women transmitted by Cuban mass media and to unveil the new needs and values related to gender that are present in Cuban ideology today. This was the main method used in studies on images of men and women in the lyrics of the traditional and the new *trova* (songs) and images of women in tourist advertising developed by Cubans. The foreign authors most often consulted were Michelle and Armand Mattelart and Maureen Honey.

Specialists in the sample also are acquainted with the life history method developed or honed by Oscar Lewis, Elena Poniatowska, Elsa Chaney, and Arlie Hochschild, but they have not used it very much. The only sociologist who has published a work based on life history is Niurka Pérez (1986), titled *El hogar de Ana* (Ana's Home).

CONCLUSIONS: METHODOLOGICAL SUGGESTIONS FOR SPECIALISTS ENGAGING IN GENDER STUDIES

I would like to conclude with several methodological suggestions that these researchers had for others interested in gender studies. They indicated that whoever decides to study gender relations must consider gender a relational category that expresses hierarchical cultural attributes of one sex in relation to the other. They must not forget this approach when they analyze the history of cultural relations in terms of power and domination at the societal and individual levels. One must study feminism in its widest conceptualization and not reduce it to the faulty interpretation of the female gender as the superior one. Gender includes both men and women, and we have to look at both. It is necessary to scientifically view men and to study their attitudes in the process of manipulating power mechanisms and the traumas they have suffered by playing these roles. This does not mean that women's studies are over. The fact is that there are more studies on women than on men. And many of the recommendations coming out of these studies aimed at equity cannot be implemented until there is enough scientific knowledge on the role of men in the social patterns used to dominate women. The new studies on men, gays, lesbians, and transsexuals should relate their findings to those available in research on Cuban women.

These scholars also said they practice epistemological vigilance, which means not imposing their own ideologies on those they are studying, to facilitate the flow of respondents' ideas. One must confer leading roles to all persons being studied, even those who play minor roles. Researchers look for meaning in unnoticed events of everyday life, like those performed by the marginalized and the forgotten. This is also important when you are studying history, and it curbs the predominance of the researcher's voice.

In contemporary studies, you must practice participative research/action whenever possible.

The researchers felt they should try to control the power they impose on their respondents throughout an investigation. Specialists admit that when they interview people and observe them, they actually invite them to, and make them, unveil parts of their lives that interest the researcher and that are usually very intimate. On the other hand, investigators never share their own experiences.

These scholars believe in multiple methods. One should learn from everything that helps one understand gender relations: Literature, lyrics of songs, and the messages contained in mass media. For example, one must be able to disentangle the most sexist manifestations conveyed in texts and images to learn what they mean and how they have been constructed. It is very useful and revealing to learn from negative experiences.

All the researchers said they must practice intuition in matters of gender, but within a process led by their skills, which are highly trained in gender issues. Specialists must be familiar with theoretical and epistemological works on gender relations and must also read research reports. They must know the social settings in which each of these works was written. By doing so, they will be able to decide how these methods can be applied in each new social setting and how they can be used to produce comparative studies to explain gender relations. They have to know the life experiences, the historical and current facts surrounding issues that they are studying, and only afterwards can they analyze them using theory. This is the only way to avoid imposing straightjackets on society, and to avoid submitting the social relations we are studying to theories that cannot explain them.

These scholars noted that a gender perspective is valuable in analyzing economic, political, and ideological relations in society.

It is impossible to study any matter concerning social behavior without a gender perspective. One has to understand gender linked to social and historical structures, linked to class, race, and generations. Therefore, one must transcend the description of what men and women do. Researchers have to rise beyond the limits of how they think of themselves to be able to understand how each of them constructs his or her truths in specific social systems.

Scholars studying gender relations cannot use a double standard. They must believe in what they are studying, and they must be able to change their most intimate conceptions and attitudes to approach their studies in an honest, genuine, and legitimate way. To commit themselves to the gender approach in their professional and personal lives means to passionately dedicate themselves to changing people's lives, policies, cultural productions, and all scopes of life. These researchers feel that they cannot be pleased just with publishing their works; they have to do everything possible to apply the recommendations of their research to the way they and others think and act. They must fight all sorts of repression toward their works and be activists.

Throughout the investigation process, they must be creative, from designing the study to concluding with recommendations.

They must pay more attention to epistemological traits in Cuban gender research, concerning questions such as research/action and participative approaches; comparative studies; case studies and macro-social structures, multidisciplinary, interdisciplinary, and trans-disciplinary trends; and involvement and detachment. It would be useful to analyze the Cuban distinctive methodological traits coming out from the Marxist training of all researchers dealing with gender studies.

Finally, a general observation: The fact that the majority of researchers in Cuba started focusing on gender in the midst of the 1980s meant that they did so once already solidly positioned in academia and living in a society where gender relations dramatically changed. This enabled them to learn from the 1960 to 1980 histories of feminist movements in Latin America, the United States, Western Europe, and Canada and to study the huge existing gender studies literature. Therefore, they could close the gap of almost two decades that had passed since their colleagues in other countries started dealing with gender topics. I suggest future analyses focus on the history of feminist thought in Cuba prior to 1959, especially on the characteristics of research done on gender. This would link the delay in the beginning of women's studies to the ways in which feminism was stigmatized up to the middle of the 1980s.

REFERENCES

Agulhon, Maurice (1983) *La ville de l'age industriel*, Paris: Editions du Seuil.

Alvarez, Mayda (1995) "Las mujeres cubanas: Problemas de estudio" (Cuban women: Problems of study), *Temas* 1.

Anuario estadístico de Cuba 1986 (1987) Havana, Cuba: National Office of Statistics.

Araújo, Nara (1996) "Otras viajeras del Caribe" (Other Caribbean women travelers), *Temas* 5.

Bengelsdorf, Carollee (1997) "Terreno en debate: la mujer en Cuba. Un ensayo bibliográfico," *Temas* 9 (January–March).

Bourdieu, Pierre ([1973] 1987) "A opinião pública nao existe" in Michel Thiollent (ed.) *Crítica metodológica, investigação social e enquete operaria*, São Paulo, Brazil: Editora Polis.

Campuzano, Luisa (1996) "Ser cubanas y no morir en el intento" (To be Cuban women and not die in the process), *Temas* 5.

Casey, James (1990) *Historia de la familia*, Madrid, Spain: Espasa Calpe.

La población de Cuba (1976) Havana, Cuba: Center for Demographic Studies of the University of Havana.

Mujeres in cifras (1975) Havana: Federation of Cuban Women.

Naples, Nancy A. (2003) *Feminism and method: Ethnography, discourse analysis, and activist research*, New York and London: Routledge.

Safa, Helen (1989) "Women, industrialization, and the federation of Cuban women," Working paper no. 133, Kellogg Institute.

Statistical profile of the Cuban woman in the threshold of the XXI century (1999) Havana, Cuba: National Office of Statistics.

Statistical yearbooks on Cuba (–1988, 1996–) Havana, Cuba: National Office of Statistics.

Vasallo, Norma (1995) "Evolución del tema mujer en Cuba" (Evolution of the woman), *Revista Cubana de Psicología* 12 (1–2).

APPENDIX

Publications by Interviewed Authors

This is a summary of up to three works on gender written by the researchers I interviewed, whether they are published or not. In each case, the interviewer respected the way in which the authors listed their work.

Alfonso Fraga, Juan Carlos: Sociologist and demographer

1. Alfonso Fraga, Juan Carlos (1975) *Características de la divorcialidad en Cuba (Análisis Monográfico)*, Havana: Editorial de Ciencias Sociales.
2. —— (2004) "Cuba: de la Primera a la Segunda Transición Demográfica," in Centro Latinoamericano y Caribeño de Demografía, CELADE y Université de París X-Nanterre, *Seminario Internacional La Fecundidad en América Latina ¿Transición o Revolución?*, Santiago de Chile: Editorial Naciones Unidas.
3. —— (2007) "Cuba: Características sociodemográficas de las mujeres de edad mediana" in *Climaterio y menopausia, Un enfoque desde lo social*, Havana: Editorial Científico-Técnica.

Alvarez Suárez, Mayda: Psychologist

1. Alvarez Suárez, Mayda (1999) "Mujer y Poder," *Revista Temas* No. 14, Havana.
2. Alvarez Suárez, Mayda, Inalivis Rodriguez Reyes, and Ana Violeta Casteñeda Marrero (2004). *Capacitación en Género y Desarrollo Humano*, Havana: Editorial Científico Técnica.
3. —— (2005) "Género, Familia y Relaciones de Poder," in VI Conferencia Iberoamericana sobre Familia. Havana, Cuba. CD ROM. ISSN 959-7164-95-7.

Artiles Visbal, Leticia: Biologist and anthropologist

1. Artiles Visual, Leticia (2005) "Disminución del deseo sexual en la mujer de edad mediana ¿Realidad o mito?" in *Boletín Electrónico del Proyecto Sexualidades, Salud y Derechos Humanos en América Latina*, No. 13. Año 2.; http://www.ciudadaniasexual.org.
2. —— (2005) "El proyecto Magisterio y la categoría género en la formación de recursos humanos en salud en la Educación Médica Superior" in *Educación Médica Superior* 19, 2 (April–June).
3. Coauthored with D. A. Navaro Despaigne and B. R. Manzano Ovies, (2007) *Climaterio y menopausia. Un enfoque desde lo social*, Ciudad de Havana, Cuba: Editorial Científico Técnica.

Araújo, Nara: Philologist, essay writer

1. Araújo, Nara (1984) *Viajeras al Caribe (Compilación, prólogo y notas)*, Havana: Casa de las Américas.
2. —— (2002) "Zonas de contacto. Narrativa a femenina de la diáspora y de la isla de Cuba" in Marli Fantini and Eduardo de Assis Duarte (eds.) *Poética da diversidade*, Belo Horizonte: Universidad Federal de Minas Gerais.
3. —— (2000) "The sea, the sea, once and again, Lo Cubano and the literature of the novísimas" in Damián Fernández and Madeline Cámara (eds.) *Cuba: The elusive nation*, Gainesville: University of Florida Press.

Barcia, María del Carmen: Historian and Professor

1. Barcia, María del Carmen (1997) "Entre el poder y la crisis: las prostitutas se defienden" in *Mujeres Latinoamericanas: Historia y cultura, siglos XVI al XIX*, Vol 1. Havana: Casa de las Américas y Universidad de Iztapalapa.
2. —— (2003) *La Otra familia (Parientes, redes y descendencia de los esclavos en Cuba)*, Havana: Fondo Editorial Casa de las Américas.
3. —— (2007) "Un catecismo para masonas perfectas," Havana, *Revolución y Cultura*, 3 (May–June): 14–19. [ISSN 0864–1315]

Campuzano, Luisa: Philologist, essay writer

1. Campuzano, Luisa (1984) "La mujer en la narrativa de la Revolución: ponencia sobre una carencia" in *Primer Forum de la Narrativa: Novela y Cuento. Ponencias*, Havana: Unión de Escritores y Artistas de Cuba, mimeographed edition.
2. —— (1992) "Las muchachas de La Habana no tienen temor de Dios" in Heloisa Buarque de Holanda (ed.) *¿Y nosotras latinoamericanas? Estudos sobre gênero e raça*, São Paulo: Memorial da América Latina. (Colección Relatórios, Eventos).
3. —— (1999) "Para empezar un siglo: antologías de escritoras cubanas" in Luisa Campuzano (ed.) *Mujeres latinoamericanas del siglo XX: historia y cultura*, Havana/México: Casa de las Américas/UAM-I.

Castañeda Fuertes, Digna: Historian and Professor

1. Castañeda Fuertes, Digna (1997) "Requetes judiciares des esclaves de sexe feminin au XIXè siècle à Cuba" in Gilbert Pago (ed.) *Actes du Colloque du 21 mai 1997*, Université des Antilles and the Guyanes: Campos Schoelcher Martinica.
2. —— (1995) "The female slave in Cuba during the first half of the nineteenth century" in Verene Sheperd, Bridget Brereton and Barbara Bailey (eds.) *Engendering History*, Kingston: Ian Randle Publishers.

Castañeda Marrero, Ana Violeta: Lawyer, diplomat, and researcher

1. —— (1998) "Capacitación de género a los participantes en el proyecto productivo No. 5686 del Programa Mundial de Alimentos en la provincia Granma, Cuba," Master's thesis in social development, Havana: FLACSO, Universidad de La Habana.
2. Coauthor. (1999) *Guía de capacitación de género*, Havana: Editorial de la Mujer.
3. —— (2001) "La capacitación en género. Una experiencia desde la educación no formal," Paper presented in Pedagogía. Havana.

Catasús Cervera, Sonia: Demographer

1. Catasús Cervera, Sonia (1996) "The sociodemographic and reproductive characteristics of Cuban Women" in *Latin American Perspective*, "Women in Latin America, Part 2." Issue 88, 23, 1 (Winter).
2. —— (1999) "Género, patrones reproductivos y Jefatura de núcleo familiar por color de la piel en Cuba," Papers de Demografía N1 151. Centre d'Estudis Demogràfics. Universitat Autònoma de Barcelona.
3. —— (2005) "La nupcialidad cubana. Características y evolución el contexto de la conclusión de la transición demográfica en Cuba," in CD of the XXV Congress of IUSSP, Tours, France.

Díaz Machado, Nayibe: Sociologist

1. Díaz Machado, Nayibe (2002) "Imagen de la mujer en la trova tradicional y en la nueva trova cubanas," Thesis for the Bachelor's degree in Sociology, Universidad de La Habana.

Díaz Vallina, Elvira: Historian and philosopher

1. Díaz Vallina, Elvira (1997) "La mujer revolucionaria en Cuba durante el período insurreccional. 1952–1958," *Revista de Ciencias Sociales de la Universidad de Puerto Rico*, 3 (June).

2. —— (1998–1999) "The self emancipation of women in Cuba," *Global Development Studies*, 1, 3–4.

Domínguez García, María Isabel: Sociologist

1. Domínguez García, María Isabel (1986) "La maternidad temprana: un freno al desarrollo de la personalidad," *Santiago* 61, Santiago de Cuba.
2. —— (1996) "La mujer joven hoy" *Revista Temas* 5, Havana.
3. —— (2000) "La mujer en el contexto de la sociedad cubana de finales de siglo," *El Gallopinto*, No. 39, Zaragoza, Spain.

Farnós Morejón, Alfonso: Economist and demographer

1. Coauthored with Fernando González Guiñones and Raúl Hernández (1984) "Cuba" in Valentina Bodrova and Richard Anker (eds.) *Working women in socialist countries: The fertility connection*, Geneva: ILO.
2. Coauthor. (1988) "Cuba: aspectos socioeconómicos de las diferencias de fecundidad. Un estudio de caso," Havana: Centro de Estudios Demográficos (CEDEM), Universidad de La Habana.
3. Coauthor. (1995) "Cuba: Transición de la fecundidad, cambio social y cultura reproductiva," Havana: Centro de Estudios Demográficos (CEDEM), Oficina Nacional de Estadísticas (ONE), Ministerio de Salud Pública, Fondo de Naciones Unidas para la Población, UNICEF.

Fernández Rius, Lourdes: Psychologist

1. Fernández Rius, Lourdes (1995) "Género y relaciones de pareja" in *Revista de la Universidad Simón Bolívar*, Barranquilla: Colombia.
2. —— (1996) "¿Feminidad versus masculinidad?" *Revista Temas* 4, Havana.
3. —— (2000) "Roles de género y mujeres académicas," *Revista de Ciencias Sociales* 42, 88, Universidad de Costa Rica.

García Pérez, Gladys Marel: Historian, Institute of History

1. García Pérez, Gladys Marel (1998) *Insurrection and Revolution: Armed Struggle in Cuba, 1952–1959*, Boulder, CO and London: Lynne Rienner Publishers.
2. —— (1999) "Género, historia y sociología. Cuba. Siglo XX: mujer y Revolución. Algunos apuntes sobre estudios de casos y familias a partir de la perspectiva de la Nación y la emigración," *Revista Santiago*, Universidad de Oriente, Santiago.

3. —— (2005) *Confrontación. Debate historiográfico*, Havana: Editorial Requeijo, S.A.

González Pagés, Julio César: Historian

1. González Pagés, Julio César (2005) *En busca de un espacio: Historia de mujeres en Cuba*, Havana. Editorial Ciencias Sociales (Segunda Edición ampliada).
2. —— (2002) "Género y masculinidad en Cuba: ¿el otro lado de una historia?" *Nueva Antropología*, 18, 61: 117–126.
3. —— (2003) "Homosexualidad, feminismo, travestismo y construcción de la masculinidad en Cuba" in *Aula de Cultura Iberoamericana. Selección de Conferencias, 2001–2002*, Havana: Cuadernos de Centro Cultural de España, Vol. 1: 78–87.

Mesa Castillo, Olga: Lawyer

1. Mesa Castillo, Olga (1993) "Participación y status jurídico-político de las mujeres en Cuba colonial (1492–1899)," *Revista de la Facultad de Derecho de la Universidad de Yucatán* 13.
2. —— (1996) "Familia, género y derechos humanos en Cuba," Speech presented at the IX World Congress on Family Rights, Panama City.
3. —— (1999) "La situación jurídica de la mujer en Cuba" in the Centro de Estudios Demográficos (CEDEM) of Universidad de La Habana and Instituto Iberoamericano de Estudios sobre Familia (eds.) *Diversidad y Complejidad Familiar en Cuba*, Santa Fe de Bogotá.

Montero Sánchez, Susana: Teacher and researcher

1. Montero Sánchez, Susana (1985) *Narrativa femenina cubana: 1923–1958*, Havana: Editorial Academia.
2. Montero Sánchez, Susana and Zaida Capote (eds.) (1999) *Con el lente oblicuo. Aproximaciones cubanas a los estudios de género*, Havana: Editorial de la Mujer.
3. —— (2003) *La cara oculta de la identidad nacional*, Santiago de Cuba: Editorial Oriente.

Miñoso Molina, Gryska: Sociologist

1. Miñoso Molina, Gryska (2000) "Estudio de personas viviendo con VIH SIDA en una comunidad de ayuda mutua," Master's thesis in Sociology, Universidad de La Habana.
2. —— (2003) "Calidad de vida: reflexiones desde la sociología," *Revista Sexología y Sociedad* 22, 9: La Habana: Centro Nacional de Educación Sexual Cuba.
3. —— (2007) "SIDA y representaciones sociales: intentos y desafíos" in *Sociedad Cubana, hoy. Ensayos de la Sociología Joven*, Havana: Editorial Ciencias Sociales.

Moro Parada, Sonnia: Historian

1. Moro Parada, Sonia (1999) "Género e historia oral. Un camino para visibilizar a las mujeres," *Revista Revolución y Cultura* 1.
2. —— (1996) "La invisibilidad de las mujeres en la historia" in *¿Di, mamá, qué cosa es género?*, Pamphlet, Havana: Magin-UNIFEM.
3. Moro Parada, Sonia, Mirta Rodríguez Calderón, Sonnia Moro, and Marta Núñez (1988) "¿Es varón la calabacita?" *Revista Bohemia* 98, Havana.

Núñez Sarmiento, Marta: Sociologist

1. Núñez Sarmiento, Marta (2001) "Cuban strategies for women's employment in the nineties: A case study with professional women," *Socialism and Democracy* 15, 1, New York.
2. —— (2005) "Changes in gender ideology among professional women and men in Cuba today," *Cleveland State Law Review*, 52, 1–2.
3. —— (2006) "Un modelo 'desde arriba' y 'desde abajo': el empleo femenino y la ideología de género en Cuba en los últimos treinta años" in *De lo Privado a lo Público. 30 años de lucha ciudadana de las mujeres en América Latina*, Mexico LASA, UNIFEM, Siglo XXI.

Pérez Rojas, Niurka: Sociologist

1. Pérez Rojas, Niurka (1986) *El hogar de Ana. Un estudio sobre la mujer rural nicaragüense*, Havana: Editorial Ciencias Sociales.
2. Pérez Rojas, Niurka, Mariana Ravenet, and Marta Toledo (1989) *La mujer rural y urbana*, Havana: Editorial Ciencias Sociales.
3. Coauthored with Miriam García (1999) "Algunas consideraciones sobre género y producción agraria en Cuba a través de estudios de caso" in Niurka Pérez Rojas, Ernel González, Miriam García (eds.) *Cambios tecnológicos, sustentabilidad y participación*, Havana: Equipo de Estudios Rurales, Universidad de La Habana.

Robledo, Luis: Sociologist

1. Robledo, Luis (2000) "Los homosexuales en Cuba: Un estudio de caso," Master's thesis in Sociology. Universidad de La Habana.
2. —— (1997) "Las representaciones sociales sobre la prostitución en Ciudad de La Habana," Havana: Centro de Estudios de la Juventud.
3. —— (1993) "Imagen de la mujer en la publicidad turística cubana: La revista Sol y Son," Course paper.

Rubiera, Daysi. Historian, and essay writer

1. Rubiera, Daysi (1997) "La mujer negra en Cuba (Mediados del siglo XVI- mediados del XIX)" in *Dos Ensayos*, Havana: Editorial Academia.
2. —— (2001) *Reyita, sencillamente*, Havana: Editorial World Data Research Center y Pro Libros, 2nd edn, Havana: Editorial Verde Olivo.
3. —— (2007) "La Iyaonifa: un problema de género en la santería cubana," *Afro-Hispanic Review* 2, Nashville: Vanderbilt University.

Vasallo, Norma: Psychologist

1. Vasallo, Norma (1993) "La influencia de la actividad laboral en la reeducación de la mujer reclusa," *NWSA Journal 5*, 3.
2. —— (1997) "SIDA y representación social. Un acercamiento a su estudio en portadores jóvenes del VIH" in *Salud Sexual y Reproductiva*, Vol. II. Havana: CEDEM.
3. —— (1999) *Subjetividad social femenina en diferentes roles y generaciones*, Havana: Editorial Ciencias Sociales.

Yáñez, Mirta: Philologist, journalist, and writer

1. Yáñez, Mirta (2000) *Cubanas a capítulo*, Santiago de Cuba: Editorial Oriente.
2. —— (1998) *Cubana*, Beacon Press.
3. Co-edited with Marilyn Bobes (1996) *Estatuas de sal. Cuentistas cubanas contemporáneas: Panorama crítico (1959–1995)*, Havana: Ediciones Unión.

CHAPTER 18

Feminist Research and Theory: Contributions from the Anglophone Caribbean [1]

Rhoda Reddock

Bailey and Leo-Rhynie's 2004 volume, *Gender in the 21st Century: Caribbean Perspectives, Visions and Possibilities*, incorporating most of the papers from the 10th Anniversary Conference of the Centre for Gender and Development Studies (CGDS) of the University of the West Indies (UWI)), and a number of other collections published by Caribbean-based scholars (e.g., Barriteau 2003b; Barrow 1998; Mohammed 2002b), are testimony to the growth and development of feminist scholarship in the English-speaking Caribbean. This chapter presents a brief historical overview of the Caribbean women's movement in its early and later phases, the key issues and conceptual ideas which have emerged in feminist theorizing and scholarship, and the key questions currently facing scholars and activists within the region at the start of this century. Although the Caribbean women's movement encompasses the entire region and working relationships exist across linguistic groupings to a limited extent, this chapter will focus on the English-speaking Caribbean,[2] referring from time to time to other parts of the region.

CONTEXT: DIVERSITY IN THE CARIBBEAN REGION

As observed by Thomas Boswell (2003), "Defining regions is not an exact science because not everyone agrees about their borders. Regions," he continues, "are like beauty—they are in the eyes of the beholder" (19). For some, the Caribbean region can be defined as all those countries washed by the Caribbean Sea and which experienced a history of plantation agriculture and African enslavement. However for many, "the Caribbean" usually includes the islands of the Caribbean archipelago ranging from Cuba in the North to Trinidad in the south, the Guianas (Guyana, Suriname and Cayenne)[3] on the north-west of the South American mainland, Belize in Central America as well as The Bahamas, Turks and Caicos Islands and sometimes Bermuda in the Atlantic Ocean. The notion of the "Greater Caribbean" also exists which includes those territories with similar historical experiences located on the South American mainland or West of the Caribbean archipelago.

There are important differences among Caribbean territories that are rooted in their historical development. For example, different colonial influences from the English/ British, French, Spanish, Dutch, Danish, or the United States, the extent and duration of the slave period, post-slavery African migration, demographic characteristics (e.g., the number of European settlers), and economic diversity are some of the factors which might distinguish one Caribbean society from another. Immigrant Asian (Indian, Chinese and Javanese) indentureship, especially in the

Southern Caribbean (Trinidad, Guyana and Surinam), and twentieth-century Middle-Eastern and Asian migration for example, have resulted in more ethnically diverse societies with consequences for political and social conflict and cultural expressions and contestations.

The English-speaking Caribbean or former British colonies comprise a majority of the countries, although the largest Caribbean populations are in Cuba, Hispañola (Haiti and The Dominican Republic), and Puerto Rico. What is common to the entire region however, is the overwhelming presence and influence of the United States, which from the mid-1800s claimed a "manifest destiny" (Erisman 2003: 157–158). The similarity in language between the U.S. North and the Anglophone Caribbean means that the cultural and other influences could be much greater. These historical and cultural factors contribute to distinguishing characteristics in the systems of gender relations within individual countries, contributing to the overall social, cultural, ethnic, religious and political diversity within the region.

The University of the West Indies, established in 1948, serves the entire English-speaking region except Guyana, which has its own University of Guyana. With campuses in Jamaica, Barbados and Trinidad and Tobago and University Centers in fourteen Anglophone Caribbean countries, it is the most extensive system of higher education in the region. Within the last decade, a number of countries established national universities in addition to the University of the West Indies, as well as other public and private colleges. Today women comprise a significant majority of those accessing higher education within the region, raising a number of issues that will be explored further in this essay.

THE WOMEN'S MOVEMENT IN THE ENGLISH-SPEAKING CARIBBEAN AND ITS SCHOLARSHIP

The Early Women's Movement in the Caribbean

Feminist organizing in the Caribbean region can be identified in the late nineteenth century (Colón and Reddock 2004). In the Anglophone Caribbean, the women's movement had its embryonic form in the self-help societies beginning with the Lady Musgrave Women's Self-Help Society formed in 1865 in Jamaica comprising primarily "white" and "highly colored" ladies. Similar organizations were formed in British Guiana, Barbados and Trinidad and Tobago with the primary aim to provide economic support to "gentlewomen who had fallen on reduced circumstances." By the early twentieth century, these were followed by middle-strata women's clubs and coteries of primarily "Black" and "colored" women that campaigned for women's political rights, girls' education and early legal reforms (French and Ford-Smith 1985; Peake 1993; Reddock 1994).

These early women's organizations combined their concern for women's status with actions related to charity and social work. The ability and opportunity to act in the interest of others, through social welfare work brought prestige to its practitioners and, for black women, it improved the status of their "race." It was also an activity that was not seen as selfish or challenging to the status quo. In 1936, therefore the First Conference of British West Indian and British Guianese Women Social Workers was held in Port of Spain, Trinidad and Tobago, under the patronage of the Coterie of Social Workers led by Audrey Jeffers. This was probably one of the first feminist conferences in the region.

Working-class women were the presumed beneficiaries of many of the activities of these organizations but they were seldom seen as active participants. But working-class women were active in their own organizations, in lodges, friendly societies, church groups, nationalist organizations like the Garvey Movement and, most importantly, workers and trade union organizations and movements. Large numbers of women participated in protest actions over work conditions, and some working-class women even founded their own worker or feminist organizations (French and Ford-Smith 1985; Reddock 1994).

Middle strata women's activists, like Audrey Jeffers in Trinidad and Tobago and Amy Bailey in Jamaica, combined a feminist consciousness *with* a concern for improving the condition of people of African descent. Many people were influenced by various strands of African nationalism and Garveyism. Indeed in the 1920s and again in the 1950s, Amy Ashwood Garvey, first wife of black nationalist leader Marcus Garvey, toured the region. A feminist, pan-Africanist and co-founder of the United Negro Improvement Association (UNIA) in Kingston, Jamaica in 1914, she established a "ladies division" and, due to her influence, the UNIA was one of the few early nationalist organizations with fixed positions for women on its executive (Ford-Smith 1987; Reddock 1994). A friend of Sylvia Pankhurst, Ashwood-Garvey was also the only woman among the organizers of the important Fifth Pan African Congress held in London in 1955 and chaired the opening session. In the session on the West Indies, she raised issues affecting black women, echoing fellow West Indian–Trinidadian Claudia Jones's famous 1949 essay, "An End to the Neglect of the Problems of Negro Women" in *The Negro Worker* (see also Boyce Davies 2007). Ashwood Garvey criticized pan-Africanist leaders for ignoring women's issues, while drawing attention to the problems faced by poor women in Jamaica (Padmore 1963).

In the transition to self-government and independence, from the 1950s through the 1970s, the women's movement was influenced by socialist and nationalist ideologies and politics, as well as a strong sense of a Caribbean identity. In April 1956, in the wake of the short-lived West Indian federation, a Caribbean Women's Conference was held in Port of Spain, instigated by Audrey Jeffers, resulting in the formation of a Caribbean Women's Association (CWA). One aim of this organization was to provide "women of the Caribbean with a representative national organization dedicated to the principle that women must play a vital role in the development and life of the Caribbean community" (Comma-Maynard 1971: 89).

In the 1970s, women were involved in the radical challenge to these nationalist governments which emerged with the failure of the Federation, first through the Black Power movements of the 1970s and then through the socialist and New Left movements which accompanied or followed in their wake.

The "Second Wave" Caribbean Women's Movement and its Context

Second-wave Caribbean feminism was the result of a number of factors: the emergence of second-wave feminism internationally in the 1960s and 1970s; the critique by women members of the socialist-oriented organizations and parties in the region; and the re-stimulation of older women activists of the 1950s, many now aligned with nationalist political parties. Additionally, through the influence of the United Nations Decade for Women (1976–1985), national and regional governmental and quasi-governmental organizations established "national machineries for women," providing some degree of legitimacy to the evolving process.

In the early 1970s, the Caribbean Women's Association (CARIWA) was established as almost a rekindling of the earlier CWA of the 1950s. In 1985, The Caribbean Association for Feminist Research and Action (CAFRA) was founded, bringing together the new organizations of the 1980s. Unlike the CWA and CARIWA, CAFRA's membership spans all cultural and linguistic areas of the Caribbean, including Cuba, Puerto Rico, Santo Domingo, the U.S. Virgin Islands, Surinam, Aruba and The Netherlands Antilles, and the other English-speaking counties as well as the Caribbean Diaspora. One of its important aims was to break down the cultural, linguistic and other barriers confronting Caribbean women.

Many of CAFRA's founders emerged from the critique of the radical, socialist and left organizations of the 1970s and 1980s, and they rejected the anti-feminist stance of many of the male leaders of these organizations and their view that "feminism divides the struggle." The "new" feminists, therefore, sought to move beyond the earlier liberal and nationalist concerns of their predecessors, which basically sought to improve the lot of their race and sex through improving rights to education, citizenship and political participation. These concerns remained, but the new feminists claimed a larger vision, which sought to come to terms with both their womanness and their Caribbeanness through a broad-based challenge to existing patriarchal, socio-cultural, economic, political and gendered structures. Among the founding members were Peggy Antrobus, Rawwida Baksh, Sonia Cuales, Joan French, Honor Ford-Smith, and Rhoda Reddock. CAFRA also drew on the experiences of the Hispanophone region in developing movement-based research as a guide to action.

Second-Wave Feminism and Feminist Scholarship

One of the most important developments of the new phase was the emergence of feminist scholarship and women's and gender studies, both within and outside of academic institutions. In the English-speaking Caribbean, the Centre for Gender and Development Studies was established in 1993 on the three campuses of the University of the West Indies. This was the culmination of eleven years of work by the Women and Development Studies groups established at the UWI in 1982.[4] These Centre units have now become the bases for systematic teaching, research and outreach in feminist scholarship and action in the region, building on the tradition which was established by the groups. They now offer undergraduate minors and a major on the Mona campus, a range of gender-based courses in different faculties of the UWI as well as graduate degrees, a summer institute and a distance diploma. Alongside the scholarship emanating within academic institutions, there has also been research emerging from activist organizations. For example in the 1980s and 1990s, CAFRA spearheaded some comprehensive region-wide research/action projects in the area of women and agriculture, women and the law and gender and human rights. More recently the Inter-American Development Bank (IDB) funded their project on police training on gender violence, again using the model of a regional action/research program. This work has the advantage of involving and reaching women's and community based organizations, especially in the smaller territories where no campus of the University of the West Indies is located.[5] While the activist-oriented work tends to be empirical and aimed at providing information for struggle and advocacy, the academic-based work may more clearly interrogate concepts and categories and contribute to theory, challenging traditional approaches in addition to supplying new knowledge. On the St. Augustine campus there has been much emphasis on cross-disciplinary teaching and research involving collaboration between the biological and physical sciences and the humanities and social sciences.

Caribbean Feminist Theorizing— Challenging the Mainstream

The current Caribbean feminist scholarship draws on the work of persons resident in the region and in the Diaspora. In the region, leading scholars include those associated with the University of the West Indies, such as Peggy Antrobus, Barbara Bailey, Eudine Barriteau, Elsa Leo-Rhynie, Patricia Mohammed, Rhoda Reddock and Tracy Robinson. U.S. and Canadian based feminist scholars of Caribbean origin include M. Jacqui Alexander and Carole Boyce Davies, both originally from Trinidad and Tobago, as well as Kamala Kempadoo, Natasha Barnes, Faith Smith, Pamela Franco, Michelle Rowley, Alissa Trotz, Ramabai Espinet, Roseann Kanhai, Linda Carty and Honor Ford-Smith. Over the past three decades (1980–2008) a rich body of scholarship has emerged, and one can discern a shift in the issues addressed that reflect the changing situation of the women's movement as well as the changing regional and global political–economic context.

Janet Momsen, in her introduction to the 1993 edited collection *Women and Change in the Caribbean*, described Caribbean feminist scholarship as heavily influenced by the metropolitan universities in the United States, Europe and Canada, where the scholars had studied. While I do not accept all of Momsen's analysis, especially her assertion about Puerto Rico re-creating American capitalist society, at that time one could safely say that Caribbean Feminist scholarship was in its early stages. Indeed in that publication, only two of the authors included, Christine Barrow and I, were resident in the region. Of the other seventeen authors, only two were of Caribbean origin while the editor herself was non-native. Today the situation is quite different. In the anthology mentioned in my introduction, *Gender in the 21st Century*, both the editors and all of contributors except one were of Caribbean background,

and thirty of these senior and emerging scholars at that time were resident in the region.

In examining Caribbean feminist scholarship published in the 1970s and 1980s, the themes were quite different from those at the start of the twenty-first century. For example, the historic Women in the Caribbean Research Project (WICP) of 1979–1982, organized by the Institute of Social and Economic Research (ISER) of the University of the West Indies and coordinated by Jocelyn Massiah, focused on four main themes: socialization and education, domestic and family life, sources of livelihood, and interactions with men and the wider society. Primarily empirical, this project aimed to provide a base of data on which to theorize and evaluate the status of women in the region. There was great resistance to introducing "external" feminist theorizing and instead the researchers sought to "let the data speak for itself."

The themes identified for this 1979–1982 study reflected the concerns of the time. They appear similar to those around which the essays in Momsen (1993) were organized: the domestic domain and the community, the intersection of reproduction and production, rural employment, and urban employment. In other words, these concerns reflected the need to establish the situation of women and their lives, to provide data which did not exist before, and to support the demands of the then strong women's movement for social, economic and political equity and visibility. In many ways this early research reflected the need to respond to the questions being put to the movement and to challenge commonly held stereotypes that stood in the way of women's emancipation.

The concern with work and labor was particularly important and it was examined in historical and contemporary perspective. A great deal of my own research focused on this area. Reflecting on this, I suggest that the influence of Marxism and socialist feminism, with their focus on a materialist analysis of work and labor, including domestic labor, was an important influence. But it was also true at that time that work and income were seen as important prerequisites, necessary although not sufficient conditions for women's autonomy. These influences also led to interest in social and political consciousness. Challenging the view that Caribbean women had been historically politically passive and apolitical, we were able to show their involvement in trade unions, political parties, labor disturbances, strikes, protests and demonstrations throughout the early part of the twentieth century (French and Ford-Smith 1985; Reddock 1994).

For those of us who were defining ourselves as "feminist," at a time when it was still seen as a dirty word and a foreign import, it was also important to establish the indigenous roots of feminism in our location. Hence research on the early feminist/women's movement was important to justify our own identification with this trend (Ford-Smith 1988; French and Ford-Smith 1985; Reddock 1994, 2005; Vassell 1993), and to critique the mainstream Caribbean historical research, which denied much of the agency now accredited to Caribbean women. This research was not limited to historians but was also carried out by social scientists (Shepherd et al. 1995; Reddock 1994). Important issues which emerged included the control of women's fertility during the slave period, slave women's rejection of child-bearing as a form of resistance, and the challenge to the myths of Indo-Caribbean women's docility and of the seamless transition of the patriarchal North Indian family to the Caribbean.

The "family" was another important issue, and the infamous "Afro-Caribbean Family" was the basis for numerous studies by North American and European scholars during the early years of the twentieth century. The female-headed household, otherwise known as the matrifocal, matrilocal, matristic, mother-centered, matricentric, grandmother and denuded family, was a logical place for the new scholarship on women to intervene. Feminist scholars sought to highlight the patriarchal character of the western conjugal family, at the same time noting that resistance to formal/legal marriage continued to be a characteristic of Caribbean family forms to the present. Some early scholars of the Caribbean family sought to locate this resistance in economic factors, such as the culture of poverty (Smith 1956),[6] but they failed to explain why similar family forms were not predominant in poor Indo-Caribbean communities.[7] As noted by Hermoine McKenzie (1993), Caribbean family forms have been strikingly consistent for a long period of time reflecting little change. In her words: "The family system emerges as 'a structure of the longue duree' (Smith 1982), linked in complex ways with the political economy and the hierarchical systems of Caribbean societies" (McKenzie 1993: 75). McKenzie (1993) cites George Roberts's observation that despite large immigration flows and the incorporation of new ethnic groups, these patterns have remained very stable. Yet, while the structures may have remained the same, the meanings attached to them and the relationships therein may have shifted.

Free unions or common-law relationships (domestic partnerships) have a long history in the Caribbean. Indeed Caribbean sociologists have long acknowledged a variety of union types including visiting relationships, common-law unions, and legal marriage. Today, countries in the region have belatedly and reluctantly sought to update legislation (such as the Cohabitational Relationships Act of 1998 in Trinidad and Tobago) to provide recognition for such unions. Meanwhile, feminist scholars continue to distinguish these unions from marriage and not to conflate them, as some well-meaning persons have sought to. Indeed, in some instances, these unions are a stage towards marriage while in others they are an alternative to marriage (Reddock 2004). In related research, Michelle Rowley has returned to the subject of motherhood, examining mothers as "maternal subjects" in their interaction with state agencies and other quasi- state agencies, in a context where many single mothers exist and motherhood is valued symbolically but not supported (Rowley 2003).

TRENDS AND ISSUES IN CONTEMPORARY CARIBBEAN THEORIZING

Feminism and the New Generation

In a 1998 presentation, "Stories of Caribbean Feminism: Reflections on the 20th Century," Patricia Mohammed noted that, for many young people, feminism is a dead "ism" like the other isms such as communism and socialism. She also noted, to the amusement of the crowd, that students at the UWI–Mona campus were surprised that I was still alive and remarked that since they had read so much of my work, I must be dead. What is clear is that feminism at the turn of the twenty-first century has been experiencing another one of its generational transitions. This emerging generation was born after the 1960s and 1970s, into a situation where courses or modules on women and gender are integrated into school and university curricula, where an institutional framework of state institutions, crisis centers and shelters for battered women exists, and where anti-domestic violence and anti-sexual offences legislation has been passed and revised. At the same time there is a climate of conservatism, a heightened and visible religious fundamentalism of all varieties (Christian, Hindu and Islamic), the overwhelming influence of U.S. cable networks and popular culture, and the pre-eminence of economic neo-liberalism with its mantra of the free market individualism and free enterprise. It is also a context where many women (and men), old and young, are questioning the continued need for a women's movement, contributing to the general backlash against the movement and the concern over the plight of men.

One can clearly discern this shift in the themes being examined as well as in the language of discourse. In this context what are the theoretical issues that emerged? As in other parts of the world, issues of ethnicity and identity have been very important, providing for the gendered analysis of diversity and difference within the region. This has been particularly important to the Southern Caribbean countries of Guyana, Trinidad and Tobago, and Suriname where there are significant South Asian (Indo-Caribbean) populations. While these discussions began in the 1980s (Mohammed 1988), they came into their own in the 1990s and early twenty-first century (Baksh-Soodeen 1998; Hosein 2004; Kanhai 1999a; Mehta 2004; Peake and Trotz 1999; Reddock 2007, 2008).

There has also been a questioning of neo-liberal economic policies and their continued deleterious effects on women and the poor (Antrobus 1989, 1990); the issue of sexuality and sexualities has emerged much more forcefully, particularly in relation to sex work and sex tourism, but more recently in the contexts of the HIV/AIDS pandemic (Kempadoo 2004; Roberts et al. 2008) and feminist legal theory (Robinson 2000). Issues of popular culture have become quite important especially in relation to performance (Barnes 2000; Cooper 1998; Franco 2000). This represents a shift from the more structuralist and materialist analyses of the 1970s and 1980s to the more post-modern and cultural studies approaches of the 1990s and 2000s. Additionally, Caribbean-based scholars have made broad conceptual contributions emerging out of the context within which we are working, as explored in more detail below.

Patricia Mohammed on Gender Negotiations

In a 2002 publication, Patricia Mohammed introduced the concept of "gender negotiations." In this study she provided a historical analysis of gender relations among migrant Indian women and men in post-indenture Trinidad and Tobago. In introducing this concept, Mohammed acknowledges its antecedents in the work of Deniz Kandiyoti on "bargaining with patriarchy" when she argued that "under conditions of apparent patriarchal control, women may not opt to openly confront the accepted norms, but continuously bargain for changes within" (Mohammed 2002a: 13). Mohammed develops this concept to interrogate the relationship between Indian women and men in the patriarchal Indo-Trinidadian family between 1917 and 1947, then being reconstituted after the "ravages of indentureship" in a hostile and distant environment. Mohammed argues that:

> despite the oppressive conditions under which women may live in any dominant patriarchy, ideologies and practices shift under pressure and the pressure points applied by women in general come from the spheres in which they have some measure of control, for instance the importance of their labour, reproduction, family life and sexuality.
>
> (Mohammed 2002a: 14)

These negotiations, Mohammed argued, were with the rules and customs carried over from India and how they were to be implemented in the new society of Trinidad and Tobago. While not revolutionary, they facilitated significant incremental changes such as education for daughters. Mohammed's notion of gender negotiations is important as it nuances the assumption of Indo-Trinidadian women's assumed docility and compliance within the patriarchy. It opens up the possibility for agency even when confronted with patriarchy and the possibility for change in social and gender relations and power.

Eudine Barriteau on Theorizing Gender Systems

In her 2001 publication, Eudine Barriteau introduces the concept of "gender systems" that she defines as:

> comprising a network of power relations with two principal dimensions: one ideological and the other material. . . . The material dimension reveals access to and the allocation of power, status and resources within a given community or society. The material dimension exposes how women and men gain access to, or are allocated, the material and non-material resources within a state and society.
>
> (Barriteau 2001: 30)

The ideological dimension involves the constructs of masculinity and femininity, and how they are shaped and maintained. She notes that the boundaries between the material and the ideological are complex and they indeed interact in unexpected ways. Central to Barriteau's idea of gender systems is her critique of the ways in which the concept of gender has come into popular usage within the Anglophone Caribbean (Barriteau 2003a). This usage neutralizes the inequalities between women and men, and the term "gender" becomes a descriptive noun that includes both women and men and ignores power relations. This understanding of gender becomes dangerous, for example in Barbados and Trinidad and Tobago, where, based on this notion of equality, men's organizations make public claims of gender discrimination.

Gender, Ethnicity and Difference

During the latter half of the twentieth century, inter-ethnic tensions were the cause of major conflicts in numerous parts of the world. These conflicts have specific impacts on women who are perceived as the bearers of culture and the protectors of the "purity" of the race. Attacks on women, such as rape or forced pregnancy, are ways through which conflicts among men take place, resulting in the violation of women and their bodies. Inter-ethnic conflict is sometimes reflected through religious divisions and religious fundamentalisms, which have specific impacts on women that become even more marked in contexts of inter-ethnic tension. In these situations, issues of women's human rights become paramount.

In the 1980s and 1990s, a discourse gradually emerged on "difference and feminism," resulting in a body of theorizing relevant not only for this region but, I would argue, for other multi-ethnic post-colonial societies of the South and for countries in the North. While the debates and discourses on "difference" in the work of post-modern feminists and U.S. or British black feminist scholars have been useful for Caribbean scholars (Barriteau 2006), they failed to provide an adequate framework for the real and distinct characteristics of this situation (Reddock 2001).

While there is no doubt that the white–black binary continues to influence everyday relations in Caribbean territories, more visible especially in the Southern Caribbean are problematic relations among people of color themselves. As noted by Brackette Williams in relation to Guyana (former British Guiana), the context is one where racial and ethnic stereotypes defined and shaped by European/Euro-American colonial and cultural hegemony continue to influence inter-ethnic relations today, including group competition for economic and political power (Williams 1991: 159).

Eudine Barriteau's early work highlighted the diversity of Caribbean women's experience and the limitations of Western/Northern constructs for its analysis and comprehension (Barriteau-Foster 1992: 25). Gemma Tang Nain took an even stronger position on North Atlantic black feminism, rejecting what she saw as the divisiveness of black feminism in North America and the United Kingdom, suggesting that its re-conceptualization as an anti-racist feminism may be more appropriate. She argued:

> White men (both local and foreign) may still control the economics of the region but black men [and I added increasingly also Indian men] have achieved political power and do exercise considerable control over the public sector. To the extent then that power changed hands, it went from white men to black men; women did not feature in that equation. Caribbean women therefore have not found it necessary to differentiate feminism into 'black' and 'white'.
>
> (Tang Nain 1991: 1)

Also important to this discourse was the work of Patricia Mohammed who, as early as 1988, began to explore some of these issues in her paper "The Creolisation of Indian Women in Trinidad." Later in her study of post-indenture Indians in Trinidad, she posited the existence of a system of competing patriarchies operating simultaneously since the colonial period. Mohammed (1994), like Tang Nain, focused on the competitions among men for political power and hegemonic control as being the defining characteristics of the multi-ethnic Trinidad and Tobago patriarchal order, an understanding which no doubt has resonance elsewhere.

This analysis put a new slant on the understanding of gendered power relations and ethnic differentiation among groups, especially historically subordinated groups. As feminist scholars have noted for some time, ethnic struggles have usually been defined in masculinist terms as struggles for the reclamation of manhood, against emasculation, etc. In this process women have both colluded with their men in the interest of the group and/or have struggled against the definitions of place and culture assigned to them. Diana Wells (2000), for example, highlights the role of women's networks in constructing unacknowledged collectivities among women of different ethnicities in Trinidad and Tobago.

At the end of the twentieth and in the early twenty-first century, new publications by Indo-Caribbean women, primarily in the area of literary theory and biography, have entered the discourse, raising questions of citizenship and belonging, and opening a new space for Caribbean feminist analysis which interrogates Indo-Caribbeaness in women-authored texts (Baksh-Soodeen 1998; Kanhai 1999b; Mehta 2004; Rampersad 1998). Commenting on these developments, Brinda Mehta (2004) observed that Indo-Caribbean women came to writing and self-expression at a much later stage than did Afro-Caribbean women, for a variety of cultural and social reasons. These writers, she suggests, are still fighting for a legitimate space and authority within the larger domain of Anglophone Caribbean Literature (Mehta 2004).

Theorizing Manhood and Masculinities in the Caribbean: A Beginning

The theorizing of masculinity and manhood and its relationship to femininity and womanhood has become an important component of recent Caribbean feminist theorizing. At the same time, the issue of masculinity has emerged as a serious intellectual and political challenge for feminist scholars and activists. This development emerged in a context of conservative politics, economic neoliberalism, and the negative impacts of free trade, increasing inequality, increasing violent crime especially among male youth, and violence against women and children. Unfortunately, the dominant issue that has emerged in Caribbean masculinity discussions has been what is popularly known as

the "male marginalization debate," begun in the 1980s and led by Errol Miller (1986). Miller argued that, beginning in the early twentieth century, colonial policy had facilitated the elevation of women over men due to colonialists' fear of black men. This resulted in black men being increasingly marginalized both educationally and economically in the Anglophone Caribbean. His general argument was further elaborated in a later publication (Miller 1991) where he states that, in patriarchal contexts, dominant males sponsor the advancement of subordinate group women to prevent the advancement of subordinate group men. Miller (1991) concludes that:

> In essence the logic seems to have been that if social advantage must be conceded to Blacks, through the teacher education and elementary school teaching, then allow black women such advancement instead of black men.... Unknowingly [therefore] the black woman was to become an accessory after the fact.
>
> (125)

In other words, the black woman was used against the black man.

This concept was attractive to many men who were growing concerned about the new visibility of women and feminist politics in public life, the improvement in women's status, and the challenge to accepted forms of male privilege. This concern was fuelled by women's predominance in institutions of higher learning and representation in the higher echelons of the public sector, a situation often contrasted with young male criminality and violence. The fact that the daily reality of the majority of women continues to be dismal is of little concern to them.

Today in the Caribbean in spite of the improvement in the conditions of women' lives and work, many structural problems still exist which affect not only women but increasingly men as well. For example, the different patterns of gender socialization of boys and girls, some suggest, contributes significantly to the differential performance of boys and girls in the education system (Figueroa 2004). However, it could be argued that the situation of young men is closely related to that of their, often single, mothers. Similarly, the centrality of violence to definitions of masculinity contributes in no small measure to the mimicking behavior of some young girls who see boys' behaviors as signs of independence and "equality."

Miller's (1991) discussion provided the intellectual basis for the regional backlash against the women's movement. Not surprisingly this masculinist discourse has sought to de-legitimize and move resources away from the women's movement and those state and quasi-state structures that support women's interests. For example, there is a call for the institutions concerned with gender developed over the past thirty years to be dismantled or to serve women and men equally and be staffed by equal numbers of women and men. Some ask the question, what more do women want? Haven't they already got enough?

Fortunately, in addition to this masculinist discourse, a pro-feminist men's movement, and scholarship on men and masculinities authored by women and men is also emerging. In many parts of the region, men's organizations and groups have been formed which have tried to reflect on the meanings of masculinity, to share experiences, to reach young boys and men, and to develop new answers to the question: What does it means to be a man?

The book, *Interrogating Caribbean Masculinities* (Reddock 2004), brings together a multi-disciplinary range of essays by Caribbean men and women. One of the articles by Hilary Beckles, for example, locates the early construction of black or Afro-Caribbean masculinity in the competitive and exploitative relationship between European and African males during the slave period. Noting that, for most of the slave period, men formed the majority of the Caribbean slave population, Beckles (2004) argues that the masculinity of enslaved blacks was constructed through its interaction with hegemonic structures of white masculinity, the principal site of interaction being the property relationship.

This process, according to Beckles (2004), occurred in a context where black men shared the same basic patriarchal values as white men and, when possible during slavery, sought to assert their masculine authority and power over women with deleterious effect. Their inability to live this reality confirmed their subordinated masculinity that they would seek to assert at any given opportunity.

In his 1993 article, Neils Sampath examines the negotiation of identities by rural Indo-Trinidadian male youth in a context of ethnic and cultural pride in an ancient Indian tradition (honor/respectability) and the hegemonic creole masculinities of the society (reputation). Sampath (1993: 245) adapts Caribbeanist scholar Peter Wilson's ideas on "reputation and respectability" to refer to the contrasting influences on young rural Indo-Trinidadian youth behaviors and identities. The discourse on inter-relations of masculinity, ethnicity, and identity therefore re-emerges in the aftermath of the 1995 Trinidad and Tobago general election where, for the first time, a predominantly Indo-Trinidadian government came to power (Reddock 1998). I argue here that inter-ethnic relations in post-colonial multi-ethnic societies were often expressed as a contest among men where control of political power and the state, serves to legitimize claims of citizenship and becomes a symbol of "manhood." No doubt the themes of gender, ethnicity, identity, and nation will continue to be significant in the continued development of Caribbean studies of masculinities and gender more generally.

Theorizing Sexualities

Although sexual innuendo is a common aspect of Caribbean popular culture, the in-depth study of sexualities has been limited. Until recently most studies of sexualities took place within the context of population and fertility studies (Chevannes 1986) and later reproductive and sexual health. More recently the HIV epidemic has opened up spaces for studies of sexualities in ways not previously possible. While epidemiological studies of sexual behaviors (knowledge, attitudes, practices and beliefs (KAPB)) have been carried out in the public health field, gendered analyses of sexualities begin to emerge at the end of the twentieth century and, in 1997, the first anthology of life stories and fiction on same-sex relations among Caribbean women was published in Canada (Elwin 1997). Important to this development has been the work of Trinidadian M. Jacqui Alexander (1991) who, in an early textual analysis, critically reviewed the debates surrounding the 1986 Sexual Offences Act of Trinidad and Tobago which criminalized same-sex relations among women and re-criminalized the same among men. In her analysis Alexander (1991) noted how discourses on morality had "become entangled with . . . practice of the power to punish" (137). In a later work, Alexander (1994) would develop this theme exploring issues of sexual citizenship in her native Trinidad and Tobago and the Bahamas.

The work of Surinamese Gloria Wekker was also significant because it raises issues of the different constructions of sexualities cross-culturally, challenging the hegemonic U.S. classifications of lesbian, gay and bi identities. In her classical exploration of "Matiwork" in Suriname, Wekker's articles (1993, 1997, 1999) complicated this construction. She traces the development of her ideas initially through her own experience of the existence of two models of same-sex relationships among women in Amsterdam.

There is "the dominant model mostly engaged in by white, middle-class women, in which the rhetoric of 'political choice, feminist chauvinism, conformity between partners,' . . . played central parts" (Wekker 1999: 121). In contrast, there is a subjugated model that she would later understand more fully in her exploration of matiwork among Creole working-class women in Suriname. Mati, Wekker (1999) observed, was part of a dual-sex system within which women and, to a lesser extent, men engage. It involves their participation in both "opposite-gendered and same-gendered relationships," sometimes simultaneously or at different periods in the lifecycle. She defines Matiwork as relationships based on a range of reciprocal social and sexual obligations, but something that is not based on a fixed identity. Wekker's (1999) profound theoretical contribution is summarized below:

> The static nature of sexual identity is in line with the ways personhood in general is envisioned within a western universe. Despite much evidence to the contrary, this culture stubbornly persists in the fictive notion that a person has a stable "core" character . . . a bounded unique, more or less integrated motivational and cognitive universe . . . organised in a distinctive whole and set contrastively . . . against such wholes.
>
> (132)

In contrast, Wekker (1999) posits a "creole universe . . . characterized by additive, inclusive, both/and thinking" where a "person is conceived of as multiple, malleable, dynamic and possessing male and female elements" (132). Interestingly Wekker's creole universe draws much of its ontological frame from the Afro-Surinamese Winti religion which, like other grassroots indigenous belief systems, is increasingly under threat from mainstream Christianity, including U.S. versions of Christian fundamentalism in which homosexuality is strongly sanctioned. In this context, Jacqui

Alexander's (2006) recent personal exploration of Afro-Caribbean spiritualities assumes even greater significance to Caribbean feminist scholarship.

Sex work has received exhaustive examination largely through the work of Guyanese scholar Kamala Kempadoo beginning with her doctoral research in Curacao (Kempadoo 1994). This continued in her coordination of a regional research project carried out with CAFRA and the Inter American Legal Services Association (ILSA) which culminated in the publication, *Sun, Sex and Gold, Tourism and Sex Work in the Caribbean* (1999). Her most recent publication, *Sexing the Caribbean* (2004), brings together at least two decades of work in this area. Kempadoo locates sex work within the context of capitalist political economy and the exoticized position of women of color in the racialized global sex economy of the Caribbean. While responding to this historically sexualized and eroticized image, which the Caribbean has evoked for centuries of colonial and neocolonial experience, this work also presents a re-imagining and claiming of Caribbean sexualization as everyday praxis, identity, and knowledge, as well as resistance (Kempadoo 2004).

In 2004, using Audre Lorde's format of "biomythography," Trinidadian Wesley Crichlow (2004) chronicled and theorized his own personal negotiations with hegemonic notions of masculinity while growing up as a "buller man" or homosexual in Trinidad and Tobago. He was able to delineate in real and concrete terms the ways in which the masculinist structures of society shape young men's identities and social and sexual agency. The Centre for Gender and Development Studies (UWI–St. Augustine), in their research projects on gender and sexuality and the implications for HIV and AIDS, continued work in this area by addressing a number of taboo issues not previously examined in the region, such as incest. This research emerged from the recognition that while HIV was a sexually transmitted disease, there continued to be limited attention to sexualities in the region. The link between this research and future policy in the region will no doubt take center stage as this century progresses.

CONCLUSION

This chapter chronicles and evaluates the developments and contributions of Caribbean feminist scholarship and its relationship to wider feminist praxis, but is by no means exhaustive. At this time, Caribbean feminist scholarship is flourishing both within the Caribbean as well as in its diaspora. Unfortunately the Caribbean women's movement has fared less well, largely through the maturing of the activists of the 1970s and 1980s and the movement of many into positions in international bureaucracies, where their energies are channeled more into policy making. This has resulted in a reduction of activism and advocacy and a break in the transition to the new generation mentioned earlier. At the same time, however, it has also facilitated the intensification of feminist research within mainstream institutions through collaborations with feminists located in academia and those in regional and international bureaucracies such as UNIFEM and the CARICOM Secretariat. In this context, the role of formal academic women's and gender studies programs in furthering the goals of the movement for gender equity needs to be continuously re-examined.

At the University of the West Indies, we seek to reach a new generation of young women trying as much as possible to keep that link between scholarship and activism, between the movement and its academic arm. We are at a point now where this may be changing, suggesting a period of renewed activism, even among a younger generation, although this may take new and different forms (Mohammed 2003). Our research and documentation project at the UWI, The Making of Feminisms in the Caribbean, seeks to create a historical memory of the movement since its inception to provide a beacon to guide the movement and by extension scholarship in the decades to come. What directions these will take however, only time will tell.

NOTES

1. This chapter is adapted from a keynote address given at the Sociologists for Women and Society (SWS) Winter Meeting, "Teaching, Method and Practice: Building and Strengthening a Global Community of Women," Miami, Florida, January 27–30, 2004.
2. Anglophone Caribbean—officially English-speaking Caribbean countries that were former British colonies—Antigua and Barbuda, The Bahamas, Barbados, Belize, Dominica, Grenada, Guyana, Jamaica, St. Lucia, St. Vincent and the Grenadines, Trinidad and Tobago. Montserrat and Anguilla are still British colonies but are served by the University of the West Indies.
3. The Guianas refer to all three Guianas—formerly British Guiana, Dutch Guiana and French Guiana. British Guiana changed its name to Guyana, Dutch Guiana to Suriname, and French Guiana to Cayenne or Guyane.
4. They emerged as a result of a 1992 meeting called together by Peggy Antrobus, then a tutor and coordinator of WAND, The Women and Development Unit of the University of the West Indies, and chaired by Jocelyne Massiah, who had recently coordinated the first regional research study of women, The Women in the Caribbean Research Project (WICP).
5. Many of these countries have now established local community colleges and the UWI, in its 2007–2012 Strategic Plan, has instituted an Open Campus to cater to the special needs of these territories and other under-served communities.
6. Raymond. T. Smith rejected this position in his later writings
7. Comparisons between Afro- and Indo-Caribbean family forms have been part of Caribbean family studies for some time, a recent example being A. Trotz (2002).

REFERENCES

Alexander, M. Jacqui (1991) "Redrafting Morality: The Postcolonial State and the Sexual Offences Bill of Trinidad and Tobago" in C. T. Mohanty, A. Russo and L. Torres (eds.) *Third World Women and the Politics of Feminism*, Bloomington and Indianapolis: Indiana University Press.

—— (1994) "Not Just Anybody Can Be a Citizen: The Politics of Law, Sexuality and Post-coloniality in Trinidad and Tobago and the Bahamas," *Feminist Review* 48: 5–23.

—— (2006) *Pedagogies of Crossing: Meditations on Feminism, Sexual Politics, Memory, and the Sacred*, Durham: Duke University Press.

Antrobus, Peggy (1989) "Gender Implications of the Development Crisis" in N. Girvan and G. Beckford (eds.) *Development in Suspense: Selected Papers and Proceedings of the First Conference on Caribbean Economists*, Kingston: Association of Caribbean Economists.

—— (1990) "Structural Adjustment Cure of Curse? Implications for Caribbean Development," *Bulletin of Eastern Caribbean Affairs* 16, 1: 1–7.

Bailey, Barbara and Elsa Leo-Rhynie (eds.) (2004) *Gender in the 21st Century: Caribbean Perspectives, Visions and Possibilities*, Kingston: Ian Randle Publishers.

Baksh-Soodeen, Rawwida (1998) "Issues of Difference in Contemporary Caribbean Feminism," *Feminist Review* 59: 74–85.

Barnes, Natasha (2000) "Body Talk: Notes on Women and Spectacle in Contemporary Trinidad Carnival," *Small Axe* 7, March: 93–105.

Barriteau-Foster, V. Eudine (1992) "The Construct of a Post-modernist Feminist Theory for Caribbean Social Science Research," *Social and Economic Studies* 41, 2: 1–43.

—— (2000) "Examining the Issues of Men: Male Marginalisation and Masculinity in the Caribbean: Policy Implications," Working Paper No. 4, CGDS-UWI, Cave Hill, Barbados.

—— (2001) *The Political Economy of Gender in the Twentieth Century Caribbean*, International Political Economy Series, Hampshire and New York: Palgrave.

—— (2003a) "Theorizing the Shift from 'Women' to 'Gender' in Caribbean Feminist Discourse" in E. Barriteau (ed.) *Confronting Power, Theorizing Gender: Interdisciplinary Perspectives in the Caribbean*, Kingston: The UWI Press.

—— (2003b) *Confronting Power: Theorizing Gender: Interdisciplinary Perspectives in the Caribbean*, Kingston: The UWI Press.

—— (2006) "The Relevance of Black Feminist Scholarship: A Caribbean Perspective," *Feminist Africa, Diaspora Voices*, 7: 9–31.

Barrow, Christine (1998) *Caribbean Portraits: Essays in Gender Ideologies and Identities*, Kingston: Ian Randle Publishers and CGDS.

Beckles, Hilary (2004) "Black Masculinity in Caribbean

Slavery" in R. Reddock (ed.) *Interrogating Caribbean Masculinities: Theoretical and Empirical Analyses*, Kingston: The UWI Press.

Boswell, Thomas D. (2003) "The Caribbean: A Geographic Preface" in Richard S. Hillman and Thomas J. D'Agostino (eds.) *Understanding the Contemporary Caribbean*, Boulder/Kingston: Lynne Rienner/Ian Randle.

Boyce Davies, Carole (2007) *Left of Karl Marx: The Political Life of Black Communist Claudia Jones*, Durham and London: Duke University Press.

Chevannes, Barry (1986) "Jamaican Male Sexual Beliefs and Attitudes: Report to the National Family Planning Board," Kingston.

Colón, Alice and Rhoda Reddock (2004) "The Changing Status of Women in the Contemporary Caribbean," UNESCO General History of the Caribbean, Volume 5, Paris: UNESCO Publishing.

Comma-Maynard, Olga (1971) *The Brierend Pattern: The Story of Audrey Jeffers and The Coterie of Social Workers*, Port of Spain: Self-published.

Cooper, Carolyn (1998) "Raggamuffin Sounds: Crossing Over from Reggae to Rap and Back," *Caribbean Quarterly* 44, 1 & 2: 153–168.

Crichlow Wesley E. A. (2004) "History, (Re) Memory, Testimony and Biomythography: Charting a Buller Man's Trinidadian Past" in R. Reddock (ed.) *Interrogating Caribbean Masculinities: Theoretical and Empirical Analyses*, Kingston: The UWI Press.

Elwin, Rosamund (1997) *Tongues of Fire, Caribbean Lesbian Lives and Stories*, Toronto: Women's Press.

Erisman, Michael H. (2003) "International Relations" in Richard S. Hillman and Thomas J. D'Agostino (eds.) *Understanding the Contemporary Caribbean*, Boulder/Kingston: Lynne Rienner/Ian Randle.

Franco, Pamela (2000) "The 'Unruly Woman' in Nineteenth Century Trinidad Carnival," *Small Axe* 7, March: 60–76.

Figueroa, Mark (2004) "Male Privileging and Male 'Academic Performance' in Jamaica" in R. Reddock (ed.) *Interrogating Caribbean Masculinities: Theoretical and Empirical Analyses*, Kingston: The UWI Press.

French, Joan and Honor Ford-Smith (1985) "Women, Work and Organisation in Jamaica: 1900–1944," Research Report, Women's Organisations and Movements, The Hague: Institute of Social Studies.

Ford-Smith, Honor (1987) "Caribbean Women and Social Change: Some Aspects of our History" in J. Wedderburn (ed.) *A Caribbean Reader on Development*, Kingston: Friedrich Ebert Stiftung.

—— (1988) "Women and the Garvey Movement in Jamaica" in R. Lewis and P. Bryan (eds.) *Garvey: His Work and Impact*, Kingston: ISER-Mona and UWI Extra Mural Studies Dept.

Glave, Thomas (ed.) (2008) *Our Caribbean: A Gather-ing of Lesbian and Gay Writing from the Antilles*, Durham: Duke University Press.

Hosein, Gabrielle (2004) "Ambivalent Aspirations: Assertion and Accommodation in Indo-Trinidadian Girl's Lives" in B. Bailey and E. Leo-Rhynie (eds.) *Gender in the 21st Century: Caribbean Perspectives, Visions and Possibilities*, Kingston: Ian Randle Publishers.

Kanhai, Rosanne (1999a) "The Masala Stone Rings: Poetry, Performance and Film by Indo-Caribbean Women" in R. Kanhai (ed.) *Matikor: The Politics of Identity for Indo-Caribbean Women*, St. Augustine: UWI School of Continuing Studies.

—— (ed.) (1999b) *Matikor: The Politics of Identity for Indo-Caribbean Women*, St. Augustine: UWI School of Continuing Studies.

Kempadoo, Kamala (ed.) (1999) *Sun, Sex and Gold: Tourism and Sex Work in the Caribbean*, Lanham: Rowman and Littlefield.

—— (2004) *Sexing the Caribbean: Gender, Race and Sexual Labor*, New York and London: Routledge.

McKenzie, Hermoine (1993) "The Family, Class and Ethnicity in the Future of the Caribbean" in J. E. Greene (ed.), *Race, Class and Gender in the Future of the Caribbean*, Kingston: ISER-Mona, UWI.

Mehta, Brinda (2004) *Diasporic Dislocations: Indo-Caribbean Women Writers Negotiate the Kali Pani*, Kingston: The UWI Press.

Miller, Errol (1986) *The Marginalization of the Black Male: Insights from the Teaching Profession*, Mona: ISER-Mona, UWI.

—— (1991) *Men at Risk*, Kingston: Jamaica Publishing House.

Mohammed, Patricia (1988) "The 'Creolization' of Indian Women in Trinidad" in S. Ryan (ed.) *The Independence Experience:1962–1997*, St. Augustine: Institute of Social and Economic Studies, UWI.

—— (1994) "A Social History of Post-Migrant Indians in Trinidad 1917–1947," Ph.D. dissertation, The Hague Institute of Social Studies.

—— (1998) "Stories in Caribbean Feminism: Reflections on the Twentieth Century," Fifth Anniversary Lecture, Centre for Gender and Development Studies, The University of the West Indies, St. Augustine Campus.

—— (2002a) *Gender Negotiations among Indians in Trinidad, 1917–1947*, Hampshire and New York: Palgrave in association with The Institute of Social Studies.

—— (2002b) *Gendered Realities: Essays in Caribbean Feminist Thought*, Kingston: The UWI Press and CGDS Mona.

—— (2003) "Like Sugar in Coffee: Third Wave Feminism and the Caribbean," *Social and Economic Studies*, 52: 5–30.

Momsen, Janet (ed.) (1993) *Women and Change in the*

Caribbean, London/Kingston/Bloomington and Indianapolis: James Currey/Ian Randle/Indiana University Press.

Padmore, George (ed.) (1963) *Colonial and Coloured Unity: History of the Pan African Congress*, London: Hammersmith Bookshop.

Peake, Linda (1993) "The Development and Role of Women's Political Organisations in Guyana" in J. Momsen (ed.) *Women and Social Change in the Caribbean*, London/Kingston/Bloomington and Indianapolis: James Currey/Ian Randle/Indiana University Press.

Peake, Linda and Alissa Trotz (1999) *Gender, Ethnicity and Place: Women and Identities in Guyana*, London: Routledge.

Rampersad, Sheila (1998) "Jahaaji Behen? Feminist Literary Theory and the Indian Presence in the Caribbean," Occasional Paper–2 in the Centre for Study of Indian Diaspora, University of Hyderabad.

Reddock, Rhoda (1994) *Women, Labour and Politics in Trinidad and Tobago: A History*, London/Kingston: Zed Books/Ian Randle Publishers.

—— (2001) "Conceptualising Difference in Caribbean Feminist Theory" in B. Meeks and F. Lindahl (eds.) *New Caribbean Thought: A Reader*, Kingston: The UWI Press.

—— (ed.) (2004) *Interrogating Caribbean Masculinities: Theoretical and Empirical Analyses*, Kingston The UWI Press.

—— (2005) "Women Workers' Struggle in the British Colonial Caribbean: the 1930s" in C. Sutton (ed.) *Revisiting Caribbean Labour*, Kingston/New York: Ian Randle Publishers/The Research Institute for the Study of Man.

—— (2007) "Diversity, Difference and Caribbean Feminism: The Challenge of Anti-Racism" in *The Caribbean Review of Gender Studies*, Issue 1, April, http://sta.uwi.edu/crgs/journals/Diversity-Feb_2007.pdf.

—— (2008) "Gender, Nation and the Dilemmas of Citizenship: The Case of the Marriage Acts of Trinidad and Tobago" in C. Elliott (ed.) *The Global Empowerment of Women*, New York: Routledge.

Roberts, Dorothy, Rhoda Reddock, Dianne Douglas and Sandra Reid (eds.) (2008) *Sex, Power and Taboo: Gender, Sexuality and HIV in the Caribbean and Beyond*, Kingston: Ian Randle.

Robinson, Tracy (2000) "Fictions of Citizenship, Bodies without Sex: The Production and Effacement of Gender in Law," *Small Axe* 7, March: 1–27.

Rowley, Michelle (2003) "Crafting Maternal citizens:

Public Discourses of the 'Maternal Scourge' in Social Welfare Policies and Services in Trinidad," *Social and Economic Studies* 52, 3: 31–58.

Sampath, Neils (1993) "An Evaluation of the Creolisation of Trinidad East Indian Adolescent Masculinity" in K. Yelvington (ed.) *Trinidad Ethnicity*, Knoxville: University of Tennessee Press.

Shepherd, Verene, Brereton Bridget and Barbara Bailey (eds.) (1995) *Engendering Caribbean History: Caribbean Women in Historical Perspective*, Kingston: Ian Randle Publishers.

Smith, R.T. (1956) *The Negro Family in British Guiana: Family Structure and Social Status in Villages*, London: Routledge and Kegan Paul.

—— (1982) "Family, Social Change and Social Policy in the West Indies" in *Nieuwe West Indische Gids* 56, 3/4: 11–142.

Tang Nain, Gemma (1991) "Black Women, Sexism and Racism: Black or Antiracist Feminism," *Feminist Review* 37: 1–22.

Trotz, Alissa (2002) "Gender, Ethnicity and Familial Ideology in Georgetown Guyana: Household Structure and Female Labour Force Participation Reconsidered" in P. Mohammed (ed.) *Gendered Realities: Essays in Caribbean Feminist Thought*, Kingston: The UWI Press.

Vassell, Linnette (1993) *Voices of Jamaican Women: 1898–1939*, Kingston: UWI-Department of History.

Wekker, Gloria (1993) "Mati-ism and Black Lesbianism: Two Ideal-typical Expressions of Female Homosexuality in Black Communities of the Diaspora," *Journal of Homosexuality* 24, 3 & 4: 145–158.

—— (1997) "One Finger Does not Drink Okra Soup: Afro-Surinamese Women and Critical Agency" in M. Jacqui Alexander and C. T. Mohanty (eds.) *Feminist Genealogies, Colonial Legacies, Democratic Futures*, London: Routledge.

—— (1999) "What's Identity Got to Do with It? Rethinking Identity in Light of Mati Work in Suriname" in E. Blackwood and S. Wieringa (eds.) *Same-Sex Relations and Female Desires: Transgender Practices Across Cultures*, New York: Columbia University Press.

Wells, Diane E. (2000) "Between Difference: Trinidadian Women's Collective Action," Doctoral Dissertation, New York University.

Williams, Brackette (1991) *Stains on my Name, Blood in my Veins: Guyana and the Politics of Cultural Struggle*, Durham and London: Duke University Press.

CHAPTER 19

Trade Unions and Women's Labor Rights in Argentina

Graciela Di Marco

Economic changes prompted by neo-liberal policies in Argentina in the 1990s brought about market reforms and industrial rationalization processes, labor precariousness, flexibilization, and the disappearance of thousands of jobs. In spite of the fact that trade unions engineered numerous strikes against the socio-economic, political and cultural model that set in between 1989 and 1995, several authors point to the gradual dismantling of the trade union based *protest matrix* in subsequent years, a fact that eventually gave way to a *civic or rights matrix* with the emergence of citizenship protests and mobilizations (Schuster and Pereyra 2001; Scribano and Schuster 2001). Whole towns in the interior of the country became immersed in a crisis related to the implementation of structural adjustment in provincial public accounts. The people came out into the streets in defense of their interests (*puebladas*).[1] *Movimientos de Trabajadores Desocupados* (MTD: Unemployed Workers' Movements) started in the interior of the country, in areas that had been affected by the cutbacks in sources of employment that ensued from privatization plans. These movements organized roadblocks that they called "pickets," which finally led people to call these workers "picketers."[2] More than one hundred enterprises were "recovered" from their owners and managed by the workers in the sectors of economic activity that were most deeply affected either by imports or the difficulties posed by exports, especially in meat packaging houses, textile factories, tractors, trailers, metal working plants, plastics, etc. (Di Marco and Palomino 2003, 2004a, 2004b).

The different stances on neo-liberal policies in Argentina during the 1990s translated into internal ruptures in the country's trade unions and this, in turn, resulted in the loss of numerous union members owing to increasing unemployment. Workers then showed their rejection of the union leaders who agreed to labor flexibilization and who looked the other way while many factories were being closed down. Two trade unions that opposed flexibilization policies broke with the *Confederación General del Trabajo* (CGT: General Confederation of Workers) in 1992, and joined in the creation of the *Congreso de Trabajadores Argentinos* (Congress of Argentinean Workers), better known as CTA. These unions were the *Asociación de Trabajadores del Estado* (ATE: Association of State Workers), composed of state workers all over the country, and the *Confederación Trabajadores de la Educación de la República Argentina* (CTERA: General Confederation of Argentinean Education Workers), composed of teachers. In 1997, the CTA was formally established as a workers' union that offered an alternative to those who did not agree with CGT. In 1994 an internal CGT sector arose, composed of trade unions that were incorporating private and public automotive transport workers. They organized the *Movimiento de los Trabajadores Argentinos* (MTA: Movement of Argentinean Workers) that fought for supremacy in the CGT throughout the decade, until they finally succeeded in achieving control in 2005.

Trade union women furthered the institutionalization of gender rights areas and, later on, of the *Trade Union Law on Female Quotas* (to be explained further on). At the same time, to a greater or a lesser degree, they joined women's movements in their claims for issues that are essential to women's lives, whether in labor or in private situations.

My goal is to describe this process, analyzing women's participation in the CGT and the CTA, and comparing the outcomes regarding women's labor rights in those organizations. For these purposes, I interviewed several women leaders in trade unions and reviewed relevant documents issued by the trade unions themselves.

The Argentine juridical corpus for the protection and advancement of women workers improved to a certain extent during a decade characterized by flexibilization and insecure employment, both of which mostly affected subordinate groups like women. The precariousness of women's labor situation was due to various factors, including sex segmentation, low wages/salaries, long working hours, insecure work conditions, lack of training for future advancement, difficulties in obtaining proper care for their children and/or shared childcare and, more often than not, lack of recognition at home or at their workplace.[3] The passing of these laws that acknowledge several women's rights has not permeated the patriarchal structures of society, as so frequently happens in spheres in which such rights are involved.[4]

TRADE UNIONS IN THE 1990s

Between 1946 and 1955, with Peronism in power, a model of economic growth emerged,

accompanied by the economic, social, and political integration of workers. They succeeded in obtaining legal enforcement for many of the claims or demands that had lain at the core of labor struggles for nearly one hundred years (Basualdo 2004). The labor movement was considered to be the very backbone of *Justicialismo* or *Peronismo*, through the *Confederación General del Trabajo* (CGT: General Confederation of Workers).[5] The CGT underwent several splits during the 1960s and 1970s, all of them resulting from the various strategies it adopted while confronting anti-Peronist governments as well as from the different stances the trade unions took regarding the *Partido Justicialista*.

The 1992 division and the establishment of the CTA were related to differences about the economic and social policies furthered by *Justicialista* President Menem's administration (Godio 2001). This division was different from others that had previously confronted anti-Peronist governments. The CTA claimed to be a new employed and unemployed Workers' Federation, different from the CGT, and founded on three main principles: direct membership, participative democracy, and political autonomy. It now is composed of over 240 organizations. Besides CTERA and ATE, there are small and medium size union groups, social organizations created in poor neighborhoods, groups of unemployed people,[6] and, notably, the *Asociación de Meretrices de la Argentina* (AMMAR: Argentine Association of Sex Workers). The CTA is consulted by the Ministry of Labor and participates in several negotiation bodies together with the CGT. The CTA's leaders demanded legal status, and they laid forth their claims at the International Labor Organization's annual Conferences. The CTA constitutes a social-and-political movement where inclusion is possible based on citizenship status rather than from belonging to some category of the labor world (Dyszel et al. 2006; Novick

2001). The fact that the CTA incorporated AMMAR may be indicative of pluralism and of a tendency to avoid discrimination on the part of the former organization. It is in this sense that some scholars regard AMMAR's inclusion as a sign of CTA's interest in gender equality. While it is remarkable that the CTA has been the first to accept sex workers, this does not close the debate regarding AMMAR members' activities. The debate is based on whether these activities should be understood as work or as slavery. Indeed, it was these differences in point of view about how women in AMMAR defined themselves and their practices that brought about a split among members of this organization. Women who parted ways with this union privileged the gender perspective and their condition as subjects of rights, not as sex workers. The argument, which ended with their separation from the original movement in 2002, was not only based on disagreements among the women, but also between themselves and the male members of the CTA's National and Federal Capital Board, who insisted on the formalization of this trade union's statutes.

Women's Areas in CGT and CTA

The most important political Secretariats, those dealing with trade union policies and organization, do not include women. Moreover, in the case of traditional trade unions, Women's Secretariats frequently operate as a place to return favors or as spaces occupied by women who uphold conventional gender notions.

There is a tension between the *model of specific structures*—female areas or departments—and the *model of main structures*—measures of affirmative action achieved through quotas that serve to access executive positions using a process that secures a given number of seats on the Executive Board.[7] Orsatti (2004) points out that in CIOSL's International Trade Unionism, the latest

strategic agreements are clearly geared to reach legitimization of the model of main structures as part of an integrative approach. The *Trade Union Law on Female Quotas*, issued in 2004, is one of the most significant policies based on this kind of positive discrimination. This law, which establishes a 30 percent quota for women's representation in union positions, was approved in 2002. In the same year, a law was passed establishing proportional participation of female delegates in collective negotiations for working conditions depending on the number of female workers in each sector or activity. In 2004 the General Confederation of Workers (CGT) amended its statutes to introduce the Female Trade Union Quota. The first direct consequence of the enforcement of this law resulted in a larger number of women appointed to the Executive Board.

One of the trade unions inside the CGT is the *Union del Personal Civil de la Nación* (UPCN: National Union of Civil Servants). Its Secretariat for Women, created in 1984, has a seat on CGT's Executive Board.[8] In 1998 UPCN joined the Tripartite Commission for Equal Treatment and Opportunity for Men and Women in the Field of Labor. As of 2008, the Institute has become the CGT's Gender Secretariat, and participated in the 1998 Equal Treatment and Opportunity Program in the First Collective Work Agreement for the National Public Sector.

In 2005, the issue of labor violence was addressed in the First Collective Work Agreement for the National Institute of Social Services to Retirees and in the Collective Agreements for the Legislature of the Autonomous City of Buenos Aires and the *Administracion Nacional de la Seguridad Social* (ANSES: National Administration for Social Security). UPCN women struggled for 15 years for sexual harassment to be included in the Criminal Code. Although it has already achieved a half-sanction in the National Senate, this shows the slow pace at which these reforms occur, in spite of the fact that they triggered a debate on one of the most urgent issues needing to be solved worldwide.[9]

CTA's women have worked in an informal environment since 1992, and were only granted recognition through a specific organizational structure in 2000. The CTA's Secretariat for Gender Equality and Opportunity was created following the 2000 statutory reform, which also included a minimum 20 percent female quota for executive positions at all levels (local, provincial, regional, and national). The Gender Secretariat was integrated into the sixteen CTA's secretariats. Both ATE and CTERA have had a Women's Department since 1987, in the first case, and the Secretariat of Gender and Equal Opportunity created in 2001, in the second (Chejter and Laudano 2001).

In both the CGT and the CTA labor Federations, male leaders' attitudes to women's rights are ambiguous. Quotas and Equal Opportunity Secretariats are accepted but, with very few exceptions, the leading strategic positions in unions tend to be kept by men.

The passing of the quota law allowed a larger number of women to be appointed to the CGT and CTA Executive Boards. At present, women hold 22 percent of the total positions in trade unions. Nonetheless, we find that the higher the position level, the lower women's participation. Regarding the General Secretary appointments in trade unions: Women hold 9.4 percent of all positions, while at the Secretary and Undersecretary level, they hold 24.6 percent of the slots. In the CGT, four out of twenty-two Secretariat positions are held by women. In the CTA, women occupy six Secretariats out of nineteen (Programa de Naciones Unidas para el Desarrollo (PNUD) 2007).

In 2004, after long negotiations, the CGT and the MTA came together in a *troika* that would stay in office for one year, composed of a MTA leader, a Sanitation Works Union leader, and a woman leader as the Health Workers trade union's delegate. A woman was included in the *troika* in an attempt to show the importance of female leadership. Some analysts understand this move as a strategy leading to unification, since the dissenting CGT (MTA) leader exercised most of the political power. At the same time, whenever the female delegate's opinions were waived aside, it was easy to blame it on gender discrimination. In July 2005, the MTA leader was appointed as the CGT's Secretary General, with the consequent dissolution of the *troika* and the vanishing of the female member's ephemeral protagonist role.

However, this woman was a "token" (Kanter 1977). It was clear that it was a ruse for the CGT leaders to boast of political correctness through declarations that women's "female conquests" had earned them outstanding positions.

Women Unionists: Between Institutional and Movement Oriented Discourses

In both union Federation organizations, women leaders are divided between those who agree that "women are usually relegated to secondary tasks" and those who support the ideas expressed by the UPCN leader, who lays emphasis on their success:

> In the CGT, we are really powerful. Let me tell you: we created the CGT's Women's Institute, and we were the first to implement the union quota.

They lean on the strengths of women's movements, but that same leader acknowledges the need for support from their male counterparts:

> without support I wouldn't have done much, wouldn't be here, wouldn't have been given this office, all of which was possible thanks to the Secretary General's [a male] support, and that is the truth.

They are also aware of the gulf between

experienced leaders in the struggle for rights and the rest of the female workers.

Two discourses co-exist: the institutional and the movement-oriented ones. Nevertheless, they should not be understood as two opposite poles to be mechanically attributed to the dichotomy existing between the *traditional* trade union Federation (CGT) and the *new* trade union Federation (CTA). Both types of discourse can be found in the two labor groups, because their approaches vary depending on the context and situation (e.g., the struggle for political space within the trade unions versus their articulation with women's movements). In the institutional discourse it is crucial that women workers bring their needs and demands into the trade union arena. Movement-oriented approaches show a wider and conceptually more "correct" pro-equity gender discourse, but face severe restrictions when women unionists intend to penetrate trade union spaces lying outside of women's traditional areas. It would seem as if the very agenda of such areas makes it difficult for women to shift from the movement's overall women's demands to women workers' priorities, because they conflict with the interests of the male trade union milieu.

When movements gathering unemployed workers and those in Recovered and Workers' Self-managed Enterprises began to emerge, they were first met with responses from CGT women leaders that followed the institutional discourse typical of trade unions. The CGT women laid emphasis on the factories' organizational aspects and left aside political and economic issues such as factory expropriations, the new characteristics of workers' co-operatives, the egalitarian distribution of money, and the workers' participation in the process of production (Di Marco and Moro 2004). It proved difficult to recognize the new social learning and leadership from this standpoint, since it did not seem likely that men and women who lacked trade union and/or political experience might run a factory or an enterprise. This view minimized the profound learning experience of the popular movement, an education that became more intense in the months and years ensuing after December 19 and 20, 2001.

Regarding women in one Recovered and Workers Self-managed Enterprise (e.g., a textile one, in which almost 90 percent of the workers are women), a female trade union leader coming from the feminist ranks declared that "the other sectors, I mean, the sectors of informal economy, have taken different ways; they have not chosen the structural path."

On the other hand, the CTA's movement-oriented approach succeeded in achieving articulation between the union and male and female workers in Recovered and Workers Self-managed Enterprises as well as in some picket movements. Women in the CTA have participated in the picket movement and joined in the struggles of a number of recovered enterprises, but have lacked the necessary strength in their claims for quality employment, working conditions, and jobs and training not segmented by sex.

In the CTA's latest conferences and communications the main issues broached by the Gender and Equal Opportunity Secretariat were sexual rights, especially the right to abortion, but there are no records of initiatives regarding further steps in the struggle against discrimination and labor segmentation. In spite of the heterogeneity of its members the CTA is ruled by ATE and CTERA, the two unions related to the service industry, and the trade union discourse overlaps with the movement and with gender discourses.

Recovered and Workers Self-managed Enterprises are good laboratories within which to observe how certain workers, on the basis of a cooperative model, can manage recovered enterprises by themselves. However, consideration of gender relations at the workplace require a process that may lead to a clearer visibility of female workers in those enterprises, so that they should not be subsumed in the uni-dimensional category of "workers." Apart from the romantic halo around some of the women who stood out in the struggle, sex segmented jobs remain, resulting in training activities that in no way enable these workers to face great technological changes that can only be tackled with the proper tools, so that women can aspire to a wider range of jobs and put their creativity and autonomy to good use (Di Marco and Moro 2004).

CONCLUSION

Both institutional and movement discourses could be found to a greater or lesser degree in both labor Federations. The CTA has been able to grasp the differentiation process within Argentinean society as well as the emergence of new, more pluralist demands. On the other hand, the CGT's Institute of the National Union of Civil Servants (UPCN) is the one that laid down tendencies, moving forward in the struggle for women's labor rights and obtaining the passage of significant laws.

The *Trade Union Law on Female Quotas* created the conditions, or the possibility, to shift the movement away from a specific structures model and into a main structures model. This transition requires women workers to familiarize themselves with union norms, procedures, channels, and spaces so that they can take full advantage of them. This process does not necessarily give rise to the appearance of women trade union leaders who can exercise power in parity with men leaders. Women occupy more Secretariat positions than ever, however it is doubtful that they have achieved leading positions in both Federations' main decision bodies. Regarding women's general rights, which encompass more than those concerning labor, it is possible to find a kind of alliance among men based on male domination

that I have named an *implicit conservative consensus* (Di Marco 2006a, 2006b), that excludes women from the most important positions of power. Therefore, women are still mostly confined to specific structures, and it is from these structures that they struggle for their rights.

Regardless of which labor Federation they now belong to, women have been working to achieve linkages between themselves and with women's movements while struggling for broadening their rights. Thus, no differences are found between CGT and CTA in this respect.

NOTES

Editors' Note: This chapter was translated from the Spanish original version by Marta Castillo. It is based on research sponsored by UNESCO, the results of which have been delivered (2006) in a modified and longer paper entitled "Gendered Economic Rights and Trade Unionism: The Case of Argentina" and will be published by UNESCO.

1. In 1993, the inhabitants of the capital city of the Province of Santiago del Estero held a *Santiagazo*. As a protest against fiscal adjustment increases, demonstrators set fire to the seat of the provincial government and tried to do the same with the buildings where the other powers of the state had their offices. They also attacked the private homes of legislators and politicians from the province.

2. Around that same time, several groups appeared, including the *Movimiento de Mujeres Agropecuarias en Lucha* (MML: Fighting Movement of Women Engaged in Rural Tasks); *Movimiento Campesino Santiagueño* (MOCASE: Rural Peasant Movement in Santiago del Estero); *Coordinadora contra la Represión Policial e Institucional* (CORREPI: Coordinating Association against Institutional and Police Repression); and *Madres del Dolor* (Grieving Mothers).

3. One example of such work is the 900,000 women working in family households as domestic help. This category comprises 16 percent of female labor in Argentina, and is equal to the average in the rest of Latin America. Fully 95 percent are not recorded, and these workers are the tip of the iceberg in terms of female irregular employment.

4. In May 2006, the Senate sanctioned a draft law to include sexual harassment in the Criminal Code. If the House of Representatives passed the

corresponding law, our national legislation would fill a legal void on this issue. Both in the private and in the public sector, labor norms establish equal opportunity in access to work positions. Still, no norms have been included that make it obligatory to establish quotas for certain jobs and positions (Faur and Gherardi 2005: 229–230).

5. CGT's organization uses the configuration of a trade union that has the exclusive representation for each branch of activity, in addition to a single, third-level confederation operating through district representatives or province located trade unions, national trade unions, or federations. Workers do not join it individually. They do so at their respective trade unions, but they can only choose the organization that they wish to join.

6. Such as the *Federación de Tierra, Vivienda y Hábitat* (Federation of Land, Housing, and Habitat); the *Federación Nacional de Salud* (National Federation of Health); *Federación de Villas y Barrios Marginados de Capital Federal* (Federation of Slums and Shanty Towns in the Federal Capital); the *Movimiento Indigenista del Chaco* (Chaco's Indigenous Movement); *the Movimiento de Ocupantes e Inquilinos* (Movement of Squatters and Tenants); and, *Asentamientos y Comunidad Eclesial de Base Solano-Quilmes* (Settlements and Church-based Community/Solano-Quilmes, Province of Buenos Aires).

7. These are the steps of the process: [1] The first step is to create specific spaces (women's areas, departments, and institutes, ultimately aiming at Gender and Equal Opportunity Secretariats) to deal with women's issues—the *specific structure model*—so that women can be involved in trade union activities and/or politics where they can exert their influence on decision making. [2] The second step is widening the already existing spaces, while promoting norms leading to mechanisms that will include more women in leadership/ decision-making positions (for example, power over the decision about the law on union quotas.) [3] The third step is an offshoot of the logic ruling the build-up of union power—the *main structure model*—where quotas are implemented and so is access to union leadership (Orsatti 2004).

8. Communication by the Argentine Republic was submitted to the Follow-up Commission of Mercosur's Social and Labor Declaration, drawn up by the Tripartite Commission of Equal Treatment and Opportunity in the World's Labor Field, Argentina, July 2001. See http://www.ispm.org.ar/ documentos/parte_2.htm.

9. According to an ILO report (Chappell and Di Martino 1998) covering 36 countries, 16.6 percent of the women they interviewed have been victims of this type of violence. This report covered 36 countries. The highest rates were shared by Argentina, France, England, Canada, and Romania. Using 1994 data from a sample survey of 302 women workers in the Government area, the National Association of Public Officials (1997) reports that 47.4 percent (143) of women declared they had been sexually harassed.

REFERENCES

Basualdo, Eduardo (2004) *Los primeros gobiernos peronistas y la consolidación del país industrial: éxitos y fracasos*, Costa Rica: Editorial La Pagina, S.A. FLACSO.

Chappell, Duncan and Di Martino, Vittorio (1998) *Violence at work*, Geneva: International Labour Office.

Chejter, Silvia and Claudia Laudano (2001) *Género en los movimientos sociales en Argentina*, Buenos Aires: Cecym.

Di Marco, Graciela (2006a) "Social justice and gender rights," Paper presented at UNESCO. International Forum on the Social Science–Policy Nexus, Buenos Aires, Argentina: February 20–24.

—— (2006b) "Igualdad de género y movimientos sociales en Argentina" in E. Maier and N. Lebon (comp.) *De lo privado a lo público: 30 años de lucha ciudadana de las mujeres en América Latina*, México: UNIFEM. LASA. Editorial Sudamericana.

Di Marco, Graciela and Héctor Palomino (2003) *Movimientos sociales en la Argentina. Asambleas. La politización de la sociedad civil*, Buenos Aires: Ediciones Baudino-UNSAM.

—— (comps.) (2004a) *Reflexiones sobre los movimientos sociales en la Argentina*, Buenos Aires: Ediciones Baudino-UNSAM.

—— (comps.) (2004b) *Construyendo sociedad y política. Los proyectos de los movimientos sociales en acción*, Buenos Aires: Ediciones Baudino-UNSAM.

Di Marco, Graciela and Javier Moro (2004) "Experiencias de economía solidaria frente a la crisis argentina: estudio desde una dimensión de género" in M. E. Valenzuela (ed.) *Políticas de empleo para superar la pobreza*, Santiago de Chile: OIT, Editorial Andros.

Dyszel, Guillermo, Juan Pablo Ferrero, and María Silvana Gurrera (2006) "El sindicalismo de movimiento social. Algunas reflexiones en torno del concepto," Sociedad Argentina de Análisis Político.

Faur, Eleonor and Natalia Gherardi (2005) "El derecho al trabajo y la ocupación de las mujeres" in Equipo Latinoamericano de Justicia y Género (ed.) *Informe sobre género y derechos humanos. Vigencia y respeto de los derechos de las mujeres en Argentina*, Buenos Aires: Biblos.

Godio, Julio and Alberto Robleso (2001) "Observatorio del movimiento y sindical argentino," *Revista Pistas* February 3.

Kanter, Rosabeth Moss (1977) *Men and women of the corporation*, New York: Basic Books.

National Association of Public Officials (Unión del Personal Civil de la Nación) (1997) *Violencia laboral. Estudio sobre Acoso Sexual*, Buenos Aires.

Novick, Marta (2001) "Nuevas reglas del juego en la Argentina, competitividad y actores sindicales" in E. De la Garza Toledo (ed.) *Los sindicatos frente a los procesos de transición política*, Buenos Aires: CLACSO.

Orsatti, Alvaro (2004) "Modelos de participación femenina en las estructuras sindicales," *Revista Pistas* December 13.

Programa de Naciones Unidas para el Desarrollo (PNUD) (2007) Objetivos del Milenio. Informe País 2007. Objetivo 4 Promover la igualdad y la equidad de género. http://www.undp.org.ar/docs/odm/odm07_obj4.pdf (accessed October 1, 2008).

Schuster, Federico and Sebastián Pereyra (2001) "La protesta social en la Argentina democrática. Balance y perspectivas de una forma de acción política" in N. Giarracca et al. (eds.) *La protesta social en la Argentina. Transformaciones económicas y crisis social en el interior del país*, Buenos Aires: Alianza.

Scribano, Adrián and Federico Schuster (2001) "Protesta social en la Argentina de 2001: entre la normalidad y la ruptura" in *Observatorio Social de América Latina*, Consejo Latinoamericano de Ciencias Sociales (CLACSO), Vol. 2, No. 5 (September), Buenos Aires.

Websites Consulted

AMMAR (Asociación de Mujeres Meretrices de la Argentina): http://www.ammar.org.ar

CTA (Central de Trabajadores de la Argentina): http://www.cta.org.ar

CTERA (Confederación de Trabajadores de la Educación): http://www.ctera.org.ar

Ministerio de Trabajo, Empleo y Seguridad Social: http://www.trabajo.gov.ar

UPCN (Union del Personal Civil de la Nación): http://www.upcndigital.org

UNDP (Programa de Naciones Unidas para el Desarrollo): http://www.undp.org.ar

Newspapers

PÁGINA|12–Supplement: Las 12|: http://www.pagina12.com.ar

CLARIN: http://www.clarin.com

LA NACIÓN: http://www.lanacion.com.ar

CHAPTER 20

In The Fabric of Brazilian Sexuality

Maria Luiza Heilborn

This article deals with the myths about and sexual behaviors of Brazilians. The objective is to demonstrate the manufactured nature of the myth of eroticized Brazilian sexuality. It is structured in three parts: first, the ideas and hypotheses that guide an anthropological view of sexuality are presented. I adopt a constructivist perspective on sexuality that looks to denaturalize this human realm (Vance 1995; Weeks 1986). The social construction argument about sexuality considers that this human dimension is not natural, nor universal in its form of expression, nor innate. Therefore, from a sociological point of view, it cannot be interpreted as a psychic impulse or a biological function. Anthropologists and sociologists believe that the expressions of sexuality take place in very specific contexts, which guide the experiences and the expressions of desire, emotions, as well as behaviors and physical practices (Gagnon and Simon 1973).

Second, the myth of Brazilian sexuality is analyzed. In various national and international contexts, the prevailing image of Brazilian culture is as sexually open, liberal, and warm. It is as if Brazilians were permanently contaminated by an atmosphere of carnival, and that we are ready to do everything in bed. The idea of an erotized national identity is very widespread, as it reverberates from an historical image that was heavily constructed. Brazilians in general take this image as a positive reference. However, there are many discontinuities between this imaginary and the actual social relations. With regards to these sexual behaviors, I will demonstrate that this image needs some repair.

The third section presents short examples of the sexual behavior and values concerning sexuality held among young Brazilians. The data come from a household survey (GRAVAD)[1] conducted in three cities of distinct regions of the country: Porto Alegre, Rio de Janeiro, and Salvador. From a cultural and regional point of view, these cities are very heterogeneous. The research was developed through collaboration among three Brazilian public universities in 2002, with 4,634 youth of both sexes participating, and whose ages varied from 18 to 24 years old.

THE SOCIO-ANTHROPOLOGICAL VIEW OF SEXUALITY

Sexuality is the subject of sociological analysis by diverse authors who contributed to understanding the historical processes that produced it as an independent dimension of human beings. Norbert Elias, in *The Civilizing Process* (Elias 1994), describes how the boundaries between bodies were constructed, creating and expanding the control of intimacy by individuals, as well as in censuring the spontaneity related to bodily gestures and demonstrations of affection (Vincent-Buffault 1988). . . .

Another important author who dedicated himself to understanding the social character of sexuality was Michel Foucault (1977). For him, sexuality was an invention of the seventeenth century, when facts connected to sexual expressions and bodily contacts, whose intentions were to procure and produce pleasure, acquired a specific social content. In the course of Western history, sexuality became an integral part of the modern self, a crucial part for the definition of the individual. According to Foucault (1977), various sorts of knowledge, established and instituted in hospitals, jails, hospices and also those fabricated by the very *dispositif* of sexuality, made sexuality the realm for articulating and expressing the individuals' *inner truth*. From this "modernity" period onward, a set of discourses about sex was created. These discourses codified the character of sexual desire, that is, its organization into the notions of heterosexuality and homosexuality. This binary classification comes from nineteenth-century psychiatry and therefore it is very idiosyncratic in Western societies.

This brief introduction allows us to argue that sex should be taken as any other *learned* human activity, such as eating manners and hygiene habits. Through culture individuals are socialized to enter sexual life, as culture guides the agendas and behaviors considered to be proper for each social group. Consequently, sexual practices are differentiated within each society, i.e. they vary in accordance to the references validated by the different social segments that compose it. Expressions and manifestations related to sexuality acquire distinct meanings, which are congruent with the current values in a given socio-cultural stratum. Therefore, sexual acts are not necessarily univocal. . . . The socialization demanded by sexuality practices is intimately related to the way in which gender relations are organized in a particular context (Heilborn 1999). . . . Differences related to sexuality are particularly noticeable according to both social class and gender (Bozon and Heilborn 1996), and it is possible to track these differences through "sexual scripts" (Gagnon and Simon 1993) followed by the individuals.

. . . Sexual scripts mirror the multiple and different socializations that a person experiences in his/her lifetime: family, types of schools, access to different forms of communication, friendship groups, and neighborhoods. Sexual scripts are especially relevant in the phase when sexuality becomes a particularly important subject: in adolescence or youth, a phase when active sexual life with a partner begins, and when the passage to adulthood occurs (Gagnon and Simon 1993). . . .

The social use of the body is a dimension of the anthropology of personhood, a field where researchers show how the ways we walk, smile or laugh, look, listen, or how we carry out many of the bodily functions that are presumably natural are actually socially constructed. When two people look at each other, there are significant differences based, for example, on national cultural contexts: Brazilians can look at someone of the same sex or the other sex in a straight-forward way, with direct eye contact. However, in European countries it is not proper to have direct eye contact with others because it could be interpreted as an attempt to seduce the other. . . . The way in which each culture considers the use of the body to be adequate reveals the dominant ideas of a society in each historical moment. Thus, the concepts of beauty can be very distinct and vary from one region to the other within the same country, from one social group to the other, and from one historical point to the other. . . .

Another relevant topic concerns the perception of sex as a legitimate activity for improving individuals' social networks and social mobility, which also varies based on gender, class, and historical context . . . [S]ex can be interpreted either as an honorable or a less acceptable alternative in establishing relations whose goals are not restricted to erotic, affective or reproductive links. In specific contexts, in Brazilian culture it is highly possible to make use of sex as a tool to attain upward social mobility. The preference of black men for white women, in inter-racial marriages (Moutinho 2004), reveals a form of moving upward in terms of social status as well as in terms of an aesthetic and racial hierarchy. This form of social and hierarchical mobility integrates a diversified repertoire for practicing and representing sexuality. This example not only illustrates one form of social ascension, but it also provides evidence of gender relations and their codification in the rules of law and customs. . . .

Sexuality can also be approached through the articulations between a wider level—the societal level—and the level of the individual biographical trajectory. Our point of departure is the thesis that sexuality is a learning process and, as such, it encompasses the conceptions of gender and anatomical sex. Thus, people would feel attraction to or interest in others based on determined parameters, as for example, the height of both men and women. In this sense, when thinking about a couple, we expect that the man usually should be taller than the woman (Bozon 1995). . . . The assumption that men should be taller than women expresses a gender hierarchical relation, disclosing a representation of gender based on masculine domination.

These unconscious rules are at work when we select our partners, guiding with whom we fall in love. Social representations are internalized by an individual, as if they were personal values and preferences. Although we are not always aware of their presence and action, all the internalized representations and patterns of behavior play an important role in how we live our sexual biographies, for these biographies are guided by sexual scripts (Gagnon and Simon 1973).

A sociological point of view about sexuality is extremely relevant because it shows that unconscious socially originated mechanisms shape an individual's subjectivity. This allows us to see that intra-psychic phenomena not only originate in individual psychology, but also in collective rules that were internalized. . . . Gender issues and asymmetry in the relationships between men and women (Heilborn 1993) continue to be powerful organizers of the way in which sexual activities are developed and of the capacity for negotiating with a partner about what is experienced during sexual intercourse. Nevertheless, I advocate for the argument that the idea of sexual revolution should be taken as a representation or parameter for praxis. People believe that there was a sexual revolution, that it referred to the liberalization of specific restricted codes of behavior— for women above all—and that it allowed more freedom to deal publicly with the issue of sexuality. At this level—the *emic* level (Bateson 1965)—the sexual revolution did take place, for it constitutes a collective cognitive achievement. In this sense, the social recognition of the sexual revolution empowers a particular field of discussion: the one that allows us to continue to address further transformations.

THE MYTH OF BRAZILIAN SEXUALITY

Generally is it believed that Brazilians are very uninhibited, "hot," warm, and always ready to experiment with anything in bed. It is as if the country were a sort of sexual paradise. This notion was historically constructed. First it deals with an image of Brazil that traces back to the narratives according to which, when the Portuguese colonizers arrived in this portion of the continent, they found native peoples who did not wear clothes and knew simple forms of social organization. According to these narratives, colonial Brazil was a land "without king and law," thus customs varied enormously. Among the Tupi tribes, for instance, men would offer their women to outsiders as proof of their hospitality and reciprocity, a custom that was very strange to Europeans. The colonizers' view was that the "new land" was a realm populated by very sensual natives who lived without sexual constraints, actually without a sexual morality. This constituted an image that was reproduced many times by European historians and travelers (Hollanda 1972). Linked to this image of a land in which sexual contacts were free, thus favoring miscegenation, an ideology of Brazilian nationality was built from and supported by the idea of the mixture of three ethnic races: European, indigenous peoples, and Africans, who came as slaves from the very beginning of Portuguese colonization. For a long time it was believed that there was a true racial democracy in Brazil, due to the total absence of racial prejudices, whose emblematic phenomenon was the mixture of races (Freyre 1933). This latter image is especially visible when comparing Brazil to South Africa, as well as to the United States. It was precisely this miscegenation between whites, indigenous peoples and blacks that was culturally elaborated in Brazil as a key factor for the dimensions of spontaneity, warmth, sensuality, and corporal ability required for dancing the samba and for a singular "ginga" [swing] in playing soccer. . . .

The idea that sensuality is due to those African roots was reinforced during the nineteenth century and now is strongly expressed in the myth of the open and uninhibited sensuality of Brazilians. This myth is very present in the dissemination of a certain way of advertising the country, as for instance in the field of tourism where a sexually charged image of the *mulata* is promoted: a woman set sexually free, "hot" and "aroused," the result of the miscegenation of a white man with a black woman. . . . More recently, Brazil has also been advertised as a paradise for gays, another indicator of the idea that it is a country where there is unrestricted tolerance and freedom for homosexuality, both masculine and feminine. In reality, these are not accurate portrayals of Brazil. To deal with the issues that are closer to what actually occurs in this "open and tolerant sexual paradise," I use data from the GRAVAD, a five-year research project about youth, sexuality and reproduction that was conducted in three Brazilian cities.

PORTRAYALS OF SEXUALITY

Much is said about the current changes in customs, and a great part of the discussion is directed toward the behaviors developed by the juvenile population. This population has always attracted the attention of researchers because it is the segment where changing trends in social processes can be observed (Abramo 1997; Sposito 1997). Currently, youth sexuality is a prominent topic internationally. In the contemporary socialization of younger generations, a decline can be observed in the importance of the family in transmitting values related to sexuality. . . . Young people have gradually achieved a more relevant role in their own socialization. Thus, a "horizontalization" occurs in socialization processes, in which young people produce new behaviors (Lhomond 1996).

The GRAVAD was a household survey that used semi-structured interviews. Initially, 123 interviews were conducted in three cities, with a system of respondent quotas according to sex, class, and maternal/paternal experience, to guarantee a reasonable representation that would offer diverse elements in elaborating the questionnaire. Also, a qualitative study was developed prior to using the questionnaire, with the goal of making it culturally appropriate to the different regions of the country. The research took into account an extremely important social problem in Brazil: "teenage pregnancy." The Brazilian government and media frequently frame teenage pregnancy as a public health and social problem whose dimensions are alarming. The media, in particular, associates teenage pregnancy as one plausible cause for the increase in crime, since the poorest of the youth are the ones who become involved with premature maternity and parenting.

The interviewees' ages varied from 18 to 24 years old, and the household sample was stratified according to three socio-economic levels. The questionnaire had 336 questions and the response time varied. If the teenager was a virgin, it would be answered in ten minutes. However, if the teenager had children, the time could surpass an hour. The average completion time for the questionnaire was 42 minutes. The first relevant finding was the median age of sexual initiation: 16.2 years old for the boys, and 17.9 years old for the girls. Therefore, there is a gap of almost 2 years between the sexes, a standard very common throughout countries in Latin America (Table 1—Not Shown). This two-year difference in the timing of sexual initiation contrasts with the standards observed in European countries, such as France and Germany, where there is an age similarity between young men and women (Bozon 2004).

Among the three cities where GRAVAD was carried out, Porto Alegre is the southernmost one, and it has a white majority population (75 percent white) of German, Italian, and Polish origins. The city of Salvador is 60 percent black and is the capital of the Brazilian state with the largest black population (IBGE 2002). Those differences can give impetus to prejudicial ideas, based on racial stereotypes. . . . However, the research showed . . . Salvador is the city with the most delayed sexual initiation, while the earliest sexual initiation was observed in the city with a population that descends in large part from white European immigrants. It is not our intention to explain the differences due to the modernization promoted by European immigrants in that region, but it is,

instead, to undo the links between race and premature or early sexuality.

To this data it is necessary to add the fact that the material conditions of life also interfere in modeling sexuality. For example, when compared to the other two cases, Porto Alegre has the best indexes of social development and education, greater coverage in terms of health services, a higher rate of contraceptive usage in the first sexual relationship, and a more equitable income distribution. This synthetic frame—where multiple variables intersect—adds auxiliary information to the interpretation of why Porto Alegre has a lower percentage of premature pregnancies, even though sexual initiation takes place comparatively early. Therefore, this brief example contributes to discrediting some of the myths around early pregnancy and Brazilian sexuality in general.

What are the ideas that teenagers have about sexuality? Their perceptions of fidelity and infidelity are useful in indicating whether there is more tolerance in regards to men's or women's infidelity. According to the interviewees, it is not possible to keep an affectionate relationship with a person and to have sex with other people, that is, being in a love relation is incompatible with experiencing sex with a person other than the beloved one. The acceptance and the dissemination of an ideal type of relationship—the one in which love joins sex—among youth show the importance of this particular stage of life as one in which learning about sexuality takes place together with the learning about sentiments (Table 2).

As for the beliefs shared by young Brazilians about the nature of sexual desire, we asked if it was possible to control the desire to have sex for a short period of time, a long one, or if it was impossible to control this desire. The answers showed that sex as a physical necessity has little acceptance among women with more schooling, but it is more accepted by young women with lower levels of schooling. However, when

Table 2 Youth between the ages of 18 and 24: Their opinions regarding the meaning of sexual activity, the possibility of controlling sexual desires, and infidelity, according to level of schooling and sex

Youth's opinion	Level of schooling: Interviewees										
	Basic Incomplete		Basic Complete		Middle Level		College Level		Total		
	n	%	n	%	n	%	n	%	n	%	p-value
Which statement better matches your opinion about sex?											
Women	435		568		785		585		2373		0.0576
Sex is a physical need like hunger and thirst		11.4		9.2		11.1		6.2		9.7	
Sex is a proof of love given by the partner		52.6		45.7		47.3		43.1		47	
Sex is a source of pleasure and personal satisfaction		36		45		41.5		50.7		43.3	
Men	495		562		629		434		2120		0.0000
Sex is a physical need like hunger and thirst		9.5		20.4		13.5		20.7		15.7	
Sex is a proof of love given by the partner		54.8		47.6		47.2		28.9		46.1	
Sex is a source of pleasure and personal satisfaction		35.7		32		39.4		50.4		38.2	
Is it possible to control the desire to have sex?											
Women	434		561		780		584		2359		0.0000
Yes, for a long period of time		41.6		47.4		59.4		59.4		53.2	
Yes, for a short period of time		42.7		44.7		35.3		35.3		39.0	
No, it is not possible		15.8		7.9		5.3		4.5		7.8	
Men	495		562		631		440		2128		0.0000
Yes, for a long period of time		16.6		25.0		31.4		41.2		27.5	
Yes, for a short period of time		54.8		58.6		58.2		45.0		55.2	
No, it is not possible		28.7		16.4		10.4		13.8		17.4	
When in a love relationship, is it acceptable to have sex with other people?											
Women	440		571		800		596		2407		0.0025
Only men can		3.5		0.8		0		0		0.9	
Only women can		0.2		0		0.3		0		0.1	
Both genders can		11.5		10.5		8.7		8.4		9.6	
No, it is not acceptable		84.8		88.7		91.0		91.6		89.4	
Men	495		566		636		449		2146		0.2199
Only men can		6.6		5.6		4.8		8.1		6.1	
Only women can		1.0		0.2		0.1		0.1		0.3	
Both genders can		15.3		16.5		11.4		12.4		14	
No, it is not acceptable		77.1		77.8		83.8		79.4		79.6	

Source: GRAVAD research, 2002.

Population: Youth between the ages of 18 and 24, Porto Alegre (RS), Rio de Janeiro (RJ) and Salvador (BA).

comparing the data provided by all those with higher levels of schooling, a very important gender difference can be observed. Middle and upper-middle-class young men with higher levels of schooling are the ones who better express masculine gender ideology, which associates sex with physical need and, for this reason, is seen as an uncontrollable force. This view was in stark contrast with what was stated by young women of the same social group. It is exactly these privileged young men who reject a more relational perspective on sexuality, upholding traditional values of the supremacy of the masculine desire.

The attitudes about homosexuality (Table 3)—mainly toward male homosexuality—are illustrative of the gender ideology that I am trying to demonstrate in this text. . . . What was initially observed was that male homosexuality is generally more tolerated among women than among men. One of the questions asked if people could have sexual intercourse with whomever they want. This question was formulated with the use of the verb "*transar*" [to get laid], a widely known

Table 3 Youth between the ages of 18 and 24: Their opinions about masculine and feminine homosexuality, according to level of schooling and sex

Opinion about homosexuality	Level of schooling: Interviewees										p-value
	Basic Incomplete		Basic Complete		Middle Level		College Level		Total		
	n	%	n	%	n	%	n	%	n	%	
With regards to men who have sex with other men:											
Women	429		561		771		572		2333		0.0000
They can have sex with whomever they want		49.4		69.8		78.7		88.2		72.7	
They are shameless		25.5		12.6		5.6		2.7		10.6	
They are sick people		25.2		17.7		15.7		9.1		16.7	
Men	488		557		621		438		2104		0.0000
They can have sex with whomever they want		27.1		50.0		60.5		74.6		51.3	
They are shameless		28.1		21.8		14.4		5.7		18.6	
They are sick people		44.8		28.2		25.1		19.7		30.1	
With regards to women who have sex with other women:											
Women	431		561		771		572		2335		0.0000
They can have sex with whomever they want		46.9		68.5		76.9		86.8		71.0	
They are shameless		27.1		12.9		7.7		3.5		11.9	
They are sick people		26.0		18.6		15.4		9.7		17.1	
Men	488		555		625		439		2107		0.0000
They can have sex with whomever they want		30.3		52.1		64.6		77.4		54.4	
They are shameless		32.0		20.3		12.8		5.7		18.7	
They are sick people		37.7		27.6		22.5		16.9		26.9	

Source: GRAVAD research, 2002.

Population: Youth between the ages of 18 and 24, Porto Alegre (RS), Rio de Janeiro (RJ) and Salvador (BA).

and socially accepted colloquial verb that means to have sexual intercourse. Other expressions used in the interviews were "shameless" and "sick people" ("homosexuality as illness"). The data are revealing: 90 percent of the women with higher levels of schooling accept homosexuality while among men this decreases to 70 percent. Thus, a marked gender difference remains among those with higher education, indicating persistence in the way in which virility is thought about in Brazil. . . .

Our analyses of the repertoire of sexual practices demonstrate a piercing difference between men's and women's practices, even when they belong to the same social category. This gap certainly reveals the effect that moral reserve has on women's answers to the questionnaire, while for men it leads us to consider the opposite, that is, the possible effects of over-valorizing all forms of sexual contact.

In this context, it is worth mentioning that men acknowledged their anal sex experiences. Such information also strongly contrasts with international research data about the same age range (Laumann et al. 1994; Spira, Majos, and the ACSF Group 1993) (Table 4—Not Shown). Besides that, qualitative material from the first stage of GRAVAD research indicated how this sexual technique is subjected to strong negotiations within couples (Leal 2004), revealing complex relations of power and persuasion in the exercise of sexuality.

The understanding provided by research data is nowhere near to the image of a country that is sexually uninhibited. Deeply rooted differences between men and women prove that a gender code establishes barriers between acceptable behaviors for each gender. Forms of meaning and accountability for sexual practices are presented as indicators of distinct universes for men and for women.

These are elements and dimensions that allow us to think further about the complex relations between social imaginary and sexual practice in general. For the specific case of Brazil, they help in addressing the distances as well as the entanglements between the "sexual paradise" and the concrete conditions (symbolic and material) that circumscribe the exercise of sexuality.

NOTE

Editors' Note: This article was translated from the Portuguese original version by Yaser S. Robles.

1. The research "Gravidez na adolescência: estudo multicêntrico sobre jovens, sexualidade e reprodução no Brasil"—GRAVAD (Adolescent pregnancy: Multicenter study on youth, sexuality and reproduction in Brazil) was conducted by three research centers: the Programa de Estudos Gênero, Sexualidade e Saúde of the Instituto de Medicina Social/UERJ; the Programa de Estudos Gênero, Mulher e Saúde of the Instituto de Saúde Coletiva/UFBA; and the Núcleo de Pesquisa em Antropologia do Corpo e da Saúde/UFRS. GRAVAD team members were Maria Luiza Heilborn (coordinator), Estela Aquino, Daniela Knauth, Michel Bozon, Ceres Victora, Fabiola Rohden, Cecilia McCalum, Tania Salem, Cristiane S. Cabral and Elaine Reis Brandão. Consultant for Statistics: Antonio Jose Ribeiro Dias (IBGE). The research was financed by the Ford Foundation, and counted on the support by the CNPq and Capes.

REFERENCES

Abramo, H. W. (1997) "Considerações sobre a tematização social da juventude no Brasil," *Revista Brasileira de Educação* No. 5–6: 25–36.

Bateson, Gregory (1965) *Naven*, Stanford: Stanford University Press

Bozon, Michel (1995) "Observer l'inobservable: la description et l'analyse de l'activité sexuelle" in N. Bajos, M. Bozon, A. Giami, V. Doré, and Y. Souteyrand (dir.) *Sexualité et sida: recherches en sciences sociales*, Paris: ANRS.

—— (2004) *Sociologia da sexualidade*, Rio de Janeiro: FGV Editoria.

Bozon, Michel and Maria Luiza Heilborn (1996) "Les caressses et les mots: initiations amoureuses à Rio de Janeiro et à Paris," *Terrain* 27: 37–58.

Elias, Norbert (1994) *The Civilizing Process*, trans. from the original German by Edmund Jephcott, Oxford: Blackwell.

Foucault, Michel (1977) *História da Sexualidade I: A Vontade de Saber*, Rio de Janeiro: Graal.

Freyre, Gilberto (1933) *Casa-grande & senzala: formação da família brasileira sob o regime de economia patriarcal*, Rio de Janeiro: Maia & Schmidt.

Gagnon, John and Willian Simon (1973) *Sexual Conduct: The Social Sources of Human Sexuality*, Chicago: Aldine.

Heilborn, Maria Luiza (1993) "Gênero e hierarquia: a costela de Adão revisitada," *Estudos Feministas* 1: 50–82

—— (1999) "Corpos na cidade: sedução e sexualidade" in G. Velho (org.) *Antropologia Urbana*, Rio de Janeiro: Jorge Zahar Editor.

Hollanda, Sérgio Buarque de (1972) *História geral da civilização brasileira*, São Paulo: Difel.

IBGE–Fundaçâo Instituto Brasileiro de Geografia e Estatística (2002) *Censo demográfico 2000: primeiros resultados da amostra*, Rio de Janeiro: IBGE.

Laumann Edward, John Gagnon, Robert Michael, and Stuart Michaels (1994) *The Social Organization of Sexuality. Sexual Practices in the United States*, Chicago: University of Chicago Press.

Leal, Andrea F. (2004) "Práticas sexuais no contexto da conjugalidade: em que implica a intimidade?" in Maria Luiza Heilborn, Luiz Fernando Dias Duarte, Clarice Peixoto, and Myriam Lins de Barros (Organizers) *Sexualidade, família e ethos religioso*, Rio de Janeiro: Garamond/CEPESC, pp. 61–85.

Lhomond, Brigitte (1996) "Qu'est ce qu'un rapport sexuel? Remarques à propos des enquêtes sur les comportements sexuels," *Mot. Les Language du Politique*, 49: 107–115.

Moutinho, Laura (2004) *Razão, cor e desejo*, São Paulo: UNESP.

Spira, Alfred, Nathalie Bajos, and the ACSF Group (1993) *Les Comportements sexuels en France*, Paris: La Documentation Française.

Sposito, M. P. (1997) "Estudos sobre juventude em educação," *Revista Brasileira de Educação* 5, 6: 37–52.

Vance, Carole (1995) "A antropologia redescobre a sexualidade: um comentário teórico," *Physis. Revista de Saúde Coletiva* 1, 5: 7–31.

Vincent-Buffault, Anne (1988) *A historia das lágrimas*, Rio de Janeiro: Paz e Terra.

Weeks, Jeffrey (1986) *Sexuality and its Discontents: Meanings, Myths and Modern Sexualities*, London: Routledge and Kegan Paul.

CHAPTER 21

Citizenship and Nation: Debates on Reproductive Rights in Puerto Rico

Elizabeth Crespo-Kebler

In this paper I analyze ways in which feminist organizations in Puerto Rico articulated their claims for political power and a concept of citizenship that includes women. I discuss how the concepts of nation and citizenship were incorporated within feminist discourses on abortion and sterilization and ways in which they reaffirmed and/or deconstructed nationalist, colonialist and patriarchal concepts of political power.

... From the point of view of nationalist discourses, the principal problem of citizenship in contemporary society is the colonial status of Puerto Rico, as a result of the U.S. invasion of the Island in 1898, ... manifest[ed] ... in ... the lack of political power to decide on local affairs and the physical and cultural genocide of Puerto Ricans.

... In the 1970s, feminist activism introduced the notion that women's full and equal membership in public life was not possible without addressing issues that had traditionally been relegated to the domestic sphere, considered private and therefore outside the scope of politics ... [T]hey introduced issues such as reproductive rights, gender role socialization, domestic work, sexuality, and sexual orientation into political debates. Feminists defined these topics as crucial elements to obtain their full rights as citizens.

... One of the most important events of [the 1970s] was the formation of "autonomous" feminist groups, that is, organizations that were formed outside political parties

and governmental structures. These organizations were of critical importance because they opened up a political space through which women could transform the notion of citizenship and gain more access to political power. In this essay I ... examine the positions of one of these groups, *Mujer Intégrate Ahora* (MIA)[1] on abortion and sterilization, and contrast these positions with other feminist points of view and various nationalist perspectives.

In the feminist debates on reproductive rights presented in this essay I find instances of both ruptures and points of convergence with nationalisms.... To explore feminist debates on nation and citizenship in the 1970s, I look at two major events: the decision of the U.S. Supreme Court in *Roe v. Wade* that legalized abortion, and the renewed efforts by the government of Puerto Rico to reduce population growth through sterilization and contraception. ...

DISCURSIVE STRATEGIES OF FEMINISMS AND NATIONALISMS

... Many times [a] ... remedy to exploitation was proposed by both nationalists and feminists in the name of a different or "true" universality that would include the groups that had been excluded. Thus, for example, many feminists reclaimed citizenship and equality as universal rights that should include women ... [while] nationalisms claimed the universal right to self-determination as an initial step to remedy the inequalities between the metropolis and the colony.

... In addition to erasing the heterogeneity of groups, this [universalism] concealed the relations between [sub-groups].... In this way, contestatory movements, which were conceived with the purpose of eliminating inequalities, reproduced and created relations of subordination of their own....

FEMINISMS AND NATIONALISMS: DEBATES ON ABORTION

One of the criticisms of feminism launched by various sectors of society on both the political right and left during the 1970s was that feminism was a result of outside influences. This perception was forcefully articulated when the U.S. Supreme Court decision on *Roe v. Wade* established the right to abortion in 1973. This right was extended to Puerto Rico because of its juridical relation with the United States. Various nationalist and pro-independence advocates immediately manifested their opposition to this decision arguing that it was a colonial imposition and another component of the genocidal population policies towards Puerto Rico....

The universalizing strategy employed here established a dichotomy between the values of the colonizer and Puerto Rican values. This dichotomy excluded feminists from the Puerto Rican national community by representing them as perverters of traditional women's roles considered here as national values (Marqués 1967; Partido Socialista Puertorriqueño 1975; Zayas and Silén 1972).... They were seen as targets of seduction by men from the imperial countries, and in this way, potential traitors. Women were not only vulnerable to men, but also to the seduction of feminist ideologies whose perceived origin was white women in the United States. The United States was often described as a matriarchal culture and its women represented with images of sexual libertinage (Partido Socialista Puertorriqueño 1975; Partido Socialista Revolucionario n.d.; *Pensamiento Crítico* 1978).

The title of an article by Nilda Aponte Raffaele (1973), a member of the feminist organization *Mujer Intégrate Ahora* (MIA), "El aborto: La mujer es la que decide" (Abortion: The woman is the one who decides), underscores the absence of a feminist standpoint in the public discussion up to that moment and seems to answer the question that no one had asked: Who should make this decision? In this article, the author examines the legal concepts that were ratified, and applauds the benefits *Roe v. Wade* would bring to women. By doing this, she places herself in open opposition to the nationalist discourse that condemned the application of the decision to Puerto Rico....

MIA denounced this [nationalist] anti-colonial stance as patriarchal, noting its hypocrisy and masculinist arbitrariness. In this way, MIA took the focus off Puerto Rico's autonomy or lack thereof to make its own laws, and made this an issue of both gender and class. In the statements made by MIA, abortion was posed as the "right of Puerto Rican women to own and make decisions about their bodies" (*Avance* 1973: 17) while recognizing at the same time that wealthy women had that right even before *Roe v. Wade*. MIA points to the fact that before *Roe v. Wade* more abortions were performed in Puerto Rico than almost anywhere else in the hemisphere, but only for the wealthy, including many women who came to Puerto Rico from the U.S. This happened in spite of the Puerto Rican abortion law that penalized the doctor with up to ten years of prison and the woman with one to five years of prison unless this procedure was necessary to save her life or health....

MIA regretted that abortion had not been addressed by the Puerto Rican legislature until the U.S. Supreme Court's decision. In 1972, a year before *Roe v. Wade*, MIA had, without success, called on the Puerto Rican legislature to approve laws that allowed abortion on demand (*MIA Informa* 1972). The decision by the U.S. Supreme Court gave the organization a renewed opportunity to present this demand. . . .

. . . The nationalist position on abortion in 1973 is reminiscent of the stance taken by the Puerto Rican legislature on women's suffrage in the early part of this century. . . . Although women in the U.S. won the right to vote in 1920, it was not until 1929 that Puerto Rican women obtained the vote.

. . . Feminist demands for reproductive rights made evident that the issue at hand was not a confrontation between two homogeneous entities: the United States and Puerto Rico. What became apparent was the lack of shared interests in the imagined community of Puerto Ricans and the patriarchal principles upon which citizenship was constructed. In both circumstances, attempts to give women the same rights of citizenship as men and the same rights as women in the metropolis (the right to vote and the right to abortion on demand) were represented by nationalists as a manifestation of colonialism. Nationalists protested any attempts by the metropolis to dictate on "local matters," in this case, the status of women. . . . [A]nticolonialist positions were, in effect, an assertion of the colony's autonomy to deny citizenship to women. The anti-colonialist discourse mobilized the binary of the metropolis versus the colony where all other forms of discrimination based on differences, including gender, were not recognized.

STERILIZATION AND THE REPRESENTATION OF WOMEN AS VICTIMS

One of the effects of the discursive strategies of universalizing paradigms is the denial of political agency to socially subordinated groups. This is achieved by presenting these groups only as victims. The examination of a nationalist framework to analyze sterilization among Puerto Rican women demonstrates this strategy. . . .

[A]s in the debates on abortion, the controversies concerning sterilization demonstrated that women's assertions of citizenship were at odds with the nationalist visions. To demonstrate this, I examine two critiques of the policy on sterilization of Puerto Rican women. The first point of view is presented through the film *La operación* (García 1982). This is an important documentary because it is a forceful and stirring exposure of the policy of sterilization as a practice of genocide. . . . Its wide distribution and its compelling presentation led it to be considered by many as required viewing material. . . . While it presents the effects of sterilization literally from the perspective of women's bodies, this is framed within a nationalist discourse.

. . . Second, . . . [a]lthough not widely known, six years prior to the release of the documentary *La operación*, MIA researched the history of the policy of sterilization and produced a document that was presented at the International Tribunal on Crimes Against Women held in Brussels (MIA 1976). This research was motivated by the campaign of zero population growth launched in the mid 1970s by the Puerto Rican government, and spearheaded by the head of the Department of Health, Antonio R. Silva. This new program of sterilization was part of the efforts to reduce the birthrate in Puerto Rico. MIA argued that this campaign was reminiscent of the one launched during the 1950s. . . .

. . . Sterilization began in the early 1930s . . . and by 1968 it had increased dramatically to 36 percent (Vázquez Calzada 1988). . . .

La Operación

Female sterilization became so common in

Puerto Rico that it was known simply as "la operación" (the operation). . . . *La operación* is above all an indictment of genocide and although its effects on women are at the center of the film, its point of view is patriarchal in very fundamental ways. It presents a policy enacted on women whose childbearing potential represents the nation and its possibilities for survival. . . .

According to the documentary, the childbearing potential of women is a longstanding value of the culture that dates back to the Taínos, the native American inhabitants of the Island at the time it was invaded by Spain. . . .

The documentary uses an expert, Dr. Helen Rodríguez-Trías, to establish a difference between population control and birth control. Birth control, she says, is an individual right. It should be built into health programs. People are given information and options. Population control, on the other hand, is a social policy instated with the thought in mind that some people should not have children or should have very few. Nonetheless, after this statement very early on, the only choice that the film advocates is the right to have children. The right *not* to have children is an important option omitted in the presentation and one that is central to establish a departure from nationalist and patriarchal views of women. The right not to have children is an important component of feminist demands for safe and accessible abortions, and more generally, for demands related to sexuality and women's right to control their own bodies. . . .

Coming from an anti-colonial perspective, this film denounces the coercive nature of the sterilization policy, and it presents misinformation as the specific mechanism through which it was enacted. Although it appeared that women had submitted voluntarily to sterilization and contraception, statements by women who underwent the procedure are used by the filmmaker to demonstrate that misinformation functioned as

coercion. . . . Many women were told that the medical procedure was a ligature of the fallopian tubes and that it could be reversed, that is, the tubes could be untied. . . .

. . . The film provides a limited and largely unidimensional narrative, one that focuses on misinformation and ignorance that led women to be manipulated by public health authorities. . . . The universalizing strategy presented in the film creates one narrative, that of a colonized subject, a Puerto Rican woman victim of an imperial strategy. . . . It fails to capture the complexity of the decision to be sterilized and a variety of individual and collective experiences. . . .

. . . [For example, one] 1976 study was a survey carried out on an island-wide sample of ever-married Puerto Rican women 20–49 years of age. One of its main conclusions was that high fertility was an important motivating factor for sterilization (Vázquez Calzada and Morales del Valle 1982). It showed that at the time of sterilization, sterilized women had an average of four children compared with three children among the non-sterilized. The island-wide sample survey performed in 1982 showed similar results: the group of women with the highest rate of sterilization was the group that had three or more children, not the women with fewest children. . . . Although rates were high among all women, older women were sterilized more than younger women, and women who had been married for a longer time were sterilized more frequently than women who were married for a short time (Vázquez Calzada 1988, 1989). In other words, these studies concluded that many women made the decision to be sterilized because they had reached or surpassed the number of children desired (Vázquez Calzada 1988). . . .

The inadequacy of methods of contraception must be considered when evaluating sterilization. The data from the 1976 survey suggests that many women, who were not successful at controlling the number of children through other methods, resorted to sterilization (Vázquez Calzada and Morales del Valle 1982). In other words, before turning to a non-reversible option as was sterilization, many women had tried methods whose effect on childbearing was temporary. . . . This was true especially among young women and among those with relatively few years of marriage. Women aged 20 to 29 who were sterilized after having used other contraceptive methods had an average of 3 children while women in this age group who had used other contraceptives and were not sterilized had an average of 1.5 children This data strongly suggests that many women actively pursued options to control the number of children they had. At the same time, it suggests discontent with the contraceptives they had used before making the decision to be sterilized.

An analysis of the 1982 data underscores the inadequacy of contraceptive methods (Warren et al. 1986), . . . [and] revealed women's dissatisfaction with the pill, intra-uterine devices and injections that are considered highly effective methods of birth control, and I would add, also life threatening as revealed in the experience of the Dalkon Shield. . . .

Data that attempts to measure women's satisfaction with sterilization also points to heterogeneity of situations and experiences that suggest choice and not only victimization. A survey conducted in 1968 indicated that a high percentage (64 percent) of sterilized women were satisfied with their decision. This degree of satisfaction has to be taken into account as well as the dissatisfaction of the 26 percent who indicated that they were not happy with sterilization because they wanted to have more children, and the dissatisfaction of an additional 10 percent because it affected their health, marital relations, or caused religious conflicts. On the other hand, 83 percent of men were satisfied with their wife's sterilization (Vázquez Calzada 1973). . . .

There is a way, nonetheless, in which *La*

operación is undeniably a departure from traditional nationalist indictments of genocide. The focus on women is deliberate throughout. . . . *La operación* presents a perspective that literally comes from a woman's body. . . . Nevertheless, the vision of this body is fundamentally patriarchal. Women are the misinformed and often ignorant victims of imperialism. The role of victim sustains the traditional view of women who need protection and are easily manipulated. Moreover, the subversion of this policy is to be found in the body of women who bear children. The final image of the documentary makes this perspective quite clear. It shows a woman wearing a T-shirt that very visibly marks her pregnancy. Bold letters on the front of her shirt read "Made in Puerto Rico." . . . Women as reproducers represent the resilience of Puerto Rican culture to withstand all attacks against the Puerto Rican nation. . . .

An alternative to a vision based on women's victimization and on their role as bearers of children is to look at sterilization and population control as policies that took advantage of and were built upon women's desire to control their reproduction. If looked at in this way, women were not passive victims. A framework that goes beyond women's victimization and genocidal attacks on the Puerto Rican nation also leads us to ask why sterilization was presented mainly as an option for women and not for men. . . .

It is significant that the same nationalist and anti-imperialist arguments used against sterilization that were adopted by nationalist feminists and presented in *La operación* are used today by anti-abortion activists trying to limit women's reproductive choices. . . .

The convergence of anti-abortion, anti-imperialist and feminist rhetoric is not surprising. It dramatizes the political effects of nationalist feminist discourses that occupied center stage in many feminist discourses of the 1970s and even today. It underscores the need to create new frameworks, a task that feminists have undertaken from a variety of perspectives (Figueroa Sarriera et al. 1994; López 1998; Lugo Ortiz 1999; Ostolaza Bey 1989; Ramírez de Arellano and Seipp 1983). . . .

Mujer Intégrate Ahora

The first feminist organization of the second wave in Puerto Rico, *Mujer Intégrate Ahora* (1973) presented a critique of population policies years earlier than the documentary *La operación* and from a perspective that departed markedly from the paradigms that dominated leftist and nationalist organizations. Presented before the International Tribunal on Crimes against Women in 1976, MIA's position was that sterilization was a patriarchal as well as a colonial policy. While nationalist frameworks identified the Puerto Rican nation as the target of genocide, MIA analyzed the effect of economic and population policies on *women. . . .*

According to MIA, these patriarchal postulates converged with the Malthusian idea that excess population causes poverty, launched by the first world as they put in place their policies of population control in the third world. The analysis of MIA shares the conspiratorial discourses of the left, but this conspiracy involved Puerto Rican male chauvinism. . . . By identifying Puerto Rican women as the target of the genocidal policy, they ruptured the unity assumed in the concept of nation. . . . This, said MIA, was a result of a male dominated society where male scientists and administrators have been in charge of contraceptive experiments and female contraceptives have always been the research priority. In this way, population control was an example of "sexual politics" ([1976] 2001: 305). The analysis made by MIA goes on to point to various actors involved in this "sexual policy": the Catholic church, various private associations that provided birth control to Puerto Rican women, the Puerto Rican government, U.S. corporations, private foundations, doctors, and Puerto Rican men. . . .

While MIA pointed to a gendered perspective of reproductive rights in a way not contemplated by the nationalist perspective of *La operación*, it retained the conspiratorial discourse of *La operación* adding the collusion of male chauvinism to the conspiracy of capitalism and colonialism. . . .

CONCLUSION

. . . As Puerto Rican women made reproductive rights a component of their demands for citizenship as colonial subjects and as women, they put into question the assumptions of universality, a fundamental principle upon which the exclusion of women was constructed. On the other hand, to the extent that feminisms adopted universalizing paradigms to understand gender, citizenship and the national question, they supported ideas and practices that upheld women's subordination and created a colonized subject stripped of agency. . . . Universalizing frameworks created woman as a unitary subject with unidimensional subjectivity whose experiences could be grasped through the concept of victimization. In light of this, the challenge is to propose another political perspective that radically questions the category woman.

NOTE

1. In addition to MIA, two other autonomous feminist groups were formed during this decade: Federación de Mujeres Puertorriqueñas and Alianza Feminista Pro-Liberación Humana. In *Documentos del feminismo en Puerto Rico: Facsímiles de la historia, 1970–1979* (2001), my co-author, Ana Irma Rivera Lassén, and I each present critical analyses of the feminist debates of the period and reproduce the unpublished documents of these organizations. In this essay I cite some of these documents.

REFERENCES

Aponte Raffaele, Nilda (1973) "El aborto: La mujer es la que decide," *Avance*, pp. 19–21. Reprinted in A. Rivera Lassén and E. Crespo Kebler, *Documentos del feminismo en Puerto Rico: Facsímiles de la historia, Vol I, 1970–1979*, 2001, pp. 260–263, San Juan: Editorial de la Universidad de Puerto Rico.

Avance (1973) "Las mujeres 'liberacionistas' y el aborto," 16 April: 16–18.

Figueroa Sarriera, Heidi, María Milagros López, and Madeline Román (1994) *Más allá de la bella (in)diferencia*, San Juan: Publicaciones Puertorriqueñas.

García, Ana María (1982) *La operación*, Puerto Rico, distributed by Cinema Guild, NY.

López, Iris (1998) "An ethnography of the medicalization of Puerto Rican women and reproduction" in Margaret Lock and Patricia Kaufert (eds.) *Pragmatic women and body politics*, Boston: Cambridge University Press.

Lugo Ortiz, Lourdes (1999) "Relatos de esterilización: Entre el acomodo y la resistencia," *Revista de Ciencias Sociales (Nueva Epoca)* 6: 208–225.

Marqués, René (1967) *El puertorriqueño dócil*, Río Piedras: Editorial Antillana.

MIA Informa (1972) "El aborto y la integración de la mujer," Número 2 (May). Reprinted in A. Rivera Lassén and E. Crespo Kebler (2001) *Documentos del feminismo en Puerto Rico: Facsímiles de la historia, Vol I, 1970–1979*, San Juan: Editorial de la Universidad de Puerto Rico.

Mujer Intégrate Ahora (MIA) (1973) "Objetivos, propósitos, reglamento, posiciones." Reprinted in A. Rivera Lassén and E. Crespo Kebler (2001) *Documentos del feminismo en Puerto Rico: Facsímiles de la historia, Vol I, 1970–1979*, San Juan: Editorial de la Universidad de Puerto Rico.

—— (1976) "La mujer puertorriqueña: Objeto del control poblacional," Presentación ante El Tribunal Internacional de Crímenes Contra la Mujer, Bruselas. Reprinted in A. Rivera Lassén and E. Crespo Kebler

(2001) *Documentos del feminismo en Puerto Rico: Facsímiles de la historia, Vol I, 1970–1979*, San Juan: Editorial de la Universidad de Puerto Rico.

Ostolaza Bey, Margarita (1989) *Política sexual en Puerto Rico*, Río Piedras: Ediciones Huracán.

Partido Socialista Puertorriqueño (Movimiento Pro Independencia) (1975) *Ponencias Suplementarias Ante-Proyecto Programa*, Puerto Rico, n.p.

Partido Socialista Revolucionario (n.d.) *Programa sobre la mujer*, Río Piedras, Puerto Rico: Ediciones PSR.

Pensamiento Crítico (1978) "La mujer trabajadora y el movimiento feminista en Estados Unidos," June–July: 27–29.

Ramírez de Arellano, Annette B. and Conrad Seipp (1983) *Colonialism, Catholicism and contraception: A history of birth control in Puerto Rico*, Chapel Hill: University of North Carolina Press.

Rivera Lassén, Ana and Elizabeth Crespo Kebler (2001) *Documentos del feminismo en Puerto Rico: Facsímiles de la historia, Vol I, 1970–1979*, San Juan: Editorial de la Universidad de Puerto Rico.

Vázquez Calzada, José L. (1973) "La esterilización femenina en Puerto Rico," San Juan: Centro de Investigaciones Demográficas, Escuela de Salud Pública, UPR (mimeo).

—— (1988) *La población de Puerto Rico y su trayectoria histórica*, San Juan, Puerto Rico: Graduate School of Public Health.

—— (1989) "El efecto de los partos por cesárea sobre la esterilización femenina en Puerto Rico," *Puerto Rico Health Sciences Journal* 8, 2: 215–223.

Vázquez Calzada, José L. and Zoraida Morales del Valle (1982) "Female sterilization in Puerto Rico and its demographic effectiveness," *Puerto Rico Health Sciences Journal* 1, 2: 68–79.

Warren, Charles W., Charles F. Westoff, Joan M. Herold, Roger W. Rochat, and Jack C. Smith (1986) "Contraceptive sterilization in Puerto Rico," *Demography* 23, 3: 351–365.

Zayas, Nancy and Juan Angel Silén (1972) *La mujer en la lucha hoy*, San Juan: Ediciones Kikirikí.

SECTION 4

*E*urope

22 Introduction to Gender Research in Europe 257

CHRISTINE E. BOSE AND MINJEONG KIM

23 Traveling Theories—Situated Questions: Feminist Theory in the
German Context 261

GUDRUN-AXELI KNAPP

24 An Overview of Research on Gender in Spanish Society 278

CELIA VALIENTE

25 At the Crossroads of "East" and "West": Gender Studies in Hungary 290

EVA FODOR AND ESZTER VARSA

26 "The Rest is Silence . . .": Polish Nationalism and the Question of
Lesbian Existence 308

JOANNA MIZIELIŃSKA

27 Collective Organizing and Claim Making on Child Care in Norden:
Blurring the Boundaries between the Inside and the Outside 315

SOLVEIG BERGMAN

28 Integrating or Setting the Agenda?: Gender Mainstreaming in the
European Constitution-Making Process 323

EMANUELA LOMBARDO

CHAPTER 22

Introduction to Gender Research in Europe

Christine E. Bose and Minjeong Kim

After the creation of the European Union (EU), an economic and political partnership that began in 1993 and now encompasses 27 democratic nations, it is easy to think of Europe as a homogenous "developed" region, but this group of countries represents a greater degree of diversity than it might appear when viewed from a U.S. perspective. Notable changes have occurred in the social, political, and economic organization of these nations since the middle of the twentieth century, all or which inevitably affected women's lives and thus, the issues that they want to study. Among those that had the most impact are the obliteration of Adolf Hitler's National Socialist German Workers Party (better known as the Nazi Party or Third Reich, a fascist regime) in Germany in 1944 and the decline of Francisco Franco's authoritarian rule in Spain, even before his death in 1975; the fall of communism in Eastern Europe in the late 1980s and early 1990s; and the unification of many European countries under a single regional government of the European Union.

MAJOR ECONOMIC AND POLITICAL SHIFTS OF THE TWENTIETH CENTURY

Gundrun-Axeli Knapp (Chapter 23) describes the impact on gender research and theory for three major political–economic time periods in Germany. First was National Socialism, including control of the nation by the Nazis from the 1930s to 1940s, which led to Germany's expansionism and invasion of a large portion of Europe, had devastating effects on the continent, and contributed to World War II. Second was the postwar division of the country into capitalist West Germany and communist East Germany. During this period, German feminists in the East and West focused on different issues, because the rights and support structures provided to women under these two economic systems left them with different benefits and problems in attaining education, jobs, and support for family life. However, after "the fall of the Wall" dividing East and West Berlin in 1989, and the unification of the former East and West Germany in 1990, entirely new issues arose as the nation needed to decide which of women's work and family rights that had existed in East Germany would be retained in the re-combined nation.

Celia Valiente (Chapter 24), writing on Spain, describes the later twentieth-century concerns of feminist researchers with issues of politics and work. This focus was chosen in reaction to almost four decades of Francisco Franco's fascist regime (1936–1975), which codified traditional women's roles into various laws that encouraged women to remain at home and have large families.

Eva Fodor and Eszter Varsa (Chapter 25) describe the post-communist political and economic trajectory in Hungary and its impact on feminist and gender research, which they analyze as being at a crossroads between the East and the West. However, the post-communist situation in Poland is somewhat different, a country that in the 1980s drew international attention for actively resisting communist domination through its Solidarity trade union movement. According to Joanna Mizielińska (Chapter 26), the Polish Catholic Church played an active role in aiding workers seeking the fall of communism. As a result, the Church's influence has been larger than it might otherwise be, and masculinist and heterosexual-based interpretations of religious catechism were built into parts of Poland's new constitution. One result is that traditional men's and women's gender roles are assumed, and that gay couples become completely invisible, both legally and socially. [Although, even in Poland, there are university courses in Queer Studies.] In contrast, post-fascist Spain now recognizes same-sex marriage, even against its backdrop of Catholicism, as do Belgium and the Netherlands—thus, religion by itself did not define the Polish outcome. Therefore, taken together, a comparative reading of the post-communist situation in the former East Germany, Hungary, and Poland reveals considerable variation in women's rights, and thus in their activism and research foci.

Finally, the most far-reaching political and economic change of recent times is the increasing economic and political coordination of the European nations through the creation of the EU, which now includes most of the former Eastern bloc socialist countries. The EU government has resulted not only in a common currency (the euro), but also in common political rules, economic rights, and the ability to move freely across the borders of EU countries. The EU has been following the global economic strategy of creating neoliberal market policies, which have helped wash away the older ideologies of state socialism, fascism, and conservative Catholic tradition, and transformed the economies of countries such as Spain and Ireland. This does not mean that the progressive agendas of socialist parties have been completely dismissed. In fact, capitalist globalization processes have not deterred some Western European countries from electing socialist prime ministers and/or parliaments in recent times (e.g., Sweden, Spain, France), and still practice some degree of socialist democratic policies and principles, especially in the areas of health, education, and other social services and benefits to their citizenry. Feminist and other backlashes to the excesses of globalization (symbolized by the World Trade Organization or WTO) are not uncommon throughout the continent, and have been characterized by transnational organized protests by civil organizations and movements, on issues such as global warming, increasing global inequality, human and workers rights, corporate abuses, the power of international financial regulatory agencies (World Bank, International Monetary Fund (IMF), WTO), and reductions in different states' support for citizen services and benefits.

Integrated into the EU constitution has been the idea of "gender mainstreaming," a change strategy described in Chapter 1. As illustrated by Emanuela Lombardo (Chapter 28), there is a risk that this approach will integrate women into EU processes, without actually allowing women to do any of their own "agenda setting" and also taking pressure off of governments to respond to further demands of women's movements. On the other hand, transnational rules have the potential of inscribing the best gender-related policies from individual countries into many other nations.

POST-COLONIALISM AND IMMIGRATION

The introductions to other regional sections of this volume—on Africa, Latin America and the Caribbean, and Asia—have emphasized the lingering effects of colonialism in those locations, perhaps leaving the impression that the post-colonial era has few impacts on the nations that were the colonizers. However, such an impression would be far from the current reality. Importantly, much of the global increase in transnational migration has come as a legacy of colonialism. There are many long-standing legal immigration paths that increasingly are being followed by residents of former colonies to enter the European nations that previously colonized their countries. Often, residents of French North Africa, Vietnam, or the French Caribbean can migrate to France, residents from Latin American and Caribbean nations can migrate to Spain, and residents of Pakistan, India or former African colonies can migrate to Great Britain, seeking education and employment or family reunification. Different patterns have surfaced in northern Europe, where migrants from parts of Asia and the Middle East, especially from Turkey, have traveled to look for service and agricultural jobs that are often available in European countries with relatively small and aging populations, high education and urbanization levels, and few native workers willing to do low-skilled labor.

European nations are making efforts to deal with the challenges of this new racial-ethnic and cultural diversity—issues that have confronted the United States, for example, for a much longer period of time. Some of these European efforts are successful, but there also have been increases in racism. For example, in the early 2000s, national demonstrations revealed the outrage of many North Africans when French school systems, which theoretically are based on principles of the separation of religion from the state (secularism), refused to allow Muslim children to wear head scarves to school. While the public felt the issue primarily was about secularism, protestors pointed out that other religious symbols (stars, crosses) had previously been allowed in classrooms. As of 2008, this controversy was still unresolved.

Several dynamics are revealed in such responses to Islam. On the one hand, European nations use gender equality as a norm to differentiate themselves from immigrants from nations with different gendered family patterns and expectations for women's lives. On the other hand, as Europeans are forced to confront racial and ethnic difference, there is also an intensification of discrimination and racism. Unfortunately, neoliberal cutbacks in state funding mean that the resources to address some of these issues are declining. European nations are combining their approaches to different forms of inequality and discrimination by merging the offices and budgets of formerly separate gender, immigrant, disability, and other government services and streamlining them into single service/policy ministries. While one might hope this would result in an intersectional approach to inequalities, it may also dilute the response to each concern. As a result of scholars struggling with these issues, there is a large body of feminist policy and legal research in Europe.

LABOR POLICIES, CHILDCARE, AND FERTILITY

Low fertility and birth rates are potentially the biggest pressure toward conservative gender relations in Europe. Because high pensions for current workers depend on taxes being paid by current and future workers, a declining base of taxpayers sows policy panic. Thus, there are pressures to increase the population through immigration or enlarging family size. In other parts of the world, lower birth rates are found in countries where women have relatively high education and more are employed in the labor force—and this is often combined with culture and laws whose goal is gender equality. Yet, within the EU, Scandinavia, with the widest scope of women's rights to childcare, has higher birth rates (e.g., Denmark 1.7, Sweden 1.6, Norway 1.9, Finland 1.7 births per woman) than in other European countries with relatively slow changes in women's equity in their family policy regimes, such as in Italy (1.2), Spain (1.2), or Portugal (1.4). While these data seem to suggest that more and better supported childcare might increase birth rates in the latter countries, European conservatives argue that the still higher birth rate in the United States (2.0), with relatively few parental or childcare services, is an example of using immigration and neo-liberal cutbacks in family services to "fix" the European birth (or labor force) shortage. Therefore, one strand of feminist activism and scholarship is focused on modifying and/or retaining social welfare provisions that support families, in the face of trends that seek to eliminate or privatize them.

As an example of these concerns, Solveig Bergman (Chapter 27) examines the variation in Scandinavian, or Nordic, childcare policies across four of these social democratic welfare states, noting the pressures in some countries to pay women to stay home and do their own childcare, rather than to pay for childcare services that allow women to return to work. Bergman's analysis reveals variation even among these most "gender progressive" countries, and unravels the links between economic trends, feminist demands, and shifting state support for family and carework.

DIVERSE RESEARCH TRAJECTORIES AND WOMEN'S STUDIES

Gender and women's studies are relatively strong in Europe. There are many academic programs and journals in the field. At the same time, the important feminist research questions for gender/women's studies have been shaped by the politics and economy of each country, or by the impact of wider globalization-related processes. Therefore, in spite of all the European diversity that we have described above, in a short volume like this one, it is impossible to cover all the European countries where gender and women's studies research is thriving. Among these are Great Britain and France (noted for their theoretical work), and the Netherlands (noted for their work on sexuality)—all of which are included in the listing of women's and gender center websites in the Appendix.

CHAPTER 23

Traveling Theories—Situated Questions: Feminist Theory [1] in the German Context

Gudrun-Axeli Knapp

The women's movement and feminism have been transnational endeavors from their very beginnings. Although the routes transnationality took in practice were more limited than claims to global sisterhood suggested, the history of feminist politics is characterized by a variety of more or less parochial transnational entanglements. In a different way, this entanglement also characterizes feminist scholarship, which cannot be described adequately from an autocentric national perspective. Realizing feminist theory's simultaneously translocal *and* situated character has undoubtedly been one of the most productive learning processes of the last three decades.

Recognizing the local forms of transnationality has drawn attention to how these encounters shape the contours of feminism quite differently across Europe and around the globe (Ferree and Tripp 2006; Griffin and Braidotti 2002). Against this background, writing about feminist theory in the German-speaking context implies outlining its constellations of encounter and collision, the traveling theories, influential traditions, and situated questions it has faced. Germanophone feminist theory also owes its basic features and development to problems always represented by constellations of concepts, not by the category of *Geschlecht* (gender) alone.

From the beginning, *Geschlecht* and *Klasse* (class), or rather, the interplay between capitalism and androcentrism in the shaping of gender relations, were at the center of much feminist theorizing. In the 1970s and 1980s, the formative years of feminism and women's studies, the foundations of a strong critical theory orientation in feminist scholarship were laid. This orientation certainly echoed the student movement in its criticism of society, but it was also rooted in the critique of modernity that is a particular tradition in German sociology. As I later show, the critical theory tradition remains important to feminist approches today, in spite of the significant shifts feminist theory underwent in the 1990s, when the constellation of *sex*, *gender*, and *sexuality* excited heated debate. Within only a few years, a whole set of different interdisciplinary approaches based in antifoundational criticism had entered Germanophone theory and changed its concerns. The strong, sometimes exclusive, focus on culture, meaning, language and discourse that then animated the debate was mainly inspired by the theories of Judith Butler (1990) and Donna Haraway (1991) and by social constructivism. (For an overview, see Becker-Schmidt and Knapp 2000.) More recently, along with older questions of intersectionality, *nationality*, *ethnicity*, and *race* have become important.

It should be kept in mind that the construct of a "Germanophone" discourse refers to countries and backgrounds that are quite divergent. Although it will not be possible to go into great detail about these differences, I would at least like to provide a brief outline of the different contexts implied by the language community of Switzerland, Austria, and Germany.

Switzerland is a small country with a population of about 7.5 million in the mountainous middle of Europe, which is not a member of the enlarged European Union (EU). It values its tradition of political neutrality and a certain kind of multiculturalism, which finds expression in the widespread multilingualism among its inhabitants. Four official languages (German, French, Italian, and Romansh) are spoken in Switzerland, and it regards itself as a place predestined for cultural translation. This self-understanding is shared by Swiss feminists, who invest great energy in working on the boundaries that both separate and connect the three universes of French, Italian, and German feminisms.

Austria has about 8.5 million inhabitants and is a member of the EU. Its historical awareness of once having been the center of the extended multi-ethnic Habsburg Empire is still very much present. This, together with the experience of sharing borders with four formerly communist countries (Hungary, the Czech Republic, Slovakia, Slovenia), constitutes a particular kind of imaginary postcolonial/post-Cold-War space. Like the Swiss with regard to the south and west, Austrian feminists have developed their own traditions of intertranslation and exchange with feminists from neighboring countries in southeastern Europe.

Last but not least, there is Germany that, with a population of about 82.5 million, is by far the largest of the three countries. Germany's "negative heritage" is one of a "belated nation" (Plessner 1982) with a relatively brief and long-neglected history of colonialism, a country that instigated two world wars and that is still coming to terms with its traumatic history of National Socialism and its subsequent Cold War division into East and West bloc states (the GDR and FRG respectively). Both Naziism and political division have unavoidably had a powerful impact on feminism.

The post-war background, in particular, makes it difficult to talk about German feminism in the singular, as the gender debates proceeded differently in eastern and western Germany. In the former German Democratic Republic (GDR), early feminist impulses were provided by writers such as Irmtraud Morgner, Maxi Wander, and Christa Wolf and not by a grassroots women's movement as in the West. (For an overview of the development of women's studies in Eastern Germany see Dölling 1994.) Yet, while some differences still remain, there are also many points of convergence. This is especially true for more recent discussions of the features of gender relations under different societal conditions in the East and West and what has been happening to them in the ongoing process of "unification" begun in 1990.

In the following three sections, I first attempt to develop a picture of the overall dimensions of the Germanophone theoretical constellation, emphasizing the local conditions that shaped this perspective as it developed from the 1970s to the 1990s, but in a context with many transnational connections. I then present some of the key lines of feminist argument developed from this basis of social-historical theorizing, emphasizing four theorists whose work is little known outside the Germanophone context but which is deeply influential there. In the final section I discuss the transnational transformations that shook this edifice of theory, particularly emphasizing how the understanding of gender and class in women's and gender studies that developed in the 1970s and 1980s moved to include more understanding of sexuality, nation and ethnicity in the 1990s. Transnational events—such as the collapse of communism, crises of reproduction and immigration, and an expansion in the scope and power of the European Union—combined with transnational theoretical currents of post-modern post-colonial cultural theories to re-frame gender issues for feminists in German-speaking countries.

GENDER RELATIONS IN CAPITALIST MODERNITY

As has been the case in other countries, Germanophone women's and gender studies developed in close interaction with the women's movement. The issues feminists put on the political agenda also became the central foci of feminist scholarship, such as questions of equal rights, political representation, abortion, labor policy and sexualized violence against women. Perhaps due to the conservative environment, hostile to calls for social change, the women's movement developed a certain radicalism in theory and practice. Feminist theorizing in the German context was driven by the strongly felt necessity to come to terms with the systemic dimension of women's oppression and to grasp the contradictory character of women's living conditions (*weiblicher Lebenszusammenhang*).

A feminist understanding of gender relations as a category of societal structuration and dominance—with its associated concepts of men, women, the heterosexual couple, masculinity and femininity—emerged through sociohistorical and cultural studies. These early researchers focused on the (re)coding and (re)structuring of the gender order in the evolving capitalist industrial society in the nineteenth century. Before discussing the individual works implied by this summary, I outline three hard-won insights about the fundamental character of gender that I believe form the core of this "German" feminist perspective.

First, the development of a bourgeois capitalist society is seen as an important turning point in gender relations. Rather than a perpetuation of "traditional gender roles," the bourgeois capitalist modernization of gender relations is characterized by a historically specific configuration of separation, differentiation, and hierarchy. Second, the normative, juridical, and factual assignment of women to the private sphere in modernity is associated with a distribution of work, roles, competences, and authority positions to women—albeit in class-specific variations—that rest on their exclusion from the public sphere. This newly institutionalized division of public and private created legal sanction for women's subordination to men, gender-typical forms of the exploitation of their labor, and their economic dependence. Dominance and inequality are therefore not only class-specific but gender-specific: Gendered positions in society are differentiated by class and also structured along lines that cut across classes.

Third, this distinctively modern configuration of separation, differentiation, and hierarchy gives rise to polarizing cultural interpretations of gender difference. Femininity in particular is seen as becoming the subject of a special anthropology that is conducted on increasingly scientist, biological–essentialist grounds. A fundamental structure of the symbolic order in Western modernity is expressed through the simultaneous particularization and feminization of gender (*Der Mensch und sein Weib*/The human being and his wife) as the objects of social scientific study. The workings of science assume a special relevance for the understanding of gender inequalities in modern and modernizing societies.

These principles can be seen as animating Karin Hausen's sociohistorically oriented reconstruction of the gender-based division of work and her analysis of the "propositional system of gender characters" (*Aussagesystem der "Geschlechtscharaktere"*), a classic, formative contribution to Germanophone feminist scholarship (Hausen 1976). Hausen explores the sociohistorical conditions in the late eighteenth and nineteenth centuries under which the understandings of "man" and "woman" lose their meaning as simply ascribed positions (*ständisch*) and polarizing attributions of masculinity and femininity become increasingly psychological essentialisms anchored inside people. Swiss sociologist Claudia Honegger's archeological investigation of "Ordering the Genders: The social sciences construct humanity and women" (*Die Ordnung der Geschlechter: Die Wissenschaften vom Menschen und das Weib* 1991) reconstructs the contemporaneous and co-equal emergence of the modern idea of the human being and the new view of gender difference anchored in biology (see also Duden 1987; von Braun 1985).

Ursula Beer's *Geschlecht, Struktur, Geschichte: Die soziale Konstituierung des Geschlechterverhältnisses*/ Gender, structure, history: The social constitution of the gender system (1990) brings together much of her explicitly social-theoretical line of argumentation. Beer reconstructs a historical entanglement of a market economy with the reproductive economy (*Versorgungs- und Fortpflanzungsökonomie*) and emphasizes the functional relevance of hierarchical gender relations for the capitalist mode of production. In doing so, she focuses on the precise examination of the historical development of this configuration from a society of ascribed positions (*ständisch*) to a bourgeois society, as well as the legally codified embedding of "secondary patriarchy" (*Sekundärpatriarchalismus*) in industrial capitalism. Beer traces this history in the continuities and changes in family and labor legislation between 1794 (*Allgemeines Preussisches Landrecht*) and 1900 (*Bürgerliches Gesetzbuch*).

Ute Gerhard's studies of the sociology of law and the development of the women's movement also belong in this category of historically oriented social theory, although with a focus on social agency. Gerhard shows how the crisis-ridden modernization of the early twentieth century enabled fraternal (*männerbündisch*) political alliances across all classes to press for new forms of patriarchal dominance in reaction to the first-wave women's movement's emancipatory demands (Gerhard 1978). In political science, the Austrian Eva Kreisky used an historical perspective to expose the androcentric and fraternal implications of concepts both central to political theory and embedded in the modern state (Kreisky 1992).

All of these studies were not merely structural in focus but also deeply cultural and historical in their implications. My emphasis on the integration of both threads comes, of course, in part from my own experience as an actor in this history as well as my placement in the disciplinary spectrum as a sociological social psychologist. But I am not alone in this view. In their 1996 study, *Out of the Shadows: Contemporary German Feminism*, the Australian German Studies scholars Silke Beinssen-Hesse and Kate Rigby write:

> German feminist thinking has been articulated in the shadow not only of the internationally dominant francophone and anglophone variants of feminist knowledge, but also of Germany's past. Indeed, the felt necessity of confronting this past has contributed to what is in our view one of the strengths of German feminist theory, namely its characteristically historical and sociological perspective and concomitant stress on the importance of understanding the origins of one's ideas and taking responsibility for their political implications.
>
> (Beinssen-Hesse and Rigby 1996: VIII)

As they point out, a sense of responsibility for history pervades the writing of Germanophone feminist scholars. Their marked social-theoretical orientation reflects their efforts to place equal weight on issues of dominance and inequality between the genders, between social classes, and in the political realm, while also tracing a historical trajectory through the social analysis and actual social relations of earlier periods into the present.

Nowhere is this clearer than in how the

history of National Socialism resonates in and influences feminist critiques. This includes a pervasive general discomfort with the term "race/*Rasse*." Although today this may also be read as a sign of a critical constructivist approach, the taboo associated with the term *Rasse* is rooted in on-going awareness of the history of racist anti-Semitism. The avoidance of notions of (collective) identities reflects not only the power of modernist individualism and psycho-analytic thought and social-theoretical traditions critical of notions of identity, but also revulsion at where the collective identity policies of the Nazi era led. Suspicion of Nazi legacies also has fueled a suspicion of affirmative understandings of femininity and motherliness. Among historians, the anxieties raised by idealizing mothers in general—and our mothers in particular—culminated in the feminist Historians' Dispute (*Historikerinnenstreit*), in which the extent to which women could be seen as actively complicit in Nazi atrocities or as powerless victims of their ideology and practices was hotly debated across the Atlantic (Bock 1982/83; Koonz 1987). In my view, the critical and self-reflexive impetus in Germanophone feminist theory borrows as much from our own historical experience as it does from deconstructionist theories traveling the transatlantic route.

Even today German feminist theory stresses the historical contextuality of both concepts and critique. Applied to reflection on the simultaneously transnational *and* locally situated character of feminist discourse, it is a demanding form of analysis. It forces me to ask what it is that is actually "traveling" when we speak of "traveling concepts"? If concepts are not to be understood abstractly, as mere cognitive representations of problems detached from any discursive context and social location, it is necessary to look at the historically situated individuals and "thought collectives" (Fleck 1999) who produce the concepts and pass

them on. When specifically located historical resonances tinge our theorizing, what happens when concepts leave one space of perception and articulation and travel to another?

Such travel could be from a context where identity politics are embedded into politico-cultural traditions and institutional opportunity structures which are open to questions of recognition of cultural "difference" or "diversity," such as the United States, to a context where there is a strong leftist tradition in articulating political interests and where the ground for collective identity claims has historically been shaken, such as Germany. To what extent do concepts separate themselves in the course of their travels not only from their cognitive–discursive framing but also from the social psychological cathexis to which they are bound? For Germanophone feminists, the specificity of experiences with respect to both the history of National Socialism and the tense relationship between the East and the West create a backdrop against which all their contextual ways of naming and framing seem immensely important. Thus, in the following section I detail some of the "thought collectives" and particular experiences with history that shaped the early development of feminist theory and women's studies in the 1970s and 1980s.

THEORETICAL TRADITIONS: FEMINIST REVISIONS

The strong Germanophone engagement with history in part reflects the young women scholars' connection to student activism in the 1970s. Like other student activists, their view of society was inseparably bound to critiquing bourgeois capitalism and dealing with the monstrosities of German history. But another important source of the distinctive direction that Germanophone feminism took lay in the interdisciplinary scholarly traditions of German sociology, which have long been oriented to social and cultural history and on which feminists were able to build in a critical way.

The development of the social sciences in Germanophone countries took a different course than it did, for instance, in the United States or the United Kingdom, even though there were numerous transnational cross-connections (Calhoun 2007; Lepenies 1981). One of the characteristics of German sociology, as developed by Ferdinand Tönnies, Georg Simmel, and Max Weber, was the close connection between theory construction and critical diagnoses of contemporary issues (*Zeitdiagnose*). At the center of these diagnostic efforts was the examination of the ambivalences and contradictions of modernization. Sociology was meant to provide a comprehensive theory of society and thus to contribute to self-reflection on contemporary processes of social change (see Habermas 1992).

The empiricist approach to social science, characteristic of the United States, was not common in Germany until after World War II, when it was frequently part of re-education programs and controversial from the start. Both conservative scholars from the humanities as well as advocates of critical sociology on the left were involved in the debates around the institutionalization of the social sciences in Germany (Nolte 2000). In the so-called positivist dispute at the Frankfurt sociologists' convention (*Soziologentag*) in 1968, Theodor W. Adorno and Jürgen Habermas defended critical social theory, as an approach based on interdisciplinary research and a theoretical concept of society as a comprehensive historical constellation against empiricist claims for the primacy of falsifiability (Adorno 1981).

Instead of embracing positivism, a whole generation of rebellious students in the German university system adopted Marxist or left-liberal theory traditions. Student critiques of authoritarianism extended to their own faculty, many of whom had been compromised by collaboration with the Third Reich. The Frankfurt School exerted a strong interdisciplinary influence, combining social philosophy with a psychoanalytically oriented social psychology and a Marxist–Weberian theory of society. Other kinds of western Marxism also played a major role: Althusser, Godelier, Gramsci, among others, and the approaches associated with the periodical *Das Argument* were especially important in the German-speaking countries. As the women's movement emerged among students, feminists critically scrutinized these competing theoretical and disciplinary perspectives on society, epistemology, and the subject, and also adopted and extended their interdisciplinary qualitative research methods. Feminist efforts to develop a complex theory of contemporary social transformation were rooted in these academic traditions but were largely not accepted by the male professoriate, helping to preserve their sense of radical outsider-critique as feminists.

The younger generation of feminist historians was oriented to the same theorists as their counterparts in the neighboring disciplines of sociology, political science, and economics. This applies above all for Karl Marx and Max Weber, the key creators of what became known as the Bielefeld School of social history. Bielefeld trained many of the feminist historians who redirected this new stream of social history more to cultural history, to questions raised by historical anthropology, and to the everyday. This laid a specifically Germanophone groundwork for the transnational *cultural turn* in feminist studies, one that preserved a social-theoretical perspective that was structural but not economistic, and historical without being limited to the discipline of history (Hark 2005; Knapp 1998; Knapp and Wetterer 1992). The development of a feminist history of gender relations is well captured in Hagemann and Quataert's overview, *Gendering Modern German History* (2007) that takes up their engagement in rethinking everything from militarism to sexuality.

As exemplifying the Germanophone perspective in the other social sciences, I focus on four empirically grounded social theorists: Regina Becker-Schmidt, whose approach developed in critical reflection on the early Frankfurt School tradition and represents the continued engagement of feminist theory with class–gender relations; Helga Krüger, whose institutionalist analysis of change over the life-course, highlights the postwar transformations of West German society; Irene Dölling, for her analysis of gender relations in the former GDR and after unification; and Hannelore Bublitz, who offers a Foucault-based social analysis of modernity. Each of these scholars represents a different set of important contextual concerns as well as distinctive theoretical contributions based on engagement with them.

These feminist approaches differ from the micro-sociological traditions of the Anglo-American approach to gender in how they build upon critical theories of modernity, analyze the constitution of gendered subjectivity and the gender system (*Geschlechterverhältnis*) dialectically, and focus on tensions, forces and counterforces within individuals and society. Despite their differences, all see society as a historically constituted relationality of individuals, collectivities, institutions, and practices. Society is understood as a "category of mediation," a functional and relational notion, and not an essentialist term with geographically definable contours, and its mediations of individuals and society, subjectivity, and social relations are permeated by power and complex modes of domination. From these premises it follows that micro-, meso-, and macro-sociological approaches are all insufficient for understanding actual societies. This understanding can only be achieved by an integrative approach that reconstructs the multifaceted dimensions, processes, and constellations involved in societal reproduction and change. The emphasis given to change in these studies is perhaps made more understandable by noting the enormous changes that German speakers experienced in the twentieth century: two world wars and the rebuilding of society after each; the political and social revolutions of fascism and socialism; the struggles around capitalism, democracy, militarism and neo-liberal globalization. Gender relations are both constitutive of and constituted by this complex history, as these theorists stress.

Regina Becker-Schmidt is the feminist theorist who has most continuously elaborated her ideas with critical reference to the earlier Frankfurt School, especially to Adorno, with whom she worked in the 1960s (Becker-Schmidt 1999; for an overview see Knapp 1999). Becker-Schmidt combines a psychoanalytically oriented social psychology and a critical theory of society. She developed her widely used concept of "dual integration/socialization" (*doppelte Vergesellschaftung*), on the basis of empirical research into the living conditions of working-class mothers and the contradictions and ambivalence that pervade their life context. The following brief outline of her influential social-theoretical perspectives, on which she continues to work, suggests both some of the distinctive insights and the common threads that inform Germanophone theorizing of gender (Treibel 2004).

Like many feminists engaging in social theory, Becker-Schmidt approaches society by applying "theories of action." These theories concentrate on *actors and their practices* with a view toward the sociostructural, institutional, and discursive conditions and outcomes of their actions (for an overview see Gottschall 2000; Knapp and Wetterer 2001, 2003). But unlike the micro-sociological "doing gender" concept, the term societal integration (*Vergesellschaftung*) accentuates the formation of constellations of power, relationships of exchange, and interdependence between social actors and *groups* of actors that evolved historically (Becker-Schmidt 1987, 1991). For Becker-Schmidt, the term "gender relations" denotes the sum total of institutionalized controls in a social structure through which the genders are put into relation to one another, and also the principles to which this placement adheres. Gender relations are both constitutive of and constituted by history. The critical social theory that Becker-Schmidt takes up also draws on Marx and Weber by explicitly engaging with conflict as core to social interaction.

Becker-Schmidt not only focuses on inequality among social *groups* but also on how societies were historically differentiated into functionally specialized, but interrelated, sectors of social *practice*. Here the concept of *Vergesellschaftung* (societal embedding/integration) refers not only to the differentiated inclusion of actors into social life processes, but to the relations of interdependence and power among differentiated spheres of societal practice themselves. The focus of her inquiry is how the different sectors of societal reproduction are interconnected as interdependent domains, how the developmental dynamic and present form of this conflicting constellation of gendered domains affects the processes and structures inside each, and how these internal dynamics affect their interrelationships with each other (Becker-Schmidt 2000, 2002, 2007).

The Bremen-based sociologist Helga Krüger, a leading exemplar of the so-called institutional approach, builds on Becker-Schmidt's work to consider gender inequality from a life-course perspective. This "institutional approach" was formulated within the multi-year, nationally funded, interdisciplinary research project "Status Passages and Risks in the Life Course." Using historical data on organizations and populations as well as life-history interviews with individuals in different social locations, Helga Krüger and her associates showed the extent to which social institutions (the educational system, the labor market, the health system, preschools, schools, the social security/welfare system, etc.) presuppose a specific form of gender relations in their temporal economy and their institutional regime. Each institution is organized around the presumption that one of the partners in a couple is set free, at least partially, to supplement and complement the institutional services. Many of the conflicts that have to be dealt with on the level of the personal relationship arise from these structural parameters and they show what kinds of different consequences this structural organization has for male and female lives over time within the framework of the heterosexual "couple."

But just as they trace the development of these constraints across the individual life course, they show how they arose in an institutional history. What today can be perceived as being merely the objective constraints (*Sachzwänge*) of institutions, without making any reference to a particular gender order, are institutionally rooted in formal decisions made in the early twentieth century in the context of an openly aggressive gender policy and reconstituted by political choices made in West Germany after World War II. Such institutional arrangements include part-day schools with irregular hours, strong age-based rules for education, jobs and retirement, and legal and tax privileges for male-breadwinner households. In German feminist discussion, these outdated institutional arrangements, which are currently coming under increasing pressure, are referred to as "Germany's special path" in social policy and welfare-state arrangements, or the *deutscher Sonderweg* (Hagemann 2006).

This general institutional framework, the structure of which makes it so difficult for women to both have a family and be gainfully employed, contributes to Germany's distinct form of gender inequality and femininization of poverty. It has been analyzed as epitomizing a "strong male breadwinner" in social policy terms in the transnational welfare state literature (Ostner and Lessenich 1998; Pfau-Effinger 2004). It has also led to concerted struggles for feminist change, both in the immediate postwar years and in the reemergence of feminism in the 1970s, with its focus on anti-authoritarian childcare, women-led local projects, and national reform of laws regulating abortion, sexuality and family life (Dackweiler 1995; Gerhard 1999; Lenz 2001).

The analysis of West German institutional development and transformation has led to important insights into the complexities of social reproduction and change. Helga Krüger and her research team point to all three levels of social organization—personal interaction, the institutional regime, and the structure of social subsystems (labor market, educational system, the sphere of private reproduction)—as mediated processes of social transformation that proceed in contradictory, non-simultaneous, and conflict-ridden ways (Born and Krüger 1993; Born et al. 1996; Krüger 2001, 2007).

Their emphasis on non-consensual and non-contemporaneous processes of social change has become an important common point of reference in feminist theory and research. Krüger's empirical studies of life-course changes and local political, social and economic developments set in motion a variety of research projects that focus on the non-simultaneities of institutional and individual change and tensions between normative change and the functional and temporal logic of institutions, in which the "silent force of history" (Marcuse 1964) finds structural expression. For example, the attitudes of women and men of the younger generation interviewed in the Bremen life-history project are without exception more egalitarian than the gender norms that underlie the institutional regimes with which they deal, and against whose demands the individuals'

good intentions wear themselves out time and again.

In its focus on life-course theory, the institutional approach highlights the significance of time—period, cohort and age—for inequalities, exposes the cumulative effects of the discrimination of women under these institutional conditions, and focuses on the social contradictions that are brought to the surface under current conditions of the erosion of the "Fordist configuration" of capitalism: the specific concatenation of welfare state provision, standard labor relations, and a breadwinner/housewife model of the nuclear family all regulated by the nation state. Wetterer (2003) particularly takes up the gendered discrepancies between rhetorical modernization and the conservatism of practices in Germany. This overall approach based in critical theory has not been without debate in recent years; Weinbach (2007), for example, bases her approach on Niklas Luhmann's systems theory and locates the reproduction of gendered inequality in interactions and organizations, but denies its relevance at the system level.

The contradictory and uneven constellation of institutional regimes and changing norms described by Helga Krüger and her colleagues is also today recognized as distinctively *West* German. From the opposite vantage point of her own experiences of institutionalized gender relations in the state-socialist *East* Germany, but also on the basis of critical theories of modernization, Irene Dölling developed an analysis of the transformation process produced within and then following the collapse of the former German Democratic Republic (GDR). Dölling showed how subjects' cultural obstinacy (*Eigensinn*) also can be asserted *against* altered general institutional frameworks. Her research demonstrates ways in which norms and attitudes persist, while all around institutions are transformed, underlining that such persistent norms need not be prejudged as "traditional." Her argument is that the special qualities continuing to characterize eastern German gender arrangements long after unification are the subliminal reverberations of the East German gender contract, which continues to be effective to this day as a "habitually anchored *longue durée*" (Dölling 2003: 80). Especially characteristic of this cultural obstinacy is how women have firmly held onto what had become for them the self-evident norm of (full-time) gainful employment.

In her attempt to place empirically observed tendencies in eastern German gender relations after unification into a comprehensive social-theoretical framework, Irene Dölling combines Ursula Beer's considerations in *Geschlecht, Struktur, Geschichte* (1990) with Peter Wagner's *Soziologie der Moderne* (1995). Wagner distinguishes three phases of modernity: severely liberal modernity (the emergence of industrial social modernity), organized modernity (the welfare state phase between the end of World War II and the 1960s), and extended liberal modernity (also known as postmodernity). State socialism is viewed as an independent variation of organized modernity. Each phase differs in its prevailing patterns of interpretation (intellectual means), institutional orders, and externalizations of those social problems that cannot be dealt with using its available cultural means and institutional forms.

Against this conceptual background, Dölling presents the rearrangements of eastern German gender relations, in the change from their version of organized modernity into the extended liberal modernity of the present, as extremely contradictory configurations. On the one hand, institutional change and neoliberal deregulation (the transition to flexible employment contracts, forms of work, and working hours) have led to the increased relevance of "gender" as a factor of social differentiation and a mediator of inequality. On the other hand, certain aspects of the gender contract typical of the

GDR, with its more shallow hierarchies between women and men, have been preserved. However, under the conditions of economic restructuring and continued neoliberal deregulation, the stubborn adherence women have to their belief in the compatibility of (full-time) gainful employment and family under these new capitalist conditions allows a less contested institutional transition to flexible working hours and undermines collective labor agreements (Dölling 2002, 2005; Nickel 2000; Ostner 1994).

These approaches have shown themselves to be fruitful in many different domains, with feminist researchers in the new millennium moving to rethink modernization (Oechsle and Geissler 2004) as well as pursue its implications in different empirical studies. Aulenbacher (2005) particularly has looked at gender and societal rationalization processes, Wetterer (2002) provides a theoretical and historical reconstruction of gender and professional work, and Gottschall (2000) offers a comparative approach to diverging sociological traditions and their ability to grasp contemporary forms of gender inequality.

A major turn in the structural, institutional approaches to gender relations that characterized Germanophone feminist social science came with the 1990s, as Foucault's work began to gain increasing importance (Bührmann 1995, 2004; Maihofer 1995). Foucault's concepts were attractive in a variety of respects. His historical epistemology as well as his emphasis on power relations as such accommodated the increasing reflexivity in women's and gender studies. Even though with different formal concepts, the apparatuses of knowledge and power and processes of normalization and subjectification had already been a primary field of feminist concern. For the relation between individuation and socialization/societal integration, so crucial to the social theories in the Western Marxist and Frankfurt School tradition, the Foucaultian "tool box" provided instruments that promised to address the action- and praxis-theoretical limitations of this tradition with which Germanophone feminists had been struggling.

One of the focal points for the feminist reception of Foucault was the research project initiated by Hannelore Bublitz: "The ordering of gender relations: The archeology and geneology of gender difference in the 1900 discourse of culture crisis" ("Die Ordnung der Geschlechterverhältnisse: Archäologie und Genealogie der Geschlechterdifferenz im Diskurs über die Kulturkrise um 1900"). This influential project again turned to historical material, this time to explore how the primary symbols of modernity are associated with an imagined "femininization of culture." Bublitz treats her discourse analysis as a historical reconstruction of a temporally bound cultural archive, but also uses this archive of historical–empirical material as a "discourse about discourses" to generate a theory of society (Bublitz 2001). These studies present gender as a central category in the constitution and regulation of "population" as a subject. By this, they contribute importantly to understanding the historical origin of the interconnection between the apparatus of sexuality (*Sexualitätsdispositiv*), denoting the cultural constitution and governance of sexuality, and the apparatus of alliance (*Allianzdispositiv*), referring to the cultural governance of gender and structures of family, kinship and belonging (Bublitz 1998; Bublitz et al. 2000).

In sum, the constellation of these four different lines of theory and research provide a window into the way that the complexity and contradictory nature of gender in the sociocultural process of reproduction was approached in Germanophone work. This theory not only reflects the tensions and transformations that run through European history in the twentieth century, but also highlight the non-simultaneities that exist within individuals, institutions, and domains

that are all multiply located and mutually constituitive. This complex and historically grounded sociotheoretical framework serves as the basis on which German-speaking feminists are building their understanding of the processes of transformation that are currently taking place. While its distinctively German concerns are evident in the questions posed and the feelings aroused by them, these approaches are also clearly situated in a long history of sophisticated transnational social theory from Marx through Foucault. The limitations of language—and the little translation done of these works—restrict their ability to travel transnationally themselves.

Although strongly based in a European social theory tradition, the transnational impetus from the Anglo-American context was also unmistakeable on feminist social science. The American social-constructivist traditions influenced gender studies on the professions (e.g., Wetterer 2002) and on organizations, the latter of which became an increasingly important field of theory and empirical research (for an overview see Müller et al. 2008). Scholars of gender, ethnicity, and migration took up postcolonial theories, sometimes relating them to critical social theory (Gutiérrez-Rodriguez 1999). Sabine Hark, among others, made queer theory known in German-speaking countries and introduced issues related to queer citizenship to the theoretical discussion of social organization (Hark 1999). As might be expected from the significance given to the scientizing impact of modernity on gender, social studies of science and the critique of the natural sciences associated with Donna Haraway became a vibrant field of Germanophone scholarship (Ebeling and Schmitz 2006; Schmitz and Schinzel 2004; Weber 2003). These developments also helped to prepare the ground for a transnationally inspired return to the considerations of class, race, sexuality and gender in a more integrated way in the new millennium.

AXES OF DIFFERENCE FROM A SOCIAL-THEORETICAL PERSPECTIVE

The shifts in feminist paradigms in the 1990s that come under the designation "cultural turn" were mainly triggered by the sex/gender debate. The so-called sex/gender, or rather, the sex/gender/sexuality debate represents an excellent example of the influence exerted on local constellations by "travelling theories." The opening for this debate was the English distinction between sex and gender, which suggests a differentiation between the bodily or biological and the socio-cultural aspects of gender. The early Germanophone feminist understanding of *Geschlecht* implicitly presupposed a biological foundation of the distinction between two gender groups, even though the gendered body was conceived as being mediated by sociohistorical life and the highly condensed German term of *Geschlecht* always included references other than biology, for example, genealogical and classificatory aspects. While Anglophone feminists started to use the distinction between sex and gender in the 1970s because of its tactical usefulness, the mistrust with respect to the category of "gender" and the "sex/gender" dualism began mounting up as early as in the mid-1980s. Accordingly, in German the distinction became popular literally at the very moment the problematical aspects of the delineation between physical and social gender or gender identity had already been exhaustively negotiated in the Anglo-American discourse.

The radical inquiry into the biological foundation of gender dualism was indeed tantamount to forcing open the earlier horizon of perception and criticism. It intervened not only in the problematic division of work between gender theories on the one hand and theories of sexuality on the other, it also represented a provocation, because in the Germanophone context there was no cultural anthropological research comparable with that conducted in Anglophone countries that could have prepared for the thought possibility of various forms of gender classification. Against this background, the questioning of a biologically founded dimorphism of the human species not only invited fierce defense reactions (Duden 1993), but rather, in a countermove, and fostered by the growing topicality of the body and sexuality in popular culture (Villa 2000), it led to a large number of primarily young scholars becoming enthusiastically involved in the debate based in antifoundational criticism of the relations between physical and social gender and their heteronormative integration.

This discussion undoubtedly contributed to raising the epistemological explication level in women's and gender studies. It also should not be underestimated how it caused more light than ever before to be cast on the systematic interrelation between sex, gender, and desire outside the fields of lesbian and queer studies. Yet, looking back to those years from today, an explanation is needed for the fact that at a time when—with the fall of the Wall and reunification—postwar Europe and Germany were experiencing incisive transformation processes at all levels of culture and society, the feminist *theory* discussion, in particular in the West, was revolving in a self-referential way around the construction-theoretical subtleties of sex and gender and only partially allowed itself to be diverted by the historical events. Could it be that the vehemence of the sex/gender debate in Germany is also due to a defensive reaction formation and encapsulation in the face of epoch-making changes whose analysis would have simply been excessively demanding at the time of their occurrence? These questions have been addressed more frequently during the last years; however, corresponding research has yet to be conducted.

More recently, this configuration in feminist theory appears to be at the same time changing and opening up again. The question of inequality and difference among women has moved to the center of much contemporary feminist theorizing, and the transnational discussion of sex, gender, and sexuality seems to re-connect to Germanophone debates about societal transformation. Joan Scott's appeal to "give sex a history," with which she set out to correct the abstract and ahistorical course the sex/gender debate had taken (Scott 2001), nowadays could be further amended to read "give sex a history and give sex, gender and sexuality more of a society." From this angle, to reconfigure both sex/gender and sexuality more coherently into a theory of society, more attention should be directed toward questions concerning the changing relations between the gendered "apparatus of alliance" and an "apparatus of sexuality" (Foucault 1981).

While the rise of the historical constellation of normal(ized) sexuality, polarized gender characters and the respective "politics of belonging" (Yuval-Davis 2006) in the structuring of family, kinship, nations for so-called "modern" society has been intensely studied with regard to the nineteenth and early twentieth century, social researchers know much less about current transformations in the social organization of sexuality, generativity, biopolitics, and population. Atina Grossman (1991) provides an historical overview of this scholarship on Germany. (For a discussion of contemporary biopolitics see Braun 2000.) Despite the accumulation of historical facts and theories about both, the gap between theorizing sexuality and theorizing gender-relations remains and needs to be closed. In my view, this can only happen when the current theoretical focus on identity formation as such is transcended. Our theories of gender must integrate other axes of difference and inequality besides gender, because the category of gender is clearly not sufficient for analyzing the conditions of women's lives, as Becker-Schmidt and others showed decades ago with regard to class, and which is apparent as well in the

historical transformations that states undergo.

An intense discussion is currently taking place in German-speaking countries about how to conceptualize the relations between various forms of dominance, inequality, difference, and normalization (e.g., Klinger et al. 2007; Klinger and Knapp 2008; Walgenbach et al. 2007). The older focus on the dual-sided mediation of capitalism and androcentrism, and on the relations of class and gender has been extended substantially and conceptually.

Already in 1995, in an important article on "gender, authority and international inequality" ("Geschlecht, Herrschaft und internationale Ungleichheit"), Ilse Lenz made an appeal to more forcefully factor in the nation-state in feminist theories of modernity's socialization/social integration (*Vergesellschaftung*) (of women). But issues related to nationality, ethnicity, and racism, which had been considered only as special fields of research (Lutz 2004), were not widely taken up in general feminist theory until the pace of European integration in the 1990s opened up a more intense examination of questions of migration, xenophobia, racism, and the legacy of colonialism and empire. In this new discussion, the subject of "cultural difference" and inequality within Europe has become acute in both theory and practical politics.

This change in the underlying paradigm guiding Germanophone social theory is taking place under conditions of dramatic societal transformation. There is a growing awareness among feminists that feminist theory will either demonstrate a stronger presence at the contested sites where contemporary social relations are being constructed or will be shaken off as irrelevant. More than any time since the rebellions of 1970s, feminist theory has to re-engage in explaining the problems of the present time. This means it must scrutinize the transformation of gender relations with regard to economic, cultural, and ecological globalization; study the transnational entanglements accelerated by technological and media-related development, by wars and by hegemonic tendencies in international politics; theorize the changing shape of inequality, the growing economization of the social sphere, the subjectification of work, and the sociostructural changes which come about as the result of new forms of migration.

My own view is that, for historical reasons, the triad of race/ethnicity, class, and gender that has been highlighted by U.S. Black feminists (Davis 2008) will be key to understanding the contradictory social constellation referred to as "European modernity" today (Knapp 2005). In the late eighteenth century, and then in a more accelerated fashion in the nineteenth and early twentieth centuries, (western) European societies emerged as industrializing, capitalistic, modern, bourgeois–patriarchal societies constituted according to the principles of the national state (or empire) and with different ethnic divisions. Analyses that concentrate on only *one* of each of the corresponding characteristics—the (industrial) capitalist economy and its relations of production, the patriarchal or androcentric forms of dominance and its related forms of normalizing sexuality, the state/territorial governance and its associated forms of ethnic/racist inclusion and exclusion—will not be in a position to grasp the specific constellation of interdependent forms of dominance, inequality, and social differentiation, whose reconfiguration we are experiencing after the collapse of Communism and in the course of European integration and globalization.

As the historical emphases of Germanophone feminist theory have always insisted, any useful understanding of current changes in culture, society and the states of subjectivity requires familiarity with the *status quo ante*. I regard the intersectional analysis of the European *status quo ante* as being the transdisciplinary "homework" that has to be done in a period of increased transnational entanglement. This historical ontology of the present should not be misunderstood as a new edition of Eurocentrism, which was frequently and justifiably criticized. Rather, it is part of a multivocal feminist effort to both de-center *and* re-appropriate Europe as a place of change. This can only happen by means of both better understanding Germany and Europe's own contradictory histories and placing them in a context of more explicitly comparative analyses of the distinctive country- and culture-specific constellations of dominance, inequality and difference.

To return to Europe and to Germany as local specific places where social theory has been and continues to be done is also to attempt to construct a deeper and truer characterization of its own diversity and its relations to others. "To become accountable for such a history requires means of revisiting it, acknowledging it, and understanding the complicity between 'difference' and 'exclusion' in the European mind-set" (Griffin and Braidotti 2002: 235). Just as the early Germanophone feminist theorists attempted to grapple with their complex location in relation to National Socialism, the issues of agency in ethical and political choices, and the extent to which social transformations liberated or oppressed them, the current generation of feminists must theorize what and who "Europe" was, is and is becoming. The historically informed critical social theory that Germanophone feminists have built is a good place to start.

NOTE

I want to thank Christine E. Bose and Minjeong Kim for their constructive comments on earlier versions of this article. My special thanks go to Myra Marx Ferree for encouraging me to write this text and for her help in the process of revision. Her thoughtful suggestions showed me, once again, the ways in which situated knowledge needs to be translated before it can enter the arena of traveling theories.

1. While the terms "women's studies" or "gender studies" refer more to the subject area of research, the adjective "feminist" places emphasis on the political impetus of this scholarly current. "Feminist theory" does not indicate a particular analytical approach; it does, however, point to an adherence to a critical perspective with respect to androcentric features in scholarly disciplines and social disparities in gender relations. In this sense, not every scholarly pursuit of the gender theme can be termed "feminist"; however, neither are non-feminist pursuits of the gender theme necessarily uncritical. From the point of view of history and the sociology of science, the designation "feminist theory" makes reference to a transdisciplinary discourse constellation that has developed since the 1960s in relation to the new women's movement.

REFERENCES

Adorno, T. W. (1981) *Positivist Dispute in German Sociology*, London: Ashgate Publishers.

Aulenbacher, B. (2005) *Rationalisierung und Geschlecht in soziologischen Gegenwartsanalysen*, Wiesbaden: VS Verlag.

Becker-Schmidt, R. (1987) "Frauen und Deklassierung, Geschlecht und Klasse" in U. Beer (ed.) *Klasse Geschlecht. Feministische Gesellschaftsanalyse und Wissenschaftskritik*, Bielefeld: AJZ Verlag.

—— (1991) "Vergesellschaftung und innere Vergesellschaftung. Individuum, Klasse, Geschlecht aus der Perspektive der Kritischen Theorie" in W. Zapf (ed.) *Die Modernisierung moderner Gesellschaften, Verhandlungen des 25. deutschen Soziologentages in Frankfurt am Main*, Frankfurt and New York: Campus.

—— (1999) "Critical Theory as a Critique of Society: Theodor W. Adorno's Significance for a Feminist Sociology" in M. O'Neill (ed.) *Adorno, Culture and Feminism*, London: Sage.

—— (2000) "Frauenforschung, Geschlechterforschung, Geschlechterverhältnisforschung" in R. Becker-Schmidt and G.-A. Knapp (eds.) *Feministische Theorien zur Einführung*, Hamburg: Junius.

—— (ed.) (2002) *Gender and Work in Transition. Globalization in Western, Middle and Eastern Europe*, Opladen: Leske & Budrich.

—— (2007) "Class, Ethnicity, Race, Gender: Logiken der Differenzsetzung, Machtmittel und gesellschaftliche Konstellationen in der Konstitution sozialer Ungleichheitsverhältnisse" in C. Klinger, G.-A. Knapp and B. Sauer (eds.) *Achsen der Ungleichheit. Zum Verhältnis von Klasse, Geschlecht, Ethnizität*, Frankfurt/New York: Campus.

Becker-Schmidt, R. and Knapp, G.-A. (2000) *Feministische Theorien zur Einführung*, Hamburg: Junius.

Beinssen-Hesse, S. and Rigby, K. (1996) *Out of the Shadows. Contemporary German Feminism*, Melbourne: Melbourne University Press.

Beer, U. (1990) *Geschlecht, Struktur und Geschichte. Die soziale Konstituierung des Geschlechterverhältnisses*, Frankfurt/New York: Campus.

Bock, G. (1982/83) "Racism and Sexism in Nazi Germany: Motherhood, Compulsory Sterilization and the State" *Signs: Journal of Women in Culture and Society* 8, 3: 400–421.

Born, C. and Krüger, H. (1993) *Erwerbsverläufe von Ehepartnern und die Modernisierung weiblicher Lebensläufe*, Weinheim: Deutscher Studien Verlag.

Born, C., Krüger, H. and Lorenz-Meyer, D. (1996) *Der unentdeckte Wandel. Annäherung an das Verhältnis von Struktur und Norm im weiblichen Lebenslauf*, Berlin and Weinheim: Deutscher Studien Verlag.

Braun, C. von (1985) *Nicht ich: Logik, Lüge, Libido*, Frankfurt: Neue Kritik.

Braun, K. (2000) *Menschenwürde und Biomedizin. Zum philosophischen Diskurs der Bioethik*, Frankfurt and New York: Campus.

Bublitz, H. (ed.) (1998) *Das Geschlecht der Moderne – Zur Genealogie und Archäologie der Geschlechterdifferenz*, Frankfurt and New York: Campus.

Bublitz, H. (2001) "Geschlecht als historisch singuläres Ereignis: Foucaults poststrukturalistischer Beitrag zu einer Gesellschafts-Theorie der Geschlechterverhältnisse" in G.-A. Knapp and A. Wetterer (eds.) *Soziale Verortung der Geschlechter. Gesellschaftstheorie und feministische Kritik I*, Münster: Westfälisches Dampfboot.

Bublitz, H., Hanke, C. and Seier, A. (2000) *Der Gesellschaftskörper. Zur Neuordnung von Kultur und Geschlecht um 1900*, Frankfurt and New York: Campus.

Bührmann, A. (1995) *Das authentische Geschlecht. Die Sexualitätsdebatte der Neuen Frauenbewegung und die Foucaultsche Machtanalyse*, Münster: Westfälisches Dampfboot.

—— (2004) *Der Kampf um 'weibliche Individualität': Zur Transformation moderner Subjektivierungsweisen in Deutschland um 1900*, Münster: Westfälisches Dampfboot.

Butler, J. (1990) *Gender Trouble: Feminism and the Subversion of Identity*, New York: Routledge.

Calhoun, C. (ed.) (2007) *Sociology in America. A History*, Chicago: The University of Chicago Press.

Dackweiler, R. (1995) *Ausgegrenzt und eingemeindet. Die neue Frauenbewegung im Blick der Sozialwissenschaften*, Münster: Westfälisches Dampfboot.

Davis, K. (2008) "Intersectionality in Transatlantic Perspective" in C. Klinger and G.-A. Knapp (eds.) *ÜberKreuzungen. Fremdheit, Ungleichheit, Differenz*, Münster: Westfälisches Dampfboot.

Dölling, I. (1994) "On the Development of Women's Studies in Eastern Germany", *Signs: Journal of Women in Culture and Society* 19, 3: 739–752.

—— (2002) "Eastern Germany: Changes in Temporal Structures of Women's Work After the Unification" in R. Becker-Schmidt (ed.) *Gender and Work in Transition. Globalization in Western, Middle and Eastern Europe*, Opladen: Leske & Budrich.

—— (2003) "Zwei Wege gesellschaftlicher Modernisierung. Geschlechtervertrag und Geschlechterarrangements in Ostdeutschland in gesellschafts-/modernisierungstheoretischer Perspektive" in Gudrun-Axeli Knapp, and Angelika Wetterer (eds.) *Achsen der Differenz. Gesellschaftstheorie und feministische Kritik II*, Münster: Verlag Westfälisches Dampfboot, pp. 73–101.

—— (2005) "Ostdeutsche Geschlechterarrangements in Zeiten des neoliberalen Gesellschaftsumbaus" in E. Schäfer et al. (eds.) *Irritation Ostdeutschland. Geschlechterverhältnisse seit der Wende*, Münster: Westfälisches Dampfboot.

Duden, B. (1987) *Geschichte unter der Haut. Ein Eisenacher Arzt und seine Patientinnen um 1730*, Stuttgart: Klett-Cotta.

—— (1993) "Die Frau ohne Unterleib: Zu Judith Butlers Entkörperung. Ein Zeitdokument," *Feministische Studien* 11, 2: 24–33.

Ebeling, S. and Schmitz, S. (2006) *Geschlechterforschung und Naturwissenschaften. Einführung in ein komplexes Wechselspiel*, Wiesbaden: VS Verlag.

Ferree, M. and Tripp, A. (2006) *Global Feminism: Transnational Women's Activism, Organizing, and Human Rights*, New York: New York University Press.

Fleck, L. (1999) *Entstehung und Entwicklung einer wissenschaftlichen Tatsache. Einführung in die Lehre vom Denkstil und Denkkollektiv*, Frankfurt: Suhrkamp.

Foucault, M. (1981) *The History of Sexuality, vol.2: The Use of Pleasure*, Harmondsworth: Penguin.

Gerhard, U. (1978) *Verhältnisse und Verhinderungen. Frauenarbeit, Familie und Rechte der Frauen im 19. Jahrhundert*, Frankfurt: Suhrkamp.

—— (1999) *Atempause. Feminismus als demokratisches Projekt*, Frankfurt: Fischer.

Gottschall, K. (2000) *Soziale Ungleichheit und Geschlecht. Kontinuitäten und Brüche, Sackgassen und Erkenntnispotentiale im deutschen soziologischen Diskurs*, Opladen: Leske & Budrich.

Griffin, G. and Braidotti, R. (2002) "Whiteness and European Situatedness" in G. Griffin and R. Braidotti (eds.) *Thinking Differently. A Reader in European Women's Studies*, London and New York: ZED Books.

Grossman, A. (1991) "Feminist Debates about Women and National Socialism" in *Gender and History* 3: 350–358.

Gutiérrez-Rodriguez, E. (1999) *Intellektuelle Migrantinnen – Subjektivitäten im Zeitalter von Globalisierung*, Opladen: Leske & Budrich.

Habermas, J. (1992) "Soziologie in der Weimarer Republik" in H. Coing, L. Gall, J. Habermas, N. Hammerstein, H. Markl and W. J. Mommsen *Wissenschaftsgeschichte seit 1900. 75 Jahre Universität Frankfurt*, Frankfurt: Suhrkamp.

Hagemann, K. (2006) *Ein deutscher Sonderweg? Welfare State Regimes, Public Education and Child Care – Theoretical Concepts for a Comparison of East and West*, http://hsozkult.geschichte.hu-berlin.de/tagungsberichte/id=1130&view=print (last visited December 20, 2007).

Hagemann, K. and J. Quataert (eds.) (2007) *Gendering Modern German History. Rewriting Historiography*, Oxford and New York: Berghahn Books.

Haraway, D. (1991) *Simians, Cyborgs and Women: The Reinvention of Nature*, London: Free Association.

Hark, S. (1999) *Deviante Subjekte. Die paradoxe Politik der Identität*, Opladen: Leske & Budrich.

—— (2005) *Dissidente Partizipation. Eine Diskursgeschichte des Feminismus*, Frankfurt: Suhrkamp.

Hausen, K. (1976) "Die Polarisierung der 'Geschlechtscharaktere.' Eine Spiegelung der Dissoziation von Erwerbs- und Familienleben" in W. Conze (ed.) *Sozialgeschichte der Familie in der Neuzeit Europas. Neue Forschungen*, Stuttgart: Ernst Klett.

Honegger, C. (1991) *Die Ordnung der Geschlechter. Die Wissenschaften vom Menschen und das Weib*, Frankfurt and New York: Campus.

Klinger, C., Knapp, G.-A. and Sauer, B. (eds.) (2007) *Achsen der Ungleichheit. Zum Verhältnis von Klasse, Geschlecht und Ethnizität*, Frankfurt and New York: Campus.

Klinger, C. and Knapp, G.-A. (eds.) (2008) *ÜberKreuzungen. Fremdheit, Ungleichheit, Differenz*, Münster: Westfälisches Dampfboot.

Knapp, G.-A. (1999) "Fragile Foundations, Strong Traditions, Situated Questioning: Critical Theory in German-speaking Feminism" in M. O'Neill (ed.) *Adorno, Culture and Feminism*, London: Sage.

—— (2005) "Race, Class, Gender: Reclaiming Baggage in Fast Travelling Theories," *European Journal of Women's Studies* 12, 3: 249–267.

Knapp, G.-A. (ed.) (1998) *Kurskorrekturen. Feminismus zwischen kritischer Theorie und Postmoderne*, Frankfurt and New York: Campus.

Knapp, G.-A. and Wetterer, A. (eds.) (1992) *Traditionen Brüche. Entwicklungen feministischer Theorie*, Freiburg: Kore.

—— (2001) *Soziale Verortung der Geschlechter. Gesellschaftstheorie und feministische Kritik I*, Münster: Westfälisches Dampfboot.

—— (2003) *Achsen der Differenz. Gesellschaftstheorie*

und feministische Kritik II, Münster: Westfälisches Dampfboot.

Koonz, C. (1987) *Mothers in the Fatherland: Women, the Familiy and Nazi Politics*, New York: St. Martin's Griffin.

Kreisky, E. (1992) "Der Staat als 'Männerbund.' Der Versuch einer feministischen Staatssicht" in E. Biester, B. Geißel, S. Lang, B. Sauer, P. Schäfter and B. Young (eds.) *Staat aus feministischer Sicht*, Berlin: Eigenverlag.

Krüger, H. (2001) "'Ungleichheit' und Lebenslauf: Wege aus den Sackgassen empirischer Traditionen" in B. Heintz (ed.) *Geschlechtersoziologie. Sonderband 41 der Kölner Zeitschrift für Soziologie und Sozialpsychologie*, Wiesbaden: Westdeutscher Verlag.

—— (2007) "Geschlechterungleichheit verstimmt: Institutionalisierte Ungleichheit in den Verhältnissen gesellschaftlicher Reproduktion" in C. Klinger, G.-A. Knapp and B. Sauer (eds.) *Achsen der Ungleichheit. Zum Verhältnis von Klasse, Geschlecht und Ethnizität*, Frankfurt and New York: Campus.

Lenz, I. (1995) "Geschlecht, Herrschaft und internationale Ungleichheit" in R. Becker-Schmidt and G.-A. Knapp (eds.) *Das Geschlechterverhältnis als Gegenstand der Sozialwissenschaften*, Frankfurt and New York: Campus.

—— (2001) "Bewegungen und Veränderungen. Frauenforschung und Neue Frauenbewegungen in Deutschland" in U. Hornung, S. Gümen and S. Weilandt (eds.) *Zwischen Emanzipationsvision und Gesellschaftskritik. (Re)Konstruktionen der Geschlechterordnung*, Münster: Westfälisches Dampfboot.

Lepenies, W. (ed.) (1981) *Geschichte der Soziologie. Studien zur kognitiven, sozialen und historischen Identität einer Disziplin*, 4 vols, Frankfurt: Suhrkamp.

Lutz, H. (2004) "Migrations- und Geschlechterforschung. Zur Genese einer komplizierten Beziehung" in R. Becker and B. Kortendiek (eds.) *Handbuch Frauen- und Geschlechterforschung*, Wiesbaden: VS Verlag.

Maihofer, A. (1995) *Geschlecht als Existenzweise. Macht, Moral, Recht und Geschlechterdifferenz*, Frankfurt: Ulrike Helmer Verlag.

Marcuse, H. (1964) *One-Dimensional Man: Studies in the Ideology of Advanced Industrial Society*, Boston: Beacon.

Müller, U., Riegraf, B. and Wilz, S. M. (2008) *Geschlecht und Organisation*, Wiesbaden: VS Verlag.

Nickel, H. M. (2000) "Employment, Gender and the Dual Transformation in Germany" in C. Flockton, E. Kolinsky and R. Prichard (eds.) *The New Germany in the East. Policy Agendas and Social Development since Unification*, London: Cass.

Nolte, P. (2000) *Die Ordnung der deutschen Gesellschaft. Selbstentwurf und Selbstbeschreibung im 20. Jahrhundert*, München: C. H. Beck.

Oechsle, M. and Geissler, B. (2004) "Modernisierungstheorien: Anregungspotenziale für die Frauen- und Geschlechterforschung" in R. Becker and B. Kortendiek (eds.) *Handbuch Frauen- und Geschlechterforschung*, Wiesbaden: VS Verlag.

Ostner, I. (1994) "Back to the Fifties: Gender and Welfare in Unified Germany" in *Social Politics* 1: 32–59.

Ostner, I. and S. Lessenich (1998) *Welten des Wohlfahrtskapitalismus. Der Sozialstaat in vergleichender Perspektive*, Frankfurt: Campus Verlag.

Pfau-Effinger, B. (2004) *Development of Culture, Welfare State and Women's Employment in Europe*, Aldershot: Ashgate.

Plessner, H. (1982) *Die verspätete Nation. Über die politische Verführbarkeit bürgerlichen Geistes*, Gesammelte Schriften. Band IV, Frankfurt: Suhrkamp.

Schmitz, S. and Schinzel, B. (2004) *Grenzgänge. Genderforschung in Informatik und Naturwissenschaften*, Frankfurt: Ulrike Helmer Verlag.

Scott, J. (2001) "Millenial Fantasies. The Future of 'Gender' in the 21st Century" in C. Honegger and C. Arni (eds.) *Gender. Die Tücken einer Kategorie*, Zürich: Chronos Verlag.

Treibel, A. (2004) *Einführung in soziologische Theorien der Gegenwart*, 6. überarbeitete und aktualisierte Auflage, Wiesbaden: VS Verlag.

Villa, P. (2000) *Sexy Bodies. Eine soziologische Reise durch den Geschlechtskörper*, Opladen: Leske & Budrich.

Wagner, P. (1995) *Soziologie der Moderne: Freiheit und Disziplin*, Frankfurt and New York: Campus.

Walgenbach, K., Dietze, G., Hornscheidt, A. and Palm, K. (2007) *Gender als interdependente Kategorie. Neue Perspektiven auf Intersektionalität, Diversität und Heterogenität*, Opladen and Farmington Hills: Verlag Barbara Budrich.

Weber, J. (2003) *Umkämpfte Bedeutungen. Naturkonzepte im Zeitalter der Technoscience*, Frankfurt and New York: Campus.

Weinbach, C. (ed.) (2007) *Geschlechtliche Ungleichheit in systemtheoretischer Perspektive*, Wiesbaden: VS Verlag.

Wetterer, A. (2002) *Arbeitsteilung und Geschlechterkonstruktion. "Gender at Work" in theoretischer und historischer Perspektive*, Konstanz: UVK Verlagsgesellschaft.

—— (2003) "Rhetorische Modernisierung: Das Verschwinden der Ungleichheit aus dem zeitgenössischen Differenzwissen" in G.-A. Knapp and A. Wetterer (eds.) *Achsen der Differenz. Gesellschaftstheorie und feministische Kritik II*, Münster: Westfälisches Dampfboot.

Yuval-Davis, Nira (2006) "Belonging and the Politics of Belonging," *Patterns of Prejudice* 40 (3): 197–214.

CHAPTER 24

An Overview of Research on Gender in Spanish Society

Celia Valiente

This article offers an overview of research on gender in Spain. The aims of this report are to describe the existing state of research, to identify the gaps in coverage, and to supply a bibliography of existing research. A main argument in this article is that the development of sociological studies on gender in Spain has been influenced more by the political evolution of the country than by the social transformation of Spanish society.

At least three factors explain the significant impact of political factors on scholarship on gender and society. First, from the mid-1930s to 1975, Spain was governed by a right-wing authoritarian regime headed by Franco that actively opposed the advancement of women's rights and status. Therefore, prior to the 1970s, very few analyses were carried out on gender and society. Second, many specialists on gender have been members of or sympathizers with the Spanish feminist movement. Thus, the topics of interest for researchers and the activist interests of participants in the movement have largely coincided. Comparatively speaking, Marxist feminism has been central in the Spanish feminist movement while the liberal and radical groups have been less important (although not negligible). Therefore, priority issues for Marxist feminists, such as women's work, have been more intensively studied than other topics, such as sexuality, which is a central concern for radical feminists. However, this article makes a conscious effort to present not only Marxist analysis but also other studies undertaken from different theoretical and empirical perspectives. Third, most of the financial support for research on gender and society comes directly or indirectly from the state. Especially since the 1990s, gender researchers have been increasingly busy writing reports for policy makers. Public authorities have thus been able to privilege their preferences and influence the field of gender analysis.

This short article is not exhaustive but rather provides a general picture of the state of sociological research on gender in Spain. I have selected works using three primary criteria. First, the works discussed here typically use gender as the main dimension in the analysis of the Spanish society in the democratic period (1975–2001). Works that deal with other topics, but use gender as one of many variables, are not included here because this type of research remains very rare in Spain. Second, only published works are included. Third, all of the publications are based on empirical research.[1]

Scholarship on gender in Spanish society differs from research on gender and society undertaken in the United States in at least six ways. As I describe below, most Spanish works (1) are macrosociological and descriptive, (2) are not comparative, (3) lack sophisticated quantitative analysis, (4) lack a systematic international perspective, (5) do not follow the American style of publication, and (6) do not have to pass severe quality filters in order to be published.

A significant proportion of studies on gender in Spanish society are macrosociological; these analyze the whole society or (more often) social institutions such as education or the economy. Very few works examine small groups where face-to-face interactions take place (such as peer groups) or individual behavior (e.g., cognitive processes). Therefore, most works commented on in this review are descriptive and limited to the documentation of the subordinate position of women in society. There are few explanatory works that analyze why and how women have unequal access to economic rewards, decision-making power, and social prestige. The majority of the studies examined are not comparative, as there is no tradition in Spain of doing comparative studies in social sciences (Uriarte 1997a: 27). Even quantitative research pieces on gender and society are usually descriptive reports (e.g., of the number of women enrolled in university education) and rarely use more complex statistical techniques such as regressions.

With relevant exceptions, most research cited in this article does not refer to international studies, discussions, and/or debates. When Spanish scholars make reference to international works, they usually do so to support their hypotheses. Spanish researchers rarely attempt to contribute to international debates and discussions. This is the case not only with research on gender but with all research in the social sciences.

I can offer some explanations for the lack of international perspective that characterizes the production of scientific knowledge. Most Spanish scholars do not master foreign languages, because these are not well taught at school. The overwhelming majority of research is published in Spanish and written by authors with the Spanish audience in mind. Generally speaking, there is not a premium in the university system for those researchers who work in international projects or publish abroad; this is especially true at the beginning of one's academic career.[2] The authoritarian regime severely limited the contacts of intellectuals and social scientists with foreign colleagues. The authoritarian government also prohibited the circulation of many international publications.

The Spanish style of publication differs from the typical U.S. pattern for a social science research article in which introduction/theory/data and methods/analysis/conclusion sections are systematically followed by most authors. Spanish pieces may lack one or more of these sections. In general, works do not have to pass strict quality tests to be published in Spain. Although the system of blind peer review is spreading among journals and book publishing houses, it is not yet the norm. In Spain, authors' connections are often as important as (or more important than) the quality of research in decisions regarding publications in the social sciences. Therefore, it is not surprising that Spanish journals generally are not included in international social sciences citation indexes. The lack of prevalent rigorous review procedures does not mean the absence of high-quality works. Some studies are excellent, but the overall quality level of publications in Spain is significantly lower than in other countries where blind peer review is firmly established.

It is important to note that in Spain, researchers on gender and society have been (and currently are) facing at least one serious difficulty while conducting research: the very negative image that gender issues have among most scholars. In Spain, people who do gender studies are usually women, and they are viewed as feminists. This is a practical obstacle for the development of research on gender and society because being a feminist is regarded negatively by society and by the academic world (Uriarte 1997a: 17–18). Gender research is a risky option for scholars, who may be denigrated by others (whether openly or not). Many mainstream sociologists think that gender is a much less important topic for study than other classical sociological issues such as socioeconomic status. Thus, it is understandable that very few Spanish scholars openly define themselves as feminist researchers. Consequently, it is often very difficult to determine which works are feminist and which are not. In this article, I have decided to review works in which the authors do not overtly or implicitly deny that women as a group occupy a subordinate position in society in comparison with men and that this subordination should be reversed. Therefore, I have included studies that in other countries would not be considered feminist. Most Spanish sociologists specializing in gender are interested in both describing and denouncing gender inequality, as is the case with most research about gender issues in Spain (Alberdi and García de León 1990). There is an elision in some pieces between scientific analysis and normative concerns (Uriarte 1997a: 15).

In spite of several difficulties, scholars have been able to develop what now constitutes an ample body of academic work on gender in Spanish society. It is to this review of the literature that I now turn. I divide the works on gender and society into six sections or topics: families, education, work, politics, sexuality, and men.[3]

FAMILIES

In general terms, (mainstream) sociology of the family is an underdeveloped subfield of sociology in Spain, although this situation has been changing slightly since the 1990s. Gender scholars have paid less attention to the study of families than to the study of other dimensions of social life, such as education or work. The relative shortage of feminist studies on families may be explained by historical factors. The earlier authoritarian political regime prescribed that women's principal role in society was full-time dedication to their families. The last goal that feminist scholars wanted to accomplish after the dictatorship was to focus their intellectual energies on the analysis of the social institution so dear to Francoist official discourse and propaganda.

However, scholars have studied decision-making processes and the division of labor within families. Regarding decision-making, dramatic changes have taken place in most Spanish families in the past three decades. Family life is currently based much less on wives' and children's obedience to husbands/fathers and more on dialogue and negotiation between family members. In contrast, equally important transformations have not happened in the gender division of labor within families. In Spain, large percentages of both sexes believe that household and caring tasks should be shared between both members of the couple. However, in practice, the main (or sole) family responsibility of many men is to serve as the breadwinner, while women (whether workers or homemakers) take responsibility for most domestic and care work. Thus, the combination of professional and family responsibilities is an acute problem for many Spanish women of working age (Alberdi 1999).

Scholars have developed a particular interest in what does not work in family life or in what is not the typical nuclear family. As a result, we can now rely on works about divorce (established in Spain only in 1981) (Domenech Almendros 1994), domestic violence (and violence against women in general) (Medina-Ariza and Barberet 2003), and families headed by an adult (usually a woman) (Madruga and Mota 2000). However, scholars' engagement by what used to be called atypical family phenomena is limited. Many of these issues are rarely studied, including families formed by people of the same sex.

We know very little if anything about many aspects of family life. Let me illustrate this point with two examples. The field of feelings, emotions, love, and intimacy is almost an unexplored territory. This is paradoxical, given that the family is usually conceived of as the private and intimate realm. Also unknown is the experience of girls within families. We know very little about this matter, apart from some basic facts such as that girls perform more domestic tasks than boys.[4]

EDUCATION

Education is one of the gender areas in which substantial research from a gender perspective has been undertaken in Spain. As in other countries, historically, girls were enrolled in the education system in considerably lower proportions than boys. Girls and boys usually attended sex-segregated schools and were taught a different curriculum. In contrast to the boys' curriculum, the girls' curriculum included a strong component of domestic skills (mainly sewing) and religious (Catholic) activities (chiefly prayers).[5] Girls' curriculum contained fewer academic subjects than did boys' curriculum. The quality of training for teachers who worked in girls' schools was lower than that of teachers in boys' schools. Since the nineteenth century, and especially during the democratic regime of the Second Republic (1931–1936), some experiments with mixed schools took place. However, in 1939 mixed schooling was forbidden by Francoist authorities, and sex-segregated schools became again the norm. It was only in 1970 that mixed schools were permitted again and in the mid-1980s that these became the established pattern. Today, only a tiny minority of schools are sex segregated in Spain (Ballarín Domingo 1994).

Because sex-segregated schools have been associated with the authoritarian period and backwardness, the overwhelming majority of social scientists, policy makers, and social actors have favored mixed schools. Therefore, in contrast with Anglo-Saxon countries, in democratic Spain, no debate has emerged on the potential usefulness of sex-segregated schools for girls. While supporting mixed schools, social scientists have studied practices in these schools that hinder girls and women. Researchers have identified at least seven areas where sexist practices exist: textbooks, curriculum, teachers' actions in the classroom, interaction among students, students' academic options, the feminization of the teaching profession, and pupils' positions in the labor market after the completion of their studies.

First, textbooks provide gender-biased views of social reality. For instance, women are mentioned and represented in textbooks much less frequently than men are. Textbooks tend to ignore women's experiences and privilege men's activities. Second, since the 1970s, the extension of mixed schooling took place by using the former boys' curriculum to teach pupils of both sexes rather than by integrating the former boys' and girls' curricula. As a result, women's traditional skills were given less importance (or no importance at all) than men's (Fernández Enguita 1991). Third, teachers (often unconsciously) interact more often with male than with female pupils, hold hostile opinions of girls, have different (and higher) expectations for the professional careers of boys than of girls, and use masculine language forms (for example "boys" or "men") when referring to female and male pupils or, even worse, when referring only to female students (Subirats and Brullet 1988). Fourth, students' own behavior contributes to gender differentiation in school. For example, male students (especially older ones) tend to use more space in the schoolyard because they play space-consuming sports such as soccer and basketball, while girls are relegated to the sides and corners of the playground (Bonal 1997).

Fifth, students tend to choose different courses depending on their sex, following the common pattern existing in other countries. In spite of the fact that on average, girls' academic performance in primary and secondary education is as good as (or even slightly better than) that of boys, girls tend to be overcrowded in studies of humanities and social sciences, while boys are in technical and scientific studies. Sixth, the teaching profession was male up until the nineteenth century, when it started to become a female profession through a process of losing prestige and pay. Finally, as in the United States, the same level of education improves women's opportunities in the labor market less than it improves men's opportunities.

As for the Spanish university system, among other topics scholars have studied is why men outnumber women in teaching or research and administrative positions, while the numbers of female and male university students are approximately the same in the university as a whole. These researchers have focused on a number of factors including sex-biased informal practices of hiring and promoting and the difficulties of combining professional and family duties.

In sum, studies on gender and education in Spain have provided us with a nuanced picture of school sexism, which is "invisible, unconscious, and subtle" (Bonal 1997: 23). However, Spanish researchers have developed a taste for the study of indirect sexism and have neglected the analysis of more open and direct practices, such as violence against girls or sexual harassment. These more overt attacks also exist in the Spanish education system and merit scholarly attention. On the other hand, more research is needed on the egalitarian dimension of education. Some scholars have argued (Fernández Enguita 1989) that schools allow women to experiment with equality of treatment to a higher degree than other social arenas such as the labor market or the

family. The impact of these comparatively higher doses of equality on girls' and women's lives is still under-analyzed.

WORK

Work is the dimension of social life that has attracted the most scholarly attention by specialists in gender. In the 1960s and 1970s, the participation of women in the labor market in Spain was among the lowest in the Western world. Since then, women's employment rates in Spain have constantly increased.[6] During the Francoist regime (especially up to the 1960s), the state established numerous policies against women's paid employment such as marriage bars, or prohibitions on entering certain professions, for instance, in the fields of medicine and law. Married women needed their husbands' permission to sign labor contracts and engage in trade. Not surprisingly, the second wave of the feminist movement has made the access to employment one of its most important demands and perhaps the most important one. Spanish feminists have tirelessly argued that women must participate in the labor market to be liberated since the majority of the people of working age acquire economic autonomy only through paid employment. The centrality of work among the demands of the feminist movement reflects the influence of Marxism.

After the dictatorship, as women were entering the Spanish labor market in increasingly higher numbers, scholars documented phenomena that had already been observed in other countries. In spite of the equality before the law achieved with democracy, on average, women's wages and salaries are lower than men's. Women are underrepresented among people who occupy decision-making positions in companies and among employers. Women are overrepresented among workers with temporary contracts, workers with shorter working records, part-time workers, workers employed in the underground economy, workers who work at home, and unemployed individuals. Women are overcrowded in some jobs and professions, while men perform a wider range of jobs and professions.

To explain women's subordinate position in the Spanish labor market, researchers have elaborated two types of explanations: supply-side and demand-side arguments. Supply-side accounts argue that women and men are different kinds of employees when they offer their working potential to employers. For instance, women have different educational backgrounds than men or have more domestic and caring responsibilities at home. As a result of these and other differences, women's and men's prospects in the labor market are dissimilar. Researchers using this supply-side perspective have mainly analyzed the aforementioned differences between women and men. In contrast, demand-side analysts propose that women and men are treated differently in the labor market. Women are discriminated against, and discrimination is the main factor that explains the unequal position of female and male workers. Scholars using this perspective have chiefly studied gender discrimination. However, some forms of discrimination (e.g., those concerning wages and salaries) have been more extensively researched than others (such as sexual harassment at work) (Cousins 1994; León 2002; Moltó Carbonell 1993).

Spanish feminist scholars have insisted that prevailing notions of work reflect male experiences of participation in the labor market in exchange for wages and salaries. Women perform enormous amounts of work that are not considered as such because they are nonpaid. The non-waged domestic and care work performed by a high proportion of Spanish homemakers (and by employed women doing their second shift) has then been analyzed. Some scholars have also tried to quantify non-waged women's work and include it into the calculation of national accounting data, such as the gross domestic product (Durán 1987).

Spain has traditionally been a country that exported its people as migrants to other countries, but it is now in the reverse situation. The appearance of a new social phenomenon (the arrival of immigrants, many of whom are women) has caught the attention of feminist researchers (Gregorio Gil 1998). Finally, the Spanish welfare state has also been studied from a gender perspective. The Spanish welfare state is of a continental type, according to the typology elaborated by Esping-Andersen (1990). In this type of welfare state, social rights are linked to occupational categories and status (e.g., there are different insurance schemes for different types of workers). Since women's experience in the labor market is less than that of men, the Spanish welfare state tends to over-benefit male citizens (Cousins 1994).

POLITICS

Three topics on politics in Spain have caught the attention of most gender researchers: women as conventional political actors (mainly as voters, candidates, and officeholders), women as nonconventional political actors (chiefly as participants in the women's movement), and gender-equality policies.

Studies on women as voters (Morales 1999) have documented that in the first democratic elections in Spain, higher proportions of women than men preferred conservative political options. This difference between the voting patterns of men and women has been eroded ever since. The almost complete disappearance of gender differences regarding voting in Spain contrasts with other countries such as the United States where the expression "the gender gap" describes a tendency for women to vote for more liberal political options than men since the 1980s. Scholars specializing in gender in

Spain have studied other gender dissimilarities in conventional political participation such as membership in political parties and trade unions.

Women's presence in conventional political positions (members of the Council of Ministers, Parliament, the senior grades of the administration and leaders of political parties), has risen throughout the whole democratic period. For instance, in the lower chamber of parliament (the so-called Congress of Deputies), the proportion of female members of parliament (MPs) has increased from 6 percent in the first democratic parliamentary term (1977–1979) to 36 percent in the current term (2004–2008). The proportion of women among members of the upper chamber (Senate) in Spain is 23 percent. In this regard, Spain is far ahead of the United States (16 percent in both chambers of Congress) (Interparliamentary Union 2007). Spanish studies have not only mapped the presence of women in conventional decision-making positions but have also attempted to explain how and why women reach (or do not) these positions (Uriarte 1997b). Several factors have been identified that hinder women's political recruitment and promotion including: the unwillingness of men to designate women for governing posts; the lack of role models; or the difficulties of combining political and family responsibilities.

With regard to women's nonconventional political mobilization, the feminist branch of the women's movement has been amply researched (Scanlon 1976; Threlfall 1996). The political environment influenced the feminist movement regarding its political allies, its goals, its organizational structures, and its activities, among other dimensions. The second wave of feminist collective activism appeared around the 1960s and 1970s in opposition to the authoritarian regime, where it encountered mainly (illegal) left-wing political parties and trade unions. These have been the political allies of the feminist movement ever since. An important proportion of the goals of the feminist movement have been instrumental (as opposed to expressive). The feminist movement has also demanded the democratization of the country. The movement has been unable to establish strong and long-lasting umbrella organizations in part because of the close links of women's groups with parties. The interest in political reform and the close alliance with the Left gave feminists incentives to use conventional forms of collective action because these were the preferred forms of action for left-wing parties and trade unions (feminists' allies) to reach political aims. The fact that the state did not provide women with some services that they needed, such as sexual information, contraceptives, and legal advice, made Spanish feminists willing to invest considerable energy in service provision since the 1970s. Service provision by feminists has been further accentuated since the 1980s (to the detriment of identity-oriented activities), when the state started giving subsidies for women's organizations that provide services.

We know much less about the non-feminist branch of the women's movement, which is formed by housewives' organizations, widows' associations, mothers' movements, and cultural and religious associations, among others. Scholars specializing in gender in Spain tend to study the social movements (and in general the topics) that they like, and not those that they do not like, even if these may be very interesting from a sociological point of view. This selection of the object of study is regrettable because the majority of women who belong to women's organizations in civil society and mobilize through them are not members of feminist groups.

With respect to studies on gender equality policies at the central, regional, and local state levels (Threlfall 1998; Valiente 1995) we now know that the establishment of most of these policies has been promoted in Spain in the past three decades by women's policy agencies[7] and/or feminists within political parties and trade unions rather than by the women's movement or by both, as in other countries. The literature has tended to study the policy-making process in relation to gender equality but has paid little attention to evaluating the effectiveness of those policies.

SEXUALITY

The sociology of sexuality is one of the topics of sociological inquiry that is least developed in Spain (Guasch 1995). Even fewer works on sexuality have been undertaken from a gender perspective. Some studies have described (and denounced) the rigid sexual mores imposed on women during the authoritarian period that allowed them to be sexually active only within marriage and exclusively while pursuing reproduction. Men's sexuality was also repressed, but to a considerably lesser degree. The liberalization period of the dictatorship and the subsequent democratization of the country were accompanied by a process of relaxation of sexual taboos and repression and a partial revision of the double moral standard, which was significantly looser for men than for women. However, we have only impressionistic accounts of these changes.

The main exception to this pattern of scarcity in studies on sexuality is the relative wealth of research on prostitution (Cebrián Franco 1977; Hart 1998). In Spain, the penal code defines as a crime both the promotion of minors' prostitution and forced prostitution of people of any age. However, prostitution itself is not defined as a crime under the law, and therefore it is not illegal. In contrast with the analysis of other areas of social reality, a significant proportion of studies on prostitution have been carried out by male scholars. Most studies analyze prostitutes, but not their pimps or clients. Most research

analyzes street prostitution, but not that which takes place in other places such as clubs, saunas, or massage parlors. Scholars have studied female prostitution but hardly that exercised by men. In general, prostitution has been only rarely conceptualized by academic studies as sexual social deviance. Many scholars have interpreted prostitution mainly as a problem of social exclusion related to the underclass and the lower classes, although most (but not all) authors have recognized that prostitutes are an internally heterogeneous group. Up to the 1980s, most Spanish feminists conceived of prostitution as an extreme form of women's exploitation that undermines the status of all women in society (whether prostitutes or not). The long-term goal to be achieved then was the eradication of prostitution. However, since approximately the late 1980s, some feminists have conceptualized prostitutes as sex workers. These feminists have demanded that the state treat prostitutes like other workers, for example, allowing them to contribute to the social security system.

Scholarly studies on gay and lesbian sexuality have developed with difficulty, and later in Spain than in other Western countries chiefly because of the former hostile political context and the former and current inhospitable academic environments. During the Franco regime, authorities used several pieces of legislation to repress homosexual behavior. For instance, the 1933 Vagrancy and Villainy Act (Ley de vagos y maleantes) was modified in 1954 to include homosexuals. In 1970, this act was again reformed and became the Social Menace and Rehabilitation Act (Ley de peligrosidad y rehabilitación social). Homosexuals were considered individuals dangerous for society, and some of them were confined in special centers where they participated in mandatory therapies to change their sexual orientation. The Social Menace and Rehabilitation Act was reformed only in 1979 (Calvo 2001). A gay and lesbian movement emerged during the transition to democracy in one of the legal scenarios most hostile to gays' rights in the Western world. The Front d'Alliberament Gai de Catalunya is considered the first mass gay organization and was formally established in 1975. It was legalized as late as 1980. The rest of the gay organizations had to wait until 1983 to be legalized (Calvo 2001). After its appearance, the gay movement immediately called the attention of researchers (Calvo 2001).

Part of the Spanish intellectual production on gays and lesbians has a general character and attempts to describe and explain the hostility toward same-sex relations in the Western world and/or in Spain (Guasch 1995; Herrero Brasas 1993a, 1993b). As a result of international influence, an interest in queer theory has been growing since the late 1990s. Spanish scholars are either popularizing queer theory produced abroad or are trying to contribute to the elaboration of this approach (Llamas 1997). Scholars familiar with the postmodern perspective have started to analyze the representation of male homosexuality in Spanish cinema and literature. Other aspects of gay sexuality, such as the gay subculture, are either little studied or are an almost unexplored territory. Another major hole in gay and lesbian studies in Spain is constituted by analyses of the sexual behavior of sexual dissidents, for instance, on polygamy or monogamy within homosexual relationships, bisexuality, sadomasochism, and risky sexual activity in the era of AIDS.

Reading academic literature on same-sex sexuality in Spain, one gets the firm impression that all Spanish people who are sexually interested in people of their own sex happen to be men. Spanish gay studies are mainly written by men and overwhelmingly focused on the experiences of men. A minority of authors add a footnote to their writings acknowledging the existence of lesbians and the possibility that lesbians' experiences and mobilization may differ from those of male homosexuals. Most scholars do not even bother to make such a small gender-sensitive gesture. The lesbian subculture and the lesbian movement have been only rarely analyzed (Llamas and Vila 1997).

MEN

In Spain, the study of gender and society is still the analysis of women and society. Men and masculinities have scarcely been researched. Anglo-Saxon anthropologists and ethnographers were the first social scientists interested in this topic. During the Francoist period, these scholars undertook studies of rural Spain, mainly in the south of the country (one of the least economically developed parts of Spain). Anthropologists described Spanish masculinity as centered on heterosexual sexuality, rejection of homosexuality, sexist attitudes, and social practices pronouncedly hostile toward women. Men were supposed to actively maintain the honor of their families. This family honor was a multidimensional feature of social life and included the preservation of the virginity of single women, the faithfulness of married women, and the sexual abstinence of widows (Brandes 1991; Gilmore 1987; Pitt-Rivers 1971). These anthropological studies have been criticized for presenting a unitary Spanish masculinity deducted only from the experiences of rural, heterosexual, middle-aged married men without taking into account other types of men. Anglo-Saxon anthropologists have also been accused of exaggerating the machismo of Spanish men (Hart 1998). Other forms of masculinity, such as those of the Gypsy community, have been less analyzed.

Studies on men with a more sociological focus started to appear in the 1980s, although the majority of them have been produced since the 1990s. Two main topics have interested researchers on men (not listed by order of importance). First, scholars have analyzed the reactions of Spanish men to the advancement of women in all areas of social life. These studies have reached opposite conclusions. For some authors, most men conceptualize women's liberation as an unstoppable process and have adapted to this social change. For other social scientists, the responses of men are more diverse. Some (or many) men have received women's advancement with ambivalence or even aversion and have actively tried to resist the improvement of women's lot and the erosion of male privileges. Second, scholars have researched the characteristics of male perpetrators of violence against women. Most other topics have been little studied, such as the representation of men in advertising and male clients of female prostitutes (Hart 1998).

In short, the study of men and masculinities is still in an embryonic stage in Spain. This is an area where more research is badly needed.

CONCLUSION

I have shown that in the past three decades, an impressive body of studies on gender and Spanish society has been developed. However, a caveat is necessary at this point. An article on existing research on any topic might give the reader the impression that the question has been closely investigated and that there are few aspects that need further research. This is definitely not the case with gender and society in Spain, where the gaps in coverage are enormous. As documented throughout this article, there are many dimensions of each issue that have not yet been researched at all. Therefore, if a scholar wants to investigate one of these dimensions, she or he will have to start from scratch and do a lot of fieldwork, which is very time and resource consuming. A related problem is the inadequate dissemination of research already done. No sociological journal on gender exists in Spain. It is often the case that some publications on gender hardly circulate and

that it is very difficult to have access to them or even to know that they exist. Therefore, there is a continual danger of replicating studies already undertaken.

To assess the merits of research on gender in Spanish society, it is important to know that the degree of institutionalization of gender studies in Spain is very low. The central organizational unit of the Spanish university system is the department. No gender studies department exists.[8] This means that all scholars who do research on gender develop their academic careers in departments dedicated to other disciplines (mainly sociology). Generally speaking, such scholars teach courses on sociological topics different from gender. This occurs because the impact of gender knowledge on the Spanish sociology curriculum has been minimal. In contrast with the United States, with very few exceptions, courses on sociology of gender are hardly taught in Spanish universities. The majority of sociology syllabi do not contain sections on gender or readings on gender. Regarding research, if scholars specializing in gender want to fit into their departments, they have to publish on areas other than gender. This institutional framework means a triple shift for gender scholars: to teach courses other than on gender, to publish on topics different than gender, and to research gender and society. This institutional framework is a powerful barrier to many scholars interested in gender (Uriarte 1997a). Future sociological analyses on the development of the sociology of gender in Spain will explain how a rich empirical literature on the topic has been built in such a challenging and nonconducive academic scenario.

NOTE

I would like to thank Kerman Calvo and Gracia Trujillo for their bibliographical advice and valuable comments on parts of an earlier draft. The staff of the library of the Women's Institute (Centro de Documentación del Instituto de laMujer) provided me with valuable help in the search of sources for this article.

1. I have analyzed all articles on gender published in the main social science journals in Spain since their first issues appeared. The journals scrutinized are *Documentación Social: Revista de Estudios Sociales y de Sociología Aplicada*, Papers: *Revista de Sociología, Política y Sociedad, Revista Española de Investigaciones Sociológicas, Revista Internacional de Sociología, Sistema: Revista de Ciencias Sociales*, and *Sociología del Trabajo*. I have also examined books and chapters mainly from the Library of the Women's Institute. This library has approximately 12,000 volumes and is probably the best library on gender in the country.

2. In Spain, most research in the social sciences is done at the university.

3. I have tried to review sociology works, although this has not always been possible since gender is an interdisciplinary field of knowledge.

4. With the exception of studies on education (see below), the analysis of girlhood and female adolescents has hardly been done in Spain (but see Maquieira d'Angelo 1989).

5. The overwhelming majority of Spaniards consider themselves Catholic (77 percent in November 2007). Although the number of practicing Catholics is much lower than the number of self-declared Catholics, it is significant: In November 2007, 15 percent of those self-declared Catholics affirmed that they attend religious services (excluding social events such as weddings, first communions, or funerals) almost every Sunday or religious festivity, and about 2 percent do so various days per week (Centro de Investigaciones Sociológicas 2007).

6. In 1960, the female labor force as a percentage of female population from 15 to 64 years was 26 percent in Spain, 43 percent in the United States, and 46 percent in the Organization for Economic Cooperation and Development (OECD) (Organization for Economic Cooperation and Development 1992: 39). Nowadays, the female employment rate is in Spain (54 percent) slightly below the European Union average (57 percent) (1st quarter 2007 data; Romans and Hardarson 2007: 3–4).

7. Since the 1970s, institutions with the explicit purpose of advancing women's rights and status have been established in all Western countries. These institutions are called "women's policy agencies" or "state feminist institutions" in the literature (Stetson and Mazur 1995).

8. Gender research has acquired a certain degree of institutionalization, for instance, with the creation of interdepartmental gender research institutes.

REFERENCES

Alberdi, Inés (1999) *La nueva familia española*, Madrid: Taurus.

Alberdi, Inés, and María A. García de León (1990) "La sociología de la mujer en España" in S. Giner and L. Moreno (eds.) *Sociología en España*, Madrid: Consejo Superior de Investigaciones Científicas and Instituto de Estudios Sociales Avanzados.

Ballarín Domingo, Pilar (1994) "La educación contemporánea de las mujeres" in J-L Guereña, J. R. Berrio, and A. T. Ferrer (eds.) *Historia de la educación en la España contemporánea: Diez años de investigación*, Madrid: Ministerio de Educación y Ciencia.

Bonal, Xavier (1997) *Las actitudes del profesorado ante la coeducación: Propuestas de intervención*, Barcelona: Universitat Autònoma de Barcelona.

Brandes, Stanley (1991) *Metáforas de la masculinidad: Sexo y estatus en el folklore andaluz*, Madrid: Taurus.

Calvo, Kerman (2001) "El movimiento homosexual en la transición a la democracia en España", *Orientaciones* 2.

Cebrián Franco, J. J. (1977) *Prostitución y sociedad*, Barcelona: ATE.

Centro de Investigaciones Sociológicas (2007) "Study number 2,742," November. Retrieved January 17, 2008 from http://www.cis.es.

Cousins, Christine (1994) "A comparison of the labor market position of women in Spain and the UK with reference to the 'flexible' labor debate," *Work, Employment & Society* 8, 1: 45–67.

Domenech Almendros, Ana (1994) *Mujer y divorcio: De la crisis a la independencia*, Valencia: Promolibro.

Durán, María Á (1987) *De puertas adentro*, Madrid: Instituto de la Mujer.

Esping-Andersen, Gosta (1990) *The three worlds of welfare capitalism*, Princeton, NJ: Princeton University Press.

Fernández Enguita, Mariano (1989) "La tierra prometida: La contribución de la escuela a la igualdad de la mujer," *Revista de Educación* 290: 21–41.

—— (1991) *Hágalo usted mismo: La cualificación del trabajo doméstico, la crisis de su aprendizaje y la responsabilidad de la escuela* (Do it yourself: Qualification for domestic work, its learning crisis and the school's responsibility), Madrid, Spain: Ministerio de Educación y Ciencia.

Gilmore, David D. (1987) *Aggression and community: Paradoxes of Andalusian culture*, New Haven and London: Yale University Press.

Gregorio Gil, Carmen (1998) *Migración femenina: Su impacto en las relaciones de género*, Madrid: Narcea.

Guasch, Òscar (1995) *La sociedad rosa*, 2nd edn, Barcelona: Anagrama.

Hart, Angie (1998) *Buying and selling power: Anthropological reflections on prostitution in Spain*, Boulder, CO: Westview Press.

Herrero Brasas, Juan A. (1993a) "La sociedad gay: Una invisible minoría. 1. Ciencia, prejuicio social y homosexualidad," *Claves de Razón Práctica* 36: 20–33.

—— (1993b) "La sociedad gay: Una invisible minoría. 2. Familia, sistema educativo, religión y Fuerzas Armadas," *Claves de Razón Práctica* 37: 26–42.

Interparliamentary Union (2007) *Women in national parliaments: Situation as of 30 November 2007*, Retrieved January 28, 2008 from http://www.ipu.org/wmn-e/classif.htm.

León, Margarita (2002) "Equívocos de la solidaridad: Prácticas familiaristas en la construcción de la política social española," *Revista Internacional de Sociología* 31: 137–164.

Llamas, Ricardo, and Fefa Vila (1997) "Spain: Passion for Life: Una historia del movimiento de lesbianas y gays en el Estado Español" in X. M. Buxán Bran (ed.) *Conciencia de un singular deseo: Estudios lesbianos y gays en el Estado español*, Barcelona: Laertes.

Madruga, Isabel, and Rosalía Mota (2000) *Las condiciones de vida de los hogares pobres encabezados por una mujer: Pobreza y género*, Madrid: Fundación Foessa and Cáritas.

Medina-Ariza, Juanjo, and Rosemary Barberet (2003) "Intimate partner violence: findings from a national survey," *Violence Against Women* 9, 3: 302–322.

Moltó Carbonell, María L. (1993) "Las mujeres en el proceso de modernización de la economía española" in J. Rubery (ed.) *Las mujeres y la recesión*, Madrid: Ministerio de Trabajo y Seguridad Social.

Morales, Laura (1999) "Participación política en España: Un análisis de las diferencias de género" in M. Ortega, C. Sánchez and C. Valiente (eds.) *Género y ciudadanía: Revisiones desde el ámbito privado*, Madrid: Universidad Autónoma de Madrid.

Organization for Economic Cooperation and Development (1992) *Historical statistics*, Paris: Organization for Economic Cooperation and Development.

Pitt-Rivers, Julian (1971) *The people of the sierra*, 2nd edn, Chicago and London: Chicago University Press.

Romans, Fabrice, and Omar S. Hardarson (2007) "Labor market trends 1st quarter 2007 data," *Eurostat DATA in Focus: Population and Social Conditions* 16.

Scanlon, Geraldine M. (1976) *La Polémica feminista en la España contemporánea (1868–1974)*, Madrid: Siglo XXI.

Stetson, Dorothy McBride, and Amy G. Mazur (1995) *Comparative State Feminism*, Thousand Oaks, CA: Sage.

Subirats, Marina, and Cristina Brullet (1988) *Rosa y azul: La transmisión de los géneros en la escuela mixta*, Madrid: Instituto de la Mujer.

Threlfall, Monica (1996) "Feminist politics and social change in Spain," in M. Threlfall (ed.) *Feminist politics and social transformation in the North*, London and New York: Verso.

—— (1998) "State feminism or party feminism? Feminist politics and the Spanish Institute of Women," *European Journal of Women's Studies* 5 (1): 69–93.

Uriarte, Edurne (1997a) "Estudios de mujeres y política en España" in E. Uriarte and A. Elizondo (eds.) *Mujeres en política: análisis y práctica*, Barcelona: Ariel.

—— (1997b) "Las mujeres en las élites políticas" in E. Uriarte and A. Elizondo (eds.) *Mujeres en política: análisis y práctica*, Barcelona: Ariel.

Valiente, Celia (1995) "The power of persuasion: The *Instituto de la Mujer* in Spain" in D. McBride Stetson and A. Mazur (eds.) *Comparative state feminism*, Thousand Oaks, CA: Sage.

CHAPTER 25

At the Crossroads of "East" and "West": Gender Studies in Hungary

Eva Fodor and Eszter Varsa

In 2007, amidst a large-scale reorganization campaign of the higher education system, the Hungarian Accreditation Board accredited the first degree-granting gender studies program in Hungary. The process was surprisingly smooth, in fact there was only one word in the accreditation documents that the learned committee took issue with: the title to appear on the transcripts. They refused to include the word "scientific discipline" (*társadalmi nemek tudománya*) in the designation of the degree and insisted on using "field of study" (*társadalmi nemek tanulmánya*) instead.[1]

This story illustrates both the progress and the obstacles along the road to institutionalizing gender studies research and education in Hungary. Two decades ago no college-level course was taught that used gender as its primary analytical perspective. Today a significant number of such classes are offered every year, the above-mentioned MA degree, and various minors have been accredited. In the past twenty years, numerous conferences have been organized in several areas of gender studies, regular lecture series are being held in Budapest, listservs connect networks of gender studies scholars, books and edited volumes have been published in Hungarian, and the importance of feminist literary analysis and considerations for gender issues in psychoanalysis have even been discussed at a very popular public lecture series on prime time

national television (Bán 2004). This chapter tracks the outlines of these recent developments and aims to familiarize the reader with at least some of the themes and ideas found in Hungarian gender studies research in the social sciences. In the first part of the article we describe the context within which gender studies developed in Hungary with occasional references to other post-state socialist countries in Europe. Then we move on to present in more detail questions raised by researchers as well as some of the characteristics, themes, problems and opportunities of gender studies scholarship in post-communist Hungary. Our goal is not necessarily to point to similarities or differences between the practice of gender scholarship in Hungary and elsewhere, but rather to depict in broad strokes the state of the art in some of its social science fields. Hungary is a small country and the history of gender studies is brief. Yet, we found it overwhelming to attempt a description that encompasses all disciplinary traditions and all the important themes researchers have published on in the past years. We were forced to make selections, and these reflect our own disciplinary and thematic interests. In general, however, the focus of our paper is the work of social science oriented gender scholars living in Hungary (regardless of what language they publish in), although occasionally, when relevant, we included Hungarian and even foreign researchers abroad if they have published on Hungarian themes and are well known and cited in the domestic literature.

We are not the first to write about this topic: in fact, Hungarian gender scholars have been quite reflexive about their "art" in recent years (e.g., Pető 2006; Timár 2007; Zimmermann 2007). In an effort to offer a somewhat different perspective and to go beyond our limited experience, between December 2007 and January 2008 we sent out an open-question survey to and received answers from close to fifty researchers who have published in Hungarian in the field of gender studies. We asked them about their contributions to scholarship as well as their views on the field. They also sent us their publication lists and most significant or recent work. In addition, in January 2008 we organized a roundtable discussion inviting the same fifty scholars to further elaborate on the emergence and status of gender studies in Hungary, its characteristics and the context that shaped it. Seventeen of us participated in the three-hour discussion. This is, thus, a joint effort even if the final analysis is ours.

As already mentioned above, by the end of the first decade of the twenty-first century, gender studies courses are taught at most major and some smaller universities, and research on gender is carried out at college departments, in research institutions as well as in a number of NGOs in Hungary. Even a cursory look at the academic landscape cannot miss the proliferation of gender studies projects and institutions in the past twenty years. Zimmermann (2007) described this period as "one of triumph for women's and gender studies in Central and Eastern Europe and the former Soviet Union." We identify three factors, which we believe have significantly contributed to shaping the field of gender studies in Hungary: (1) the history of the study of women before and under state socialism, (2) the particular organization and political dynamics of Hungarian academia as it is being reshaped by the "harmonization"

process of higher educational institutions in the European Union, and (3) our geo-political position in the global hierarchy of knowledge production. We review each in the next section, and discuss their impact on the discipline.

THE SOCIAL CONTEXT OF DOING RESEARCH IN GENDER STUDIES

The History of the Study of Women

Scholarly attention devoted to the "woman question" dates back to the middle of the nineteenth century in Hungary. The first authors were primarily educated upper and upper middle-class women, who set out to demonstrate and develop women's capabilities in the male-dominated sphere of intellectual life: they argued and advocated for women's right to schooling. Middle-class intellectuals, Éva Takáts and her daughter, Teréz Karacs, were, for example, active contributors to the first Hungarian scholarly journal, *Tudományos Gyűjtemény* (Scientific Collection). The editors of the journal published a series of Takáts' writings in the 1820s arguing against differentiation by gender in educational issues (Fábri 1999). Another well-known aristocratic supporter of women's education was Mrs. Pál Veres. She became known for spearheading a wider movement for the higher education of women, but she also wrote a more academic tract published in 1868, entitled "*Nézetek a női ügy érdekében*" (Views in favor of the issue of women).

By the end of the nineteenth and the beginning of the twentieth century women's suffrage emerged as another significant political issue among Hungarian activists. Representatives of different social classes voiced their views on women's right to vote, their position in society, and offered suggestions for future political action. Writings by the leading members of the two largest women's organizations, Mariska Gárdos and

Rózsa Bédy-Schwimmer of *Magyarországi Munkásnők Országos Egyesülete* (National Association of Women Workers in Hungary), and *Feministák Egyesülete* (Feminist Association), respectively are good examples.

The political take-over of the communist Hungarian Workers' Party (*Magyar Dolgozók Pártja*, MDP) in 1948 meant strict limitations to open scholarly and public discussions on the "woman question" for decades. The communist party formulated its particular version of women's emancipation, and alternatives were not tolerated. The first codified constitution of Hungary in 1949 granted women "equal rights with men" and, as the crucial element of the emancipation project, extended the obligation of paid work to both men and women, framed in terms of social rights as citizens of the Hungarian People's Democracy. In 1952 the Family Law ensured women's legal equality in marriage. Women were officially granted equal access to education and political decision making as well. Since the state appropriated all these demands, women's movements and feminism were labeled as unnecessary, and were discursively connected to the bourgeois pre-World War II past from which the state was eager to distance itself.[2]

In this vein, the official and only organization for women during the second part of the communist era, *Magyar Nők Országos Tanácsa* (National Council of Hungarian Women), commissioned scholars to research and analyze issues of importance to policy makers (e.g., Turgonyi and Ferge 1969). Subject areas primarily covered were women's contributions to the production process, women in leadership positions, questions about the situation of female agricultural workers, etc. While some of these pieces provide excellent analysis of the work conditions and life chances of working women, the topics chosen as well as the final political messages communicated were carefully selected to fit the party's limited emancipation agenda. Later in the 1970s and 1980s, when Hungary's declining birth rate became a pressing political concern and called for further analysis of the "woman question," research was published on a wider range of topics, such as, how women can balance work and family responsibilities, the feminization of certain occupational areas or women's roles as mothers (e.g., Koncz 1982). Judit H. Sas's book on social stereotypes (1984) was in many ways a groundbreaking piece as it argued, against the pronounced convictions of the communist party, that women's subordinate position in the family was being reproduced consistently even when women actively participated in paid work. In a politically careful way the book attempted to redirect attention away from the productive sphere to "culture" and the household as areas where gender inequality should also be considered. This was particularly important, as towards the end of the state socialist period a growing pool of conservative intellectuals sought to renegotiate women's reproductive rights and reintroduced the thesis that women's nature was rooted in, and determined by, biology. A number of sociologists, including H. Sas, and Zsuzsa Ferge (1985), argued for the social construction of gender and pointed out that even communist social institutions function—regardless of the oft repeated intentions of the party decrees—to maintain male dominance.

In sum, research that may be classified as women's studies has been carried out in Hungary since the mid-nineteenth century. Writing about women's issues, however, had different political implications throughout these decades. In the late nineteenth century the work of educated and mostly middle-class women represented enlightened modernity, in contrast to the remnants of the feudal conditions prevalent elsewhere in Hungary. Under state socialism research for the party was carried out for a number of reasons: a true commitment to the emancipation project as laid out by the party programs; a desire to reform the system from within and affect change where it is most likely to be influential; a need for survival; fear of political retribution, etc. At the same time, writing that may have been considered feminist criticism before 1989 implied a political opposition to the communist system. Bollobás, for example, tells the story of her arriving back to Hungary in the 1980s after a conference in the "West" and crossing the border with feminist literary analysis in her luggage. She was stopped by the border patrol and the books were confiscated as politically dangerous material (Bollobás 2006). While other avenues of dissent were no doubt more popular and visible, the rare voices of feminist criticism represented a social critique in the Western intellectual tradition and a way to distance oneself from what was seen as a backward and oppressive political regime. Doing feminist research in the post-communist era may in fact have quite similar connotations: it represents identification with "Western" traditions rather than reaching back to the Hungarian nationalist past. Only now "Western" signifies a range of different positions: from the neo-liberal technocratic one through the more moderately liberal equal opportunity bound to everything "alternative," queer, anti-capitalist, neo-marxist, etc.

The Structure of Hungarian Academia in a Changing Europe

Research topics and an older generation of researchers represent the continuity from the state socialist era to the present. Yet, in addition to this legacy, the practice of gender studies has been shaped by the Hungarian educational system and its ongoing transformations. Sociologist Maria Schadt describes a recent academic year opening ceremony at a large university in a rural town in Hungary where the dean of humanities and social sciences urged the (predominantly female) student body to work hard during the semester so that at the end of the year they could say "We have had a good time—we've done a man's (sic) work!"[3] (Schadt 2006: 93). Hungarian institutions of higher education and research are dominated by men: not one of the 24 state and private universities is headed by a woman, and a mere six of all the 69 higher educational institutions in Hungary have female presidents (three of these are tiny religious colleges), even though almost 42 percent of Ph.D. students are female. Men dominate elsewhere at the top of the academic hierarchy as well: less than 4 percent of members of the Hungarian Academy of Sciences, 10 percent of Doctors of the Academy, 13 percent of full professors and 29 percent of associate professors, but 41 percent of all assistant professors and almost half of all teaching assistants are women (Hrubos 2002; Timár 2007). The large research universities are organized in a rigidly paternalistic and hierarchical structure; change is slow and new ideas are difficult to introduce. Even more importantly, funding is limited thus significant political leverage and networking is necessary to gain access to some of the scarce resources. Women, and gender studies scholars in particular, are less likely than scholars in more mainstream fields to possess the social and political capital necessary. It is thus not surprising that none of the large public research universities so far has dedicated sufficient resources to establish gender studies as a department in its own right. (The exception is the Central European University, a private graduate school with both U.S. and Hungarian accreditations, where the source of funding is a private endowment and not the national budget.) Instead, a handful of committed academics initially "snuck in" class sessions and later courses on gender studies in a curriculum unfriendly or at least indifferent to these ideas and later developed, with none to minimal resources, specializations and research centers within already existing departments or at universities at large.

Major changes have been affected by a handful of researchers through sheer perseverance. But the legitimacy of gender studies scholarship is not fully established either inside or outside of academia. Findings on gender inequality, discrimination, the social construction of gender and sexuality are barely acknowledged by politicians, decision makers, media outlets or public intellectuals, even though this is considered important by Hungarian scholars for both intellectual and political reasons. The lack of legitimacy also means that it is difficult to obtain grants for projects whose explicit aim is the study of gender issues, and researchers are thus forced to try to obtain funding by "hiding" their interest in gender in larger research questions. This leads to a situation in which there is excellent scholarship in some areas but basic research is missing in others.

The relaxation of political surveillence at universities after the collapse of the communist regime in 1989 opened up space for committed academics to introduce teaching and research on gender into their classrooms and, as a consequence, the higher education curriculum. Hungary joined the European Union in 2004 and is thus collaborating in the efforts to harmonize the national systems of higher education as part of what is called the "Bologna process." This has, by some accounts, accelerated change but has also created a lot of confusion and uncertainty in the regulation of higher education, at least in the short run. The long-term effects remain to be seen and evaluated.

Geopolitical Location

In 1989 the communist party in Hungary relinquished its power. Following the guidelines of the IMF's and World Bank's structural adjustment policies, and with the eager help of local liberal technocrats, Hungary's economy was quickly transformed to suit the demands of global capitalism. With much hope and enthusiasm the institutions of a multi-party democracy were also introduced within years.

A surge of scholarly interest from the more developed world accompanied this "velvet" revolution, opening up new opportunities for many local scholars, including those studying gender in the region. Along with the curious "Western" academics came invitations to conferences, calls to write for edited volumes, and opportunities to participate in research projects. Yet, the inequalities embedded in these exchanges quickly became obvious for all those involved. Scholars in post-communist countries found themselves used as sources for ideas which turned into research papers, with no more than a brief nod of thanks to the originator of the idea. At conferences or in research consortiums, participants from post-communist countries felt they were invited to represent "Euro-diversity" but their contributions were barely heard. Scholars found it impossible to publish in international outlets without a willingness to submit to the hegemonic Euro-American linguistic and theoretical toolkit of scholarly writing, and no similar effort at adaptation or at least accommodation was detectable on the part of Western scholars (for a detailed discussion, see Cerwonka 2008; Gal 1997; and for the experience of a Hungarian feminist researcher, Timár 2007).[4] In this context of cross-national economic and intellectual inequalities, the questions arise: What can we contribute to knowledge production? How can our own voices be heard? These questions have preoccupied scholars including gender scholars from the post-communist region.

One solution offered to avoid the oppressive hegemony of Western academic thought and practice has been to emphasize the unique experience of writing from the post-communist periphery and, thus, to strive to create theories that explain East

European-ness and gender relations under the post-communist condition as profoundly different and unintelligible when seen through what is often called a "Western" lens (e.g., Tóth 1993). Other researchers tend to emphasize the need for a "constant interchange between East and West" (Pető and Szapor 2007), as well as the need for "redistributive politics" to alleviate inequalities (Timár 2007). In an altogether different turn, Cerwonka, an American academic resident in Hungary at the cross-border position of the Central European University, questions whether the concept of "hegemony" is the most useful one to describe the relationship between Western feminist theory and post-communist gender research. Instead, she claims theories are "transculturated"—adapted, modified, rethought in each specific context, and when Western feminist theories are made to "travel" to Eastern Europe they become more sophisticated and refined (Cerwonka 2008). This may be the challenge and contribution of East European scholarship.

Zimmermann (2007) also sees opportunities (and dangers) embedded in the process of doing research on the peripheries of the global capitalist system. Examining the reasons why foreign funding has been so keen to contribute to the rapid institutionalization of gender studies in a number of post-state socialist countries she argues that "gender studies [played] the role of a 'symbolic marker' of Westernization and the compliant incorporation of the Central and Eastern European/former Soviet region into the Western-dominated global system" (Zimmermann 2007: 9). She thus argues that instead of emphasizing our unique experience and focusing on the local or even regional, some are calling on gender studies scholars to adopt a critical stance and examine *systems* of global inequality in order to understand our own specific locations within them.

GENDER STUDIES IN HUNGARY

After the collapse of the communist regimes in 1989 along with a growing number of feminist civil organizations, the first centers of women's/gender study appeared in the region and individual courses on gender proliferated at universities. In Hungary feminist analysis was first taught and researched in departments of English/American language and literature.[5] This was so for both practical and intellectual reasons. On the one hand, reading British and U.S. literary and cultural criticism, especially of the post-structuralist, postmodern kind popular at these departments (Barát and Marinovich 2006) "naturally" brought with it an affinity to Western feminist theories. On a more practical level, students and scholars in these departments had easier access to books written by British and American feminist scholars, and were more likely to have had a chance to travel to countries with a tradition of feminist research. Finally, and not negligibly, British and American visiting professors brought with them their feminist political affiliations as well as feminist texts to read and ideas to share sometimes under the guise of foreign language courses. Indeed, a non-negligible number of the younger generation of feminist academics and activists in Hungary encountered feminist ideas for the first time at a series of English language and linguistics courses taught at the Department of English and American Language and Culture at ELTE University in Budapest by Antonia Burrows, a British feminist activist and language teacher in the early to mid 1990s. These courses served as consciousness-raising experiences and Antonia Burrows was the first feminist role model for a surprisingly large cohort of later feminist scholars (including both co-authors of this chapter, if in different ways). Departments of English and American literature are still major bastions of gender studies scholarship in Hungary both in literary criticism (e.g.,

Friedrich 2006; Séllei 2007), visual cultural criticism (Bán 2000; Hock 2002), cultural studies (Csapó 2003; Joó 2005; Wessely 2004) and linguistics (Barát and Sándor 2007; Boronkai 2006).

By the late 1990s, scholars researching gender in social science disciplines were more successful in creating institutions for gender studies teaching and research. The largest such center, The Center for Gender and Culture, operates in the Department of Sociology at Corvinus University. Its directors have organized several large interdisciplinary conferences, run a lecture/seminar series, and produced a growing number of MA and Ph.D. students yearly who write theses and dissertations in the broad field of gender studies. Another large conference series has been organized annually since 2005 by the Department of English Studies at the University of Szeged in the field of linguistics, entitled "Language, Ideology and the Media" (Barát and Sándor 2007).

The establishment of the Regional Gender Studies Seminar, then the Program on Gender and Culture in 1994, and later a Department of Gender Studies at the Central European University represented a new phase in the development of gender studies in the second part of the 1990s. The first and only such department in Hungary, it operates in a private, primarily U.S. funded graduate school, with English as the language of instruction and students from all over the post-communist world and beyond.[6]

Importantly, research on gender is carried out in research institutes (e.g., in the Research Institute of Sociology of the Hungarian Academy of Sciences, or the Center for Policy Studies at the CEU) and increasingly in NGOs as well. For example, SEED (Kisvállalkozás-fejlesztési alapitvány) a foundation promoting small-scale entrepreneurship has done extensive research on gender discrimination in the labor market as well as on women and entrepreneurship in Hungary. Using grants from the Ministry of Social Affairs, FIONA, Foundation for Young Women financed a project entitled "Men Talking" (Férfibeszéd) in which researchers analyzed the views of male executives on equal opportunity politics and women's paid work. FIONA also organized a conference and exhibition on gender and advertising in collaboration with researchers from a number of post-communist countries. Amnesty International in Budapest has commissioned and published a report on domestic violence in Hungary also.

We are providing this list as an illustration of the point that in a resource-poor research community, intra-governmental agencies (such as the European Commission, UN agencies, etc.) and government organizations are important initiators of basic research on gender, especially in fields considered relevant for domestic and international policy makers. Commissioned research has some advantages: as these projects are not written for an academic audience, they are more accessible for lay people and the research findings are more likely to find their way into the national media and public knowledge. In addition, these commissioned pieces provide a way for academics to get involved in more policy-oriented work and to exchange ideas with NGO activists about social issues. At the same time, however, these types of funding opportunities may limit the questions that are available for research.

Below we review in more depth three areas traditionally and more recently considered important research sites in Hungarian gender studies: (1) changing gender relations in women's work opportunities and participation in the public sphere, (2) domestic violence and rape, and (3) reclaiming women's history.

THREE POPULAR THEMES IN HUNGARIAN GENDER STUDIES RESEARCH IN THE SOCIAL SCIENCES

1. What Happened to Women and Gender Relations after 1989?

Even before the last bricks of the Berlin wall hit the ground questions started pouring in from concerned feminists in Western Europe and North America: What will now happen to the emancipation project underway during state socialism? Will women suffer disproportionately in the newly emerging market economies? Will abortion rights be revoked? And finally, most vehemently, why, oh why are Hungarian women seemingly unconcerned about these issues? Researchers arrived to study the revolution *in situ* and while most East Europeans were unreflexively rejoicing over their new found freedoms, Western feminist scholars forcasted imminent doom for women and the end to any semblance of gender equality (Corrin 1994). International NGOs and transgovernmental agencies also arrived and, in preparation for conducting development projects to promote gender equality, commissioned reports to describe the current "position of women in Hungary."

Weathering the Storms: Women and Work
In fact, a number of excellent and much needed exploratory and analytical pieces were born out of these concerns and opportunities. While the Hungarian Statistical Office had been collecting data disaggregated by gender for decades, new publications gave access to information on gender inequality to the larger public (e.g., KSH 2006). A slew of research reports on women summarized these findings in outputs entitled "Women in the Transition" (e.g., UNICEF 1999) or some variation thereof. A volume entitled "Changing Roles" (for the latest edition, see Nagy I. et al. 2005) has been published in English and in Hungarian in four subsequent years with different sets of

articles on women's position in the labor market (Bukodi 2005), in management (Nagy B. 2005), and politics (Ilonszki 2005), as well as on a number of other related issues (such as women's health, Roma women, gender differences in migration, and fertility issues, etc.) in the most recent issue. Assembling and making sense of the data available was important both politically and academically, comparing them to similar information from Western European countries proved occasionally eye opening.

In studying labor markets, however, it soon became clear that using the indicators harmonized with the European Union's labor force statistics occasionally hides rather than reveals women's experience. For example, a key concern for researchers and politicians alike in Hungary has been the exceptionally low level of employment among Hungarian women, especially compared to the European Union's averages. These numbers, given the political direction of the EU and funding allocated to serve these goals, have implications for research and policy making. Indeed, when using the international measurement for the population between 15 and 64 years of age, the employment rate of women in Hungary is about 5 percent lower than the EU average. This "harmonized" indicator, however, ignores the fact that Hungary has had a historically low retirement age threshold for women, thus, unlike in most EU countries, a vast majority of those over 55 years of age are not in the labor force because they are retired, explaining at least partially the large gap. Indeed, when comparing those in the 24–55 year-old category, women's employment rates are comparable to EU averages. When taking into account another point that mainstream international reports ignore, i.e., that women in Hungary tend to work full time, and calculating employment rates in full-time equivalents, Frey (2005) has found that the employment rate for women in fact exceeded the EU averages.

In response, researchers started to develop ways of thinking about changing gender relations that more adequately describe women's everyday experience. They found that a lot of women had lost their jobs, became unemployed or withdrew from the labor force altogether (Frey 1999), they identified barely changing patterns of job segregation both vertically (Nagy B. 2001) and horizontally (Bukodi 2005), and found a significant wage gap. Yet, at least in the first decade after the transition, relative to men, women's position did not decline in quantifiable ways, contrary to the expectations of a number of less optimistic analysts. So researchers raised the question of what explained women's ability to at least stay on course against many odds? Júlia Szalai (2000) pointed out that much of women's work in the gray or underground economy is hidden in national accounts and in labor force surveys, yet their income keeps families afloat and contributes to the national budget. Women, she argues, used to participate in feminized segments of the informal economy and exchanged care-work for similar services in kind under state socialism. Now they use these skills and experience to gain access to formal and especially informal jobs in the growing service sector, which provides subsistance. In a somewhat similar vein, Fodor (1997) argues that women gained resources under state socialism which became revalued in the newly emerging market economies, contributing to their surprising—and relative—success in retaining some of their labor market advantages. Szalai, however, calls attention to the fact that vast social differentiation is emerging among women, and later studies moved away from discussing women as a broad category and researched ways in which the transition from state socialism affected different groups of women in different ways. Kovács and Várady (2000), in an ethnographic study of middle- and working-class women in a small rural town in Hungary, trace this process of "restratification," or the emergence and renegotiation of class differences among women, and differing notions of femininity in each social stratum. Ethnic differences have also been identified by researchers studying Roma women (Durst 2002).[7] Specificities in the lives of women in rural areas, and especially the ways in which rural women negotiate care work obligations have been the focus of Ildiko Asztalos's (2007) research. In addition to class, ethnic, religious, and geographical differences, generational distinctions also make sense. Mária Neményi (2000) interviewed women in midlife to explore how they constructed their identity as women, mothers, and workers under state socialism, in a context when the experience of their parents was made moot by the radical changes in the social system they witnessed. Then in a later project, Neményi and Kende (1999) added the views of the youngest generation, who again find themselves in a position where their mothers' experience is of little help in yet another radically different social world.

In sum, analysis in the realm of paid and unpaid work tended to move from testing hypotheses and expectations on a broad general level to the production of more nuanced reflections on the experience of women growing up at different times and in different social and geographic locations in Hungary.

Rethinking Women's Political Action
Under state socialism quotas ensured a reasonable representation of women in high level political bodies, such as the parliament or the Central Committee of the Communist Party. The new political parties after 1989, in an effort to distance themselves from the communist past, eliminated quotas of all kinds and, as a result, the proportion of women in political office declined precipitously to a level well below the European Union's average (Koncz 2006;

Lévai and Kiss 1997).[8] What explains this drop and especially women's inability to gain these positions back in the two decades after the fall of the communist regime—a phenomenon quite unlike in most other postcommunist countries? One answer may be found in an article by Olga Tóth (1997) comparing attitudes among Hungarians to people in other European countries and finding that although Hungarians do not necessarily behave in more traditional ways, they certainly hold more conservative views on family life and gender roles than people elsewhere. Exploring the sources of these attitudes educational researchers have found that school textbooks, along with pedagogical practice, project stereotypical roles for boys and girls at all levels of schooling and do not encourage young women to participate in public life (Kereszty 2008; Rédai 2006; Thun 2001). Montgomery and Ilonszki (2003) also suggest that antifeminist political attitudes explain women's failure to gain proportional representation at high levels of power, but also add the lack of a pro-women political lobby and characteristics of the electoral system, where parties have little incentive to promote women. Recently, researchers have started to explore women's political participation in a historical context (Palasik 2007; Szapor 2004), outside national level politics, (e.g., in women's NGOs, see Fábián 2007) and in behind-the-scene roles in local politics (Kovács and Várady 2000).

To some extent at the prompting of Western feminists, marvelling at the lack of organized resistence put up by women following the destructions of the transition, and amidst the emergence of political discourse promoting the importance of civil society in a democracy, researchers addressed the question of why it was so difficult to mobilize women for political action in Hungary. Some have argued that while the state socialist regime did not achieve equality between men and women, women did not become conscious of themselves as women and did not experience discrimination in gender terms (Neményi 1994). Others point to the unfavorable political atmosphere as a possible explanation. Acsády (2006) emphasized the fact that women in positions of authority tended to have negative images tied to the notion of emancipation, while Barát et al. (2004) pointed to hate speech elements in the Hungarian media in discussions on feminism. Susan Gal (1997) notes the dearth of available linguistic tools for feminist organizing in the sea of neo-liberal and neo-conservative voices, and in a later work analyzes the process of "translating" and "recontextualizing" feminist ideas using postcommunist Hungary as an example (Gal 2003). Fábián (2007), on the other hand, disagrees with those who are dissatisfied with the shape and size of the feminist movements in Hungary and analyzes instead the themes and dynamics through which the existing organizations are attempting to influence political decision making.

While rejecting the notion that women have been victimized by the collapse of state socialism, researchers have nevertheless started to identify some of the mechanisms through which gender discrimination has become institutionalized in the post-communist workplace. Two areas have been researched in more depth: organizational culture and political discourse. Beáta Nagy and Lilla Vicsek (2008) conducted in-depth interviews and focus group discussions in a local government agency, a workplace dominated by women, to find out how office and organizational culture is shaped and in turn shapes gender relations. They found that both men and women hold stereotypical and often negative views about female workers and especially female managers, which is likely to make conducting daily business as well as workplace advancement difficult for women. The fact that primarily women work in this office and most managers are also women does not seem to matter. The presence of women, the fact that women were not merely in token positions any more, did not change the discourse. Conversely, according to Herta Tóth (2007), in the male dominated context of international corporations the promotion of seemingly women friendly policies, targeting "work-life" balance tended to function as a mechanism to blur the line between home and workplace, contributing to an overall increase in work hours and stress. In the field of political culture, Dombos et al. (2007) as part of QUING, a large EU-funded research project analyzed policy debates on anti-discrimination and identified the discursive frames utilized in public talk. They find, among other things, that over time, politicians have become less and less likely to talk specifically about gender discrimination and more likely to talk in general about discrimination on a variety of different grounds. This means that gender discrimination itself remains unaddressed in specific terms in political culture. Hungary's joining the European Union and adopting its anti-discrimination policies does not seem to help either, as the "EU requirements" are seen as external, remain unreflected and have not become an integral part of Hungarian policy-making discourse.

In sum, Hungarian social scientists with an interest in gender studies have done considerable research on how women's lives have changed after the fall of the communist regime and what is to be expected in the future. They have looked for answers in a number of areas of social life: work, politics, language, the law and other social institutions, and used a variety of methodologies, from quantitative analysis, through discourse analysis, to interviews and ethnographies to reveal and make public how gender inequalities and gender relations are produced and reproduced in Hungarian society.

2. Emerging from the Silence: The Body, Sexuality, and Violence

Unlike the topics described above, on how women fared in the world of work and politics, the second theme has no tradition or history in Hungary under state socialism. Issues of the body, sexuality and sexual violence were surrounded by silence in the official Hungarian party circles: these questions were not raised in research and barely touched upon by legislation. After the fall of the regime, the first order of business became, therefore, to define a set of phenomena as social problems: homophobia, compulsory heterosexuality, new forms of masculinity, prostitution and trafficking, domestic and sexual violence, and sexual harrassment against women. International aid agencies participated in, some would say initiated, this enterprise, which is still ongoing.

On the theme of prostitution, gender studies scholars have contributed to both academic and media debates (Betlen 2007), but interest in this topic is surprisingly low, especially given the fact that Hungary has been labeled the porno capital of Europe. Masculinity studies was initiated by sociologist Miklós Hadas, who explores the construction of maleness in historical studies of exercise and sports (Hadas 2007). Much needed books and reports have been published on various aspects of domestic violence (most notably, Morvay 2003), as well as on abortion rights (Sándor 1992). Gay and lesbian communities also became the subject of scholarly interest. Judit Takács's work (2004; Kuhar and Takács 2007) calls attention to homophobia in the law and the popular media as well as the wide-spread discrimination and harrassment experienced by gay, lesbian, transexuals and bisexuals in all walks of life. By utilizing a wide array of research methods, from surveys through in-depth interviews to content analysis, Takács persuasively shows the drastic degree of social exclusion imposed on gays and lesbians in Hungarian society. Others have conducted research on clothing style among Hungarian lesbians (Béres-Deák 2007), on bisexuality (Borgos 2007) or have used book reviews to introduce elements of queer theory into the Hungarian discourse on literature and history (Csapó 2003).

It is perhaps in this area of research where an ongoing exchange between academia and NGOs is most easily observable, both on the personal and intellectual levels. Many of the founders and early activists of LABRISZ, the first and most significant lesbian NGO in Hungary, later received degrees in gender studies. Some are teaching courses on gender studies at universities, many are working as experts or researchers for local or international NGOs, some are doing both. Indeed, for many, volunteering at LABRISZ may have created the consciousness-raising experience from which they developed an academic interest in gender studies. In addition, and possibly not unrelated, this NGO, along with other gay rights organizations in Hungary, has been able to secure funding to produce a significant volume of publications on gay and lesbian rights and discrimination (e.g., Sándor 2001). These pieces are available for both the research community and the general public.

With notable exceptions, studies on the body, sexuality, and violence tend to be empirically focused and motivated by a genuine desire to shed light on phenomena perceived as unjust and oppressive. Many of the projects have built on, but also contributed to, the efforts of political organizations who lobby policy makers to rewrite Hungary's legislation in more inclusive and women friendly ways.

3. Reclaiming our History

In *Rajk Júlia* (Júlia Rajk) Andrea Pető (2007) creates the life story of a woman who had so far been only identified as the wife of the first communist Minister of the Interior in Hungary, executed in the country's most famous political show trial in 1949. On the basis of oral histories and archival research, Pető presents the story of Júlia Rajk not merely through the mythical figure of her husband, but by tracing her personal development from a Party politician to a woman politician in her own right. A large number of monographs have been continuously published on famous (or undeservedly less famous) women since the mid 1980s in Hungary (e.g., Balogh and Nagy 2000; Borbíró 2002; Dizseri 1994; Mona 1997; Toronyi 2002; Turai 2002) in an effort to reinsert women and women's voices into mainstream history writing. In addition to "adding women back in," these books introduce previously under-utilized methodologies of writing about the past (e.g., oral histories) and new ways in which people can make a difference and become "important" from a historical point of view.

Perhaps the most important source of biographical information on Hungarian women who were part of national and/or international women's movements and feminisms is provided by the recently published *Biographical Dictionary of Women's Movements and Feminisms: Central, Eastern, and Southeastern Europe, 19th and 20th Centuries* (de Haan et al. 2006). Among the main goals of the dictionary, that includes biographical information on more than 150 women and men who participated in women's movements and feminisms in 22 countries of the region, is to challenge the widely held belief that "there was no feminism in this part of Europe." The dictionary therefore undermines the notion that feminism in this part of Europe is simply a "Western import" and reflects on "continuities between feminisms past and present." In writing about the Hungarian women's movements at the turn of the twentieth century, Acsády (2007), among a number of other researchers (see also Szapor 2004) is motivated by similar goals: to describe the ways in which feminists of this period thought about the role of women in society and the arguments, ideas, and commitments they contributed to Hungarian political and social life. Indeed, these works demonstrate that for the past hundred years just like in the first decade of the twenty-first century, women's groups have been heroically active, yet weak and relatively isolated, in the Hungarian political landscape. Then and now they have been largely unable to mobilize women to fight for improvements in their lives.

A number of historians have focused on the relationship between the construction of gender, social welfare and legislation in Hungary. Susan Zimmermann (1994) for example, analyzes the beginnings of state-provided welfare services and the development of social policy making and poor relief in the Austro-Hungarian Monarchy. In "Municipal Welfare and Social Policy as Gender Politics. Budapest and Vienna, 1870–1914," she draws attention to the asymmetries embedded in and sexual discrimination practiced through officially gender-neutral criteria for access to or exclusion from municipal welfare provisions in the twin capitals of the Dual Monarchy (Zimmermann 1994). Looking at political discourses on and eventual legislation of marriage, Loutfi (2006) traces the influence of nineteenth- and early twentieth-century international feminist and reform movements, which allowed a more woman friendly formulation of marriage laws in Hungary. Studying a later period, Szikra (2008) explores the intersections of gender and anti-semitism in the working of a national level social welfare institution in the 1940s.

The more recent, state socialist past has also been analyzed, interpreted and re-interpreted by feminist scholars. The 1950s was a particularly fascinating time in Hunga-ry's history: a period of rapid social change, when the communist regime introduced its most basic reforms, crushed an uprising and stabilized its rule. The role of women in this process has been the focus of a number of studies: their participation in the policing of others (Pető 2003), in the production process as members of an award-winning female socialist brigade in a Budapest textile factory (Tóth 2007), working in the mines (Schadt 2002), as revolutionaries in 1956 (Juhász 1998), or as Roma (Gypsy) mothers, whose access to state maternity benefits was denied (Varsa 2005). The collapse of the communist regime in 1989 allowed a new light to be shed on women's history during the early periods of state socialism, as previously classified materials from party archives became available and new research methods (especially qualitative research) have been gaining momentum.

Overviews of the state socialist period have also been published. In a much cited piece, Lynne Haney (2002) analyzes the gendered construction of "need" in state policies, welfare offices, and families in Hungary in three periods between 1945 and the early 1990s. Mária Adamik (2000) explores different public discourses on gender and on the relationship between men and women during 30 years of state socialism, with special emphasis on one stream of discourse that posited women primarily as mothers, thereby reconstructing the actual process of women's emancipation. In yet another effort, which tries to embrace the whole stretch of state socialism, Fodor (2003) compares the process, principles and outcome of Hungarian policy making on gender to that in Austria in the same fifty years between 1945 and 1995. These three books, and others like them, attempt to show how gender was constructed, "done," and talked about in state socialist Hungary, as well as how this changed over time, and was carried out in many social locations by people of different political orientations.

They support the general argument that ideas and practices about gender profoundly shaped the way social life was imaged and regulated in Hungary, with consequences for both men and women, which lingered on well after 1989.

CONCLUSION

Gender studies scholars and scholarship in this country share many similarities with those in other former state socialist countries: For example, the scholars' unequal position in terms of access to international publications and grants vis-à-vis their Western colleagues; the debilitating backlash against women's emancipation brought about by decades of state socialism; the legacy of themes which revolve around women's position in the public sphere, etc. Indeed, gender scholars in the region have collaborated and networked amongst themselves, especially in the field of developing educational programs in gender studies. Yet, important differences among the countries should also be noted and analyzed: differences in primary disciplinary orientations; the history of institutionalization; differences in the power of feminist NGOs to disseminate research results; differences in the researchers' positions from which to join international research projects, etc.

In Hungary, while research *on women* pre-dates the state socialist era, it was only in the early 1990s that scholarship and teaching *on gender* has started to gain popularity. In addition, gender studies as a discipline, although gradually and willy-nilly acknowledged by university administrators and educational policy makers, lacks full legitimacy as a veritable scientific endeavor. Related and similarly troubling is the fact that gender studies scholars have difficulty making their voices heard in public contexts where their opinions may be relevant. To some extent this is linked to the relative powerlessness of women's civil organizations as well as to the popularity of conservative attitudes regarding gender roles, and a low tolerance for change in this area. The fact that Hungary's position is peripheral in the global knowledge market may open up critical space for interesting ways to interpret ("transculturate") gender theory, but it also brings with it the daily struggle to make a living and an impact. Recent changes in the structure of academia are just as likely to reproduce inequalities, as they could potentially reshape them. The achievements of Hungarian gender studies scholars are numerous but much work remains to be done.

NOTES

Direct all correspondence to Eva Fodor, fodore@ceu.hu. We would like to thank members of the Hungarian gender studies community for their contributions and fighting spirit.

1. It may be argued that this is in fact the literal translation of the term "gender studies" into Hungarian. This, however, was hardly the main reason behind the Accreditation Committee's decision. "Media studies," for example, was translated using the Hungarian term for "scientific discipline" ("*médiatudomány*"), rather than "field of study," an indication that members of the committee did not consider gender studies quite worthy of the label "science."

2. Equality defined in terms of equal access to work was at the core of the state's approach to the "woman question." This emancipation project was to be enhanced by state-provided welfare services ensuring the socialization of reproductive work, such as child-care, cooking or the care of the elderly. In practice, however, the state's emphasis on catch-up industrialization meant a reliance on women as a "flexible (and cheap) reserve army of labor" (Lampland 1989: 315) without the accompanying provision of adequate social services. Women's "double burden" in the spheres of both productive and reproductive labor did not ease significantly even at times of economic decline when, as numerous historians and sociologists have pointed out, women were seduced back to motherhood (Adamik 2000). Pro-natalist concerns were characteristic of the state socialist period exemplified by the 1953 ban on abortion, the introduction in 1967 of a three-year long, flat

rate maternity leave benefit and its income differentiated version in 1985.

3. This is a popular quotation from a Hungarian poem, Vörösmarty Mihály's "Gondolatok a könyvtárban" written in 1844.

4. Inequalities among researchers within each country also emerged: those who spoke English and were positioned at more visible and better equipped institutions could utilize the opportunities and make a living selling East European "difference," while the majority of university professors and researchers continued to make do on below-subsistence salaries and had very limited access to books, libraries or research grants.

5. Then, the first interdisciplinary gender studies course was organized in 1990 at ELTE in Budapest by Maria Adamik as a university-wide co-taught course.

6. For a detailed review of the institutionalization of gender studies education in Eastern Europe and the former Soviet Union, see Zimmermann 2007.

7. Hungary's largest ethnic minority, the Roma (Gypsy), represent about 4 percent of the population. They are subject to increasing racial discrimination and are on average less educated, less healthy and poorer than the rest of the population.

8. Indeed, this process started to happen already in the 1980s when the communist party first allowed people to choose between carefully selected and largely similar candidates, indicating people's long-standing convictions that men are more fit for political office, and as a result women's representation in Parliament declined.

REFERENCES

Acsády, J. (2006) "A varázstalanító emancipáció mítosza" in J. Bíró, F. Hammer and I. Örkény (eds.) *Tanulmányok Csepeli György 60. születésnapjára*, http://www.csepeli.com/tanulmanyok.html (accessed February 9, 2008).

—— (2007) "In a Different Voice: Responses of Hungarian Feminism to the First World War" in A. Fell and I. Sharp (eds.) *The Women's Movement in Wartime: International Perspectives, 1914–1919*, London: Palgrave.

Adamik, M. (2000) "Az államszocializmus és a 'nőkérdés.' A legnagyobb ígéret – a legnagyobb megaláztatás," Budapest: ELTE Szociológia Tudományok Doktori Iskola, Ph.D. Dissertation.

Asztalos Morrell, I. (2007) "Care Work in Hungarian Agrarian Entrepreneur Families during the Post-Socialist Transition" in I. Asztalos Morell and B. Bock (eds.) *Gender Regimes, Citizen Participation and Rural Restructuring*, Elsevier: Rural Development Series.

Balogh, M. and S. Nagy, K. (eds.) (2000) *Asszonysorsok a 20. században*, Budapest: BME Szociológia és Kommunikációs Tanszék, Szociális- és Családvédelmi Minisztérium Nőképviseleti Titkársága.

Bán, Zs. (2000) "Women on the Verge of a Semiotic Breakdown: The Work of Cindy Sherman, Jenny Holzer and Barbara Kruger" in T. Alves, T. Cid and H. Ickstadt (eds.) *Ceremonies and Spectacles – Performing American Culture*, Amsterdam: VU University Press.

—— (2004) "Van-e az irodalomnak neme?," *Mindentudás Egyeteme* 4, Budapest: Kossuth.

Barát, E. and Marinovich, S. (2006) "Is There Space for Teaching Gender Studies in Hungarian Higher Education?" in A. Pető (ed.) *A társadalmi nemek oktatása Magyarországon*, Budapest: ICSSZEM.

Barát, E. and Sándor, K. (eds.) (2007) "A nő helye a magyar nyelvhasználatban," Proceedings from the conference *Nyelv, ideológia, média*, September 8–9, 2005, Szeged: JATE Press and Szegedi Egyetemi Kiadó.

Barát, E., Pataki, K. and Pócs, K. R. (2004) "Gyűlölködni szabad," *Médiakutató*, Spring.

Béres-Deák, R. (2007) "Values Reflected in Style in a Lesbian Community in Budapest" in R. Kuhar and J. Takács (eds.) *Beyond the Pink Curtain. Everyday Life of LGBT People in Eastern Europe*, Ljubljana: Mirovni Institut.

Betlen, A. (2007) "A férfi ősi jussa: társadalompolitikai érvek a prostitúció legalizálása ellen," *Ezredvég* 2–3.

Bollobás, E. (2006) "From Consciousness-Raising to Intellectual Empowerment: Teaching Gender Since the Early 1980s" in A. Pető (ed.) *A társadalmi nemek oktatása Magyarországon*, Budapest: ICSSZEM.

Borbíró, F. (2002) "Történelmi lecke lányoknak" in A. Pető, (ed.) *Társadalmi nemek képe és emlékezete Magyarországon a 19–20. században*, Budapest: A Nők Valódi Esélyegyenlőségéért Alapítvány.

Borgos, A. (2007) "The Boundaries of Identity: Bisexuality in Everyday and Theoretical Contexts" in R. Kuhar and J. Takács (eds.) *Beyond the Pink Curtain. Everyday Life of LGBT People in Eastern Europe*, Ljubljana: Mirovni Institut.

Boronkai, D. (2006) "A 'genderlektusokról' egy szociolingvisztikai diskurzuselemzés tükrében," *Szociológiai Szemle* 16, 4: 64–87.

Bukodi, E. (2005) "Női munkavállalás és munkaidőfelhasználás" in I. Nagy et al. (eds.) *Changing Roles*, Budapest: Tárki.

Cerwonka, A. (2008) "Traveling Feminist Thought: 'Difference' and Transculturation in Central and Eastern European Feminism," *Signs: Journal of Women in Culture and Society* Forthcoming.

Corrin, C. (1994) *Magyar Women: Hungarian Women's Lives, 1960s–1990s*, London: Palgrave Macmillan.

Csapó, C. (2003) "Görög homoszexualitás – demitologizálva (Kenneth James Dover: *Görög homoszexualitás* című könyvéről)," *Kalligram*, December.

De Haan F., Daskalova, K. and Loutfi, A. (eds.) (2006) *A Biographical Dictionary of Women's Movements and Feminisms: Central, Eastern, and Southeastern Europe, 19th and 20th Centuries*, Budapest and New York: Central European University Press.

Dizseri, E. (1994) *Zsindelyné, Tüdős Klára*, Budapest: Magyarországi Református Egyház Kálvin János Kiadója.

Dombos, T., Horváth, A. and Krizsán, A. (2007) "Where Did Gender Disappear? Anti-Discrimination Policy in the EU Accession Process in Hungary" in M. Verloo (ed.) *Multiple Meanings of Gender Equality: A Critical Framework Analysis of Gender Policies in Europe*, Budapest and New York: CEU Press.

Durst, J. (2002) "Fertility and Childbearing Practices Among Poor Gypsy Women in Hungary: The Intersections of Race, Class and Gender," *Communist and Post-Communist Studies* 35, 4: 457–474.

Fábián, K. (2007) "Making an Appearance: The Formation of Women's Groups in Hungary," *Aspasia* 1, 1.

Fábri, A. (ed.) (1999) *A nő és hivatása. Szemelvények a magyarországi nőkérdés történetéből, 1777–1865*, Budapest: Kortárs.

Ferge, Zs. (1985) "Biologikum és nemek közti egyenlőség" in K. Koncz (ed.) *Nők és férfiak*, Budapest: Magyar Nők Országos Tanácsa, Kossuth.

Fodor, É. (1997) "Gender in Transition: Unemployment in Hungary, Poland and Slovakia," *East European Politics and Societies* 11, 3: 470–500.

—— (2003) *Working Difference: Women's Working Lives in Hungary and Austria 1945–1995*, Durham, NC: Duke University Press.

Frey, M. (1999) "Nők a munkaerőpiacon" in T. Pongrácz and I. Gy. Tóth (eds.) *Szerepváltozások*, Budapest: Tárki.

—— (2005) *Nők munkaerőpiacon – a rugalmas foglalkoztatási formák iránti igények és lehetőségek*, Budapest: Foglalkoztatási Hivatal, Manuscript.

Friedrich, J. (2006) "My Feminist Critical Thinking" in A. Pető (ed.) *A társadalmi nemek oktatása Magyarországon*, Budapest: ICSSZEM.

Gal, S. (1997) "Feminism and Civil Society" in J. Scott, C. Kaplan and D. Keats (eds.) *Transitions, Recognition Struggles and Social Movements: Contested Identities, Power and Agency*, Cambridge: Cambridge University Press.

—— (2003) "Movements of Feminism: The Circulation of Discourses about Women" in B. Hobson (ed.) *Environments, Translations: Feminisms in International Politics*, New York: Routledge.

H. Sas, J. (1984) *Nőies nők és férfias férfiak: a nőkkel és férfiakkal kapcsolatos társadalmi sztereotípiák élete, eredete és szocializációja*, Budapest: Akadémiai Kiadó.

Hadas, M. (2007) "Gentlemen in Competition: Athletics and Maculinities in Nineteenth-Century Hungary," *International Journal of the History of Sports* 24, 4: 480–500.

Haney, L. (2002) *Inventing the Needy: Gender and the Politics of Welfare in Hungary*, Berkeley, CA: University of California Press.

Hock, B. (2002) "Vector Art", *Praesens* 1: 69–74.

Hrubos, I. (2002) "Nők a Tudományban- Európai dimenzióban," *Magyar Tudomány* 3.

Ilonszki, G. (2005) "Nők a politikában: Az Európai Unió és Magyarország" in I. Nagy et al. (eds.) *Changing Roles*, Budapest: Tárki.

Joó, M. (2005) "Simone de Beauvoir in the Post-Socialist Condition" in E. Barát (ed.) *Spaces in Transition*, Szeged: JATE Press.

Juhász, B. (1998) "The Memory of 1956: A Gendered Transcript," MA Thesis, Budapest: Central European University, Department of History.

Kereszty, O. (2008) "Társadalmi nem az oktatásban – Kezdeményezések Magyarországon" in A. Kende (ed.) *Pszichológia és feminizmus*, Budapest: L'Harmattan.

Koncz, K. (1982) *Nők a munka világában*, Budapest: Kossuth Könyvkiadó.

—— (2006) *Nők a politikai hatalomban: Számvetés a rendszerváltástól napjainkig*, Budapest: Magyar Női Karrierfejlesztési Szövetség.

Kovács, K. and Várady, M. (2000) "Women's Life Trajectories and Class Formation in Hungary" in S. Gal and K. Gail (eds.) *Reproducing Gender: Politics, Publics, and Everyday Life After Socialism*, Princeton: Princeton University Press.

KSH (2006) *Nők és Férfiak Magyarországon*, Budapest: Központi Statisztikai Hivatal.

Kuhar, R. and Takács, J. (eds.) (2007) *Beyond the Pink Curtain. Everyday Life of LGBT People in Eastern Europe*, Ljubljana: Mirovni Institut.

Lampland, M. (1989) "Bibliographies of Liberation: Testimonials to Labor in Socialist Hungary" in S. Kruks, R. Rapp and M. Young (eds.) *Promissory Notes: Women in the Transition to Socialism*, New York, NY: Monthly Review Press.

Lévai, K. and Kiss, R. (1997) "Nők a közéletben" in K. Lévai and I. Gy. Tóth (eds.) *Szerepváltozások. Jelentés a nők helyzetéről*, Budapest: Munkaügyi Minisztérium Egyenlő Esélyek Titkársága, Tárki.

Loutfi, A. (2006) "The European Norm: Hungarian Family Law and Paralysis in Hungarian Civil Rights Feminism in the Late 19th and Early 20th Centuries" in E. Frysak, M. Lanzinger, and E. Saurer (eds.) *Networks and Debates in Post-Communist Countries in the 19th and 20th Centuries*, L'Homme Schriften 13. Reihe zur Feministischen Geschichtswissenschaft, Cologne, Weimar and Vienna: Böhlau Verlag.

Mona, I. (1997) *Slachta Margit*, Budapest: Corvinus.

Montgomery, K. A. and Ilonszki, G. (2003) "Weak Mobilization, Hidden Majoritarianism, and Resurgence of the Right: A Recipe for Female Under-Representation in Hungary" in R. E. Matland and K. A. Montgomery (eds.) *Women's Access to Political Power in Post-Communist Europe*, Oxford: Oxford University Press.

Morvay, K. (2003) *Terror a családban*, Budapest: Kossuth.

Nagy, B. (2001) *Női menedzserek*, Budapest: Aula kiadó.

—— (2005) "Nők a vezetésben" in I. Nagy, et al. (eds.) *Changing Roles*, Budapest: Tárki.

Nagy, B. and Vicsek, L. (2008) "The Evaluation of Male and Female Managers at a Local Municipality in Hungary," *Gender in Management: An International Journal* 23, 1.

Nagy, I., Pongrácz, T. and Tóth, I. Gy. (eds.) (2005) *Changing Roles*, Budapest: Tárki.

Neményi, M. (1994) "Miért nincs Magyarországon nőmozgalom?" in M. Hadas (ed.) *Férfiuralom. Írások nőkről, férfiakról, feminizmusról*, Budapest: Replika.

—— (2000) *Csoportkép nőkkel*, Budapest: Új Mandátum Könyvkiadó.

Neményi, M. and Kende, A. (1999) "Anyák és lányok," *Replika* 35: 117–141.

Palasik, M. (2007) "A nők a Parlamentben" in M. Palasik (ed.) *A Nő és a Politikum*, Budapest: Napvilág Kiadó.

Pető, A. (2003) *Hungarian Women in Politics 1945–1951*, New York, NY: Columbia University Press, East European Monographs Series.

—— (2007) *Geschlecht, Politik und Stalinismus in Ungarn. Eine Biographie von Júlia Rajk. Studien zur Geschichte Ungarns*, Bd. 12, Herne: Gabriele Schäfer Verlag.

Pető, A. (ed.) (2006) *A társadalmi nemek oktatása Magyarországon*, Budapest: ICSSZEM.

Pető, A. and Szapor, J. (2007) "The State of Women's and Gender Studies in Eastern Europe: The Case of Hungary" in T. Fernández-Acenes and K. Hagemann (eds.) *Gendering Trans/national Historiographies: Selection of Papers for the History Practice Section of the Journal of Women's History* 19, 1: 160–166.

Rédai, D. (2006) "Gender in Hungarian Educational Discourse: Democratic Transition since 1990" in J. Sempruch, K. Willems and L. Shook, Laura (eds.) *Multiple Marginalities: An Intercultural Dialogue on Gender in Education across Europe and Africa*, Hamburg: Ulrike Helmer Verlag.

Sándor, B. (2001) *Összefoglaló a leszbikusok, melegek és biszexuálisok diszkriminációjáról Magyarországon*, http://www.hatter.hu/kiad/osszefoglalo.htm (accessed February 9, 2008).

Sándor, J. (1992) *Abortusz és jog*, Budapest: Literatura Medica.

Séllei, N. (2007) *Miért félünk a farkastól? Feminista irodalomszemlélet itt és most*, Debrecen: Kossuth Egyetemi Kiadó.

Schadt, M. (2002) "Nők határokon kívül. A bányásznők emlékezete" in A. Pető (ed.) *Társadalmi nemek képe és emlékezete Magyarországon a 19–20. században*, Budapest: A Nők Valódi Esélyegyenlőségéért Alapítvány.

—— (2006) "Men's Work" in A. Pető (ed.) *A társadalmi nemek oktatása Magyarországon*, Budapest: ICSSZEM.

Szalai, J. (2000) "From Informal Labor to Paid Occupations: Marketization from below in Hungarian Women's Work" in S. Gal and G. Kligman (eds.) *Reproducing Gender: Politics, Publics, and Everyday Life After Socialism*, Princeton: Princeton University Press.

Szapor, J. (2004) "Sisters or Foes: The Shifting Frontlines of the Hungarian Women's Movement, 1896–1918" in B. Pietrow-Ennker and S. Paletschek (eds.) *Women's Emancipation Movements in the Nineteenth Century: A European Perspective*, Palo Alto, CA: Stanford University Press.

Szikra, D. (2008) "Social Policy and Anti-Semitic Exclusion before and during World War II in Hungary: The Case of Productive Social Policy" in D. Schulte and G. Hauss (eds.) *The Dual Mandate: Social Work between Serving the State and Serving the Client*, Opladen and Farmington Hills: Barbara Budrich Publishers.

Takács, J. (2004) *Homoszexualitás és társadalom*, Budapest: Új Mandátum Kiadó.

Thun, É. (2001) "Gender Representation in Educational Materials in the Period of Transition in Hungary" in S. Webber and I. Liikanen (eds.) *Beyond Civic Society: Education and Civic Culture in Post-Communist Countries*, Houndsmills UK: Palgrave.

Tímár, J. (2007) "Gender Studies in the Gender-blind Post-socialist Geographies of East Central Europe," *Belgeo* 3: 349–369.

Toronyi, Zs. (ed.) (2002) *A zsidó nő*, Budapest: Magyar Zsidó Múzeum és Levéltár.

Tóth, E. Zs. (2007) '*Puszi Kádár Jánosnak': Munkásnők élete a Kádár-korszakban mikrotörténeti megközelítésben*, Budapest: Napvilág Kiadó.

Tóth, H. (2007) "Struggle for Life" in B. Nagy (ed.) *Szervezet, Menedzsment, Nemek*, Budapest: Aula.

Tóth, O. (1993) "No Envy, No Pity" in N. Funk and M. Mueller (eds.) *Gender Politics and Post-Communism: Reflections from Eastern Europe and the Former Soviet Union*, New York: Routledge.

—— (1997) "Working Women, Changing Roles, Changing Attitudes," *Hungarian Quarterly* 38:147, http://www.hungarianquarterly.com/no147/p69.shtml (accessed February 9, 2008).

Turai, H. (2002) *Anna Margit*, Budapest: Szemimpex Kiadó.

Turgonyi, J. and Ferge, Zs.(1969) *Az ipari munkásnők munka - és életkörülményei*, Budapest: Kossuth.

UNICEF (1999) *Nők a rendszerváltásban*, Regional Monitoring Report 6, UNICEF: International Children Development Center.

Varsa, E. (2005) "Class, Ethnicity and Gender – Structures of Differentiation in State Socialist Employment and Welfare Politics, 1960–1980" in K. Schilde and D. Schulte (eds.) *Need and Care – Glimpses into the Beginnings of Eastern Europe's Professional Welfare*, Opladen and Bloomfield Hills: Barbara Budrich Publishers.

Wessely, A. (2004) " 'Nőkérdés' a XVIII. század végén" in D. Helmich and Z. Szántó (eds.) *Módszertan,* *gazdaság, társadalom. In Memoriam Bertalan László*, Budapest: Közgazdasági Szemle Alapítvány.

Zimmermann, S. (1994) "Municipal Welfare and Social Policy as Gender Politics. Budapest and Vienna, 1870–1914" in A. Pető (ed.) *CEU History Department Yearbook, 1994*, Budapest: Central European University.

—— (2007) "The Institutionalization of Women and Gender Studies in Higher Education in Central and Eastern Europe and the Former Soviet Union: Asymmetric Politics and the Regional–Transnational Configuration," *East-Central Europe/L'Europe du Centre-Est: Eine wissenschaftliche Zeitschrift* 33, 1–2.

CHAPTER 26

"The Rest is Silence . . .": Polish Nationalism and the Question of Lesbian Existence [1]

Joanna Mizielińska

There is not one but many silences and they are an integral part
of the strategies that underlie and permeate discourse.

(Foucault 1980: 27)

. . . The major focus of this article is on topics rarely spoken of openly or written about in history. Thus, the article investigates what is behind the silence and discusses invisibility. The silence regarding lesbians in Poland is significant and tells a lot about the concept of the Polish nation and Polish citizenship (its male and heterosexual character). This article examines the Polish nationalistic discourse, which largely avoids the question of homosexual orientation. Moreover, heterosexual orientation is taken for granted as the only possible and natural course. And so, invisibility is a major focus in this article. I show this invisibility by examining two texts: the latest edition of the Catechism of the Catholic Church and the new Polish Constitution. Both discourses are interwoven, and both contain a very rigid concept of the Polish nation. I go on to focus on how these discourses are perceived by Polish lesbians, and how this concept of the Polish nation affects their daily lives. I argue that the silence and invisibility of lesbians in official discourse influence Polish opinion about them, thus reinforcing homophobia and increasing the pressure on lesbians to remain invisible.

NATIONALISM AS A CONSTRUCTIVE TOOL

. . . Scholars dealing with the concept of nation and nationalism point out the discursive nature of both . . . [and] it is important to ask how nations are constructed and by whom.

In order to establish a national identity, an authority uses different discursive tools and deploys various rhetorical styles. Hence, the concept of the nation is reflected in language and popular images/symbols of nations. Although it is important to investigate the content of these images, it seems to be even more indispensable to study what has been excluded and the reasons why some images have been chosen instead of others.

Many scholars point out that the nation is always constructed in opposition to the Other. The Other can be external, i.e. other nations, or the Other can live within the nation, somewhere on the margins—the internal or inner Other. In this sense, women are considered to be the inner Other. Both exclusions are reflected in the concept of the nation, which is a male construct. Women can belong to it only on condition that they accept the place in society that male discourse has allotted to them. Moreover, according to the country's needs, images of both inner and outer Others are introduced and appear in daily propaganda. Therefore, in times of peace the inner Other will be more important in order to keep national homogeneity ... Mechanisms of this control vary, from rigid rules of sex roles to more subtle ways which serve to keep the Other in its right place. The latter include the myths about women. These myths are used to assure women of the inevitability of their position as mothers and wives. Consequently, when women appear in the concept of a nation they appear to have a very rigid and prescribed role connected with their "natural," "biological" function. They are presented in national discourse as mothers and housewives as well as keepers of national values and reproducers of citizens. (see Milic 1993) ...

Because they are not considered to be mothers, lesbians are completely excluded from the concept of nation: they are double outsiders. They are women, but they are not mothers and are useless to the nation. Moreover, because they resist the traditional and "natural" position of women, they threaten the "universal" patriarchal order emphasized in national discourse. ... Therefore, for the sake of the nation, lesbian existence must be either kept quiet or presented as deviant.

POLISH NATIONALISM AND ITS IMAGES

... Polish scholars point out the changes in Polish nationalistic discourse throughout history (see Andrzej Walicki in Hauser [n.d.] for more on Polish nationalisms). At the same time they emphasize that because of the history of the Polish nation—obliteration of the Polish state and later Poland's submission to the Communist regime—the strongest influence on the Polish national consciousness has been the romantic tradition. This trad-

ition presents Poland as a nation chosen by God and compares its suffering to that of Christ. Thus, not only is Polish Catholicism the weapon to resist other's power, but it is also dominant in Polish national symbols. ...

As soon as religious symbols became national symbols, the whole notion of these symbols was incorporated into the concept of the Polish nation. Therefore, women's role in this concept is strongly connected to the Church's teaching. The Black Madonna as a symbol of the Polish nation holds in its notion a very rigid premise for all Polish women and strongly determines their role. *Matka Polka* (Polish Mother) reflects the sacred duty to bear children/sons who are doomed to fail. Strong but passive, she defines the destiny of all Polish mothers. The roots of this concept can also be found in the romantic tradition (see Adam Mickiewicz's poem *To a Polish Mother*[2]). From this tradition a slightly different image of Polish women emerged which stresses their active role as heroic warriors. Both women's roles were present in Polish history. Polish women were active in acts of resistance, but disappeared from the public scene in more stable times.[3] ...

The concept of the Polish Mother that dominates nationalistic discourse nowadays stresses such attributes as passivity, self-sacrifice, self-fulfilment in domestic duties, natural nursing and maternal instinct. Anybody who does not fit into the concept of true Polish femininity, as lesbians or non-mothers do not, is therefore excluded and punished for not being feminine. One method of exclusion is the disguise or neglect of other options, including a strong pressure to accept the "natural" and "inevitable" female role. This pressure ranges from mass media transmissions showing women only in relation to men and children, to family's or neighbour's pressure to get married (Buczkowski 1997; Mizielińska 1997a). The absence or erasure of other options in mainstream discourses can be considered a means of exclusion that renders lesbian existence even more invisible and impossible to accept in Polish society.

POLISH CHURCH AND THE QUESTION OF LESBIANS

. . . The teachings of the Catholic Church, which strongly influence Polish nationalistic discourse, promote women's role as mothers and wives. This rhetoric denies women any choices other than the dominant tenet, such as that on abortion. In the Church's statements about family and the role of women as mothers, lesbians are not mentioned. Women are always described as the foundation of the family and the primary caretakers of children. In its instructions, the Church promotes the traditional and patriarchal model of a family with many children. Although the question of homosexuality rarely arises, the Church included this problem in its Catechism. Therefore, it is important to examine this in order to reveal the Church's attitude towards lesbians.

In the chapter on the Sixth Commandment, "Do not commit adultery," which in the Church's opinion "comprises the wholeness of human sexuality" (Catechism 1994: 528), the question of homosexuality appears among other sins to be against the purity and nature of human sexuality as such. First of all, the whole commandment refers to men, and is based on the identification of men with mankind. . . . Hence, the reference to homosexuality treats it as a male sin. Although women are mentioned, an unwritten assumption exists which states that they are less inclined to participate in homosexual acts. Women prescribed the role of mother are simply absent from other roles.

Moreover, the lesbian issue as such appears less often in mass media not only because, as some scholars point out, female homosexuality is less visible, but also because it is made less visible by the rigid compulsory natural role which has been imposed on women and presented everywhere. . . . Lesbians in Poland neglect and weaken the image of the Polish Mother, therefore they are more absent in mainstream discourse than male homosexuals. Hence, it is worth noting that when lesbians do appear they are always associated with deviance, and the very word "lesbian" has mostly clinical connotations.

The Church's opinions about homosexuality presented in the Catechism determine how homosexuals should be treated by society. First of all, it stresses the natural and inevitable complementary relationship between man and woman (man is always mentioned first!). Moreover, this "differentiation and complementary physical, spiritual and moral aim brings welfare to the family and develops family life" (Catechism 1994: 527). Because of this natural complementariness, marriage is strongly defined as a relation between man and woman, and its aim is dominated by procreation. "Fertility is a gift, a goal of marriage, because conjugal love by its nature tends to be fertile" (Catechism 1994: 534).

Consequently, any other sexual orientation is considered to be unnatural and deviant because these people cannot take part in the saintly duty of giving life. . . .

Moreover, homosexuality is seen as an illness which can be cured. Although it is stated that homosexuals do not choose their condition, at the same time it is stressed that they can resist it and maybe in the future become "normal." Under no condition can they fulfil their life as homosexuals and be engaged in any relationship with a person of the same sex. That would be considered a sin against purity. . . .

This teaching is reflected in Catholic magazines and programmes on homosexuality. Aneta Krzewinska (1996), who analyzed the presence of homosexuality within Catholic magazines, points out that homosexuality always appears to be associated with illness and is strongly disapproved of. . . .

THE POLISH CONSTITUTION AND THE QUESTION OF HOMOSEXUALS

Marriage as a relationship between woman and man; motherhood and parenthood are under the protection and care of the Polish Republic.

(Polish Constitution 1997: Article 18)

The drawing up of the new Polish Constitution was accompanied by a very vivid and grave discussion on the concept of nation. Because this constitution was to replace that drawn up by the Communist government in 1956, there was strong pressure to establish a new one based on traditional Polish values, which right-wing politicians believe to be inseparably connected to Polish Catholicism. . . . On the other hand, left-wing politicians stressed the fact that if the Preamble evoked as a principle only Christian values, people who did not believe in God or who followed other religions but considered themselves to be Polish citizens would be discriminated against. Finally a compromise was reached and the Preamble, prepared by Tadeusz Mazowiecki, a politician from the centre-left party Unia Wolnosci (Union of Freedom), was reluctantly accepted. It tries to arbitrate between both arguments and includes statements which stress both Catholic traditional beliefs and values rooted in "other sources." But statements regarding belief in God are always mentioned first. . . .

The whole text of the Polish Constitution reflects the Church's concept of family as a communion between father and son. Consequently, the Polish Constitution becomes a communion between the state and its male citizens. In many places in the text, the male form of the word "citizen" is used (the Polish for male citizen is *obywatel*, and for female citizen, *obywatelka*). . . . There is no instance where only the female form is used. In conclusion, one can say that the Constitution favours male citizens and is mostly addressed to them.

In the citation at the beginning of this section, "motherhood" is mentioned together with "parenthood" and not with fatherhood. In Article 71, regarding the welfare of the family, once again a woman appears as a mother: "A mother before [How is it possible to be a mother before bearing a child?] and after bearing a child has a right to special help from public authorities whose scale is defined by the act." These are the only instances where the woman's role is defined so definitively. In other parts of the Constitution, the authors are far less explicit about women's role. Consequently, Polish lesbians are not only excluded or less valued as citizens because they are women, but they are doubly excluded as non-mothers, i.e. they are both juridically and socially invisible.

The concept of marriage and the very rigid definition of marriage as a relationship between woman and man were introduced in this way due to the pressure of the Catholic Church, which is very concerned about legislation in some other countries allowing marriages between homosexuals. In consequence, any attempt to legalize a homosexual relationship is considered an act against the Polish Constitution . . .

The whole process of working out the new Constitution as well as its final form has been strongly influenced by nationalistic discourse, stressing Polish traditional religious values "shared by the Polish population, which is 99 percent Catholic."[4] At the same time, its final form is the result of a compromise, which makes it very open to manipulation. There are gaps which can be used in the future, as in the case of abortion legislation.[5] . . . According to the Constitution, . . . marriage is only valid between man and woman. This strict and discriminating definition in practice renders it impossible to demand an equal right to marriage for gay people.

THE OTHER SIDE, OR THE LESBIAN VIEW ON POLITICS AND THE CATHOLIC CHURCH

. . . Despite a lack of lesbian organizations and the invisibility of the lesbian issue in the mass media, an invisibility which would suggest that there are no lesbians in Poland at all, lesbians *do* exist and are highly critical towards politics and the power of the Church. First, in the interviews I conducted in February 1997[6], six lesbians pointed to the immensely strong influence of the Church's stance on homosexuality on society as a whole; they believe that to a large extent the social bias against homosexuals is a reflection of the Church's point of view. . . .

Homosexuals have to deal with these biases and stereotypes on a daily basis. All respondents emphasized that they feel strong pressure from family, friends and even neighbours to get married:

> . . . As a young girl in a big foreign city I really needed my parents' help. My parents were steadfast. They helped my brother and sister, and they started to help me when I brought home a male partner. Then all the simple-minded people in the neighbourhood, who can't wait to call someone's boyfriend or girlfriend a fiancé as soon as they see a girl and a boy together, would start asking about the wedding date. Or even worse, they would ask with a sneer: "Oh, so you are a lesbian, are you?" Generally, the majority of people are unaware of this problem—and it is terrifying to think that heterosexuality is considered to be the norm.
>
> (Interview 7)

This pressure is particularly intense in the case of motherhood. A woman does not have to be a wife, but she has to be a mother in order to fulfil her purpose in life. It reflects the social opinion, strongly influenced by the Church, that true femininity is totally embodied in the figure of the Polish Mother:

> I tried very hard not to give into the pressure of my parents and my immediate family, which at first concerned clothes. But then it was not only clothes—it was having a child. I could not have a husband, but I should have a child, because a woman's role is to be a mother. A woman is considered a woman when she bears a child.
>
> (Interview 6)

The Church's influence was seen as ranging from reinforcing certain stereotypes in society to shaping politicians' opinions and politics as such. Many lesbians in Poland perceived themselves as being discriminated against by law. They pointed out the new Constitution and Article 18, which is de facto against any homosexual marriage. They noted the discrepancy between rights and duties. They pay taxes as other citizens, but they do not have the same rights. Therefore, they are second- or even third- (when we consider women as second-) class citizens:

> What is going on in the Church is of course very alarming, and its influence on legislation in this country should not exist. It is inadmissible in a free country where the Constitution takes such a form. It is a phenomenon on a world scale that in the Constitution it is written who should love whom and who has to have a relationship with whom. The marriage institution is not an institution which exists only on paper. If the marriage is a community of feelings, thoughts and property, then not the Church or the Constitution or family law should define whether a marriage should be heterosexual or homosexual.
>
> (Interview 2)

Lesbians experience the consequences of "compulsory heterosexuality" imposed on them by the Constitution in their daily lives. Even when some of them are against marriage as an institution, they perceive that the illegal status of their relationship could be a real problem, for example when inheritance of property is concerned. . . . In fact, only as mothers can women become rightful members of society. In the new Polish Constitution this role has been doubly emphasized. The real problem is that even when lesbians want to be mothers, the possibility is rather limited. They face both the power of the Church's resistance towards in vitro fertilization, which strongly influences mainstream discourse, and strict laws defining who is allowed to go through this process. Moreover, they are afraid of the fact that they will not be able to bring up a child together with their partner in such an intolerant society.

THE CONSEQUENCES OF EXCLUSION

. . . Besides the legal consequences of nationalistic discourse (i.e. constitutional laws), the real drama of lesbians' daily lives is even more serious and painful. They deal with prejudices and biases on a daily basis, ranging from abandonment by the family to discrimination at school or in job-hiring practices. Therefore, the majority of them choose not to disclose their sexuality. Some have come out to a small circle of friends, but they prefer not to inform their family because of their family's traditional opinions about a woman's proper future.

> I stay in the closet at work. I know that the majority of young Poles (I work with such) have been brought up in the cult of the ideal of Christian family. My free-thinking, my aversion to marriage and bearing children is troublesome enough during conversations. It is so troublesome that I do not want to add that apart from all of this I am a lesbian.
>
> (Interview 4)

Some consider staying in the closet to be a survival tactic. . . . Of course this tactic has its consequences. A fear is always present, fear of being recognized and rejected and also excluded. They must be always very careful when leading their "double life." They lie and tell stories about their boy-friends, instead of the pronoun "she" they use "he." Some of them express sadness that they cannot truly share their feelings with family or friends. Moreover, they cannot bring their partners along to any family gatherings or holidays. . . .

In gay magazines in Poland many advertisements regarding so-called "white marriages" often appear. One can consider these marriages a kind of cooperation between gays and lesbians in Poland. "White marriages" are more popular among people who have important and official jobs: being more high profile or having an official career make marriage even more obligatory (see Piatek 1997). Nevertheless, this kind of strategy reflects the amount of pressure put on lesbians and gays. . . .

INSTEAD OF A CONCLUSION, OR ABOUT THE NATURE OF SILENCE

. . . Silence regarding homosexuality is a strategy that reinforces "compulsory heterosexuality," which then in the dominant social mentality becomes the only possible and natural way of life. This leads to the problem of social ignorance and intolerance, which is probably the most serious effect of this kind of nationalistic discourse. This lack of knowledge in society of other life options which can be considered normal makes the gap between lesbians and the rest of society wider and more difficult to cope with on a daily basis. What is even worse is that this silence makes lesbian existence even more invisible. . . . The lack of more collective activism[7] renders the issue of lesbianism even more invisible. Silence strengthens silence. It seems that this vicious circle of invisibility and exclusion will never end.

NOTES

1. In the article's title I use the last words spoken by Hamlet in Shakespeare's tragedy. The term "lesbian existence" comes from the famous article by

Adrienne Rich "Compulsory Heterosexuality and Lesbian Existence" written in 1980 (see Rich 1993).

2. See Mickiewicz (1944: 237–238). Adam Mickiewicz (1798–1855), the Polish national bard, wrote this poem after the tragedy of the November Insurrection (1830). This poem has inspired many generations of Poles, and played a particular role in building Polish national identity. In the poem, a Polish mother sacrifices her sons on the altar of national freedom. Her role is very passive, as was the role of Christ's mother, who had to suffer patiently while watching her son die.

3. A good example of this would be women's role within the Solidarity movement. Women organized it because the men were in prison, but after 1989 they disappeared from the Polish political scene and men took all the credit. See Penn 1994.

4. Sweeping generalizations like this statement are commonplace in the Polish mass media.

5. It is worth mentioning that in 1997 the paragraph of the Constitution stating that the "Polish Republic secures the legal protection of every human being's life" was used by the Constitutional Tribunal to annul the new, less restrictive abortion law. They stated that the amended law was not consistent with the Constitution. Hence, the real threat lies in how other inconsistencies in the new Constitution can be interpreted in the future.

6. In this section I use excerpts from interviews and questionnaires gathered during my research project in February 1997 on lesbian existence in Poland. My research consisted of two parts. In the first part, I participated in several meetings and talked with lesbians at the Rainbow Centre for Gays and Lesbians in Warsaw. During those meetings I distributed about 50 questionnaires and I got back about 20. Since then I have been in contact with lesbian organizations in Warsaw, for example the OLA Lesbian Archive, and I must say that the situation has not changed much. More extensive extracts from the interviews were used in my article "Lesbianism in Poland—Between Consciousness and its Lack" (Mizielińska 1997b).

7. Most analyses of homosexuality in Poland emphasize the lack of organizations. Moreover, lesbians are less willing to organize themselves in comparison to gay men. The Lambda Association stopped functioning quite recently (although a few groups in some cities are still in existence, for instance in Warsaw) as did the Gay and Lesbian Movement, mainly because of a lack of support. One recent exception in this field, which can give us hope that something is changing, is the Lesbian OLA Archive. It welcomes more and more lesbians. It is also trying to introduce the feminist issue by publishing the first feminist lesbian magazine in Poland, *Furia pierwsza* (Fury First). Since 1997, eight issues have been published. The seventh issue was devoted to the question of queer theory.

REFERENCES

Buczkowski, Adam (1997) "Dwa rozne swiaty, czyli jak socjalizuje sie dziewczynke i chlopca" in J. Brach-Czaina (ed.) *From a Woman to a Man and Back: Consideration about Sex in Culture*, Bialystok: Trans Humana.

Catechism of the Catholic Church (1994) Poznan: Pallotinum.

Foucault, Michel (1980) *The History of Sexuality*, trans. Robert Hurley, Vol. 1. New York: Vintage.

Hauser, Ewa (n.d.) "Polish Nationalism and Gender," unpublished manuscript.

Krzewinska, Aneta (1996) "Lesbijki w polskich warunkach kulturowych" (Lesbians in Polish Culture), unpublished MA thesis.

Mickiewicz, Adam (1944) "To a Polish Mother" in G. R. Noyes (ed.) *Poems by Adam Mickiewicz*, New York: The Polish Institute of Arts and Sciences in America.

Milic, Andjelka (1993) "Women and Nationalism in the Former Yugoslavia" in N. Funk and M. Mueller (eds.) *Gender Politics and Post-communism: Reflections from Eastern Europe and Former Soviet Union*, New York and London: Routledge.

Mizielińska, Joanna (1997a) "Matki, zony, kochanki, czyli tak nas widza" in J. Brach-Czaina (ed.) *From a Woman to a Man and Back: Considerations about Sex in Culture*, Bialystok: Trans Humana.

—— (1997b) "Lesbianizm w Polsce—pomiedzy swiadomoscia a jej brakiem," *Furia Pierwsza* 1: 23–52.

Penn, Shana (1994) "Tajemnica panstwowa," *Pelnym Glosem* 2: 3–16.

Piatek, Tomasz (1997) "Milosc nie jest happy endem," *Gazeta Wyborcza Magazyn* 24–25 Oct.: 39–40.

Rich, Adrienne (1993) "Compulsory Heterosexuality and Lesbian Existence" in H. Abelove, M. Barale and D. Halperin (eds.) *The Lesbian and Gay Studies Reader*, New York and London: Routledge.

CHAPTER 27

Collective Organizing and Claim Making on Child Care in Norden [1]: Blurring the Boundaries between the Inside and the Outside

Solveig Bergman

During the past few decades, a political will has existed in all the Nordic societies to pursue gender equality through child care and parental policies that encourage mothers to take up paid work. More recently, this "working mothers' policy" (Lindvert 2002) has been complemented by an emphasis on fathers' rights and duties in respect to child care and shared parenthood. Mainstream welfare state research tends to underplay the significance of women's own actions and organizing when it comes to the making of welfare policies. . . .

. . . In fact, Nordic women's organizations have been active participants in the process behind policy interventions and the construction of welfare policies throughout the twentieth century. Public child care has largely been seen as a "women's issue" (Bergqvist et al. 1999: 141) and even as a "feminist issue" (Anttonen 2003: 160). This article relates the development of Nordic child care policies to the political rationales and actors behind the policies and analyzes the major debates and significant "collective voices" that have helped shape the formation of child care policies, as well as the role of collective organizing and agency in the process. . . .

INSIDE–OUTSIDE ORGANIZING

The issue of strategic choice relates to the long-standing debate within the feminist movement about which strategy is more efficient: working inside or outside mainstream organizations and institutions. . . . In this article I emphasize that "inside" and "outside" as well as "autonomous" and "integrated" must be understood in relational and contextual terms and as being in constant and complex interplay. Fully independent or autonomous organizing and claim making never became a dominant strategy in Nordic women's movements, but rather complemented activity in mixed-gender organizations and institutions (Bergman 2002). I argue that this kind of combined strategy, which is based on a mixture of inside and outside organizing, is advantageous particularly in countries—such as the Nordic ones—where women's participation and representation in state politics has been at a comparatively high level internationally. . . .

The issues will be explored in relation to two much debated examples of recent Nordic child care policies, namely, the issue of home care allowance versus institutional day care in nurseries, and the issue of earmarked entitlements for fathers in the parental leave schemes. I begin this discussion with an overview of the major features of Nordic child care policies that emphasizes both the similarities and the variety to be found across the region. I use Finland as my primary case, contrasting it to its Nordic neighbors, particularly Sweden but also Norway. . . .

IS THERE A NORDIC CHILD CARE MODEL?

Prior to the 1970s, child care policy in Norden was formulated in terms of social welfare services. Since then, this narrow definition has been challenged, not least by gender equality activists and feminists who have advocated a publicly funded and universal child care system, which they have seen as being necessary for the achievement of equality and social justice (compare Dobrowolsky and Jenson 2002). In all Nordic countries, child care has been identified as a universal citizenship right, as a key issue affecting women's economic independence and well-being, as well as a cornerstone of gender equality. . . .

. . . From an international perspective, Nordic child care systems differ from child care regimes found elsewhere. The extensive public care provision for the youngest group of children (under three years of age) is especially distinctive. The generous parental leave schemes, where income substitution is tied (partly or fully) to previous income levels, are internationally unique (see Bergqvist et al. 1999; Leira 2002).[2] The duration of entitlements to parental leave is one year or more in all Nordic countries. Thus, despite the universality of wage work for mothers, child care arrangements are not normally needed for the youngest children. In fact, a significant proportion of preschool children are cared for at home by a parent, mostly the mother.[3] The Nordic "state interventionism," as pointed out by Keith Pringle (1998: 95), seems therefore somewhat overstated in respect of child care. . . .

Since the early 1990s, differences in the child care and parental policies between the Nordic countries seem to have increased (Leira 2002; Rantalaiho 2001). The issue of institutional care versus subsidized home care of children has been controversial and has divided women's organizations. . . .

HOME CARE ALLOWANCE VERSUS INSTITUTIONAL DAY CARE

The issue of a home care allowance has been a continuing controversy among Nordic feminists. In an international perspective, home care of children (following a period of statutory maternity/parental leave) is seldom subsidized by the public sector, except through family taxation rules. In recent years, however, some European countries have introduced care leave with low benefits (Heinen and Martiskainen de Koenigswarter 2001; Morgan and Zippel 2003).[4] It is interesting that two Nordic countries—Finland and Norway—belong to the countries that have introduced public allowances for the home care of the smallest children as a complement or an alternative to public day care. These countries differ clearly from Sweden and also Denmark, which have continued to address women first and foremost as citizen-workers with the focus on developing day care institutions (Bergqvist et al. 1999).

As such, the issue of monetary compensation for the care of one's own children is by no means new. In the 1970s, parts of the new women's movement in Western Europe were reluctant to identify women's independence with full-time employment and demanded "wages for housework" (e.g., Ostner 1993). . . .

Among other feminists, such a maternalist line was less valued. The idea of wages for mothers or—as it was renamed later—home care allowance was much less popular in these circles. . . .

During the 1980s, the issue of institutional day care versus home care reemerged into public debate. These opposing and competing discourses and policy strategies divided the women's movement. The issue was both a political–ideological conflict and a question of different gender discourses and different needs in rural and urban Finland. The shortage of day care places, particularly in the larger towns, was a further impetus for the advocates of the home care allowance. . . . The trade union movement, the political left, and parts of the liberal parties (in practice, women activists and the women's federations) fought for the statutory right of children to municipal day care. The home care allowance was created as an alternative, above all following pressure from the agrarian-conservative Center Party and its women's federation. In connection with the reform of the public day care system (fully implemented in 1990), a law on home care allowance was adopted as part of a historical compromise. . . .

The [child care] package was framed as promoting parents' options in respect [to] child care arrangements. The contents of the compromise guaranteed public day care as a statutory right for all children less than three years of age. As an alternative option, a home care allowance was introduced for the same age group to be paid after the parental leave (which lasts approximately 11 months in Finland). Thus, since the 1990s all parents in Finland with children under age three have a statutory right to public support for the type of care that they prefer, that is, public day care or a home care allowance. The home care allowance can be regarded as a public compensation for those families who do not wish to use their right to a place in a municipal nursery or in supervised family day care. Contrary to the relatively generous entitlements (tied to a wage-earner's previous income) during parental leave, the home care allowance is flat rate and modest. The system is built on the idea that the recipient is supported by a spouse/partner. The parent who stays at home receives the right to care leave and a full workplace guarantee (Bergqvist et al. 1999; Morgan and Zippel 2003). . . .

In 1995 the unconditional right to municipal day care (but not to the home care allowance) was extended to all preschool children, irrespective of parents' income or whether they are employed (Bergqvist et al. 1999). The actors behind the bill on the absolute right to day care were linked to the Women's Network in Parliament. This network crosses party lines, and women deputies from all political parties participate in it. The network works closely with women's organizations and the gender equality apparatus. Its goals are to promote gender equality and to highlight a women's perspective in legislative work. One of the major political victories of the network was the decision to recognize the statutory right to day care despite resistance from the major parties and the finance minister, who strongly wanted such an expensive reform to be postponed (Ramstedt-Silén 1999).

In Sweden a similar statutory right to public day care was introduced in 1985. The Swedish right also concerns afternoon care for school children less than 12 years of age. In contrast to the Finnish universal system, Swedish parents have to be in employment or students or the children have to have a special need for day care. . . . However, [in 1994] the new government introduced a home care allowance as an option for parents. The reform was harshly criticized by left-wing women activists and [by] the feminist movement, who claimed it marked "the end of the consensus on the dual-breadwinner model in Sweden" (Bergqvist et al. 1999: 144). When the Social Democrats regained power, the home care allowance was immediately abolished and has not been reintroduced since then.

Norway introduced a home care allowance or, as it is called in Norway, a cash-for-care scheme in 1999. . . . The allowance was first introduced for children under two years of age, and later it was extended to children under three years of age. The scheme has become very popular. Currently more than 70 percent of the age group are cared for through this allowance. It can also be used for purchasing private care or part-time public day care (Leira 2002). Unlike in Finland, a subjective right of children to nursery places does not exist in Norway. For this reason, critics argue that the Norwegian home care allowance effectively postpones the development of day care institutions and there is no real parental choice as there is in Finland (e.g., Andenaes 1998).

WOMEN'S MOVEMENTS DIVIDED

. . . Two opposing standpoints on the question of home care allowance can be discerned. One approach emphasizes that women's invisible care work has to be acknowledged, that is, women should be paid for such work. These kinds of policies have also been interpreted as a means of liberating women, at least partially, from their economic dependence on male breadwinners. The opposite view is that although being formally gender-neutral, the home care allowance is in practice gendered, reinforcing the traditional division of labor in the labor market and in the home. In both Finland and Norway women make up around 95 percent of the beneficiaries. A care wage accommodates gender differences as long as no pressure is put on men to do care work. Because, according to the critics, it is difficult to argue for a substitution level much higher than the minimum income level, women's economic situation can be only marginally improved through such an allowance. For many women their economic dependence on a husband will increase. Reentering the labor market will be difficult, and the risk of increased discrimination against women during child-bearing years is evident (compare Sundström 2003; see also Morgan and Zippel 2003).[5] Like other policy reforms created to increase the possibilities to combine employed work and the care of children, this system may in practice strengthen the traditional gender order of society by creating a trap for women. Undoubtedly, the ideological principle behind the home care allowance constitutes a break with the established Nordic strategy of focusing on women as paid employees . . . and reshapes women's citizenship. . . .

In Finland the beneficiaries of the home care allowance are mostly low-income, low-educated, and semi- or unemployed women (compare Anttonen 2003). In many cases the allowance has turned into an alternative source of livelihood, particularly at times of high unemployment, so it will have a negative effect on these women's pension rights. A new class division may thus emerge with the middle classes preferring public day care and the poorly educated the home care allowance. . . . Another crucial issue that has hardly been discussed is children's right to high-quality care: Who controls the quality of home care? . . .

However, there is strong popular support for subsidized home care in Finland and this attitude is partly reflected among women activists and scholars, while a more critical view seems to have been dominant among feminists in Sweden and Norway (Andenaes 1998; Leira 1998). . . .

DECLINE IN WOMEN'S EMPLOYMENT?

In Norway, women's labor market participation has only modestly been affected by the cash-for-care scheme. It seems as if the benefit is predominantly used by those groups of women who earlier carried out unremunerated care work (Gender Equality Barometer 2002; see also Morgan and Zippel 2003). In Finland, mothers' employment rate has dropped during the 1990s. Finland no longer tops international statistics on women's share of the labor force.[6] Participation rates are somewhat higher elsewhere in Norden and the United States, and some European countries are not far behind (Lehto 1999).

Anneli Anttonen (2001, 2003) has argued that the decline in women's employment rates has shifted the emphasis of the Finnish gender model from traditional "wage-earner motherhood" to a "temporary homemaking model" that resembles the continental European gender model. . . . Thus the image of a good mother that takes care of her child for two or three years is increasingly being adopted in Finland. . . .

In other words, women continue to be strongly committed to waged work in Finland, but—because there is a public subsidy for it—they devote themselves more than before to home care of the smallest children. For example, only 22 percent of children under age three and 63 percent of children over three years of age were in public child care in 1996 (compare Anttonen 2001; Julkunen 1999). . . .

For most women, the home care allowance is a buffer in the shift from maternity leave back to waged work. The majority of mothers remain at home for a relatively short period of time (one to six months) after their maternity/parental leave. . . .

QUOTAS FOR FATHERS

. . . [I]n some Nordic countries, a third policy approach has sought to support care-sharing parenthood through the idea of a father's quota in the parental leave scheme (Leira 2000, 2002).

It has been a guiding principle of Nordic family policies since the mid-1970s to encourage fathers to take up paternity and parental leave as a means of promoting gender equality, both in the home and in society at large. In Sweden a system of a parental leave was introduced as early as 1974 that offered parents the choice of sharing the leave. At the same time fathers received the right to individual paternity leave for 10 days, simultaneously with the mother. Similar reforms were carried out in Finland, Norway, and Denmark during the 1970s and early 1980s (Rantalaiho 2003).

In addition to this traditional form of paternity leave and shared parental leave,

several Nordic countries have more recently introduced a special "daddy month," that is, a period of the parental leave scheme that has either to be taken by the father or is lost altogether. The scheme was created to encourage or "gently force" (Leira 2000) men to take (a small) part of the parental leave. It represents a departure in Nordic care policies because it explicitly addresses fathers and is an active strategy aiming at redivision of care work in families through enticements or obligations (Leira 1998). Such entitlements earmarked to fathers reflect the strong Nordic faith in men as carers, and the scheme is framed as a means of creating a discourse of "new fatherhood" or "new masculinity." Current research in Norway shows that many fathers interpret the leave as a right instead of as an obligation (e.g., Brandth and Kvande 2003).

The father's month was introduced first in Norway (1993), preceded by a rather lively debate since the idea was introduced in 1988 (Oftung 1993). . . . The paternal quota became an immediate success in Norway, and the scheme is currently used by more than three-quarters of those fathers who have an entitlement to it. The example set out by Norway was followed by Sweden (one month 1995, since 2003 two months) and Denmark (1997, but abolished in 2002). In Iceland, a radical change took place over the period 2000–2003, when parental leave was extended to nine months, of which one-third is reserved for the mother, one-third for the father, and the remaining three months can be shared according to individual wishes (Leira 2002). . . .

Both in Norway and Sweden the father's quota was preceded primarily by demands from women's organizations (particularly from Social Democrats and Liberals) but also from some influential men. . . . However, there were hardly any signs of organized grassroots-level action in the issue of fathers' rights, although men activists and researchers participated in the committees and working groups set up by public equality bodies at governmental level. In Finland, too, suggestions for increased paternity leave or the introduction of a father's quota in the parental leave legislation originated in women's organizations, political parties, the state gender equality apparatus, and a state committee on the status of fathers. The labor market organizations in Finland have also been active in promoting men's take-up of parental leaves through special campaigns (Haataja 2004).

Yet despite public campaigns and political pressure the parental leave systems have only managed to alter the traditional gendered pattern of care of the youngest children to a limited extent. The number of fathers as full-time carers has grown only slowly, and care of small children is still one of the most gendered spheres of activity in Norden. At the end of the 1990s, Swedish fathers used about 12 percent of all leave days, Norwegian fathers 7 percent, Danish fathers almost 6 percent, and Finnish fathers 4 percent. The care of small children is still overwhelmingly a "women's world" (Rantalaiho 2003). One reason for the popularity of fathers' leave in Sweden is that there is no home care allowance system. In Finland . . . most Finnish fathers take the leave simultaneously with the mothers (Rantalaiho 2003). . . .

CONCLUSIONS

In child care claim making and organizing Nordic women activists have preferred to combine independent or autonomous action with working through the established organizations and institutions, including the state. . . . The Nordic tradition renders the women's movement outwardly open, sometimes to the extent that the boundary between movement activists and women inside the power structures (e.g., women politicians and "femocrats" within the gender equality machinery) is blurred (compare Bertone

2003). There is a stronger convergence between state and civil society than is expected or accepted elsewhere in Europe. . . .

. . . Not all feminists are interested in child care policies or have an identical approach to child care and parental policies. On the whole, the relationship of the women's movement to mothering, or the politics of motherhood and care, is a complex issue. Since the 1990s, an internal critique of the "false universality of womanhood" has increasingly spread within the feminist movement. As a consequence, the notion that all mothers need, want, or prefer the same child care services has also become a point of contention. . . .

. . . For my part, I want to challenge generalized assessments that argue that integrationist strategies are always more efficient than a feminist politics that operates outside of the state and political institutions. The organizational form and the repertoires of action do matter, but so do political identity and strategy, as well as the general political culture. . . .

NOTES

1. I use the terms Norden and Nordic to refer to what in Anglo-American context is often called Scandinavia(n).

2. In Sweden parental leave currently consists of 450 days, which the parents can share between them. Both parents have a quota of 60 personal days of leave, which can only be given to the other parent in exceptional circumstances. In Finland, fathers have the right to 18 days of paternity leave to be taken simultaneously with the mother (this leave can be taken in periods). Altogether the parental leave is 263 days, out of which the mother's quota is 105 days. The rest can be divided between the parents. In Norway the leave is 52 weeks altogether, out of which the maternity leave is 9 weeks, the paternity leave 4 weeks, and the rest can be shared between the parents (Rantalaiho 2003).

3. In Sweden, 86 percent of mothers of preschoolers belonged to the labor force (as registered job seekers or as being on temporary parental leave) in 1988, but their actual rate of presence in the workplace was 55 percent (Jonung and Persson

1993). In 1998, 74 percent of Finnish mothers with children under three years of age were counted as part of the labor force, but only 30 percent of them were in paid work (Julkunen 2001).

4. Some countries (e.g., the United Kingdom, the Netherlands) have introduced a care allowance for single mothers/parents to facilitate home care of small children (Hobson 1994). . . .

5. Swedish parental leave is not only longer than Finnish leave, it is also extremely flexible, allowing parents to share the leave period, divide it up in shorter periods, and so on, until the child is eight years old.

6. This development is clearly reflected in the difficulties that young women experience in obtaining permanent employment in today's Finland. Some 43 percent of women under 30 years of age have time-limited employment contracts, compared with one-third of men in the same age group (Salmi 2000).

REFERENCES

Andenaes, Agnes (1998) "Faglige premisser i politiske diskusjoner: Fra kontantstøttedebatten 1997–1998," *Kvinneforskning* 22: 12–26.

Anttonen, Anneli (2001) "The Female Working Citizen: Social Rights, Work and Motherhood in Finland," *Kvinder, Køn og Forskning* 2: 33–44.

—— (2003) "Lastenhoidon kaksi maailmaa" in H. Forsberg and R. Nätkin (eds.) *Perhe murroksessa: Kriittisen perhetutkimuksen jäljillä*, Helsinki: Gaudeamus.

Bergman, Solveig (2002) *The Politics of Feminism: Autonomous Feminist Movements in Finland and West Germany from the 1960s to the 1980s*, Åbo, Finland: Åbo Akademi University Press.

Bergqvist, Christina, Jaana Kuusipalo, and Audur Styrkarsdóttir (1999) "Family Policy in the Nordic Welfare States" in C. Bergqvist, A. Borchorst, A-D. Christensen, V. Ramstedt-Silén, N. Raaum, and A. Styrkarsdóttir (eds.) *Equal Democracies? Gender and Politics in the Nordic Countries*, Oslo: Scandinavian University Press.

Bertone, Chiara (2003) "Claims for Child Care as Struggles over Needs: Comparing Italian and Danish Women's Organizations," *Social Politics* 10: 229–255.

Brandth, Berit, and Elin Kvande (2003) *Fleksible fedre*, Oslo: Universitetsforlaget.

Dobrowolsky, Alexandra, and Jane Jenson (2002) "Shifting Patterns of Representation. The Politics of 'Children,' 'Families,' 'Women,'" Paper presented to the meeting of Care, Values and the Future of Welfare, CAVA, Leeds University, November 1.

Gender Equality Barometer (2002) *Likestillingsbarometeret*, Oslo: Likestillingssenteret.

Haataja, Anita (2004) "Pohjoismaiset vanhempainvapaat kahden lasta hoitavan vanhemman tukena," *Janus* 12: 25–48.

Heinen, Jacqueline, and Heini Martiskainen de Koenigswater (2001) "Framing Citizenship in France and Finland in the 1990s: Restructuring Motherhood, Work, and Care," *Social Politics* 8: 170–181.

Hobson, Barbara (1994) "Solo Mothers, Social Policy Regimes and the Logics of Gender" in D. Sainsbury (ed.) *Gendering Welfare States*, London: Sage.

Jonung, Christina, and Inga Persson (1993) "Women and Market Work: The Misleading Tale of Participation Rates in International Comparisons," *Work, Employment and Society* 7: 259–274.

Julkunen, Raija (1999) "Gender, Work, Welfare State," in S. Apo et al. (ed.) *Women in Finland*, Helsinki: Otava.

—— (2001) "Naistutkimuksen identiteetti," *Naistutkimus-Kvinnoforskning* 13: 44–49.

Lehto, Anna-Maija (1999) "Towards Equality in Working Life?" in A-M. Lehto and H. Sutela (eds.) *Gender Equality in Working Life*: Labour Market, 22. Statistics Finland: 7–46.

Leira, Arnlaug (1998) "Caring as Social Project: Cash for Child Care and Daddy Leave," *Social Politics* 5: 362–378.

—— (2000) "Combining Work and Family: Nordic Policy Reforms in the 1990s" in T. P. Boje and A. Leira (eds.) *Gender, Welfare State and the Market: Towards a New Division of Labour*, London: Routledge.

—— (2002) "Updating the 'Gender Contract'? Childcare Reforms in the Nordic Countries in the 1990s," *NORA* 10: 81–89.

Lindvert, Jessica (2002) "A World Apart. Swedish and Australian Gender Equality Policy," *NORA* 10: 99–107.

Morgan, Kimberly J., and Kathrin Zippel (2003) "Paid to Care: The Origins and Effects of Care Leave Policies in Western Europe," *Social Politics* 10: 49–85.

Oftung, Knut (1993) *Menn og endring: En analyse av argumenter om mannsrollen og omsorgspraksis i den offentlige debatt. 2nd ed.*, Department of Sociology and Human Geography, University of Oslo.

Ostner, Ilona (1993) "Slow Motion: Women, Work and the Family in Germany" in J. Lewis (ed.) *Women and Social Policies in Europe: Work, Family and the State*, Aldershot, UK: Edward Elgar.

Pringle, Keith (1998) *Children and Social Welfare in Europe*, Buckingham, UK: Open University Press.

Ramstedt-Silén, Viveca (1999) *Riksdagsutskott eller kvinnoförening? Det kvinnliga nätverket i Finlands riksdag*, SSKH Notat 4/1999.

Rantalaiho, Minna (2001) "Welfare State for Children?"

Paper presented to the 5th Conference of the ESA, "Visions and Divisions: Challenges to European Sociology," Helsinki, August 28.

—— (2003) "Pohjoismaisen isyyspolitiikan isäkuva" in H. Forsberg and R. Nätkin (eds.) *Perhe murroksessa: Kriittisen perhetutkimuksen jäljillä*, Helsinki: Gaudeamus.

Salmi, Minna (2000) "Kotihoidon tuki ja naisten asema: tutkimushaasteita ja tulkintaongelmia," *Yhteiskuntapolitiikka* 65: 46–56.

Sundström, Eva (2003) "Gender Regimes, Family Policies and Attitudes to Female Employment: A Comparison of Germany, Italy and Sweden," Department of Sociology, Umeå University.

CHAPTER 28

Integrating or Setting the Agenda?: Gender Mainstreaming in the European Constitution-Making Process

Emanuela Lombardo

Is gender mainstreaming in European Union (EU) politics applied with an integrationist or an agenda-setting approach? This question is explored with reference to the EU constitution-making process, which includes both the European Constitutional Convention, held from February 2002 to July 2003 as a preparation for the 2004 Intergovernmental Conference (IGC), and its product, the Constitutional Treaty (CT). The adoption of either of the two approaches to gender mainstreaming affects the process in different ways. An "agenda-setting" approach may have a stronger impact on the decision-making structures and process, as it aims at reorienting the mainstream political agenda from a gender perspective. By contrast, an "integrationist" approach may achieve a formal introduction of gender mainstreaming but not an effective implementation of it in policy practice, as it does not aim at challenging existing policy paradigms (Jahan 1995).

This article examines the convention's approach to gender mainstreaming, taking as a starting point five indicators of application of the strategy: a broader concept of gender equality, the incorporation of a gender perspective into the mainstream, equal representation of women, the prioritization of gender policy objectives, and a shift in institutional and organizational culture. It concludes that an "integrating" rather than an "agenda-setting" approach to mainstreaming has been

adopted and provides tentative explanations for this finding.

The study of the EU conventions[1] offers an opportunity for observing how gender has been mainstreamed in the EU policy-making process, in this case in foundational debates. . . .

GENDER MAINSTREAMING IN THE EU: A STRATEGY TO SUIT ANY VISION?

Since it appeared in the European political arena after the 1995 United Nations (UN) World Conference on Women in Beijing, gender mainstreaming has raised high expectations, though also doubts, on the part of institutional and academic feminism, and low resistance, though also misunderstanding, on the part of policy-makers. The enormous potential of the strategy was both a strength and a weakness. . . .

EU policy-makers, who did not feel as threatened by gender mainstreaming as they had been with positive actions, waxed eloquent about the importance of integrating equality in all policies but then did little to implement the strategy. As a result, many of the gender policies implemented in European countries after 1995 were a mere continuation of previous policies (Behning and Serrano Pascual 2001). In the worst cases gender mainstreaming was interpreted as a replacement for specific gender policies and structures, in spite of warnings by the group of experts of the Council of Europe that this was a misunderstanding of the concept. . . . The fact that gender equality was now included in the mainstream led many to assume, incorrectly, that specific funds and programs for women should disappear, as there was no further need for them.

THE DILEMMA OF "INTEGRATING" VERSUS "SETTING THE AGENDA"

European policy-makers did not perceive the revolutionary potential of gender mainstreaming, either because the definition of the concept is so vague that actors untrained in gender cannot grasp all its implications or because of the way in which gender mainstreaming campaigners have framed the strategy in their effort to persuade decision makers to accept it. . . . Gender campaigners adopted the strategy of "selling" gender mainstreaming to the most reluctant Directorate Generals (DGs) "as an effective means to the ends pursued by policy-makers, rather than as an overt challenge to those ends," emphasizing the gains in "efficiency" rather than in equality that would derive from the introduction of gender in their policy areas (Hafner-Burton and Pollack 2000: 452–453).

However, the undesired effect of this strategic framing process was the adoption of an "integrationist" approach to gender mainstreaming that subverts the innovative meaning of the strategy, diluting its revolutionary character. Integrationist approaches to gender mainstreaming introduce a gender perspective into existing policy paradigms without questioning them (Jahan 1995). . . . The strengths of this approach are an emphasis on the role of gender experts in policy formulation and the possibility to produce effective integration once the concept is accepted by regular policy-makers. Its focus on bureaucratic processes and the

danger of "rhetorical entrapment" (Verloo 2001) are among its weaknesses (Squires 2005). Furthermore, integrationist approaches may succeed in formally introducing gender mainstreaming in EU policy, but they are not necessarily successful in effectively implementing the strategy in policy-making practices.

Jahan (1995) introduces another interpretation of gender mainstreaming, more faithful to its revolutionary potential: the "agenda-setting" approach. It implies a transformation and reorientation of existing policy paradigms, by changing decision-making structures and processes, prioritizing gender objectives among competing issues, and reorienting the mainstream political agenda by rethinking and rearticulating policy ends and means from a gender perspective. In this approach "women not only become part of the mainstream, they also reorient the nature of the mainstream" (Jahan 1995: 13). Recognition of women's voices via consultation processes is one of its strengths, though the approach risks reifying identities and thus undermining solidarity across groups (Squires 2005).

Scholars have also discussed a third "transformative" approach, whose strengths are its ability for addressing mainstreaming in the context of diversity and its emphasis on processes of democratic deliberation for bringing the concerns of different groups to the public agenda (Squires 2005). Its lack of gender specificity and concrete articulations is among its weaknesses. . . . This article will limit itself to assessing the extent to which an "integrationist" or an "agenda-setting" approach to gender mainstreaming has been adopted in the EU constitution-making process.

GENDER MAINSTREAMING IN THE EUROPEAN UNION

When the first convention began its work on the Charter in 1999, gender mainstreaming was already reflected in EU law, and it seemed difficult to ignore in a constitution-making process. According to the Council of Europe (1998: 15), gender mainstreaming required, in fact, "the (re)organisation, improvement, development and evaluation of policy processes, so that a gender equality perspective is incorporated in all policies at all levels and at all stages, by the actors normally involved in policy-making." . . .

The main guarantee of the *acquis* on gender equality is Article 141 EC on the "principle of equal pay for male and female workers for equal work or work of equal value,"[2] which in its paragraph 141.4 allows member states to introduce positive actions. Finally, the Amsterdam Treaty (European Union 1997) introduced Article 13, which allows the council to take action "to combat discrimination based on sex, racial or ethnic origin, religion or belief, disability, age or sexual orientation."

[. . . The definition of gender mainstreaming by the Council of Europe (1998) and a number of reflective studies (Beveridge et al. 2000; Hafner-Burton and Pollack 2000; Jahan 1995; Shaw 2000; Verloo 1999) provide us with a set of [following] criteria for recognizing gender mainstreaming. These will serve as reference points for exploring how it has been applied in the constitutional convention.] . . .

MAINSTREAMING GENDER IN THE EU CONSTITUTION-MAKING PROCESS

A Broader Concept of Gender Equality

The Charter of Fundamental Rights (CFR) includes equality as a European Union value and refers to equality between women and men and nondiscrimination on grounds of sex in Article II-83 and II-81.1, respectively, while it also mentions the sharing of work and family responsibilities in Article II-93. In the same way as it opens opportunities for a broader concept of gender equality,

the ambiguous framing of Article II-83 also raises doubts concerning the scope of equality provided by the Charter. Its first paragraph states, "equality between women and men must be ensured in all areas, including employment, work and pay." The extension of gender equality to all areas represents progress compared with an *acquis* mainly centered on equality at work. However, the added clause "including employment, work and pay" reorients the application of equality to the usual labor-related areas of EU gender policy. The way in which judges will interpret the article will determine the scope of the provision.

Moreover, Article II-83's mismatch with the *acquis* reveals some of the limits of the Charter's concept of equality. Unlike Article 141 EC on equal pay, Article II-83 CFR is not directly effective; it is a "general statement of intent" rather than a "rights conferring measure" (León et al. 2003: 13), and it does not include any positive obligation to promote gender equality as Articles 2 and 3.2 EC do (McCrudden 2003). . . .

Further reference to gender equality can be found in Article II-81.1 CFR, which prohibits discrimination on several grounds, including sex. The list of types of discrimination prohibited in the Charter is wider than that of Article 13 Treaty of the European Union (TEU) (Article III-124 CT). Despite this progress, decisions based on Article II-81.1 CFR are subject to unanimity in council and European Parliament consultation, which makes agreement on a proposal difficult to achieve and gives the parliament a weaker decision-making role.

. . . After months of lobbying by conventioneers, representatives of civil society, the European Parliament Committee on Women's Rights, and gender experts, "equality" (but not between women and men) was added to the European Union's values in one of the last drafts of the Constitutional Treaty (European Convention 2003) in June 2003. The fact that the value of equality had to be fought for instead of being taken for granted shows that Convention II had embraced a remarkably limited concept of gender equality. . . .

In sum, the *acquis* is safe, but the concept of gender equality has not broadened so as to cover other policies beyond employment; neither the legal basis of gender policy nor the strategy of gender mainstreaming have been strengthened. The inclusion of a general clause of nondiscrimination shows a shift in the concept of equality toward an emphasis on nondiscrimination policies, with developments that are currently difficult to foresee, also due to the weak legal instruments provided to decide on measures and to claim rights.

Incorporating a Gender Perspective into the Mainstream

To satisfy this requirement we should encounter not only a reference to gender mainstreaming like Article 3.2 TEU (Article III-116 CT) but also the application of a gender perspective to all areas and a gender-sensitive reorientation of the political agenda. Both the Charter and the Constitution contain relevant omissions at least in the areas of violence, asylum, sharing of work and family responsibilities, health, culture and education, budgeting, and security and defense policy.

Violence against women has not been explicitly addressed in the Constitution. Article II-64 of the Charter prohibits "torture, inhuman or degrading treatment or punishment." However, the adoption of a gender perspective on violence would have also specified that female genital mutilation, rape, or domestic violence are forms of "inhuman or degrading treatment or punishment." . . .

Provisions against trafficking have received a more explicit treatment by both conventions. Article II-65.3 CFR prohibits trafficking in human beings, and the explanations provided in the Constitution clarify that the article will be used to combat trafficking in women and children. In section 4 on judicial cooperation on criminal matters of the Constitution, Article III-271 (Article 17 TEU) allows the introduction of rules for combating the traffic "of human beings and sexual exploitation of women and children." . . . No analogous progressive treatment was provided to grant the right of asylum to women who seek to escape from gender-specific forms of persecution imposed by law, religion, or social norms. . . .

A gender perspective is also absent in policies such as health, culture, and education, where the EU can take "coordinating, supplementary or supporting action," but which are mainly of national competence. . . .

Finance is a policy area where the integration of a gender perspective could have a substantive impact on women's conditions. Gender budgeting has been introduced in the guidelines of the European Structural Funds 2000–2006, . . . [which] aims to produce a budget in which gender has been "mainstreamed" by analyzing public expenditure and methods of raising public revenue from a gender perspective and identifying the implications for women as compared to men (Elson 2003). In "The Multiannual Financial Framework" and "The Union's Annual Budget" of the Constitution, there is no reference to gender budgeting or gender equality considerations.

Finally, a gender perspective has not been incorporated in the "Common Foreign and Security Policy" and "Common Security and Defence Policy" of the Constitution. . . .

With the exceptions of trafficking and, only in a marginal way, the sharing of family and work responsibilities, all other areas of the Constitutional Treaty considered do not show any consistent integration of a gender perspective. Nevertheless, the text includes formal provisions on gender mainstreaming. The convention appears committed to promoting gender mainstreaming but not yet ready for putting it into practice in the context of its own constitution-making process.

Women's Representation in Decision Making

Expectations that women would be better represented in the more open and democratic process of the conventions were soon undone. The percentage of female representatives in the convention that drafted the Charter was 16 percent. The criticisms of gender campaigners regarding the underrepresentation of women in the Charter did not affect selection procedures of Convention II: in February 2003 women represented only 17.14 percent (18 of 105 members) of the body that drafted the document. . . . [The actual] figures are nowhere near the 40 percent recommended by Commission Decision 2000/407 (Commission 2000b). . . .

. . . These scant results reveal that one of the greatest obstacles that gender mainstreaming must face is the fact that the decision-making process, be it deliberative or based on traditional methods of negotiating, takes place in an environment in which power mechanisms are not gender-neutral.

Prioritizing Gender Equality Objectives and Policies of Relevance for Women

The inclusion of provisions on gender equality and nondiscrimination in the Charter and in the Constitution indicates that gender objectives have been integrated in both constitution-making processes. Social policy provisions were included in Chapter III on equality and Chapter IV on solidarity of the Charter, and the Constitution maintains the social measures contained in the *acquis*. In spite of their inclusion, the type of guarantees that have been granted to gender equality provisions is not very strong. . . .

The struggle over the inclusion of the value of equality during the process of Convention II reveals that gender was not especially prioritized. . . . Whether the risk of losing existing equality rights in the Constitution was real, the fact that equality was added to the values of the Union in one of the last drafts (CONV 797/03, European Convention 2003) speaks volumes regarding the consideration of gender as a priority for Convention II. . . .

A Shift in Institutional and Organizational Culture

The fifth requirement of gender mainstreaming is a shift in institutional and organizational culture that should be observed in three aspects of EU constitution-making: policy process, mechanisms, and actors.

Policy Process

. . . The president of the Committee on Women's Rights of the European Parliament (2002), Anna Karamanou, in a letter addressed to the president of Convention II, Valéry Giscard, and distributed to all conventioneers in June 2002, made . . . proposals for reorganizing the policy process "to compensate for the under-representation of women amongst the conventionals and to aim at an outcome of the Convention that reflects the aspirations of societies composed of active and concerned women as well as men." . . .

. . . In spite of the efforts of gender advocates, Convention II did not bring evidence of a shift toward a reorganization of the policy process so that institutional actors could take a gender perspective into account.

Policy Mechanisms

Evidence of a shift in policy mechanisms can be found in the use of horizontal cooperation on gender issues across policy areas and of tools for integrating a gender perspective and then monitoring and evaluating its integration in the policy process. Horizontal cooperation has been relatively easy in the conventions due both to the fact that these bodies had sufficiently defined tasks to perform (more precise in the first than in the second convention) within a limited time span, and to the method of deliberation, based on the need to achieve consensus and a certain autonomy enjoyed by the members, that facilitated internal communication and debate. . . . An analysis of the final reports of the working groups[3] (none of which concerned gender equality, as the Committee on Women's Rights had recommended) reveals that gender was not a transversal issue across the groups. Gender equality was debated only by the Working Group on Social Europe (2003) . . .

Policy Actors

. . . Actors of civil society could send their contributions to the debate via the Internet, and both conventions organized hearings with representative organizations of civil society. . . . (Conference of the Representatives of the Governments of the Member States 2004). However, it is not clear that this change has occurred to comply with gender mainstreaming, as it is part of the moves toward governance that the EU is making to open the policy-making process to a wider range of actors (Commission 1998, 2000a, 2001).

Civil society groups in both conventions were active on gender. . . . However, gender equality could become a priority for civil society but not for EU institutional actors. . . . Rather then being mainstreamed into the political agenda, gender equality could run the risk of becoming a marginalized issue in the hands of equally marginalized actors. Moreover, the few women's groups who were actively engaged in the convention process were European-based organizations, more familiar with the EU institutional context and language. . . .

CONCLUSIONS

The foregoing analysis provides evidence that gender mainstreaming has been integrated in Convention II but has not managed to reorient the mainstream of the constitution-making process, as an "agenda-setting" approach to the strategy would recommend (Jahan 1995). In spite of the supposedly more democratic character of the European constitution-making process that produced the Charter and the Constitution, the convention has maintained strong patriarchal elements typical of most political contexts. Except for the integration of formal concepts of gender mainstreaming in the text, the EU constitutional convention has failed to effectively apply the strategy to its own policy-making experience. Different hypotheses can be advanced to explain this failure.

Stratigaki (2005) argues that the reasons for the failure of a deeper incorporation of gender mainstreaming in the European political process lie in the resistance by EU dominant policy frames, which are based on a hierarchical gender distribution of power. . . . Although this could be part of the explanation, the resistance to mainstreaming gender in the EU constitution-making process seems rather a case of prioritization of some other goal in the contested process of "norm-setting" (Elgström 2000) that took place in the constitutional convention. . . .

The fact that the convention discourse was more institutionally driven has limited wider debates about the nature of the EU project and has marginalized actors who are willing to discuss more substantive questions regarding the type of polity aimed at and the extent to which gender is being mainstreamed in EU policy-making. The passive role granted to civil society and the unfair treatment of social policy, with regard to both the late creation of a working group on the issue and the lack of consideration of its conclusions on the part of the Presidium, exemplify this attitude (Lombardo 2007). In addition, . . . issues and perspectives that accepted the existing neoliberal trend were prioritized, while social and gender issues that challenged this model were marginalized, and the actors defending them were constrained to adopt "realistic" (that is, within the dominant paradigm) standpoints to participate in the debate.

. . . [T]he focus of the convention mandate on institutional reform contributed to diverting attention from substantive issues such as gender equality; the priority given to debates on EU competence and the principle of subsidiarity encouraged the perception that gender equality provisions could be limited in the constitutional text (since gender equality is a national competence). . . .

Another reason for explaining the gender blindness of the constitution-making process could be the low number of female members of the convention. As Agnès Hubert made clear, only 18 women out of 105 conventioneers is a small number to make your voices heard. . . .

Competing frames, "norm-setting," and male-dominated EU institutions are . . . tentative reasons offered to explain the observed resistance to adopting gender norms in the EU constitution-making process. In view of the treatment reserved to gender mainstreaming in the latest EU foundational debates, gender advocates need both to deepen the reflection on the obstacles opposed to the strategy and to devise ways for effectively implementing gender mainstreaming in the European political arena. The challenge of letting gender set the mainstream political agenda of European policy-making processes still needs to be taken on.

NOTES

1. Though the main focus of this article is on the EU Constitutional Convention, the EU Charter of Fundamental Rights is taken into account both because it sets an institutional precedent for the establishment of Convention II, and it has been incorporated in the Constitution. Reference to articles of the charter will respect the numbering established in the Constitution.
2. Article 141 EC is "directly effective," which

means that it is enforceable by individuals in domestic courts both against the state and against private employers.
3. The eleven working groups of Convention II included Subsidiarity, Charter of Fundamental Rights, Legal Personality, National Parliaments, Complementary Competencies, Economic Governance, External Action, Defence, Simplification, Freedom, Security and Justice, and Social Europe.

REFERENCES

Behning, Ute, and Amparo Serrano Pascual (2001) *Gender Mainstreaming in the European Employment Strategy*, Brussels: ETUI.

Beveridge, Fiona, Sue Nott, and Kylie Stephen (2000) "Mainstreaming and Engendering of Policy-Making: A Means to an End?" *Journal of European Public Policy* 7, 3: 385–405.

Commission (1998) "Communication of the Commission 'Promoting the Role of Voluntary Organisations and Foundations in Europe'," No. COM (97) 241 final. March 30.

—— (2000a) "The Commission and Non-Governmental Organisations: Building a Stronger Partnership," Commission discussion paper no. COM (2000) 11 final. January 18.

—— (2000b) No. COM 2000/407/EC. June 19.

—— (2001) "The White Paper on European Governance," No. COM (2001) 428 final. July 25.

Conference of the Representatives of the Governments of the Member States (2004) "Treaty Establishing a Constitution for Europe," IGC 87/2/04 REV 2, Brussels. October 29.

Council of Europe (1998) *Gender Mainstreaming: Conceptual Framework, Methodology and Presentation of Good Practices: Final Report of Activities of the Group of Specialists on Mainstreaming*, EG-S-MS. Strasbourg: Council of Europe.

Elgström, Ole (2000) "Norm Negotiations: The Construction of New Norms Regarding Gender and Development in EU Foreign Aid Policy," *Journal of European Public Policy* 7, 3: 457–476.

Elson, Diane (2003) "Gender Mainstreaming and Gender Budgeting," Paper presented at the Conference of the Jean Monnet Project on "Gender Equality and Europe's Future," European Commission, Brussels. http://ec.europa.eu/education/programmes/llp/jm/more/confgender03/elson.pdf (accessed October 1, 2008).

European Convention (2003) "Text of Part I and Part II of the Constitution," CONV 797/03 REV 1. June 12. http://register.consilium.eu.int/pdf/en/03/cv00/cv00797-re01en03.pdf (accessed October 3, 2005).

European Parliament. Committee on Women's Rights and Equal Opportunities (2002) "Highlights of

Debate" and "Letter of Anna Karamanou, President of Committee on Women's Rights of the European Parliament, to Valéry Giscard d'Estaing, President of the European Convention, June 3, 2002," *Le fil d'Arianne* No. 1. Gender Equality Newsletter.

European Union (1997) "Treaty Establishing the European Community," http://eur-lex.europa.eu/en/treaties/dat/11997E/htm/11997E.html#0173010078 (accessed October 25, 2005).

Hafner-Burton, Emilie, and Mark A. Pollack (2000) "Mainstreaming Gender in the European Union," *Journal of European Public Policy* 7, 3: 432–456.

Jahan, Rounaq (1995) *The Elusive Agenda: Mainstreaming Women in Development*, London: Zed Books.

León, Margarita, Mercedes Mateo Diaz, and Susan Millns (2003) "Engendering the Convention: Women and the Future of the European Union," http://www.fedtrust.co.uk/constitutionalpapers (accessed October 3, 2005).

Lombardo, Emanuela (2007) "The Participation of Civil Society" in D. Castiglione et al. (eds.) *Constitutional Politics in the European Union. The Convention Moment and its Aftermath*, Houndmills, UK: Palgrave.

McCrudden, Christopher (2003) "Gender Equality in the Constitutional Treaty: Drafting Suggestions,"

Lecture given at the Albert Borschette Conference Centre, Brussels, March 4, 2003.

Shaw, Jo (2000) "Importing Gender: The Challenge of Feminism and the Analysis of the EU Legal Order," *Journal of European Public Policy* 7, 3: 406–431.

Squires, Judith (2005) "Evaluating Gender Mainstreaming in the Context of EU Diversity Strategies," Paper presented at European Consortium for Political Research Joint Sessions of Granada, Workshop on "The Future of Gender Equality in the European Union." April 14–19, Granada.

Stratigaki, Maria (2005) "Gender Mainstreaming versus Positive Action: An Ongoing Conflict in EU Gender Equality Policy," *European Journal of Women's Studies* 12, 2: 165–186.

Verloo, Mieke (1999) "Gender Mainstreaming: Practice and Prospects," Report prepared for the Council of Europe, No. EG 99, 13.

—— (2001) "Another Velvet Revolution? Gender Mainstreaming and the Politics of Implementation," IWM Working Paper No. 5/2001. Vienna: IWM.

Working Group XI on Social Europe (2003) "Final Report of Working Group XI on Social Europe," February 4. http://register.consilium.eu.int/pdf/en/03/cv00/CV00516-re01en03.pdf (accessed October 3, 2005).

Websites of International Women's Research Centers

Compiled by Nicole Lamarre, Minjeong Kim, and Christine E. Bose

The increasing number of women's research centers around the world illustrates growing interest in women's issues. In the following 84 countries, and others not included here, numerous women's research centers and institutes have been established. To create this list, we located major women's research centers, in countries across the regions analyzed in this volume, which created their own websites and had their own web addresses. As of the book's completion in Summer 2008, these addresses were accurate and the links to their sites were functioning. Given the nature of the World Wide Web, and the uneven support for global gender research, we cannot know how often the web page contents will be updated. We wish to thank many of the book's contributors for their ideas on the appropriate websites to incorporate.

Afghanistan

Afghan Women's Network (AWN)
  http://www.afghanwomensnetwork.org/
Revolutionary Association of the Women of Afghanistan (RAWA)
  http://www.rawa.org/index.php

Argentina

Area de Genero del Instituto de Investigaciones Gino Germani
  http://www.iigg.fsoc.uba.ar/
Area de Investigacion del Consejo Nacional de la Mujer
  http://www.cnm.gov.ar/
Centro de Encuentros Cultura y Mujer
  http://www.cecym.org.ar [in Spanish]
Centro de Estudios sobre Democratización y Derechos Humanos (CEDEHU) Universidad Nacional de San Martin
  http://www.unsam.edu.ar/escuelas/posgrado/cedehu/cedehu.asp?m=1&s=5&s1= 150&s2=222
Centro de Estudios de Estado y Sociedad (CEDES)
  http://www.cedes.org/ [in Spanish]
Centro de Estudios de Poblacion (CENEP) (Center for Population Studies)
  http://www.cenep.org.ar/index2.html [in Spanish]
Fundación para Estudio e Investigación de la Mujer (FEIM)
  http://www.feim.org.ar/somos.htm [in Spanish]

Fundacion Alicia Moreau de Justo
   http://www.geocities.com/fmoreaudejusto/ [in Spanish]
Instituto Hannah Arendt
   http://www.institutoarendt.com.ar/
Instituto Interdisciplinario de Estudios de Genero
   http://www.filo.uba.ar/contenidos/investigacion/institutos/aiem/home2.htm
Instituto Social Y Politico De La Mujer
   http://www.ispm.org.ar/ [in Spanish]
Interdisciplinary Centre for Historical Studies on Women (CEHIM), National University of Tucumán
   http://www.filo.unt.edu.ar/centinti/cehim/cehim_investigacion.htm [in Spanish]

Australia
Australian Women's Research Centre (AWORC), Deakin University
   http://acqol.deakin.edu.au/introduction/perspectives/klein.htm
Gender Research Department, The University of Sydney
   http://www.arts.usyd.edu.au/departs/gcs/
Institute for Women's Studies, Macquarie University
   http://www.iws.mq.edu.au/
Office of the Status of Women: Department of Prime Minister and Cabinet
   http://www.dpmc.gov.au/
Research Centre for Gender Studies, University of South Australia
   http://www.unisa.edu.au/cgs/
Research Centre for Women's Studies, University of Adelaide
   http://www.arts.adelaide.edu.au/socialsciences/gls/

Barbados
Centre for Gender and Development Studies, Dame Nita Barrow Unit, University of the West Indies
   http://gender.uwichill.edu.bb/

Belgium
Centre for Women's Studies Theology
   http://www.theo.kuleuven.be/page/centr_women/
RoSa Documentatiecentrum (Rosa Documentation Centre)
   http://www.gelijkekansen.vlaanderen.be/rosa [in Dutch]

Benin
Association Des Femmes Juristes Du Benin (AFJB)
   http://afjb.courantsdefemmes.org/ [in French]
Bibliothèque et Centre de Documentation de la Faculté des Sciences Agronomiques
   http://www.agricta.org/partners/bidoc/fsa.html [in French]

Bolivia
Centro de Información y Desarrollo de la Mujer (CIDEM)
   http://www.cidem.org.bo/ [in Spanish]

Brazil

Fundação Carolos Chagas
  http://www.fcc.org.br/ [in Portuguese]
Centro Feminista de Estudos e Assessoria (CFEMEA)
  http://www.cfemea.org.br/quemsomos/presentation.asp
Special Secretary of Policies for Women
  http://www.presidencia.gov.br/spmulheres/
University of Sao Paulo NEMGE – The Center for the Study of Women & Gender
  http://www.usp.br/nemge/nemge.htm
Núcleo de Estudos Interdisciplinares sobre a Mulher (NEIM)
  http://www.neim.ufba.br/site/ [in Portuguese]

Bulgaria

Center of Women's Studies and Policies
  http://www.cwsp.bg/htmls/home.php
Ministere de la promotion de la femme
  http://www.mpf.gov.bf/ [in Bulgarian]

Canada

Atlantic Centre of Excellence for Women's Health (ACEWH/CESF)
  http://www.acewh.dal.ca/
British Columbia Centre of Excellence for Women's Health (BCCEWH), British Columbia's Women's Hospital
  http://www.bccewh.bc.ca/about-us/default.htm
Canadian Research Institute for the Advancement of Women
  http://www.criaw-icref.ca/
Center for Research in Women's Studies and Gender
  http://www.wmst.ubc.ca
Centre for Feminist Research, York University
  http://www.yorku.ca/cfr/default.htm
Centre for Girls' and Women's Health and Physical Education (CGHHPA), University of Toronto
  http://www.ac-fpeh.com/academic/research/centres.php
Centre for Research on Violence Against Women and Children, University of Western Ontario
  http://www.crvawc.ca
Centre for Women's Studies and Feminist Research, University of Western Ontario
  http://www.uwo.ca/womens/
Centre for Womens Studies in Education, Ontario Institute for Studies in Education (OISE), University of Toronto
  http://www1.oise.utoronto.ca/cwse/
Feminist Research, Education, Development, and Action (FREDA) Centre for Research on Violence against Women and Children, collaboration of Simon Fraser University and the University of British Columbia
  http://www.vancouver.sfu.ca/freda/
Institute for the Study of Women, Mount Saint Vincent University
  http://www.msvu.ca

International Development Research Centre (IDRC), Women' Rights and Citizenship (WRC)
http://www.idrc.ca/womensrights/
McGill Center for Teaching and Research on Women
http://www.mcgill.ca/mcrtw/
National Network on Environments and Women's Health (NNEWH)
http://www.nnewh.org/
Simone de Beauvoir Institute, Concordia University
http://artsandscience1.concordia.ca/wsdb/
Women and Gender Studies Institute (WGSI), University of Toronto
http://www.utoronto.ca/iwsgs/

Chile
Centro de Estudios de la Mujer
http://www.cem.cl/english.htm

China
All China Women's Federation
http://www.women.org.cn/english/index.htm
Center for Women's Law and Legal Services of Peking University
http://www.woman-legalaid.org/
Center of Gender Studies, Dalian University
http://202.199.159.238/edoc/default.asp
China Women's University
http://www.cwu.edu.cn/english/index.htm
Chinese Society for Women's Studies
http://www.csws.org/
Chinese University of Hong Kong Gender Research Centre
http://www.cuhk.edu.hk/hkiaps/grc/
Gender and Development in China
http://www.china-gad.org/english.asp
Gender and Law Research Center, Institute of Law, CASS
http://www.genderandlaw.org.cn/english/aboutus_english.asp
Hong Kong University of Science and Technology: Centre For Cultural Studies
http://www.ust.hk/~webccshs/rfoci.htm
Media and Gender Institute, Communication University
http://mgi.cuc.edu.cn/web/englishversion.htm
National Working Committee on Children and Women Under the State Council
http://www.nwccw.gov.cn/index.jsp [in Chinese]
Network of Women/Gender studies
http://www.chinagender.org [in Chinese]
Sex/Gender Education Forum at Sun Yat-sen University
http://genders.zsu.edu.cn/ [in Chinese]
Shaanxi Research Association of Women and Family
http://www.westwomen.org [in Chinese]
Tianjin Normal University – Center for Women's Studies
http://www.gendercommunity.org [in Chinese]

Women Resources
  http://www.womenresources.org/public/main [in Chinese]
Women's Academy at Shandong
  http://www.cwcsb.com/Eng/Main.htm
Women's Studies Center of Peking University
  http://www.pku.edu.cn/academic/wsc [in Chinese]
Women's Studies Institute of China
  http://www.wsic.ac.cn/ENGLISH/ENGLISHMain.html

Colombia
Center of Economic Development Studies (CEDE)
  http://ingles.uniandes.edu.co/ECO/ResearchFacultyEconomy.php?Menu=29
Universidad del Valle – Centro de Estudios de Género, Mujer y Sociedad (Center of General, Women's, and Social Studies) Universidad Nacional de Colombia (National University of Colombia)
  http://www.univalle.edu.co/~cgenero/ [in Spanish]

Congo (Republic)
Ministère chargé de la Promotion de la Femme et de l'Intégration de la Femme au développement
  http://www.ministere-femme.dj/index2.php?option=com_content&task=view&id=
    51&pop=1&page=0&Itemid=53 [in French]

Costa Rica
National Institute of Women
  http://www.inamu.go.cr [in Spanish]
Universidad de Costa Rica – Centro de Investigación en Estudios de la Mujer (CIEM)
  http://www.ciem.ucr.ac.cr [in Spanish]
Universidad Nacional – Instituto de Estudios de la Mujer
  http://www.una.ac.cr/iem/principal.htm [in Spanish]

Cuba
Centro Nacional de Educación Sexual, Ministerio de Salud Pública
  http://www.cenesex.sld.cu [in Spanish]
Women's Studies Program at the Casa de las Américas
  http://www.casadelasamericas.com/programamujer/programaestudiosmujer.php?pagina=
    mujer [in Spanish]

Cyprus
The Mediterranean Institute of Gender Studies
  http://www.medinstgenderstudies.org/

Czech Republic
Centrum pro Gender Studies
  http://www.ecn.cz/gender [not in English]
Prague Gender Studies Centre
  http://www.en.genderstudies.cz/gender-studies/who-we-are.shtml

Denmark

Feminist Research Centre in Aalborg, Department of Development and Planning
http://www2.ihis.aau.dk/freia/uk/index.php
The Danish Centre for Information on Women and Gender, University of Aarhus
http://www.kvinfo.dk/side/225/ [in Danish]
University of Aarhus – CEKVINA: Centre for Gender Studies in Aarhus
http://www.hum.au.dk/cekvina/web/study_committee.html

Djibouti

Ministère chargé de la Promotion de la Femme, du Bien-être Familial et des Affaires Sociales
http://www.ministere-femme.dj/ [in French]

Dominican Republic

Instituto Tecnológico de Santo Domingo – Centro de Estudio del Género
http://www.intec.edu.do/grupos/genero.html [in Spanish]

Ecuador

Centro de Estudios y Investigaciones de la Mujer Ecuatoriana (CEIME)
http://www.ceime.org [in Spanish]
Instituto Ecuatoriano de Investigaciones y Capacitación de la Mujer
http://www.iecaim.org/

Egypt

The American University at Cairo, Institute for Gender and Women's Studies
http://www.aucegypt.edu/ResearchatAUC/rc/IGWS/Pages/default.aspx
The National Council for Women in Egypt
http://www.ilo.org/public/english/employment/gems/eeo/law/egypt/i_ncw.htm

Eritrea

National Union of Eritrean Women
http://www.nuew.org/

Finland

Christina Institute for Women's Studies (Kristina-instuutti), University of Helsinki
http://www.helsinki.fi/kristiina-instituutti/english/
Institute for Women's Studies in Abo, Abo Akademi University
http://www.abo.fi/instut/kvinnis/ifkvhems.htm [in Finnish]
University of Tampere Department of Women's Studies
http://www.uta.fi/laitokset/naistutkimus/reasear.htm

France

Association Nationale des Etudes Feministes
http://www.anef.org/ [in French]
CEDREF (Centre d'Enseignement de Documentation, de Recherche et d'Etudes Feministes),
Université of Paris VII Jussieu
http://www.cedref.univ-paris7.fr/ [in French]

Centre de Recherches en Etudes Feminines
http://www.univ-paris8.fr/ef/ [in French]
Research Group on the Social and Gender Division of Labor, National Center for Scientific Research (CNRS)
http://www.cnrs.fr/index.html

Germany
Cornelia Goethe Centrum in Frankfurt
http://www.cgc.uni-frankfurt.de/english-cgc-home.shtml
Federal Ministry for Family, Seniors, Women and Youth
http://www.bmfsfj.de/Politikbereiche/gleichstellung.html [in German]
Humboldt University of Berlin: Center for Interdisciplinary Sex Studies
https://www.gender.hu-berlin.de/
Rheini Friedrich William University Bonn – working group woman research
http://www.frauengeschichte.uni-bonn.de/ [in German]
University Centre for the Promotion of Women's Studies and Research on Women: Free University of Berlin
http://www.fu-berlin.de/zefrauen/en/index.html
University of Applied Sciences: Institute for Women and Gender Studies
http://www.frauenforschung.fh-kiel.de/ [in German]
University of Bielefeld : The interdisciplinary center for woman and sex research
http://www.uni-bielefeld.de/IFF/ [in German]
University of Bremen: Center for Women's Studies
http://www.zfs.uni-bremen.de/ [in German]
University of Hanover: Gender Studies
http://www.gps.uni-hannover.de/gender/ [in German]
University of Kiel: Gender Research Group
http://www.uni-kiel.de/zif/index-e.shtml

Ghana
Centre for Gender Studies and Advocacy at the University of Ghana
http://cegensa.ug.edu.gh/

Greece
Mediterranean Women's Studies Institute
http://www.kegme.org.gr/

Guatemala
Centro de Estudios de Guatemala (Center of Guatemalan Studies)
http://ceg.org.gt/index.asp

Guinea
Ministere des Affaires Sociales, de la Promotion Feminine et de l'Enfance
http://www.cauri.com/guinee/maspfe/ [in French]

Honduras

Centro de Estudios de la Mujer-Honduras (CEMH)
  http://www.cemh.org.hn/ [in Spanish]

Hungary

Center for Gender and Culture at Corvinus University
  http://gender.uni-corvinus.hu/index_en.php
Department of Gender Studies, Central European University
  http://www.ceu.hu/gend/
Gender Studies at ELTE
  http://gender.tatk.elte.hu/ [in Hungarian]
Gender Studies and Equal Opportunity Center
  http://www.uni-miskolc.hu/bolgender/english/events.htm
Institute of English and American Studies (University of Szeged)
  http://www.arts.u-szeged.hu/ieas/03-programs.html
MONA- Foundation for Women in Hungary
  http://www.mona-hungary.hu/eindex.ivy

Iceland

Center for Women's Studies, Haskola Islands University of Iceland
  http://www.rikk.hi.is/Apps/WebObjects/HI.woa/wa/dp?id=1008411

India

Centre for Development Studies
  http://www.cds.edu/
Centre for Women's Development Studies in New Dehli
  http://www.cwds.org/
Maharaja Sayajirao University Baroda: Women's Studies Research Centre
  http://www.msubaroda.ac.in/newdepartmentinfon.php?ffac_code=9&fdept_code=10
Ministry of Human Resource Development: Department of Women and Child Development
  http://wcd.nic.in/
Sakhi Women's Resource Center
  http://sakhikerala.org/
Shreemati Nathibai Damodar Thackersey Women's University (SNDT) Women's Research
Center in Mumbai
  http://sndt.digitaluniversity.ac/
South Asian Women's Network (SAWNET)
  http://www.sawnet.org/
Tamil Nadu Corporation for Development of Women
  http://www.tamilnaduwomen.org/
University of Calcutta: Centre for Women's Studies (CWS)
  http://www.caluniv.ac.in/academic/academic_frame.htm
University of Delhi: Women's Study Development Centre
  http://www.du.ac.in/centerdetails.html?center_id=Women+Study+Development+Centre

Indonesia

Atma Jaya Research Center
http://puslit.petra.ac.id/links/centre-indonesia4.htm

Iran

Center of Women and Family Affairs
http://www.women.gov.ir [in Farsi]
Institute for Women's Studies and Research
http://www.iwsr.org/en/index.html
Rahyab Institute
http://www.rahyabiran.org [in Farsi]
University of Tehran: Center for Women's Studies
http://cws.ut.ac.ir/
Women's Research Center (Alzahra University)
http://www.alzahra.ac.ir/faculty/research.htm
Women's Socio-Cultural Council
http://www.iranwomen.org/Zanan/English/home.htm
Women's Studies Group of Iran Sociology Association
http://www.isa.org.ir/framework.jsp?SID=214 [in Farsi]

Iraq

Al – Amal Iraqi Association
http://www.iraqi-alamal.org/ [in Arabic]
The Organization of Women's Freedom in Iraq
http://www.equalityiniraq.com/english.htm

Ireland

Centre for Gender and Women's Studies, University of Dublin, Trinity College
http://www.tcd.ie/cgws/research_centre/
Women's Education Research and Resource Centre (WERRC), University College, Dublin
http://www.ucd.ie/werrc/

Israel

Bar Ilan University: Gender Studies
http://www.biu.ac.il/LIB/gender.htm
Ben Gurion University – Gender Studies Program
http://www.bgu.ac.il/gender/index.html [in Hebrew]
Israel Women's Network
http://www.iwn.org.il/indexEn.asp
Knesset Committee: The Committee for the Advancement of the Status of Women
http://www.knesset.gov.il/committees/eng/committee_eng.asp?c_id=11
Tel Aviv University: The NCJW Women and Gender Studies Program
http://www.tau.ac.il/humanities/ncjw/about_us.heb.html [in Hebrew]

Italy

Centro Italiano Femminile (CIF)
http://www.cifnazionale.it/ [in Italian]

Centro Studi e Documentazione Pensiero Femminile
  http://www.pensierofemminile.org/centro.htm [in Italian]
Italian Association for Women in Development (AIDOS)
  http://www.aidos.it/ [in Italian]
Pari e Dispari, University of Milan
  http://www.pariedispari.it [in Italian]

Ivory Coast

Institute for Education of Women in Africa and the Diaspora IEWAD
  http://iewad.tripod.com/africanwomen/index.html

Jamaica

Centre for Gender and Development Studies, University of the West Indies
  http://www.uwi.edu/cgds/index.html

Japan

Aichi Shukutoku University, Institute for Gender and Women's Studies
  http://www2.aasa.ac.jp/org/igws/english/
Center for Gender Studies, International Christian University
  http://olcs.icu.ac.jp/mt/cgs/e/
Gender Law and Policy Center, Tohoku University.
  http://www.law.tohoku.ac.jp/gelapoc/
Institute for Gender and Women's Studies, Josai International University
  http://www.jiu.ac.jp/igws/index.html
Institute for Women's Studies, Ochanomizu University
  http://www.igs.ocha.ac.jp/igs/indexE.html
National Women's Education Centre (NWEC)
  http://www.nwec.jp/English/

Kenya

African Women Development and Communication Network
  http://www.femnet.or.ke/
Forum for African Women Educationalists FAWE
  http://www.fawe.org/home/index.asp

Korea, South

Asian Center for Women's Studies, Ewha Woman's University
  http://ewhawoman.or.kr/acws_eng/index.php?PHPSESSID=dca3d13e883d6a121ba
    4a2413068aa32
Center for East Asian Women & Politics
  http://www.eawp.re.kr/ [in Korean]
Hanyang Institute for Women, Hanyang University
  http://i.hanyang.ac.kr/jcommunity/index.jsp?community_id=hiwomen [in Korean]
Institute for Gender Research, Seoul National University
  http://igender.snu.ac.kr/ [in Korean]
Korean Association of Women's Studies
  http://www.kaws.or.kr/ [in Korean]

Korean Women's Institute, Ewha Woman's University
http://ewhawoman.or.kr/kwi_eng/index.php
Korean Women's Institute, Sungshin Women's University
http://www.sungshin.ac.kr/~kowoin/ [in Korean]
Korea Women's Studies Institute
http://www.kwsi.or.kr/ [in Korean]
Research Institute of Asian Women, Sookmyung Women's University
http://riaw.sookmyung.ac.kr/
The Catholic Women's Research Institute of Korea
http://songsim.catholic.ac.kr/~cwrik/index.html [in Korean]
Women's Studies Center under Pusan National University
http://mypage.pusan.ac.kr/women/index/ [in Korean]
Women's Studies Digital Information Center, Dongduk Women's University
http://210.121.133.152/women/english/center_index.html
Women's Studies Institute, Seoul Women's University
http://family.swu.ac.kr/~swsi/aboutus.htm [in Korean]

Malaysia
Asian Pacific Resource and Research Centre for Women (ARROW)
http://www.aworc.org/org/arrow/arrow.html
Women's Development Research Centre (a.k.a. KNITA), University of Science Malaysia
http://www.usm.my/kanita/

Mauritius
Ministry of Women's Rights, Child Development, and Family Welfare
http://women.gov.mu/

Mexico
Centro de Estudios des Género, Universidad de Guadalajara
http://www.cucsh.udg.mx/mxdivdep/phpdees/indexceg.php [in Spanish]
Centro de Información y Documentación Programa Universitario de Estudios de Género, UNAM-México
http://www.pueg.unam.mx/Biblioteca_v2/bib_quienes.php [in Spanish]
Centro de Investigación y Capacitación de la Mujer (CICAM)
http://www.cicam.org.gt/index.php?ID=1573 [in Spanish]
Interdisciplinary Program for Women's Studies, El Colegio de Mexico
http://piem.colmex.mx/ [in Spanish]

Mozambique
WLSA (Women and Law in Southern African Research and Education Trust)
http://www.wlsa.org.mz/

Netherlands
International Information Centre and Archives of the Women's Movement
http://www.iiav.nl/eng/index.html
Netherlands Research School of Women's Studies
http://www.genderstudies.nl/index.php?pageid=52

Nijmegen Institute for Social Cultural Research
http://www.ru.nl/socialewetenschappen/nisco/

New Zealand
Department of Women's and Gender Studies, University of Waikoto
http://www.waikato.ac.nz/wfass/subjects/societies-cultures/womens-gender-stds/
Society for Research on Women
http://www.nram.govt.nz/record.php?id=9143&parent=nramindexbyvolume&volume=Y

Nicaragua
Movimiento Autonomo de Mujeres de Nicaragua
http://www.movimientoautonomodemujeres.org/ [in Spanish]
Puntos de Encuentro
http://www.puntos.org.ni/english/

Nigeria
Center for Gender Studies, University of Benin
http://www.uniben.edu/genderstudies.html

Norway
Center for Research on Women, University of Oslo
http://www.skk.uio.no/English/frontpage.html
Nordic Institute for Women's Studies & Gender Research
http://www.nikk.uio.no/index_e.html

Pakistan
Centre of Excellence for Women's Studies, University of Karachi
http://www.uok.edu.pk/research_institutes/Women_Studies/Research_Info.php

Pan-African Research Centers
http://minfam.netangola.com/conferencia/html/introducao.htm [in Portuguese]

Panama
Centro de Estudios y Accion Socioal Panameno (CEASPA)
http://www.ceaspa.org.pa/ [in Spanish]
Centro para el Desarrollo de la Mujer (CEDEM)
http://www.cedem.cl/ [in Spanish]
Instituto De Investigaciones Y Capacitacion Para La Promocion De La Mujer
(ICAPROMUPA)
http://www.un-instraw.org/fr/index.php?option=content&task=view&id=
784&Itemid=87

Paraguay
Centro Paraguay de Estudios Sociales (CPES)
http://www.cpes.org.py/ [in Spanish]

Peru
Centro de la Mujer Peruana Flora Tristan (Flora Tristan Peruvian Women's Center)
 http://www.flora.org.pe/ [in Spanish]
Women's Documentation Centre CENDOC-Mujer
 http://www.cendoc-mujer.org.pe/lechuza.html [in Spanish]

Philippines, The
Institute of Women's Studies, St. Scholastica's College
 http://www.ssc.edu.ph/sscweb_content/iws_iwsgoals.htm
Women's Resource and Research Center, Miriam Maryknoll College Foundation, Inc.
 http://www.asha-foundation.org/

Poland
eFKa Women's Foundation
 http://www.efka.org.pl/en/
Feminoteka
 http://www.feminoteka.pl/viewpage.php?page_id=10
Fundacja OŚKA
 http://www.oska.org.pl [in Polish]
Women's Studies Centre, University of Lodz
 http://www.gender.uni.lodz.pl/enver/index.html

Portugal
Centro de Investigação e Estudos de Sociologia
 http://www.cies.iscte.pt/ [in Spanish]

Puerto Rico
Centro Interdisciplinario de Investigacion y Estudios del Genero at the Inter-American
University
 http://www.metro.inter.edu/directorio.htm
Promujeres in Cayey
 http://promujeres.cayey.upr.edu/historia.htm [in Spanish]
SaludPromujer Project
 http://www.saludpromujer.org [in Spanish]
University of Puerto Rico: Research Center on Women's Health
 http://rcmi.rcm.upr.edu/
Women's Studies Project in the University of Puerto Rico
 http://www.cayey.upr.edu/proyecto-de-estudios-de-la-mujer [in Spanish]

Russia
Center for Integration of Women's Studies, St. Petersburg University
 http://www.owl.ru/eng/women/aiwo/tsizhi.htm
Moscow Center for Gender Studies
 http://www.gender.ru/english/index.shtml

Rwanda
Forum for African Women Educationalists
http://www.fawe.org/home/index.asp

Saudi Arabia
King Abdullah University (KAUST), center for research
http://www.kaust.edu.sa/research/at-kaust.aspx

Senegal, Republic of
Association of African Women for Research and Development
http://www.afard.org/ [in French]

South Africa
Commission on Gender Equality
http://www.cge.org.za/
University of Cape Town: African Gender Institute
http://web.uct.ac.za/org/agi/
University of Pretoria: Centre for Gender Studies
http://www.gender.up.ac.za/
University of South Africa – Institute for Gender Studies
http://www.unisa.ac.za/default.asp?Cmd=ViewContent&ContentID=175
University of the Western Cape – Women's and Gender Studies Programme
http://www.uwc.ac.za/arts/gender/index.htm

Spain
Autonomous University of Madrid: Institute for Women's Studies
http://www.uam.es/otroscentros/institutomujer/default.html [in Spanish]
Basque Institute of the Woman
http://www.emakunde.es/indice_i.htm [in Spanish]
Complutensian University of Madrid: Institute of Feministas Investigations
http://www.ucm.es/info/instifem/a_investig.htm [in Spanish]
Department of Employment and Social Affairs: Canarian Institute of Women
http://www.icmujer.org/ [in Spanish]
Navarran Institute of Women
http://www.cfnavarra.es/inam/INDEX.HTM [in Spanish]
University of Alicante Centre for Women's Studies
http://www.ua.es/cem/ [in Spanish]
University of Grenada: Institute of Women's Studies
http://www.ugr.es/%7Eiem/ [in Spanish]
Women's Institute (Instituto de la Mujer) of the Ministry of Labor and Social Affairs
(Ministerio de Trabajo y Asuntos Sociales)
http://www.mtas.es/mujer/ [in Spanish]

Sweden
Center for Women Scholars and Research on Women, Stockholm University
http://www.kvinfo.su.se/ [in Swedish]

Centre for Women in Research and Working Life, Lulea University
http://www.luth.se/depts/arb/genus_tekn/index.htm [in Swedish]
Centre for Women's Studies in Lund, Lund University
http://www.genus.lu.se/o.o.i.s/4737

Switzerland
Center for Gender Studies, University of Basel
http://www.genderstudies.unibas.ch/ [in German]
Center for Women and Gender Research, University of Bern
http://www.izfg.unibe.ch/

Taiwan
Center of Research on Women, Kaohsiun Medical College
http://www.kmu.edu.tw/en
Women Research Program, Population Studies Center, National Taiwan University
http://homepage.ntu.edu.tw/~psc/e_pub.htm

Tanzania
Tanzania Gender Networking Program
http://www.tgnp.org/

Thailand
National Commission on Women's Affairs
http://web.sfc.keio.ac.jp/~thiesmey/ncwa.html
National Council of Women of Thailand
http://www.thaiwomen.or.th/ [in Chinese]

Trinidad and Tobago
Caribbean Association for Feminist Research and Action (CAFRA)
http://www.cafra.org/
Centre for Gender and Development Studies, University of the West Indies
sta.uwi.edu/cgds

Turkey
Ankara University Women's Studies Center
http://kasaum.ankara.edu.tr/index.php [in Turkish]

Uganda
Department of Women and Gender Studies Makerere University
http://www.makerere.ac.ug/womenstudies/
National Association of Women Organizations in Uganda
http://www.nawou.interconnection.org/

United Kingdom
Cambridge University Centre for Gender Studies
http://www.gender.cam.ac.uk/

Centre for Gender & Religions Research
  http://www.soas.ac.uk/academics/centres/grr/centre-for-gender-and-religions-
    research.html
Center for the Study of Women and Gender
  http://www2.warwick.ac.uk/fac/soc/sociology/gender/
Institute for Feminist Theory and Research
  http://www.iftr.org.uk/
LSE Gender Institute – Research Institute and Graduate Programs in Gender Studies
  http://www.lse.ac.uk/collections/genderInstitute/

Uruguay

Comité de América Latina y el Caribe para la Defensa de los Derechos de la Mujer
(CLADEM)
  http://www.cladem.org/espanol/nacionales/uruguay/uycddapoyo.asp [in Spanish]
Red de Educación Popular entre Mujeres (REPEM)
  http://www.repem.org.uy/ [in Spanish]

Venezuela

Universidad Central de Venezuela – Centro de Estudios de la Mujer
  http://www.ucv.ve/cem/ [in Spanish]

Yugoslavia

Belgrade Women's Studies Center
  http://www.zenskestudie.edu.yu/pages/about.htm
Gender Training and Research Centre
  http://www.gtrcenter.org/

Zimbabwe

Ministry of Youth Development, Gender & Employment Creation
  http://www.mydgec.gov.zw/
Women of Zimbabwe Arise Action Group
  http://wozazimbabwe.org/
Zimbabwe Women's Resource Centre & Network
  http://www.zwrcn.org.zw/

CONTRIBUTORS

Edna Acosta-Belén is a Distinguished Professor of Latin American, Caribbean, and U.S. Latino Studies, with a joint appointment in the Department of Women's Studies, at the University at Albany, State University of New York (SUNY) in the United States. She is editor and co-founder of the *Latino(a) Research Review*. Her publications are in the areas of Hispanic Caribbean, Puerto Rican, and U.S. Latino(a) cultural studies and women's studies. She is the editor of the volume *The Puerto Rican Woman: Perspectives on Culture, History, and Society* and co-edited with Christine E. Bose the volumes *Researching Women in Latin America and the Caribbean* and *Women in the Latin American Development Process*.

Akosua Adomako Ampofo is an Associate Professor at the Institute of African Studies and Head of the Centre for Gender Studies and Advocacy at the University of Ghana, Legon. She is the recipient of several international awards and has been co-convenor of the Women's Caucus of the African Studies Association (2004–2006), and member of the Ghana AIDS Commission. Her current scholarship and activism focus on gender in higher education, constructions of masculinity and femininity, and gender-based violence. She is currently working on a co-edited volume (with Signe Arnfred) titled, *Paid by the Piper and Playing the Tune? Tensions, Challenges and Possibilities in African Feminist Research and Scholarship*.

Josephine Beoku-Betts is an Associate Professor of Women's Studies and Sociology at Florida Atlantic University in the United States. She has been Book Review co-editor for *Gender & Society*, regional co-editor of *Women's Studies International Forum*, the U.S. representative for the RC 32 Committee of the International Sociological Association, and is a member of the Editorial Board of the *Journal of African and Asian Studies*. Her recent research focuses on the educational and career experiences of African women scientists. She co-edited *Women and Education in Sub-Saharan Africa: Power, Opportunities and Constraints* and published articles in journals including *Gender & Society*, *Meridians*, *NWSA Journal*, *Journal of African and Asian Studies*, *Journal of Women and Minorities in Science and Engineering*.

Solveig Bergman is Director of the Nordic Institute for Women's Studies and Gender Research (NIKK) in Oslo, Norway. Previously, she was the first Nordic Coordinator for Women's Studies and a researcher–teacher in sociology and women's studies at Åbo Akademi University in Finland, and she served as President of the Finnish Association of Women's Studies. Her publications focus on women's movements in Finland and Germany, new social movements in the Nordic countries, gender and politics, Nordic childcare policies, and the institutionalization of women's studies in Nordic countries.

Kristen Bini is a Ph.D. student in French Studies at the University at Albany, SUNY in the United States. Her research interest is in Francophone literature, specifically immigrant writing. She is currently a lecturer of French at Siena College in Albany, New York.

Christine E. Bose is a Professor of Sociology, with joint appointments in the Department of Women's Studies and the Department of Latin American, Caribbean, and U.S. Latino Studies at the University at Albany, SUNY in the United States. She has been the President of Sociologists for Women in Society (2006) and Editor of the journal *Gender & Society* (2000–2003). She has published seven books in the areas of women's paid and unpaid employment in the U.S. and in Latin America, the most recent of which is *Global Dimensions of Gender and Carework* (with Zimmerman and Litt 2006).

Sunita Bose is an Assistant Professor of Sociology and an active member of the Asian Studies Program at State University of New York at New Paltz in the United States. A native of India, her undergraduate degree in Economics is from the University of Calcutta. Her substantive areas of interest include gender and families with a regional focus on South Asia. Her current research includes fieldwork in India on girl's education, as well as other research on gender discrimination, marriage and families, and HIV/AIDS in India.

Marta Castillo (Marta Merajver-Kurlat) is an Argentinian trained psychoanalyst with a degree in literature and translation, and is a winner of the 2004 Dunken Poetry Prize. She lectures at several psychoanalytic institutions in Buenos Aires, and has translated over thirty major works from and into Spanish, *El hombre que inventó a Fidel* by American journalist Anthony DePalma, among others. Her first novel, *Gracias por la muerte*, was published in 2006 and translated into English under the title *Just Toss the Ashes* in 2007. Her latest book, *El Ulises de James Joyce: una lectura posible* (2008) intends to guide readers through the Joycean labyrinth.

Esther Ngan-ling Chow is a Professor of Sociology at the American University in Washington, D.C., in the United States. Her major research interests are in the intersectionality of race/ethnicity, class, gender and sexuality, work and family, social inequality, migration and citizenship, gender and development, globalization, transnationalism and social change, economic sociology, feminist theory and pedagogy, policy studies, and Chinese and Asian American studies. She is a feminist activist and scholar and her major publications include *Women, the Family, and Policy: A Global Perspective, Race, Class and Gender: Common Bonds, Different Voices*, and *Transforming Gender and Development in East Asia*. She has co-edited special issues of *Race, Class and Gender* and *Gender & Society*, and guest-edited "Globalization, Gender, and Social Change in the 21st Century" in *International Sociology*. She has a forthcoming co-edited volume, *Women and Citizenship in Local/Global World*.

Alice E. Colón Warren is a researcher and sociologist, working at the Social Science Research Center of the University of Puerto Rico, Río Piedras. She has coordinated various feminist academic projects, was Co-chair of the Gender and Feminist Studies Section of the Latin

American Studies Association (2004–2006), and has published in the areas of women's employment and poverty, and reproductive health and rights.

Elizabeth Crespo-Kebler is a Professor of Sociology at the University of Puerto Rico at Bayamón and Dean of Academic Affairs at the Centro de Estudios Avanzados de Puerto Rico y el Caribe in San Juan, Puerto Rico. She publishes and teaches in the areas of gender, sexuality, race, ethnicity and feminism in Latin America and the Caribbean. She is currently working on the second volume of her work on feminist activism in Puerto Rico.

Thi Minh An Dao is lecturer and Doctor of Philosophy in the Faculty of Public Health, Epidemiology Department at the Hanoi Medical University in Vietnam. She is also a researcher in HIV/AIDS Studies at the Centre for Research and Training on HIV/AIDS. She has conducted research on injected drug users, youth at risk, models of HIV counseling, testing and referral in rehabilitation centers, gender and HIV/AIDS, and medical education. Her research interests also include global gender issues, tobacco smoking among health professionals and medical students, second-hand smoking, risk behaviors and HIV/AIDS, and behavior change communication.

Akosua K. Darkwah is an Assistant Professor of Sociology at the University of Ghana. She serves on various committees of the Centre for Gender Studies and Advocacy at that institution and her research interests include gender, sexuality, globalization, and the changing nature of work in the African context.

Manisha Desai is the Director of Women's Studies and an Associate Professor of Sociology at the University of Connecticut in the United States. She served as the President of SWS (2007), was the senior program specialist in the Gender, Equity, and Development Section at UNESCO in Paris, and has served as the SWS representative to the U.N.'s ECOSOC in New York City. Her areas of research include gender and globalization, transnational feminisms, and contemporary Indian society.

Graciela Di Marco is a Professor of Democratization, Citizenship, and Human Rights at the Humanities School and Director of the Center of Studies on Democratization and Human Rights at the Universidad Nacional de San Martín in Buenos Aires, Argentina. She has organized and co-ordinates a Master's Degree in Human Rights and Social Policies, based on Gender Equality and Children's Rights. She has been a guest lecturer at Emory University, Vassar College, the University of Maryland, Toronto University and Hunter College (NY). Her current research is on the impact of participation in social movements and the development of rights discourses and practices among women and men. She has served as Co-chair of the section on Gender and Feminist Studies in the Latin American Studies Association (LASA).

Ana C. Escalante is a Full Professor Emeritus and researcher on Gender, Organizational Change and Leadership at the University of Costa Rica. She serves as a consultant in the fields of gender, human rights, cultural diversity and human development for national and international organizations such as the Inter-American Institute for Human Rights; the International Union for the Conservation of Nature; the National Institute for the Advancement of Women; the United Nations Development Program; and UNIFEM. She is a member of the Editorial Board of the *Social Science Review* at the University of Costa Rica.

Shahla Ezazi is a Professor of Sociology and Women's Studies at Alame Tabatabaee University located in Tehran, Iran. She is the president of Women's Studies Group of the Iranian Sociology Association (since 2000), a scientific member of the Family Research Institute of the Ministry of Education (1997), board member of the Iran Sociology Association (1998–2000), and a board member of Independent Researchers on Women's Issues (2000). She edited a special issue of the *Journal of Education* on gender education. She has published in the areas of family, socialization process in the family and the educational system, and family violence in Iran.

Eva Fodor is an Associate Professor of Gender Studies at the Central European University in Budapest, Hungary. Her work explores how the meaning, ideology, practice, and social consequences of women's work change under shifting social conditions. Her first book, *Working Difference: Women's Working Lives in Hungary and Austria, 1945–1995*, theorizes the differences between state socialist and capitalist gender regimes of paid work. She has conducted research on the feminization of poverty in post socialism, and currently is working on a project that explores social and gender inequalities in work, leisure, and political participation in a comparative international context.

Lydia Gregg holds a faculty position as the divisional Medical Illustrator and Research Associate of Interventional Neuro-radiology at The Johns Hopkins University School of Medicine in Baltimore, Maryland in the United States. She provided the cover illustration for this volume. Her research, illustrations, and animations focus on vascular malformations, interventional treatments, and effective design of electronically distributed patient education for parents of pediatric patients. She also is the proud niece of this volume's co-editor, Christine E. Bose.

Jacqueline Hayes is a doctoral student in the Department of Latin American, Caribbean, and U.S. Latino Studies at the University at Albany, SUNY in the United States. She is the recipient of the University's Bread and Roses Award for her activism in the "Killer-Coke Campaign" to persuade the University not to renew its contract with Coca Cola because of its history of human rights violations against Latin American workers and their communities.

Maria Luiza Heilborn is a Professor at the Institute of Social Medicine, State University of Rio de Janeiro in Brazil, where she coordinates the Latin American Center on Sexuality and Human Rights and the program on Gender, Sexuality, and Health. Her academic work has focused on issues of gender, sexuality, youth, and family.

Minjeong Kim is an Assistant Professor of Women's Studies at Virginia Tech (Virginia Polytechnic Institute and State University) in the United States. She was a 2007 Woodrow Wilson Dissertation Fellow in Women's Studies for her dissertation research on "Gendering Marriage Migration and Fragmented Citizenship Formation: 'Korean' wives from the Philippines." Her research interests include global gender issues, international migration and family, Asian American Studies, and the Mass Media.

Gundrun-Axeli Knapp is a Professor of Sociology and Social Psychology at the Institute of Sociology and Social Psychology, Leibniz University of Hannover, Germany. She is also Director of the Interdisciplinary Program in Gender Studies at the Faculty of Philosophy.

She has published articles on feminist issues in various journals and books and has edited and co-authored several books on developments in international feminist theory, with a focus on social theory and interlocking structures of inequality and dominance.

Insook Kwon is an Associate Professor in the College of Basic Studies at Myongji University in South Korea, where she teaches Women's Studies. She has published a book, *South Korea is the Military: Peace, Militarism and Masculinity with Gender Perspective*, and several articles about militarism, sexual violence and masculinities, including the most recent one on "Sexual Violence among Men in the Military in South Korea" (*Journal of Interpersonal Violence*). Currently, she is working on several new projects: militarized college culture, female conscription, and conscientious objectors.

Emanuela Lombardo is *Ramón y Cajal* researcher at the Department of Political Science and Public Administration at the Complutense University in Madrid, Spain, and a researcher in the European QUING (FP6) and TARGET (Atlantis) projects. Her research and publications concern theoretical and empirical aspects of gender equality policies, especially in the European Union and Spain. She is co-editor (with Petra Meier and Mieke Verloo) of *The Discursive Politics of Gender Equality. Stretching, Bending and Policymaking*.

Joanna Mizielińska is an Assistant Professor at the Institute for Sociology at the Warsaw School for Social Psychology, where she also teaches gender and queer studies. She has been a CIMO researcher at the Christina Institute in Helsinki University (2004–2005) and a Fulbright Scholar at Princeton University (2001–2002). She is author of *(De)Contructions of Femininity* (2004) and *Gender/Body/Sexuality: From Feminism to Queer Theory* (2007). She has contributed articles to several journals, including *The European Journal of Women's Studies, Respublica Nova, OŚKA, Pelnym Glosem, Katedra, Przegl12d Filozoficzno-Literacki, Pogranicza, Czas Kultury*, and *Krytyka Polityczna*.

Van Huy Nguyen works as a lecturer and researcher in the Faculty of Public Health at Hanoi Medical University in Vietnam. He holds a Medical Doctor Degree from Hanoi Medical University. He has significant experience and expertise in conducting quantitative, qualitative, and interpretive research across the broad field of population, health, public health, social issues, gender, and human development including HIV. He has been a consultant in projects/NGOs both locally and internationally, and with governmental agencies. He obtained several research and academic awards for his work and publications.

Wairimũ Ngarũiya Njambi is Associate Professor of Women's Studies and Sociology at the Harriet L. Wilkes Honors College, Florida Atlantic University in the United States. Her research and teaching areas include science and technology studies, feminist science studies, postcolonial studies, cultural studies, and critical race and sexuality studies. Her work has appeared in edited collections such as *Burden or Benefit? Imperial Benevolence and its Legacies and African Gender Studies*, and in journals such as *Feminist Theory, NWSA Journal, Meridians, Gender & Society, Critical Sociology*, and *Australian Feminist Studies*.

Marta Núñez Sarmiento is a sociologist, professor, and researcher at the Center for Studies of International Migrations at the University of Havana in Cuba. She teaches Methodology of Sociological Research, Gender Relations in Cuba, and Gender and Knowledge. Her research and publications deal with gender relations in Cuba, mainly in employment, ideology, and international migrations, as well as with the application of a gender approach to political discourses.

Mary Johnson Osirim is Professor and Chair of the Department of Sociology, Co-Director of the Center for International Studies, and Faculty Diversity Liaison at Bryn Mawr College in the United States. Her teaching and research interests focus on gender and development, race and ethnic relations, immigration, the family and economic sociology in Sub-Saharan Africa, the English-Speaking Caribbean, and the United States. During the past twenty years, she has conducted fieldwork on women, entrepreneurship and the roles of the state and non-governmental organizations in the microenterprise sectors of Nigeria and Zimbabwe and published extensively in this area including the book, *Enterprising Women in Zimbabwe: Identity, the State and Globalization* (forthcoming 2009). Her current research project examines transnationalism, civil society, and urban redevelopment among African immigrants in the northeastern U.S.

Conceição Osório is a feminist, presently conducting research for the Mozambique-based regional organization, Women and Law in Southern Africa (WLSA), which fights for women's human rights, focusing on their legal protection in African society. Until 2007, she was a Professor of Research Methods in the Social Sciences at Eduardo Mondlane University in Maputo, Mozambique. She has published several works based on research in various provinces and districts of Mozambique, and in 2007 published "Subverting Political Power?" a gender analysis of the 2004 legislative elections in Mozambique.

Bandana Purkayastha is Associate Professor of Sociology and Asian American Studies at the University of Connecticut in the United States. She has published more than 25 journal articles and chapters on race, gender, immigration, and human rights issues. Her books are *The Power of Women's Informal Networks: Lessons in Social Change in South Asia and West Africa* (2004, with Mangala Subramaniam), *Negotiating Ethnicity: Second-Generation South Asian Americans Traverse a Transnational World* (2006), *Living Our Religions: Hindu and Muslim South Asian American Women Narrate their Experiences* (2008, with Anjana Narayan), and *Armed Conflict and Conflict Resolution: Sociological Perspectives* (with Giuseppe Caforio, and Gerhard Kuemmel, forthcoming 2008). She currently serves on the Executive Board of Research Committee-1 on Armed Forces and Conflict Resolution, as well as RC-32 on Women in Society of the International Sociological Association. She is Deputy Editor of *Gender & Society*.

Rhoda Reddock is Professor and Head of the Centre for Gender and Development Studies at the University of the West Indies, St. Augustine campus. She is a founder of the Caribbean Association for Feminist Research and Action (CAFRA) and a former president of Research Committee-32 (Women and Society) of the International Sociological Association. She is an editor of the *Journal of Latin American Ethnic Studies*, and has researched and published in the areas of women's labor and labor movement activism, feminism and women's movements, gender and environment, Caribbean masculinities, gender, ethnicity and identity and most recently gender and sexualities.

Yaser S. Robles is a Ph.D. student in the Department of Latin American, Caribbean, and U.S. Latino Studies at the University at Albany, SUNY in the United States. He teaches a course on the Cultures of Latin America. His dissertation work deals with the Honduran invisibility in the Central American 1970s/1980s conflict. Other research interests include police brutality in Brazil, and peace negotiations and conflict resolution.

Montserrat Sagot is Professor of Sociology and Women's Studies at the University of Costa Rica. She has been Director of the Regional Master's Program in Women's Studies (1995–2001), Associate Dean for Graduate Studies (2002–2004) and member of the University Council (2004–2008). She is the author of *The Critical Path of Women Affected by Family Violence in Latin America: Case Studies from 10 Countries* (2000) and co-author of *Femicidio en Costa Rica: 1990–1999* (2001).

Udoy Sankar Saikia is the Associate Director of Population Studies Programme at Flinders University, South Australia. His area of research broadly covers population, gender, and development issues with a special focus on developing countries. His current research and publications focus on women's empowerment and fertility relationships in transitional societies, such as Timor Leste, and in various ethnic communities in India. He worked as an international consultant for UNDP (United Nations Development Programme) and Oxfam.

Ki-young Shin is an Associate Professor in the Institute for Gender Studies and the School of Humanities and Social Sciences at Ochanomizu University in Japan. Her research interests include comparative women's legal mobilizations, feminist analysis of the state and family laws, and transnational women's activisms in East Asian countries. She publishes in English, Japanese and Korean journals.

Fatou Sow is a Senegalese Professor of Sociology and is Research Director of Habilitation (University Paris Denis Diderot, France). She spent her career at the University Cheikh Anta Diop (Senegal) and the University Paris-Diderot/CNRS (France). She researched, published, and taught on African Sociology and about women and gender relations in African societies and cultures and related issues. Professor Sow is a member of several research and activist organizations, including DAWN (Development Alternatives with Women for a New Era). She is the current Coordinator of Women Living under Muslim Laws Solidarity Network.

Mangala Subramaniam is an Associate Professor of Sociology and affiliated faculty member of Women's Studies at Purdue University, West Lafayette in the United States. Her main interests and publications are in the areas of gender, social movements (including transnational movements), and international political economy. She is currently working on a project on HIV/AIDS and gender in India.

Eulália Temba is a feminist teacher, psychologist, and activist in the women's movement in Mozambique. She is the President of WLSA-Mozambique, and is currently working as a manager of Social Community Development at Sasol, a South African petrochemical company working on the exploration of natural gas. Sasol has a social department that supports the development of communities living around their operations. Some of the department's social initiatives include the building of schools and clinics, supplying potable water, and the development of job creation projects.

Celia Valiente is an Associate Professor in the Department of Political Science and Sociology at the Universidad Carlos III de Madrid in Spain. Her main research interests are gender equality policies and the women's movement in Spain from a comparative perspective. She has published articles in *Gender & Society*, *European Journal of Political Research*, *Politics & Gender*, and *South European Society & Politics*. Her most recent books are *Gendering Spanish Democracy* (with Monica Threlfall and Christine Cousins 2005) and *El feminismo de estado en España: El Instituto de la Mujer (1983–2003)* [State Feminism in Spain: The Women's Institute (1983–2003)] (2006).

Eszter Varsa is an advanced Ph.D. student in the Department of Gender Studies of the Central European University in Budapest, Hungary. Her Ph.D. research focuses on the social history of residential care for children during the early communist period in Hungary. She is interested in exploring how social inequalities along the lines of gender, race, and class are recreated and reproduced in social policy.

Wang Jinling is a Professor of Sociology, Director of the Sociology Institute and the Center of Women of Family Studies at Zhejiang Academy of Social Sciences in China. She also was the first director of the Department of Women's Studies at the Women's College of China—the first Department of Women's Studies in China. Her research has focused on gender sociology, women sex workers, women and crime, and women in rural development. She is working on a project, "Research on Trafficking Women in Mainland China," and recently concluded a project on "Women's Crime and Social Change in Contemporary China," supported by the National Social Sciences Foundation of China. She has published the books *Women Sociology: Research and Experience in Mainland China*, *Women, Family and Policy—Global Perspectives* (translated from English), and the textbook *Women Sociology*.

Naihua Zhang is an Associate Professor of Sociology at Florida Atlantic University in the United States. Her research and publications are in the areas of social movements and gender and development, in particular, the contemporary women's movement and women's organizations in China.

REPRINT PERMISSION LIST

SECTION 1: AFRICA

3. Beoku-Betts, Josephine, Akosua Adomako Ampofo, Wairimũ Ngarũiya Njambi, and Mary Osirim "Women's and Gender Studies in English Speaking Sub-Saharan Africa: A Review of Research in the Social Sciences," *Gender & Society* 18 (6): 685–714. Copyright © 2004 by the Sage Publications, Inc. Used by permission of the Sage Publications and the authors.

4. Darkwah, Akosua K. "Trading Goes Global: Ghanaian Market Women in an Era of Globalization," *Asian Women* 15: 31–49. Copyright © 2002 by the Research Institute of Asian Women. Used by permission of RIAW and the author.

5. Conceição Osório and Eulália Temba "A justiça no feminine" in *Conflito e Transformação Social: Uma Paisagem das Justiças em Moçambique, Vol II*, edited by B.S. Santos and J. C. Trindade. Copyright © 2003 by Afrontamento. Used by permission of Afrontamento and the authors. [Translated from Portuguese by Yaser S. Robles.]

6. Fatou Sow "Les femmes, L'État et le sacré" in *L'Islam politique au Sud du Sahara. Identités, discours et enjeux*, edited by Muriel Gomez-Perez. Copyright © 2005 by Karthala Editions. Used by permission of Karthala and the author. [Translated from French by Kristen Bini.]

SECTION 2: ASIA AND THE MIDDLE EAST

8. Esther Ngan-ling Chow, Naihua Zhang, and Wang Jinling "Promising and Contested Fields: Women's Studies and Sociology of Women/Gender in Contemporary China," *Gender & Society* 18 (2): 161–188. Copyright © 2004 by the Sage Publications, Inc. Used by permission of the Sage Publications and the authors.

9. Bandana Purkayastha, Manisha Desai, Mangala Subramaniam, and Sunita Bose "The Study of Gender in India: A Partial Review," *Gender & Society* 17 (4): 503–524. Copyright © 2003 by the Sage Publications, Inc. Used by permission of the Sage Publications and the authors.

11. Insook Kwon "Hegemonic Masculinity and Conscription: Focusing on the Masculinity of KATUSA (Korean Augmentation to the U.S. Army)," *Korean Journal of Women's Studies* 21 (2): 223–253. Copyright © 2006 by the Journal of Korean Women's Studies. Used by permission of the Journal of Korean Women's Studies and the author.

12. Van Huy Nguyen, Udoy Sankar Saikia and Thi Minh An Dao "Gender, Development and HIV/AIDS in Vietnam: Towards an Alternative Response Model among Women Sex Workers," *Asian Journal of Women's Studies* 14 (1): 98–119. Copyright © 2008 by the Ewha Womans University Press. Used by permission of the Asian Center for Women's Studies, Ewha Womans University Press and the authors.

13. Ki-young Shin "*Fufubessei* Movement in Japan: Thinking About Women's Resistance and Subjectivity," *F-GENS Journal* 2: 107–114. Copyright © 2004 by the *F-GENS Journal*. Used by permission of the *F-GENS Journal* and the author.

SECTION 3: LATIN AMERICA AND THE CARIBBEAN

16. Alice E. Colón Warren "Puerto Rico: Feminism and Feminist Studies," *Gender & Society* 17 (5): 664–690. Copyright © 2003 by the Sage Publications, Inc. Used by permission of the Sage Publications and the author.

17. Marta Núñez Sarmiento "Gender Studies in Cuba: Methodological Approaches, 1974–2001," *Gender & Society* 17 (1): 7–32. Copyright © 2003 by the Sage Publications, Inc. Used by permission of the Sage Publications and the author.

20. Maria Luiza Heilborn "Entre as Tramas da Sexualidade Brasileira," *Estudos Feministas, Florianópolis* 14 (1): 43–59. Copyright © 2006 by the Revista Estudos Feministas. Used by permission of Revista Estudos Feministas and the author. [Translated from Portuguese by Yaser S. Robles.]

21. Elizabeth Crespo-Kebler "Ciudadanía y nación: Debates sobre los derechos reproductivos en Puerto Rico," *Revista de Ciencias Sociales, Nueva Época* 10: 57–84. Copyright © 2001 by *Revista de Ciencias Sociales*. Used by permission of *Revista de Ciencias Sociales* and the author.

SECTION 4: EUROPE

24. Celia Valiente "An Overview of Research on Gender in Spanish Society," *Gender & Society* 16 (6): 767–792. Copyright © 2002 by the Sage Publications, Inc. Used by permission of the Sage Publications and the author.

26. Joanna Mizielińska " 'The Rest is Silence . . .': Polish Nationalism and the Question of Lesbian Existence," *European Journal of Women's Studies* 8 (3): 281–297. Copyright © 2001 by the Sage Publications, Inc. Used by permission of the Sage Publications and the author.

27. Solveig Bergman "Collective Organizing and Claim Making on Childcare in Norden:

INDEX

abandoned women 51, 53, 54, 99
abortion 19–20, 179; Puerto Rico 189, 249–50
Abrahams report 43
academic positioning 77–9
academics/academia: conflict and cooperation
  with feminist activists in Central America 156,
  158–77; Hungary 293–4; India 103–4; linkages
  between feminist activism and 1–3, 5–6; *see
  also* women's studies
Acevedo, L. del A. 186
activism 210; feminist *see* feminist activism;
  student 265
Adamik, M. 302
advancement of women, men's reactions to 286–7
advocacy 21, 115
affirmative action Africa 12, 26, 31, 32; quotas
  31, 166, 298
Afghanistan 331
Africa 5, 11–15; English-speaking Sub-Saharan
  Africa 16–40; *see also under individual
  countries*
African Charter on Human and People's Rights
  23, 31, 62
African Journal of Reproductive Health 19
African Platform for Action 17
African Union 7, 11, 62
agenda-setting approach to gender mainstreaming
  323, 324
agriculture 28
Alame Tabatabee University 114
Alexander, J. 226–7
Alfonso, J.C. 202, 204
All-China Women's Federation (ACWF) 71, 73,
  74, 76–7, 81, 82, 83, 86–7; Institute of
  Women's Studies (WSIC) 74, 78, 87
All India Democratic Women's Association
  (AIDWA) 71, 97
Almanac of Chinese Women's Studies 87
Alvarez, S. 170

Ampolo, A. 19
anal sex 246
Annual of Sociology 78, 79
anthropology: masculinity in Spain 286; view of
  sexuality 239–41
anti-abortion activism 252
anti-Americanism 125–32
anti-Westernization 94
Anttonen, A. 318–19
Argentina 331–2; trade unions and women's
  labor rights 156, 231–8
Armed Forces Revolutionary Council (AFRC) 43
Ashwood Garvey, A. 217
Asia 67–72; financial crisis 45; *see also under
  individual countries*
Asociación de Meretrices de la Argentina
  (AMMAR) 232, 233
Asociación de Trabajadores del Estado (ATE)
  231, 232, 234, 235
Association of African Women for Research and
  Development (AAWORD) 16, 25
Australia 332
Austria 262
authoritarian government 278, 279, 281
autonomous women's groups: India 98, 99–100;
  Puerto Rico 248
axes of difference 272–4

Bachelet, M. 154
Baerga, M. del C. 185
Bailey, A. 217
bandwagon, jumping on the 170
BAOBAB for Women's Human Rights 32
Barbados 332
Barcia, M. del C. 204, 206, 207
Barriteau, E. 222, 223
Basic Law (Mozambique) 49
Becker-Schmidt, R. 267–8
Beckles, H. 225

Beer, U. 264
Beijing World Conference on Women (1995) 71, 74, 75, 84, 112, 167, 323; Cuban Government Plan of Action 199
Beinssen-Hesse, S. 264
Belgium 258, 332
Benin 332
Benjamin, S. 28
Bielefeld School of social history 266
Biological Dictionary of Women's Movements and Feminisms 301
birth control 61, 188–9, 251–2
birth rates 259–60
body 300–1
Bolivia 332
Bollobás, E. 293
Bologna process 294
Botswana 15, 32
Bourdieu, P. 197
bourgeois capitalist society 263
Bradford, H. 20
brain drain 14
Brazil 5, 333; sexuality 156, 239–47
Bublitz, H. 267, 271
Bulgaria 333
Burrows, A. 295

Cabellero, J.A. 206
Camacho, L. 166
Campuzano, L. 203, 204
Canada 333–4
capacity building 139
capitalism 2; gender relations in capitalist modernity 263–5
Caribbean 151–7; English-speaking 155–6, 215–30; *see also under individual countries*
Caribbean Association for Feminist Research and Action (CAFRA) 155, 190, 218
Caribbean Studies Association (CSA) 154
Caribbean Women's Association (CARIWA) 217–18
Caribbean Women's Association (CWA) 217–18
case-based research 97–8
Casey, G.J. 186
Casey, J. 207
Castañeda, D. 202, 204
Catholicism 5, 180; Catholic universities 162; Poland 258, 309, 310–13
Center for Gender and Culture, Corvinus University 296
Center for Gender and Development Studies (UWI) 218, 227

Center for International Development, Beijing University 80
Center for Studies on Women, Cuba 200
Center for Women's Studies Research, University of Costa Rica 163
Central America 156, 158–77; *see also under individual countries*
Central American Women 161
Central European University 293; Department of Gender Studies 296
Cerwonka, A. 295
Chacha, K. 24
Charter of Fundamental Rights (CFR) 325
child abuse 51–2
child care 259–60, 315–22
child prostitution 30
children: discrimination against illegitimate children 141, 146; impact of HIV/AIDS on 136
Chile 334
China 67, 68, 71, 73–91, 334–5
China Women's College 77
Chinese Academy of Social Sciences (CASS) 73, 75, 78, 79, 86; Institute of Sociology 78
Chinese Communist Party (CCP) 74, 75, 81, 82, 83
Chinese Society for Women's Studies (CSWS) 71, 75, 84
'Chinese Women and Development – Status, Health and Employment' conference 84
Chinese Women's News 75, 84
Chinese Women's Research Society (CWRS) 86, 87
citizenship: Puerto Rico 248–54; rights 166–7
Ciudad Juárez 154
civil code: Japan 142; Senegal 56–7, 59–60
class 25, 83, 274; Puerto Rico 183–4
Coca-Cola 151
cohabitation: Caribbean 220–1; Japan 145–6
Cold War era 68, 69
Collection of Women's Studies 75, 84
Colombia 335
colonialism 67, 151, 259; Africa 11, 14, 21, 25, 28; Brazil 241–2; and education 25; Puerto Rico 248, 250; Senegal 56–7, 58
comfort women 69
Commission on the Status of Women (CSW) 3, 6
commissioned research 17, 296
communism: Hungary 292–3, 294, 302–3; *see also* Chinese Communist Party (CCP)
community 94–5
community courts 49, 53
comparative research 279
compiled data 97

condoms 135, 138
Confederación General del Trabajo (CGT) 231–2, 232, 235, 236; women's areas 233–4
Confederación de Trabajadores de la Educación (CTERA) 231, 232, 234, 235
conflict management 52–4
Congo (Republic) 335
Congreso de Trabajadores Argentinos (CTA) 231, 232–3, 235, 236; women's areas 233–4
consciousness-raising 83
Consejo Superior Universitario de Centroamérica (CSUCA) 161
consensus theories 114
constitution: EU constitution-making process 323–30; Poland 311, 312–13
Constitutional Revolution (Iran) 110
content analysis 208
contraception 61, 188–9, 251–2
Convention on the Elimination of All Forms of Discrimination Against Women (CEDAW) 22–3, 31–2, 70, 158, 199
Costa Rica 159–60, 161, 162, 163, 335; current trends in women's and gender studies 164–8
Costa Rican Women's Movement, The: A Reader 168
Cott, N.F. 147
Council for the Development of Social Science Research in Africa (CODESRIA) 12
creole universe 226
Crespo Kebler, E. 184
Crichlow, W. 227
critical theory 261, 266, 267–8
Cuba 155, 196–214, 335
cultural obstinacy 269–70
cultural relativism 94
culture 33; analysis of violence in India 103–4; feminization of 271; *fufubessei* groups as cultural space 143–5; KATUSA, masculinity and 126–8; spread of HIV/AIDS in Vietnam 135
currency devaluations 47
curriculum 281
Cyprus 335
Czech Republic 335

dahira 58, 63
decision making: families in Spain 280; women's representation in EU 327
delays, justice system and 53
demand-side analysis 283
democracy 58
Denmark 316, 319, 320, 336
deserted women 51, 53, 54, 99

Developing China's Women/Gender Studies Project 77
Development Alternatives with Women for a New Era (DAWN) 190
developing countries, fieldwork in 95
developmentalism 18
Diallo, A. 23
diaspora 71; Iranian scholars 120–2
Dietrich, G. 98–9, 100–1
difference: axes of difference from a socio-theoretical perspective 272–4; gender, ethnicity and in the Caribbean 222–4
Dignas, Las (*Mujeres por la Dignidad y la Vida*) 162
Diouf, A. 58, 59
discipline building 75, 76–7, 86
discourse analysis 182
dissemination of research 4–5, 287
diversity 259; in the Caribbean 215–16
Division for the Advancement of Women (DAW) 3
division of labor: global 153–4; within families 280
divorce: Japan 146–7; Mozambique 51, 52
Djibouti 3336
'Doi moi' reform policy 134–5
Dölling, I. 267, 269–70
Dombos, T. 300
domestic violence 21–2: India 102–3, 103, 104; Iran 119; *see also* violence against women
Domínguez, M.I. 201–2
Dominican Republic 336
donor-driven research 17, 296
dowry deaths 102, 103–4
Du, Fangqin 77, 85, 88

economic conditions 4, 5, 167
economic development 185–7
economic reform 134–5
Ecuador 336
education: Africa 13–14, 25–7; Cuba 199; level and opinions on sexuality in Brazil 243–6; Senegal 59; Spain 281–2; Vietnam 137–8
Egypt 336
El Salvador 161, 162
electivism 206
Elias, N. 239
empowerment 12–13
Enchautegui, M. 186
'*Encuentro Mesoamericano de Estudios de Género*' 162
'Engendering China' conference 84

English/American language and literature departments 295–6
English-speaking Caribbean 155–6, 215–30
English-speaking Sub-Saharan Africa 16–40
epistemological bases of gender research 94
Eritrea 336
ethnicity *see* race/ethnicity
Europe 257–60, 273–4; *see also under individual countries*
European Union (EU) 257, 258, 294, 297; gender mainstreaming 258, 323–30
excision 59; *see also* female genital mutilation
exclusion of lesbians 309–10, 313
exploitation 100
export-oriented industrialization (EOI) 68
Ezazi, S. 118

Fábián, K. 299
family 70, 165, 207; Caribbean 220; impact of HIV/AIDS in Vietnam 136; Mozambique 50; Puerto Rico 187–8; Spain 280–1
family honour 286
family law: Iran 115; reform movement in Japan 141–8; Senegal 58, 59–62
family name 70; Japan 70, 141–8
Fasl-e Zanan 118
fathers' quotas 319–20
Federal Republic of Germany (FRG) 257, 262, 268–9
Federation of Cuban Women 155, 199, 205
female genital mutilation 21, 23, 59, 119
female-headed families 186
femininity discourse, China 83
feminism: Caribbean feminist scholarship 218–21; Iran 114, 116–17; and Marxist theory in China 80–5, 88; motivations of Cuban researchers 204; and nationalism in Puerto Rico 248–50; new generation 221; research approaches 4–5; and roots of gender scholarship in India 94; as a social movement 170–2
feminist activism 6; Africa 16, 31; conflict and cooperation with academics in Central America 156, 158–77; India 98–101; linkages with academic women's studies/gender research 1–3, 5–6; Spain 284; *see also* women's movement
Feminist Africa 12, 14
feminist economics 97
'Feminist Perspectives in the Social Sciences' Conference 159
femocracy 30–1
Fernández de Kirchner, C. 154
fertility 259–60; control 19, 20, 61, 188–9

fieldwork 95–6
Finland 316, 317, 318–19, 320, 336
FIONA 296
'First Central American–Mexican Seminar on Women's Research' 159
first ladies' programs 12, 18
'First Latin American Seminar on Women's Research' 160
flexibilization 231
Flores, L. 166
Fodor, É. 298, 302
food pension, request for 51
foreign authors 206–8
foreign specialists 205–6
formal and informal sociability 207
formal sector 28, 41
Forum for African Women's Education 25
Foucault, M. 240, 270–1
France 11, 58, 259, 336–7
Frankfurt School 266, 267
French Suez water company 152
Front d'Alliberament Gai de Catalunya 286
fufubessei movement 141–8
functionalism 114, 116
fundamentalism 105; Islamic 57–8, 68

Gaidzanwa, R.B. 26
Gal, S. 299
Gandhi, N. 99
García, G.M. 204
Gays and Lesbians of Zimbabwe 24
gender budgeting 326
gender and development perspective 134–5
gender and development (GAD) units 79
gender equality 172; broader concept in EU 325–6; Hungary 292; policies in Spain 284–5; prioritizing gender equality objectives in EU 327; Senegal 62; Vietnam 137–8
gender identities 167
gender mainstreaming 6; China 86, 87; EU 258, 323–30
gender negotiations 222
gender neutrality 79
gender perspective: distinctive traits of Cuban researchers' 201–3; incorporating into the mainstream 326–7
gender roles 202
gender systems 222
geopolitical location 294–5
Gerhard, U. 264
German Democratic Republic (GDR) 257, 262, 269–70
Germany 257, 262, 265, 266, 268–9, 337

Germophone feminist theory 261–77
Ghana 13, 29, 32, 337; market women 14, 41–8
Ghasemzade, F. 118
global gender order 69
global processes 95
global trends 5–6
globalization 2, 46–7, 153, 190, 258; Africa and 13–14, 29–30; dowry demands and 104
government posts, women in 31, 154, 200, 284, 298–9
GRAVAD household survey 242–6
Greece 337
Grupo Dinamizadores 52
Guatemala 161, 162, 337
Guinea 337

Haney, L. 302
Hausen, K. 263–4
He, Zheng-shi 76
health 5, 15; reproductive 18–20, 188–9; Sub-Saharan Africa 18–21; see also HIV/AIDS
health promotion 138
hegemonic masculinity 131, 132
Hindu nationalism 100, 101
Historian Women Scholars 118, 120
Historians' Dispute 265
historical approach 17–18, 202; Central America 164–5; Germanophone feminism 263–4; India 96–7, 97–8; Iran 120; Puerto Rico 182
history, reclaiming in Hungary 301–3
HIV/AIDS: Africa 15, 20, 26; global trends 133; sex workers in Vietnam 69, 133–40
home care allowance 316–18, 319
homosexuality 205; Brazil 245–6; Caribbean 226; lesbianism in Poland 308, 309, 310–13; Spain 285–6; Sub-Saharan Africa 24–5
Honduras 161, 163, 338
Honegger, C. 264
Hong Kong 68
'housecleaning exercise' 43
Hubert, A. 329
human rights 62, 165
human trafficking 14, 30, 326
Hungarian Workers' Party (MDP) 292
Hungary 258, 290–307, 338
husbands, killings of 119

Iceland 319, 338
'ideologues' 170, 171
idiothematic analysis 207
ie (family institution) 142, 145
illegitimate children, discrimination against 141, 146

Imam, A. 18
implicit conservative consensus 236
in-depth interviews 208
income gaps 134
income tax 61–2
independence 11, 151; India 93; Mozambique 49; Sub-Saharan Africa 28, 30
Independent Researchers on Women's Issues 118
India 67, 68, 70, 71, 92–109, 338
Indian School for Women's Studies and Development 97
individuality, subversive 145–7
Indonesia 339
inferiority, sense of 125
infidelity 243, 244
informal sector 13–14; Ghanaian market women 41–8; Puerto Rico 187
injecting drug users (IDUs) 133
inside-outside organizing 315
insider status 169–70
Institute for Women, University of Panama 163
Institute of Women Studies, National University of Costa Rica 163
institutional approach: Germanophone feminist theory 268–9; institutional discourse and trade unions in Argentina 234–6
institutional culture 327–8
institutional day care 316–18
institutional factors in spread of HIV/AIDS 135
Institutional Regulatory Board (IRB) 98
institutionalization of women's/gender studies: Central America 161, 162–4; China 86–7; Hungary 295–6; Spain 287
integrationist approach to gender mainstreaming 323, 324
intellectuals 111–12
Intercontinental Hotel, Lusaka 31
Interdisciplinary Gender Studies Program, UCA 163
inter-ethnic conflict 222–3
International Center for Research on Women 97
international conferences 3, 84, 199, 294; Beijing see Beijing World Conference on Women (1995)
International Monetary Fund (IMF) 153
international perspective 279
international treaties 22–3, 31–2
International Tribunal on Crimes Against Women 250, 253
intersectionality 170, 273–4; Africa 28; India 93–4; Puerto Rico 180, 183–5, 187, 188, 190
Iran 68, 70, 71, 110–24, 339
Iran-Iraq war 111

Iranian Sociology Association Women's Studies Group 118, 119
Iraq 60, 339
Ireland 339
Islam 5, 13, 68, 259; diasporic Iranian scholars 121, 121–2; and sexuality 24–5; women, state and in Senegal 56–63
Islamic fundamentalism 57–8, 68
Islamism 57–8
Islamic revolution, Iran 111
Israel 339
Italy 339–40
Ivory Coast 340

Jack, J. 154
Jahan, R. 324
Jamaica 340
Japan 68, 340; family names and women's resistance 70, 141–8
Jeffers, A. 216, 217
Jense-Dovom 118
Jiang, Zemin 81, 83
Jin, Yihong 85
jokes 205
Jorge, A. 184
Juridical Journal 188
justice system, Mozambique 49–55

Kane, M. 60
Kang, Keqing 81
Karacs, T. 291
Karamanou, A. 327
KATUSA (Korean Augmentation to the United States Army) 69, 125–32
Kempadoo, K. 227
Kende, A. 298
Kenya 15, 29, 31, 340
Kishwar, M. 102
Koran 57, 59
Korea, South 68, 69, 340–1; KATUSA and masculinity 69, 125–32; Korean women and US soldiers 128–30; military culture 127–8
koseki (family registration system) 142–3, 145–7
Kovács, K. 298
Kreisky, E. 264
Krüger, H. 267, 268–9
Krzewinska, A. 310
Kumar, R. 99

labor policies 259–60; *see also* work
labor rights 231–8
LABRISZ 301
Lady Musgrave Women's Self-Help Society 216

language 4, 182; and diasporic scholars' works in Iran 121; and fieldwork in India 96; translation between English and Chinese 73, 85
large-scale surveys 97
'latecomers' 170
Latin America 151–7; conflict and cooperation between academia and the feminist movement in Central America 156, 158–77; *see also under individual countries*
Latin American Studies Association (LASA) 154
law/legal systems: Africa 13, 22; civil codes 56–7, 59–60, 142; India 103; Iran 115; justice system in Mozambique 49–55; repressive legal policies in Vietnam 135, 137; *shari'a* 13, 57, 58, 60; women's resistance in Japan 141–8
Lenz, I. 273
lesbians in Poland 308, 309, 310–13; *see also* homosexuality
Li, Xiaojiang 74, 76, 82, 83
Li, Yinhe 78, 80
life history approaches 169, 208; Africa 17–18; Germanophone feminist theory 268–9; Ghanaian market women 41–6; Hungary 301
Lin, C. 85
local-global interaction 74–6
local groups 143–5
Longwe, S. 31
'lost decade' 152–3
Loutfi, A. 302

macrosociological research 279
Magyar Nök Országos Tanácsa 292
Making of Feminisms in the Caribbean project 227–8
Makola market (Ghana) 41, 43, 45, 46
Malaysia 341
male breadwinner model 269
male marginalization debate 224
Mama, A. 16, 21, 23, 30–1
manhood 224–5
Manushi 71, 102
maquiladoras 154
marital naming 70, 141–8
market traders 14, 41–8
marriage: Poland 311, 313; registration system in Japan 142–3, 145–7; temporary 122; white marriages 313
Marx, K. 266
Marxism 203, 206; China 77, 80–5, 88; Germanophone feminist theory 266; perspective on women 75
Marxist feminism 278

masculinity 4; Caribbean 224–5, 227; Costa Rica 167–8; KATUSA 69, 125–32; Spain 286–7
maternal benefits 78
Matiwork 226
matriarchal systems 54
Mauritania 56, 58
Mauritius 341
May Fourth feminism 81
Mazowiecki, T. 311
media 119–20
Mehta, B. 224
men: Iran 117; manhood in the Caribbean 224–5; need to study 204, 209; Spain 286–7; see also masculinity
Menchú, R. 161
Mesa, O. 204
Mexico 154, 341
microenterprise sector 28–9
Middle East 67–72; see also under individual countries
migration 283; Central America 168; Europe 259; from Puerto Rico 181; refugees 14, 153
militarization 69; KATUSA and masculinity 69, 125–32
military discipline 126–7
Millennium Development Goals (MDGs) 3
Miller, E. 224, 225
miscegenation 242
misinformation 251
mixed schools 281
Moazemi, S. 119
modernity: gender relations in capitalist modernity 263–5; phases of 270
modernization: GDR 269–70; Iran 111
Mohammed, P. 221, 222, 223
Momsen, J. 219
Montero, S. 203, 207
Moro, S. 204
motherhood 221, 311, 312, 320; Polish Mother 309, 312
motivations for studying gender issues 204–6
movement-driven analysis 100–1, 102–3
movement-oriented discourse 234–6
Movimiento de los Trabajadores Argentinos (MTA) 231, 234
Movimientos de Trabajadores Desocupados (MTD) 231
Mozambique 13, 341; justice system 49–55
Mujer 160
Mujer Intégrate Ahora (MIA) 248, 249–50, 250, 253

Nagy, B. 299–300

Nairobi Strategies 159
nakama 144
names, family 70, 141–8
National Center for Sexual Education (Cuba) 200
National Council on Women and Development (Ghana) 45
National Council of Women of Kenya 31
national economic status 4
national identity: KATUSA conscripts 127–8; Puerto Rico 183, 190
national machineries for women 12, 32
National Organization for Women (NOW) 154
national organizations 71
National Socialism (Nazism) 257, 262, 264–5
nationalism 273; China 81; as a constructive tool 308–9; Hindu 100, 101; Polish 309–10, 311; Puerto Rican 248–54
needle and syringe exchange program 138
Negrón-Muntaner, F. 184
Neményi, M. 298
neo-conservative backlash 179
neo-liberal policies 153, 258; Argentina 231
Netherlands, The 258, 341–2
'new' social movements 100
New Zealand 342
newly industrializing countries (NICs) 68
Newmont Mining 151–2
newsletters 144
Nicaragua 160, 161, 163, 342
Nigeria 13, 15, 31–2, 32, 56, 342
non-governmental organizations (NGOs): China 87; Hungary 301; Iran 117–118, 123; Sub-Saharan Africa 30–2
non-waged work 283
Nordic countries 260, 315–22; see also under individual countries
norms of masculinity 130
Norway 316, 317–18, 319–20, 342
Nzomo, M. 30, 31

observation techniques 207–8
Office of the Women's Advocate (Puerto Rico) 179, 181, 190
OMM (Women's Organization of Mozambique) 52, 53
Omvedt, G. 98–9, 100
Operación, La 250–3
Organization of African Unity 11
organizational culture: Hungary 299–300; shift in EU 327–8
Other 308–9

Pakistan 342

Pan-African research centers 342
Panama 161, 163, 342
paper divorce 146–7
Paraguay 342
parental authority law 61
parental leave 316; quotas for fathers 319–20
parents-in-law 103, 104
Parliwala, R. 104
participant observation 207–8
participatory research 80, 182, 209
patriarchy 105; Asia and the Middle East 70;
    China 83; India 103; Mozambique 49–50;
    sterilization in Puerto Rico 253
peace-making process 161–2
peer education 138
Pereira, C. 32
Perez, N. 207, 208
personal context 198–201
Peru 343
Petö, A. 301
Philippines 68, 69, 343
'pioneers' 170
Poland 5, 258, 308–14, 343
policy actors 328
policy mechanisms 327–8
policy process 327
Polish Mother 309, 312
political discourse 300
political movements 12–13, 152
political office, women in 31, 154, 200, 284,
    298–9
political participation 166–7, 190
political parties 52
political will 137, 138
politics: Africa 12–13, 30–2; gender perspective
    and 203; Hungary 298–300; India 101; Spain
    283–5
polygamy 51, 60, 122
popular tribunals 49, 50
population control 19, 20; Puerto Rico 180,
    188–9, 251, 253
Porto Alegre 243
Portugal 11, 343
positivist dispute 266
postcolonialism 30, 259
post-communist periphery 294–5; see also
    Hungary, Poland
postmodernism 114, 116
post-structuralism 114
poverty: feminization of in Iran 120; poor
    women's movements in India 98–9; Puerto
    Rico 180, 186–7; Vietnam and HIV/AIDS
    136

power differences, and fieldwork 95–6
Prada, G. 164
Prah, M. 26
Pratunam market (Thailand) 46
Presidents' reports 163–4
preventive health programs 138
prioritization of gender equality objectives
    327
production of life 101
Programa Regional La Corriente 166
proportional representation 31
prostitution see sex work/workers
public and private spheres 263
public sector 28, 45
publication style 279
Puerto Rico 343; citizenship, nation and
    reproductive rights 156, 248–54; feminism and
    feminist studies 155, 178–95
pupils, school 281–2
purchasing trips 46

qualitative research 4, 17; China 80; Cuba 206–7;
    India 97; Puerto Rico 182
quality of research 279
quantitative research 4, 17, 206; China 80; India
    97, 104; Iran 116; Spain 279
queer theory 286
quotas: fathers' and parental leave 319–20;
    political representation 31, 166, 298

race/ethnicity 25, 273, 274; gender, difference and
    in the Caribbean 222–4; Puerto Rico 180–1,
    184–5, 186
racism 259
Rajk, R. 301
Randall, M. 160–1
rank, formalities of 126
rape 22; anti-rape campaign 99–100; India
    99–100, 102, 103
Ratele, K. 24
recovered and workers' self-managed enterprises
    235
redistribution 138
Reformism, Iran 112
refugees 14, 153
regional languages 105
regional trends 5–6
regulation of research procedures 98
rehabilitation centers 135
religion 5; Indian women and 100–1; and
    sexuality 24–5; teaching of 59; women, state
    and in Senegal 56–63; see also Catholicism,
    Islam

Report of Unnatural Deaths with Special Reference to Dowry Deaths 97
reproductive health: Puerto Rico 188–9; Sub-Saharan Africa 18–20
reproductive rights 19; Puerto Rico 156, 188–9, 248–54
research institutes (Hungary) 296
research networks 294
research units (China) 76
reserved-seat policies 31, 166, 298
resistance, women's 141–8
resource limitations 138–9
Reza Shah 111
Rigby, K. 264
right-wing fundamentalism 105
rights: human 62, 165; labor 231–8; reproductive 19, 156, 188–9, 248–54; sexual 20
Rivera Lassén, A.I. 184
Robledo, L. 202, 208
Rodriguez-Trías, H. 251
Roe v. Wade 249–50
romantic tradition 309
Rooshangaran and Women's Studies 118
Rowley, M. 221
Rubiera, D. 205
runaway girls 112, 119
rural women 99, 100
Russia 343
Rwanda 344; War Crimes Tribunal 21

Salvador 243
same-sex relationships *see* homosexuality
Sampath, N. 225
Sas, J.H. 292
Saudi Arabia 344
Scandinavia 260, 315–22; *see also under individual countries*
Schadt, M. 293
School of Social Work, Universidad de Costa Rica 160
school textbooks 119, 123, 281
scientific approach 204
SCOFI (*Scolarisation des Filles*) program 59
Scott, J. 273
second-wave feminism 217–18, 284
secularism 259; and religion in Senegal 56, 57–8
SEED 296
Sen, I. 98–9, 100
Senegal 344; women, religion and the state 56–63
Senghor, L.S. 60
sensuality 242
SEWA 101

sex/gender debate 272–3
sex-segregated schools 281
sex work/workers 69–70; Africa 14, 29–30; Caribbean 227; comfort women 69; Cuba 200; KATUSA conscripts and 129–30; Spain 285; trade unions in Argentina 232, 233; Vietnam and HIV/AIDS 69, 133–40
sexual desire 243–5
sexual harassment 26–7, 233
sexual initiation 243
sexual orientation 202
sexual revolution 241
sexual rights 20
sexual scripts 240
sexuality: Africa 14–15, 23–5; Brazil 156, 239–47; Caribbean 226–7; Hungary 300–1; KATUSA conscripts 128–30; Puerto Rico 180, 184; Senegal 61; socio-anthropological view 239–41; Spain 285–6; *see also* homosexuality
Shaanxi Women's Federation 83
Shah, N. 99
shari'a law 13, 57, 58, 60
shelters for battered women 118
Shen, Tan 80
Singapore 68
slavery 225
social context: Cuba 198–201; Iran 112–14
social history approach 263–4, 266–7
social mobility 240–1
social model of justice 52
social movements: feminism as a social movement 170–2; Japan 141–8; Latin America and the Caribbean 152; movement-related scholarship in India 100–1, 102–3, 104; 'new' 100; *see also* women's movement
social roles 20–1
social stratification 79
social theory: and axes of difference 272–4; Germanophone feminist theory 267–71
social tranformations 62, 273–4
socialism 258
societal integration 267–8
socio-anthropological view of sexuality 239–41
Sociological Research 78, 79
sociology 115; China 77–8; German 266; of women/gender in China 77–80, 85–7
Sociology of Women and Gender Research Committee (SWGRC) 86
Sojo, A. 166
Sood, S. 102
South Africa 28, 344
South Korea *see* Korea, South

Sow, F. 60
Spain 5, 257, 258, 278–89, 344
state: Africa 12–13, 30–2; Chinese and women 81, 82, 83; feminist activism and in Puerto Rico 190; and gender scholarship in India 94–5; Spain 278; and traders in Ghana 43; and violence against women 22; women, religion and in Senegal 56–63
statistical data 204–5
Status of Women, 2001 97
sterilization 180, 189, 250–3
stratification, social 79
Stratigaki, M. 328
Strengthening Gender and Women's Studies for Africa's Social Transformation 33
structural adjustment policies (SAPs) 153; Africa 13, 26, 29, 41; Ghana 44, 47; Hungary 294
structural perspective 21–3
student activism 265
Suárez Findlay, E.J. 184
subjectivity 202–3
Sub-Saharan Africa 16–40
subversive individuality 145–7
Sudan 56
suicide 112–13
Sun, Liping 78
sunnah 57
superiority, sense of 125–6
supply-side analysis 283
Sweden 316, 317, 318, 319–20, 344–5
Switzerland 262, 345
'Symposium on Female Education' 159
Szalai, J. 298
Szikra, D. 302

Taiwan 68, 345
Takács, J. 300–1
Takáts, É. 291
Tamale, S. 31
Tang Nain, G. 223
Tanzania 27, 28, 345
teachers: feminization of teaching 281; interactions with pupils 282
teenage pregnancy Africa 19, 26; Brazil 242–3
Tehran University 116
television 119–20
temporary marriage 122
testimonial literature 160–1
textbooks, school 119, 123, 281
Thailand 68, 69, 138, 345
theories of action 267–8
Tóth, H. 300

Tóth, O. 299
trade liberalization policies 47
Trade Union Law on Female Quotas 232, 233, 234, 236
trade unions 156, 231–8
traders, market 14, 41–8
traditional authorities 52–3
trafficking in humans 14, 30, 326
Tran Duc Luong 137
transformative approach to gender mainstreaming 324
translation of books/articles 118
transnational corporations 154
transnational feminism 5–6, 12, 71, 75, 101, 190, 261, 271
transnational traders 13–14, 41–8
'traveling concepts' 265
Trinidad and Tobago 225, 345; Sexual Offences Act (1986) 226
Tudományos Gyüjtemény 291
Turkey 345

Uganda 26, 29, 31, 32, 345
Union of African States 11
Union del Personal Civil de la Nación (UPCN) 233, 236
United Kingdom (UK) 11, 345–6
United Nations: CSW 3, 6; DAW 3; Decade for Women 2, 158, 159; Platform for Action 75
United Nations Development Fund for Women (UNIFEM) 3
United Nations Fund for Population Activities (UNFPA) 61, 199–200
United Negro Improvement Association (UNIA) 217
United States (US) 7; and the Caribbean 151, 216; KATUSA 69, 125–32; and Latin America 151; militarization and Asia 69; and Puerto Rico 155, 178, 181, 248, 249–50; *Roe v. Wade* 249–50; war on terrorism 56
universality 253
Universidad Centroamericana (UCA) (Central American University) 161, 163
Universidad de Panamá Workshop for Women's Studies 161
universities: Central America 161, 162–4; China 86; Hungary 293–4; Iran 112; Spain 287; Sub-Saharan Africa 26–7
University of Cape Coast 26
University Congress on Women 160
University of Szeged Department of English Studies 296
University of the West Indies 216, 218, 227–8

University of Zimbabwe 14
'unmet need' 19
urban autonomous women's groups 99
urbanization 134–5
Uruguay 346

Vallina, E.D. 204
Várady, M. 298
Venezuela 346
Ventana 160
Veres, P. 291
Vergesellschaftung (societal integration)
  267–8
Vicsek, L. 299–300
victims, representation of women as 250–3
Vietnam 68; sex workers and HIV/AIDS 69,
  133–40
violence against women 5, 105, 326; Africa 15,
  21–3; Central America 165–6; Ciudad Juárez
  154; Hungary 300–1; India 70, 101–4; Iran
  117, 118–19; Mozambique 51, 52, 53; Puerto
  Rico 179, 182, 187–8
voting patterns 283–4

Wagner, P. 270
Wal-Mart 151
Wang, Jinling 78, 79, 80, 86
Wang, Zheng 77, 83
war/conflict 69; Africa 14, 22; inter-ethnic 222–3;
  Latin America 153; Mozambique 50; and rape
  22
Washington Consensus 153
Weber, M. 266
Wekker, G. 226
welfare state: child care in Scandinavia 260,
  315–22; Germany 268–9; Hungary 302; Spain
  283
white marriages 313
Williams, B. 223
witchcraft 52
'wives' strategy 12, 18
woman-to-woman marriage 24
women, representation as victims 250–3
women-centered standpoint 79
Women in the Caribbean Research Project
  (WICP) 219
Women in Development consultancies 17
Women/Gender Studies Research and Training
  Bases 86–7
Women and Law in South Africa 22
Women Living under Muslim Laws (WLUML)
  22, 57
women unionists 231–8

Women's Bureau (Iran) 71, 112, 118
women's liberation 80–1
Women's Manifestos 32
women's movement: Caribbean 216–18, 227;
  conflict and cooperation between academia and
  activism in Central America 156, 158–77; Iran
  110–13, 117–18, 122; movement-oriented
  discourses in Argentina 234–6; Puerto Rico
  178–81, 190; Scandinavia and child care
  controversy 316, 318; scholarship in India
  98–101; Spain 284
Women's Network in Parliament (Finland)
  317
Women's Organization (Iran) 111
women's resistance, Japan 141–8
Women's Secretariats 233–4
women's studies: Central America and
  establishment of 159–64; development in
  China 73–7, 85–7; Europe 260; Iran 70, 71,
  110–24; links between feminist activism and
  1–3, 5–6
women's studies centers 74, 75
Women's Studies Institute of China (WSIC) 74,
  78, 87
women's suffrage 291–2
Women's World Conferences 3; Beijing *see* Beijing
  World Conference on Women (1995)
work: Africa 13–14, 27–9; Caribbean 219–20;
  Central America 160; China 78; Cuba 199;
  decline in women's employment in Scandinavia
  318–19; Ghanaian market women 14, 41–8;
  Hungary 297–8; job opportunities for sex
  workers in Vietnam 137–8; labor policies
  259–60; male control of women and work in
  Senegal 60–1; Mozambique 50; Puerto Rico
  179–80, 185–6; Spain 282–3; women's labor
  rights and trade unions in Argentina 156,
  231–8
World Bank 153
World Social Forum 101
World Trade Center attacks 56
World Trade Organization (WTO) 28, 153

Yáñez, M. 203, 206
young people, and opinions on sexuality 242–6
Yugoslavia 346

Zambia 32
Zanan 71, 113, 118, 121, 123
Zhao, J. 80
Zheng, Yefu 78
Zimbabwe 13, 15, 26, 28, 346
Zimmermann, S. 295, 302